Korea

Robert Storey

Korea

4th edition

Published by
Lonely Planet Publications
Head Office: PO Box 617, Hawthorn, Vic 3122, Australia
Branches: 150 Linden St, Oakland, CA 94607, USA
               10a Spring Place, London NW5 3BH, UK
               1 rue du Dahomey, 75011 Paris, France

Printed by
Craft Print Pte Ltd, Singapore

Photographs by

Adrian Buzo	Rusty Carter	Geoff Crowther	Mason Florence
H. Goosens	Patrick Horton	Choe Hyung Pun	Richard I'Anson
David Mason	Martin Moos	Robert Storey	Deanna Swaney
Chris Taylor			

Front cover photography by Grant V Faint, The Image Bank

First Published
1988

This Edition
July 1997

Although the authors and publisher have tried to make the information as
accurate as possible, they accept no responsibility for any loss, injury or
inconvenience sustained by any person using this book.

National Library of Australia Cataloguing in Publication Data

Storey, Robert.
Korea.

4th ed.
Includes index.
ISBN 0 86442 494 9

1. Korea – Guidebooks. I. Title. (Series : Lonely Planet travel survival kit).

915.190443

text & maps © Lonely Planet 1997
photos © photographers as indicated 1997
Cheju-do climate chart compiled from information supplied by Patrick J Tyson, © Patrick J Tyson, 1997

Robert Storey

Robert has had a chequered past, starting with his first job (a monkey keeper at a zoo) and continuing with a stint as a slot machine repairman in a Las Vegas casino. Robert has been involved in 14 Lonely Planet books to date, and has written a number of English-teaching textbooks including *Creative Conversation* and *The Travellers' Guide to English*. He updated the South Korea chapters of this 4th edition and the 3rd edition of this book.

David Mason

David fled from the Detroit (USA) area as soon as he could. After obtaining university degrees in Oriental Philosophy and Education while a hippie-Deadhead resident of San Francisco, he took off for East Asia. David obtained a second Master's Degree in Korean Studies from Yonsei University in Seoul. He has been living in South Korea since 1986 and has authored several books and academic articles about Korea. David updated the North Korea chapter for this edition.

From the Authors

Several local Koreans, expats and foreign visitors to Korea generously donated time and useful information to this project. Special thanks go to Yoon Kil-sup, Athol Yates, Patrick Horton, Otfried Schwarzkopf, Bruce Arnold, Laurie Notch, Charles A Smith, Rob Housley, Heather Todd, George O McCarten and Gary Rector.

From the Publisher

Back in the Melbourne office of Lonely Planet, this edition of Korea was edited by David Andrew with help from Carolyn Papworth and Peter Cruttenden, who also helped with the proofing. The maps were drawn by Mark Germanchis, Adam McCrow and Andrew Tudor. Ann Jeffree toiled over layout and illustrations, and Trudi Canavan helped out at the 11th hour with some nice drawings. Sally Gerdan and Dan Levin proved invaluable with their timely advice.

Last, but not least, we'd like to thank the many travellers who used the last edition of Korea on the road and took the time to write to us with helpful comments or criticisms. The many to whom we are grateful include:

R Allen, Rick Attenburg, Jacqui Bauer, Qani Belul, David Burns, Aaron Butt, Tess Camagna, Craig Campbell, Rose Chessman, Jan Christoffersen, Dan Costello, Tom Delaney, Jennifer Depto, Audra Dewhurst, M Errico, Lisa Fairbrother, William Fink, M Folkesson, Nigel Foster, Dan Free, Doug French, Robert Gardner, Greg Giaccio, Jane Gindin, Eugene Gleser, G Gustafsson, Sven Haakon Kristensen, Roger Hannaker, Katya Hayes, Di Head, Kim Hoyle, Vanessa Huth, Mark Irwin, Chris Jae-Seok Ahn, Mary Jean Chan, Gary Jennings, Andrew Karkus, Russell Kenny, Laura Kluthe, Leslie Kodish, Eddie Koh, Jenny Kotauskos, Terence Langdon, Deryk Langlais, Robert Langridge, Julie Larson, Keith A Leitich, John Leyva, Tonya Lowe, Derek Martin, Rick Marusyk,

Angela Masrud, Ben Masters, Craig McLeman, John McNeil, Bev McPhail, Brett Meyer, Michael & Rosemary Murray, Kyung Nam Masan, Peter Oram, Steve Oszewski, Alex Pasquali, Stan Paulic, Gary & Charlene Peterson, E Pukpundang, Lance Reeher, Daphne Rosenzweig, Rick Ruffin, Michelle Sale, Kampbell Salehi, Roger Satterthwaite, Duncan Schofield, Florence & Peter Shaw, Shannon Smith, Jason Strauss, J T Errico, Erik Tschopp, Pierre van den Heuvel, Peter Wall, Tori Watson, Richard Watson, Cy West, Stephen Whelan, Madeline Wilks, William Wise, Clayton Wood, Rachel Wright, Jay Yoo, Graham Young, David Young

Warning & Request

A travel writer's job is never done. Prices go up, new hotels open, old ones degenerate, some burn down, others get renovated and renamed, bridges collapse and recommended travel agents get indicted for fraud. Remember, this book is meant to be a guide, not the oracle – things change. If you find that Korea is not identical to the way it's described herein don't get upset, just get out your pen or word processor and write to Lonely Planet.

Your letters will be used to help update future editions and, where possible, important changes will also be included in an Update section in reprints. Excerpts from correspondence may also appear in our newsletter, *Planet Talk*, or in the postcards section of our Web site – so please let us know if you don't want your letter published or your name acknowledged.

We greatly appreciate all information that is sent back to us from travellers. Back at Lonely Planet, Julie Young co-ordinates a small but hard-working team who read and acknowledge every reader's letter, postcard and email, and ensure that every morsel of information finds its way to the appropriate authors, editors and publishers.

Everyone who writes to us will find their name in the next edition of the appropriate guide and will also receive a free subscription to our quarterly newsletter, *Planet Talk*. The very best contributions will be rewarded with a free copy of the next edition, or another Lonely Planet guide if you prefer. We give away lots of books, but unfortunately not every letter/postcard receives one.

Contents

Map Legend

BOUNDARIES

International Boundary

Regional Boundary

ROUTES

Freeway

Highway

Major Road

Unsealed Road or Track

City Road

City Street

Railway

Underground Railway

Metro

Walking Track

Walking Tour

Ferry Route

Cable Car or Chairlift

AREA FEATURES

Parks

Built-Up Area

Pedestrian Mall

Market

Cemetery

Beach or Desert

Rocks

HYDROGRAPHIC FEATURES

Coastline

River, Creek

Intermittent River or Creek

Rapids, Waterfalls

Lake, Intermittent Lake

Canal

Swamp

River Flow

SYMBOLS

CAPITAL		National Capital
Capital		Regional Capital
CITY		Major City
City		City
Town		Town
Village		Village
		Place to Stay, Place to Eat
		Cafe, Pub or Bar
		Post Office, Telephone
		Tourist Information, Bank
		Transport, Parking
		Museum, Youth Hostel
		Caravan Park, Camping Ground
		Church, Cathedral
		Mosque, Synagogue
		Buddhist Temple, Pagoda
		Hospital, Police Station

		Embassy, Petrol Station
		Airport, Airfield
		Swimming Pool, Gardens
		Shopping Centre, Zoo
		Ski Field, Picnic Site
	A25	One Way Street, Route Number
		Stately Home, Monument
		Castle, Tomb
		Cave, Hut or Chalet
		Mountain or Hill, Lookout
		Lighthouse, Shipwreck
		Pass, Spring
		Beach, Surf Beach
		Archaeological Site or Ruins
		Ancient or City Wall
		Cliff or Escarpment, Tunnel
		Railway Station

Note: not all symbols displayed above appear in this book

Introduction

South Korea is still very much off the beaten track to travellers. Quite a few reach Seoul, the capital, en route to somewhere else and a few intrepid individuals make it to Kyŏngju and the island province of Chejudo, but hardly anyone seems to take the time to explore the other attractions of the country. Undoubtedly the magnets of Japan and China serve to distract most people's attention, yet Korea is one of the most fascinating enigmas of the Far East. Its history is one of the world's most turbulent sagas of a small nation's struggle for survival against what would appear to be impossible odds. Sandwiched between vastly more powerful neighbours who for at least two millennia have frequently attempted to absorb it, it has nevertheless preserved its own unique character and cultural identity.

You might be forgiven for thinking that the most coveted gems of oriental culture are to be found in either Japan or China, and that Korea merely offers a pale reflection of these, but you would be wrong. Korea has some of the world's most enchanting countryside: beautiful, forested mountains offer endless trekking possibilities which, while seen at their most colourful either in the spring or autumn, are misty and romantic even during the wet season. In the forests you will find sublimely crafted temple complexes whose origins stretch back 1500 years. A visit to any one of these hauntingly beautiful places will leave an indelible impression. Many of them are still functioning monasteries and anyone expressing an interest in delving beneath the surface will find the monks not only very friendly but also hospitable. Then there are Korea's innumerable islands scattered like confetti off its southern and eastern shores, many of them with intriguing variations on mainland culture. Very few of them have ever seen a visitor from abroad let alone had their paths tramped bare by tourist hordes.

And what of the people? Koreans are a proud, romantic, spontaneous and friendly people. You will not encounter that feeling of disinterest which westerners often experience in China. Even in cosmopolitan Seoul you'll be regarded with curiosity. Wherever you go, but especially in the smaller places, you'll constantly be approached by people who want to strike up a conversation, whether they be soldiers, hotel proprietors, students, businesspeople or whatever. They will try their best – regardless of language or cultural differences – to establish some rapport with you, yet always with humour and never in an overbearing manner. If you respond with friendship and a little imagination you will often find yourself the recipient of the most unexpected and often disarming hospitality. It's not that Koreans don't have fairly rigidly defined rules of social conduct and public behaviour in common with other Oriental people; they do – and you will often be aware of this – but for a foreigner they'll bend the rules double to spare you involvement and make you feel at home.

Not surprisingly, history lies heavily on these people. At times the cost of their survival as a nation has been devastating (the most recent example of this was, of course, the Korean War in the early 1950s). Continually on the alert and prepared for invasion, the armed forces have always been an important element of Korean society. This is no less true today than it has ever been. It would be fatuous to ignore the ubiquitous presence of the army – in South Korea conscription is a two-year stint – but it would also be a grave mistake to allow these realities to prejudice your view of the country and its people. Koreans have felt the cold wind of superpower rivalry for centuries.

Perhaps that's why they're so keen to establish friendships and exchange views with foreign visitors, but then again maybe it's just their natural disposition. Whatever the reasons, the line drawn between guest and lifelong friend is very much a question of your own attitude.

There's one last plus which ought to put Korea firmly on the travellers' route and that is its safety and cleanliness. Public transport is well organised and all but the most rural of roads are paved. True, you can find similar conditions in Japan, but at two to three times the price.

Korea is one of the unexplored gems of Asia. It acquired the nickname of the 'Hermit Kingdom' after it closed its borders to all foreigners in the late 19th century as a result of what seemed like insuperable pressures from the outside. That name still fits North Korea, but South Korea is certainly one of the most open and rapidly changing societies in Asia.

Facts about the Country

HISTORY

Korean folk legends fix the date of the nation's birth from a semi-deity named Tangun at around 2333 BC. But according to the latest research, its origins go back even further into the mists of time to 30,000 BC, when migrating tribes from Central and Northern Asia first arrived in the peninsula.

The earliest outside influences assimilated by these nomadic tribes came from the Chinese, who had established an outpost near present-day P'yŏngyang during the Han dynasty. Constant wars with the Chinese forced an early alliance between the tribes of the north; this eventually led to the formation of the first Korean kingdom – Koguryo – around the 1st century AD, and the uniting of the northern half of the peninsula four centuries later after the collapse of the Han dynasty. Not being subject to the same immediate pressures the related tribes of the south were slower to coalesce, but by the 3rd century AD two powerful kingdoms – Shilla and Paekche – had emerged to dominate the southern half of the peninsula. Sandwiched between them for a while in the south was the loose confederacy of Kaya, but this had a relatively brief existence since the leaders of its constituent tribes were rarely able to present a common front when threatened with invasion.

Three Kingdoms Period

The next four centuries – known as the Three Kingdoms Period (Koguryo, Paekche and Shilla) – witnessed a remarkable flowering of the arts, architecture, literature and statecraft as Chinese influences continued to be absorbed, reinterpreted and alloyed with traditional Korean beliefs. Probably the single most formative influence was Buddhism which, in time, became the state religion of all three kingdoms.

The Three Kingdoms Period also marked the first exports of Korean cultural developments to Japan. Architects and builders from Paekche, for instance, were primarily responsible for the great burst of temple construction which occurred in Japan during the 6th century. This transmission of cultural developments naturally accelerated during periods of conflict and there were times in Japan's early history when there were more Koreans involved in influential secular and religious positions than Japanese.

There was, of course, much rivalry between the three kingdoms and wars were fought constantly in attempts to gain supremacy. But it was not until the 7th century that a major shift of power occurred.

Shilla Dominance

The rise of the Tang dynasty in China during the 7th century provided Shilla with the opportunity to expand its dominion over the whole peninsula. An alliance of the two was formed and the combined armies first attacked Paekche (which quickly fell), then Koguryo in 668 AD.

However, the alliance was short-lived since it turned out to have been a convenient ruse by the Tang ruler to establish hegemony over Korea. The Shilla aristocracy had no intention of subscribing to such a plan and so, in order to thwart Tang designs, switched allegiance to what was left of the Koguryo forces. Together, the two Korean forces were eventually able to drive out the Chinese. Shilla thus united the peninsula for the first time and this unification was to last through various changes of regime right up until partition after WWII. Yet Shilla was to learn, as all Korean dynasties have had to, that this often precarious independence depended on the recognition of the vastly superior forces of China and its acknowledgment in the form of tribute. This relationship with China has more than once thrown Korea between contending armies from China at times of dynastic change and left it vulnerable to Japanese military adventurism.

A unified Shilla presided over one of

Korea's greatest eras of cultural development and nowhere is this more apparent than in the countless tombs, temples, pagodas, palaces, pleasure gardens and other relics which dot the countryside in and around present-day Kyŏngju, the former Shilla capital. Buddhism, in particular, flourished: state funds were lavished on the construction of temples and images, and monks were dispatched to China and India for study.

The cohesiveness of Shilla society was based on the twin pillars of *kolpum* (a rigid hierarchy of rank based on ancestry) and the *hwarang* (a kind of paramilitary youth organisation for the training and education of the sons of the Shilla elite). Yet the very rigidity of this system brought about its eventual downfall. By the beginning of the 9th century, discontent among those who were excluded from power had reached such a pitch that the kingdom began to fall apart. Threatened by rival warlords to the north and west, the end came surprisingly bloodlessly when the last king of Shilla, unwilling to contemplate further destruction, offered his kingdom to the ruler of Later Koguryo in the northern half of the peninsula. As a result, the capital was moved to Kaesŏng, north of Seoul, and the peninsula reunited.

The last king of Shilla was allowed to live out the rest of his days as an honoured guest in his rival's capital. Kyŏngju sank into obscurity and remained that way until 'rediscovered' in the 20th century. This was a blessing in disguise, since recognition of its value would have caused the city's priceless artefacts to have been looted, destroyed and lost forever.

Koryŏ Dynasty 918–1392

The new dynasty, which took the name of Koryŏ, abolished kolpum and restructured the government. Koryŏ emphasised a Confucian examination system for state officials, similar to that which prevailed in China except that eligibility for the examination was limited to the sons of the oligarchy. With stability restored the new dynasty prospered; Buddhism, through royal patronage, reached the height of its development and acquired

considerable secular power through the acquisition of land and accumulation of wealth.

In time, however, the Koryŏ government became as despotic and arrogant as that of Shilla, except that in this case it was the literati who monopolised the top positions rather than warrior-aristocrats. Disaffected military officers eventually reduced the power of these bureaucrats by assassinating one of the Koryŏ kings and installing his son as a puppet ruler. At the same time events were taking place on Korea's northern borders which would radically affect the nation's survival as an independent kingdom.

Throughout its later years marauding Khitan tribes began to make life difficult for the Koryŏ kingdom. The Khitans were only kept in check by an alliance with the Mongols of China. This alliance was a reluctant one on the part of Koryŏ, since it involved the payment of considerable annual tribute, and eventually it was broken off.

The reckoning didn't come until 1231 because the Mongols were preoccupied with their own problems, but when it did the decision to rescind the treaty proved to have been a disastrous one. The Mongols invaded with vastly superior forces, quickly took Kaesŏng and forced the king to take refuge

Statuary from the Koryŏ Dynasty, at the Royal Tomb in Kaesŏng

on Kanghwado. There he remained relatively safe but totally powerless while the Mongols laid waste to the peninsula for the next 25 years. A bitter truce was arranged in 1259. The Koryŏ monarch was restored to his kingdom (minus Cheju Island, which the Mongols used for rearing horses) on condition that Koryŏ crown princes would be held hostage at Beijing until the deaths of their fathers; that they would be forced to marry Mongol princesses; and that the tribute would be restored.

The tribute demanded by the settlement was a heavy one for Korea to shoulder. It included gold, silver, horses, ginseng, hawks, artisans, women and eunuchs. There were also demands to provide soldiers and ships for the ill-fated Mongol invasion of Japan between 1274 and 1281. These various exactions, plus the powerful influence which the Mongol princesses wielded at the Koryŏ court, placed intolerable strains on the fabric of Korean society and were the root cause of the eventual downfall of Koryŏ.

Still, Koryŏ survived for a little while longer and reasserted its independence when rebellions in China led to the replacement of the Mongols by the Ming dynasty. There were reforms and wholesale purges of pro-Mongol aristocrats, but the rot had spread too far: rebellions broke out which climaxed in the overthrow of the Koryŏ monarch and the foundation of a new dynasty by one of the king's former generals, Yi Song-gye.

Yi (Chosŏn) Dynasty 1392–1910

The new regime staked its future on the ideals and practices of Neo-Confucianism. These combined the sage's original ethical and political ideas with a quasi-religious practice of ancestor worship and the idea of the eldest male as spiritual head of the family. At the same time, Buddhism, regarded as an enemy and rival, was suppressed. The monasteries' estates were confiscated, their wealth sequestered and the building of monasteries limited to rural areas. Buddhism has never recovered its former dominance, but it still wields considerable influence and its economic clout is definitely on the rise. Neo-Confucianism remains the moral foundation of the nation, though few Koreans would actually acknowledge it as their 'religion'.

The next 150 years were a time of relative peace and prosperity, during which great strides were made under a succession of enlightened kings. The most beloved of these was Sejong (1418-50), who presided over the invention of a phonetic script – hangŭl – for the Korean language. The new script was an outstanding achievement and, since it was infinitely simpler than Chinese, led to a vast increase in literacy. However, it was not introduced without considerable opposition among the intelligentsia, many of whom regarded it as subversive and worried about the reaction of the Ming court.

A master tactician, Admiral Yi Sun-sin outwitted a far greater Japanese navy.

Japanese Invasion of 1592

The period of peace came to a dramatic end in 1592: following Korea's refusal to join an invasion of China, it was invaded by a newly united Japan under Toyotomi Hideyoshi. With superior weaponry, including muskets supplied by the Portuguese, the Japanese overran the peninsula in just one month. At sea, however, they were soundly defeated by Korea's most famous admiral, Yi Sun-sin, the inventor of the world's first ironclad ships (known as 'turtle ships' or *gobugson*). In their encounters with Admiral Yi Sun-sin, the Japanese lost more than 500 ships in less than six months. Unfortunately, the admiral fell foul of the Yi court and was dismissed (not the last time the Korean bureaucracy has bungled) only to be recalled at a later date when his successor failed to match up.

The war dragged on for four years until Korean guerrilla resistance and Chinese intervention forced a conclusion. The Japanese invaded again the following year; this time the war was confined to the southern provinces and came to a speedier end when Hideyoshi died and the invaders withdrew.

The Japanese invasion was an unprecedented disaster for Korea. Many craftspeople and intellectuals were taken prisoner and transported to Japan, and almost all of Korea's temples and palaces were burnt to the ground. There was to be no early respite.

Manchu Invasion

The early 17th century was a time of conflict in China. The Manchus were in the process of overthrowing the Ming court, with whom the Koreans had treaty obligations. Although unsure which side to declare for the Korean court decided to side with the Ming, thus incurring the wrath of the Manchus who, as soon as they had consolidated their hold over China, turned to invade Korea. The Korean forces were routed and severe restrictions placed on the country's sovereignty.

The Hermit Kingdom

Profoundly shocked and exhausted by this series of events, Korea folded its wings and withdrew into itself over the next century.

Meanwhile, the spread of western ideas and contacts caused the pace of change to accelerate all around. Nowhere was this more apparent than in the number of converts to Catholicism and, later, to various sects of Protestantism. Frightened by the growing influence of these groups, the Yi court panicked and in the repression which followed hundreds of people were executed. But the event which most shook their confidence was the occupation of Beijing by the French and British in 1860. In a vain attempt to shut off these dawning realities, the country was closed to all foreigners and Korea acquired the name of the 'Hermit Kingdom'.

It was a policy doomed to fail. The late 19th century was no time to turn a blind eye to the increasing industrial and military might of the European maritime nations, the USA and Japan. Sooner or later, one or more of them would force the Koreans to open their doors. This happened some 25 years later as a result of independent occupations of Kanghwa Island by the French and Americans, and a naval skirmish engineered by the Japanese which led to a so-called treaty of 'friendship'. The treaty was biased in favour of the Japanese: Korean ports were opened to Japanese traders and the policy of excluding foreigners was abandoned. Suddenly, very ill prepared, Korea found itself blown like a leaf in the winds of imperial rivalry.

Japanese Control

The Tonghak uprising in 1894 – by followers of a religious sect founded in 1860 by Choe Che-U – set off a chain of events which led to the Sino-Japanese War, the defeat of China and the installation of a Japanese-controlled government in Seoul. With China eliminated, Russia quickly jumped into the political arena and the Koreans became pawns in yet another struggle between giants.

During this time pro-Japanese and pro-Russian governments followed each other in rapid succession in Seoul. Queen Min – the real power behind the Yi throne – was assassinated by Japanese agents and for a year and a half King Kojong took refuge inside the Russian legation. In the end, the struggle for supremacy was settled by the Russo-Japanese War of 1904 and Korea was occupied by the Japanese. Shortly after, in 1910, following public riots and serious guerrilla activity by elements of the disbanded Korean army, the Japanese annexed the country and abolished the monarchy.

Annexation by Japan was not something the Koreans took lightly. After the failure of a Korean delegation to gain the right of self-determination at the Versailles Conference following WWI, an independence movement was formed by a group of patriots. They leafleted Seoul and provoked public demonstrations against the Japanese occupation. The unrest quickly spread to the rest of the country. The Japanese troops and police panicked; in the brutal repression which followed over 7000 Koreans were shot and many thousands more seriously injured. Cosmetic reforms were brought in to try and contain the uprising, but at the same time the ranks of the secret police were rapidly expanded and censorship tightened.

As WWII drew near, Japan's grip over Korea was tightened even further: Japanese was made the mandatory language of instruction in schools; all public signs had to be in Japanese; the teaching of Korean history was banned; and hundreds of thousands of Korean labourers were conscripted to assist the Japanese army both in Korea and in China. It was a time which the Koreans rightly regard as one of attempted cultural genocide and the scars are a long way from being healed even today.

Post WWII

When the Americans dropped the atomic bombs on Japan in 1945 most Koreans thought two weren't enough. But as much as they rejoiced at being freed of Japanese rule, hopes for a new era of peace were soon dashed. A deal had been struck between the USSR, USA and Britain over the fate of post-war Korea: the USSR was to occupy the peninsula north of the 38th parallel and the USA the country south of that. Though never intended as a permanent division, it became so once the occupying troops were in position.

Negotiations for a provisional government floundered because neither side was willing to make concessions which would result in the loss of its influence over the proposed new government. A UN commission was set up to try and resolve the problem and to oversee elections for a united government, but it was denied entry to the north and was forced to confine its activities to the south. The new government which was elected in the south declared its independence. The stage was set for the Korean War.

Korean War

By 1948 Soviet and American troops had been withdrawn, but while the Americans supplied only arms considered necessary for self-defence to the regime in the south, the USSR provided the north with a vast array of weaponry with which to create a powerful army. On 25 June 1950 the North Korean army invaded. The Americans responded by sending in troops and they were soon joined by contingents from 16 other countries following a UN resolution supporting the American action. The USSR absented itself from the Security Council deliberations.

The war went badly for the UN at first and its troops were soon pushed into a small pocket around Pusan. Following a daring landing at Inch'ŏn under the command of General MacArthur, its fortunes changed and within a month the North Korean army had been thrown back to the borders of Manchuria.

Having lost the war, the North Koreans decided to outsource the job to the Chinese. In November 1950 Communist Chinese troops poured into the war and the UN forces were pushed back below the 38th parallel. The conflict continued for the next six months, with both sides alternately advancing and retreating until a stalemate was reached just north of the 38th parallel.

Negotiations for a truce were started, but dragged on for two years, eventually leading to the creation of the Demilitarised Zone (DMZ) and the truce village of P'anmunjŏm, where both sides have met periodically ever since to exchange heated rhetoric.

At the end of the war Korea lay in ruins.

Seoul had changed hands no less than four times and was flattened. Millions of people were left homeless, industry destroyed and the countryside devastated. In the south, 47,000 Koreans had lost their lives and around 200,000 were wounded. Of the UN troops, 37,000 had been killed (mostly Americans) and 120,000 wounded. Combined military and civilian casualties were estimated at over two million.

Post Korean War

North Korea went on to become one of the most closed countries in the world, ruled by the eccentric and uncompromising Kim Il-sung (see the North Korea chapter for more details).

In South Korea, economic recovery was slow, and the civilian government of President Syngman Rhee weak and corrupt. In 1961, following blatantly fraudulent elections, massive student demonstrations and the resignation of Rhee, a military dictatorship was established and General Park Chung-hee emerged as its strongman. Pressures soon mounted for the return of a civilian government and so, in 1963, Park retired from the army and stood as a candidate for the Democratic Republican Party. The party won the elections and Park was named president. He was re-elected in 1967 and again in 1971, when he narrowly missed defeat at the hands of his rival, Kim Dae-jung.

On the positive side, Park created an efficient administration and was the architect of South Korea's economic 'miracle', which he modelled on Japan. But in October 1972, in an attempt to secure his position, he declared martial law, clamped down on political opponents and instituted an era of intensely personal rule. Like Kim Il-sung, he created his own personality cult and his record on human rights grew progressively worse. A botched assassination attempt in 1975 killed his wife. A rigged poll in 1978 resulted in Park's 're-election', but this only further fuelled discontent. Finally, on 26 October 1979, he was assassinated by Kim Chae-kyu, the chief of the Korean Central Intelligence Agency.

The 1980s

After 18 years of Park's tyrannical rule, Koreans were ready for a change. The brief period of political freedom which followed his death aroused popular desire for free elections and the dawning of Korean democracy.

Unfortunately, such hopes were soon dashed. On 17 May 1980 a group of army officers, headed by General Chun Doo-hwan, re-established martial law and arrested leading opposition politicians, including Kim Dae-jung. Student protests erupted the next day in Kim's home town of Kwangju and were brutally put down – about 200 civilians were killed, over 1000 injured and thousands more arrested. The 'Kwangju Massacre' has haunted the nation's conscience ever since.

In the rigged elections held shortly afterwards Chun secured his position as president, but since more than 500 former politicians were banned from political activity during the campaign the result was a foregone conclusion. Kim Dae-jung was tried for treason and sentenced to death, but so transparent were the charges against him that Chun was forced to commute the sentence to life imprisonment after worldwide protests. Probably the single most important factor which saved Kim was Chun's need for a continued and substantial American military presence in South Korea. Although US President Reagan had just come to power and was intent on keeping American forces there, Chun's insistence on going through with Kim's execution was jeopardising Congressional approval for Reagan's wishes. Kim Dae-jung was eventually released to go to the USA for medical treatment. He stayed on there as a lecturer at Harvard University until his return to Korea in 1987.

Having consolidated his power base, Chun lifted martial law, granted amnesty to quite a few detainees and allowed the National Assembly to debate issues somewhat more freely than was ever possible during Park's presidency. Press censorship, nevertheless, remained tight under a 'voluntary restraint' system.

During an official visit to Burma in late

CHOE HYUNG PUN

CHRIS TAYLOR

MARTIN MOOS

CHRIS TAYLOR

A
B	C
D

People

A: Resting the traditional way, Hahoe Folk Village

B: Guest at a traditional wedding

C: Old man at Sŏkkuram Grotto

D: Colourful costumes, Kyŏngbokkung Palace

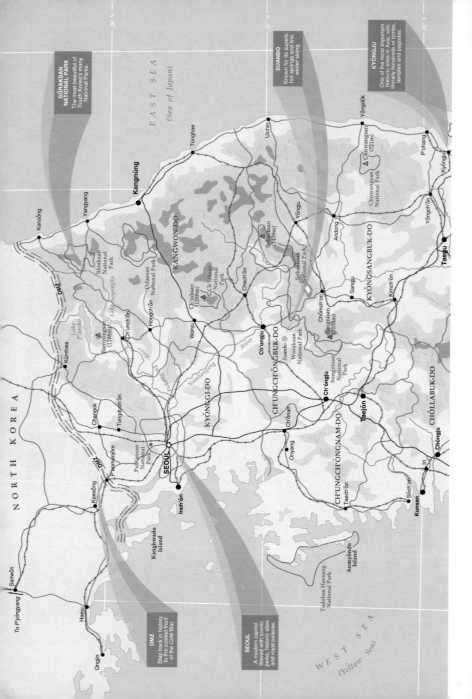

E A S T   S E A
(Sea of Japan)

N O R T H   K O R E A

W E S T   S E A
(Yellow Sea)

To P'yŏngyang
Sariwŏn
Haeju
Ongjin

Kansŏng
Yangyang
Kangnŭng
Tonghae

Kŭmhwa
Samyangsan
(1198m)
Ch'unch'ŏn
Hongch'ŏn
Wŏnju

DMZ
Kaesŏng
P'aenmunjŏm
Changgok
Tongduch'ŏn

Sŏraksan
National
Park
Lake Soyangho
Lake
P'aroho
Odaesan
National Park

KANGWŎN-DO

Ch'iaksan
(1280m)
Ch'iaksan
National
Park
Chech'ŏn

Sŏbaeksan
(189m)
Yŏngju

Uchin

Yŏngdŏk

Chuwangsan
(721m)
Chuwangsan
National
Park

P'ohang

Kyŏngju

Andong
Yŏngch'ŏn

KYŎNGSANGBUK-DO

Sangju
Kimch'ŏn

Taegu

PukKansan
National Park
SEOUL
Inch'ŏn

Kanghwado
Island

KYŎNGGI-DO

Nambangang
River

Ch'ŏnan
Onyang

CH'UNGCH'ŎNGBUK-DO

Ch'ungju
Suanbo
Woraksan
National Park

Songnisan
(1058m)
Songnisan
National
Park

Ch'ŏngju
Taejŏn

Sŏbaeksan
National Park
Ch'ungch'ŏn

CH'UNGCH'ŎNGNAM-DO

Taech'ŏn

Iri
Sŏch'ŏn
Kunsan

Chŏnju

CHŎLLABUK-DO

Annyŏndo
Island

Tadohae Haesang
National Park

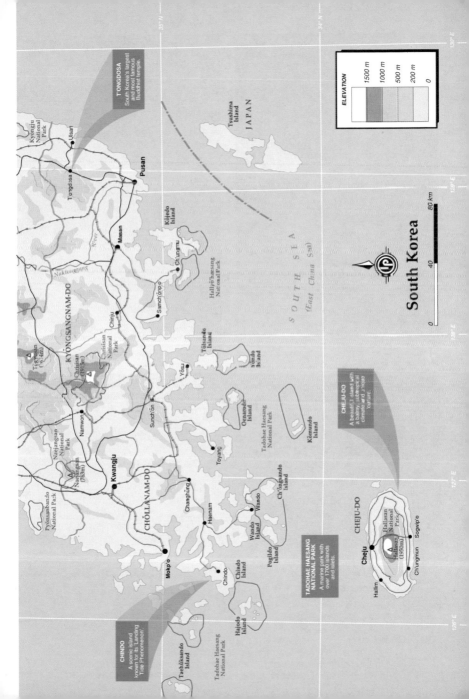

TONGDOSA
South Korea's largest and most famous Buddhist temple.

ELEVATION
1500 m
1000 m
500 m
200 m
0

Kyongju National Park
Ulsan
Tongdosa
Pusan

Tsushima Island
JAPAN

Naktong River

Masan
Kojedo Island

KYŎNGSANGNAM-DO
Chinju
Chungmu
Samch'ŏnp'o

Taegsan (1915m)
Chirisan (1915m)
Chirisan National Park

Hallyŏ-Haesang National Park

SOUTH SEA
(East China Sea)

Namwon
Naejangsan National Park

Sunch'ŏn
Tŏksando Island
Yŏsu
Yŏmdo Island

Pyŏnsanbando National Park
Naebyŏn (763m)

Kwangju

CHŎLLANAM-DO
Changhŭng
Haenam

Toyang
 Onarodo Island
Tadohae Haesang National Park
Kŏmundo Island

Ch'ŏngsando Island

CHEJU-DO
A beautiful island with a balmy subtropical climate and a huge tourist.

Mokp'o
Wando
Wando Island
Poglido Island

Chindo
Chindo Island

TADOHAE HAESANG NATIONAL PARK
A marine park with over 1700 islands and islets.

Hajodo Island
Taehŭksando Island
Tadohae Haesang National Park

CHINDO
A scenic island known for its 'Landing Tide Phenomenon'.

CHEJU-DO
Hallim
Cheju
Hallasan National Park
Hallasan (1950m)
Chungmun
Sogwip'o

South Korea

0   40   80 km

CHRIS TAYLOR

CHRIS TAYLOR

DAVID MASON

Ceremony
A: Traditional costume for a Farmers' Dance, Korean Folk Village
B: On the tightrope between past and present, Korean Folk Village
C: Massed ranks of dancers at the fascinating Sŏkchŏnje Ceremony, Seoul

1983, Chun miraculously escaped assassination at the hands of North Korean agents. In 1987, two North Koreans posing as Japanese tourists bombed a Korean Air flight, causing 115 deaths. Hopes of reunification of the two Koreas remained as remote as ever.

Because of continued opposition to his rule, Chun announced his intention to step down from the presidency in February 1988. Shortly afterwards, Roh Tae-woo, a classmate and confidant of Chun's, was nominated by the ruling party to succeed him. For a while it seemed that real democracy was still just a distant dream.

What happened next took the world by storm. Overnight, thousands of students in every city across the nation took to the streets to demonstrate. They were met by riot police, tear gas and mass arrests and within a matter of days the country was at a flashpoint. The students were quickly joined by tens of thousands of industrial and office workers and even Buddhist monks. Although he threatened Draconian measures to quell the disturbances, Chun largely took a back seat and left Roh to negotiate.

Under intense pressure from America to compromise, and well aware that the government wasn't just confronted with a bunch of radical students, Roh invited the opposition Reunification Democratic Party to talks. The two leaders of the opposition were Kim Young-sam and Kim Dae-jung.

Kim Dae-Jung had returned from exile in the USA the year before; he had been kept virtually under house arrest since then, but the two opposition leaders suddenly found themselves on centre stage. A deal with the government proved to be elusive. Free, direct, popular presidential elections; the release of political prisoners, freedom of the press; and a number of other reforms were all being demanded. However, Roh felt he could not concede to these demands and negotiations were broken off.

But not for long. While massive demonstrations continued on the streets, the country was convulsed by a wave of strikes by industrial workers. Civil war and a military coup were getting dangerously close. Realising this, Chun gave Roh the go-ahead to concede to all of the opposition's demands. The country reeled with a mixture of disbelief and ecstasy and the demonstrations stopped.

The deal set in motion campaigns for the coming presidential elections by both the ruling Democratic Justice Party and the opposition Reunification Democratic Party. At first, it seemed that the two Kims of the opposition party would form an alliance and agree to one of them running for president in order not to split the opposition vote. A lot of pledges were made in this respect early on in the campaign but, in the end, they both announced their candidacy. This proved to be an ill-fated decision.

In the elections which followed (judged to have been the fairest ever held in Korea), neither of the Kims was able to match Roh's share of the vote (37%) though their combined total (55%) was considerably more than Roh's. Roh therefore became the next president and his party the government. There was a good deal of sabre-rattling during the election campaign: various army officers threatened a coup should Kim Dae-jung win, but they were probably restrained by the thought that the 1988 Olympics, scheduled for Seoul, might have to be cancelled if such an event occurred. As a matter of national pride, few people in South Korea wanted to see that happen.

Following the elections there were the inevitable accusations of vote-rigging and electoral fraud, but much of this was simply sour grapes on behalf of the opposition. By failing to compromise and running against one another, the opposition was doomed from the start. Even Kim Young-sam admitted as much when, after the result was announced, he publicly apologised to the country for having failed to reach an agreement with Kim Dae-jung and field a single opposition candidate.

With Roh's power restrained by two powerful opposition parties, some of the heat went out of South Korean politics. The students continued violent demonstrations every spring (coinciding with mid-term exams which were cancelled as a result), but the radicals began to look increasingly out of touch. Roh's government brought forward numerous democratic reforms, giving South Koreans an unprecedented level of freedom to voice their opinions without fear of imprisonment. Restrictions on South Koreans travelling abroad were also lifted.

While the students achieved widespread support for their courageous opposition to the repressive Chun regime, renewed violent protests quickly squandered this goodwill and even produced a strange nostalgia for Chun's military dictatorship. Public disgust sharply increased in 1989 after students set a fire trap which killed seven policemen and injured 30 others at Tongui University in Pusan. The police were on campus at the time to rescue another policeman who had been kidnapped by the students.

The 1990s

Seoul made considerable progress on the diplomatic front by establishing relations with the Soviet Union in September 1990. Another milestone was the re-establishment of diplomatic relations with China in 1992, an act which greatly angered North Korea.

On 18 December 1992 the DLP candidate Kim Young-sam (who had merged his opposition party with the DLP in 1990) won the general election, soundly defeating his old opposition rival, Kim Dae-jung, and the billionaire head of the Hyundai company, Chung Ju-yung.

Immediately after the election, President Kim embarked on his promised anti-corruption campaign. He publicly stated his own net worth at US$2.1 million (almost poverty level for a South Korean president) and then pushed through legislation forcing other government officials to reveal their assets. Revelations of ill-gotten gains forced a number of politicians to resign and senior prosecutor Lee Kun-kae was given an 18-month prison term for accepting bribes. A widely-used loophole for hiding wealth was closed by the passing of a real-name financial transaction act; previously, politicians could hide their income simply by using a fictitious name.

After evidence surfaced in 1995 that former presidents Chun and Roh had pocketed million of dollars in illicit 'campaign contributions', there was a massive public outcry to prosecute both men for bribery and their role in the 1980 'Kwangju Massacre'. Although he resisted at first, President Kim finally supported the necessary legislation to extend the statute of limitations. In August 1996 Chun was given the death sentence and Roh was sentenced to 22 years in prison. Another 14 military officers were prosecuted for their role at Kwangju and nine businessmen were convicted on bribery charges. At the time of this writing, Chun's death sentence had not been carried out and there is much speculation that President Kim will pardon the convicted men just before he leaves office in 1998.

As an opposition politician Kim Young-sam was revered by the student movement, but within a month of being elected president students were denouncing President Kim as the worst dictator in South Korean history. It was at this point that many people came to realise that the student movement organisation Hanchongnyon had fallen under North Korea's sway. As a result, the student movement was reduced to a small, hard-core faction which is unabashedly pro-North Korea.

Korea also has a militant and somewhat leftist union movement that is prone to going on strike – street battles between workers and police have occasionally made world headlines. This hasn't gone unnoticed by the students, who have tried to ally themselves with the unions. Indeed, the media is fond of publicising 'worker/student unrest'. But the student movement has lurched sharply toward North Korea and these alliances have become badly strained. For all their militancy, few workers are enamoured of the students' main cause – reunification with the North.

Nonetheless, the workers showed their mettle in early 1997 when the unions organised crippling nationwide strikes in response to a new labour law that would make it much easier to fire workers. The new law was passed in a secret parliamentary session which rattled the public's nerves – after all, South Korea claims to be a democracy. The strikes and public hostility to the way in which the legislation was passed caused the government to at least partially back down and agree to modify the law.

GEOGRAPHY

The Korean peninsula borders China and Russia in the north, faces China in the west across the Yellow Sea (which the Koreans call the West Sea) and Japan to the east and south across the Sea of Japan (which Koreans label the East Sea). The peninsula is divided roughly in half just north of the 38th parallel between the two countries, North and South Korea.

South Korea's land area is 98,500 sq km, making it slightly larger than Portugal. Its overall length from north to south is approximately 500 km while at its narrowest point it's 216 km wide. Much of the country is mountainous, particularly the east coast. South Korea's highest peak is Hallasan (1950m) in the island province of Cheju-do.

CLIMATE

Korea has four distinct seasons. Autumn is the best time to visit – the forests are riotously colourful – and is at its best in late October and early November. April, May and June are generally good months, before the summer monsoon rains. Winter, from November to March, sees temperatures hovering around both sides of 0°C and it can be bitter in the mountains, where temperatures drop to – 15°C. However, the snow is picturesque.

Cheju-do off the south coast is the warmest place in South Korea and also the wettest. Winter is particularly dreary and will leave you wondering why the whole island doesn't wash away.

ECOLOGY & ENVIRONMENT

Various wars took a serious toll of Korea's environment. The Japanese were not the least bit squeamish about exploiting Korea's resources for their war effort and this meant chopping down trees and digging up useful minerals. Today, however, South Korea is

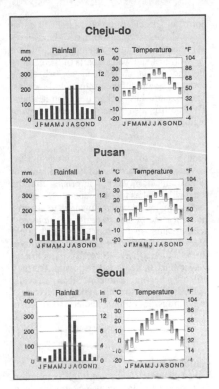

one of the world's leading nations in reafforestation and this effort has paid off.

South Korea is a throwaway-packaging, consumer-oriented society with a heavy emphasis on industrialisation. In recognition of this problem, the use of officially designated rubbish bags has been mandatory for households since 1995. Not using these could result in a fine. The profits from selling these high-priced bags are supposed to be used for government-sponsored environmental projects.

FLORA & FAUNA
Flora

The northern part of South Korea is the coldest region and in this area the flora tends to be alpine. Trees typically found in the north are beech, birch, fir, larch, oak and pine. Moving further south, deciduous trees dominate. The south coast and Cheju-do are the warmest and wettest parts of the country and the vegetation tends to be lush. Some common species of the south include aralias, azaleas, camellias, ginkgo trees and heathers. The south is also Korea's ginseng growing region.

Fauna

Given Korea's history of war and recent industrialisation, it's not surprising that the local wildlife has taken a beating. Nevertheless, some hardy species manage to survive in the remote mountain regions. The largest wild creature in the country is the Korean black bear and deer are reasonably common in the national parks. Siberian tigers are no longer found in Korea and it's possible that they will even become extinct in Siberia as well.

Birds do a reasonably good job of surviving alongside human society. Biologists have identified 379 species of birds in Korea, of which 266 are migratory.

National Parks

Given Korea's small size, high population and booming economy, one would expect to find every tree felled, every beach polluted and every mountainside covered with industrial and housing estates. In fact, the situation is much the opposite. The South Koreans have done a first-rate job of protecting scenic areas and the whole country is dotted with beautiful parks. A lot of travellers have commented that the national parks are perhaps the best of Korea's many fine attractions.

The three most popular national parks are Sŏraksan, Hallasan and Chirisan. In fact, they are so popular that you'd better avoid them during holiday times. The government has already closed a number of walking trails in the most popular parks for up to three years in order to give the wilderness some time to recover from the crush of hikers. Fires and cooking are prohibited in most national parks except in designated camping grounds.

At present there are 20 national parks, listed here in alphabetical order:

Ch'iaksan is in Kangwon-do, east of Wŏnju, and is the site of Kuryongsa (a temple). The summit of Ch'iaksan reaches 1288m.

Chirisan straddles the border of three provinces – Chŏllanam-do, Chŏllabuk-do and Kyŏngsangnam-do. The summit of Chirisan reaches 1751m, making it South Korea's second highest peak. Hwaŏmsa is the most important temple in this park.

Chuwangsan is in Kyŏngsangbuk-do near Ch'ŏngsong.

Hallasan is on Cheju-do. The park is dominated by an extinct volcano, South Korea's highest peak.

Hallyŏ Haesang is off the southern coast near Pusan. There are approximately 400 small islands within the park's boundaries.

Kayasan is in Kyŏngsangbuk-do and Kyŏngsangnam-do, 64 km west of Taegu. The highest peak in the park is 1430m and a temple, Haeinsa, is located here.

Kyeryongsan is in Ch'ungch'ongnam-do, just west of Taejŏn.

Kyŏngju is near the city of the same name in Kyŏngsangbuk-do. Unlike the previously mentioned parks, the attractions here are mainly cultural. Kyŏngju was the capital of the ancient Shilla kingdom and there are many historical relics and temples here.

Naejangsan is just north of Kwangju, straddling the border of Chŏllanam-do and Chŏllabuk-do.

Odaesan is in Kangwon-do, south of Sŏraksan NP.

Puk'ansan is in the northern suburbs of Seoul and is therefore very accessible from the city.

Pyŏnsanbando is on a peninsula in the western part of Chŏllabuk-do. It's dotted with temples such as Naesosa and Kaeamsa.

Sobaeksan straddles the border between Kyŏngsangbuk-do and Ch'ungch'ŏngbuk-do, just to the north of Yŏngju.

Songnisan is 15 km east of Poŭn in Ch'ungch'ŏngbuk-do. Within the park is Pŏpchusa, a famous temple.

Sŏraksan is in Kangwon-do near the city of Sokch'o. This is perhaps South Korea's most beautiful and popular park.

Tadohae Haesang is a huge marine park consisting of hundreds of islands along the south-western tip of Korea. The westernmost part of the park is spectacular Hondo Island.

T'aean Haean is a coastal park at the western end of Ch'ungch'ŏngnam-do.

Tŏgyusan is in Chŏllabuk-do, south-east of Taejŏn.

Wolch'ulsan is known for rugged rock formations. It's in the south-west corner of Chŏllanam-do.

Woraksan is in Ch'ungch'ŏngbuk-do; it is a large and uncrowded park with scenic valleys, forests and temples.

Provincial Parks

There are 19 provincial parks in South Korea and some of them are easily as spectacular as the national parks. Furthermore, provincial parks tend to be relatively uncrowded simply because they are less well known. They are listed here by province:

Kyŏnggi-do

Namhansansŏng This old mountain fortress is about 26 km south-east of central Seoul and makes a good day trip from the city.

Kangwon-do

Kyŏngp'o is another beachside park, but it's very developed and touristy. It's six km north of Kangnŭng.

Taebaeksan (elevation 1568m) is the sixth highest peak in South Korea and is one of the country's three sacred mountains.

Tonghae is also known as Naksan Provincial Park. It's a beachside park offering fine facilities for swimming. Other major sights in the park include Naksansa temple and Uisangdae pavilion.

Kyŏngsangbuk-do

Ch'ŏngnyangsan (elevation 870m) also boasts 11 other scenic peaks, eight caves and a small temple, Ch'ongnyangsa.

Kŭmosan is just outside Kumi City. Kumi is a major industrial area and the park is mostly a recreational area for the local workers.

Mun-gyŏng Saejae straddles the mountain pass connecting Ch'ungch'ŏngbuk-do and Kyŏngsangbuk-do. It's not spectacular, but does feature pleasant scenery.

P'algongsan is north of Taegu and has a big temple called Tonghwasa. There is also a big standing Buddha on the peak of a mountain.

Kyŏngsangnam-do

Kajisan has a collection of major temples, including Sŏngnamsa (right at the mountain), Unmunsa (to the north of the mountain), P'yoch'ungsa (south of the mountain and just outside the park boundary). Nearby (but outside the park) is T'ongdosa, one of the five big temples of Korea.

Yŏnhwasan (477m) is home to one moderate-sized temple, Okch'onsa, and several hermitages.

Chŏllanam-do

Chogyesan (elevation 884m) is the home of Songgwangsa, the main temple of the Chogye sect of Korean Buddhism.

Mudŭngsan (elevation 1187m) is just east of Kwangju City. There are numerous hiking trails and it's a popular walking area for residents of Kwangju. Otherwise it's not spectacular.

Turyunsan (elevation 703m) is the most southwestern peak in Korea and the location of Taehŭngsa, a major Zen meditation temple.

Chŏllabuk-do

Maisan (elevation 685m) means 'horse ears mountain', which roughly describes the shape of the two rocky outcrops which make up the peaks. T'apsa (pagoda temple) is stuck right between the two 'horse ears'.

Moaksan (elevation 794m) is where you'll find Kŭmsansa, a temple famous for Shamanism. It's south-west of Chŏnju.

Sŏnunsan is a beautiful place which boasts a temple (Sŏnunsa) and small sub-temples perched all around a gorge near the sea.

Taedunsan (elevation 878m) is a very small and compact place, but spectacularly beautiful. It's notable for granite spires, cliffs, great views and hiking trails.

Ch'ungch'ongnam-do

Ch'ilgapsan (elevation 561m) is a small but very steep mountain. Temples in this thickly-forested park include Changgoksa and Chonghyesa.

Tŏksan is known for its waterfalls, valleys and hot springs. The largest temple here is Sudoksa. The park is to the west of Ch'ŏnan.

GOVERNMENT & POLITICS

Power emanates from the Blue House (the president's residence and office), which is behind Kyŏngbokkung in Seoul. In theory, the president shares power with the legislative and judicial branches, but in practice the president is far stronger than the entire 299-member National Assembly. The president is democratically elected. There has been no vice-president since the 1960s. The president and members of the National Assembly serve five-year terms.

The prime minister – the head of the cabinet – in theory wields considerable power, but in practice is mostly a figurehead. In the National Assembly, there is one elected member from each constituency and up to 10 non-elected members 'at large' for each party. All the parties have been known to sell the 'at large' seats to the highest bidder

A Perfectly Balanced Flag

The South Koreans may well have the most philosophical flag in the world. The white background represents Confucian 'purity' or the Buddhist concept of 'emptiness'. In the centre lies a *T'aegŭk*, the Taoist symbol of the balance of, or harmony between, opposites. It was adapted from the Chinese, who usually depicted it in black and white and divided it vertically. The Korean version is more colourful and divided horizontally, with the red top half representing Yang (Heaven, day, male, heat, active, construction, etc). The blue lower half represents Yin (Earth, night, female, cold, passive, destruction, etc). These twin cosmic forces cycle perpetually in perfectly balanced harmony, despite their superficial opposition; wisdom doesn't see them as fighting each other, but as two sides of the same coin.

The three lines at each corner, known as trigrams, were borrowed from the most important ancient book of Chinese thought, the *Classic of Changes* (Korean: the Chu Yŏk; Chinese: the I Ching). The

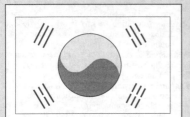

three unbroken bars symbolise Heaven-Creative, while the opposite three broken bars symbolise Earth-Receptive. The trigram in the upper right corner is Water-Treacherous Danger, and in the opposite corner lies Fire-Loyal Love.

Something similar to this flag was created in 1882 by a team of reformist envoys to Japan, as they realised they had no modern standard to represent Korea as an equal among nations. The current design was adopted by the Shanghai-based government-in-exile and became the national flag of the Republic of Korea in 1948. It is called the T'aegŭkki. One may well wonder whether the top half of the horizontally-divided T'aegŭk being red was some sort of omen of the north half of Korea becoming communist. ∎

---

as a means of raising money, but this practice is being increasingly criticised.

Federal judges are appointed by the executive branch and confirmed by the National Assembly. As time goes on South Korea's judiciary has become increasingly independent of politicians.

In early 1990 several parties merged to form the ruling Democratic Liberal Party (whose name was unabashedly cloned from Japan's ruling Liberal Democratic Party). The party has been riven by factions, which has made governing the country a delicate balancing act. The Democratic Party is the main opposition party and has also become factionalised.

ECONOMY

South Korea is one of Asia's 'little tigers' (also called 'little dragons'). In the 1950s Korea began an industrial revolution based on the polluting, low-wage and labour-intensive manufacture of cheap goods for export. These industries are now dying as the country moves upmarket into high technology and service industries. South Korea now enjoys a standard of living approaching that of Hong Kong, Singapore and Taiwan – with significant differences. Unlike the other tigers, South Korea's economy is dominated by huge, corporate conglomerates *(chaebol)*. These companies are concentrated around Seoul, but there are some manufacturing plants in Taegu and Pusan. In more or less descending order, the 'big 10' are: Hyundai, Daewoo, Samsung, LG (Lucky-Goldstar), Sunkyong, Hanjin, Ssangyong, Kia, Hanhaw and Lotte.

Complaining about bureaucracy and high labour costs, most large Korean companies have started to move manufacturing facilities abroad. At the same time, the chaebol have been trying to grab a larger slice of foreign markets and acquire foreign technology. One way to do this is to buy foreign companies and the chaebol have gone on a shopping spree over the past few years. For example, Samsung has purchased AST Research (an

American computer manufacturer) and FGT (a German glass bulb company), though their attempt to buy Fokker (a bankrupt Dutch airline manufacturer) fell through. Hyundai has bought AT&T GIS, a US chip maker. Daewoo purchased FSO, a Polish car manufacturer and at the time of writing was trying to buy Lotus, a British car company. LG bought Zenith, the last American TV maker.

Critics of the chaebol say this strategy is fraught with risks: leading edge companies are seldom for sale and the Koreans have had difficulty retaining the loyalty of their newly acquired foreign staff. Late in 1996 an attempt by Daewoo to buy a French electronics firm, Thomson Multimedia, met with strong opposition from French workers. The French government bowed to domestic pressure and cancelled the deal, which caused the Koreans considerable loss of face and led to accusations of racial discrimination. The jury is still out on the success or failure of this latest corporate buying binge, but for now it seems certain that the chubby chaebol will continue to grow even bigger.

South Koreans often decry the centralisation of wealth into so few channels. The chaebol have not only enormous wealth but also considerable political power; their 'charitable' contributions to the government have raised more than a few eyebrows. The trail of the Hanbo scandal in early 1997, whereby political connections ensured that the bankrupt steel company was kept afloat with bank loans, led perilously close to the door of the Blue House itself.

Not surprisingly, the cosy relationship between big business and government has often provided fertile ground for corruption. Many large companies admit having to pay bribes in order to avoid tax audits, price controls and other problems. Those companies which have offended the government (as happened in 1992 when Hyundai chief Chung Ju-yung ran for president) have suddenly seen their access to cheap credit cut off.

If all this sounds vaguely similar to the Japanese system, that's because it is. Former president Park Chung-hee based the formula for Korea's economic development on the Japanese model (Park was educated in Korea, but studied in a Japanese-run military academy). Indeed, the notion of 'Korea Inc' seems even more valid than the familiar 'Japan Inc'.

As in Japan, the South Korean economic model is *not* a true freewheeling capitalist system. Rather, the government is heavily involved in all sectors of the economy and has built up a formidable bureaucracy to regulate everything from the price of automobiles to the types of snacks restaurants can serve. Bureaucratic controls extend through the chaebol and the banking system, right down to the smallest enterprises. The regulations are often used to keep imports out — one importer of foreign ice cream was told he could only import flavours that were already being produced by Korean manufacturers because 'foreign flavours might hurt Korean stomachs'.

Bureaucratic meddling is widely believed to be doing far more harm than good to South Korea's economy. Many foreign firms have also found Korea's investment climate too harsh and pulled out. This alarmed the Korean government and there were calls for reform. Kim Young-sam's government has committed itself to follow the more liberal trading policies set by the General Agreement on Tariffs & Trade (GATT) and hopes to have South Korea admitted to the OECD (Organisation for Economic Cooperation and Development), which has even stricter rules about economic liberalisation. The government is gradually trying to ease up on regulations governing land use, the banking system, interest rates, foreign exchange controls, price controls and import barriers.

Korean farmers can be very vocal about defending their interests and can generate a good deal of political heat. In 1994, Korea opened 1% of its rice market to imports; farmers protested and students quickly took up their cause, leading to riots. Although the government has bent over backwards to protect domestic farmers from cheap imports, agriculture is clearly declining and import barriers are not likely to save it. If you travel through the countryside at times other than school holidays, you will notice that it seems to be populated almost entirely by the elderly. Indeed, most Korean farmers are over the age of 60; young people flock to the cities in search of a better life. South Korea will almost certainly have to import food in ever larger quantities in the years ahead.

Despite its paternalistic approach to the economy, the government goes light when it comes to social welfare programs. Given the large amounts that South Korea must by necessity spend on defence, there is little cash left over to shovel into free medical care, unemployment benefits and retirement schemes.

Happy Seouls

POPULATION & PEOPLE

The population of South Korea stands at 45.2 million with an annual increase of 0.9% (one of the lowest rates of population growth in Asia). Population density is 458 per sq km – in other words, it's crowded. However, people are very unevenly distributed: over 70% live in urban areas while some mountainous regions remain nearly pristine. About 25% of South Koreans live in the capital, Seoul, but this figure rises to 35% when you include the surrounding suburbs.

Koreans as a group show remarkably few cultural or physical differences. Their origins probably lie in the assimilation of local aboriginal tribes with newcomers of central Asian origin who migrated into the peninsula from around 5000 to 1000 BC.

Korean creation myths suggest that the Koreans are of divine origin: the issue of a heavenly king and a woman who started life as a bear. The bear became human by living on 20 cloves of garlic in a cave for 100 days. (The Korean obsession with the pungent garlic clove apparently started early.) The bear element in the myth is shared by Siberian creation myths, backing up the hypothesis of the central Asian origins of the Koreans.

There are no real ethnic minorities in Korea other than foreign expats. Well over 100,000 expats live in South Korea at the moment, with a nationality breakdown as follows: Americans 20.2%, Chinese 17.5%,

Canadians 17.3%, Japanese 8.5%, Filipinos 8.2%, Vietnamese 5.2%, Indonesians 3.1%, Germans 0.9%, Britons 0.8% and other nationalities 18.3%.

EDUCATION
Korean Education

Needless to say, the han'gŭl alphabet (as opposed to the old system of writing in Chinese characters) has been a boon and the literacy rate in South Korea has now reached 96%. For most Koreans, 12 years of education is the norm (from age 6 through 18 years).

As in Japan, gaining entrance to a university is a formidable task and students are pushed, pulled and badgered for years by their parents to prepare for the much-feared entrance exams. Preparation begins at an early age, so getting into a good elementary school is important. One reason why virtually all Koreans want to live in Seoul is because the best schools are there. The 'examination hell' has profound effects on Korean society. Pity the poor middle school students who must spend all evening, weekends and holidays studying. For those who don't commit suicide, the final irony is that if they pass the entrance exams they can look forward to a four-year study-free holiday –

university students are practically guaranteed to graduate no matter how poor their academic performance.

In the past, academically unqualified children from well-to-do families simply bribed their way into universities, but this is now highly illegal and parents who indulge in this practice can be imprisoned. However, wealthy families can still hire private tutors, in the process creating lucrative jobs for foreign English teachers.

Schools for Foreigners

There are several schools in Seoul catering to the children of expat workers. If this interests you, try contacting one of the following:

Centennial Christian School, 2-22 Namsan-dong, Chung-gu (☎ 773-8460)

French School, San 85-24, Panp'o-dong, Soch'o-gu (☎ 535-1158)

Hanyong School of Foreign Language, 166 Sang-il-dong, Kangdong-gu (☎ 429-0360)

Samyuk Foreigners' School, San 6-2, Hwigyong-dong, Tongdaemun-gu (☎ 248-8682)

Seoul Academy, 988-5 Taech'i-dong, Kangnam-gu (☎ 554-1690)

Seoul Foreigners' Academy, 55 Yonhui-dong, Sodaemun-gu (☎ 335-5101/5)

Seoul German School, 4-13 Hannam-dong, Yongsan-gu (☎ 792-0797)

Seoul International School, San 32-16, Pokchong-dong, Chung-gu (☎ 233-4551/2)

Seoul Liberty Foreigners' School, 260-7 Pogwang-dong, Yongsan-gu (☎ 792-4116/7)

ARTS
Music

Korean traditional music *(kugak)* resembles the traditional music of China and Japan. There is much emphasis on stringed instruments, such as the *kayagum*, and other popular instruments include chimes, cymbals, drums, horns and flutes.

Traditional music can be divided into two categories: court music *(chŏngak)* and folk music *(minsogak)*. Court music was the favourite of the upper crust, much as opera and classical orchestras were the province of Europe's aristocrats in the 19th century. Its melodies tend to be slow and serious.

Folk music (you might call it 'traditional pop music') was for the masses. It's definitely played faster than court music and is more lively. In times past it was a favourite of farmers and today is still played to accompany Shamanistic rituals.

Dance

Traditional Korean folk dances take a wide variety of forms. The most popular ones include drum dances *(sungmu)*, mask dances *(t'alchum)* and solo improvisational dances *(salpuri)*.

Of the three, the drum dances are definitely the most exciting and require a great deal of skill to execute. The dancers perform

Korean music resembles other East Asian music in that it emphasises tone rather than melody, but it differs in having its own rhythm.

in brightly coloured costumes while twirling a very long tassel from a cap on their heads. Making it all the more difficult is the fact that the drums are not set on the ground, but are instead suspended from a cloth strap draped around the dancer's neck and shoulder. Tremendous co-ordination is required to dance, twirl and play the drums at the same time without falling flat on one's face. Not surprisingly, drum dance shows are a big hit with foreign visitors and you should definitely try to catch one while you're in Korea. Audience participation is often welcome at the end – much fun!

Pottery

Archaeologists have unearthed bits and pieces of Korean pottery dating back 10,000 years. Glazing is a skill the Koreans seem to have learned from the Chinese between about 200 and 600 AD; it wasn't long before they introduced their own innovations. During the Koryŏ dynasty (918 to 1392 AD), Korea turned out celadon pottery with a blue-green tinge which the Chinese sought at high prices.

The pottery business took a turn for the worse when the Mongols invaded: during the 12th century the Koreans mostly produced *p'unchŏng* ware, which was greyish with simple folk designs. Nevertheless, it was admired by the Japanese and led to the Imjin War (sometimes called the 'Pottery War') – during which whole families and villages of Korean potters were abducted and resettled in Japan to produce the goods for their new masters. This is still something of a sore point with the Koreans.

Perhaps the perfection of Korean pottery came during the Chosŏn period (1392 to 1910) when the country started turning out stunning white porcelain. This was much admired by both the Chinese and Japanese elites.

Literature

The monk Illyŏn wrote *Samguk Yusa* ('Myths & Legends of the Three Kingdoms') in the 12th century; it remains the most important work of early Korean literature. It's also a good read in English.

Beginning with the Chosŏn dynasty, Korean literature gets more interesting. There were many forms of poetry based on Chinese models (and still written in Chinese characters) and the first real Korean novel, *The Legend of Mr Hong Kil-dong*, dates from this time.

The han'gŭl writing system (introduced in the 14th century) gave a major boost to Korean literature, but it wasn't widely adopted until the late 19th century because most of the nation remained illiterate.

The Japanese takeover (1910-45) had a huge impact on Korean literature. After the occupation ended, there was a sharp turn away from Chinese and Japanese influence of all kinds. Western influence – especially after the Korean War – was dramatic.

One of the best known novelists of the 20th century is Ahn Cheong-hyo. Ahn is notable because he writes the same novel in both Korean and English! Two famous ones are *Silver Stallion* (about the Korean War) and *White Badge* (about Koreans fighting in the Vietnam War). Both have been made into Korean movies.

The 1970s and 1980s produced much dissident literature which was popular with Korea's youth. The 1990s have seen a Taoist-style ecological consciousness literary movement. Cho Chong-nae's 10-volume novel *The Taebaek Mountains* covers the period 1945-55 and has been popular in this decade. A lot of recent works are now being translated into English. Much of the best poetic energy these days goes into the lyrics of popular songs.

Architecture

Good examples of Korean traditional architecture can be found in temples, shrines, palaces and gates. This style is characterised by massive wooden beams set on stone foundations; they are often built with notches instead of nails and thus can be dismantled and moved. Roofs tend to be made from heavy clay tiles.

Seoul can boast the nation's best architecture, both traditional and modern. The best Chosŏn remains would have to be Kyŏngbokkung Palace, renovated in loving detail.

Ondol the Floor

Korea's architectural gift to the world is its unique underfloor heating system known as *ondol*. In winter the entire floor is heated, turning it into a giant radiator. In traditionally constructed houses coal was burned in an oven under a clay floor. The problem with this design was the real danger of carbon monoxide poisoning if the floor developed any cracks. Concrete floors more or less solved the problem, but modern houses use an even safer system - hot water pumped through pipes in the floor. The older style ondol is very rare now and there is little likelihood that you'll encounter the carbon monoxide problem.

Traditionally, Koreans slept on the floor, though these days western-style beds are catching on. Not surprisingly, many Koreans (and for that matter, foreigners too) abandon their bed for the floor during the winter months. There's nothing quite so cosy, nor quite so Korean, as sleeping on a hot floor in the dead of winter! ■

Of course, the great gates of the city, such as Namdaemun and Tongdaemun, are worth a mention. The Korean Folk Village in Suwon gives a good idea of traditional village architecture for the masses. The Japanese left their mark too (eg Seoul City Hall and the former National Museum), but Korean nationalists are intent on removing these symbols of an unhappy past.

Sculpture

Traditional sculpture mainly comprises stone Buddhist statues and pagodas. The best free-standing Buddha is at Sŏkkuram (see the Kyŏngju section in the Kyŏngsangbuk-do chapter). The best relief carving is the 11-head Kwansŭm Posal just behind him!

Kyŏngju also chips in with excellent Shilla pagodas, such as the ones at Pulguksa. Shilla pagodas are three storeys high, simple and elegant; those of Koryŏ have a different style; and those from the Chosŏn dynasty are in a variety of overly fancy styles.

The best stone sculptures are found on mountain temples and hermitages; cast bronze was more common for Buddhas and bells in urban temples.

Shamanist wood carvings (used as spirit guardian posts in villages) are found all over the country and modern versions are increasing in popularity (even leftist radicals have adopted them to their cause). Stone versions of spirit-guardians can sometimes be seen. The 'grandfather stones' of Chejudo are a variation on the theme.

Confucianists didn't create sculpture – it was considered 'too Buddhist'.

Modern sculpture is burgeoning and the Seoul area is rich in newly developed 'art sculpture parks' such as Taehangno (University St) and Olympic Park. In Kyŏnggi-do try the National Museum of Modern Art (in Seoul Grand Park) or the Hoam Art Museum inside Yong-in Everland. On Chejudo there's the Cheju Art Park.

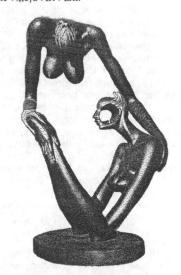

Modern sculpture in Seoul's
Taehangno Art Street

Film

Korea produces plenty of films, but there are no multi-million dollar budgets, as in Hollywood, and consequently no big box office hits like *Rambo* and *Terminator* (which could be a blessing in disguise). In fact, financing Korean films has been a big problem, in part because the government has forbidden the chaebol (who have all the cash) to finance studios for fear of 'cultural hegemony'.

Western films are so popular that the government encourages the production of Korean films by forcing cinemas to limit foreign movies to 60% of the total shown. The problem is that even the 40% of the movies which must be Korean have not been able to break even. Indeed, cinemas have had no choice but to subsidise the Korean film industry with box office revenue from showing foreign films – otherwise, there would simply not be enough Korean films to fill the quota.

Most Korean cinema resembles western-style soap operas – low-budget stories of romance, jealousy, violence (decidedly mild) and people's everyday lives. There is very little sex in Korean movies largely thanks to government censorship, though this is now being relaxed.

If you travel much in Korea, you'll probably get to see a Korean movie even if you never set foot inside a cinema. This is because Korean-made videos are often shown on long-distance buses and ferries, not to mention the TV set in your hotel room. Unfortunately, it's hard for westerners to follow the story line because the dialogue is entirely in Korean and English subtitling is extremely rare. Nonetheless, a few films are subtitled in English because the producers hope to enter international film festivals – you can occasionally see these films in Seoul so check the English-language newspapers for announcements.

Theatre

Modern theatre is one area in which Koreans excel, be it adaptations of western drama or locally written and produced plays. Seoul, in particular, has a large number of theatres, mostly concentrated in the area known as Taehangno (University St). If you go to Taehangno, it's easy enough to find out what's on: posters pasted on ubiquitous noticeboards advertise current offerings.

The big problem for foreigners is, of course, language. Virtually no plays are performed in any other language but Korean. Unless you bring along your own translator, you'll have to be satisfied admiring the costumes rather than the dialogue.

Opera

Traditional operas also take different forms. A solo storyteller singing to the beat of a drum while telling a story (and sometimes waving a paper fan) is called *p'ansori*. Somewhat more similar to western opera is *ch'ang*, which can involve a large cast of characters.

Calligraphy

The art of writing with brush pens and ink originated in China, but the Koreans have adopted this skill to suit their own needs. Calligraphy can be done in both traditional Chinese *(hanja)* characters or in the Korean phonetic alphabet (hangŭl). Calligraphy is most common in temples, art galleries and museums, but you could stumble across it anywhere – in souvenir shops, people's homes and on the decorative signs that some shops hang out, for example.

Painting

Chinese influence is definitely visible in traditional Korean paintings. The basic tools (brush and water-based ink) are those of calligraphy, which influenced painting in both technique and theory. The brush line, which varies in thickness and tone, is the important feature of a Korean painting.

The first westerners to visit both China and Korea criticised Oriental watercolour paintings, finding them flat and lacking in depth, shading and realism. The Koreans in turn were astonished by the oil paintings brought in from the west, which to them resembled mirror images: in the end they rejected them as art because they were devoid of expressive brushwork and imagination.

Hanja

Before the invention of the hangŭl alphabet in the 15th century, Korean was written exclusively in Chinese characters known as *hanja*. Around 70% of all Korean dictionary entries are of Chinese origin, although the two languages are completely unrelated. The words borrowed from Chinese are apparent to anyone who has studied both languages. For example, 'mountain' is *shan* in Chinese and *san* in Korean; 'south' is *nan* in Chinese and *nam* in Korean.

Hangŭl is much easier to learn than hanja, so in 1970 President Park Chung-hee banned hanja in an attempt to increase literacy. Furthermore, the hangŭl alphabet is Korea's own invention, while Chinese characters are an exotic import and thus an insult to national pride. The Koreans were further infuriated by the fact that the Japanese (who also use Chinese characters) tried to force Korea to abandon hangŭl and adopt hanja during their occupation of the peninsula.

The South Koreans had a sudden change of heart in 1975. Hanja was restored to high school textbooks, but placed in parentheses after the hangŭl words. The Ministry of Education drew up an official list of 1800 hanja characters which Korean students had to learn. Korean dictionaries identify 4888 characters, but very few Koreans know even half of these. Ironically, the ban on hanja remains in elementary schools, though it is not enforced and private elementary schools often teach hanja.

Interest in the learning of Chinese characters was boosted in 1993 when Korea established diplomatic relations with China. However, it has been complicated by the fact that communist China simplified 2238 characters in the 1950s, thus making them look very different from hanja (which is based on traditional Chinese). The traditional characters are still used in Hong Kong and Taiwan, and now there is a serious movement afoot in mainland China to return the characters to their original complex form.

Nowadays, very few South Koreans are functionally literate in hanja. The use of the traditional Chinese characters is usually restricted to maps, small sections of newspapers, restaurant signs and occasionally the writing of names (as in name cards).

North Korea banned the use of Chinese characters until 1964. Officially, North Korean students are expected to learn around 2000 Chinese characters, though it's questionable how many of them really do. Certainly the shortage of reading material in the North would mean that few have the opportunity to practice hanja. ■

The function of traditional landscape painting was to substitute for nature, allowing the viewer to wander imaginatively. The painting is meant to surround the viewer, and there is no 'viewing point' as there is in western painting.

Of course, times change and modern Korean artists study both traditional Oriental and western techniques. Examples of both traditional and modern painting can be seen at galleries all over Korea; Insadong in Seoul is particularly good.

SOCIETY & CONDUCT
Traditional Culture
Meeting the Koreans Koreans don't bow as frequently as the Japanese, but a short nod or bow is considered respectful when greeting somebody or departing.

Korea is probably the most Confucian nation in North-East Asia and even more so

than China, where Confucianism originated. This makes for some behaviour that many westerners take time to get used to. At the heart of Confucian doctrine are the so-called Five Relationships. These prescribe behaviour between ruler and subject, father and son, husband and wife, old and young, and between friends. This structuring of relationships is very important in making sense of Korean society, as well as the nearby cultures of China and Japan.

Newly arrived visitors to Korea may remark on the jostling of the crowds, the queue jumpers, inconsiderate driving and the tendency of the locals to be late for appointments. However, to put it down to plain rudeness would be somewhat off the mark. All relationships require a placement in some sort of hierarchy for one party to determine how to behave with respect towards another. The middle-aged male office worker thrusting ahead of you to pay for a Coke at the 7-Eleven store does not even register your presence. You, as a foreigner, have not been introduced and he has nowhere to place you on the scale of relationships. An introduction and an exchange of business cards would immediately place you into a category that would demand certain behaviour from him.

Once contact has been established everything changes. Most Koreans are extremely courteous and will go out of their way to accommodate you. Korean rules of etiquette are fairly complex, but allowances will be made for foreigners.

Koreans are a proud people who enjoy boasting of their 5000 year cultural heritage and ethnic uniqueness. This pride is complicated by what many Koreans feel to be the indignity of their turbulent recent history: the occupation by the Japanese, the carving up of the country by foreign powers and the presence of American armed forces personnel. This means you should be aware in your dealings with Koreans that they are very sensitive to any perceived slights of their culture. It is a good idea to behave pleasantly when bargaining over prices, and to avoid contentious remarks regarding Korea and its culture when chatting with Koreans.

You are likely to encounter peculiar kinds of strongly held opinions from Koreans themselves. Examples might be that the han'gŭl script is the most perfect writing system in the world or that there is no such thing as homosexuality in Korea. There is probably not much point arguing about these kinds of issues.

Social Hierarchy Korean relationships are much complicated by the social hierarchy – persons with higher status may well act arrogant and demeaning towards persons with lower status. High status is governed by many factors – for example, who is the older of the two? Who has the more prestigious job? Who attended the better university or primary school?

This notion of social status is one aspect of Korean culture that many foreigners (who

prefer equality) find unpleasant. Especially if you're working in Korea, your employer could possibly make it all too clear that he or she is on the top of the social totem pole and you are at the bottom. But for simple tourists, this is seldom a problem – indeed, the Koreans are most anxious to make a good impression and therefore visitors are accorded considerable respect. Then again, it does depend on which country you're from – people from rich countries have a higher position in the social hierarchy than those from developing nations.

The Family The ideal of the Confucian household is 'five generations under one roof'. In times past, the mortality rate rarely allowed this to happen, but when the old people hung on, it was common for grandparents, parents and their children to live together. Koreans find the idea of packing off their parents to an old people's home abhorrent. Usually it is the responsibility of the eldest son to live with the parents, even after marriage. Today, despite the increasing prevalence of the nuclear family, this tradition still exerts a lot of pressure on young Korean men.

In the past, marriages were always arranged. Traditionally the young couple had no contact until the night of the wedding. In modern Korea couples generally marry for romantic reasons, but this should not obscure the fact that family approval remains of paramount importance. Parental choice is based on more 'practical' considerations (such as background, education, job prospects and, in the case of women, ability to fulfil the domestic duties of marriage).

Men & Women Korea is still very much a male-oriented society and women's rights have been slow in becoming an issue. There is traditionally a clear delineation in the respective responsibilities of men and women. In general terms it can be said that the male preserve is public, while women cater to the private, personal world of the home. These values have lingered into the 1990s, with Korean public life very much

Desperately Seeking Kim

There are only a few hundred surnames in Korea. More than 20% of the population use the surname 'Kim' and 15% are named 'Lee', though there are some variations in the Romanised spellings. In traditional Confucian culture, it is considered incest to marry someone with the same surname (thus, the same clan), which certainly limits marriage prospects among Koreans! Some Koreans have ignored the law and have lived together for years (and even had children) despite a legal ban. A temporary law was passed in 1988 (and expired at the end of 1996) permitting these cohabiting couples to legalise their union. There is talk of repealing the law that bans people of the same clan from marrying, but this legal change is bitterly opposed by the Confucianists (who seem to wield considerable political power).

The vast majority of Korean surnames are only one syllable in length, while the given name is usually (but not always) a two-syllable word separated by a hyphen (in Romanised form). Thus, a name like Kim Chung-hi would be typical. However, for the benefit of foreigners, some Koreans reverse the order on their namecards; thus, the preceding example would become Chung-hi Kim. Just look for the hyphen to figure out which is the given name. Most Koreans will insist that you call them by their family name until you get to know them very well, so it's just 'Kim' or 'Lee'. This means that if you stay in the country for any length of time, you will soon have dozens of friends with the same name – it's quite a drag when you get a written message saying 'Kim called at 4 pm and wants you to call back'.

With few exceptions, Koreans will not assume English nicknames even for the purpose of taking an English class. This means that if you teach English in Korea and say, 'Kim, please answer the question', you can expect about a dozen answers at once. In general, students will not appreciate any attempts to give them English names, so don't even try. This is in sharp contrast to China, where every student wants an English nickname. ■

---

dominated by men. Even the traditional separation of male-female education lingers in some of the women's universities in Seoul.

Nevertheless, compared to the Yi dynasty of not so long ago, a woman's lot has improved considerably. There is virtual equality in access to education and women, admittedly in very small numbers, have entered politics. As in many other nations, the corporate world is mostly a male domain, but many women do attain lower-level managerial positions. Furthermore, young Koreans often participate in non-segregated activities, such as evenings out and hikes, that were rare even 10 years ago.

Although two-worker families are becoming more common in South Korea, and particularly in Seoul, women usually accept lower paid, more menial positions. Many working women are also expected to retain their traditional household responsibilities, putting an additional strain on them. Korean male office workers are expected to make frequent appearances in after-hours drinking bouts and spend much of their free time in the company of male colleagues. Such situations exclude women. When guests visit the men will often sit and eat together, separately from the women who will grab a bite together between preparing food. The younger generation is starting to challenge these customs.

The one area where Korean women have some authority is in the control of family finances. A husband is expected to hand over his salary (at least most of it) to his wife, and she is then supposed to pay all the bills.

Women do not assume their husband's family name when getting married. This has nothing to do with women's rights; rather, it's because Koreans traditionally consider families to be based on 'blood ties'.

Women are still expected to be virgins when they marry and many Korean girls will go so far as to have their virginity 'restored' surgically if they've already lost it. The idea that women should be capable of enjoying sex is also a somewhat new and radical idea in Korea. Not so long ago wives were regarded as little more than domestic help and men were as likely as not to seek female companionship elsewhere.

Where Have All the Girls Gone?

A dire shortage of marriageable women is looming over South Korea's social future and, by the early 21st century, many Korean men will find it almost impossible to win a Korean bride.

It was recently reported in the press that 115.6 male babies were born for every 100 girls in 1993. In 1995 just 47.9% of primary school pupils were female, meaning that there were already about 200,000 'extra' boys aged 6 to 11, and in some classes less than 30% of students were female. By the year 2010 it is estimated that there will be 128 single men at 'peak marriage age' (27 to 30 years old) for every 100 single women at peak eligibility (age 24 to 27). And the mismatch in numbers gets worse every year.

What's going wrong? Most young families these days want only two children and one of each gender is seen as ideal. Two sons are acceptable and if the second child is a boy they'll usually stop having children. But two daughters are not. If the first born child is a girl, ultrasound scans are used to discover the gender of the foetus of any further pregnancies. If female, there is a good chance she will be aborted. This may continue until a son is produced or the couple gives up (usually at the woman's insistence). This pattern results in the increasing gender imbalance – and severe marital stress for those yet without a son.

It is now illegal in South Korea for doctors to inform prospective parents of the sex of their foetus following sonagram or other tests, but this restriction has been widely ignored. A cash 'gift' generally loosens the physician's tongue and then may lead to a nominally illegal abortion if the foetus is reported as female. Although these laws have been on the books for over a decade, the very first arrest of any doctor for violating them was carried out in September 1996. The busted doc was a woman.

So why don't Koreans want daughters? The answers lie mostly in the strong residual Neo-Confucianism of their social mores. It remains all-important that a man's family name be passed on to future generations. Only males can properly perform the ancestor worship ceremonies that are still widely practised. Economic security in the golden years is a further concern, despite the rise in western-style pension systems and the sharp decline in the actual practice of sons caring for aged parents. Ironically, there is a growing awareness that in adult life, daughters, married or not, do much more for mum and dad than sons ever do. Modern wags acknowledge modern sons' lack of 'filial piety' by saying 'Every set of Korean parents needs a son, so they'll have a daughter-in-law to take care of them in their old age'.

The growing gender imbalance is now well known, but there seems to be an element of selfishness among young parents: they all want *other* couples to supply future brides for their sons, but don't wish to supply more than one bride themselves. A factor in this is the expense of marrying a daughter off; this was traditionally minor, but it has grown exponentially since the Korean War.

This is expected to change radically in the next decade or two. It may start costing a whole lot of money to marry a son to an attractive, well-educated Korean woman, presuming he can find one. Many other worrisome social trends now predicted by the Korean media include rises in involuntary bachelorhood, rapes, prostitution, kidnapping and harassment of young women, and a sharp population drop (baby bust) in the next century.

Exacerbating the trend is the continuing gender imbalance of marriage to foreigners. About three weddings of Koreans and foreigners are registered with the government every day; more than 80% of them involve Korean women and foreign men. No one has yet seriously proposed legally banning Korean girls from marrying non-Korean men, but it would be no surprise if a 'social movement' discouraging such unions suddenly materialised.

Theoretically, South Korea could 'import' young women from other countries as Japan is now doing for their own lonely bachelors. However, only fair-skinned North-East Asian brides are usually seen as acceptable to Korean men. Darker skinned brides from South-East Asia are likely to be disqualified by most Korean families because of racial and cultural considerations. North Korea may prove to be a treasure-trove of eligible (and willing) girls, since genders seem to be in fair balance there, but it cannot be tapped until the current regime falls. Further, most of Korea's north-east Asian neighbours such as Japan, China and Taiwan have similar bride shortages. The final factor against an import solution is that few non-Korean women can endure the behaviour typical of Korean men.

This points to what may be the biggest social change to come from the rising gender imbalance: Korean men may start treating 'their' women much better than ever before. Look for gentlemanly behaviour to increase while most kinds of physical, emotional and mental abuse decline sharply. As South Korean men have to compete ever more fiercely to gain and keep their brides the social status of Korean women may make a historic leap forward! ∎

Lunar Calendar

Rat	1924	1936	1948	1960	1972	1984	1996
Ox/Cow	1925	1937	1949	1961	1973	1985	1997
Tiger	1926	1938	1950	1962	1974	1986	1998
Rabbit	1927	1939	1951	1963	1975	1987	1999
Dragon	1928	1940	1952	1964	1976	1988	2000
Snake	1929	1941	1953	1965	1977	1989	2001
Horse	1930	1942	1954	1966	1978	1990	2002
Goat	1931	1943	1955	1967	1979	1991	2003
Monkey	1932	1944	1956	1968	1980	1992	2004
Rooster	1933	1945	1957	1969	1981	1993	2005
Dog	1934	1946	1958	1970	1982	1994	2006
Pig	1935	1947	1959	1971	1983	1995	2007

Geomancy *(pungsu)* Derived from the Chinese characters meaning 'wind and water', geomancy is the art of remaining in proper physical harmony with the universe. If a Korean person finds that their business is failing, a geomancer might be consulted. Sometimes the solution will be to move the door of the business establishment, at other times the solution may be to relocate an ancestor's grave.

Korea's former and present rulers have all understood the importance of geomancy. When one empress died, 16 hours were spent arranging the feet of her corpse to get them into an auspicious position before the funeral could commence. The palaces and temples of Seoul have all been correctly arranged according to the laws of geomancy. When the Japanese came to conquer Korea, they deliberately constructed their Capitol building to obstruct the geomantic 'axis of power' on which the nation's fate was hinged.

In this day of modern high-rises and housing estates, most Koreans have had to push aside concerns about which direction their home or business is oriented. However, the position of an ancestor's grave is still taken very seriously.

Zodiac *(shipijikan)* The Korean zodiac is the same as that used by the Chinese. As in the western system of astrology, there are 12 signs of the Korean zodiac. Unlike the western system, your sign is based on which year rather than which month you were born, though the exact day and time of your birth are also carefully considered in charting your astrological path.

Fortune tellers are common in Korea. Making use of astrology, palmistry and face reading, fortune tellers claim they can accurately predict the future. If you are so inclined, you can try out this service, though you are almost certain to need an interpreter since few can speak English.

If you want to know your sign in the Korean zodiac, look up your year of birth in the above chart (future years are given so you know what's coming). However, it's a little more complicated than this because Korean astrology goes by the lunar calendar. The lunar New Year usually falls in late January or early February, so the first month will be included in the year before.

It's said that the animal year chart originated when Buddha commanded all the beasts of the earth to assemble before him. Only 12 animals came and they were rewarded by having their names given to a specific year. Buddha also decided to name each year in the order in which the animals arrived – the first was the rat, then the ox, tiger, rabbit and so on.

Lunar Calendar The Korean lunar calendar is another borrowing from China and it's also used by other countries in the region, including Japan, Taiwan, Vietnam and Mongolia.

Lunar dates do not correspond exactly with solar dates because a lunar month is slightly shorter than a solar month. The Koreans add an extra month every 30 months to the lunar calendar, essentially creating a lunar leap year. Thus, the lunar New Year can fall anywhere between 21 January and 28 February on the Gregorian calendar (the calendar westerners are familiar with). Were it not for the lunar leap year, the solar and lunar seasons would get totally out of synchronisation.

The Koreans believe that their race was born precisely in the year 2333 BC. Therefore, the year 1997 is 4330 in the traditional calendar and you'll find this date printed on Korean-made calendars even now.

Dos & Don'ts

Losing Face The one thing to bear in mind is the Korean concept of *kibun*, a sense of well-being or harmony between people. In practice this is very similar to the idea of 'face'. Efforts are made to smooth over potential problems, such as remarks that could lead to political disagreements. If you say something silly, there will be, at the most, an embarrassed laugh before someone steers the topic on to safer ground. Arguments, or any situation that is going to lead to one party having to back down, will involve a loss of face and this is a big no-no in East Asian cultures. Be sure not to accidentally put yourself in a situation where you cause someone else to lose face.

Unlucky Numbers When the Koreans borrowed the Chinese counting system, they also borrowed the 'unlucky' number four. It's unlucky because it also sounds just like the Korean word for death *(sa)*, which was also borrowed from Chinese. If you have any Korean friends coming to visit you in your own country, you probably should not check them into a 4th floor hotel room. This will not be a problem in Korea itself, because most hotels have no 4th floor and hospitals *never* do.

Body Language Beckoning someone is done with the palm down and fluttering

fingers – avoid pointing or gesturing with one finger at somebody as this is considered impolite.

Deadly Chopsticks Sticking your chopsticks upright into rice is a definite no-no. This is a gesture of symbolic significance when making offerings of food to the dead. Like other peoples in this part of the world, the Koreans are extremely superstitious when it comes to anything relating to death and a faux pas like this one would create extreme embarrassment to your hosts or fellow diners.

Don't Touch One thing worth bearing in mind is that a foreign man with a Korean woman (or a woman who looks Korean) runs a particularly high risk of being the recipient of Korean male belligerence. The woman will also be given a hard time. If you are male accompanying a Korean female friend, you are advised not to get intimate (like holding hands) in public.

Red Ink Don't write a note in red ink. If you want to give someone your address or telephone number, write in any colour but red. Red ink conveys a message of unfriendliness. If you're teaching in Korea it's OK to use red ink to correct students' papers, but if you write extensive comments or suggestions on the back of the paper use some other colour.

Proper Dress In general, Koreans dress very well and very neatly, even in hot weather. Shorts can be worn, but again the emphasis is on dress shorts, not cut-offs. A new trend is high-tech 'sports sandals', but thongs are never worn outdoors. Long hair on men is very rare, as is any facial hair. Men never wear earrings. Male travellers who show up wearing a ragged T-shirt, shorts, a beard, long hair and earrings are asking to be treated like circus freaks. In recent years, women have been showing more skin – the government has threatened to recruit a special police force to fine women who dress 'too provocatively'!

RELIGION

There are four broad streams of influence in the Korean spiritual and ethical outlook: Shamanism, which originated in central Asia; Buddhism, which entered Korea from China around the 4th century AD; Confucianism, a system of ethics of Chinese origin; and Christianity, which first made inroads into Korea in the 18th century. To a certain extent Shamanism has been stigmatised by modern education as a form of superstition and about half of all Koreans nowadays profess to be religious sceptics. But Shamanism continues to be an active cultural force and official records claim that there are 40,000 registered Shamanist priests (mudang) in South Korea. Anthropologists maintain that, as many mudang do not register, the actual figure is perhaps closer to 100,000.

Shamanism is thought to have had a significant influence on other religions entering Korea. Buddhism certainly made itself more accessible to the common people by incorporating Shamanistic rites and identifying Buddhist saints with Shamanistic gods. Similarities have been noted between Pentecostal Christian services and certain elements of Shamanistic ritual, which could help explain the popularity of Christianity in Korea.

Shamanism

Shamanism is not an organised religion. It has no temples, no body of scriptures or written texts. Nonetheless, it is an important part of the Korean religious experience. Central to Shamanism is the mudang, whose role is to serve as an intermediary between the living and the spirit worlds. The mediating is carried out through a kut, a ceremony that includes dance, song and even dramatic narrative. Mudang are almost always female and find their calling in one of two ways. The most common is through inheritance of the skill from ancestors, but mudang may also acquire their spiritual connections after being possessed by a spirit themselves. After the spirit has been 'enshrined' in the body of the mudang, she can then go on to study kut rituals with an experienced mudang. This period of study can take anywhere from two to 10 years.

Shamanist ceremonies are held for a variety of reasons. At a most basic level they might be held on the occasion of a minor illness or before setting out on a journey. In this case the arrangements will be a simple affair of some food offerings and a prayer offered by a mudang. While praying the mudang simply rubs her hands together. Strictly speaking, a ceremony of this kind is known as a pison. More serious matters, such as deep financial problems, will require a more elaborate ceremony known as a kosa. In ceremonies of this kind the mudang is required to communicate human wishes to the spirit world by dance and song accompanied by drums and cymbals. Finally, the kut itself is a more elaborate affair with many participants. It might be held to send a deceased family member safely into the spirit world, or it might be held by a village on a regular basis to ensure the safety and harmony of its members.

It is remarkable that Shamanism has survived as long as it has. It has been subject to persecution since early in the Yi dynasty. Its practitioners are female and usually uneducated and for this reason it is scorned most by educated urban males. Yet many Koreans continue to turn to mudang for solace and assistance.

Buddhism

The founder of Buddhism was Siddhartha Gautama. He was born around 563 BC at Lumbini, on the border of present-day Nepal and India. Born of a noble family, he questioned the comforts of his existence and for many years led the life of an ascetic. He was to turn his back on this life, too. After a period of intense meditation, he achieved 'enlightenment', which is the essence of Buddhahood.

Buddhism has been greatly complicated because it has fractured into a vast number of schools of thought. Basically these can be divided into the Hinayana (Lesser Vehicle) and the Mahayana (Greater Vehicle) schools; the former emphasising personal enlightenment and the latter seeking the salvation of all beings. Nevertheless, the teachings of Gautama are at the heart of all Buddhism.

Buddhism in Korea, as in Japan and China, belongs to the Mahayana school. Since its arrival it has split into a great number of smaller schools of thought, the most famous of which is Sŏn – better known to the outside world by its Japanese name Zen.

There are 18 Buddhist sects in Korea; the largest by far is the Chogye sect, which has its headquarters in Seoul's Chogyesa (Chogye temple). It is an amalgamation of two Korean schools of Buddhism: the Sŏn sect, which relies on meditation and the contemplation of riddles, among other things, to achieve sudden enlightenment; and the Kyo school, which relies more heavily on extensive scriptural study. The major temples of the Chogye sect are located as follows (by province):

Seoul: Chogyesa, Hwagyesa, Pongŭnsa, Tosŏnsa

Kyŏnggi-do: Chŏndŭngsa, Pongsonsa, Shillŭksa, Yongjusa

Kangwon-do: Ch'ŏngp'yŏngsa, Kukhyangsa, Kuryongsa, Naksansa, Pobhungsa, Sangwonsa, Shinhŭngsa, Sut'asa, Wolchŏngsa

Kyŏngsangbuk-do: Chikchisa, Huibangsa, Hungyungsa, Kounsa, Namsan Mountain (five temples), Paekyunsa, Pulguksa, Punhwangsa, Pusŏksa, Shinsonsa, Tonghwasa, Ŭnhaesa, Unmunsa

Kyŏngsangnam-do: Haeinsa, Kuwolsa, Pŏmŏsa, P'yoch'ungsa, Sŏknamsa, Ssanggyesa, T'ongdosa

Chŏllanam-do: Chungshimsa, Hwaŏmsa, Mihwangsa, Paekyangsa, Sŏnamsa, Songkwangsa, T'aeamsa, Taehŭngsa, Unjusa

Cheju-do Kimnyongsa, Kwanumsa

Chŏllabuk-do: Anguksa, Kŭmsansa, Miruksa-ji, Naejangsa, Naesosa, Shilsangsa, Songkwangsa, Sŏnunsa, T'apsa (Unsusa)

Ch'ungch'ŏngnam-do: Kapsa, Kwanch'oksa, Magoksa, Shinwonsa, Sudŏksa, Tonghaksa

Ch'ungch'ŏngbuk-do: Tukjusa, Kosansa, Miruksa-ji, Pŏpchusa, Toduksa

The Chogye sect represents around 90% of Korean Buddhists; next in size is the T'aego sect, representing about 7%. The T'aego sect distinguishes itself by permitting its monks to marry. The Japanese installed this system of married monks during their occupation of Korea. Apparently, married monks were easier to control than other-worldly medita-

tive monks. Headquarters for the T'aego sect is in Seoul at Pongwonsa, a temple close to Ehwa Women's University. This magnificent temple is noted for its paintings.

Buddhism, a remarkably adaptive faith, has co-existed closely with Shamanism in Korea. Almost all Buddhist temples have a *samsŏng-gak* ('three spirit hall') on their grounds which houses Shamanistic deities. Buddhist priests also often carry out activities associated with Shamanism, such as fortune telling and the sale of good luck charms.

Buddhism suffered a sharp decline after WWII. This was partly because of the Japanese occupation during which Buddhist monks were coerced to support unity with Japan. Those who proved unco-operative simply disappeared. Furthermore, as South Korea's post-war economic boom got under way, Buddhism seemed to have little to offer – Koreans were not about to cast off their pursuit of worldly desires to become a nation of fasting monks and nuns.

Ironically, South Korea's recent status as a developed nation has caused Buddhism to suddenly revive. Westernisation has gone so far in South Korea that the country is suffering from an identity crisis; the last thing Koreans want to be called is westernised Asians. As national pride reasserts itself, more and more South Koreans are seeking to rediscover their cultural roots and these include Buddhism. Pilgrimages to temples have increased enormously and a huge amount of money is now flowing into temple reconstruction. It is estimated that approximately 25% of South Koreans now call themselves Buddhists, about equal to the number of practising Christians.

Maps produced in Korea mark temple sites with what appears to be a swastika. You will also see this symbol on the temples themselves. But if you look more closely, you'll see that it's actually the reverse image of a swastika. This is, in fact, an old Buddhist religious symbol with which you should become familiar.

Confucianism

Confucianism is a system of ethics rather than a religion. Confucius (551 to 479 BC) lived in China during a time of great chaos and feudal rivalry known as the Warring States Period. He emphasised devotion to parents and family, loyalty to friends, justice, peace, education, reform and humanitarianism. He also emphasised respect and deference to those in positions of authority, a philosophy later heavily exploited by emperors and warlords. However, not everything said by Confucius has been universally praised – it seems that he was a male chauvinist who firmly believed that men are superior to women.

Confucius preached the virtues of good government, but his philosophy was used to justify the horrifying bureaucracy which

It is still possible to meet elderly gentlemen garbed in traditional white robes and the *kat* – a hat made of horsehair.

exists in China to this day. On a more positive note, his ideas led to the system of civil service and university entrance examinations where one gained position through ability and merit, rather than from noble birth and connections. Confucius preached against practices such as corruption, war, torture and excessive taxation. He was the first teacher to open his school to all students on the basis of their eagerness to learn rather than their noble birth and ability to pay for tuition.

As Confucianism trickled into Korea it evolved. Religious evolution produced Neo-Confucianism, which combined the sage's original ethical and political ideas with a quasi-religious practice of ancestor worship and the idea of the eldest male as spiritual head of the family.

Confucianism was viewed as being enlightened and radical when it first gained popularity. However, over the years it has become very paternalistic and conservative. It's even fair to say that many younger Koreans regard Confucianism as something of an embarrassment, which explains why many of them have defected to Christianity. Yet Confucianism lives on as a kind of ethical bedrock (at least subconsciously) in the minds of most Koreans. South Korea is frequently described as the most Confucian society in the world and most Korean social behaviour confirms this.

Christianity

Korea's first exposure to Christianity was through the Jesuits from the Chinese imperial court of the late 18th century. A Korean aristocrat was baptised in Beijing in 1784. When it was introduced to Korea the Catholic faith took hold and spread quickly; so quickly, in fact, that it was perceived as a threat by the royal family and vigorously suppressed, thus creating Korea's first Christian martyrs.

Christianity got a second chance in the 1880s with the arrival of American Protestant missionaries. The founding of schools and hospitals won them many followers.

Nowhere else in Asia, with the exception

Smashing Skulls with the Iron Bars of Democracy

'Reverend' Moon Ik-kwan was never a practising minister and few doubt that he exploited the church to lend respectability to his own political campaign. He made no secret of the fact that he intended to run for president. He ran afoul of South Korean law when he travelled to North Korea and appeared on public TV hugging Kim Il-sung. He was arrested upon his return to South Korea and spent two years in prison before being let out on an amnesty. Unrepentant, he continued to travel around South Korea blatantly encouraging students to violence. In one of his famous speeches, he proclaimed 'We will smash the skulls of dictatorship with the iron bars of democracy'. The Reverend promised that if he became president, he would reunify Korea and jointly govern with Kim Il-sung. These plans were cut short when Reverend Moon died suddenly in 1993. Although the church wants nothing to do with him, he has since been unofficially 'canonised' by both leftists in South Korea and the North Korean leadership. ■

of the Philippines, have the efforts of proselytising missionaries been so successful; today about 25% of all Koreans consider themselves Christians.

Young people have been particularly eager to make the jump to Christianity. Those with political ambitions have used the church to catapult themselves into prominence and a number of church leaders have assumed major roles in anti-government protests. It's only fair to point out that most of these self-proclaimed leaders adopt the label 'reverend' even though they have no official church backing.

Church Services For those who are interested in attending English-language church services, there is a listing every week in the Saturday edition of the *Korea Times* newspaper.

LANGUAGE

Korean is a knotty problem for linguists. Various theories have been proposed to explain its origins, but the most widely accepted is that it is a member of the Ural-Altaic family of languages, specifically belonging to the Tungusic branch. This is not particularly enlightening in itself, though it helps to know that other members of the same linguistic branch are Turkish and Mongolian. In reality, Korean shares much more

with Japanese and Chinese than it does with either Turkish or Mongolian. This should come as no surprise given all the contact (not always happy) between these three countries. Korean suffixes indicating time, place and relationship are piled on the end of verbs, much the same as in Japanese. Basic sentence order is subject-object-verb, unlike the English subject-verb-object ordering.

In the past, Korean was written using Chinese characters. Given that the average person had neither the time to study nor the money for tuition, most Koreans remained illiterate. Reading and writing were the pursuit of the elite and monks, and conservative Confucianists wanted to keep it that way. This all changed with the introduction of hangŭl, a cursive alphabet developed under King Sejong in the 15th century.

Hangŭl originally consisted of 28 characters, but this has been reduced to 24. Not surprisingly, it's very easy to learn. However, the formation of words using hangŭl is very different from the way that western alphabets form words. The emphasis is on the formation of a syllable in such a way that it resembles a Chinese character. Thus the first syllable of the word 'hangŭl' is formed by an 'h' in the top left corner, an 'a' in the top right corner and an 'n' at the bottom, the whole syllabic group forming what looks like a Chinese character. In total, it's possible to create 2350 'characters' this way. These syllabic characters are strung together to form words. Spaces should appear between written words, but these are often randomly deleted, causing great confusion for foreign students of Korean. Traditionally the language was written top to bottom and right to left as in Chinese, but now the western practice of writing horizontally from left to right is standard.

Despite the best efforts of conservative education systems, all languages change over time. The pronunciation of Korean words has changed a bit in the 500-plus years since hangŭl was introduced, with the result that you will often encounter words which are not pronounced as they are spelled. To be fair, English is one of the world's most notorious offenders in this respect (what happened to the 'gh' sound in 'night' or in 'through'?).

Like most non-European languages, the Romanisation of Korean has been applied in fits and starts with all sorts of confusing irregularities. Officially, the McCune-Reischauer system is supported by the Korean government as the standard Romanisation system and it is used in this book. However, the government previously supported the Ministry of Education Romanisation scheme, which in many ways was better and is still used by the majority of Koreans. Furthermore, many Koreans have never understood either system and therefore use all kinds of mismatched transliterations. You'll find that most Koreans write their names in Romanised spellings of their own fancy, so Mr Chae and Miss Choi might be brother and sister. There are also wide divergences in the spelling of place names. You might for example see Taejŏn spelled as Daejeon, or Poshingak as Bosingag. The thing to do is to stay on your toes and try to anticipate these discrepancies. Best of all, learn enough hangŭl to be able to double-check place names.

A feature of the McCune-Reischauer system is the use of apostrophes to indicate aspirated (accompanied by a puff of air) consonants, as in P'yŏngyang. A hyphen is optionally used to separate syllables. Thus 'han-gŭl' could be written with a hyphen to be sure it is not pronounced 'hang-ŭl'. A final feature of the McCune-Reischauer system is the use of diacritics on the 'o' and 'u' sounds to fully represent the values of Korean vowels. Under this system the capital city should be spelled 'Sŏul' rather than 'Seoul', but it's difficult to change an accepted standard so 'Seoul' remains the official spelling. In practice, most Koreans simply omit the apostrophes or diacritics, which causes great confusion.

Korean is much complicated by the degrees of status codified into the grammar. Those of higher status need to be spoken to in a more polite manner than those of lower status. You can easily offend someone by using the wrong level of politeness, especially when you are talking to an older person. One reason why Koreans like to learn English is because it frees them of the formality of their own language. Indeed, young Koreans tend to use the very polite forms a lot less than the generations before them did, but for safety's sake the sentences in this section all employ polite forms.

Aside from grammar, the Korean notion of social hierarchy demands that you use certain terms to address people according to their social rank. The Koreans you most often deal with are likely to be the owners of the hotel where you're staying or the restaurant where you eat. Woman who look old enough to be married should always be addressed as *ajumma*. If talking to her husband, he is *ajŏssi*. If the woman is young looking and doesn't seem to be married, then she's an *agassi*. Young unmarried men and teenagers are *haksaeng*, though if you're dealing with a young man who is obviously a blue collar worker then call him *ajŏssi* even if he's not married. A child under age 10 of either sex is addressed as *kkomaya*. For the really old folks, call them *halabŏji* (grandfather) or *halmŏni* (grandmother). And for someone older than you whom you want to be *very* respectful to (a Customs officer?), the polite term is *sŏnsaengnim*.

It's well worth your while to learn hangŭl in alphabetical order since this will enable you to use a Korean-English dictionary.

Vowels

ㅏ	a	like the 'a' in 'shah'
ㅑ	ya	like the 'ya' in 'yard'
ㅓ	ŏ	like the 'e' in 'open'
ㅕ	yŏ	like the 'yo' in 'young'
ㅗ	o	like the 'o' in 'law'
ㅛ	yo	like the 'yo' in 'yoke'
ㅜ	u	like the 'u' in 'flute'
ㅠ	yu	like the word 'you'
ㅡ	ŭ	like the 'oo' in 'look'
ㅣ	i	like the 'ee' in 'beet'

Combination Vowels

ㅐ	ae	like the 'a' in 'hat'
ㅒ	yae	like the 'ya' in 'yam'
ㅔ	e	like the 'e' in 'ten'
ㅖ	ye	like the 'ye' in 'yes'
ㅘ	wa	like the 'wa' in 'waffle'
ㅙ	wae	like the 'wa' in 'wax'
ㅚ	oe	like the 'wa' in 'way'
ㅝ	wo	like the 'wo' in 'won'
ㅞ	we	like the 'wa' in 'wet'
ㅟ	wi	like the word 'we'
ㅢ	ŭi	'u' plus 'i'

Consonants

Apostrophes are used to indicate consonant sounds that are aspirated (accompanied by a puff of air). Consonants that are not marked with an apostrophe are unaspirated and are generally difficult to render for English speakers. To those unfamiliar with Korean, an unaspirated 'k' will sound like 'g', an unaspirated 't' like 'd' and an unaspirated 'p' like 'b'.

Single Consonants

Korean Letters	Initial Position	Medial Position	Final Position
ㄱ	k	g	k
ㄴ	n	n	n
ㄷ	t	d	t
ㄹ	r	r/n	l
ㅁ	m	m	m
ㅂ	p	b	p
ㅅ	s/sh	s	t
ㅇ	silent	ng	ng
ㅈ	ch	j	t

ㅊ	ch'	ch'	t
ㅋ	k'	k'	k
ㅌ	t'	t'	t
ㅍ	p'	p'	p
ㅎ	h	h	ng

ㅅ is pronounced *sh* if followed by the vowel ㅣ. Medial ㄹ is pronounced *n* when it follows ㅁ *(m)*, ㄴ *(n)* or ㅇ *(ng)*.

Double Consonants

Double consonants are said with more stress than single consonants.

Korean Letters	Initial Position	Medial Position	Final Position
ㄲ	kk	gg	k
ㄸ	tt	dd	–
ㅃ	pp	bb	–
ㅆ	ss	ss	t
ㅉ	tch	tch	–

Complex Consonants

These occur only in a medial or final position in a word.

Korean Letters	Initial Position	Medial Position	Final Position
ㄱㅅ	-	ks	k
ㄴㅈ	-	nj	n
ㄴㅎ	-	nh	n
ㄹㄱ	-	lg	k
ㄹㅁ	-	lm	m
ㄹㅂ	-	lb	p
ㄹㅅ	-	ls	l
ㄹㅌ	-	lt'	l
ㄹㅍ	-	lp'	p
ㄹㅎ	-	lh	l
ㅂㅅ	-	ps	p

Greetings & Civilities

Hello.
annyŏng hashimnigga (formal)
안녕하십니까
annyŏng haseyo (less formal)
안녕하세요
Goodbye. (to person leaving)
annyŏnghi kaseyo
안녕히가세요

Goodbye. (to person staying)
  annyŏnghi kyeseyo
  안녕히계세요
Please.
  put'ak hamnida
  부탁합니다
Thank you.
  kamsa hamnida
  감사합니다
Yes.
  ye/ne
  에 / 네
No.
  anyo
  아니요
Excuse me.
  shillye hamnida
  실례합니다

Getting Around
I want to get off here.
  yŏgiyae naeryŏ chuseyo
  여기에 내려 주세요
National Timetable
  shigakp'yo
  시각표
I want to go to...
  e kago shipsŭmnida
  에 가고싶습니다
Where can I catch the bus to...?
  ...haeng bŏsŭnŭn ŏti e sŏ tapnigga?
  ... 행 버스는 어디에서 탑니까?

airport	*konghang*	
	공항	
bus	*bŏsŭ*	
	버스	
airport bus	*konghang bŏsŭ*	
	공항버스	
bus stop	*bŏsŭ chŏngnyujang*	
	버스 정류장	
express bus	*kosok bŏsŭ*	
	고속버스	
inter-city bus	*shi'oe bŏsŭ*	
	시외버스	
terminal	*t'ŏminŏl*	
	터미널	
taxi	*t'aekshi*	
	택시	
bullet taxi	*ch'ong'al t'aekshi*	
	총알택시	

train	*kich'a*	
	기차	
railway	*kich'a yok*	
station	기차역	
ferry pier	*pudutga*	
	부둣가	
one-way	*p'yŏndo*	
(ticket)	편도	
return	*wangbok*	
(ticket)	왕복	
refund	*hwanbul*	
ticket	환불	
subway	*chihach'ŏl yŏk*	
station	지하철역	
lockers	*lakk'a*	
	락카	

stored-value subway ticket
  chŏngaek ch'agwin
  정액승차권
lost & found office
  punshilmulpo kwansaenta
  분실물보관세타
immigration office
  chul'ibkuk kwali so
  출입국관리소

Necessities
toilet	*hwajangshil*	화상실
toilet paper	*hwajangji*	화장지
tampons	*tempo*	템포
sanitary pads	*saengnidae*	생리대
condoms	*kondom*	콘돔
pharmacy	*yak*	약
anti-diarrhoeal	*sŭlsa yak*	설사약
laxative	*pyunbi yak*	변비약
pain killer	*chintongche*	진통제
incense	*chŏnja mugihyang*	
	전자 모기향	

Communication
post office	*uch'eguk*	우체국
stamp	*u'pyo*	우표
aerogramme		
hanggong sŏ gan		항공서간
International Express Mail		
kokje t'ŭkgŭ pop'yŏn		국제특급우편
telephone office		
chŏnhwa kuk		전화국

telephone card
chŭnhwa kadŭ   전화카드
I'd like to know the telephone number here.
yŏgi chŏnhwapŏnho jom karŭch'yŏ chuseyo
여기 전화번호 좀 가르쳐 주세요

Money

May I have change please?
chandonŭro pakkwo chuseyo?
잔돈으로 바꿔 주세요?
How much does it cost?
ŏlmayeyo?   얼마예요?
Too expensive.
nŏmu pissayo   너무 비싸요
Can I have a discount?
chom ssage hae juseyo?
좀 싸게 해 주세요?

Accommodation

hotel	*hot'el*	호텔
guesthouse	*yŏgwan*	여관
cheapest guesthouse	*yŏinsuk*	여인숙
home stay	*minbak*	민박
single room	*singgul lum*	싱글룸
double room	*tobul lum*	더블룸
towel	*sugŏn*	수건
bathhouse	*mok yok t'ang*	목욕탕

with shared bath
yokshil omnun pang chuseyo
욕실 없는 방 주세요
with private bath
yokshil innun pang chuseyo
욕실 있는 방 주세요
May I see the room?
pang'ŭl polsu issŏyo?
방을 볼 수 있어요?
Do you have anything cheaper?
tŏ ssan kot sun ŏpsŭmnigga?
더 싼 것은 없습니까?
May I have a namecard?
myŏngham jom ŏtŭl su issŭlkkayo?
명함 좀 얻을 수 있을까요?
I will pay you now.
chigŭm chibulhago ship'ŭn teyo
지금 지불하고 싶은 데요
Please give me a receipt.
yŏngsujŭng jom katda chuseyo
영수증 좀 갖다 주세요

I want to stay one more night.
hangru tŏ mukgo shipsŭmnida
하루 더 묵고 싶습니다
Please give me my key.
yŏlsoe jom chuseyo
열쇠 좀 주세요
Could you clean my room please?
bangchyŏngso jom hae chuseyo?
방청소 좀 해 주세요?
Can you have my clothes washed?
setak ssobisŭ taemnikka?
세탁 써비스 됩니까?

Emergencies

Help!	*saram sallyŏ!*	사람살려!
Thief!	*todduk iya!*	도둑이야!
Fire!	*pul'iya!*	불이야!
hospital	*pyŏngwon*	병원

Call a doctor!
ŭisarul pulŏ chuseyo!
의사를 불러 주세요!
Call an ambulance!
kugŭpch'a chom pullŏ chuseyo!
구급차 좀 불러 주세요!
Call the police!
kyŏngch'alŭl pulŏ chuseyo!
경찰을 불러주세요!
I'm allergic to penicillin.
penishillin allerugiga issŏyo
페니실린 알레르기가 있어요
I'm allergic to antibiotics.
hangsaengche allerugiga issŏyo
항생제 알레르기가 있어요
I'm diabetic.
tangnyopyŏngi issŏyo
당뇨병이 있어요

Numbers

Korean has two counting systems. One is of Chinese origin and the other a native Korean system. Korean numbers only go up to 99 and are used to count days, minutes and mileage (as long as the total doesn't exceed 99). The Chinese system is used to count money, which is not surprising since the smallest Korean banknote is W1000.

Number	Chinese		Korean	
0			yŏng	영
1	il	일	hana	하나
2	I	이	tul	둘
3	sam	삼	set	셋
4	sa	사	net	넷
5	o	오	tasŏt	다섯
6	yuk	육	yŏsŏt	여섯
7	ch'il	칠	ilgop	일곱
8	p'al	팔	yŏdŏl	여덟
9	ku	구	ahop	아홉
10	ship	십	yŏl	열

Number	Combination	
11	ship'il	십일
20	i'ship	이십
30	sam'ip	삼십
40	sa'ip	사십
48	sa'shippal	사십팔
50	o'ship	오십
100	paek	백
200	i'paek	이백
300	sampaek	삼백
846	p'alpaek saship'yuk	팔백사십육
1000	ch'ŏn	천
2000	i'ch'ŏn	이천
5729	o'ch'ŏn ch'ilpaek i'shipku	오천칠백이십구
10,000	man	만

Facts for the Visitor

PLANNING

When to Go

The best time of year for a visit is autumn, from September through November. The sight of leaves turning red and yellow in autumn is considered one of Korea's great splendours. Even though there is always a possibility that a late typhoon could interfere with some of your sightseeing plans in September, autumn is generally a time of sunny skies and little rain.

Winter is dry and cold, but some travellers enjoy this season. There is no question that this is a very picturesque time in Korea, with brilliant skies and snow draping the roofs of temples. There are also opportunities to enjoy skiing. Except during the Christmas and Lunar New Year holidays, you can look forward to a scarcity of crowds almost everywhere you go. However, you'll have to deal with sub-zero temperatures.

April and May is a beautiful time, with mild temperatures and flowers blooming everywhere. However, it's important to note that Japan has a holiday during the first week of May, called 'golden week', and Japanese tourists flood into Korea at this time. The Japanese tend to book out all the top-end and mid-range accommodation, but the budget hotels don't seem to be heavily affected.

Summer is not a particularly good time to be in Korea. While it's the only time for the beach, you will have to deal with hot and muggy weather and jumbo crowds in all scenic areas. What's more, hotels raise their prices at this time. This is also the wet season, in which Korea gets some 70% of its annual rainfall. Occasional typhoons during summer can hole you up in your hotel room for a couple of days and play havoc with a tight travel itinerary.

Maps

The various tourist offices have a number of give-away maps which are certainly worth picking up. Do this in Seoul because they are not readily available elsewhere.

Korea's largest retail outlet for maps is Chung'ang Atlas Map Service (☎ 720-9191), 125-1 Gongpyeong Dong, Chongno-gu, Seoul. Maps here come in two sizes – big and enormous. If you are planning to do any serious hiking this is the place to come and stock up.

If you plan on driving or cycling in South Korea, take a look at the *Korea Road Atlas* (Chung'ang Atlas Company). This contains detailed road maps showing all major points of interest, plus many reasonably detailed city maps. It's partially in English, but the rest is in Chinese characters (rather than hangŭl script); you'd do better to get an atlas with hangŭl script. A good one is entitled *Road Maps to Tourist Attractions in Korea*. These atlases and fold-out maps can be readily bought at major bookstores.

The city hall in almost every large town has excellent detailed maps. These usually contain both Korean and English script, and are often given away. Unfortunately, the staff at most city halls can't speak English and they often run out of maps. Still, it could be worth a try if you want something more detailed than what is available in atlases.

The Koreans have a hard time emotionally dealing with their country's division. Consequently, very few maps produced in Korea (both North and South) show the heavily-fortified DMZ. The idea is to maintain the illusion that Korea is an undivided nation. Unaware of Korea's politics, a few travellers have been misled by the maps to such an extent that they thought they could travel north all the way to China. You can rest assured that this is impossible – despite the creative map-making, the border between the two Koreas does indeed exist and you cannot cross it.

What to Bring

Almost anything you forget to bring along can be purchased inexpensively in Seoul. If you plan to do any camping or hiking – popular activities among the Koreans – the markets in Seoul are excellent places to pick up anything you need and prices will generally be lower than at home. However, mosquito repellent and sun block (UV) lotion are hard to come by; shaving cream, vitamins and medicines tend to be expensive (though not prohibitively so); and deodorant is only available from big tourist hotels, such as the Lotte Hotel pharmacy in Seoul. Tampons *(tempo)* are available from some pharmacies and supermarkets.

HIGHLIGHTS

The royal palaces and museums of Seoul will give you an excellent introduction to Korea's intricate culture and history. Kyŏngju in south-east Korea has an overwhelming collection of historical sights. The Korean Folk Village at Suwon is a tasteful re-creation of Korea's traditional culture.

Outstanding mountainous beauty spots include the national parks at Sŏraksan, Puk'ansan and Naejangsan. Temple enthusiasts should visit Songnisan and Kayasan National Parks. Spectacularly beautiful islands include Cheju-do, Ullŭngdo and the hundreds of islands which make up Tadohae Haesang National Park.

TOURIST OFFICES
Local Tourist Offices

The Korean National Tourism Office, or KNTO, deserves a plug for being one of the most helpful and best organised tourist offices in Asia, if not the world. KNTO produces an extensive range of well-illustrated booklets and maps, and you can pick up some of these at the three international airports: Kimp'o (☎ 665-0088), Cheju (☎ 420032) and Kimhae (☎ 973-1100). KNTO has an excellent information centre (☎ 757-0086) in Seoul – see the Seoul chapter for details. You can also call their main office in Seoul (☎ 757-0086; fax 757-5997) or write to them at KPO Box 1879, Seoul 110-618.

Almost every city has a tourist information office located in the city hall. In large cities these offices are well equipped with English-speakers and maps, but in the backwaters the staff might only speak Korean and have scant literature to offer you. Not surprisingly, Seoul has the biggest and best of these offices, but you'll also find a decent one in Pusan city hall.

In some large cities, information booths with English speakers are located in crucial spots such as tourist sights and some railway or bus stations. Again, these information booths are most numerous in Seoul, but they can be found elsewhere. The level of spoken English is sometimes close to zero, but the friendly staff will at least try to help you even if communication is in sign language. See the relevant chapters of this book for directions on where to find these booths.

If you have trouble with transport, food, shopping or accommodation, there is a KNTO Tourist Complaint Centre (☎ 735-0101), KPO Box 1879, Seoul 110-618. Outside Seoul, the provincial governments have offices to assist travellers experiencing difficulties: Taegu (☎ 422-5611); Ch'ŏngju (☎ 520202); in all other cities, dial the area code followed by 0101.

KNTO Overseas Offices

KNTO has representatives in the following countries:

Australia
17th floor, Tower Building, Australia Square, George St, Sydney 2000 (☎ (02) 9252-4147; fax 9251-2104)

Canada
Suite 406, 480 University Ave, Toronto, Ontario M5G 1V2 (☎ (416) 348-9056; fax 348-9058)

China
Room 1142, Beijing Hotel, 33 Chang'an Donglu (☎ (010) 513-7766; fax 513-7703)

France
Tour Maine Montparnasse, 33 Avenue de Maine, Paris (☎ (01) 4538-7123; fax 4538-7471)

Germany
Baseler Strasse 48, 60329 Frankfurt am Main (☎ (069) 233226; fax 253519)

Hong Kong
Suite 3203, 32nd floor, Citibank Tower, 3 Garden Rd, Central (☎ 2523-8065; fax 2845-0765)

Japan
Room 124, Sanshin building, 4-1 1-chome, Yuraku-cho, Chiyoda-ku, Tokyo (☎ (03) 3580-3941; fax 3591-4601). There are branch offices in Fukuoka (☎ (092) 471-7174), Nagoya (☎ 933-6550), Osaka (☎ (06) 266-0847) and Sapporo (☎ (011) 210-8081)

Singapore
    24 Raffles Place, 20-01 Clifford Centre, Singapore 0104 (☎ 533-0441; fax 534-3427)
Italy
    Via Larga 23, 20122 Milano (☎ (02) 5831-6009; fax 5831-6637)
Taiwan
    Room 1813, International Trade Centre Building, 333 Keelung Rd, Section 1, Taipei (☎ (02) 720-8049; fax 757-6514)
Thailand
    15th floor, Silom Complex, 191 Silom Rd, Bangkok 10500 (☎ 231-3895; fax 231-3897)
UK
    20 Saint George St, London W1R 9RE (☎ (0171) 409-2100; fax 491-2302)
USA
    3435 Wilshire Blvd, Suite 1110, Los Angeles, CA 90010 (☎ (213) 382-3435; fax 480-0483)
    205 North Michigan Ave, Suite 2212, Chicago, IL 60601 (☎ (312) 819-2560; fax 819-2563)
    2 Executive Drive, 7th floor, Fort Lee, NJ 07024 (☎ (201) 585-0909; fax 585-9041)
    1188 Bishop St, Ph 1, Honolulu, Hawaii 96813 (☎ (808) 521-8066; fax 521-5233)

VISAS & DOCUMENTS
Passport

A passport is essential and if yours is within a few months of expiry get a new one now – Korea and many other countries will not issue a visa if your passport has less than six months of validity remaining. Also, be sure it has plenty of space for visas and entry and exit stamps.

Losing your passport is very bad news – getting a new one means a trip to your embassy or consulate and usually a long wait while they send faxes or telexes (at your expense) to confirm that you exist. If you're going to be in Korea for a long period of time, it might be wise to register your passport at your country's consulate in Seoul. This will expedite matters should you need a replacement.

Visas

Transit Visa With an onward ticket, visitors from almost anywhere – except countries not recognised by South Korea (Cuba, Laos and Cambodia) – will be granted a transit stay of up to 15 days without a visa. Some other countries which don't qualify include the Philippines, Nepal, India, Sri Lanka, the former Soviet republics and a few odd places in Asia and Africa. But be warned, the 15-day stay cannot be extended and there are steep fines for overstaying.

Visa Exemptions In addition, South Korea has reciprocal visa-exemption agreements with numerous countries. There are visa exemptions for nationals of all west European nations except Ireland. If you fall into this category you'll be given a 90-day or three-month permit; 60 days in the cases of Italy and Portugal. Canadians get 180 days.

Tourist & Business Visas Nationals of all other countries – including Australia, New Zealand and the USA – require visas for stays of over 15 days. If your nationality does not permit you a visa exemption and you need more than 15 days, apply for a visa before you go to South Korea.

South Korean embassies and consulates are notoriously fickle. Many of them require that your visa photos be 6x6 cm (a size used nowhere else in the world) and they can be slow in issuing visas; allow at least three working days no matter what they tell you. On the other hand, some of the consulates will accept 3x5 cm photos and issue the visa the same day you apply.

Visas are usually issued for a stay of 90 days. Onward tickets and/or proof of 'adequate funds' are not normally required. If you apply for a visa in your own country, you might get a multiple-entry visa – you usually *cannot* get this if you apply at a South Korean embassy in a nearby Asian country.

If you're coming to South Korea on business, then say so on the application. Most countries do not care if you do business on a tourist visa, but the South Koreans do. The immigration authorities are known to fine foreigners who 'violate' the terms of their visa.

Work Visas Applications can be made inside Korea and are processed in as little as one week, but you must leave the country to pick up the visa. You can also apply for a work visa before entering Korea, though in this case it may take two to four weeks for the visa to be issued.

Your contract has to be turned in to the Korean authorities by your prospective employer. The employer does all the bureaucratic processing, then just mails you a visa-confirmation paper. The contract is unsigned by the worker at that point (and there might be a penalty if it was!). After getting the visa and entering Korea, the worker signs the contract and takes it with passport to the immigration office to get a residence permit. There are penalties for starting work *before* getting the visa, or if the starting date on the contract is before the date of obtaining the visa.

Visa Extensions As a general rule tourist visas cannot be extended. About the only exceptions are for emergencies, such as accidents or illness, cancelled flights, loss of passport, etc. You are supposed to apply for this extension at least one day before the visa expires and overstaying your visa can result in a stiff fine.

Working visas are valid for one year and can be extended for at least a further year. This process has recently been simplified.

Alien Registration If you are working or studying in South Korea on a long-term visa it is necessary to apply for a residence certificate within 90 days of arrival. This must be done at the immigration office for your province of residence. This may not be the closest immigration office to where you live and you won't necessarily find it in the provincial capital. The local police station in the town where you live should be able to direct you to the immigration office, or ask a Korean-speaking friend to make a couple of phone calls.

Re-Entry Visas If you don't want to forfeit your working visa you should apply for a multiple re-entry visa before making any trips out of the country. This must be done at the immigration office of whichever province you happen to be living in.

Photocopies
Prudent travellers keep photocopies of vital documents separate from the originals. You should also leave a copy of all these things with someone at home.

Useful things to photocopy include your passport (data pages only), credit cards, airline tickets, educational and employment qualifications (if you plan to work) and driver's licence (if you plan to drive). Keep a list of the serial numbers of your travellers' cheques separate from the cheques themselves and, while you're at it, throw in an emergency stash of about US$100. If you're travelling with your spouse, a copy of your marriage certificate could come in handy in case you get involved with hospitals, the police or various bureaucratic authorities.

Travel Insurance
Whatever insurance you have at home is probably not valid in Korea. There are various types of international travel insurance policies. Some will cover losses caused by theft, accident, illness and death (when at least your relatives benefit).

Travel insurance is something you should arrange before you venture abroad. You can, of course, purchase an insurance policy after arrival in Korea, though finding one written in English may be tricky. Rates vary, so shop around. Travel agents and insurance sales people should be able to give you the inside scoop on these policies. The international travel policies handled by STA Travel or other travel organisations are usually good value. Carefully read over any policy before you sign on the dotted line, and check the small print:

- Some policies specifically exclude 'dangerous activities' which can include scuba diving, motorcycling, even trekking. If such activities are on your agenda you don't want that sort of policy. A policy might even specify than you need a licence for a certain activity (such as driving a motorcycle) and a locally acquired motorcycle licence may not be valid under your policy!
- You may prefer a policy which pays doctors or hospitals direct, rather than you having to pay on the spot and claim later. If you have to claim later make sure you keep all documentation. Some policies

ask you to call back (reverse charges) to a centre in your home country where an immediate assessment of your problem is made.

• Check if the policy covers ambulances or an emergency flight home. If you have to stretch out you will need two seats and somebody has to pay for them!

Driving Licence & Permits

Driving Licence If you intend to drive in Korea, you must be at least 21 years old, have one year's driving experience, have your passport and an international driving permit. A national licence from your own country is not acceptable. It is possible to obtain a temporary Korean driving licence valid for three months against your national licence in Seoul, but you'll waste a day doing so.

If you have to get one, here's the procedure: there are three places in Seoul where you can get this licence, but you must make sure that the address you are going to give is covered by the office where you apply. Seoul's three offices are:

Kangnam, near Samsŏng subway station on line 2
  (☎ 555-0855)
Kangso, near Kimp'o Airport (☎ 664-3610)
Tobong, near Nowon subway station on line 4
  (☎ 975-4710)

All the licensing centres have a counter which deals exclusively with temporary licences for foreigners. You will need your passport plus photocopies of the relevant front pages and your Korean visa page; your national driving licence plus a copy of both sides; six photographs of a size suitable for the Korean licence (about half the size of a normal passport photograph); money to pay for the licence (approximately W10,000, depending on nationality and visitor status).

Photographs, photocopies and fiscal stamps can all be obtained at the licensing centres. The forms you will be given are entirely in Korean, but the staff can help you fill them in. Once you've done this and obtained photographs, photocopies and fiscal stamps, you must take a compulsory eye test (the chart has numbers on it, not Korean characters). Assuming you pass it, you can pick up your licence 24 hours later.

The procedure for getting a permanent driving licence (valid for five years) is much the same, but you'll need a Korean residence permit to qualify. Furthermore, you must surrender your own country's driving licence to the Korean authorities in order to obtain the Korean licence. If you don't have a licence from your home country, then you'll have to undergo the whole unpleasant procedure of taking a driving course, written examination and driving test.

International Driving Permit If you plan to be driving abroad get an International Driving Permit. These *cannot* be issued to you in Korea unless you've first obtained a Korean licence – in other words, get it before you leave home.

In some countries these permits are issued by the local motor vehicle department, but in other places you have to get it from your local automobile association. The validity varies from country to country: in some places you only get one year, while other countries will give you three years. If you can only get a one year permit, then obviously there's no sense getting one far in advance of departure.

Make sure that your permit states that it is valid for motorcycles if you plan to ride one.

Vehicle Documents As in most Asian countries, when purchasing a motor vehicle you are issued only a registration certificate. There is no separate ownership certificate as is typically used in western countries.

If renting a vehicle, keep a copy of the rental agreement in your possession when you drive.

Hostel Card

An International Youth Hostel (IYH) card can be of some use in South Korea but is considerably more useful in nearby Japan. However, the vast majority of travellers will not need one in Korea because they stay in private hotels or guesthouses. For information on Korea's hostels, see the Accommodation section in this chapter.

Student Cards

Full-time students can often get good discounts on tickets with the help of an International Student Identity Card (ISIC). This card entitles the holder to a number of discounts on air and train fares, and entry to museums, etc. To get this card, inquire at your campus. These can be issued in Korea at the Korean International Student Exchange Society (KISES) (☎ 733-9494; fax 732-9568) in room 505 of the YMCA building on Chongno 2-ga (next to Chonggak subway station) in Seoul. A student ID card or a university letter of acceptance is required.

International Health Card

Useful (though not essential) is an International Health Certificate to record any vaccinations you've had. These are normally issued by hospitals, vaccination clinics or public health departments. These can also be issued in Korea.

Photos

A collection of small photos (3x5 cm, *not* 3x5 inches!) for visas will be useful if you're planning to visit several countries, but will also come in handy if you apply for work. Of course, these can be obtained in Korea and most other countries, but you'll save yourself some time by having a few in reserve (10 should be sufficient). Visa photos must have a neutral background so forget about using snapshots from your last birthday party.

EMBASSIES
South Korean Embassies Abroad

There are South Korean embassies and consulates in the following countries (places listed are embassies unless otherwise specified):

Australia
113 Empire Circuit, Yarralumla, Canberra ACT 2600 (☎ (06) 273-3044)
Consulate, 8th floor, Challenge Bank, 32-36 Martin Place, Sydney, NSW 2000
(☎ (02) 9221-3866)
Canada
5th floor, 151 Slater St, Ottawa, Ontario K1P 5H3
(☎ (613) 232-1715)
Consulate, 555 Avenue Rd, Toronto, Ontario,

M4V 2J7 (☎ (416) 920-3809)
Consulate, 830-1066 West Hastings St, Vancouver, BC V6E 3X1 (☎ (604) 681-9581/2)
China
3rd & 4th floor, China World Trade Centre, 1 Jianguomenwai Dajie, Beijing
(☎ (010) 505-3171)
Consulate, 4th floor, Shanghai International Trade Centre, 2200 Yan'an Xilu, Shanghai
(☎ (021) 219-6917)
France
125 Rue De Grenelle, 75007 Paris
(☎ (01) 4753-0101)
Germany
Adenauerallee 124, 5300 Bonn 1
(☎ (0228) 267960)
Consulate, Kurfuerstendamm 180, 1000 Berlin 33 (☎ (030) 885-9550)
Consulate, Eschersheimer-Landstrasse 327, 6000 Frankfurt (☎ (069) 563051/3)
Hong Kong
5th floor, Far East Finance Centre, 16 Harcourt Rd, Central (☎ 2529-4141)
Indonesia
57 Jalan Gatot Subroto, Jakarta Selatan
(☎ (021) 520-1915)
Ireland
20 Clyde Rd, Ballsbridge, Dublin 4
(☎ (01) 608800)
Japan
2-5 Minami-Azabu, 1-Chome, Minato-Ku, Tokyo 106 (☎ (03) 3452-7611)
Fukuoka Consulate (☎ (092) 771-0461)
Kobe Consulate (☎ (078) 221-4853/5)
Nagoya Consulate (☎ (052) 935-4221)
Naha, Okinawa Consulate (☎ (0988) 676940/1)
Niigata Consulate (☎ (025) 230-3400)
Osaka Consulate (☎ (06) 213-1401)
Sapporo Consulate (☎ (011) 621-0288/9)
Sendai Consulate (☎ (022) 221-2751)
Shimonoseki Consulate (☎ (0832) 665341/4)
Yokohama Consulate (☎ (045) 621-4531)
Malaysia
22nd floor, Wisma Mca No 163, Jalan Ampang 50450, Kuala Lumpur (☎ (03) 262-2377)
Mongolia
Baga Toyruu St 37, Ulaan Baatar (☎ 23541)
New Zealand
11th floor, ASB Bank, Tower Building, 2 Hunter St, Wellington (☎ (04) 473-9073)
Philippines
Alpap 1 Building, 140 Alfaro St, Salcedo Village, Makati, Manila (☎ (02) 817-5703)
Russia
Ul Spiridonobka Dom 14, Moscow
(☎ (095) 956-1474)
Consulate, Room 512-529, 45A October 25th St, Vladivostok 690009 (☎ (4332) 227729)

Singapore
    101 Thomson Rd, United Square, 10-03, 13-05, Singapore 1130 (☎ 256-1188)
Thailand
    23 Thiam-Ruammit Rd, Ratchadpisek, Huay Kwang, Bangkok 10310 (☎ (02) 247-7537)
UK
    4 Palace Gate, London W8 5NF (☎ (071) 581-0247)
USA
    2450 Massachusetts Ave, NW, Washington DC (☎ (202) 939-5600)
    Consulate, 305 GCIC Building, Agana, Guam 96910 (☎ (671) 472-6488)
    Consulate, 101 Benson Blvd, Suite 304, Anchorage, AL 99503 (☎ (907) 561-5488)
    Consulate, 229 Peachtree St, Cain Tower, Suite 500, Atlanta, GA 30303 (☎ (404) 522-1611/3)
    Consulate, 15th floor, Financial Center 1, Boston, MA 02111 (☎ (617) 348-3660)
    Consulate, 455 North Cityfront Plaza Drive NBC Tower 27th floor, Chicago, IL 60611 (☎ (312) 822-9485/8)
    Consulate, 2756 Pali Highway, Honolulu, HI 96817 (☎ (808) 595-6109)
    Consulate, 1990 Post Oak Blvd, Suite 1250, Houston, TX 77056 (☎ (713) 961-0186)
    Consulate, 3243 Wilshire Blvd, Los Angeles, CA 90010 (☎ (213) 385-9300)
    Consulate, Suite 800, Miami Center 201, South Biscayne Blvd, Miami, FL 33131 (☎ (305) 372-1555)
    Consulate, 460 Park Ave at 57th St, 5th floor, New York, NY 10022 (☎ (212) 752-1700)
    Consulate, 3500 Clay St, San Francisco, CA 94118 (☎ (415) 921-2251)
    Consulate, Suite 1125, United Airline Building, 2033 6th Ave, Seattle, WA 98121 (☎ (206) 441-1011)
Vietnam
    3rd floor, Boss Hotel, 60-62 Nguyen Du St, Hanoi (☎ (04) 269160)

Foreign Embassies in South Korea

Foreign embassies are concentrated entirely in Seoul, although a few countries also maintain consulates in Pusan. Seoul's embassies include the following:

Australia
    11th floor, Kyobo Building, 1-1 Chongno 1-ga, Chongno-gu (☎ 730-6490)
Canada
    10th floor, Kolon Building, 45 Mugyo-dong, Chung-gu (☎ 753-2605)
France
    30 Hap-dong, Sŏdaemun-gu (☎ 312-3272)

Germany
    4th floor, Daehan Fire & Marine Insurance Building, 51-1 Namch'ang-dong, Chung-gu (☎ 726-7114)
Indonesia
    55 Yŏŭido-dong, Yŏngdŭngp'o-gu (☎ 783-5675)
Ireland
    Daehan Fire & Marine Insurance Building, 51-1 Namch'ang-dong, Chung-gu (☎ 774-6455)
Japan
    18-11 Chunghak-dong, Chongno-gu (☎ 733-5626)
Malaysia
    4-1 Hannam-dong, Yongsan-gu (☎ 794-0349)
Mongolia
    1-104 Riverside Village, 300-24 Tongbuich'on-dong, Yongsan-gu (☎ 794-6249)
Myanmar (Burma)
    724-1, Hannam-dong, Yongsan-gu (☎ 796-9858)
New Zealand
    18th floor, Kyobo Building, Chongno 1-ga, Chongno-gu (☎ 730-7794)
Philippines
    641-11 Yŏksam-dong, Kangnam-gu (☎ 568-6141)
Russia
    1001-13 Taech'i-dong, Kangnam-gu (☎ 552-7094)
Singapore
    7th floor, Citicorp Building, 89-29, Shinmunno 2-ga, Chongno-gu (☎ 722-0442)
South Africa
    1-37 Hannam-dong, Yongsan-gu (☎ 792-4855)
Taiwan
    6th floor, Kwanghwamun Building, Chung-gu (☎ 399-2767)
Thailand
    653-7 Hannam-dong, Yongsan-gu (☎ 795-3098)
UK
    4 Chŏng-dong, Chung-gu (☎ 735-7341)
USA
    82 Sejongno, Chongno-gu (☎ 397-4114)
Vietnam
    28-58 Samch'ŏng-dong, Chongno-gu (☎ 739-2065)

CUSTOMS

Because of high duties on many imported goods, Customs is very thorough with Koreans returning from overseas. But for visiting foreigners Customs is very easy. Although it's not mandatory, Korean Customs advises travellers to declare any items worth more than W300,000 (US$375) so you won't get taxed when you try to depart with these goods. In reality you may be wiser not to do so, since they will stamp your passport and you'll have to pay duty if you do not depart with the goods. You are required to declare foreign currency worth over US$10,000 (and this includes travellers' cheques). By not doing so you could risk having the balance confiscated when you try to leave with it.

There is a duty-free allowance of 200 cigarettes (or 50 cigars), two ounces of perfume and one bottle of spirits (not exceeding a total of one litre). It's prohibited to bring in two-way radios (walkie-talkies) or any literature, cassette tapes or motion pictures that are deemed 'subversive to national security or harmful to public interests'. You can leave any prohibited items in bonded baggage for about US$2 per day.

If you bring in a dutiable item (expensive jewels or furs, for example), Customs may stamp the back page of your passport. In this case, you'll have to be sure to bring the items out with you on departure – otherwise, you'll be liable for import duty.

If you have any further queries there is a Customs Information Service (☎ 665-3100) at Kimp'o International Airport.

For those leaving the country with antiques purchased in South Korea, take note of the Cultural Properties Preservation Law. The law forbids the export of items deemed 'important cultural properties'. If there is any doubt whether one of your purchases might fall into this category, you should contact the Art & Antiques Assessment Office (☎ 662-0106) in Seoul.

Needless to say, customs will not be amused if you try to import explosives, guns or narcotics. While most budget travellers leave their dynamite and AK-47s at home, more than a few foreigners have run into trouble with drugs. Unless you wish to research living conditions inside Korean prisons, it would be wise to leave any recreational chemicals at home.

MONEY
Costs
Korea is steadily shouldering its way into the big league when it comes to costs. In many respects it is already on a par with Australia, Europe and the USA. On the other hand, it offers far more value for money than Japan.

So how much can you reckon on spending a day in Korea? Of course this depends on where you stay and how you spend your time. Budget travellers could get by on US$30 per day, but this means going for the cheapest accommodation and doing a fair bit of self-catering. Transport costs can be reduced by not doing much travelling around beyond hiking.

Korea is much kinder to the visitor with a few more dollars to throw around. Spending a few extra dollars allows you to eat well, sleep well, move around a fair bit, enjoy some simple nightlife and buy some souvenirs. It is possible to do all this quite comfortably on US$40 to US$50 a day.

There is a modest entry fee to most museums, historical sites and national parks which goes towards a worthy cause (maintenance, reconstruction and archaeological research); nevertheless it can burn quite a hole in your pocket. Admission fees are typically in the range of W1000 to W2000. You can get a sizeable discount if you've got a student card, if you're below age 24, or if you're in the military or police (or CIA?) and have the ID to prove it. Many places offer discounts for seniors as well.

To save money on haircuts, men should go to a women's beauty shop – barbershops do manicures and massage, and some are fronts for prostitution. A haircut costs around W3000 in a beauty shop while a barbershop charges about W10,000.

Carrying Money
Korea has its share of pickpockets. Rather than lose your precious cash and travellers' cheques (not to mention passport), large amounts of money and other valuables should be kept far from sticky fingers. Various devices which can usually thwart pickpockets include pockets sewn on the inside of your trousers, Velcro tabs to seal pocket openings, a money belt under your clothes, or a pouch under your shirt. In

winter a vest (waistcoat) worn under your coat will do very nicely, but this isn't such a good option in summer when it's just too hot to wear an extra layer.

Cash

Within all US military bases (including the USO and DMZ) you can use US currency, including coins. Occasionally you'll find shops near the bases (particularly in It'aewon) which will accept US currency. Otherwise, you'll have to use Korean money for all transactions.

US dollars (paper money) are easiest to exchange at banks, but changing other major currencies (especially Japanese yen) should not prove problematic. Coins (except Korean ones) cannot be exchanged. Also, bills which are dirty, tattered and wrinkled could be difficult to exchange.

Travellers' Cheques

Apart from the benefit of safety, another advantage of travellers' cheques is that the exchange rate is more favourable than for cash. Cheques denominated in US dollars will be easiest to change.

If you're legally working in Korea you can purchase travellers' cheques, although you'll need your passport. There's a US$10,000 limit on how many cheques you can purchase in a year and your passport will be stamped to make sure you don't exceed this limit. At least, that's the official rule. In practice, this rule gets stretched because banks compete for foreign exchange business (which is lucrative) and because many bank employees simply don't care. If you often buy travellers' cheques in Korea, it's worth shopping around for a bank that has the 'right attitude'.

ATMs

You'll find 24-hour cash advance machines all over Seoul, Pusan and some other major cities, such as Kyŏngju. Some of these machines are marked 'Cirrus' or 'Star' and will therefore accept most foreign-issued credit cards and ATM cards. You may need local help to use them since all the instruc-

tions are in Korean only and there is no option for switching the display to English.

Credit Cards

You will have no problem finding opportunities to put your credit cards to use in Seoul, where international cards such as American Express, Diners Club, Visa, MasterCard and JCB are widely accepted. The main offices of credit card companies are:

American Express
    181-1 Puam-dong, Chongno-gu
    (English, ☎ 394-4100; Korean, ☎ 287-0114)
Diners Club
    2-191 Hankongro, Yongsan-gu (☎ 596-4100)
Visa
    50 Sogong-dong, Chung-gu
    (☎ 524-8000, 752-6523)

International Transfers

Sending money either into or out of Korea poses no special difficulty. Inquire at any foreign exchange bank for the exact procedure. Even non-resident foreigners are permitted to send money out, purchase travellers' cheques and open bank accounts.

Officially, you need to have your passport when you wire money out of Korea – the amount you send is stamped into the passport to make sure you don't exceed the US$10,000 limit. As with travellers' cheques, finding a bank with a business-oriented attitude can solve this problem.

Currency

Some shops near US military bases will accept US dollars if you don't have any Korean money. Otherwise, the only currency for use in South Korea is the won (W). Notes come in denominations of W1000, W5000 and W10,000. Coins are issued in units of W1, W5, W10, W50, W100 and W500, but the W1 and W5 coins are only seen in banks.

Theoretically you should have your exchange receipts when reconverting won back to foreign currency. In practice, you can change up to US$2000 worth of won at the airport exchange services without showing receipts.

Currency Exchange

Exchange rates in March 1997 were:

Country	Currency		W
Australia	A$1	=	650
Belgium	Bfr1	=	27
Canada	C$1	=	596
China	Y1	=	98
France	F1	=	161
Germany	DM1	=	550
Hong Kong	HK$1	=	106
Japan	¥1	=	7.5
Netherlands	G1	=	491
New Zealand	NZ$1	=	567
Singapore	S$1	=	581
Sweden	Kr1	=	123
Switzerland	Sfr1	=	678
Taiwan	NT$1	=	30
UK	UK£1	=	1280
USA	US$1	=	818

Changing Money

Big cities are thick with banks offering foreign exchange services and these are the best places to change your money. Most Korean post offices are also banks, but these do not handle foreign exchange. It's also convenient to change money at any of the three international airports.

Banking hours are from 9.30 am to 4.30 pm on weekdays and 9.30 am to 1.30 pm on Saturdays. They are closed on Sundays and public holidays.

Tipping & Bargaining

Tipping is generally not necessary or expected in South Korea. A 10% service charge which is added to the bill at tourist hotels could be thought of as a mandatory tip. In the international hotels, international standards apply with regard to tipping.

Big department stores have fixed prices and the low-paid employees are in no position to offer you a discount even if they want to. It's a different story in small street markets and small stores where you can talk directly to the shop owner; this is particularly the case in It'aewon.

Some visitors to the tourist shopping zones get a bit intimidated by the fact that they are in what looks to be a shop with fixed prices. Don't be. Most of the shops that cater to foreigners – and this is all the shops in It'aewon and many in Pusan – will offer some leeway in their prices. Elsewhere, it doesn't hurt to ask politely for a discount.

The Koreans don't take kindly to nastiness when bargaining – always remember to be polite and smile. If your bargaining gets too persistent and the shopkeeper starts to get angry, that is a sign to end the negotiation swiftly – either pay up and take the goods, or graciously depart the scene. Always smile and say 'thank you'.

Taxes & Refunds

Most items purchased in South Korea are subject to a 10% value added tax (VAT) which is included in the selling price. At upmarket hotels, there is also a 10% VAT on top of a 10% service charge, making for a steep 20% surprise surcharge when you go to pay your bill. However, VAT is not normally charged at the budget hotels.

LUGGAGE STORAGE

International airports have bonded baggage facilities, but airports have no left-luggage rooms after you've passed through customs. If you do place something into bonded baggage, you will not be able to gain access to the luggage until you depart the country. Needless to say, it will also be necessary to depart from the same airport.

Left-luggage rooms are exceedingly rare in Korea. A few national parks have baggage rooms where you can store things while you go hiking. There are lockers at most major railway, subway and bus stations which can be used for a maximum of three days – don't go over the limit or your goods could be confiscated and you'll have to pay a fine to get them back. The price for renting a locker varies from W700 to W1200 and the machines accept W100 coins only. You feed money into the coin slot for the first day, but if you leave things overnight you must put in more coins to get them out again.

POST & COMMUNICATIONS
Postal Rates
Domestic rates are W130 for a letter up to 50g (W930 if registered) and postcards cost W100. International rates vary according to region. The Korean postal service divides the world into four zones: Zone 1 is East Asia; Zone 2 is South-East Asia; Zone 3 is Australia, New Zealand, the USA, Canada, Middle East, Europe and Oceania; Zone 4 is Africa and Latin America. The rates in won are as follows:

Postal Rates	Zone 1	Zone 2	Zone 3	Zone 4
aerograms	350	350	350	350
postcards	300	300	300	300
letters (10 g)	370	400	440	470
letters (20 g)	400	460	540	600
registered letter (10 g)	1170	1200	1240	1270
printed matter (20 g)	200	220	250	300

Sending Mail
Post Office Post offices are open from 9 am to 6 pm on Monday to Friday (9 am to 5 pm during winter) and from 9 am to noon on Saturday. Public mail boxes are always coloured red. Domestic mail can be delivered in about two days if it bears an address in Korean characters – if written in English, figure on a week.

If you're sending parcels or printed matter, don't worry about chasing around for cardboard boxes and the like. Major post offices like the Seoul CPO have excellent, inexpensive packing services.

Sending printed matter is about 40% cheaper than letters, but to get this discount you must seal the envelope with string rather than with tape or glue. The postal packing services know just how to prepare printed matter so you can get this discount, so it's worth your while to let them do it.

If speed is of the utmost importance, you can send documents and small packets by Express Mail Service (EMS) Speedpost (*kokje t'ŭkgŭ pop'yŏn*).

Private Couriers If you need to send things too large or valuable to trust to the post office, or you're simply in a hurry, there are a number of foreign private courier services available. Courier services include Federal Express (☎ 664-2611) and United Parcel Service (☎ 601-3300); both have their main offices near the airport, but offer a pick-up service.

Packing & Shipping A number of companies in Seoul can pack, ship and move large items (household goods, furniture, etc) to or from Korea. They include Saejin Express (☎ 752-9462; fax 756-5681) and Korea Transport Moving & Storage (☎ 358-5411; fax 355-6451).

Receiving Mail
Poste restante is available at all central city post offices, but only in Seoul and Pusan will you find a counter dealing exclusively with poste restante. Elsewhere such letters may go astray because few postal workers speak English.

At poste restante counters, all incoming mail is entered into a logbook which you have to sign when you pick it up – check carefully for your name because letters are often misfiled. Hotels will hold mail for a limited period and perhaps longer if you let them know you are expecting it.

Telephone
There is a 30% discount on calls made from 9 pm to 8 am daily and for 24 hours on Sundays and public holidays.

Pay phones accept three types of coins, W10, W50 and W100 (but *not* W500). Pay phones can be used for local and long distance calls, and there is no time limit as long as you keep feeding money into the machine. The cost for local calls is W40 for three minutes.

You will often find local-call phones are

left off the hook with a credit remaining. This is because it is not possible to get change from a W50 or W100 coin, although you can use the credit after a W40 call to make further calls as long as you don't hang up. To make another call, simply press the green button on the phone (it doesn't always work).

Korea abounds with card phones and these can be used for local, long-distance and international calls. The magnetic telephone cards come in denominations of W3000, W5000 and W10,000, but you get a discount and only have to pay W2900, W4800 and W9500 respectively. The phone cards (*chŏnhwa kadŭ*) can be bought from banks, shops near the card telephones and at 24-hour convenience stores. The cards are notoriously poor quality – the charge on the cards will often disappear a week or two after you've broken the seal on the plastic packet! If this happens, try flexing the card (not too vigorously) and it *might* reappear again. If not, take the card to any phone company office and it will be exchanged free. Needless to say, this is a hassle best avoided, so try to purchase the minimum denomination (W3000) cards and use them up quickly before they go bad.

Of course, you will need to know the area codes when dialling outside your local calling area. It's worth noting that the first two digits of an area code gives a hint as to what part of the country you're calling: 03 is the northern region, 04 is west-central, 05 is south-east and 06 is south-west. The following area codes (listed by province) cover all the major cities and towns in Korea:

Major Cities
  Seoul 02, Inch'ŏn 032, Kwangju 062, Pusan 051, Taegu 053, Taejŏn 042
Kyŏnggi-do
  Ansan 0345, Ansŏng 0334, Changhŭng Resort 0351, Hwasong 0339, Ich'ŏn 0336, Kanghwa 0349, Kapyong 0356, Kimp'o 0341, Koyang 0344, Kuri 0346, Kwangju 0347, Namyangju 0346, Paengnyŏngdo 032, P'aju 0348, P'och'ŏn 0357, P'yŏngt'aek 0333, Sanjŏng Lake 0357, Sŏngnam 0342, Suwon 0331, Uijŏngbu 0351, Yangp'yŏng 0338, Yonchon 0355, Yong-in Farmland 0335, Yŏju 0337

Kangwon-do
  Ch'unch'ŏn 0361, Cholwon 0353, Chŏngson 0398, Hoengsŏng 0372, Hongch'ŏn 0366, Hwach'ŏn 0363, Inje 0365, Kangnŭng 0391, Naksan 0396, Osaek Hot Springs 0396, P'yŏngch'ang 0374, Samch'ŏk 0397, Sokch'o 0392, Sŏrak-dong 0392, T'aebaek 0395, Tonghae 0394, Wŏnju 0371, Yangyang 0396, Yanggu 0364, Yŏngwol 0373
Kyŏngsangbuk-do
  Andong 0571, Ch'ŏngdo 0542, Ch'ŏngsong 0575, Chŏmch'on 0581, Ch'ilgok 0545, Chuwangsan 0575, Hayang 0541, Kimch'ŏn 0547, Koryŏng 0543, Kumi 0546, Kunwi 0578, Kyŏngju 0561, P'ohang 0562, Ponghwa 0573, P'yŏnghae 0565, Sangju 0582, Sŏngju 0544, Uljin 0565, Ullŭngdo 0566, Ŭisŏng 0576, Waegwan 0545, Yŏngch'ŏn 0563, Yŏngdŏk 0564, Yŏngju 0572, Yŏngyang 0574
Kyŏngsangnam-do
  Ch'angnyŏng 0559, Ch'angwon 0551, Ch'ungmu 0557, Chinhae 0553, Chinju 0591, Hadong 0595, Haman 0552, Hamyang 0597, Hapch'ŏn 0599, Kimhae 0525, Koje 0558, Kŏch'ang 0598, Kosŏng 0556, Miryang 0527, Namhae 0594, Pugok 0559, Samch'ŏnp'o 0593, Sanch'ŏng 0596, Taewonsa 0596, Ulsan 0522, Ŭiryŏng 0555, Yangsan 0523
Chŏllanam-do
  Changhŭng 0665, Changsŏng 0685, Chindo 0632, Haenam 0634, Hamp'yŏng 0615, Hongdo 0631, Hŭksando 0631, Hwasun 0612, Kangjin 0638, Kohŭng 0666, Koksŏng 0688, Mokp'o 0631, Wando 0633, Yŏng-am 0693, Yŏnggwang 0686, Yŏsu 0662
Cheju-do
  Cheju 064
Chŏllabuk-do
  Changsu 0656, Chinan 0655, Chŏngŭp 0681, Chŏnju 0652, Imshil 0673, Iri 0653, Kimje 0658, Koch'ang 0677, Kunsan 0654, Moaksan 0658, Muju 0657, Namwon 0671, Puan 0683, Sŏnunsan 0677, Sunch'ang 0674
Ch'ungch'ŏngnam-do
  Ch'ŏnan 0417, Choch'iwan 0415, Chongyang 0454, Hongsŏng 0451, Kongju 0416, Kŭmsan 0412, Nonsan 0461, Onyang 0418, Puyŏ 0463, Sosan 0455, Sŏch'on 0459, Taech'ŏn 0452, Tangjin 0457, Yesan 0458
Ch'ungch'ŏngbuk-do
  Ch'ŏngju 0431, Ch'ungju 0441, Chech'ŏn 0443, Chinch'ŏn 0434, Koesan 0445, Okch'ŏn 0475, Poŭn 0433, Songnisan 0433, Suanbo 0441, Tanyang 0444, Umsong 0446, Yongdong 0414

International Direct Dialling (IDD) calls can be placed through Korea Telecom (by dialling 001) or Dacom (by dialling 002). Calls placed through Dacom are 5% cheaper, but you can only do this from a private phone – Korea Telecom owns the public phones and their phones will not connect to Dacom. To make an IDD call, first dial 001 (or 002), then the country code, area code (minus the initial zero if it has one) and then the number you want to reach.

To place an international call through an English-speaking operator dial 0077. For information about international dialling (country codes, rates, time differences, etc) dial 0074. Placing a call through an international operator means that you must pay for a three-minute minimum call, though the actual rate per minute is the same as IDD. There are four types of operator-assisted calls: station to station, person to person, reverse charges and credit card calls.

The Korean phone company divides the world into four zones: Zone 1 is East Asia; Zone 2 is North America and Oceania; Zone 3 is Europe, Central & South America, the Middle East, South-West Asia and Africa; and Zone 4 is the UK. The following are the daytime IDD rates in won when dialling the 001 prefix:

	First Minute	Each Additional Minute
Zone 1	1150	860
Zone 2	1500	1130
Zone 3	1770	1330
Zone 4	1480	1100

Another dialling option is called 'home country direct', which allows you to talk directly to an operator in the country which you are calling. This system is useful only for collect calls or if you want to charge to a credit card and it's not available for every country. There are special home country direct telephones at Kimp'o airport and at the KNTO in Central Seoul. You can also access home country direct at any card phone – insert the card, dial 0090 (or 0091 for the USA) plus the country direct number (see the boxed list).

If you will be staying in Korea for more than a few months and plan to make frequent

Country Direct Codes

Country	Dial
Australia	0090+61
Canada	0090+015
France	0090+33
Germany	0090+049
Guam	0090+671
Hawaii	0090+012
Hong Kong	0090+852
Indonesia	0090+62
Japan	0090+081
Macau	0090+853
Malaysia	0090+06
New Zealand	0090+64
Philippines (Philcom)	0090+631
Philippines (PLDT)	0090+63
Singapore	0090+65
Taiwan	0090+886
Thailand	0090+660
UK (BT)	0090+44
UK (Mercury)	0090+441
USA (AT&T)	0091+1
USA (MCI)	0091+4
USA (Sprint)	0091+6

calls abroad, it would be worthwhile to sign up for callback services. These companies are almost entirely based in the USA (because of the low phone rates), though it is possible to use their services to call elsewhere. Some American-based callback companies include:

Justice	☎ (310) 335-5262; fax 335-5255
Kallback	☎ (206) 284-8600; fax 270-0009
NewWorld	☎ (201) 996-1670; email: economist@newworldtele.com
PrimeCall	☎ (800) 698-1233; email: primecal@compumedia.com
Ultra comm	☎ (206) 251-0325; fax 251-0326; email: sales@ultracomm.com

Useful Phone Numbers The *Korea Yellow Pages* is published annually in English, and is available from major bookstores in Seoul. There are no white pages available in English, so you'll have to manage with hangŭl. A few useful telephone numbers and prefixes include the following:

Ambulance	☎ 119
Directory Assistance (toll-free)	☎ (080)-211-0114
English-speaking Operator	☎ (080) 211-0114
Fire	☎ 119
IDD (Dacom)	☎ 002
IDD (Korea Telecom)	☎ 001
Immigration (Seoul)	☎ 653-3041
International Dialling Assistance	☎ 0074
International Operator	☎ 0077
Korea's Country Code	☎ 82
Local Directory Assistance	☎ 114
Long-distance Directory Assistance	☎ area code + 114
Phone Repairs	☎ 110
Police	☎ 112
Report A Spy	☎ 113
Telegram (domestic)	☎ 115
Telegram (international)	☎ 005
Time	☎ 116
Toll-free Prefix	☎ 080
Weather (local)	☎ 131
Weather (long-distance)	☎ area code + 131

Cellular Phones If you take up permanent residence in Korea, you could purchase a cellular phone. The new digital models use the controversial CDMA technology, which is compatible with the USA but incompatible with Europe's GSM system.

For those trying to keep expenses down, there is a service in Seoul called 'city phone'. City phones are cheaper than standard cellular service; the difference is that you can only dial out – you cannot receive calls.

Pagers Everyone seems to have a pager these days in Korea, including many short-term expat English teachers. The cost of buying a pager and setting up an account varies from W45,000 to W110,000. The cheaper pagers can only be used in the Seoul metropolitan area, while the pricier models work throughout South Korea. Maintaining your account costs about W11,000 per month for the Seoul area only, or W16,000 to W21,000 per month for Korea-wide service.

Even if you don't have your own pager, it's still useful to know how to contact somebody by this method. The system is fully automated – you don't speak to an operator at all. All Korean pager numbers start with

012 or 015 and are followed by at least seven digits. Simply dial this number (no area code is necessary) and you will hear either a beep or a recorded voice message followed by a beep. At this point you have two options – you can punch in your phone number or leave a voice message. For the first option, after the beep press 1, dial your phone number, finish by pressing the asterisk (or pound sign) and wait a couple of seconds before hanging up. To leave a voice message, after the beep press 2, start talking (maximum 25 seconds) and again press an asterisk or pound sign before hanging up. If you forget to press the asterisk or pound sign, it still seems to work (despite the fact that the paging companies say it won't)!

Naray Mobile Telecom and Seoul Mobile Telecom have both announced that they will soon offer operator-assisted paging systems.

Fax, Telegraph & Email

Fax A fax service is available at major post offices and at business centres in tourist hotels. Many small shops also offer photocopying and a fax service – these are most numerous in the vicinity of universities.

Telegraph If you want to send a telegram, it's probably easiest to go to the telephone office and write it out on paper. However, you can call one in if you have your own phone by dialling 115 (domestic) or 005 (international). Domestic telegrams are of two types, ordinary and express. If sent in English, ordinary telegrams cost W80 per word and express cost W160 per word. For international telegrams, the cost per word is as follows:

Australia	W660	Japan	W240
Canada	W430	Taiwan	W240
France	W450	UK	W610
Germany	W430	USA	W280
Hong Kong	W270		

Electronic Mail Electronic mail *(chonja meil)* and Internet surfing have both become very chic in Korea. There are several ways to get online whether you are a permanent resident or just a short-term visitor to the country.

If you don't happen to have your own computer, you can still go online by visiting a cyber cafe. Failing that, a few super-deluxe hotels have business centres equipped with computers and modems. However, the fees for using these can add up fast.

Things are more straightforward if you have your own portable computer. If you're a member of CompuServe, you can simply plug in your modem and dial up Hanjin-Net (☎ 786-5501) or Info-Net (☎ 795-1002) in Seoul. If you need assistance or wish to sign up as a new member, CompuServe's representative in Korea is Hanjin Information Systems & Telecommunications (☎ 318-1435; toll-free (080) 090-1435; fax 753-8666), 17th floor, 51 Sogong-dong, Chung-gu, Seoul.

Members of America Online can gain access by dialling one of the AolGlobalnet Access numbers (Seoul ☎ 775-6647; Pusan 462-5408).

If you take up residence in Korea, you can establish a local Internet account and do your email on the cheap. Korea's four most popular network service providers are (in more or less descending order): Hitel (☎ 764-0001, 743-0223) which is run by Korea Telecom; Chollian (☎ 790-1522, 797-7555) which belongs to Dacom; Unitel (☎ 528-0114) which is run by Samsung; and Nownuri (☎ 590-3800) by Nowcom. These networks are mostly in hangŭl, but they provide Internet gateways in English.

If you can't read hangŭl and Internet surfing is your main interest, the best thing to do is sign up with a direct Internet service provider (ISP). Prices vary considerably, but typically average W25,000 to W40,000 per month and some companies offer big discounts to students. All ISPs are based in Seoul; most (though not all) offer local calling numbers throughout Korea. ISPs come and go – new ones are opening up all the time while others go bust. The situation will no doubt be different by the time you read this, but among the current crop you will find:

AmiNet	☎ 398-4867; http:// www.aminet.co.kr
CRENET	email: info@cre.co.kr;
	http:// www.cre.co.kr
ELIMnet	☎ 3149-4800; http:// www.elim.co.kr.
Hinet-P	☎ 753-0200
I-Net	☎ 538-6941; fax 538-6942;
	email: info@nuri.net; http:// www.inet.co.kr
Interpia	http:// www.interpia.net
Ivy Net	http:// www.hansol.net
Nextel, also called Uriel	☎ 202-9300;
	http:// www.nextel.net or www.uriel.net

BOOKS

There are some excellent books in print covering Korea's history, religion and culture. Unfortunately, most are hard to obtain outside Korea. Seoul is really the only place to go hunting for books printed in English, although you might stumble across something in Pusan. Outside Korea you will probably have to obtain books by special order.

Lonely Planet

For those with more time to explore Korea's capital, Lonely Planet publishes the *Seoul city guide*. On the opposite extreme, *North-East Asia on a shoestring* gives a condensed overview of both North and South Korea.

The guidebook you now hold in your hands only covers the very basics of the Korean language. For a more in-depth look, see Lonely Planet's *Korean phrasebook*.

Guidebooks

The Berlitz *Korean For Travellers* has extensive vocabulary lists, but doesn't offer much help with the grammar. Be prepared to spend some time working through it. To delve even further into the language, *An Introductory Course in Korean* by Fred Lukoff is a popular textbook available within Korea.

Korea Guide – A Glimpse of Korea's Cultural Legacy by Edward B Adams is highly informative and colourful. If you want to appreciate the splendour of Kyŏngju, the same author has done a magnificent job in *Korea's Golden Age*.

Discovering Seoul: An Historical Guide by James Grayson & Donald Clark is strong on historical Seoul, for those who want to identify every nook and cranny of the palaces. *Seoul* by Rose E Lee is a good introduction to the city.

For illuminating background reading and good photographs, turn to the Insight Guide to *Korea*.

History & Politics

One of the most up-to-date histories is *Korean Old and New – A History.* Also very current is *Korea, Tradition & Transformation* by Andrew C Nahm.

The entire Chosŏn dynasty is well-covered by *The Confucian Transformation of Korea* by Martina Deuchler. The same author also did a fine earlier work called *Confucian Gentlemen and Barbarian Envoys* which covers the opening of Korea between 1875 and 1885.

General

A good primer in Korean culture is *Korea's Cultural Roots* by Jon Carter Covell, which covers Shamanism, Confucianism and Buddhism. Sequels by the same author include *Korea's Colorful Heritage* and *The World of Korean Ceramics*. Teaming up with her son Alan, the Covells produced *Korean Impact On Japanese Culture – Japan's Hidden History*. Alan Covell went on to write *Folk Art and Magic – Shamanism in Korea*. All these books are published by Hollym Publications in Seoul.

Those interested in South Korea's economy should pick up a copy of *The Chaebol* by Steers, Shin & Ungson.

Korea, A Religious History by James Huntley Grayson is a fine scholarly work.

To understand the heart and soul of Korean Confucianism, the book to read is *To Become A Sage – The Ten Diagrams on Sage Learning* by Yi T'oegye.

Two intellectual works are *Introduction of Buddhism to Korea* and *Assimilation of Buddhism in Korea* by Lancaster & Yu.

To Dream of Pigs by Clive Leatherdale is an excellent travelogue of both North and South Korea.

ONLINE SERVICES

The Internet changes so fast that almost anything one can say about it will probably be obsolete tomorrow. With that caveat in mind, the following attempts to provide some general insight on where to start searching the Net for information on Korea.

The KNTO provides plenty of useful online data of interest to travellers. Check out their web site (http://www.knto.or.kr). Alternatively, you can telnet to the KNTO IP address (203.236.107.10).

Log-In Seoul has an interesting web site (http://www.login.co.kr).

The *Korean Herald* has some online news (http://zec.three.co.kr/koreaherald)

A good all-round web site – especially for business travellers – is Korealink (http://www.korealink.co.kr).

The KRNIC, or Korea Network Information Centre (http://www.krnic.net), is another place to look. KRNIC aims to provide information service to the Internet within Korea and to provide a primary contact point for inquiries on Korean Internet.

There is an emailing list called 'KEXPAT' which provides a discussion forum for expats living in Korea. To subscribe, send a message to *kexpat-d request@uriel.net.* Place the words *subscribe kexpat* in the subject line. To post a message, email it to kexpat@uriel.net.

And, of course, there's the award-winning Lonely Planet website (http://www.lonely planet.com).

NEWSPAPERS & MAGAZINES

Two locally produced English-language newspapers are available: the *Korea Times* and the *Korea Herald*. These papers are published six days a week – the day on which they're not published alternates between Sunday and Monday. Both perhaps glean their news from Korea's official Yonhap news agency, which is why they report identical news. The *Herald* has a better TV listing and seems to be more popular with expats than the *Times*.

Log-In Seoul is a weekly freebie geared towards counter-culture and cyber-punks. In

Seoul, look for copies at various cyber-cafes, trendy restaurants or the KNTO tourist office. For subscription information try sending email to login@elim.net or write to Seodaemoon, PO Box 113, Seoul 120-600.

Seoul Scope is a monthly magazine in English which ostensibly costs W2000 per issue but is in fact free at the KNTO tourist office. You can order a subscription for W18,000 per year by ringing up the office in Seoul (☎ 743-7784; fax 743-7078).

Koreana magazine is the best source on arts and culture. It's published quarterly by the Korea Foundation and costs W4500 per issue or W18,000 per year by subscription. There are great photos, essays, translations of stories and poems, plus theme issues covering temples, music, novels, painting, sports, songs and pottery.

The *Korea Economic Report*, *Korea Post* and *Business Korea* are locally published monthly magazines; people who find these most interesting are mainly Koreans learning to speak English.

Large bookstores in Seoul and most of the large hotels sell imported publications. The best coverage of Korea in foreign publications seems to be in the *Asian Wall Street Journal*, *Far Eastern Economic Review* and *The Economist*.

RADIO & TV

There are four Korean-language TV networks: KBS, MBC, SBS and EBS. A few programs are bilingual, but a special TV is needed to switch between Korean and English. Korean TV broadcasts on week days from 6 am to 10 am and from 5.30 pm until midnight; on Saturdays from 6 am to 10 am and from 1 pm until midnight; and on Sundays from 6 am until midnight.

AFKN is an English-language cable TV station run by the US military. It features typical US shows, but sex scenes are judiciously censored to avoid offending Korean sensibilities. Advertising is also axed – and replaced with military advice and safety tips like 'wear your uniform proudly' and 'driving and alcohol don't mix'. AFKN broadcasts 24 hours a day, although it's mostly trash between midnight and 6 am. Outside military bases AFKN is only available on cable TV.

Satellite TV is now widely available, even at some budget hotels. The most popular stations are CNN, Hong Kong's STAR TV and Japan's NHK.

AFKN radio broadcasts in English 24 hours a day on AM (549 kHz) and FM (102.7 MHz). A complete schedule of TV and radio programs is listed in the daily English-language newspapers.

VIDEO SYSTEMS

South Korea has adopted the NTSC video standard. This is the same standard used in the USA, Canada and Japan, but is incompatible with the PAL standard (used in Australia, Hong Kong, New Zealand, the UK and most of Europe) and SECAM (France, Germany and Luxembourg). Video rental shops are abundant and many foreign movies are in English with Korean subtitles.

PHOTOGRAPHY & VIDEO

All the big-name brands of print film are readily available in Korea and at reasonable prices. Photoprocessing facilities are of an international standard and not expensive. Slide film is a little more difficult to come by and easiest to find in Seoul. Blank video cassettes are readily available.

For processing slide film, prices seem to vary depending on where you ask. Professional photoprocessing shops are usually cheapest and fastest – most offer one-day service. Ordinary camera shops can take three days and charge double.

Korea is not a particularly good place to buy photographic or video equipment because of prohibitive import taxes. For this reason, there is a large market in second-hand cameras, but even these are not cheap. Korean-made point-and-shoot cameras exist, but the lack of competition ensures that they are also overpriced. If you want a Japanese-made camera it would be better to pick one up in Hong Kong, Singapore, Taipei or even Tokyo.

Beware the traditional Korean *ondol* (underfloor heating system), which can slowly cook your film if you leave it or your camera on the floor.

Be careful about taking liberties when photographing monks. South Korea is a country still technically at war and photographing military installations or anything of a military nature is prohibited. Student rioters are not particularly fond of being photographed. Photographs can be taken around airports but do not try to photograph the airport security procedures.

TIME

The time in South Korea is GMT/UTC plus nine hours. When it's noon in South Korea it is 7 pm the previous day in San Francisco, 10 pm the previous day in New York, 3 am in London and 1 pm in Sydney. Daylight savings time is *not* observed.

ELECTRICITY

Both 110V and 220V, both 60Hz (60 cycles per second), are in common use. The way to tell the difference in voltage is from the design of the electrical outlets – two flat pins is 110V and two round pins is 220V. There is no third wire for ground (earth).

WEIGHTS & MEASURES

In former times, Korea used the traditional Chinese system of weights and measures. Nowadays, the international metric system is in use for everything except the measurement of real estate. When buying or renting a flat, area is measured in *p'yŏng*, where one p'yŏng is equal to 3.3 sq metres.

LAUNDRY

Most hotels, including bottom-end yŏgwan, can do laundry if you prefer not to do it yourself. Charges for this service are usually reasonable, but ask first.

There are laundromats in large cities (especially Seoul); they are most common around universities. Charges are typically W4000 for a large load.

Many travellers wind up doing their own laundry in the nearest sink. This can work OK, but dark coloured clothing is preferred because the dirt won't show up so clearly. Most yŏgwan try to discourage this – they seldom provide more than two coat hangers per room so it's difficult to find a place to hang things up to dry. Still, you can manage with a little creativity (some string and clothes pins usually will do the job).

HEALTH

No vaccinations are required to enter South Korea. This doesn't mean you shouldn't get any: it isn't a bad idea to get a few prophylactic jabs in the arm if you will be travelling to neighbouring Asian countries (such as China). It's probably a good idea to get a hepatitis A vaccination and polio, tetanus and diphtheria boosters. Other shots to consider are rabies, hepatitis B, tuberculosis and typhoid.

That having been said, South Korea is a very healthy country – you are unlikely to encounter any of the things that might have you running for the nearest pharmacy in India, the Philippines or Indonesia.

Opinions are divided as to whether you can drink the tap water – some South Koreans do, some don't. It might be best to drink only boiled water until your body adjusts to the local microbes. If you drink unboiled water it's unlikely you'll suffer any illness more serious than diarrhoea, although there is some risk of hepatitis A.

Emergency medical care in hospitals is excellent and reasonably cheap, but normal outpatient care leaves much to be desired. Westerners are liable to become very frustrated with most Korean doctors because they will not answer questions from patients regarding illness, laboratory tests or the treatment being given. Questions are regarded as insults to the doctor's competence, thus causing a loss of face. If you are dying, Korean doctors will not even tell you this since it would imply that the doctor is too incompetent to cure you. Doctors who have studied and worked abroad may be more accustomed to western ways.

Getting the Point

Acupuncture, the traditional Chinese system of healing in which needles are inserted into specific points of the body, is widely practised in Korea. The procedure itself is hardly appealing, but is known to relieve an amazing range of symptoms.

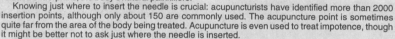

The exact mechanism by which acupuncture works is not fully understood, but practitioners suggest that the needle stimulates energy channels, meridians or deep sensory nerves which connect the insertion point to the organ, gland or joint being treated. This needle stimulation is also thought to cause the pituitary and midbrain to release endorphins, the body's natural painkillers.

Knowing just where to insert the needle is crucial: acupuncturists have identified more than 2000 insertion points, although only about 150 are commonly used. The acupuncture point is sometimes quite far from the area of the body being treated. Acupuncture is even used to treat impotence, though it might be better not to ask just where the needle is inserted.

As with herbal medicine, the fundamental question asked by a sceptical patient is: 'Will it really work?'. Unfortunately, the answer is far from clear. Not only does it depend on the skill of the acupuncturist, but also on what condition is being treated. Like herbal medicine, acupuncture tends to be more useful for those who suffer from lingering conditions (like chronic headaches) rather than sudden emergencies (like an acute appendicitis).

However, there are times when acupuncture has been used for an immediate condition. Major surgical operations have been performed using acupuncture as the only anaesthetic. Again, it is not understood just how or why this works.

Suction is a related form of healing; a piece of alcohol-soaked cotton is set alight in a cup made of bamboo. When the cup is placed directly onto the patient's skin, the flame is extinguished and a partial vacuum is produced, sucking the area up into the cup. Suction leaves a nasty-looking, but harmless, red circular mark on the skin which goes away in a few days.

Moxibustion is similar. Various types of herbs, rolled into what looks like a ball of fluffy cotton, are held just near the skin and ignited. Another method is to place the herb on a slice of ginger then ignite it. The idea is to apply the maximum amount of heat possible without burning the patient. This heat treatment is thought to be good for diseases such as arthritis. ∎

An embassy or consulate can usually recommend a good place to go for medical advice. So can five-star hotels, although they often recommend doctors with five-star prices. (This is when that medical insurance really comes in useful!)

Self-treatment poses some risks, but Korean pharmacists are willing to sell you all sorts of dangerous drugs over the counter without a prescription. Be careful about abusing over-the-counter drugs – many people do, sometimes with serious consequences. Korean pharmacists know the English names of most drugs but can't pronounce them. However, they can generally read English well, so try writing down what you want to avoid misunderstandings. Pharmacies seem to be everywhere and can be found in most bus terminals. To find a Korean pharmacy, simply look for the character:

Environmental Hazards

Sunburn You can get sunburnt surprisingly quickly, even through cloud, at the beach or while skiing. Use a sunscreen and take extra care to cover areas which don't normally see sun – eg your feet. A hat provides added protection, and you should also use zinc cream or some other barrier cream for your nose and lips. Calamine lotion is good for mild sunburn.

Remember that too much sunlight, whether its direct or reflected (glare) can damage your eyes. If your plans include being near water, sand or snow, then good sunglasses are doubly important. Good quality sunglasses are treated to filter out ultraviolet radiation, but poor quality sunglasses provide limited filtering, allowing more ultraviolet light to be absorbed than if no sunglasses were worn at all. Excessive ultraviolet light will damage the surface structures and lens of the eye.

Heat Exhaustion Dehydration or salt deficiency can cause heat exhaustion. Take time to acclimatise to high temperatures and make sure you drink sufficient liquids. Wear loose clothing and a broad-brimmed hat. Do not do anything too physically demanding.

Salt deficiency is characterised by fatigue, lethargy, headaches, giddiness and muscle cramps and in this case salt tablets may help. Vomiting or diarrhoea can deplete your liquid and salt levels.

Hypothermia Too much cold is just as dangerous as too much heat and can lead to hypothermia. You should always be prepared for cold, wet or windy conditions if you're walking in national or provincial parks, or climbing scenic peaks.

Hypothermia occurs when the body loses heat faster than it can produce it and the core temperature of the body falls. It is surprisingly easy to progress from very cold to dangerously cold with a combination of wind, wet clothing, fatigue and hunger, even if the air temperature is above freezing. It is best to dress in layers; silk, wool and some of the new artificial fibres are all good insulating materials. A hat is important, as a lot of heat is lost through the head. A strong, waterproof outer layer is essential because keeping dry is vital. Carry basic supplies, including food containing simple sugars to generate heat quickly and lots of fluid to drink. A space blanket is something all travellers in cold environments should carry.

Symptoms of hypothermia are exhaustion, numb skin (particularly toes and fingers), shivering, slurred speech, irrational or violent behaviour, lethargy, stumbling,

dizzy spells, muscle cramps and violent bursts of energy. Irrationality may take the form of sufferers claiming they are warm and trying to take off their clothes.

To treat mild hypothermia, first get the person out of the wind and/or rain, remove their clothing if it's wet and replace it with dry, warm clothing. Give them hot liquids – not alcohol – and some high-kilojoule, easily digestible food. Do not rub victims, instead allow them to slowly warm themselves. This should be enough to treat the early stages of hypothermia. The early recognition and treatment of mild hypothermia is the only way to prevent severe hypothermia, which is a critical condition.

Motion Sickness If you'll be taking a ferry to one of the islands, or farther to Japan or China, and you're prone to seasickness, you must prepare yourself before departure. Eating lightly before and during a trip will reduce the chances of motion sickness. If you are prone to motion sickness try to find a place that minimises disturbance – near the wing on aircraft, close to midships on boats, near the centre on buses. Fresh air usually helps; reading and cigarette smoke don't. Commercial motion sickness preparations, which can cause drowsiness, have to be taken before the trip commences; when you're feeling sick it's too late. Ginger (available in capsule form) and peppermint (including mint-flavoured sweets) are natural preventatives.

Infectious Diseases
Diarrhoea A change of water, food or climate can all cause the runs; diarrhoea caused by contaminated food or water is more serious. Despite all your precautions you may still get a mild bout of travellers' diarrhoea but a few rushed toilet trips with no other symptoms is not indicative of a serious problem. Moderate diarrhoea, involving half-a-dozen loose movements in a day, is more of a nuisance. Dehydration is the main danger with any diarrhoea, particularly for children for whom dehydration can occur quite quickly. Fluid replacement

remains the mainstay of management. Weak black tea with a little sugar, soda water, or soft drinks allowed to go flat and diluted 50% with water are all good. With severe diarrhoea a rehydrating solution is necessary to replace minerals and salts. Commercially available oral rehydration salts (ORS) are very useful; add the contents of one sachet to a litre of boiled or bottled water. In an emergency you can make up a solution of eight teaspoons of sugar to a litre of boiled water and provide salted cracker biscuits at the same time. Stick to a bland diet as you recover.

Lomotil or Imodium can be used to bring relief from the symptoms, although they do not actually cure the problem. Only use these drugs if absolutely necessary – eg if you *must* travel. For children under 12 years Lomotil and Imodium are not recommended. Under all circumstances fluid replacement is the most important thing to remember. Do not use these drugs if the person has a high fever or is severely dehydrated.

Hepatitis A This is a very common disease in countries with poor standrds of santitation, but the risk of contracting it in Korea is no more than in other deveoped nations. Hepatitis A only poses a threat to the traveller who may have been exposed to it while passing through a developing countries.

The symptoms are fever, chills, headache, fatigue, feelings of weakness and aches and pains, followed by loss of appetite, nausea, vomiting, abdominal pain, dark urine, light-coloured faeces and jaundiced skin, and the whites of the eyes may turn yellow. In some cases you may feel unwell, tired, have no appetite, experience aches and pains and be jaundiced. You should seek medical advice, but in general there is not much you can do apart from resting, drinking lots of fluids, eating lightly and avoiding fatty foods. People who have had hepatitis must forego alcohol for six months after the illness, as hepatitis attacks the liver and it needs that amount of time to recover.

The routes of transmission are via contaminated water, shellfish contaminated by sewage, or foodstuffs sold by food handlers with poor standards of hygiene.

Taking care with what you eat and drink can go a long way towards preventing this disease. But this is a very infectious virus, so if there is any risk of exposure, additional cover is highly recommended. This cover comes in two forms: Gamma globulin and Havrix 1440. Gamma globulin is an injection where you are given the antibodies for hepatitis A, which provide immunity for a limited time. Havrix 1440 is a vaccine, where you develop your own antibodies, which gives lasting immunity.

Sexually Transmitted Diseases
Sexual contact with an infected sexual partner spreads these diseases. While abstinence is the only 100% preventative, using condoms is also effective. Gonorrhoea, herpes and syphilis are among these diseases; sores, blisters or rashes around the genitals, discharges or pain when urinating are common symptoms. In some STDs, such as wart virus or chlamydia, symptoms may be less marked or not observed at all in women. Syphilis symptoms eventually disappear completely, but the disease continues and can cause severe problems in later years. The treatment of gonorrhoea and syphilis is with antibiotics.

There are numerous other sexually transmitted diseases, for most of which effective treatment is available. However, there is no cure for herpes and there is also currently no cure for AIDS. Any exposure to blood, blood products or bodily fluids may put the individual at risk of AIDS. Transmission can be through heterosexual sexual activity, but in industrialised countries it is mostly through contact between homosexual or bisexual males, or via contaminated needles shared by IV drug users. Apart from abstinence, the most effective preventative is always to practise safe sex using condoms. It is impossible to detect the HIV-positive status of an otherwise healthy-looking person without a blood test.

Officially, at least, the incidence of AIDS and IV drug use is low in Korea. It's easy enough to buy condoms (same word in Korean) at any pharmacy. Unlike in western countries, they are not sold in supermarkets or convenience stores. In some hotels you may well find a condom machine in your room (so if you forgot to bring the condoms, then at least bring two W500 coins).

AIDS can also be spread by dirty needles – vaccinations, acupuncture, tattooing and ear or nose piercing can be potentially as dangerous as intravenous drug use if the equipment is not clean.

Fear of HIV infection should never preclude treatment for serious medical conditions. Although there may be a risk of infection, it is very small indeed.

Insect Bites & Stings

Thanks to Korea's cold climate, insects are not the major threat to your health they can be in tropical countries. Nevertheless, insect bites can be a nuisance if you do much summer hiking. For those with allergies, certain types of insect bites can even be life threatening.

Mosquitos are an annoyance during summer, especially in the far south, but in Korea they do not carry malaria. Electric mosquito zappers are useful, but are too heavy for travelling. Mosquito incense coils are also effective, but these put out a large amount of nasty smoke and the incense coils break easily when travelling. The Korean solution to these problems is 'electric mosquito incense' (chŏnja mugihyang); this consists of a small plastic bottle of insecticide which is slowly vapourised by an electric heater. The entire unit (bottle and electric heater) only weighs a few grams and is easy to travel with. You can purchase both the heater and bottles of insecticide in Korean pharmacies. A variation on the theme is a cardboard pad (soaked in insecticide) and an electric heater - this design is perhaps superior since there is no possibility of a leaky bottle making a mess out of your backpack. The long-term health effects of breathing the vapourised insecticide are unknown; at the very least it seems to irritate the nasal passages, but all the manufacturers

of this stuff insist that it's safe. However, if you're going to resort to such chemical weapons, it might be prudent to keep a window partially open.

If you are allergic to red ant bites or bee and wasp stings, it is prudent to carry some epinephrine in your first-aid kit.

Emergencies

To contact the police in an emergency dial ☎ 112 and for the fire department dial ☎ 119. If no English is spoken, keep trying. On a public phone just push the red button before dialling these emergency numbers – you won't need a phone card or coins.

If you need urgent medical attention, Asia Emergency Assistance (☎ 790-7561) in Seoul is an organisation that operates 24 hours a day and will act as an intermediary between foreigners and Korean hospitals. There is a fee involved for the latter.

If an emergency occurs on the street look for a police box. There seems to be one on every second street corner.

TOILETS

Kudos to the Koreans for their fine public toilets. You'll find these facilities everywhere you need them – in parks, railway stations, bus stations, department stores and museums. Korea's public toilets are kept universally clean and are free of charge. Even in Seoul's congested subways you can find clean and uncrowded rest rooms. It's a sharp contrast to other cities in the region (shame on you, Hong Kong).

Public toilets come in two flavours – typical Asian squat-style and western throne-style. Keeping your balance while using a squat toilet is a little tricky for uninitiated westerners. Don't leave your wallet in your back pocket at such times, lest it disappear forever into the abyss. Using one of these toilets while standing up can take considerable skill – one male traveller compared it to those water-pistol games at the amusement park!

What to do with used toilet paper can be an important issue. In general, if you see a waste basket next to the toilet, that is where you should throw the toilet paper: the plumbing system in many older buildings cannot cope with toilet paper. Also, in rural areas there is seldom a sewage treatment plant – the waste empties into an underground septic tank and toilet paper will really create a mess in there. For the sake of international relations, be considerate and throw the paper in the waste basket if one is provided.

Another toilet tip – keep a small stash of tissue paper with you at all times, since it's not always available.

WOMEN TRAVELLERS

In general, Korea is a safe place for women travellers, but sexual assaults seem to be on the increase and a few foreign women have been raped. There's no need for excessive paranoia, but think twice before taking late-night solo sojourns down dark alleys.

Koreans tend to be big drinkers and you may meet some fairly aggressive drunks late at night. At least in Seoul, it's quite common from 10 pm onwards for the streets to be crowded with swaying packs of drunken office workers.

Korea remains very much a male-dominated society. Korean women complain of furtive groping on crowded trains and buses – some carry pins and umbrellas for the express purpose of deterring probing hands.

TRAVEL WITH CHILDREN

As in most of Asia, children are highly prized in Korea. Everywhere you go, adults will want to play with your children. For the most part this is harmless – kidnapping of children is rare and almost unheard of when the kids are foreigners. Still, use common sense as you would anywhere else. By far the biggest danger to children is from the traffic.

Toddlers under age two can generally travel free on public transport; kids aged two through 12 typically get a 50% discount on tickets and admission fees.

USEFUL ORGANISATIONS

In Seoul the Foreign Community Service (FOCUS) (☎ 798-7529, 797-8212) provides referrals to hospitals, doctors, lawyers, schools and other services in South Korea.

This place could be good for advice on activities, renting apartments, etc, but it's mostly oriented to long-term foreign residents rather than short-term travellers. The office is open Monday to Friday, 9 am to 5 pm, and there's a 24-hour answer phone for emergencies. The address is 5th floor, B Building, Namsan Village Apartments, San 1-139, It'aewon-dong, Yongsan-gu.

To complain about taxis and other transport you can also try the Transportation Complaint Centre (☎ 392-4745), 122 Pongnae-dong 2-ga, Chung-gu, Seoul 100-162.

Business travellers might find it useful to contact one of the following organisations:

Federation of Korean Industries (FKI),
    28-1 Yŏŭido-dong, Yŏongdŭngp'o-gu, Seoul
    (☎ 780-0821; fax 782-6425)
Korea Chamber of Commerce & Industry (KCCI),
    45 Namdaemunno 4-ga, Chung-gu, Seoul
    (☎ 316-3114)
Korea Exhibition Centre (KOEX),
    159-1 Samsŏng-dong, Kangnam-gu, Seoul
    (☎ 551-0114; fax 555-7414)
Korea Foreign Trade Association (KFTA),
    159-1 Samsŏng-dong, Kangnam-gu, Seoul
    (☎ 551-5114; 551-5100)
Korea Trade Promotion Corporation (KOTRA),
    159-1 Samsŏng-dong, Kangnam-gu, Seoul
    (☎ 551-4181; fax 551-4477)
Korea World Trade Centre (KWTC),
    159-1 Samsŏng-dong, Kangnam-gu, Seoul
    (☎ 551-5114; fax 551-5100)

DANGERS & ANNOYANCES
Crime

Korea is one of the safest countries in Asia, but this does not mean that foreigners never encounter trouble. There are very strict gun control laws and almost no drug addicts – both these factors undoubtedly keep the crime rate down. Unfortunately, Korea is no longer the crime-free country it once was. In Seoul, burglaries have become common while muggings and rapes are on the rise. It's still much safer than Third World cities like Manila or New York, but you should keep your valuables secure. The back alleys of any large city are best avoided late at night, but you can walk major streets after dark without fear. Pickpockets work in all crowded areas.

Riots

Student rioting is a seasonal sport most common in late spring or early summer. Although fatalities are rare, injuries are common. It's best to avoid riots unless your idea of a good time is getting clubbed or tear-gassed (by police), fire bombed (by students) or stoned (with rocks).

Macho Posturing

The Korean Health & Welfare Ministry estimates about one in five Korean men over the age of 20 has a serious drinking problem. Most drinkers are 'friendly drunks' whose worst habit is puking in the gutter (you'll see plenty of that if you wander around Seoul at night). However, more than a few men can become quite hostile after they've drunk enough to lose their inhibitions. And it's then that Korea's famous xenophobia can boil to the surface.

In other words, foreign males who head out for a night on the town should watch out for aggressive locals (and this particularly applies to It'aewon). Some of the bumps you get on the street late at night may not be accidental. The thing to do is to stay cool and keep walking. It's no use arguing with a drunk and if you try to fight your way out of a situation there's a good change that you'll get pounced upon by incensed passers-by. If things get violent, the foreigner is usually seen to be in the wrong.

One thing worth bearing in mind is that a foreign man with a Korean woman (or a woman who looks Korean) runs a particularly high risk of being the recipient of Korean male belligerence. The woman will also be given a hard time. If you are male and with a Korean female friend, at least take the precaution of not holding hands or showing any other intimacy.

I came across two Korean men fighting in an alley and a few other Koreans were watching. But when the brawling duo saw me, the foreigner, they immediately stopped fighting. First there was embarrassed silence, then friendly smiles and I was escorted out of the alley. I was really tempted to sneak back to see if the fighting had resumed, but I didn't dare.

Marie Scott

War Games

Air-raid drills are held occasionally, but never more than once a month. When you hear the sirens you must get off the streets and keep away from doors and windows. If you're on a bus during an air raid, the bus will stop and you'll have to get off and seek shelter. After the all-clear signal is given, you are permitted to get back on the bus again without paying an additional fare – some people take advantage of this to get a free ride.

While in Seoul we experienced an air-raid drill and were fascinated to see a busy 14-lane highway become deserted in three minutes flat.

R Allen

LEGAL MATTERS

Outside of getting busted for drugs or caught working illegally, resident foreigners are most likely to become involved in the law by suing their employer after being cheated on wages. In Seoul, you can try ringing up Volunteer Lawyers (☎ 522-9100) or the Association for Foreign Workers' Human Rights (☎ 795-5504). Otherwise, contact your embassy.

BUSINESS HOURS

For most government offices, business hours are from 9 am to 6 pm Monday to Friday, and from 9 am to 1 pm on Saturdays. From November to February, government offices close at 5 pm.

Private businesses normally operate from 8.30 am until 7 pm on weekdays, and from 8.30 am to 2 pm on Saturdays. Department stores are open from 10.30 am to 7.30 pm daily, while small shops may stay open from dawn until late at night.

PUBLIC HOLIDAYS & SPECIAL EVENTS

There are two types of public holidays – those that are set according to the solar calendar and those that follow the lunar calendar. Solar holidays include:

1 & 2 January
New Year's Day
1 March
Independence Movement Day Anniversary of the 1919 Independence Movement against the Japanese.
5 April
Arbor Day Trees are planted across the nation as part of South Korea's ongoing reafforestation program.
5 May
Children's Day
6 June
Memorial Day
17 July
Constitution Day
15 August
Liberation Day In memory of the Japanese acceptance of the Allied terms of surrender in 1945.
3 October
National Foundation Day
25 December
Christmas Day

Lunar holidays, of course, fall on different dates in different years. There are three lunar festivals which are designated public holidays, as follows:

Lunar New Year *(sŏlnal)*
The 1st day of the 1st moon. You can expect Korea (and the rest of North-East Asia) to grind to a halt at this time. This holiday will fall on the following dates: 28 January 1998; 16 February 1999; 5 February 2000; 24 January 2001.
Buddha's Birthday
Also called the 'Feast of the Lanterns', this is held on the 8th day of the 4th moon, which will fall on the following dates: 3 May 1998; 22 May 1999; 11 May 2000; 30 April 2001. It's celebrated in Seoul with an evening lantern parade from Yŏŭido Plaza to the temple of Chogyesa, starting around 6.30 pm. On the same evening, there is a similar lantern parade at Pŏpchusa, a temple in Songnisan National Park in the central part of the country.
Harvest Moon Festival *(chusŏk)*
Also known as the 'Korean Thanksgiving'. It falls on the 15th day of the 8th moon and is the most important of South Korea's lunar holidays. At this time Seoul becomes almost deserted as most city dwellers return to their family homes and prepare offerings for their ancestral tombs. As in other North-East Asian countries, moon viewing is another feature of the festival. This holiday will fall on the following dates: 16 September 1997; 5 October 1998; 24 September 1999; 12 September 2000; 1 October 2001.

A large number of festivals are held annually throughout the country and there are also smaller festivals held only in particular locations. These may not be public holidays but they are nonetheless interesting. Some of the more notable festivals include:

Sŏkchŏnje
This fascinating ceremony is held twice a year according to the lunar calendar (1st day of the 2nd moon and 1st day of the 8th moon). The 1st day of the 1st moon will fall on the following dates: 27 February 1998; 18 March 1999; 6 March 2000; 23 March 2001. The 1st day of the 8th moon will fall on the following dates: 2 September 1997; 21 September 1998; 10 September 1999; 29 August 2000; 17 September 2001. The ceremony is staged in the courtyard of the Confucius Shrine at Sungkyunkwan University in the north of Seoul, and at a few other Confucian shrines in other cities. Performances are done by a traditional court orchestra and full-costume rituals are enacted. To get to the university, take the subway to Hyehwa subway station.

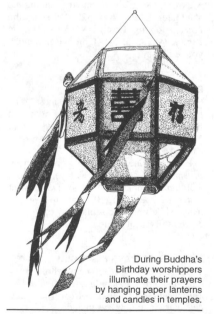

During Buddha's Birthday worshippers illuminate their prayers by hanging paper lanterns and candles in temples.

Chyongmyo T'aeje
    Called the 'Royal Shrine Rites' in English, this is a homage to the kings and queens of the Chosŏn kingdom. Full costume parades are held along with court music. It takes place in Seoul's Chongmyo Shrine on the first Sunday of May.

Tano Festival
    This is held throughout South Korea on the 5th day of the 5th lunar month, which will fall on the following dates: 30 May 1998; 18 June 1999; 6 June 2000; 25 June 2001. The festival features processions of shamans and mask dance dramas.

National Folk Arts Festival
    The date and the venue for the National Folk Arts Festival changes from year to year, but falls around September. It is an excellent opportunity to see traditional Korean festival activities, and includes real crowd pullers like the wagon battle and torch-hurling events. Check with KNTO to find out when it's scheduled.

Cherry Blossom Festival
    This week-long event is held in the southern city of Chinhae and is usually held in the first half of April. An exact date is hard to give because the weather (and thus, the cherry blossoms) won't always co-operate.

ACTIVITIES

Archery (kungdo)

Both traditional Korean style archery and the western form are practised in South Korea. Archery ranges are usually out of town. More information can be obtained by contacting the Korea Amateur Sport Association (☎ 420-3333), 888 Oryun-dong, Songp'a-gu, Seoul.

Billiards & Bowling (tanggu, polling)

The Koreans are keen on bowling and even keener on billiards. Billiard halls are to be found everywhere – an unmistakable sign identifies these places. Koreans can advise you on the location of bowling alleys, though they are not difficult to find. Operating hours are approximately from 10 am until midnight.

Canoeing & Rafting (k'anu, kǔmnyut'agi)

Korea has only three rivers which attract white water enthusiasts: the Naerinchŏn River near Inje in Kangwon is considered the best; in the southern part of Kangwon near Yŏngwol there's the Tong River; and the Hant'angang Resort, about 50 km north of Seoul, also has some rafting activities.

For further information, contact the Pine River Canoe School (☎ 3473-1659) in Seoul, or ring their office in Inje (☎ 461-4586).

Cycling (ssaik'ǔlling)

Riding a bike is almost suicidal in cities, but is a reasonable form of recreation in the countryside. Bikes are usually only available for rent in tourist areas.

The Seoul-based Korean Mountain Biking Association, or KMTBA (☎ 967-9287) is a friendly organisation that arranges outings. If you don't already have a mountain bike, the KMTBA can direct you to a shop that rents them. This organisation is very 'foreigner friendly', though you might want to have a Korean ring up to avoid any language problems.

Golf (golpǔ)

Japanese golfers are enthralled with South Korea because green fees are so much cheaper than at home. But for many western visitors, prices won't seem like such a bargain. You can expect to pay W50,000 to W65,000 for a game and club rental will set you back somewhere in the vicinity of W20,000. Golf clubs should be declared at Customs when you enter the country.

There are over 60 golf courses in Korea and the number continues to grow, with some serious consequences for the natural environment. To see the current complete list of golf courses, visit the KNTO (☎ 757-0086) in Seoul.

Under the administration of President Kim Young-sam, members of parliament and bureaucrats have been discouraged from playing golf. Their fellow golfers tend to be rich business people and golf courses offer plenty of privacy for cooking up deals and conspiracies. However, it's hard to believe they couldn't find other places to make back-room deals.

Hang Gliding (haeng gǔllaiding)

This sport is just starting to catch on. The most popular venue seems to be around the base of Hallasan on the island of Chejudo.

Paragliding – a variation on the theme – is even more popular.

Several companies run paragliding trips. In Seoul contact Mirae (☎ 773-4267) or KRA (☎ 585-3002).

Hash House Harriers

This is mainly for expats, so if you're just passing through you might not be enthusiastically welcomed. Hash House Harriers is an informal, loosely-strung international club with branches all over the world. It appeals mainly to young people, or the young at heart. Activities typically include a weekend afternoon easy jogging session followed by a dinner and beer party which can extend until the wee hours of the morning.

There is no club headquarters, but every branch of the Hash is supposed to have a 'Grandmaster' who can be contacted for information. It would be useless for us to publish the Grandmasters' phone numbers here since this information changes quickly. Finding the Grandmaster or the Hash meeting place is a matter of asking around. Some embassy employees know about it, otherwise check the noticeboards at expat pubs.

The Seoul Hash is run every week from the Mug Club in It'aewon (across from the fire station and almost next to the Hollywood Club). The Pusan Hash is currently run from the Westin Chosun Beach Hotel – the American manager is a Hash-head (but that could change). There are Hash chapters at every large US military base. Some industrial-complex cities like Ulsan, Kumi & Taejŏn have small Hash chapters oriented to expat engineer types.

Hiking *(tŭngsan)*

Every province of Korea offers outstanding opportunities for hiking. Indeed, you'll find many challenging walking and climbing areas right in suburban Seoul.

Perhaps the biggest problem with hiking in Korea is the crowds: at times it feels as if you're riding the Seoul subway rather than visiting the wilderness and some areas are so popular that you sometimes have to stand in line to reach the summit of a peak. Fortunately, this predicament can be bypassed if you simply avoid the most popular spots during weekends and holidays.

If you want to travel with a group, Korean friends can help you join a mountaineering club *(san ak hoi)*. Don't expect hikers at the Korean clubs to be able to speak much English.

The USO in Seoul operates an English-speaking hiking club. Although geared towards US military personnel, civilians are welcome to participate. You can ring up the club (☎ 795-0392) for information.

Koreans are serious about the great outdoors; any excursion away from the concrete of Seoul is prepared for with a thoroughness worthy of an expedition primed to assault Everest. This includes ice axes (in summer) and ropes (for walking up a gentle slope). Koreans also must be the best-dressed hikers in the world – check out the red vests, yellow caps and multi-coloured knee-high socks. All the equipment and fancy clothing makes for heroic photos – a camera is *de rigueur*.

While the Koreans no doubt overdo it, there are a few things which you should bring. Useful, if not fashionable, items include sun protection (sunglasses, sunscreen lotion and hat), rain gear, food, maps, compass, mosquito repellent and warm clothing. The most important item you can bring is water – no less than two litres per person per day in summer.

Mountainous areas have notoriously fickle weather and this problem should not be taken lightly – at high altitudes, it can go from sunny and mild to dangerously cold and wet in remarkably little time. It's best to dress in layers – shirts, sweaters and nylon windjackets can be peeled off and put on as needed. Bring proper rain gear or you may live (or may not) to regret it.

As for purchasing mountaineering equipment, you'll find everything you need in Korea so it's not imperative to bring anything from abroad.

A serious issue for hikers is something called 'declination' – the angle between true north and magnetic north. The problem gets more severe the further you are from the equator, and South Korea lies very far to the north. Declination is Korea is about 20° north-east – that is, when you look at your compass dial, true north is about 20° to the north-east of where the compass needle is pointing.

Horse Riding
Cheju island is without a doubt the prime location for this hobby, though there are commercial stables in the countryside around Seoul.

Hot Springs *(onch'ŏn)*
Korea has plenty of health spas where you can soak away your aches and pains. The drawback is that every single usable hot spring has been developed – forget about frolicking nude in a large outdoor pool surrounded by trees and boulders. In Korea the hot water is piped into hotels and guests are expected to do their frolicking in private pools, usually located in the hotel's basement. Nudity is acceptable but the pools are segregated by sex. For those too shy to be naked in front of 100 Koreans (or if you want to bathe with a member of the opposite sex), hotel rooms can usually be rented with hot spring water piped directly to the bath tubs (but check that out before you pay!). Even if you are not staying at the hotel, you can normally use the big pools for about W1000 to W8000 – a private room will easily cost 10 times more.

Despite the lack of natural outdoor settings, soaking in a steaming hotel public pool isn't the worst way to spend a cold winter evening. All sorts of health benefits are claimed of the mineral content of natural hot baths. Since mineral content varies from one spring to the next, each has its own reputation for curing a particular ailment. The Japanese are most enthusiastic about pursuing this hobby; large tour groups from Japan often spend a full week going from one spa to another to sample the mineral water of each.

Perhaps the most enjoyable hot springs are those found in ski resorts. You can get in a full day of skiing and soak those tired muscles in the evening. Even when there's a lack of snow, a good day's hiking followed by a hot water soak is positively heavenly.

The following is a list (by province) of hot spring resorts in Korea. Remember that they can be extremely crowded on weekends and holidays:

Kyŏnggi-do
Ich'ŏn, the closest hot spring resort to Seoul; in a suburban setting; expensive hotels; water temperature 30°C

Kangwon-do
Ch'ŏksan, major hot spring four km west of Sokch'o and just inside Sŏraksan National Park; a rural setting and very popular with hikers
Hongch'ŏn, a minor hot spring, now undergoing development; in a rural setting on highway 5 south-east of Ch'unch'ŏn
Osaek, the best hot spring resort in Korea; located in the southern part of Sŏraksan National Park; spectacular scenery and popular with hikers

Kyŏngsangbuk-do
Kyongsan, also known as Sangdae hot springs; at Sangdae-ri 30 km south-east of Taegu; water temperature 30°C
Paegam, in a very rural setting 14 km from P'yŏnghae (which is by the East Sea); water temperature 46°C

Relaxing in hot springs is a popular pastime in Korea, although the uninitiated may take a while to adjust to the high water temperatures.

Kyŏngsangnam-do

Haeundae, Korea's only hot spring resort by the sea; urban setting at a crowded beach, close to central Pusan

Magumsan, a minor resort; water temperature 35°C–55°C; north of Ch'ang-won close to the Chunam Lake bird sanctuary

Pugok, major resort developed for mass tourism; scalding hot water (58°C–78°C) in outdoor and indoor pools; a rural setting west of Miryang

Tongnae, another urban hot spring 14 km north of central Pusan; this spring has been overdeveloped and the water temperature has fallen

Chŏllabuk-do

Chukrim, a minor hot spring resort, newly developed; 11 km from Chŏnju along highway 17 to Namwon

Hwashim, a minor hot spring, also known as Hwasun hot springs, 20 km from Chŏnju on highway 26 towards Chinan (near Maisan Provincial Park)

Sokchong, in a semi-rural setting just outside the city of Koch'ang, 20 km from Sŏnunsan Provincial Park

Ch'ungch'ŏngnam-do

Onyang, a major, intensively developed, hot spring with over 150 hotels; in a small city setting close to Seoul; water temperature 50°C

Togo, a small hot spring with a lot of tourist development, just 16 km from Onyang; semi-rural setting; water temperature not very hot

Tŏksan, in a rural setting close to Tŏksan Provincial Park; water temperature a steamy 52°C

Yusŏng, major hot spring development 10 km west of central Taejŏn; good-quality water at 42°C–55°C; numerous hotels and high prices

Ch'ungch'ŏngbuk-do

Nung-am, also known as Tonsan and Ch'ung-on hot springs; currently under development; close to Suanbo hot springs

Suanbo, Korea's largest hot springs resort, in a rural setting 21 km south of Ch'ungju near Woraksan National Park; close to the ski area

Korean Chess *(paduk)*

This game is virtually identical to the Japanese *go*, though it originated in China. Flat black and white stones are moved around on a playing board. As with western chess, the rules are simple but the techniques can be very complex.

It's easy to find partners who can teach you the art of Korean chess – try the local pubs. Frequently, a fair bit of alcohol is consumed during these games and wagers often change hands. As with western chess, major championships are followed in the news media.

Skating *(sŭk'eit'ŭ)*

Both roller skating and ice skating are popular pastimes. A few large cities have good indoor ice-skating rinks, but in most other areas it's outdoors and therefore strictly a winter sport.

Skiing *(sŭk'i)*

Although Korea's mountains don't compare with the Swiss Alps, there are some good places where you can practise the art of sliding downhill. The ski season is from about early December through mid-March. Facilities include hotels, artificial snow and equipment hire. These places can get pretty crowded at weekends – get there early if you need to hire equipment. Since ski resorts are on remote mountaintops some don't have a regular bus service; numerous travel agencies run tour buses up to these places as part of a package tour. Otherwise, hire a taxi for the last leg of the journey or hitchhike.

For half a day of skiing at the Alps resort, prices for equipment hire are W11,800 and lift tickets are W9900. For a full day, equipment hire costs W16,000 and lift tickets are W16,700.

The USO runs inexpensive weekend ski trips to Bear's Town, Alps and Yongpyeong resorts. They also sell tickets for the daily shuttle bus to Bear's Town and Yongpyeong. In Seoul, Korea Travel Bureau (☎ 778-0150) organises full-day trips to the Bear's Town resort for W27,000 which includes transport from Seoul, equipment, lift tickets and lunch – KTB is on the 3rd floor of the Lotte Hotel.

All ski resorts have a representative office in Seoul that you can call for information. They claim to have English speakers on duty who book buses and hotels at the resorts. The eight ski areas and their phone numbers in Seoul are as follows:

Alps (☎ 756-7210), eight slopes, about 45 minutes north-west of Sokch'o and just north of Sŏraksan National Park in Kangwon-do. This area gets the most snow and has the longest season. There are eight slopes, five chair lifts, several condominiums (500 rooms) and one hotel (34 rooms).

Bear's Town (☎ 546-7210), 11 slopes, 11 chair lifts, two T-bars. It's about 40 minutes north-east of Seoul in Kyŏnggi-do.

Chonmasan (☎ 744-6019), three slopes, seven chair lifts, one hotel (38 rooms). It's about 50 minutes north-east of Seoul in Kyŏnggi-do.

Daemyung (☎ 222-7000), eight slopes, five chair lifts, one condominium (1080 rooms) and one hotel (168 rooms). It's at Hongch'ŏn in Kangwon-do, about two hours from Seoul.

Muju (☎ 597-5500), 19 slopes, six chair lifts, two J-bars. It's in Tŏgyusan National Park (south-east of Taejŏn in Chŏllabuk-do), about four hours from Seoul.

Seoul (☎ 561-1230), eight slopes, three chair lifts, one hotel (66 rooms), 40 minutes by bus from Seoul at Paekpongsan in Kyŏnggi-do.

Yangji (☎ 511-3033), seven slopes, six chair lifts, two J-bars, one hotel (60 rooms). It's east of the Korean Folk Village in Kyŏnggi-do, about one hour from Seoul.

Yongpyŏng (Dragon Valley) (☎ 561-6255), 16 slopes, 16 chair lifts, two T-bars, two hotels (257 rooms), condominiums (825 rooms) and a youth hostel (54 rooms). It's just south of Odaesan National Park in Kangwon-do about 3½ hours from Seoul. This is South Korea's premier resort – the slopes are lit for night skiing.

Swimming *(suyŏng)*

In crowded South Korea, most urban residents do their swimming in shallow pools in which there is no chance of drowning. The short warm season also makes indoor pools more practical than the outdoor variety. There are a number of inexpensive public pools, which get very crowded, and private ones which cost quite a bit more. Super-deluxe hotels usually have pools and even non-guests can generally use these facilities if they pay. If you live in Korea long-term, it may be worthwhile joining a health club (also at major hotels) where you can use the pool and exercise equipment.

Most of South Korea's lakes are in fact reservoirs where swimming is not permitted because it is drinking water. It's a different story at the seashore, but the season is basically July and August and during the rest of the year most beaches are not even open to the public. As you will soon discover, South Korea's beaches are lined with barbed-wire fences. These are partially removed during the summer months to give the public access,

but all coastal areas are heavily guarded and that particularly applies to areas close to North Korea. You are not supposed to be on the beach at night and soldiers enforce this rule strictly. In case you're wondering, North Korea has fences along the beach too (though in the north the fences are electrified).

The better-known beaches near urban areas can be extremely crowded. The best all-round beaches are found on the island of Chejudo, which also has the warmest weather. The water around the peninsula tends to be calm and shallow on the west coast, while the eastern seaboard has deep water and rough surf.

Tennis *(t'enisŭ)*

There are public tennis courts in city parks. They tend to be very crowded, but you can sometimes get on if you go during normal working hours. Forget it on weekends and holidays.

Not surprisingly, deluxe tourist hotels offer even better facilities, but you can expect to pay deluxe prices.

Windsurfing *(windŭsŏping)*

The art of windsurfing is just starting to take off in southern areas such as Pusan and Cheju-do. Championships are sometimes held at Haeundae Beach in Pusan. For more information, you can contact the Korean Windsurfing Association (☎ 511-7522; fax 511-7523), Room 402, Songhŏn Building, 55-3 Nonhyŏn-dong, Kangnam-gu, Seoul.

COURSES

It is very important that you obtain a student visa *before* enrolling in any kind of course – the schools will not tell you this! Even if you already have a work visa, you cannot legally enrol in a school without first getting permission stamped into your residence permit by immigration. The fine for breaking this rule is at least W100,000.

Language

The most popular courses for foreigners are language courses. Most foreigners study in Seoul, though you can certainly study at schools elsewhere. There are several large government-run language schools in Seoul, such as the Yonsei University Foreign Language Institute (FLI), Sogang University and Ehwa Women's University. The Language Research Teaching Centre (LRTC) in Seoul is a well-known private language school. Other language schools advertise in the *Korea Times* and *Korea Herald* ; the *Korea Herald* itself operates a language school at its branch off Myŏng-dong. Just remember that the school must be government-approved in order to sponsor you for a student visa.

WORK

One unusual method of fund-raising is to turn in a North Korean spy – the government pays from W1,000,000 to W5,000,000 for each one you report. The telephone number for the Korean CIA hotline is 113.

Failing that, you just might need to get a job. Korea in general, and Seoul in particular, is becoming a popular place to look for work – mainly teaching English at private language schools *(hagwon)*. Although it is illegal to work on a tourist visa many people still do (and some get deported for doing so).

Of course, if you are suitably qualified (ie have graduated with a degree in *something)*, and are prepared to spend a bit of time in Korea, there is no need to run the risks of working illegally. Many schools in Korea are willing to sponsor English teachers on one-year contracts. Remuneration for English teaching on this basis can be quite lucrative, but there are several drawbacks.

The first problem is that many written agreements include ways to keep you to the end of your contract (a fine of two months wages for early resignation is common and schools usually only pay once monthly so this is easily enforced). The second is that many schools (including public universities) simply cheat on wages. If you are being paid less than your contract stipulates or being forced to work overtime without pay, there isn't a whole lot you can do other than quit. Unfortunately, you will lose your work visa within just a few days of quitting, which means you must leave the country. A work

visa is valid for one job only – if you quit and want to seek other employment, you must apply for a new work visa. In theory, if you've been cheated by an employer, you can take the case to court – in practice, this seldom works.

The truth is that South Korea has a sordid reputation. As more foreigners come here to work, pay is going down, cheating is becoming more common and many employers are becoming outrageously arrogant and abusive towards their employees. Concerned by the damage that this is doing to South Korea's image, the government has been considering changes to the law that will give foreign workers better legal protection – these changes are desperately needed and long overdue. Whether or not this is really going to happen, or all the rhetoric is simply a public relations exercise, only time will tell.

One suggestion – secretly tape record all your conversations with your South Korean employer. This could be of some use in a lawsuit (or maybe some use in the classroom when you do a lesson on 'dishonesty') and even without going to court a tape can have a powerful effect on the outcome of a dispute.

If you are working illegally, you have no legal rights and are very likely to be cheated. At the end of the month your employer may tell you that he's short on cash, but will promise to pay you next month. Come next month and it's the same story. You may never see more than a fraction of your promised wages and you can rest assured that you'll be fired if you grumble too loudly. If you complain to the authorities you will be deported for working illegally.

Despite these drawbacks it can all pay off. Korea is filled with foreign workers – legal and illegal – and the jobs are not only in Seoul. If at all possible, try to do things legally. If you feel you can guarantee your employer a year of your time and are willing to run the risk of working for someone who might cheat you, then it would be worth your while scouting around for a school in Korea that is willing to offer you sponsorship.

So how do you find teaching work in Korea? The obvious place to look is the classifieds section of the daily English-language newspapers. Some people maintain that the best jobs are never advertised here, and that it is only the schools that consistently lose staff that need to advertise. Nevertheless, it is possible to meet teachers who have found jobs through the newspaper and are happy with their work – it would not be a good idea to write the newspapers off entirely. Recently, some schools have started advertising on the Internet. You could also pop down to the British Council Library next to the Tŏksugung Palace in Seoul and ask at the counter for their list of English-language schools. You can also simply walk door to door and talk to the schools. The other way to find work is to book yourself in to the Inn Daewon in Seoul (see the Places to Stay section for Seoul). This is where most destitute backpackers end up and it's a standby for English-language schools that need to find a substitute teacher in a hurry.

ACCOMMODATION

Camping

Korea is a paradise for campers, at least when the weather co-operates. Every national park has camping grounds and most are free. When a fee is charged, it's usually no more than W3000 and this buys you access to fine facilities like hot showers and flushing toilets. There are a few private camping grounds, but most are government-run.

Seoul is a good place to stock up on camping equipment such as tents, sleeping bags and stoves (see the Things to Buy section for Seoul).

Because Korea is a crowded place the wilderness really takes a beating. Therefore, campers should be extra diligent about protecting the environment. If you intend to cook, you should carry is a portable gas stove. Building wood fires in the forest is not recommended – it's environmentally ruinous, not to mention hazardous when the weather is dry. Human waste and used toilet paper should be buried at least 50m from surface water. However, other paper and plastic rubbish should not be buried – if you packed it in, you can pack it out. Remember the old

wilderness explorers' slogan: take nothing but pictures, leave nothing but footprints.

The national park service has closed a number of back-country areas to camping and cooking in order to give the wilderness a badly needed rest. If you have any questions about where camping is prohibited, make local inquiries.

Mountain Huts & Shelters

Strategically-located shelters *(taepiso)* or huts *(sanjang)* are placed along the hiking trails in many national parks. Don't expect luxurious facilities – basically, you only get a wooden floor on which to roll out a sleeping bag. Toilets tend to be the smelly latrine style. Drinking water is almost always available and some huts have basic items for sale like food and drinks, although you should not count on this.

The huts and shelters are almost certain to be open during the busy summer hiking season and often in autumn when Koreans head for the hills to watch the leaves turn colours. A few (but not many) huts and shelters are open in the springtime, but you can forget it in winter.

The better-appointed places charge a basic fee of W1000 to W2000 for use of the facilities.

Rental Accommodation

An increasing number of foreigners (especially English teachers) are basing themselves in Korea for long periods. In many cases they come to an agreement with the owners of a yŏgwan for a better monthly deal on a room. However, this has drawbacks, like not being able to cook for yourself and not having your own telephone. Alternatives are to find an apartment or rent a room in a boarding house; the latter are known locally as *hasukchip* and cost around US$200 a month in Seoul.

The Korean government copied its land use policy from Japan, with the same result – a housing shortage. Building permits were difficult to obtain and bank loans for aspiring home owners were virtually non-existent. For tenants this translates into high rents, outrageous deposits and long-term leases that heavily favour the landlord. Needless to say, the housing shortage became a hot political issue, arousing popular demands for reform. Recent amendments to the land use law are making it easier to build apartments, and government-controlled banks have loosened up somewhat on issuing loans (though they are still not easy to obtain). The government has also embarked on a program of building public housing estates. You can see these all around Korea now – row after row of ugly, identical buildings.

All of which means that apartment hunting is quite an expedition and the help of a Korean friend is practically mandatory. The biggest problem is the requirement of astronomical deposits (known as 'key money') – another obnoxious custom borrowed from Japan. A figure of 20 times the monthly rent is not uncommon and in choice neighbourhoods of Seoul this can add up to over US$40,000! Most Koreans do not have this kind of money and many are forced to borrow it and pay interest.

There are actually several approaches to this key money story – basically, the higher the deposit, the lower your rent will be. You can even pay a sky-high deposit with no monthly rent – this system is called *jŏnse*. Or you can pay a relatively small deposit plus fixed monthly rent – this is called *walse*. Rental contracts generally run for one year. Legally, your landlord must refund the deposit at the end of your rental contract. As locals point out, however, this is a dangerous system. In some cases your money will be channelled into dodgy investments (or in some cases, even gambled away) and there is always the risk that you will never see it again. In theory, you can sue if this happens, but as a foreigner you are always at a legal disadvantage.

Boarding houses are probably a better alternative to the expense of renting an apartment, but conditions in these houses are not always ideal. It's wise to look around for a while before committing yourself to anything. Check to see that there are cooking facilities and whether there is a curfew in effect. Best of all, if you're working in Korea, inquire as to whether the provision of accommodation can be built into your contract. Many jobs provide accommodation for their foreign staff and there's no reason why your employer shouldn't make some effort towards helping you to get set up as well.

Fed up with high rents and outrageous deposits, some long-term foreign residents have wondered if they could simply buy a house in Korea. In most cases, the answer is a resounding 'no'. The only foreigners who are permitted to buy real estate in Korea are veterans of the Korean War.

Homestays

Another form of traditional accommodation is homestays *(minbak)*. Essentially, a minbak is a room in a private house. Bathing and cooking facilities are shared with the family, although occasionally you may find separate facilities for guests. Some of these places will be signposted but many are not. Souvenir shops, teashops and small restaurants can usually point you in the right direction and may actually be minbak themselves. In many rural areas, minbak may be the only accommodation available.

Prices are always on a 'per room' basis and should cost roughly W10,000, except in Seoul where they charge around W12,000. Meals generally can be provided on request. Minbak offer considerable discounts if you plan to stay for a month or more.

Hostels

There are 19 youth hostels scattered around the country. Unlike some of their counterparts in Europe, America and Australia, South Korean hostels are generally huge, luxurious places with incredible facilities and some private rooms. Unfortunately, there aren't very many hostels and their locations are often inconvenient. Dorm beds vary between W5000 and W9900 but the private rooms cost as much as W35,000. All the hostels have their own restaurants with meals at reasonable prices.

For more information and reservations contact the Korean Youth Hostel Association (☎ 725-3031; fax 725-3113), Room 409,

Chŏksŏn Hyŏndae Building, Chŏksŏn-dong, Chongno-gu, Seoul 110-052.
The following is the complete line-up of hostels, listed here by province:

Seoul
Olympic Parktel 88 Bangyi-dong, Songpa-gu, Seoul (☎ 410-2114; fax 410-2100); take subway line No 2 to Songnae station & walk ½ km; 1234 beds, W9900 per bed

Kyŏnggi-do
Bear's Town, 295 Sohak-ri, Naech'on-myŏn, P'och'ŏn (☎ 322534); 600 beds
Koyang, 278-3 Koyang-dong, Koyang City (☎ 629049; fax 629579); 700m from Koyang Market; 200 beds, W5000 per bed
Kyŏng-in, San 253-1, Kyŏngso-dong, Sŏ-gu, Inch'ŏn (☎ 379-7195), 560 beds
Pulam, 99 Hwajŏp-ri, Byŏlrae-myŏn, Namyangju (☎ 658081); take Seoul subway line No 1 to Ch'ŏngnyangni, then train to Sŏkkye, walk 15 minutes towards Pulam Mt; 200 beds, W5000 per bed

Kangwon-do
Kangch'ŏn, 366 Kangch'on-ni, Namsan myŏn, Ch'unch'ŏn (☎ 262-1201, fax 262-1201); from Kangch'on walk one km towards Kugok Falls; 264 beds
Naksan, 30-1 Chŏnjin-ni, Yangyang (☎ 672-3416; fax 672-3418); 200m from Nakansa; 300 beds, W5000 per bed
Yongp'yŏng 130 Yongsan-ni, Toam-myŏn, P'yŏngch'ang (☎ 355757); in Yongpyŏng Ski Resort; 580 beds, W5500 per bed

Kyŏngsangbuk-do
Academy 349-1 Namyul-ri, Sokchŏng-myŏn, Ch'ilgok (☎ 972-8866); 200 beds
Kyŏngju 407-2 Ch'unghyo-dong, Kyŏngju (☎ 421771); 400 beds

Kyŏngsangnam-do
Fantasia 13-2 Sunji-ri, Habuk-myŏn, Yangsan (☎ 812591); 800 beds
Namhae 140-1 Kŭmsong-ri, Samdong-myŏn, Namhae (☎ 867-4510); 309 beds
Pusan Tongsŏng 206-11 Songjŏng-dong, Haewudae-gu, Pusan City (☎ 743-8466; fax 743-7564); east of town, take train to Songjŏng station & walk 10 minutes; 141 beds, W5000 per bed

Ch'ungch'ŏngnam-do
Samjung Puyŏ, 105-1 Kugyo-ri, Puyŏ-ŭp, Puyŏ (☎ 835-3102); 450 beds

Ch'ungch'ŏngbuk-do
Hanal, 730 Onch'ŏn-ni, Sangmo-myŏn, Chungwon (☎ 846-3151; fax 846-3159); one km from Suanbo; 980 beds
Hanal Tanyang San 23-6, Ch'ŏngdong-ri, Tanyang-ŭp, Tanyang (☎ 223151); 1121 beds
Hwayang 153-1 Hwayang-ri, Ch'ŏngch'ŏn-myŏn, Koesan (☎ 328801); 500 beds
Songnisan, 3-8 Sangp'an-ni, Naesongni-myŏn, Poŭn (☎ 425211); ½ km from bus stop at Songni-dong near Pŏpchusa; 1200 beds, W6600 per bed
Sajo Maŭl, 52 Onch'ŏn-ri, Sangmo-myŏn, Ch'ungju (☎ 846-0750); 426 beds

Guesthouses
Yŏinsuk & Yŏgwan Western-style accommodation in the major centres is generally very expensive so budget travellers usually head for the traditional Korean inns known as *yŏlnsuk* or *yŏgwan*. The more upmarket yŏgwan are called *jang yŏgwan* (sometimes just abbreviated to *jang*).

The name gives an indication of what facilities you can expect and the price you'll pay. Yŏgwan usually have at least some rooms with private bath, while yŏinsuk almost never do. Rooms in the jang yŏgwan all have a private bath. Basic yŏinsuk rooms generally cost W10,000 to W12,000. Prices in yŏgwan start at around W15,000, but W20,000 or more is typical in jang yŏgwan. In smaller towns (especially resort areas) you get charged more than in major cities, at least during the summer tourist season – figure on about W30,000.

The yŏinsuk and cheaper yŏgwan are becoming an endangered species, while relatively pricey jang yŏgwan are rapidly multiplying. To judge from some of the sounds coming through the paper-thin walls, many of the cheaper yŏinsuk are surviving primarily as short-time love hotels, or else Koreans are afflicted with severe breathing problems.

Probably the easiest way to save money on accommodation is to double up. Doubles and singles are usually the same price, though a third person might be charged extra.

The proprietors are highly unlikely to speak English, but they'll expect you to want to see the room and bathroom facilities before you decide to stay. If they don't offer to show you the room, then ask to see it (*pang'ŭl polsu issŏyo*).

Yŏinsuk and yŏgwan are usually clustered around bus and railway stations. If you can't read Korean, at least learn the symbol for bath, which is as follows:

You'll find this symbol on the signs of all jang yŏgwan and it indicates that all rooms have a private bath. But be forewarned: the same symbol is used on public bath-houses (*mokyokt'ang*).

Since yŏinsuk have such primitive bathing facilities, you might indeed want to visit a bath-house. This can be a very pleasant experience – it's a great way to get the winter chill out of your bones. Men and women have separate facilities, and you can rent towels and soap and bathe for as long as you like for around W2000 to W3000. Many bath-houses employ staff to give massages (legitimate massage, not prostitution), but inquire about the price first. In large cities, bath-houses are typically open from 5 am to 9 pm; most shut down for a 10-day break in early August.

Many of the old bath-houses have recently been converted into saunas (*tchimjilbang*). This is a relatively new trend and it should catch on because many Koreans believe sweating is good for you. However, the vast majority of these places (so far) are for women only. At W5000, they cost more than bath-houses, but you get more for your money. For one thing, they are usually open all night, which means you can sleep in a lounge chair wearing a bathrobe (supplied by the sauna) and thus save a night's accommodation at a hotel.

At all yŏgwan, never wear your shoes into the room – take them off and leave them outside or place them on a sheet of paper so they don't touch the floor.

The KNTO tourist information booth at Seoul's Kimp'o Airport has information on yŏgwan in the form of hand-outs and individual business cards (usually including an abstract map for finding the place).

Many older yŏgwan and yŏinsuk seem to have been designed for midgets, and the low doorways are a real hazard to travellers over 150 cm tall. Some swear these are booby-traps left over from the Korean War. One Lonely Planet writer (we won't mention any names) suffered a mild concussion after cracking his skull on one of these doorways when searching for the toilet in the middle of the night.

Motels

The word 'motel' doesn't have quite the same meaning in Korea as it does in the west: generally these are upmarket yŏgwan, although prices are still very reasonable – perhaps W25,000 to W35,000 per night. They tend to be a little more spacious than yŏgwan and many double as love hotels. But if you don't mind frilly pink beds with well-placed mirrors and a condom machine on the wall, 'motels' are quite all right.

Hotels

The KNTO divides Korea's hotels into categories: super deluxe (equivalent to five-star), deluxe (four or five-star), 1st class (four-star), 2nd class (three-star), 3rd class (two-star). Yŏinsuk, yŏgwan and youth hostels are excluded from the ratings, though you could probably call the jang yŏgwan one-star hotels (the plush ones could be considered two-star). In many respects the lower end mid-range hotels are less of a bargain than jang yŏgwan, but they offer amenities such as English-speaking staff and business facilities.

Exactly how much you'll pay varies by location and season, but as a rough guide rates for the different classes are approximately as follows:

Class	Rates (W)
3rd	40,000–50,000
2nd	51,000–80,000
1st	81,000–110,000
Deluxe	111,000–160,000
Super Deluxe	161,000–300,000

In addition to the foregoing rates, many mid-range places and all top-end ones will charge an extra 10% tax plus another 10% service charge. As a minor compensation, tipping is not expected in these places.

FOOD

The four generic cuisines available in South Korea are Korean, Chinese, Japanese and western.

Korean Food

The one element of Korean cooking which receives the most comments, both positive and negative, is that staple of the Korean diet, *kimch'i*. Kimch'i is basically grated or chopped vegetables mixed with various other ingredients – notably chilli, garlic and ginger – and left to ferment in an earthenware pot. The result is served up as a side dish or as the principle component of any Korean meal, even breakfast. It has a raw, tangy taste and most varieties are very spicy.

While most Westerners can't face kimch'i at 7 am, it does make a tasty addition to lunch or dinner. Some foreigners simply can't get used to kimch'i at all and if you fall into this category, you'll have to be more picky about what you eat. But you won't starve – there is always something good to eat on virtually every street corner.

An omelette with rice *(omŭ raisŭ)* is a cheap dish which has sustained many a backpacker. Perhaps even better is veal cutlet with rice and vegetables *(tonggasŭ)*. Another budget travellers' special is *kimbap*, the Korean version of Japanese *sushi*. Thanks to the liberal use of spices, the Korean 'sushi' is usually tastier than the Japanese variety. Low-grade kimbap is usually filled with rice, ham, egg and pickles, but the premium class variety can include cheese, beef or tuna. Kimbap is always served with some yellow-coloured pickled daikon radishes as a side dish. In big cities, the best place to find cheap kimbap stalls is in the underground arcades around subway and railway stations.

Unless you're vegetarian, you should definitely try *pulgogi*, which is almost certainly the favourite dish of foreign visitors.

Pulgogi, which literally means 'fire beef', is often translated as 'Korean barbecue'. Strips of beef marinated in soy sauce, sesame oil, garlic and chilli are grilled on a hot plate right on the dining table. Basically, you do your own table-top cooking. Eating this way is a leisurely social affair and it makes sense to have at least two persons, rather than do it solo. Prices vary, but should be in the W6000 to W10,000 range.

Similar to pulgogi is *kalbi*, which uses short ribs instead of strips of beef. Most pulgogi restaurants also serve kalbi.

A dish that uses kimch'i as an ingredient is *pibimbap*. Basically it's a bed of rice with kimch'i, vegetables, meat and a dollop of hot chilli on top; variations on the theme exclude meat – a boon to vegetarians. Pibimbap is usually served in a thick, heated iron bowl, and the dish is still cooking when it is placed in front of you. The whole thing should be stirred up with a spoon before eating.

Shinsŏllo is similar to Japanese *shabu-shabu*. Meat, fish, vegetables and bean curd are simmered together in a broth at your table. This is another dish that most foreigners enjoy.

Koreans also like noodle soup dishes: a notable speciality is *naeng myŏn*, or 'cold noodles'. The noodles are made of buckwheat and are very healthy. *Kong kuksu* is a

Kujŏlp'an is a colourful first course that consists of meat and vegetables attractively arranged around a pile of Korean pancakes.

The Fine Art of Making Kimch'i

Mastering the ins and outs of kimch'i making is something only acquired through experience. Virtually every woman in Korea considers the making of kimch'i an essential skill that must be learned if she hopes to find a good husband! But even if you're male and not in the market for marriage, producing your own kimch'i can be a reward in itself. Just remember, the longer you allow kimch'i to sit, the spicier it will be.

You'd be wise to find a Korean (probably female) to teach you, but if you'd like to take a stab at it yourself, here is a basic recipe:

- In a colander, mix five cups roughly chopped Chinese cabbage with 6 teaspoons sea salt. Set aside for three hours then rinse thoroughly and drain.
- Place the drained cabbage in a bowl with two tablespoons sugar, crushed red chilli to taste, 1/4 teaspoon chopped ginger, one clove finely chopped garlic and two finely chopped green onions. Mix thoroughly, preferably with your hands.
- If you don't have a special ceramic kimch'i pot, cover the mixture with plastic wrap and let sit at room temperature for two days.
- Chill before serving. ■

noodle dish made in a soy milk broth. More appealing to western tastes is *mak kuksu*, a combination of vegetables and meat slices with noodles in chicken broth.

Korean *haute cuisine* is best represented by *hanjŏngshik*, a banquet meal with a vast array of dishes. At the other end of the spectrum are cheap but filling dishes like *mandu guk*, a Korean equivalent of Chinese *wonton* soup. It's a lot more filling than the Chinese variety and is a cheap way to satisfy large appetites.

Stews Korean stews (*tchigae*) are very tasty and inexpensive. There seems to be an almost endless variety of stews, but one of the most delicious is *tobu tchigae*, or bean curd stew. A variation of it is bean paste stew (*toenjang tchigae*). The broth is made with a bean paste mixture that is very similar to Japanese *miso*.

Another excellent, although more expensive, stew is *kalbi-tchim*, in which the main ingredient is kalbi short ribs. These dishes come with rice and a serving of kimch'i.

Cow intestine stew generally gets mixed reactions from westerners – it's definitely an acquired taste. There is also kimch'i stew for those who can't get enough of the stuff in the side dishes provided.

Soups Korea's cold winter climate has given rise to a number of interesting soup dishes. Probably the most famous of these is *samgye t'ang* or 'ginseng chicken soup'. A small, whole chicken stuffed with ginseng and glutinous rice is served with a soup in a clay pot. It is believed to be an extremely nutritious meal and, in keeping with this thinking, many of the restaurants around town that specialise in this dish tout themselves as 'nutrition centres'.

Kalbi t'ang is beef short rib soup served with rice and kimch'i. *Sŏllŏng t'ang* is a hearty beef stock soup with rice mixed in. Beef soup (*kom t'ang*) is simple beef with bones cooked in a broth. Ox-tail soup (*kkorikom t'ang*) is self-explanatory. Spicy beef soup (*yukkaejang*) often contains the cows' entrails, which doesn't always cheer western diners. Pepper pot soup (*maeun t'ang*) is excellent but *very* spicy.

Street Stall Food Street stalls are a good option, both for the traveller on a tight budget and for others interested in sampling the full gamut of Korean cuisine. A very palatable example is *t'oekim*, a slightly Koreanised version of Japanese tempura – vegetables, seafood and mandu deep fried in batter.

Stalls specialising in Korean pancakes are also very common. These come in various forms, the most basic being *p'ajŏn*, or green onion pancakes. *Pindaeddok* is a pancake which contains bean sprouts and pork.

Ttŏkbukgi is a popular snack consisting of rice dough rolled into the shape of hot dogs and simmered in hot sauce. You can find these tasty morsels everywhere, but be warned – the chilli sauce is as hot as it looks.

Desserts Korean junk food is prime stuff and has become a major export item. Read the small print and you'll find the 'made in Korea' label on packages of cakes, cream puffs and frozen ice cream bars in such disparate locations as Hong Kong, Vietnam, Taiwan and even in the ethnic grocery stores of San Francisco and Melbourne. The lion's share of this market belongs to food-giant Lotte, Korea's 10th largest chaebol. Another biggie is Haitai, maker of top-grade chocolate candy and pies.

Koreans seldom eat dessert after a meal, as is the common practice in the west. Junk food is usually for snacks.

Of course, there's all the usual stuff like ice cream, pies and donuts, but you might want to try something distinctly Korean. A popular dessert which seems to be a Korean-Chinese-western hybrid is known as red bean parfait *(p'atbingsu)*. It's made with sweetened red beans mixed with crushed ice, fruit cocktail, milk and ice cream. It can be bought in numerous places, but is most accessible at western-style fast food restaurants. This dish is usually only sold during the summer months.

Push-carts all over the country sell *hoddŏk*, a fried sweet roll (resembling a doughnut without the hole). It usually has a cinnamon and honey paste in the centre and is delicious.

Chinese Food
Seoul's Chinese restaurants cater mostly to the lower end of the dining market, although there are some upscale places as well. The smaller and dingier the restaurant, the more likely it is to be cheap.

If you don't know what to order, start with *tchajang myŏn*, a northern Chinese special-

ity that is a little similar to spaghetti bolognese. Virtually all of Korea's Chinese restaurants have this dish on the menu and the price is universally low. Most Chinese restaurants also have fried rice, which is *poggŭm bap* in Korean. Another time-honoured delicacy is *t'angsu yuk*, more familiarly known to westerners as sweet and sour pork.

Japanese Food
Japanese food typically costs twice as much as an equivalent Korean meal, although there is no reason why it should. Despite the price and the fact that most Koreans will claim to hate Japanese food, there seems to be no shortage of clientele in the Japanese restaurants.

The Koreans have adopted sushi *(kimbap)* as their own, but if you order it in a Japanese restaurant you get the privilege of paying double. A variation on the theme is *yubu ch'obap*, which is prepared in a similar way

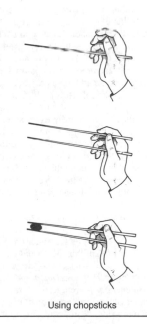

Using chopsticks

to kimbap except bean curd and rice mixed with vinegar are wrapped up into a roll with a very thin omelette.

Another famous Japanese cold dish is *saengsŏn hoe (sashimi* in Japanese) or raw fish. In Japan it gets served with hot green horse radish *(wasabi)*, but the Koreans prefer it with either soy or hot chilli sauce and rice.

The cheaper Japanese hot dishes include tempura *(twigim)* – battered, deep-fried cuisine. The most common are shrimp tempura with vegetables *(sae'o twigim)*, fish tempura *(saengsŏn twigim)* and vegetable tempura *(yach'ae twigim)*.

Western Food

Koreans have their own tastes when it comes to western food. Or to put it another way, Koreans do Korean food much better than foreign cuisine. Notorious examples of what passes as 'western food' include mayonnaise-drenched sandwiches, 'porkburgers' and pizzas with sweet corn topping.

On the other hand, foreign joint-venture restaurants have invaded Seoul and other large cities. Korean chefs have been packed off to European chef schools for intensive training courses and the results are good. Fine western restaurants dishing up steak, salad, French bread and wine are not hard to find, at least in Seoul. But the bad news is that most places specialising in deluxe western cuisine are absurdly expensive. No matter if the restaurant's theme is Italian, French or American, you will pay a bundle for the luxury of good cooking dished up on fancy plates and wooden tables.

The good news is at the lower end of the market: Seoul, at least, has yielded itself to the razzle dazzle of the fast-food industry with apparent abandon. Pusan is far behind, but trying to catch up. It probably won't be long before an assiduous Korean archaeologist unearths a Neolithic McDonald's and proves that the Big Mac was actually a Korean invention. Hot dogs *(hat dogŭ)*, hamburgers *(haem bŏgŏ)*, French fries, pizza and other staples of western fast-food culture are very much in evidence in Seoul. Prices at the

familiar chain stores are in line with what you'd pay in the west.

It can be debated whether or not fried or barbecued chicken is really a western food, because this is one thing the Koreans do very well. Nor do you need to seek out a foreign chain like KFC or Hardees; small Korean pubs dish up this stuff throughout the country. But if you want chains, Korea has its own home-grown brand names, examples being *Pelicana* and *Lim's Chicken*. You'll often encounter small shops with signs (in English) above the door advertising 'Mexican chicken', which is chicken roasted or fried in fiery hot spices (excellent stuff, but not for the meek).

Self-Catering

Given the expense of eating out, self-catering is not a bad idea at all. One great feature of Korea is the existence of little hole-in-the-wall grocery stores open from early morning to late at night. These are found everywhere, so you'll never have to walk far to pick up that package of noodles, ham, bread, tuna in a tin, biscuits or coffee.

By contrast, large western-style supermarkets are a rarity. Mostly these are found in the basements of large department stores. Also, any city or town of significant size has an Agricultural Cooperative Supermarket, a government-sponsored scheme that offers some good bargains.

The biggest problem with self-catering is simply finding cooking facilities. Some yŏgwan have boiling hot water available from an electric urn, but this is the exception rather than the rule. If you ask politely, the ajumma might boil some water for you, but don't count on it – most yŏgwan try to discourage travellers from eating in their rooms because they don't want to clean up the mess.

An alternative is to carry a small electric heating coil or electric teapot for boiling water. Of course, you can avoid this hassle by living on foods that don't need to be cooked (peanut butter and bread, for example), but most travellers grow tired of this *very* quickly.

In many cities 24-hour convenience stores

re a possibility for a cheap lunch or dinner.
These places invariably sell instant noodles
ackaged in a styrofoam bowl. Most (but not
ll) have hot water, disposable chopsticks
nd a table (no chairs though), so you can
onsume your instant banquet on the prem-
ses. This should cost between W500 and
W700 in 7-Eleven or Family Mart, but a
taggering W1000 to W1500 in Bestore.

If you're in the vicinity of a large univer-
ity, you can eat well for about W1500 to
W2000 at the student cafeterias. This doesn't
pply at some of the aristocratic schools (like
hwa Women's University in Seoul) where
ne food is pricey and the portions are stingy.
University cafeterias are normally only open
rom about 10 am to 6 pm, but some only
erve food from noon to 1 pm and 5 to 6 pm.

Useful Phrases

m a vegetarian.
ch'aeshik juwi imnida
채식주의 입니다.
want to eat spicy food.
mae'un ŭmshikyu   매운 음식요!
can't eat spicy food
mae'un ŭmshikun   매운 음식은
mukji motamnida   먹지 못합니다.
estaurant
shikdang   식당
Which of the following items do you have?
igŏt chungesŏ toenayo?
이것 중에서 뭐가 되나요

Korean Food   한국음식

melette with rice
omŭ raisŭ   오므라이스
eal cutlet with rice & vegetables
tonggasŭ   돈까스
arbecued beef & vegetables grill
bulgogi   불고기
arinated beef/pork ribs grill
bulgalbi   불갈비
arbecued beef ribs grill
kalbi kui   갈비구이
eef ribs soup
kalbi t'ang   갈비탕
alted beef ribs
sogŭm kui   소금구이

stew
tchigae   찌개
barbecued beef ribs stew
kalbi tchim   갈비찜
bean curd stew
tubu tchigae   두부 찌개
fried bean curd
yubu ch'obap   유부초밥
chicken stew
talgtchim   닭찜
kimch'i stew
kimch'i tchigae   김치찌개
bean paste stew
toenjang tchigae   된장찌개
cow intestine stew
kopch'ang chŏnggol   곱창전골
roasted chicken
t'ongdalggui   통닭구이
fried chicken
t'ongdak   통닭
rice, egg, meat & vegetables with hot
sauce
pibimbap   비빔밥
meat, fish & vegetables broth cooked at
table
shinsŏllo   신선로
noodles
myŏn or kuksu   면, 국수
cold buckwheat noodles
& broth
naeng myŏn   냉면
cold noodle kimch'i soup
yŏlmu mul naeng myŏn   열무물냉면
cold noodles without soup
pibim naeng myŏn   비빔 냉면
noodle dish & soy milk broth
kong kuksu   콩국수
fried ramen noodles
ramyŏn boggi   라면볶이
soup ramen noodles
shin ramyŏn   신라면
mixed vegetables & beef
with soybean noodles
chapch'ae   잡채
vegetables, meat, noodles & chicken broth
mak kuksu   막국수
soup
kuk or t'ang   국 / 탕
ginseng chicken soup
samgye t'ang   삼계탕

beef & rice soup
sŏllŏng t'ang　　설렁탕
beef soup
kom t'ang　　곰탕
ox tail soup
kkorikom t'ang　　꼬리곰탕
spicy beef soup
yukkaejang　　육개장
pepper pot soup
maeun t'ang　　매운탕
boiled silkworm snack
ppŏndaegi　　뻔대기
dumplings
mandu　　만두
soup with meat-filled dumplings
mandu guk　　만두국
fried dumplings
yakki mandu　　야끼만두
seafood & vegetables fried in batter
t'oekim　　튀김
pickled vegetables, garlic & chilli
kimch'i　　김치
corn on the cob
oksusu　　옥수수
green onion pancake
p'ajŏn　　파전
bean sprouts & pork pancake
pindaeddŏk　　빈대떡
pickled daikon radish
tongchimi　　동치미
seasoned raw beef
yukhoe　　육회
dog meat soup
poshin t'ang　　보신탕
live octopus tentacles
munŏbal　　문어발
banquet
hanjŏngshik　　한정식
Korean sushi
kimbap　　김밥
beef sushi
soegogi kimbap　　쇠고기 김밥
cheese sushi
ch'ijŭ kimbap　　치즈 김밥
tuna sushi
ch'amch'i kimbap　　참치 김밥
kimch'i sushi
kimch'i kimbap　　김치 김밥
assorted sushi
modŭm kimbap　　모듬 김밥

Chinese Food　　중국음식
Chinese Restaurant
chungkuk chip　　중국집
noodles with hot beef sauce
tchajang myŏn　　짜장면
thick noodles with sauce
udong　　우동
spicy seafood noodle soup
tchambbong　　짬뽕
vegetables with noodles & hot beef sauce
kan tchajang myŏn　　간짜장면
soupy noodles
ul myŏn　　울면
noodles & spicy sauce
samsŏn tchajang　　삼선짜장
noodles & flavoured sauces
samsŏn ganjajang　　삼선간짜장
spicy noodles with vegetables
samsŏn tchambbong　　삼선짬뽕
seafood noodles
samsŏn udong　　삼선우동
seafood soupy noodles
samsŏn ul myŏn　　삼선울면
fried rice
poggŭm bap　　볶음밥
fried rice with noodles
chapch'ae bap　　잡채밥
assorted seafood, meat,
vegetables & rice
chapt'ang bap　　잡탕밥
rice with mushroom sauce
song'idŏp bap　　송이덮밥
shrimp fried rice
sae'u poggŭm bap　　새우볶음밥
fried dumplings
kun mandu　　군만두
fried vermicelli, meat & vegetables
chapch'ae　　잡채
sweet & sour pork
t'angsu yuk　　탕수육
pork & green pepper rice
koch'u chapch'ae　　고추잡채
pork & scallions rice
puch'u chapch'ae　　부추잡채
seafood & vegetables
p'albo ch'ae　　팔보채
chicken dish
kkanp'unggi　　깐풍기
spicy chicken dish
rajogi　　라조기

spicy pork & beef dish
  rajouk 라조육

minced pork or beef balls
  nanjawansŭ 난자완스

shrimp dish
  sae ut'wikim 새우튀김

prawns
  k'ŭnsae ut'wikim 큰새우튀김

Sichuan dish
  sach'ŏn t'angyuk 사친탕육

cold Chinese salad
  samp'um naengch'ae 심품냉채

sliced meats
  ohyang jangyuk 오향잔육

egg soup
  kyeran t'ang 계란탕

assorted soup
  chap t'ang 잡탕

Japanese Food 일식

Japanese Restaurant
  Ilshikchib 일시집

shrimp tempura with vegetables
  sao'o twigim 새우뒤김

fish tempura
  saengsŏn twigim 생선튀김

vegetable tempura
  yach'ae twigim 아채튀김

sashimi (raw fish)
  saengsŏn hoe 생선회

sushi
  kimbap 김밥

egg-wrapped sushi
  yubu ch'obap 유부초밥

Western Food 양식

cheeseburger
  ch'ijŭ bŏgŏ 치즈버거

hamburger
  haem bŏgŏ 햄버거

hot dog
  hat dogŭ 핫도그

fried chicken
  takt'ikim 닭튀김

French fries
  kamjat'ikim 감자튀김

steak
  sŭt'eik'ŭ 스테이크

salad
  saellŏdŭ 샐러드

bread
  ppang 빵

roll
  roulpang 로울빵

toast
  t'osŭt'ŭ 토스트

ham
  haem 햄

sandwich
  saendŭwich'i 샌드위치

boiled egg
  salmŭn kyeran 삶은계란

fried egg
  keranhufurai 계란후라이

Seafood 생선요리

clam
  taehap 대합

crab
  ke 게

fish
  saengsŏn 생선

oyster
  kul 굴

shrimp
  saeu 새우

eel
  paemjangŏ 벰장어

Meat 육류

beef
  sogogi 소고기

chicken
  takkogi 닭고기

mutton
  yanggogi 양고기

pork
  taejigogi 돼지고기

Vegetables 아채요리

cucumber
  oi 오이

garlic
  manŭl 마늘

onion
  yangp'a 양파

potato
  kamja 감자

mushroom
  pŏsŏt 버섯

radishes	
muu	무우
green or red pepper	
koch'u	고추
spinach	
shigumchi	시금치
dried seaweed	
kim	김
soybean sprouts	
k'ongnamul	콩나물
beans	
k'ong	콩
lotus root	
yŏn'gŭn	연근
rice	
pap	밥

Desserts	디저트
ice cream	
aisŭk'ŭrim	아이스크림
cake	
k'eik'ŭ	케이크
pie	
p'ai	파이
pastry	
kwaja	과자
waffles	
wap'ŭl, p'ulbbang	와플, 풀빵
red bean parfait	
p'atbingsu	팥빙수

Condiments	양념
salt	
sogŭm	소금
butter	
pŏt'ŏ	버터
jam	
chaem	잼
black pepper	
huch'u	후추
sugar	
sŏltang	설탕
hot chilli pepper	
koch'u karu	고추가루
hot sauce	
koch'ujang	고추장
ketchup	
k'ech'ŏp	케찹
mayonnaise	
mayonejŭ	마요네즈

mustard	
kyŏja	거자
soy sauce	
kanjang	간장
soybean paste	
toenjang	된장
vinegar	
shikch'o	식초

DRINKS

Non-alcoholic Drinks

Tea or coffee rooms *(tabang)* are great social centres. No food is served (by government edict), but it is possible to take sandwiches in. Coffee shops *(k'ŏp'i syop)* are numerous in Seoul. These are good places to grab breakfast and they usually have cakes and sandwiches at reasonable prices. Prices for a coffee in coffee shop chains like Doutor or Caravan are around W1000.

Korea produces what are arguably the best herb teas in the world. Ginseng tea *(insam ch'a)* is the most famous, but also check out herb tonic tea *(ssanghwang ch'a)*, made from three different roots and often served with an egg yolk or pine nuts floating in it. Ginger tea *(saengkang ch'a)* is also excellent.

Alcoholic Drinks

Koreans love their liquor and there is no shortage of drinking establishments. Boozing it up is mostly a male group activity in Korea. Visit a typical pub in Seoul and you'll see plenty of Koreans (mostly men) getting drunk, often with a great deal of boisterous toasting and, as time passes, collective singing. Anyone with an aversion to mixing drinks will be made to suffer by these gatherings. Korean drinkers frequently switch from beer to whisky to potato vodka, and from there to anything they can get their hands on short of paint thinner – a perfect recipe for a killer hangover the next morning.

A traditional drink is *makkoli*, a caustic, milky-white rice brew which is cheap but, like kimch'i, can make your hair stand on end. It's sold in raucous beverage halls known as *makkoli jip*. *Soju* is the local firewater; it's a potent drink made from potato and similar to bad vodka. Makkoli and soju are often drunk with various snacks known as *anju*. They include fresh oysters, dried squid, salted peanuts and *kim* (seaweed).

Korea's best wine is *Kyŏngju Beobjoo*. Some drinkers try to mitigate the effects of indulgence by slaking their thirst with ginseng wine *(insamju)*. Beer *(maekju)* comes in three brands – OB, Crown and CASS. If you drink in a beer hall the management expects you to buy some snacks (peanuts, etc) along with it. All of these drinks can also be bought in the 24-hour convenience stores at a fraction of the price you'd pay in a club. Korean beers are generally around W1300 a bottle, while soju can be bought for as little as W400 for a small waxed carton.

Korean beer can be bought cheaply by the keg. You'll get the best deal simply by stopping one of the beer delivery trucks and negotiating directly with the driver.
Craig Jensen

Drinks Glossary

hot water	*toun mul*	너운물
cold water	*ch'an mul*	찬물
mineral water	*sengsu*	생수
	kwangch'ŏnsu	광천수
tea	*ch'a*	차
arrowroot tea	*ch'ik ch'a*	칡차
barley tea	*bori ch'a*	보리차
black tea	*hong ch'a*	홍차
Chinese matrimony vine tea	*kugija ch'a*	구기자차
citron tea	*yuja ch'a*	유자차
ginger tea	*saengkang ch'a*	생강차
ginseng tea	*insam ch'a*	인삼차
green tea	*nok ch'a*	녹차
honey tea	*kkul ch'a*	꿀차
honey-ginseng tea	*kkul sam ch'a*	꿀삼차
Job's Tears tea	*yulmu ch'a*	율무차
jujube tea	*taech'u ch'a*	대추차
lemon tea	*remon ch'a*	레몬차
mugwort tea	*ssuk ch'a*	쑥차
pine nuts, walnuts & adlay tea	*yulmu ch'a*	율무차
herb tonic tea	*ssanghwa ch'a*	써회자
coffee	*kŏpi*	커피
hot cocoa	*k'ok'oa*	쿠코아
juice	*chyusŭ*	쥬스
orange juice	*orenji chyusŭ*	오렌지쥬스
milk	*oyu*	우유
Coca-Cola	*k'ok'a k'olra*	코가콜라
beer	*maekju*	맥주
wine	*p'odoju*	포도주
Kyŏngju Beobjoo (wine)	*Kyŏngju pŏbju*	경수법주
milky white rice brew	*makkŏli*	막걸리
'potato vodka'	*soju*	소주
ginseng wine	*insamju*	인삼주

ENTERTAINMENT

Cinemas *(yŏnghwa gwan, kukjang)*

Young Koreans are certainly fond of movies, and the cinemas tend to pack out on weekends and holidays. Indeed, you might even have to buy a 'black market' ticket from scalpers who hang around the cinemas on Sundays. However, there are seldom problems on weekdays.

Imported western films are extremely popular; they retain their dialogue in English, French or whatever and have Korean subtitles.

Discos *(tisŭk'o chang)*

Discos certainly exist in Korea, but they have declined somewhat. Apparently, the karaoke business has offered formidable competition.

A pretty steep 'table charge' gets you your first few beers and the anju (snack) at the Korean-style places. This system may differ in places that cater to foreigners, such as in Seoul's It'aewon neighbourhood.

The discos at the big tourist hotels are flashy and very good for meeting people, but these places cost big money. If it helps any, they accept credit cards.

Drinking

Korea's nightlife is significantly dampened by government-imposed midnight closing. This restriction has its roots in a curfew which was enforced back when Korea was a military dictatorship. The dictatorship is gone, but the government feels the need to shut down bars at midnight to protect the morals of the nation. An exception is made for bars inside officially-designated tourist hotels: some are allowed to operate until 2 am, the logic being that guests in the hotel needn't go out on the street for a long drunken commute home. Of course, this doesn't stop non-guests from visiting the hotel bars and staying until 2 am, only then to begin the lengthy drunken commute home.

Pre-dawn revellers can also get sozzled at 'after-hours bars'. This practice is illegal, but it goes on. The way it works is that the bar simply keeps the door locked and the windows shuttered, but inside everyone is partying. If you arrive after midnight, they may not allow you to enter, but if you're already inside before the clock strikes 12, you won't get thrown out. We can't specify which clubs mentioned in this book keep late hours because to do so would invite raids by the police. You'll just have to make your own inquiries.

Pubs are known as 'hofs' *(hop'ŭ)* or soju parlours *(soju bang)* but can be expensive.

Generally hofs double as restaurants and it is expected that patrons buy something to eat, even if it is just some nibbles. These small dishes of finger food (anju) are where the hofs make a lot of their money. Just going in for a couple of beers is usually frowned upon.

One Korean innovation with a long history are soju tents *(taep'otjip)*. These are usually set up in the evening along the bank of a river, and feature inexpensive drinks and snacks. The government frowns on these places, believing they are a relic from the poverty-stricken past which have no place in modern Korea. They are also extremely popular! Soju tents are now banned in Seoul, though they can still be found in most other cities and towns. If the government ever gets serious about cracking down soju tents will become a thing of the past.

Gambling *(norŭm)*

The only forms of legal gambling available to the average Korean is the national lottery (tickets can be bought everywhere) and horse racing (see 'Seoul Horse Race Track' in the Kyŏnggi-do chapter).

It's a different story for foreigners. If you're a compulsive gambler and can't wait to get to Las Vegas, then you can lose your fortune in South Korea at one of the special casinos *(k'ajino)* which are designed to milk foreign tourists only (no Koreans allowed). Japanese and Arabs are the most favoured customers, but all non-Koreans with excess cash are welcome.

The casinos are in major tourist hotels; these include:

Sheraton Walker Hill Hotel, Seoul (☎ 456-2121); Olympos Hotel, Inch'ŏn (☎ 762-5181); Grand Hotel, Cheju City (☎ 432121); Oriental Hotel, Cheju City (☎ 528222); Nam Seoul, Cheju City (☎ 424111); Hyatt Regency, Sŏgwip'o, Cheju-do (☎ 385353); Shilla Hotel, Sŏgwip'o (☎ 388822); KAL Hotel, Sŏgwip'o (☎ 329851); Sŏrak Park Hotel, Sŏraksan (☎ 347111); Paradise Beach Hotel, Pusan (☎ 742-2121); Kolon Hotel, Kyŏngju (☎ 771-2121).

Karaoke *(norae bang, KTV)*

Karaoke (empty music) is a Japanese invention. For the uninitiated, it's basically one big amateur singing contest to the accompaniment of a video tape (or laser disk). The idea is to give you the chance to be a star, even if nobody but you gets to hear the performance.

There are variations on the theme. One type of karaoke is a bar or lounge in which you sing in front of others. In this type of place there will usually be no cover charge, although you are expected to buy drinks and snacks. Another type is a little booth (around W12,000 per hour) in which you sit by yourself (or with a friend) and sing along with a video tape and record your performance. You can take home your recorded tape to enjoy at your leisure.

Korea is unusual in that the karaoke business is somewhat organised. Songs (some of which are in English) are numbered and all the clubs use the same numbering system – if you ask for song No 112 it will be the same at every karaoke place in Korea.

In general, karaoke gets the thumbs down from westerners, while most Koreans (along with most other Asians) love it. There appears to be a clear cultural difference here. If checking into a hotel for the evening, it's worth looking next door to make sure you aren't next to a karaoke club – the music and awful singing typically goes on until midnight.

Theatres *(sokŭk jang)*
Most of Korea's theatres are concentrated in Seoul, especially in the Taehanro entertainment district (see the Seoul chapter). Unfortunately, performances are almost entirely in Korean.

Video Parlours *(pidio bang)*
These are supposedly illegal, which explains why they try to maintain a low profile. Video parlours are no different from video rental shops except that you watch the movies on their equipment. There is no reason why they should be illegal, except that movie producers (ie Hollywood) fear they compete against cinemas. The dispute over video parlours has boiled over into trade negotiations between South Korea and the USA, thus the need for the Koreans to at least maintain the appearance of illegality. Legal or not, you can find these places easily enough if you ask a local to assist you.

SPECTATOR SPORT
Traditional Korean sports have a heavy tendency to be based on martial arts and hunting. These days, Korea's mass media focuses on western-style sports. Baseball is a long-time favourite and Koreans are fanatical about soccer. Basketball appeals to the affluent westernised class in Seoul.

One of the best places to contact for information about traditional and modern sports is the Korean Amateur Sport Association (☎ 420-3333; fax 414-5583), Oryun-dong, Songp'a-gu, Seoul.

Archery
The traditional Korean wooden bow has gradually given way to more modern fibreglass models. Competitions are most common during festivals and this is one of the few traditional sports in which women can participate.

For further information, contact the Korean Amateur Sport Association.

T'aekwondo
An effective form of self-defence, *t'aekwondo* was developed in Korea. The original form of t'aekwondo is called *t'aekkyŏn* and is still practiced by enthusiasts. If you're interested in either observing or studying, call the Korea T'aekwondo Association (☎ 420-4271).

International competitions are hosted by the World T'aekwondo Federation (☎ 566-2505; fax 553-4728), 635 Yŏksam-dong, Kangnam-gu, Seoul.

Wrestling
Ssirŭm is a traditional form of Korean wrestling. Two opponents face off each other and one loses if any part of the body other than the feet touch the ground. Ssirŭm bears some resemblance to the better-known Japanese *sumo* style. Indeed, some of Japan's best sumo wrestlers are in fact ethnic Koreans, though the Japanese are loath to admit this. For their part, the Koreans say the Japanese borrowed the idea of sumo wrestling from them. The Korean Amateur Sport Association can give you information about competitions and classes.

THINGS TO BUY

One of Korea's main exports is sporting equipment. There are good deals to be had on tents, sleeping bags, hiking boots, backpacks, rock climbing equipment, tennis rackets and other such items. Indoor sports enthusiasts will find various sorts of springs, weights, trampolines and various other contortionist devices.

Korea is the ginseng capital of the world, and for many Asians this root is a magical cure-all. Japanese and Chinese tourists buy as much as they can get their hands on, and as result the government restricts how much an individual can take out of the country (three kg in its raw state).

Lacquercraft is one of Korea's ancient arts and lacquerware boxes are just one example of this tradition. It also encompasses furniture, from tables and chairs to wardrobes and storage chests. The latter can be stunning and a great deal of attention is also given to the brass fittings. Naturally, these larger items are bulky – and more expensive – so, if you were to buy them, you'd have to arrange for them to be shipped to your home country. Most retailers can make these arrangements for you.

In most shops which sell lacquerware there is usually a wide selection of brassware as well. Hand-hammered and moulded brassware is made into everything, including paperweights, plates, goblets, lamps, vases and even beds. Much draws its inspiration from Buddhist statuary. Prices are reasonable.

Ceramics are another Korean craft with a long pedigree – going back to the days of the Koryŏ dynasty, when the pale blue-green, crackle-glazed celadon pottery was regarded as perfection itself.

There are heaps of antiques on sale, most of them fake. Of course, there's nothing wrong with buying a reproduction, provided you aren't paying 'genuine antique' prices. Theoretically, it's illegal to take rare antiques and other 'cultural treasures' out of Korea. In practice this is seldom a problem because you aren't likely to find many cultural treasures on sale in the marketplace. However, it would be useful to get a receipt when buying anything that looks antique just in case customs wants to give you a bad time when you depart.

Much cheaper, and well within the range of a budget traveller's pocket, are the carved wooden masks which you'll come across in many a souvenir shop in country areas. Only

Name Chops

When the Koreans adopted the Chinese writing system, they also borrowed the concept of *tojang* – a name chop or seal. The traditional name chop has been used in China for thousands of years: it's likely that people began using them because Chinese characters are so complex and few people in ancient times were able to read and write. Back then there was no other form of identification, such as fingerprinting, picture ID cards and computer files. A chop served both as a form of identification and as a valid signature. All official documents in both Korea and China needed to be stamped with a chop to be valid. Naturally, this made a chop quite valuable, for with another person's chop it was possible to sign contracts and other legal documents in their name.

Today, most Koreans have abandoned the use of Chinese characters, preferring the much simpler hangŭl system. Furthermore, chops are no longer recognised as a valid signature on legal documents in Korea, although they are in China. But traditions die hard and you will still find plenty of shops in Korea which carve name chops. Normally, highly-decorative Chinese characters are used to produce a name chop, though you can have one carved in hangŭl. Only red ink is used when stamping your 'signature' with a name chop. On traditional Korean watercolour paintings and decorative scrolls, you will always find the tell-tale red chop mark which identifies the artist.

There are many different sizes and styles of chops. Inexpensive small chops can be carved from wood or plastic for about W2000 or so. Chops costing W50,000 and up can be carved from ivory, jade, marble or steel. ∎

rarely do these resemble the Shamanistic spirit posts found at the entrance to rural villages. Instead they concentrate on exaggerated facial expressions and range from the grotesque to the humorous. They're easily carried in the average backpack and usually cost around W10,000, though the detail determines the price.

Visit any Korean home and you'll see scores of examples of embroidery. It's a national hobby among the women and highly regarded as a decorative art. Many fabric shops specialise in this and incredibly ornate brocades: you can pick up everything from handkerchiefs and pillow cases to room-size screens. Many such shops do personalised embroidery either to their own or to the customer's designs. Another similar national hobby is macramé. Common items are colourful wall hangings and the long *no-ri-gae* tassels which adorn the front of every Korean woman's traditional costume. The latter always hang from a painted brass headpiece which itself is often very colourful.

Korea produces a wide range of precious and semiprecious stones, including amethyst, smoky topaz, rubies, sapphires, emeralds and, of course, jade. Korean jade is lighter in colour than Chinese green jade and is often almost white, but it's a lot cheaper.

Getting There & Away

AIR

Airports & Airlines

Most major international airlines fly into South Korea. The Koreans also operate two airlines of their own, Asiana Airlines and Korean Air (KAL).

Seoul's Kimp'o Airport is the principal gateway to South Korea, but there are international airports at Pusan and Cheju-do which mostly serve the Japanese market.

Buying Tickets

There are plenty of discount tickets and those which allow multiple stopovers with open dates provide a great deal of flexibility. The best tickets give up to 12 months from the date of purchase to complete the journey.

Your date of departure can affect the ticket price: the year is divided into 'peak' (expensive), 'shoulder' (less expensive) and 'low' (relatively inexpensive) seasons. For Korea, summer (July and August) is the peak season. Some airlines may also count major public holidays as peak season (ie Christmas, the Korean Lunar New Year and Harvest Moon Festival).

APEX (Advance Purchase Excursion) tickets are sold at a discount but will lock you into a rigid schedule: they must be purchased two or three weeks ahead of departure; they do not permit stopovers and may have minimum and maximum stays; and there are fixed departure and return dates. There are stiff cancellation fees if you decide not to use your APEX ticket or try to change the dates.

'Round-the-world' tickets are usually offered by an airline or combination of airlines, and let you take your time (six months to a year) to move from point to point on their routes for the price of one ticket. The main restriction is that you have to keep moving in the same direction and there are some drawbacks: you usually book individual flights as you go; you can't switch carriers; you can get caught out by flight availability;

and the whole exercise might not even save you any money.

'Frequent flyer' plans are offered by most airlines, including some budget ones. Basically, these allow you a free ticket if you chalk up so many km with the same airline. However, the plans aren't always as good as they sound – some airlines require you to use all your frequent flyer credits within one year or you lose the lot. Sometimes you find yourself flying on a particular airline just to get frequent flyer credits, but the ticket is considerably more expensive than what you might have gotten from a discount airline without a frequent flyer bonus. Many airlines have 'blackout' periods – peak times when you cannot use the free tickets you obtained under the program.

Some airlines offer discounts of up to 25% to student card holders. In some countries an official-looking letter from the school is also needed. You also must be aged 26 or younger. These discounts are generally only available on ordinary economy-class fares. You wouldn't get one, for instance, on an APEX or a round-the-world ticket, since these are already discounted.

Courier flights can be a bargain if you're fortunate enough to find one. The way they work is that an air freight company takes over your entire checked baggage allowance. You are permitted to bring a carry-on bag, but that's all, and in return you get a steeply discounted ticket. These arrangements usually have to be made a month or more in advance and are only available on certain routes. Also, such tickets are sold for a fixed date and schedule changes can be difficult or impossible to make. Courier flights are occasionally advertised in newspapers, or you can contact air freight companies listed in the phone book.

Buying plane tickets from a travel agent is almost always cheaper than buying directly from the airline because airlines don't give discounts. It's a good idea to call the airline first and see what their cheapest ticket costs; use that as your starting point when talking to travel agents.

Use common sense before handing over the cash and always get a receipt. Whenever possible, try to avoid handing over the cash until they hand over the ticket, or else pay only a deposit and be sure your receipt clearly states the total amount due.

It's important to understand that when you buy an air ticket from a travel agent, you must also go back to that agent if you want to obtain a refund – the airlines will not refund to you directly unless you purchased the ticket from the airline yourself. While this is no problem if you don't change your travel plans, it can be quite a hassle if you decide to change the route halfway through your trip. In that case, you'd have to return to the place where you originally purchased the ticket to refund the unused portion of the journey. It's also true that some travel agents (and airlines) are notoriously slow to issue refunds – some travellers have had to wait up to a full year!

After you get to Korea, you may see some advertisements on noticeboards or in the newspapers by foreigners who decide to sell the return portion of their ticket home. Do *not* buy these second-hand tickets as you cannot use them. The immigration staff check your boarding pass on departure, and if your passport name doesn't match what's on the boarding pass you don't go anywhere.

Travellers with Special Needs

Most international airlines can cater to special needs – travellers with disabilities, people with young children and even children travelling alone.

Special dietary needs (vegetarian, kosher, etc) can also be catered to with advance notice. However, the 'special meals' usually aren't very special – basically you get a salad and fruit plate.

Airlines usually carry babies up to two years of age at 10% of the relevant adult fare and a few may carry them free of charge. Reputable international airlines usually provide nappies (diapers), tissues, talcum and all the other paraphernalia needed to keep babies clean, dry and half happy. For children between the ages of two and 12 the fare on international flights is usually 50% of the regular fare or 67% of a discounted fare.

Australia

Among the cheapest regular tickets available in Australia are APEX tickets. The cost depends on your departure date from Australia: peak season is December to January. It's possible to get reductions on the cost of APEX and other fares by going to the student travel offices and/or some of the travel agents in Australia that specialise in discounting.

The weekend travel sections of papers like *The Age* (Melbourne) or the *Sydney Morning Herald* are good sources of information. STA Travel has numerous offices in Australia and worldwide. They have a toll-free number (☎ (1800) 637 444) and main offices at 855 George St, Ultimo, Sydney 2007 (☎ (02) 9212-1255), and at 222 Faraday St, Carlton, Melbourne 3053 (☎ (03) 9349-2411).

Also well worth trying is the Flight Centre (☎ (03) 9670-0477), 386 Little Bourke St, Melbourne. They have numerous branches in Sydney (☎ (02) 9233-2296) and Brisbane (☎ (07) 3229-9958), and around the country.

Bottom-end one-way/return tickets between Seoul and either Sydney or Melbourne cost US$612/765.

Canada

CUTS is Canada's national student bureau and has offices in a number of Canadian cities, including Vancouver, Edmonton, Toronto and Ottawa – you don't necessarily have to be a student to use their services. There are a number of good agents in Vancouver for cheap tickets. Budget one-way/return fares between Vancouver and Seoul are US$870/1100.

China

Asiana Airlines, Korean Air and Air China operate routes between Seoul and Beijing. The fare is US$270/540. In Beijing, Asiana

---

Air Travel Glossary

Apex Apex (advance purchase excursion) is a discounted ticket which must be paid for in advance. There are penalties if you wish to change it.

Bucket Shop An unbonded travel agency specialising in discounted airline tickets.

Bumped Just because you have a confirmed seat doesn't mean you're going to get on the plane (see Overbooking).

Cancellation Penalties If you have to cancel or change an Apex or other discount ticket, there may be heavy penalties involved; insurance can sometimes be taken out against these penalties. Some airlines impose penalties on regular tickets as well, particularly against 'no show' passengers (see No Shows).

Check In Airlines ask you to check in a certain time ahead of the flight departure (usually two hours on international flights). If you fail to check in on time and the flight is overbooked, the airline can cancel your booking and give your seat to somebody else.

Confirmation Having a ticket written out with the flight and date you want doesn't mean you have a seat until the agent has checked with the airline that your status is OK or 'confirmed'. Meanwhile, you could just be 'on request' (see Reconfirmation).

Cross-Border Tickets Sometimes it is cheaper to fly to countries A, B and C rather than just B to C, usually because country A's airline is desperate to sell tickets or because the currency in country A is very weak. Authorities in B can get very unhappy if you turn up for the flight from B to C without having first flown from A to B. Be cautious about discounted tickets which have been issued in another city, particularly in Eastern European countries.

Discounted Tickets There are two types of discounted fares – officially discounted (see Promotional Fares) and unofficially discounted. The lowest prices often impose drawbacks like flying with unpopular airlines, inconvenient schedules, or unpleasant routes and connections. A discounted ticket doesn't necessarily have to save you money – an agent may be able to sell you a ticket at Apex prices without the associated Apex advance booking and other requirements. Discounted tickets only exist where there is fierce competition.

Full Fares Airlines traditionally offer 1st class (coded F), business class (coded J) and economy class (coded Y) tickets. These days there are so many promotional and discounted fares available that few passengers pay full economy fare.

Lost Tickets If you lose your airline ticket, an airline will usually treat it like a travellers' cheque and, after inquiries, issue you with a replacement. Legally, however, an airline is entitled to treat it like cash, so if you lose a ticket, it could be gone forever. Take good care of your tickets.

No Shows No shows are passengers who fail to show up for their flight for whatever reason. Full-fare no shows are sometimes entitled to travel on a later flight. The rest of us are penalised (see Cancellation Penalties).

On Request An unconfirmed booking for a flight.

Open Jaws A return ticket which allows you to fly to one place but return from another, and travel

---

Airlines (☎ 506-1118) is in room 134, Jianguo Hotel, 5 Jianguomenwai Dajie. Air China is in the Aviation Building, 15 Xichang'an Jie (☎ 601-6667) and there is another branch in the China World Trade Centre.

Asiana and China Eastern Airlines fly Seoul-Shanghai for US$283/566. Seoul-Shenyang costs US$240/480.

There are also flights between Seoul and several other Chinese cities, including Dalian, Guangzhou, Qingdao, Shanghai, Shenyang and Tianjin.

Travel agents cannot give discounts on China-Korea tickets and return tickets cost exactly double the one-way fare.

Europe

The Netherlands, Brussels and Antwerp are good places to buy discount air tickets. In Antwerp, WATS has been recommended. In Zurich, try SOF Travel and Sindbad. In Geneva, try Stohl Travel. In the Netherlands, NBBS is a reputable agency. Typical bottom-end one-way/return fares between Seoul and western European cities are US$580/970.

Guam & Saipan

For the Koreans, Guam and nearby Saipan have emerged as fashionable honeymoon and vacation spots. Guam is just 4½ hours from Seoul by air. KAL flies into Guam and Asiana flies into Saipan. One-way/return between the two 'jaws' by any means of transport at your own expense. If available, this can save you backtracking to your arrival point.

Overbooking Airlines hate to fly with empty seats and since every flight has some passengers who fail to show up (see No Shows), they often book more passengers than they have seats available. Usually the excess passengers balance those who fail to show up, but occasionally somebody gets bumped. If this happens, guess who it is most likely to be? The passengers who check in late.

Promotional Fares Officially discounted fares like Apex fares which are available from any travel agent or direct from the airline.

Reconfirmation You must contact the airline at least 72 hours before departure to 'reconfirm' your intention to be on the flight. If you don't do this, the airline can delete your name from the passenger list and you could lose your seat. You don't have to reconfirm the first flight on your itinerary or if your stopover is less than 72 hours. It doesn't hurt to reconfirm more than once.

Restrictions Discounted tickets often have various restrictions on them – advance purchase is the most usual one (see Apex). Others are restrictions on the minimum and maximum periods you can stay away, such as a minimum of 14 days or a maximum of one year (see Cancellation Penalties).

Standby This is a discounted ticket where you only fly if there is a seat free at the last moment. Standby fares are usually only available on domestic routes.

Tickets Out An entry requirement for many countries is that you have an onward or return ticket – in other words, a ticket out of the country. If you're not sure what you intend to do next, the easiest solution is to buy the cheapest onward ticket to a neighbouring country or a ticket from a reliable airline which can later be refunded if you do not use it.

Transferred Tickets Airline tickets cannot be transferred from one person to another. Travellers sometimes try to sell the return half of their ticket, but officials can ask you to prove that you are the person named on the ticket. This may not be checked on domestic flights, but on international flights tickets are usually compared with passports.

Travel Agencies Travel agencies can vary widely and you should ensure you use one that suits your needs. Some simply handle tours, while full-service agencies handle everything from tours and tickets to car rental and hotel bookings. A good one will do all these things and can save you a lot of money, but if all you want is a ticket at the lowest possible price, then you really need an agency specialising in discounted tickets. However, a discounted ticket agency may not be useful for other things such as hotel bookings.

Travel Periods Some officially discounted fares, Apex fares in particular, vary with the time of year. There is often a low (off-peak) season and a high (peak) season. Sometimes there's an intermediate (shoulder) season as well. At peak times, when everyone wants to fly, both officially and unofficially discounted fares will be higher, or there may simply be no discounted tickets available. Usually the fare depends on your outward flight – if you depart in the high season and return in the low season, you pay the high-season fare. ■

---

fares begin at US$300/360. There are also Pusan-Guam and Pusan-Saipan flights, which cost the same as those from Seoul.

Hong Kong

Buying tickets in Hong Kong requires some caution because there are quite a few tricky travel agents. The most common trick is a request for a non-refundable deposit on an air ticket: you pay a deposit for the booking, but when you go to pick up the tickets they say the flight is no longer available. However, there will be another flight available at a higher price, sometimes 50% more!

It is best not to pay a deposit. Rather, pay for the ticket in full, and get a receipt clearly showing that there is no balance due and that the full amount is refundable if no ticket is issued. Tickets are normally issued the day after booking, but you must pick up the really cheap tickets (actually group tickets) yourself at the airport from the 'tour leader' (who you will never see again once you've got the ticket). One caution: when you get the ticket from the tour leader check it carefully for errors. Occasionally you may be issued with a ticket on which the return portion is valid for only 60 days when you paid for a ticket valid for one year, etc.

Some agents we've found to be cheap and reliable in Hong Kong include the following:

Phoenix Services
  in Room B, 6th floor, Milton Mansion, 96 Nathan Rd, Tsim Sha Tsui, is scrupulously honest and gets good reviews from travellers (☎ 2722-7378; fax 2369-8884)
Shoestring Travel
  Flat A, 4th floor, Alpha House, 27-33 Nathan Rd, Tsim Sha Tsui (☎ 2723-2306; fax 2721-2085)
Traveller Services
  Room 1012, Silvercord Tower 1, 30 Canton Rd, Tsim Sha Tsui (☎ 2375-2222; fax 2375-2233)

The lowest one-way/return prices on the Hong Kong-Seoul route are US$201/272.

Indonesia

Garuda Airlines and KAL fly Jakarta-Seoul direct. Discount air tickets out of Indonesia can be bought from travel agents in Kuta Beach in Bali and in Jakarta. There are numerous airline ticket discounters around Kuta Beach and several on the main strip, Jalan Legian. You can also buy discount tickets in Kuta for departure from Jakarta. In Jakarta, there are a few discounters on Jalan Jaksa. Bottom-end one-way/return prices for Jakarta-Seoul are currently US$555/737.

Japan

Japanese tourists comprise the vast majority of foreign visitors to Korea – an odd state of affairs considering how much the Koreans purport to hate their powerful neighbours. Despite the heavy volume of tourist traffic, airfares between the two countries are anything but cheap. However, they are definitely lower if you purchase your ticket in Korea. The following are the cheapest prices (in $US) you can expect on tickets booked in Seoul:

Route	Fares (in US$)	
	One Way	Return
Fukuoka-Seoul	83	166
Hiroshima-Seoul	146	292
Nagoya-Seoul	140	280
Okinawa-Seoul	153	306
Osaka-Seoul	169	338
Sendai-Seoul	257	514
Takamatsu-Seoul	158	316
Tokyo-Seoul	176	352
Toyama-Seoul	199	398

There are also direct flights between Pusan and five Japanese cities – Tokyo, Nagoya, Osaka, Fukuoka and Sendai.

If you must buy an air ticket in Japan, Tokyo is the best place to shop around for discounts. You should start your search by checking the travel ad section of the *Tokyo Journal*. Three long-standing travel agencies where English is spoken and discounted tickets are available are: Across Traveller's Bureau (☎ (03) 3374-8721) in Shinjuku and (03) 5391-2871) in Ikebukuro); STA (☎ (03) 5269-0751 in Yotsuya, (03) 5485-8380 in Shibuya and (03) 5391-2922 in Ikebukuro); and Just Travel (☎ (03) 3207-8311) in Takadanobaba.

Macau

KAL has announced plans to begin a service on the new Macau-Seoul route. Details were sketchy at the time of writing, but prices should be similar to flying Hong Kong-Seoul.

New Zealand

Both KAL and Air New Zealand can shuttle you between Auckland and Seoul. Tickets are not especially cheap. Rock-bottom one-way/return fares begin at US$850/1350.

The Philippines

Bottom-end one-way/return fares between Seoul and Manila are US$262/452.

Singapore

A good place for buying cheap air tickets in Singapore is Airmaster Travel Centre. Also try STA Travel. Other agents advertise in the *Straits Times* classified columns. One-way/return Singapore-Seoul tickets start at US$400/673.

Taiwan

Discount travel agents advertise in Taiwan's two English-language newspapers, the *China News* and *China Post*. Don't believe the advertised rock-bottom fares – many are elusive 'group fares' which are not accessible to the individual traveller. Another thing to be cautious of is sending money through the mail – this never seems to work as well as visiting the travel agent with cash in hand.

A long-running discount travel agent with a good reputation is Jenny Su Travel (☎ 594-7733, 596-2263; fax 592-0068), 10th floor, 27 Chungshan N Rd, Section 3, Taipei. Wing On Travel and South-East Travel have branches all over the island; both have good reputations and offer reasonable prices.

Bottom-end tickets on the Taipei-Seoul route start at US$180/315.

Thailand

Check out the travel agents on Khao San Rd in Bangkok and shop around a little for the best price. The Bangkok-Seoul run is served by numerous carriers, and it's often possible to get a stopover in Hong Kong for a little extra. Bangkok-Seoul one-way/return fares start at US$400/550.

The UK

Both British Airways and KAL offer a London-Seoul service at competitive prices. Ticket discounting is a long-running business in the UK and it's wide open. The various agents advertise their fares. Discount tickets are most readily found in London. You may find discounters in various smaller cities, but forget it elsewhere. The danger with discounted tickets in Britain is that some of the 'bucket shops' (as ticket discounters are known) are unsound. Sometimes the backstairs over-the-shop travel agents fold up and disappear after you've handed over the money and before you've received the tickets. Get the tickets before you hand over the cash.

Two reliable London bucket shops are Trailfinders (☎ (0171) 437-7767), 194 Kensington High St, London W8 7RG, and STA Travel, which has several offices. Another place to try is Regent Holidays (UK) Ltd (☎ (0117) 211711; telex 444606; fax 254866), 15 John St, Bristol BS1 2HR.

The lower end of the market for London-Seoul one-way/return tickets is US$580/970.

The USA

There are some very good open tickets which remain valid for six months or one year (opt for the latter), but don't lock you into any fixed dates of departure and allow multiple stopovers. For example, there are cheap tickets between the US west coast and Hong Kong with a stop in Seoul for no extra money – the departure dates can be changed and you have one year to complete the journey. However, be careful during the peak season (Christmas, Lunar New Year and summer holidays) because seats will be hard to come by on short notice.

San Francisco is the air ticket discounters' capital of America, though some good deals can be found in Los Angeles, New York and other cities. Travel agents can be found in the Yellow Pages or the major daily papers; those listed in both Roman and Oriental scripts are invariably discounters. A more direct way is to wander around San Francisco's Chinatown where most of the shops are – especially in the Clay St and Waverly Place area. Many of these are staffed by recent arrivals from Asia who speak little English. Inquiries are best made in person. A good place to try is Wahlock Travel in the Bank of America Building on Stockton St.

It's not advisable to send money (even cheques) through the post unless the agent is very well established – some travellers have reported being ripped off by fly-by-night mail order ticket agents. Nor is it wise to hand over the full amount unless the travel agent can give you the ticket straight away – most US travel agencies have computers that can spit out the ticket on the spot.

Council Travel is the largest student travel organisation and although you don't have to be a student to use them they do have specially discounted student tickets. Council Travel has an extensive network in all major US cities and is listed in the telephone book.

One of the cheapest and most reliable travel agents on the west coast is Overseas Tours (☎ (800) 222-5292), 475 El Camino Real, room 206, Millbrae, CA 94030. Another good agent is Gateway Travel

(☎ (214) 960-2000, (800) 441-1183), 4201 Spring Valley Rd, suite 104, Dallas, TX 75244. Both these places seem to be trustworthy for mail-order tickets.

Some quotations for one-way/return tickets are: Honolulu-Seoul US$450/700; Los Angeles-Seoul/San Francisco-Seoul US$800/743; New York-Seoul US$870/1050.

Vietnam

Vietnam Airlines, Asiana and Korean Air all fly Seoul-Ho Chi Minh City for US$350/632. Vietnam Airlines also offers a direct Seoul-Hanoi flight.

LAND

Digging invasion tunnels under the so-called 'Demilitarised Zone' is a favourite preoccupation of the North Koreans, but *you* can forget about entering South Korea by land.

SEA
Japan

Several ferries link Japan with South Korea. Purchasing a round-trip ticket gains you a 10% discount on the return half, but fares from Japan are higher and there is a ¥600 departure tax in Japan. Korea-Japan-Korea tickets work out to be the same or less than a straight one-way Japan-Korea ticket. So for the numerous travellers who work in Japan and need to make visa runs, consider taking a one-way to Korea the first time if you intend to cross the waters more than once a year. You must arrive at the ferry terminal at least one hour before departure (two hours is preferable) or you won't be allowed to board.

If you'll be doing much travelling in Japan, it's worth buying a Japan Rail Pass before you depart Korea. This can be bought from travel agencies in Seoul or even at the port office. There is also a cheaper Kyushu rail pass if you'll be confining your rail journeys to the island of Kyushu.

Pusan-Shimonoseki Run by the Pukwan Ferry Company, this used to be the most popular boat; its popularity is in decline now because of competition from the Camellia

Line (see next listing). The one-way journey takes 14½ hours. Daily departures from Pusan (South Korea) or Shimonoseki (Japan) are both at 6 pm and arrival is at 8.30 am. Fares for 1st class tickets bought in Korea are US$90 to US$100; 2nd class costs US$60 to US$70. Students can receive a 20% discount and bicycles are carried free. Tickets are available in Shimonoseki (☎ (0832) 243000), Pusan (☎ 466-7799) or Seoul (☎ 738-0055).

Pusan-Hakata (Fukuoka) Camellia Line operates modern ferries thrice weekly between Pusan and Hakata. The journey takes 16 hours and costs US$62–US$125, but students can enjoy a 20% discount. Departure from Hakata is at 5 pm on Monday and Wednesday and at 7 pm on Friday. Departures from Pusan are at 5.40 pm on Tuesday, Thursday and Sunday. Call Camellia Line for bookings in Pusan (☎ 466-7799), Seoul (☎ 775-2323) or Hakata (☎ (092) 262-2324).

Note that in Hakata, the name of the wharf for Pusan (and for boats to Okinawa) is *Chuo Futoh* and it is across the bay, a long walk from *Hakata Futoh* (bayside place) which has other domestic boats.

Hydrofoils also connect Pusan with Hakata (three hours, US$70) – the boat is called the *Beetle*. Departures from Hakata are at 8.45 am and 3.45 pm on Tuesday and Thursday; at 10 am on Monday, Saturday and Sunday; and at 12.15 pm on Wednesday

---

A Sticky Cure

On ferries heading into or out of Korea you'll almost certainly notice a few people who seem to have small pieces of plaster stuck behind their ears. This is *kwimit'ae*, touted as a cure for seasickness. It's available from almost any pharmacy in Korea. The locals claim it works wonders and there's no harm in trying it, but if you're really prone to seasickness you could consider the virtues of flying. ■

and Friday. Departures from Pusan are at 8.45 am and 3.45 pm on Wednesday and Friday; 12.15 pm on Tuesday and Thursday; and at 2 pm on Monday, Saturday and Sunday. These hydrofoils are operated by Korea Marine Express in Hakata (☎ (092) 281-2315), Pusan (☎ 465-6111) and Seoul (☎ 730-8666).

Seoul-Osaka There is a wonderful combination ferry-train ticket: super-express train to Pusan, ferry to Shimonoseki, plus a rail ticket to Osaka (or someplace else in Japan). Seoul-Osaka costs US$195 and Pusan-Osaka costs US$175. Tickets are sold at Aju Tours in Korea and Nippon Travel in Japan. Tickets can be obtained as late as two days in advance. Aju Tours has an office in Seoul (☎ 753-5051, 754-2221) and Pusan (☎ 462-6661). Nippon Travel has its office in Osaka (☎ (06) 312-0451).

China

International ferries connect the South Korean port of Inch'ŏn with three cities in China: Weihai, Qingdao and Tianjin. Weihai and Qingdao are in China's Shandong province (the closest province to South Korea) and boats are operated by the Weidong Ferry Company. Tianjin is near Beijing and boats are run by the Jinchon Ferry Company. The boats have (horrors) a karaoke lounge.

The phone numbers for the Weidong Ferry Company are: Seoul (☎ 711-9111); Inch'ŏn (☎ 886-6171); Weihai (☎ (0896) 522-6173); Qingdao (☎ (0532) 280-3574). Phone numbers for the Jinchon Ferry Company are: Seoul (☎ 517-8671); Inch'ŏn (☎ 887-3963); Tianjin (☎ (022) 331-6049). In Seoul, tickets for any boats to China can be bought from Universal Travel Service, otherwise known as UTS (☎ 319-5511; fax 737-2764), room B-702, Dongyang Building (west of the KAL Building – see the Seoul map). For the Tianjin ferry only, you can also get tickets in Seoul from Taeya Travel (☎ 514-6226, 3442-4200) in Kangnam-gu by the Shinsa subway station. In China, tickets can be bought cheaply at the pier, or from China

International Travel Service (for a very *steep* premium).

To reach the International Ferry Terminal, take the Seoul-Inch'ŏn commuter train (subway line 1 from downtown) and get off at Tonginch'ŏn station. The train ride takes 50 minutes. From Tonginch'ŏn station it's either a 45-minute walk or five-minute taxi ride to the ferry terminal.

Inch'ŏn-Weihai The trip takes approximately 17 hours. Departures from Weihai are Wednesdays and Fridays at 5 pm. Departures from Inch'ŏn are on Tuesdays and Thursdays at 5.30 pm. The fares are 2nd class US$100; 1st class US$140; royal class US$180 and royal suite class US$300. There is a 5% discount on a round-trip ticket.

Weihai is no place to hang around, so if you arrive there it's best to hop on the first bus to Qingdao. If that's not available, take a bus to Yantai and then to Qingdao.

Inch'ŏn-Qingdao This trip takes about 24 hours. Departures from Qingdao are on Mondays at 11 am. Departures from Inch'ŏn are on Saturdays at 5.30 pm. Fares are exactly the same as for the Inch'ŏn-Weihai route.

Inch'ŏn-Tianjin The schedule for this ferry is a little irregular. It departs once every four or five days, usually Monday, Wednesday or Friday. The journey takes a minimum of 28 hours. Departures from Tianjin are at 10 am. The boat departs Inch'ŏn at 1 pm. The fares are 3B class US$120, 3A class US$140, 2B class US$150, 2A class US$160, 1st class US$180 and VIP class US$230.

The boat doesn't dock at Tianjin proper, but rather at the nearby port of Tanggu. Accommodation in Tianjin is outrageously expensive, but Tanggu has at least one economical accommodation, the *Seamen's Hotel*. Tanggu has trains and minibuses directly to Beijing.

Third class on the boat is a huge vault with around 80 beds and horrid toilets.

Russia

A weekly passenger boat service between Pusan (South Korea) and Vladivostok (Russia) began operations in 1996. The 817 km journey takes 46 hours. Departures from Pusan are at 3 pm on Saturday; departures from Vladivostok are at 7 pm on Tuesday. Second class fares are US$270; first class US$390; super class US$370; royal class US$490. Further information can be obtained by calling the Korea-Russia Maritime Service (☎ 463-7000) in Pusan. If the service does not prove economically successful it may be cancelled.

DEPARTURE TAXES

All departure taxes must be paid in Korean won. Airport departure tax on international flights is W9000. Children under age two and military personnel stationed in Korea are exempt from paying. If departing by ship it's W3000. There is also a W3000 airport tax on domestic flights but this is included in the ticket price. For children age 12 and under, the departure tax on domestic flights is W1000.

ORGANISED TOURS

Booking organised tours outside Korea is possible, but you'll get a much better deal if you book something after you've arrived in Korea. See the Organised Tours section in the following Getting Around chapter for additional information.

WARNING

Korea's continued economic growth has been accompanied by steadily advancing inflation. Please be aware that prices quoted in this book are subject to sudden change.

Getting Around

In terms of public transport, South Korea is a dream come true: apart from being frequent, on time and comfortable, it's also reasonably cheap. But finding an address can be a real chore.

Koreans are very helpful to lost-looking foreigners, so if you stand around looking bewildered with a map in your hands someone will probably come up and offer to assist you. However, If you hand a Korean your map and ask directions, be sure that they don't have a pen in their hands – they will draw and write directions all over the map until it becomes illegible (the same applies to dictionaries or your Lonely Planet book).

Just Give Me the Fax

There's a good reason why most hotel namecards in Korea include a map on the reverse side – it's because addresses are impossible to find. Consequently, fax machines have become very popular because Koreans often have to fax maps to each other to locate addresses.

In Korea, an 'address' exists in name only. In the entire country, there are almost no signs labelling street names. Indeed, most streets do not have names at all. Nor do houses have numbers on the outside, though every house does in fact have an official number. Unfortunately, even these 'secret numbers' mean little – numbers are assigned to houses when they are built, so house No 27 could be next to house No 324, and so on.

Even Koreans find it close to impossible to locate an address. Pity the poor postal workers who must actually track down these buildings! On the other hand, the system (or lack of a system) provides a form of job security for letter carriers – no one dares to fire them since only they can interpret the otherwise meaningless addresses which appear on envelopes.

The city of Seoul is considering reforming the system. There is a proposal to give all streets real names and consecutive numbers. However, the process is expected to take years and is by no means certain to happen at all.

In the meantime, there is a skeletal addressing system of sorts and it helps if you learn it. A province is a *do*. Thus we have Kangwon-do, Kyonggi-do, etc. *Buk* means 'north' and *nam* means 'south', and there are a few provinces where knowing this is useful – Chôllabuk-do is 'Chôlla North Province' and Chôllanam-do is 'Chôlla South Province'. Provinces are subdivided into counties, or *gun*; for example, Ch'unch'ôn-gun. A *ri* is a small village. Thus, we can have an address like this: 366 Kangch'on-ri, Namsan-myôn, Ch'unch'ôn-gun, Kangwon-do.

It gets a lot more complicated in cities. A *gu* is an urban district only found in large cities like Seoul and Pusan. A *dong* is a neighbourhood smaller than a gu. Seoul presently has 22 gu and 494 dong. Thus, an address like 104 Itaewon-dong, Yongsan-gu, means building No 104 in the Itaewon neighbourhood of the Yongsan district. However, you could wander around Itaewon for hours in search of this building with no hope of finding it, even with the help of a Korean friend. This is the time to make a phone call to the place you are looking for and get instructions; or find a local police box, tourist information booth; or – best of all – a fax machine.

The word for a large street or boulevard is *no* or *ro*. So Chongno means Chong St, Ulchiro is Ulchi St, etc. Also worth knowing is that large boulevards are divided into sections called *ga*. Thus, you'll see on the Seoul subway map that there is a station for Ulchiro 3-ga and Ulchiro 4-ga - these are just different sections of Ulchi St. A *gil* is a smaller street than a no/ro – Sambonggil is one such example. Many larger buildings have names and knowing the name of the building will often prove more useful than knowing the address.

You might speculate as to how or why the Koreans ever came up with such a chaotic system for addressing houses. The simple answer is that the Koreans borrowed the system from Japan during the colonial era. Given the fact that the Koreans are not generally fond of the Japanese, one also has to wonder why they would want to borrow such a dysfunctional system from their former colonial masters. Posing this question to Koreans, we've received the surprising answer that it was actually the Japanese who borrowed the system from Korea. If this is true, then the Koreans have gotten their revenge against Japan after all. ■

AIR

There are two domestic carriers – Korean Air *(taehan hangkong)* and Asiana Airlines *(ashiana hangkong)*. Korean Air is currently slightly cheaper than Asiana, though that could change. Asiana claims to offer better service (debatable). Amazingly, the fares have not been raised in years – indeed, they have actually dropped slightly in price during the last couple of years.

The airlines offer a 10% discount to students; children under two years old travel free; and those between two and 13 years old travel at 50% of the adult fare. Military personnel get a 30% discount. There is no financial penalty for cancellation if you do so at least three hours before departure time.

The following are the routes and fares available. Where the fares between the two airlines differ the lower of the two is shown. To all these fares you must add a domestic departure tax of W3000, which will be included in the price when you purchase a ticket.

Route	Fare (W)	Airline
Cheju-Chinju	25,000	(K)
Cheju-Kunsan	25,600	(A, K)
Cheju-Kwangju	17,000	(A, K)
Cheju-Mokp'o	13,900	(K)
Cheju-P'ohang	39,100	(A)
Cheju-Pusan	28,100	(A, K)
Cheju-Taegu	34,700	(A, K)
Cheju-Ulsan	33,300	(A, K)
Cheju-Yech'ŏn	48,800	(K)
Cheju-Yŏsu	20,000	(K)
Pusan-Kangnŭng	29,100	(A, K)
Pusan-Kwangju	18,900	(A)
Pusan-Mokp'o	23,300	(K)
Seoul-Cheju	44,000	(A, K)
Seoul-Chinju	35,500	(A, K)
Seoul-Kangnŭng	18,900	(A, K)
Seoul-Kunsan	18,400	(A, K)
Seoul-Kwangju	26,900	(A, K)
Seoul-Mokp'o	31,100	(A, K)
Seoul-P'ohang	27,900	(A, K)
Seoul-Pusan	34,400	(A, K)
Seoul-Sokch'o	23,300	(K)
Seoul-Taegu	25,700	(A, K)
Seoul-Ulsan	30,900	(A, K)
Seoul-Yech'ŏn	16,100	(A)
Seoul-Yŏsu	34,900	(A, K)

A = Asiana Airlines
K = Korean Air

Reservations

The telephone numbers for domestic reservations and ticket offices are as follows:

Asiana

Andong/Yech'on (☎ 544000), Cheju (☎ 434000), Chinju (☎ 747-4000), Ch'ŏngju (☎ 234-4000), Chŏnju (☎ 252-4000), Ch'unch'ŏn (☎ 241-4000), Inch'ŏn (☎ 872-4000), Kangnŭng (☎ 434000), Kunsan (☎ 614000), Kwangju (☎ 226-4000), Masan (☎ 224000), Mokp'o (☎ 424000), P'ohang (☎ 774000), Puch'ŏn (☎ 651-4000), Pusan (☎ 465-4000), Seoul (☎ 774-4000), Sunch'ŏn (☎ 742-4000), Suwon (☎ 216-4000), Taegu (☎ 421-4000), Taejŏn (☎ 284-4000), Ulsan (☎ 614000), Yŏsu (☎ 666-4000)

Korean Air

Andong/Yech'on (☎ 532000), Ansan (☎ 497-2000), Anyang (☎ 742000), Cheju (☎ 522000), Chinju (☎ 572000), Ch'ŏngju (☎ 522000), Chŏnju (☎ 872000), Ch'unch'ŏn (☎ 512000), Inch'ŏn (☎ 885-2000), Kangnŭng (☎ 653-2000), Koyang (☎ 967-2000), Kumi (☎ 522000), Kunsan (☎ 471-2000), Kwangju (☎ 222-2000), Masan (☎ 972000), Mokp'o (☎ 732000), P'ohang (☎ 722000), Puch'ŏn (☎ 656-2000), Pusan (☎ 463-2000), Seoul (☎ 756-2000), Sokch'o (☎ 322000), Sŏngnam (☎ 756-2000), Sunch'ŏn (☎ 744-2000), Suwon (☎ 332000), Taedŏk (☎ 862-2000), Taegu (☎ 423-2000), Taejŏn (☎ 252-2000), Ulsan (☎ 712000), Ŭijŏngbu (☎ 432000), Wonju (☎ 731-2000), Yŏsu (☎ 412000)

BUS

South Korean bus travel is fast, frequent and on time. Buses depart even if there's only one passenger aboard.

In some parts of Korea – particularly in the southernmost provinces – you are likely to encounter extremely annoying ticket machines. Rather than buying tickets from people, you must first feed notes into a machine and then press buttons (which in most cases are all in Korean) for your destination. The machines accept W1000, W5000 and W10,000 notes. This contraption gives change, though you may need to press the coin return button (also labelled in Korean) before it will cough up your cash. You may find that half your notes are rejected because they have a few creases or dirt on them. The whole procedure is complicated and error-prone if you can't read hangŭl. There is now an effort under way to add English to these

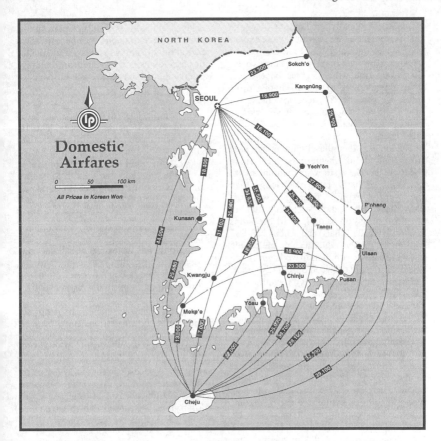

Domestic Airfares

0   50   100 km

All Prices in Korean Won

NORTH KOREA

Sokch'o
Kangnŭng
SEOUL
Yech'ŏn
P'ohang
Kunsan
Taegu
Ulsan
Kwangju
Chinju
Pusan
Mokp'o
Yŏsu
Cheju

23,300
18,900
16,100
18,400
34,500
35,500
31,100
26,600
44,000
25,900
19,800
27,900
30,400
25,300
34,400
18,900
23,300
29,100
18,500
7,100
75,200
62,700
29,100
15,700
39,100
22,000

machines (P'ohang inter-city bus terminal deserves kudos for making this effort), but in most cases foreigners will require the assistance of a local when buying a ticket from these machines.

If the bus driver doesn't take the ticket off you when you board the bus hang onto it – some bus companies want you to turn in the ticket to the driver when you disembark. Smoking is prohibited on all buses and the rules are generally enforced.

Sitting in the rear of the bus might help you escape the infernal karaoke music that some drivers like to play on their beloved

cassette players. However, the newer buses have rear speakers too – in which case there is no escape. If you find the music unappealing (most westerners do), you might try carrying a few music cassettes and see if you can persuade your driver to play them. In general, Korean bus drivers won't play hard rock but something mellow might go down well.

Classes

Most Korean cities and even some obscure towns have at least two bus stations, an express bus terminal (*kosok bŏsŭ t'ŏminŏl*) and an inter-city bus terminal (*shi'oe bŏsŭ t'ŏminŏl).* Logically, you might conclude that express buses are faster and more expensive, while inter-city buses are slower and cheaper. However, in most cases the express doesn't save much time. Express buses travel point to point, with no stop-offs to pick up or discharge passengers, except of course for 10-minute rest stops about once every two hours. Express buses do not accept standing passengers.

By contrast, the inter-city buses will stop to pick up and discharge passengers along the route, but these stops are combined with rest stops so it hardly takes much longer than the so-called 'express'. Inter-city buses typically make at least three stops en route, but they can also stop at designated bus stops (not only bus terminals) and accept standing passengers for short distances. Some people use these buses to commute to work, which can make them quite crowded during rush hour.

Express buses come in two flavours – 1st class *(udŭng)* and 2nd class *(chikhaeng).* The 1st class coaches are luxurious, with plenty of leg-room, and some are even equipped with cellular pay-phones, though none as yet have on-board toilets.

Local *(wanheng)* buses constitute the 3rd class. These buses operate on short, set routes and will pick up and drop off anywhere. There are no reserved seats, often as many standing as sitting passengers, and all but the bulkiest of freight may also be squeezed on. You will not be using these for long-distance travel, but you might occasionally need to take one to a remote spot.

Reservations
On the express buses you'll be sold a ticket with a reserved seat and a guaranteed time and date of departure. Miss the bus and you're out of luck.

Inter-city bus tickets are *usually* not sold with a particular time and seating is open. If you miss your bus you can board the next one on a space available basis. However, you are supposed to use the ticket the same day you bought it.

In most cases, you won't need an advance ticket, but seats are hard to come by on weekends and holidays. At such peak times, you might have to queue for hours to buy a ticket in Seoul. Things are easier in smaller cities and towns, but travel during holidays is synonymous with packed-out buses.

Costs
Given the high standard of service, bus fares are certainly reasonable in Korea. The 1st class coaches cost about 50% more than regular inter-city buses – you pay a lot for those comfortable seats. Just about the longest bus ride you can take in the entire country is Seoul-Pusan (428 km), which costs W11,500 for 2nd class and W17,200 for 1st class.

TRAIN
South Korea has an excellent railway network connecting all major cities and the ticketing system is computerised. Smoking is prohibited on trains, but there is usually a smoking car.

Few ticket clerks speak any English. Some of the larger stations have English signs indicating special ticket windows for foreigners. They were installed for the 1988 Olympics and subsequently went to pot, but were revived once again for the 1993 Taejŏn Expo. At the moment, it seems that these places function, at least part-time, so they're worth trying. The stations which have these special ticket windows are as follows:

Seoul station	☎ 392-7811
Seoul Ch'ŏngnyangni	☎ 966-0018
Iri	☎ 527788
Kyŏngju	☎ 438052
Mokp'o	☎ 427788
Pusan	☎ 463-5782
Tongdaegu (east Taegu) station	☎ 955-8877
Taejŏn	☎ 253-7451
Yŏsu	☎ 626491

With advance notice, you can buy train tickets from the KNTO in Seoul and you can also buy them from numerous travel agencies.

There's a monthly timetable available from bookstores – this contains schedules for all forms of transport throughout the country, but only the rail portion is in English. The Korean name for the timetable is *shigakp'yo*.

Classes
There are four classes of trains. The fastest are called *saemaul-ho*. Then come the limited stop *mugunghwa-ho*. Similar, but not air-con, are the *t'ongil-ho* trains – the best deal for budget travellers. Finally there are the incredibly slow 4th-class (local) trains known as *pidulgi-ho* – avoid these! Seats on the 4th-class trains cannot be booked; on the saemaul trains there are 1st and 2nd class carriages; on the two middle-range trains there are 1st and economy class seats and standing tickets.

Reservations
There are no reservations as such, but you can purchase train tickets up to three months in advance. As long as you don't need to travel during weekends or holidays, there should be no need to buy a ticket in advance. However, the situation is much the opposite during non-working days. Departing Seoul on a Friday night or Saturday is almost impossible if you haven't bought a ticket in advance. Indeed, even the standing-room tickets sell out on holidays! The moral of the story is either get a train ticket well in advance or don't plan to move around at all during holidays. If you get stuck, your only alternative will be to queue for the buses.

Costs
The longest trip you can do by train is Seoul-Pusan, a distance of 445 km. The schedule and price breakdown is as follows:

Class	Duration	Price (W)
Saemaul-ho	4 hrs 10 min	29,000
Mugunghwa-ho	5 hrs	15,400
T'ongil-ho	5 hrs 20 min	10,600

BULLET TAXI
Long-distance share taxis are affectionately known as 'bullet taxis' *(ch'ong'al t'aekshi)* because the drivers tend to drive like maniacs. These taxis can be found at two places – at some major tourist sites and at bus or train stations. They often meet incoming ferries such as the boat on Lake Soyangho near Ch'unch'ŏn. You can also find them around the Seoul Express Bus Terminal at night when the regular buses stop running.

Meters are not used, so you must negotiate the fare in advance. Try to find a group of Koreans and let them do the bargaining.

CAR & MOTORCYCLE
The car revolution has arrived in Korea. Visitors in the 1980s can remember Seoul as a city almost free of pollution and traffic – no longer! The vast increase in cars brings with it all the usual environmental problems, including a severe shortage of parking spaces in Korea's crowded cities. The Koreans – who in former times got along well with their neighbours – often come to fisticuffs with the family next door about who can park in front of whose house.

It makes little sense to rent a car in South Korea – the cost will burn a hole in all but the deepest pockets, while public transport is cheap and excellent (though getting worse because cars are plugging up the crowded highways). Driving in the larger cities is particularly not recommended. However, if you confine your driving to rural areas, having a car allows you the freedom to explore the backwaters at a leisurely pace. Rural roads are generally excellent and have little traffic, except during holiday times when Koreans head for the hills.

Korean drivers seem to be totally oblivious to the presence of motorcycles – ride one at your peril! This is not intentional – they just simply don't expect motorcycles to be there and therefore don't see them. Your chances of getting squashed by a car or taxi are reduced if you keep your headlight on even during the day – at least this makes you more visible. Rural roads are certainly safer and more enjoyable than the mean streets of Seoul. Motorcycles are seldom available for hire, so if you need one you'll probably have to buy your own.

Signposting inside cities and large towns is inadequate, especially if you're trying to find your way out. Most of the sign-posting is for the various *dong* (suburbs) and such things as 'railway station', 'city hall' or 'express bus terminal'.

A detailed road atlas is essential and these are readily available from major bookshops.

Road Rules

The speed limits vary considerably and there are not too many signs indicating what they are. In general, the limits are 100 km/h on expressways, 80 km/h on main highways, 60 km/h on provincial roads and 50 or 60 km/h in urban areas. Speed cops make a small fortune stopping offenders, and they're out in force at weekends and holidays, but this doesn't stop drivers routinely exceeding the limits by considerable margins. Drivers coming in the opposite direction will often indicate the presence of a speed trap ahead of you by flashing their lights. Foreigners should not consider themselves above the law in Korea, but sometimes you can talk your way out of a fine – try to look ignorant and be friendly, apologetic and humble.

Bikini Wars

The sale of petrol was once monopolised by the government, but the last few years have seen many private companies enter the market. Fierce competition has not produced the 'price wars' so common in western countries; instead, it has led to periodic 'service wars'.

In this competitive free-for-all, Korea's petrol stations must do their best to maintain a picture-perfect image – they're spotlessly clean, brightly painted and often decorated with flowers. The staff, selected for their good looks (half are male, half are female), are immaculately groomed and queue up by the station entrance to bow to customers as they drive in. While one person puts in the petrol, another attendant brings the customer free tea or coffee and then cleans the vehicle's windows. After paying, the customer receives a hearty *kamsa hamnida* and more polite bows. Some petrol stations give a free car wash as well.

At times when the service wars reach a fever pitch, petrol stations are known to employ bikini-clad dancing girls (not in winter though). ■

The police do spot checks for drunk drivers. If you're stopped and there's evidence that you've been drinking, they'll put the bag on you and the fines are heavy. When sober, driving is on the right side of the road.

Accidents and traffic jams are disturbingly frequent and it is wise not to expect any consideration from other road users. In major cities there is virtually no legal parking other than in private garages. However, you would never know that to look around – there appear to be no *enforced* rules for parking, and if there's a space then someone will park there. Drivers *do* respect traffic lights, and they are supposed to respect pedestrian crossings even when these are not controlled by lights. If a car hits a pedestrian, bicycle or even a motorcycle, the police (and courts) usually blame the driver of the car regardless of fault.

The driver and front seat passengers are required by law to wear seat belts. Safety helmets are mandatory for motorcyclists (though you'd never know it) and life insurance wouldn't be a bad idea either.

Rental

Cars are available for hire in Seoul, Cheju, Inch'ŏn, Kwangju, Pusan, Taegu and Taejŏn; see the relevant sections for details.

Only Korean cars are available for hire, but they aren't cheap; imported cars are virtually banned in Korea. Inquire about discounts for long-term rentals. The following rental rates (in won) will give you some idea of what to expect:

Model	10 hours	24 hours	1 week
Tico	32,000	44,400	248,640
Espero 1.5	49,600	68,900	384,840
Grandeur 3.0	114,800	145,300	813,680
Minibus	70,900	89,700	502,320

BICYCLE

While riding a bicycle in Seoul is almost certain death, it's not a bad way to move around in rural areas if you're experienced in this kind of travel. Besides urban traffic, there are a few other obstacles to consider – remember that Korea has four seasons and summer can sometimes be very wet. Korea is also fairly hilly, so you'll need to be athletically inclined.

Long-term rentals are impossible to find, but good 10-speed bikes can easily be purchased in Korea.

HITCHING

Hitchhiking is not customary among Koreans, and indeed, there is no particular signal for it. In other words, if you stand by the side of the road with your thumb out, many Koreans will just think you're weird. Then again, they expect madness from foreigners so you probably won't turn heads.

Nevertheless, hitching is a possibility. Koreans are generally kindly disposed to foreigners, and if you stand by the roadside waving and looking like you need assistance drivers will usually stop to help. However, they may not be amused if they think you're just hitching to save money – after all, bus transport is not that expensive. Public transport is poor in parts of Korea, especially during the off-season when rural backwaters (including the national parks) may be devoid of visitors. In such a situation, hitching may be your only option.

The issue of hitching begs the question, 'Is it safe?' Unfortunately, there is no clear-cut answer. Hitching is probably safer in Korea than in many western countries. Most Koreans are reasonably prosperous and needn't resort to robbery, though this doesn't mean the country is free of thieves. Rape is also a possibility – a single woman hitching by herself is no doubt taking a much greater risk than a man. In general, hitching is *usually* safe, but there are no guarantees and we don't recommend it. Hitching in pairs is safer, but it's also more difficult to get rides. Use your judgement, just as you would in your own country.

BOAT

Korea has an extensive network of ferries that service the offshore islands as well as several lakes.

You can travel by boat to numerous islands off the west and south coasts, and to Ullŭngdo off the east coast. Chejudo, Korea's largest island, can be reached by both car and passenger ferry from Mokp'o, Wando and Pusan. There are daily departures and a wide choice of ferries from each of these towns. If you want to explore the smaller islands of the south-west then Mokp'o and Wando are the main departure points. All these ferries are dealt with in detail in the Getting There & Away sections of each town.

For those seafaring souls who prefer the rolling of the waves to the bumping of a bus, a ferry connects the mainland towns of Wando and Mokp'o (seven hours), and the *Angel* hydrofoil plies between Pusan and Yŏsu. The latter is a popular trip as it goes through the beautiful Hallyŏ Haesang National Park, and stops at the islands and main towns along the way. The journey takes only about three hours, though some trips only go between Pusan and Ch'ungmu.

You can get ferries to Ullŭngdo from P'ohang, Hup'o and Tonghae, but those from Hup'o and Tonghae only operate on a daily basis during the summer months. During rough weather ferries can be cancelled, and it is wise to book in advance during the summer months.

As well as the sea ferries there are boats on several large lakes. These can be found on two lakes in the province of Kangwon-do (Paroho and Soyangho), and further south on Ch'ungju Lake, in Ch'ungch'ŏngbuk-do.

LOCAL TRANSPORT
City Bus

Inside cities and their outlying suburbs, buses are classified as ordinary *(ipsŏk)* and seat *(chwasŏk)*. The former generally cost W400 regardless of distance (or W390 if you buy tokens from a booth beforehand) but they get incredibly crowded at rush hours. A chwasŏk bus over the same route will cost W900. All city buses carry a route number and destination on the front and sides. Bus stops, likewise, carry panels on the post indicating the route served. None of these will be in English so you need to be able to recognise the name of your destination in Korean.

Underground
Seoul and Pusan have underground railways, which are a very convenient and cheap way of getting around. All signs for both the trains and the stations are in Korean and English. Tickets are bought at vending machines or at ticket windows. For more details, see the Getting Around sections for those two cities.

Taegu is also building a subway system which might be open by the time you read this (don't count on it though).

Taxi
Until very recently, Korea had a severe shortage of taxis. Locals solved this problem by creating unofficial 'share taxis'. Though now supposedly illegal, the practice (called *hapsung*) is still common so it's worth knowing how the system works. Once the driver has a passenger and is following a major boulevard, he will continue to slow down to listen out for the calls of other hopefuls as long as there is spare seating in the taxi. If he does pick up another passenger, this won't make your fare any cheaper, although it does make sorting out exactly how much it should be a bit more complicated. If there are already passengers in the taxi when you get in, the meter will already be running. Make a mental note (or better yet, write down) what the meter says when you get in and subtract it from the meter fare when you disembark. If two or more of you get in the taxi at the same time for the same destination, you should pay a single fare, not the same fare multiplied two or more times. Single women travelling late at night should be especially wary about getting into a taxi with other passengers – rapes have occurred when the driver and other 'passengers' turn on the unsuspecting victim.

The two official types of taxis are 'medium-sized taxis' and 'deluxe taxis' ('small taxis' disappeared some time ago). Flagfall for medium-size taxis is W1000, which takes you two km, and W100 for every 247m. At speeds under 15 km per hour, W100 for every 60 seconds is added to the basic fare. Fares are raised 20% between midnight and 4 am – this is automatically calculated by the meter (which has its own internal clock) so you needn't add more to what the meter says.

A deluxe taxi *(mobŏm t'aekshi)* is black with a yellow sign on the roof and the words 'Deluxe Taxi' written in English on the sides. These special taxis were originally created for foreigners, though there is nothing to prevent locals from making use of them. The designation 'deluxe taxi' not only means that the vehicle is very comfortable inside (some have cellular pay phones!), but also that the driver wears a crisp uniform, speaks some English and is polite to a fault. All this luxury does not come cheaply. Flagfall is W3000, which takes you three km, then W200 for each additional 250m or each 60 seconds when the speed drops below 15 km per hour. On the other hand, there is *no* late-night surcharge for the deluxe taxis. When you pay, the driver will issue you a receipt. In theory, the deluxe taxis will only stop at officially designated taxi stands, but in practice they'll stop wherever they see a chance to make a few won.

Complaint forms are available from the Ministry of Transport and the public have been encouraged to record details of taxi drivers who drive dangerously or attempt to charge more than the amount on the meter. However, the authorities won't entertain any complaint about taxis not stopping for you.

In the countryside, many taxis are not metered so you'll have to negotiate the fare before you set off. On the positive side, taxi drivers in rural areas and small towns are generally more co-operative than their urban counterparts. That is, they are willing to stop when you try to flag them down, rather than thumbing their nose at you while driving away.

If you take a metered taxi to a place where the driver won't necessarily get a return fare (to a temple outside a town, for instance), the driver may insist on a flat fare which will inevitably be higher than the metered fare.

ORGANISED TOURS
The Royal Asiatic Society (☎ 763-9483; fax 766-3796) in Seoul operates tours every weekend. The day tours are reasonably

priced, but overnight trips are somewhat expensive because they stay in good hotels rather than cheap yŏgwan. The RAS is in Room 611 of the Korean Christian Building (also called the CBS Building) on Tae-hangno. Office hours are 10 am to 5 pm, Monday to Friday. Take subway line 1 to Chongno 5-ga station.

The USO (☎ 795-3063, 795-3028) runs tours at bargain prices and you don't have to be a member of the US military to join. The Seoul office is opposite Gate 21 of the Yongsan military compound. There is also a USO in Pusan (☎ 462-3732).

There are, of course, plenty of commercial travel agents which can arrange tours to almost anywhere for a fee. While some of these tours are not horribly expensive, few could be regarded as cheap. Large groups can bargain for a reduced price. If any of this

interests you, the following are some of the travel agents (all in Seoul) recommended by the KNTO:

Global Tour, Global Building, 186-43 Tongkyo-dong, Map'o-gu, Seoul (☎ 335-0011; fax 333-0066)
Korea Travel Bureau, 1465-11 Sŏch'o-dong, Sŏcho-gu, Seoul (☎ 585-1191; fax 585-1187)
Seojin Travel Service, Seojin Building, 149-1 P'yŏng-dong, Chongno-gu, Seoul (☎ 732-4400; fax 732-1285)
Seoul Travel Service, Room 508, Kumjung Building, 192-11 Ŭlchiro 1-ga, Chung-gu, Seoul (☎ 754-6831; fax 753-9076)

Just to give an idea of what's available, Seoul Travel Service charges US$1600 for a 'Korea In Depth' tour which includes Seoul, Korean Folk Village, Sŏraksan, Songnisan, Pŏpchusa, Haeinsa, Kyŏngju, T'ongdosa, Pusan, Chejudo and then back to Seoul by air.

Seoul

The capital of South Korea, Seoul is a city of incredible contrasts. It was flattened during the Korean War but has risen from the ashes to become a modern metropolis with a population of 10.8 million; by some estimates Seoul rates as the fifth largest city in the world. Seoul now boasts high-rise buildings, 12-lane boulevards and urban problems to match, but the centuries-old royal palaces, temples, pagodas and imposing stone gateways set in huge traditional gardens remain timeless and elegant.

Seoul is the political, economic and educational hub of the country to a dangerous degree. So much of the country's wealth, industry and technology is concentrated here that it's a prime target for attack by North Korea. Even the Defence Ministry is headquartered in Seoul. With this in mind, former president Chun Doo-Hwan made an attempt to move some government ministries out of the capital. However, Chun met with fierce opposition and had to drop the plan. As far as Koreans are concerned, Seoul is *the* place to live because of its educational and economic opportunities. Another factor is prestige – in the face game, you gain a lot of points by having a Seoul address.

Seoul is also a magnet for foreigners, most of whom are more interested in economic opportunities than prestige. If the motive for your visit is sightseeing rather than job-hunting, Seoul is still certainly worth your time. But once you've taken in the major sights, you'd be well advised to get down to a bus or railway station and get out of town. Many travellers never do.

HISTORY

Seoul dates from the establishment, in 1392, of the Yi dynasty, which ruled Korea until 1910. During this time, when Korea was largely closed to the outside world, the shrines, palaces and fortresses that still stand today were built.

ORIENTATION

The Han-gang (Han River) flows from east to west and bisects the city. There are 12 urban districts on the north side of the river and 10 districts on the south. The city is further subdivided into 494 neighbourhoods *(dong)*.

Chung-gu is the central district, comprising the City Hall area south to Namsan Park. Chongno-gu is from Chongno (Chong Rd) northwards to the Kyŏngbokkung Palace area; this district has most of the budget hotels and the city's best sights. It'aewon-dong is a neighbourhood in Yongsan-gu on the south side of Namsan Park famous for its shopping, bars and nightlife.

Kangnam-gu is the district on the south side of the Han River and includes two of Seoul's most modern neighbourhoods – Yong-dong and Chamshil-dong. For Koreans this is the most prestigious area to live, but foreigners usually prefer the north side of the river.

INFORMATION
Tourist Offices

The best source of information about Seoul itself is the Seoul City Tourist Information Centre (☎ 731 6337, 735-8688) inside City Hall. It's open every day from 9 am to 6 pm, but closed from noon to 1 pm.

The municipal Seoul Tourist Information kiosks around town are as follows:

Chongno 5-ga: in front of the Cheil Bank (☎ 272-0348)
It'aewon: in front of Wendy's Hamburgers (☎ 794-2490)
Kwanghwamun: in front of the Kyobo Building (☎ 735-0088)
Myŏng-dong: in front of the Hanil Bank (☎ 757-0088)
Namdaemun: in front of the Shinsegae department store (☎ 779-3644)
Seoul express bus terminal: in front of the terminal (☎ 537-9198)
Seoul station (☎ 392-7811)
Tŏksugung: in front of the palace (☎ 756 0045)

You can get information about Seoul and the rest of Korea by visiting the KNTO Tourist Information Centre (☎ 757-0086) in the basement of the KNTO Building, 10 Ta-dong, Chung-gu. There are touch-screen computers here where you can choose a destination and find out about transportation, accommodation, things to see, etc. KNTO is open daily from 9 am until 6 pm (9 am to 5 pm from November through February).

The KNTO also operates the information counter at the international terminal of Kimp'o airport (☎ 665-0086). The Seoul City

government operates an information counter (☎ 664-5197) in the domestic terminal.

It's also worth trying the USO (☎ 792-3028/3063), 104 Galwol-dong, Yongsan-gu, (just opposite Gate 21 of the Yongsan US army base down the road past Seoul railway station). The USO is an information, entertainment and cultural centre that serves the US army base here, though you don't have to be with the military to get in. Take subway line No 1 to Namyong station (one stop south of Seoul station) and walk south for five minutes. Office hours are daily from 8 am to 6 pm.

Money

You can change money seven days a week at Kimp'o airport. Money exchange counters open two hours before the first aircraft departure and close one hour after the last arrival.

But a big warning – on departure, do *not* believe anyone when they tell you that there's a money changer in the airport transit area (the boarding area after you've passed through immigration). Yes, there is a money changing booth there, but it's closed 50% of the time and cannot be relied on.

During regular business hours, any one of Seoul's ubiquitous foreign exchange banks can accommodate you.

Post & Telecommunications

Poste Restante is on the third floor of the Central Post Office (CPO). All incoming letters are entered into a logbook which you have to sign when you pick up a letter or package – look over this logbook carefully for your name because they often misfile letters.

The telecommunications building is just behind the CPO – fax, telephone and telex services are available.

Travel Agencies

There are hundreds of travel agencies in Seoul, but English is not spoken in many of them and they are unlikely to be accustomed to westerners' preoccupation with getting the cheapest price. Highest recommendations go to Joy Travel Service (☎ 776-9871; fax 756-5342), 10th floor, 24-2 Mukyo-dong,

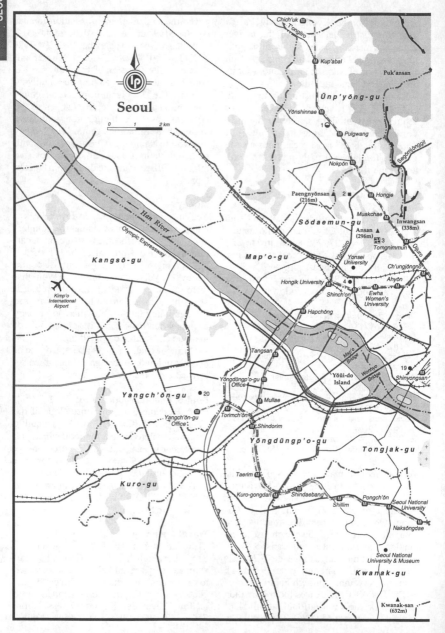

Seoul

0   1   2 km

Han River

Olympic Expressway

Ŭnp'yŏng-gu

Chich'uk Ⓜ
Tongjiro
Ⓜ Kup'abal
Puk'ansan

Yŏnshinnae Ⓜ
1 Ⓜ Pulgwang

Nokpŏn

Paengnyŏnsan ▲ 2 ■
(216m)
Ⓜ Hongje
Muakchae

Sŏdaemun-gu
Ansan ▲
(296m)
■ 3
Inwangsan
(338m)
Tongnimmun

Yonsei
University
Ch'ungjŏngno

Hongik University Ⓜ 4 ●
Shinch'on
Ewha
Women's
University
Ahyŏn

Map'o-gu

Kangsŏ-gu

Ⓜ Hapchŏng

Kimp'o
International
Airport

Tangsan Ⓜ

Mapp'o
Bridge

Wŏnhyo
Bridge

Yŏŭi-do
Island

19 ●
Shinyongsan

Yŏngdŭngp'o-gu
Office Ⓜ

Ⓜ Mullae

Yangch'ŏn-gu
● 20

Yangch'ŏn-gu
Office Ⓜ
Torimch'ŏn Ⓜ
Ⓜ Shindorim

Yŏngdŭngp'o-gu

Tongjak-gu

Taerim Ⓜ

Kuro-gu
Kuro-gongdan Ⓜ
Shindaebang Ⓜ
Shillim
Pongch'ŏn Ⓜ
Ⓜ Seoul National
University
Naksŏngdae

Seoul National
University & Museum

Kwanak-gu

Kwanak-san ▲
(632m)

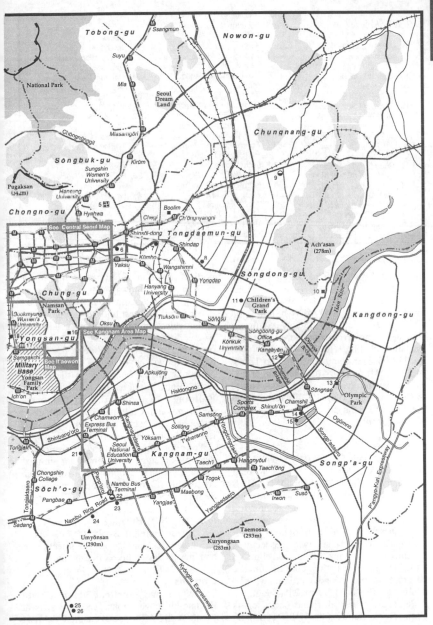

Chung-gu, Seoul, which is directly behind City Hall.

You'll also find two good discounters on the 5th floor of the YMCA building on Chongno 2-ga (next to Chonggak subway station): Korean International Student Exchange Society (KISES) (☎ 733-9494; fax 732-9568) in room 505; and Top Travel (☎ 739-5231; fax 736-9078) in room 506.

In It'aewon, you can try O&J Travel (☎ 792-2303; fax 796-2403). It's on the 2nd floor just above the Honey Bee Club (see the It'aewon map).

Bookshops

The Royal Asiatic Society (☎ 763-9483; fax 766-3796) is in Room 611 of the Korean Christian Building on Taehangno. The RAS is not really a bookshop – it's dedicated to those with an interest in Korea's culture, history, economy and geography. However, the society has the best collection of books about Korea. The RAS also sponsors free lectures and runs weekend trips. Take subway line No 1 to Chongno 5-ga station. Office hours are 10 am to 5 pm, Monday to Friday. The mailing address is CPO Box 255, Seoul.

Perhaps the best all-round bookshop is Ŭlchi Book Centre (☎ 757-8991) in the north-east section of the underground arcade at Ŭlchiro 1-ga subway station (at the intersection of Namdaemunno & Ŭlchiro). This is *not* Seoul's largest bookstore, but it's got a great selection, prices are lower than elsewhere, the manager speaks English and you can even special order books (the other bookstores will never do that for you).

Seoul's largest bookstore is the Kyobo Book Centre in the basement of the Kyobo Building (on the north-east corner of Sejongno and Chongno); you can enter through the pedestrian underpass. This place is a good source of Lonely Planet books.

Youngpoong Bookstore is similar to Kyobo – a huge underground complex. There is a good selection of textbooks which are useful if you're teaching English in Seoul. The bookstore is in Chonggak subway station, directly across the street from the KNTO Building.

It'aewon Foreign Books (☎ 793-8249), 533 It'aewon-dong, has a wide selection of both new and used books in English.

Libraries

There are two excellent libraries with English-language books. The largest is at USIS (☎ 397-4185), opposite the USO near

Namyŏng station on subway line 1. It's open Monday through Friday from 11 am to 5 pm. Expect it to be closed on all American and all Korean holidays.

The other good library is the British Council, just north of Tŏksugung and east of the British Embassy.

Campuses

Three of Korea's biggest universities arc just west of the centre and easily reached by subway linc 2. The big three in this neigh-bourhood are Ehwa Women's University, Hongik University and Yonsei University. This is also a very active nightlife district.

In the centre near Namsan Park is Dong-guk University, which boasts a couple of interesting museums on campus. Take subway line 3 to Dongguk University station.

Down in the south end of town and also reached on subway line 2 is Seoul National University; it has a museum and some hiking areas nearby.

Medical Services

Seoul has a number of good hospitals with English-speaking doctors, but most arc hor-ribly overcrowded. All the useful hospitals seem to be at least one km from the nearest subway station, which means you'll have to get a taxi, walk or crawl the last 1000m.

For emergencies, one of the biggest, best and jam-packed is Seoul National University Hospital (☎ 762-5171) – it's about one km from Hyehwa subway station (line 4).

For normal outpatient treatment one of the two best places to go is the Foreigners' Clinic at Severance Hospital (☎ 361-6540), which is attached to the Yonsei University Medical School. Take subway line 2 to Shinch'on station. The other is on the south side of the Han River, the Asan Medical Centre (☎ 480-3025) – also known as Seoul Chung-ang Hospital. Like Severance, there is a foreigners' clinic here too. Take subway line 2 to Sŏngnae station.

To avoid the crowds, visiting a small private clinic is not a bad idea at all. Seoul's It'aewon neighbourhood has two clinics catering to foreigners: the International Clinic (☎ 790-0857) at 5-4 Hannam-dong, Yongsan-gu, and the Seoul Foreign Clinic (☎ 790-0075, 796-1871).

Other hospitals with English-speaking doctors include Cheil (☎ 269-2151), Ewha (☎ 762-5061), Soonchunhyang (☎ 794-7191) and Saint Mary's (☎ 789-1114).

Emergency

Asia Emergency Assistance (☎ 353-6475/6) has English-speaking staff on duty 24 hours daily. This organisation will relay your request for help to the proper authorities, but charges a fee for this service.

During office hours, you might be able to get a call for help relayed through the Seoul City Tourist Information Centre (☎ 735-8688) or KNTO (☎ 757-0086). However, don't count on it if your life (or someone else's) is in danger.

If you want to try your luck with someone who probably won't speak English, the emergency telephone number for police is ☎ 112; for an ambulance or fire it's ☎ 119.

Lost & Found

If you leave something in a taxi or bus, there is a chance of recovering it from the lost & found at the Seoul Metropolitan Police Bureau (☎ 298-1282, 299-1282). There is a subway lost & found number for line 1 (☎ 869-0089) and lines 2-4 (☎ 753-2408).

Immigration

The headquarters of the Seoul Immigration Office (☎ 653-3041/8) covers both Seoul and the province of Kyŏnggi-do. It's incon-veniently located in Yangch'ŏn-gu out near the airport. You can get there by taking subway line 2 to Shindorim station, and then transferring to a spur subway line to Yangch'ŏn-gu Office station. From there you have to walk two blocks to the north.

Fortunately, there is also a much more convenient branch in the city centre (☎ 732-6214) on the 5th floor of the Chŏksŏn Hyŏndae Building. This is easily reached by taking subway line 2 to Kyŏngbokkung station. When walking out of the station, take exit No 7 (the sign says 'Seoul Metropolitan Police Administration').

THINGS TO SEE & DO
Kyŏngbokkung Palace

Kyŏngbokkung, at the far north end of Sejongno, has had its ups and downs. Built by the first Yi dynasty king when he relocated the capital to Seoul, this palace was the hub of royal power and the royal residence for around 200 years. Before 1592 the grounds housed some 500 buildings, but the Japanese onslaught saw most of these destroyed. The palace was then neglected until an ambitious reconstruction scheme commenced during the reign of King Kojong (1864-1907). By 1872 some 200 buildings had been completed. Another Japanese occupation (1910-1945) and the Korean War resulted in wholesale destruction – only 10 buildings at Kyŏngbokkung survived these disasters.

In 1995 the Koreans started a major effort to restore the entire complex to the splendour it enjoyed during the time of King Kojong. The only part which could not be completely restored was the front of Kwanghwamun Gate because doing so would have blocked traffic on the street in front of the palace.

The palace grounds and buildings are open for viewing from 9 am to 6 pm from March to October, 9 am to 5 pm November to February, and is closed on Tuesdays. Admission for adults costs W700; for persons aged 19 to 24 it's W300; and it's free for persons under age 19.

National Folk Museum

This is on the grounds of Kyŏngbokkung Palace. Unlike the National Museum it will not be demolished, but it may be undergoing renovation at the time of your visit.

The collection displays items from the daily lives of Koreans through history – everything from kitchen utensils to relics

---

National Pride Museum

While arguably the best museum in Korea, the main problem with the National Museum is figuring out where it is. Until 1995 it was housed in the former Capitol building on the grounds of Kyŏngbokkung Palace. In 1996 the building closed its doors for good and work crews began tearing it down.

There is a story behind all this. The Japanese built their Capitol building in 1926 on the grounds of Kyŏngbokkung for a specific purpose: to symbolically intersect the axis of power that flowed from the throne hall through the Kwanghwamun Gate (Gate of Radiant Transformation). To make matters worse, the building was constructed in the shape of the Japanese character for Japan. All this was to enforce the notion that Korea was now part of Japan. Needless to say, many Koreans were less than happy about this and have long vowed to get rid of this symbol of Japanese imperialism.

However, not everyone felt that demolishing the National Museum was a great idea: the preservationist lobby argued that the building was an important part of Korea's history and that much post-liberation history happened here (it was the Capitol for the Rhee, Park and Chun administrations); taxpayers noted that building a new National Museum would be very costly; and pragmatists suggested it would be wise to preserve the old museum at least until a new one could be built to take its place.

In the end national pride won the day. As demolition of the National Museum began, its priceless collection of art and treasures was shifted around between various annexes in the Kyŏngbokkung compound. Unfortunately, those buildings have also been undergoing renovation and none is large enough to display the museum's entire collection. As a result, displays of selected art objects have had to be rotated.

And the new National Museum? It's supposed to be built at the Yongsan Family Park, the former golf course of the US military base at It'aewon. A ground-breaking ceremony has been held, but at the time of writing construction was yet to begin. The project has been hampered by financial questions and arguments over the choice of architect. Some wanted to open the design competition to international bidding, but after lengthy haggling, a Korean architect was chosen.

Optimists hope to have the new museum open by the year 2000. Meanwhile, the national treasures keep getting shifted between temporary quarters, just like a game of musical chairs. To find out just where this mobile collection might be at any given time, ask the KNTO. The museum – wherever it is – is closed on Monday. ■

Frescoes such as this one in Kyŏngbokkung Palace depict items such as animal and plant life to assist the departed in the afterlife.

associated with Shamanistic rituals. Altogether there are about 10,000 items housed in nine display rooms. Admission costs W550 and the museum is closed every Tuesday and on New Year's Day (1 January).

The Blue House

One could say that Kyŏngbokkung is actually still the seat of power in South Korea. Just beyond Shinmumun (the north gate of Kyŏngbokkung) is the Blue House *(Ch'ŏngwadae)*, where South Korea's president lives.

On 21 January 1968, a squad of 31 North Korean commandos were caught just 500m from the Blue House – their mission was to assassinate South Korean President Park Chung-hee. Obviously, security remains tight and the Blue House itself is not open to the general public. However, the tree-lined street in front of the Blue House has been open to the public ever since President Kim Young-sam was inaugurated in 1993.

Samch'ŏng Park

In the hills just north of the Blue House is Samch'ŏng Park. It is thought to be of Taoist origin, but during the Chosŏn dynasty Confucian rites were also performed here. The park would be a much more pleasant place for a stroll if it wasn't for a nearby military installation. As it is, many of the paths in the park are fenced on both sides.

Kwanghwamun Intersection

The intersection just north of the Koreana Hotel is Kwanghwamun, named for a gate one block to the north near Kyŏngbokkung Palace. It's the only intersection in Seoul from which each of the four radiating roads has a different name. Slightly to the north of the intersection, in the middle of Sejongno, is a bronze statue of **Admiral Yi Sun-shin** (1545-98), possibly the most revered figure in Korean history. Yi Sun-shin was a masterful military strategist and the inventor of the so called 'turtle ship' *(kŏbuksŏn)*. By cladding the wooden ships of the time in sheets of armour, he was able to achieve stunning victories over Hideyoshi's numerically and militarily stronger Japanese navy.

To the right of the statue is the Kyobo Building. The building is not particularly interesting in itself, but the basement is home to the vast Kyobo Book Centre. Huddled in the shadow of the Kyobo Building is the tiny **Pigak Pavilion**. It was built in 1903 to commemorate the coronation of King Kojong.

Chogyesa Temple

Buried in the alleys south-east of Kyŏngbokkung Palace is Chogyesa. It is the only major Buddhist temple in Seoul and is named after the Chogye sect (the major Buddhist sect in Korea) to which it belongs. In the vicinity of Chogyesa, out on the main road, are a number of Buddhist supply shops selling everything from bowls for alms to tapes of Buddhist meditation chants.

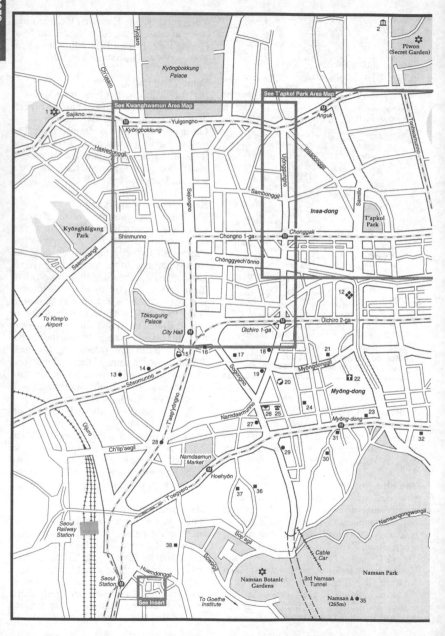

See Kwanghwamun Area Map

See T'apkol Park Area Map

Kyŏngbokkung
Palace

Piwon
(Secret Garden)

HyoJaro

Ch'usaro

Sajikno

Kyŏngbokkung

Yulgongno

Haejedonggil

Anguk

Insadonggil

Ujŏnggukno

Sambonggil

Insa-dong

Kyŏnghŭigung
Park

Samilro

T'apkol
Park

Saemunangil

Shinmunno

Chongno 1-ga

Chonggak

Sajongno

Chŏnggyech'ŏnno

To Kimp'o
Airport

Tŏksugung
Palace

City Hall

Ŭlchiro 1-ga

Ŭlchiro 2-ga

12

Sŏsomunno

14

13

T'aep'yŏngno

15 16

17

18

19

20

21

Myŏngdonggil

22

Myŏng-dong

24

25

26

Namdaemunno

27

Myŏng-dong

23

Sogongno

31

32

Ch'ilp'aegil

28

Namdaemun
Market

29

30

Hoehyŏn

T'oegyero

37

36

Seoul
Railway
Station

38

Namsangongwongil

Ojuro

Cable
Car

Namsan Park

Seoul
Station

Huamdonggil

See Insert

Sop'agil

Sowolgil

Namsan Botanic
Gardens

3rd Namsan
Tunnel

Namsan ▲ ●35
(265m)

To Goethe
Institute

Tonhwamunno

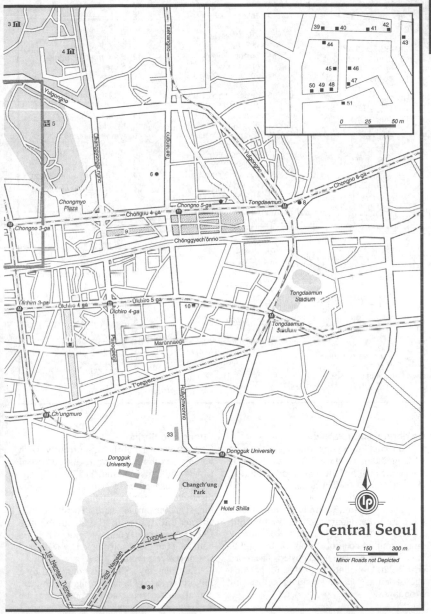

Central Seoul

0   150   300 m

Minor Roads not Depicted

Central Seoul
서울중심부

PLACES TO STAY
10 Chonji Hotel
    천지호텔
11 Poongjun Hotel
    풍전호텔
16 Seoul Plaza Hotel
    서울프라자호텔
17 Westin Chosun Hotel
    조선호텔
21 Royal Hotel
    서울로얄호텔
23 King Sejong Hotel
    세종호텔
24 Savoy Hotel
    사보이호텔
30 New Oriental Hotel
    뉴오리엔탈호텔
31 Pacific Hotel
    퍼시픽호텔
32 Astoria Hotel
    아스토리아호텔
33 Sofitel Ambassador Hotel
    소피텔앰배서더호텔
36 Seoul Rex Hotel
    서울렉스호텔
37 Palace Hotel
    파레스호텔
38 Hilton Hotel
    힐튼호텔
39 Hanwŏn Yŏinsuk
    한원여인숙
40 Shinhŭng Yŏinsuk
    신흥여인숙
41 Kwangju Yŏinsuk
    광주여인숙

42 Tŏksŏng-jang Yŏgwan
    덕성장여관
43 Choil Yŏgwan
    조일어관
44 Sŏjŏng Yŏinsuk
    서정여인숙
45 Sŏngnam Yŏinsuk
    성남여인숙
46 Kwangshin Yŏinsuk
    광신여인숙
47 Migyŏng Yŏinsuk
    미경여인숙
48 Songrim Yŏinsuk
    송림여인숙
49 Hyŏndae Yŏinsuk
    현대여인숙
50 Kyŏnggi Yŏinsuk
    경기여인숙
51 Myŏngshin Yŏinsuk
    명신여인숙

OTHER
1 Sajik Park
   사직공원
2 Korean Buddhist
   Art Museum
   불교미술관
3 Ch'angdŏkkung Palace
   창덕궁
4 Ch'anggyŏnggung Palace
   창경궁
5 Chongmyo Shrine
   종묘
6 Royal Asiatic Society
   로얄아시아협회
7 Herbal Medicine Arcade
   한약상가

8 Tongdaemun Gate
   동대문
9 Tongdaemun Market
   동대문시장
12 Printemps Department
    Store
    쁘렝땅백화점
13 Universal Travel Service
    유니버살여행사
    (동양빌딩)
14 Korean Air (KAL)
    대한항공
15 Airport Bus Stop
    정류장 (공항)
18 Lotte Department Store
    롯데백화점
19 Midopa Department Store
    미도파백화점
20 Chinese Embassy
    중국대사관
22 Myŏng-dong Cathedral
    명동성당
25 Central Telephone Office
    중앙전화국
26 Central Post Office (CPO)
    중앙우체국
27 Shinsegae Department
    Store
    신세계백화점
28 Namdaemun Gate
    남대문
29 Asiana Airlines
    아시아나항공
34 National Theatre
    국립극장
35 Seoul Tower
    서울타워

Ch'angdŏkkung Palace

To the east of Kyŏngbokkung Palace is Ch'angdŏkkung Palace. There are tours of the area which include a visit to Piwon (the 'Secret Garden'). Tours take around 90 minutes, and although tours in English are only available at 11.30 am, 1.30 and 3.30 pm, there are Korean language tours on the hour from 9 am to 5 pm. Joining a Korean-language tour is no problem as all the sights have English explanations posted. The tours cost W2200 for adults or W1100 for persons age 24 or under. Ch'angdŏkkung is closed on Mondays.

Chongmyo Shrine

Chongmyo was built concurrently with Kyŏngbokkung to enshrine the ancestral tablets of the first Yi king, Yi T'aejo. Today, with the exception of two kings of some disrepute, the ancestral tablets of all 27 Yi kings are enshrined here. There are two shrine buildings on the grounds: the Chŏngjŏn and the Yŏngnyŏngjon. They are both long buildings surrounded by walls and flagstoned courtyards.

The Chongmyo Shrine is connected by a footbridge to the Ch'anggyŏnggung Palace, and it makes sense to continue into the grounds of the latter. The Chongmyo Shrine is open from 9 am to 6.30 pm March to October, and 9 am to 5.30 pm November to February; it is closed on Tuesdays. Admission for adults is W700; W300 for people age 19 to 24; and free for persons under age 19.

Ch'anggyŏnggung Palace

Built in 1104, Ch'anggyŏnggung was originally a Koryŏ summer palace. In the early 1390s the first Yi king, T'aejo, lived here while Kyŏngbokkung Palace was being completed. During the Japanese occupation, the palace was demoted to a park, a colonial-style red building constructed, and a botanic garden and zoo moved here. The zoo has since been relocated to Seoul Grand Park.

Ch'anggyŏnggung is open daily from 9 am to 6 pm from March to October, and 9 am to 5 pm November to February; it's closed on Tuesdays. Admission for adults is W700; W300 for persons aged 19 to 24; and free for persons age 18 and younger.

Korean Buddhist Art Museum

The museum (☎ 766-5000/6000) has interesting displays of Buddhist paintings, ceramics and sculpture. Most of the items date back to the Chosŏn dynasty. The museum is open from 10 am to 5 pm and admission costs W1000. The address is Chongno-gu, Wonsuh-dong 108-4, which is about 300m up the alley that runs between the Hyundai Building and the front gate of Ch'angdŏkkung Palace (along the palace wall near Piwon).

Unhyŏn-gung Palace

This small palace is the former residence of Regent Hŭngsŏn T'aewongun (father of the last Chosŏn king, Kojong), an important figure in Korea's history between 1850 and 1890. After the Korean War Unhyŏn-gung became the site of Duksung Women's University; when the campus moved to north-east Seoul in the early 1980s the palace was kept as a school annexe. It was finally renovated to 1866 standards and reopened for public viewing in 1996.

The palace is open daily except Monday and displays royal relics in six separate buildings. There are plans to host public re-enactments of the 1866 Royal Wedding on an annual basis, but no details were available at the time of writing on just when this will happen – ask the KNTO for details.

The palace is on a small alley to the west of the Chongmyo shrine.

T'apkol Park

On the corner of Insadonggil and Chongno is T'apkol Park. There are always crowds of friendly elderly people sitting around here and it's very easy to strike up a conversation with someone. In the vicinity of the park are roadside vendors selling maps of Korea and copies of the Declaration of Independence. In the evenings fortune tellers set up shop in small candle-lit tents in the same area.

T'apkol ('pagoda') Park is named after the 10-tier marble pagoda inside. The statue in the park is Sun Pyong-Hui, leader of the independence movement. On 1 March 1919 Sun Pyong-Hui and other Korean dissidents drew up a Declaration of Independence. The declaration was read aloud in the park two days later. It unleashed a torrent of anti-Japanese feeling, and the sam il, or 1 March Movement, was born. The entire contents of the Declaration of Independence are reproduced on a brass plaque alongside Sun Pyong-Hui's statue. Look also for the murals along the wall of the park depicting the activities of the independence movement.

Poshingak Pavilion

Poshingak Pavilion is on the south-east corner of Chongno and Ujŏnggungno. Chongno, which means 'Bell Street', derives its name from its city bell. The old city bell, dating from the mid-15th century, is in the National Museum and a new city bell is now hung in the Poshingak Pavilion. The bell, once struck daily at dawn and dusk to signal the opening and closing of the city gates, is now only sounded to usher in the new year and mark Independence Movement Day and National Liberation Day. The pavilion area is fenced off and there's not a lot to see, but the place is packed on New Year's Eve.

SEOUL

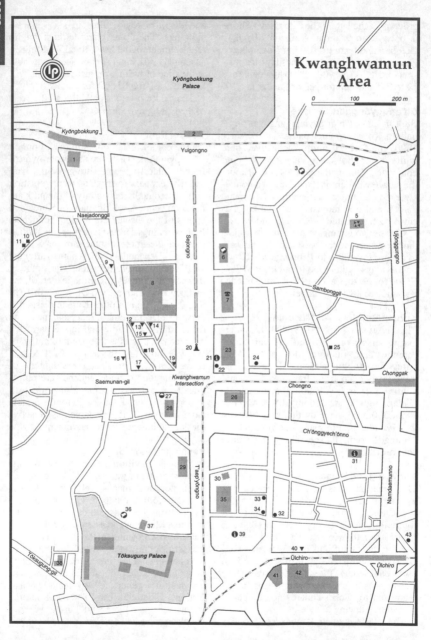

Kwanghwamun
Area

0   100   200 m

Kyŏngbokkung
Palace

Kyŏngbokkung

Yulgongno

Naejadonggil

Sejongno

Sambonggil

Ŭlchiro

Kwanghwamun
Intersection

Saemunan-gil

Chongno

Chonggak

Ch'ŏnggyech'ŏnno

T'aep'yŏngno

Namdaemunno

Tŏksugung Palace

Tŏksugung-gil

Ŭlchiro

Ŭlchiro

Kwanghwamun Area
광화문

PLACES TO STAY
10 Inn Sung Do
   성도여관
11 Inn Sam Sung
   삼성여관
18 Inn Daewon
   대원여관
25 Seoul Hotel
   서울관광호텔
29 Koreana Hotel
   코리아나호텔
30 New Kukje &
   New Seoul Hotels
   뉴국제호텔,
   뉴서울관광호텔
41 President Hotel
   프레지던트호텔
42 Lotte Hotel
   호텔롯데

PLACES TO EAT
9 Tonghwaru Chinese
   Restaurant
   동화루
12 Pizza Inn
   피자인
13 Paris Baguette &
   Milim Kimbap
   부산회집, 미림김밥
14 Sapporo Pub
   & Restaurant
   삿뽀로우돈

15 Tongsŏnggak Chinese
   Restaurant
   동성각
16 Koryŏ Supermarket
   고려쇼핑
17 Hardee's Hamburgers
   & Bakery
   하디스
19 Wendy's
   웬디스
40 La Cantina Restaurant
   라 칸티나 레스토랑

OTHER
1 Immigration Office
   & KYHA
   적선현대빌딩
2 Kwanghwamun Gate
   광화문
3 Japanese Embassy
   일본대사관
4 Korea Ginseng Centre
   고려인삼중심
5 Chogyesa Temple
   조계사
6 US Embassy
   미국대사관
7 Kwanghwamun
   Telephone Office
   광화문전화국
8 Sejong Cultural Centre
   세종문화회관
20 Yi Sun-shin Statue
   이순신장군동상
21 Tourist Information Booth
   관광안내소

22 Pigak Pavilion
   비각
23 Kyobo Building & Kyobo
   Book Centre
   교보빌딩, 교보문고
24 Net Cyber Cafe
   넷카페
26 Kwanghwamun Post
   Office
   광화문우체국
27 Airport Bus Stop
   정류징 (공항)
28 Kwanghwamun Building
   광화문빌딩
31 KNTO
   한국관광공사
32 Fax & Photocopy
   가뤼문화시
33 Kodak Photo Shop
   코닥양행
34 Joy Travel Service
   조이한공
35 Seoul Press Centre
   신문회관
36 British Embassy
   영국대사관
37 British Council Library
   영국문화원
38 Chŏngdong Theatre
   정독
39 City Hall & Tourist
   Information Centre
   시청
43 Ŭlchi Book Centre
   을지서적

Tŏksugung Palace

The palace was built in the mid-15th century by King Sejo for his grandson, Prince Wolson. Even though it is the smallest of Seoul's palaces it has twice served as a temporary royal residence: once for 15 years after Hideyoshi sacked Seoul in 1592; and on a second occasion, from 1897 to 1907, when King Kojong made it his residence after a year-long asylum in the Russian legation. After his son King Sunjong took power in 1907, Kojong remained in Tŏksugung Palace until his death in 1919.

The entrance to Tŏksugung Palace is through the Taehanmun Gate, opposite the Seoul Plaza Hotel. It's open from 9 am to 6 pm from March to October, and 9 am to 5 pm November to February; the entrance fee is W700. It is closed on Mondays.

Namdaemun Gate

South of the City Hall down T'aep'yŏngno, the Namdaemun Gate was once Seoul's chief city gate, in keeping with the geomantic principles that determined the layout of the Yi palaces. It's still an impressive sight, although surrounded by tall office buildings and knots of jostling traffic. It was originally built in the late 14th century and has now been designated National Treasure No 1. The most recent reconstruction work – to repair damage sustained in the Korean War – was completed in the 1960s.

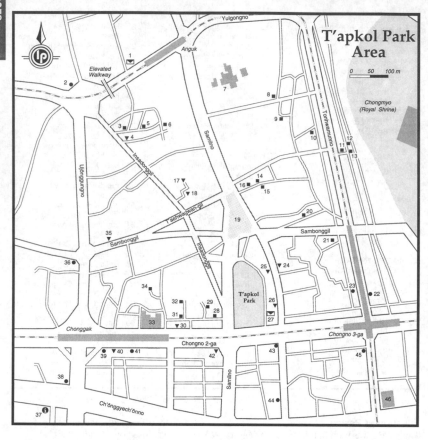

T'apkol Park Area

Postal Museum

Strictly for the keen philatelist, the Postal Museum is on the 4th floor of the CPO. It has a reasonably extensive collection of 19th-century stamps and items related to the postal industry. The museum is closed on Sunday and public holidays.

Namsan Park

Namsan once marked the southern extent of old royal Seoul, and remains of the city walls can still be seen in the park's wooded grounds. The peak was also once crowned

with defensive fortifications, though these have now been replaced by Seoul Tower.

In the western section, not far from Namdaemun market, there is the **Namsan Botanic Gardens**, a library and the odd statue.

At the top of Namsan is **Seoul Tower**. With the help of Namsan, the tower reaches 483m, though minus the mountain it's a mere 240m. Still, it's the third tallest tower in the world and one of Seoul's most notable landmarks.

There's a revolving restaurant, but most visitors settle for the observation deck. There's also a booth where you and your beloved can have a photograph printed onto a T-shirt inscribed with the words 'for the precious love' – at only W30,000, this is one of Seoul's bargain highlights. Other attractions in the tower include the Aquarium, Marine Life Museum, Fancy World, Game Room and Natural Stone Exhibits. If you enjoy this kind of tourist-oriented action, the B ticket for the tower includes all the attractions and the observation deck for W4500. For those content with the view and a T-shirt, the A ticket at W1600 will suffice.

You can get up to the tower either by walking from the botanic garden area (a short walk from Namdaemun market) or by way of the cable car. The latter runs at 10-minute intervals from 9 am to 10 pm. To get back into town, it's a pleasant downhill walk

through a residential area to Myŏng-dong subway station on line 4.

Dongguk University Museum

The Dongguk University Museum (☎ 260-3462) has a small collection of Buddhist art. The museum is open for public viewing every day except public holidays, and admission is free.

Also within the campus is the **Suk Ju-son Memorial Museum of Korean Folk Art** (☎ 709-2188). This has a collection containing more than 6000 items of traditional clothing and shoes. The museum is only open on Tuesday and Thursday.

To reach the campus, take subway line 3 to Dongguk University station.

T'apkol Park Area
탑골공원

PLACES TO STAY
3 Hanhung-jang Yŏgwan
   한흥장여관
5 Kwanhun-jang Yŏgwan
   관훈장여관
6 Shingung-jang Yŏgwan
   신궁장여관
8 Munhwa Yŏgwan
   문화여관
9 Motel Jongrowon
   종로원여관
10 Seahwa-jang Hotel
   세화장여관
11 T'aeyang-jang Yŏgwan
   태양장여관
12 Taerim-jang Yŏgwan
   대림장여관
13 Sun Ch'ang Yŏgwan
   순창여관
14 Yongjin Hotel
   용진여관
15 Hwasŏng-jang Yŏgwan
   화성장여관
16 Emerald Hotel
   애머랄드호텔
20 Sŏngbo-jang Yŏgwan
   성보장여관
21 Tongnam-jang Yŏgwan
   동남장여관
28 Insŏng Yŏgwan
   인성여관

29 Unjong-jang Yŏgwan
   운종장여관
31 Chongno Yŏgwan
   종로여관
32 Wongap Yŏgwan
   인갑여관
33 YMCA
   와이엠씨에이
34 Taewon Yŏgwan
   대원여관
46 Central Hotel
   쎈쥬럴호텔

PLACES TO EAT
4 Youngbin Garden
   Restaurant
   영빈식당
17 Sanch'on Vegetarian
   Restaurant
   산촌식당
18 Airirang Restaurant &
   Yet Ch'at Chip Teashop
   옛찻집다실
24 Doutor Coffee Shop
   도토루
25 P'ungch'a Hof
   풍차호프
26 Kentucky Chicken
   켄터키후라이드
30 Iga Kimbap
   이가김밥
35 Hanaro Mart
   하나로마트
40 Popeye's Chicken
   파파이스

42 McDonald's
   맥도날드

OTHER
1 Anguk Post Office
   안국우체국
2 Paek Sang Memorial Hall
   백상기념관
7 Unhyŏngung Palace
   눈현궁
19 Nakwon Elevated Arcade
   낙원상가
22 Dansŏngsa Cinema
   단성사극장
23 Picadilly Cinema
   피카디리극장
27 T'apkol Post Office
   탑골우체국
36 Chung-ang Map & Atlas
   중앙지도
37 KNTO
   한국관광공사
38 Youngpoong Bookstore
   영풍문고
39 Poshingak Pavilion
   보신각
41 Chongno Book Centre
   종로서적
43 Musicland
   뮤직랜드
44 Cine Plaza Cinema
   시네프라자극장
45 Seoul Cinema Town
   서울시네마타운

Changch'ung Park

At the eastern end of Namsan Park and just behind the Hotel Shilla is Changch'ung Park. The park is unusual in that it's well-adorned with magnificent sculptures set among the woods.

The park is open daily. Take subway line 3 to Dongguk University station.

Tongdaemun Gate

At the east end of Chongno 6-ga is the Tongdaemun Gate. It dates from 1869, though it had to be repaired after the Korean War.

Pongwonsa Temple

North-east of Yonsei University, Pongwonsa Temple dates back to the late 9th century. It was destroyed during the Korean War and has been subsequently rebuilt. It is now the headquarters of the T'aego sect of Korean Buddhism. The T'aego is an interesting sect, insofar as it allows its monks to marry; this is a vestige of the Japanese administration and a controversial issue among Korean Buddhists. To get to the temple take bus No 135 from the Kyobo Building on Chongno.

War Memorial

Despite the name, this is a fully-fledged museum and certainly one of the best in Seoul. The War Memorial traces the history of war in Korea from the Three Kingdoms Period to the Korean War. Many younger travellers are surprised by the exhibit on the Vietnam War – it's often forgotten that the South Koreans participated in this war at the urging of their No 1 ally, the USA.

This large museum houses over 13,000 items and a number of large aircraft are parked outside. All the 'great victories' are discussed in the few English translations. The defeats suffered at the hands of the Japanese are only mentioned in hangŭl script.

Operating hours are 9.30 am to 6 pm (9.30 am to 5 pm in winter) and the museum is closed on Mondays. Admission costs W2000. The War Memorial is in the Yongsan area, very close to Samgakchi subway station on line 4.

King Sejong University Museum

This is a museum of folklore with some 3000 exhibits and an emphasis on traditional dress and furniture. The university and museum are close to Children's Grand Park, and can be reached by a 10-minute walk from Kŏnkuk University subway station on line 2.

Kimch'i Museum

Really the only thing worth doing in the enormous Korea World Trade Centre is to pop into the Kimch'i Museum in the basement. The museum has an interesting collection of exhibits related to kimch'i making; a lifestyle room that illustrates the connection between kimch'i and the everyday life of an average Korean; and a kitchen for attempting your own kimch'i experiments. The museum is open from 9 am to 6 pm from April to October and from 9 am to 5 pm from November to March. Entry is free. The museum is closed on Sundays and public holidays. Take the line 2 subway to Samsŏng station.

Agricultural Museum

This museum has seven rooms displaying 1600 agricultural implements that date from the Stone Age to modern times. It's in the old National Agricultural Cooperative Federation (NACF) Building on Chungjongno 1-ga. Admission costs W300. Take subway line 5 to Sŏdaemun station.

Pongŭnsa Temple

Slightly north of the Korea World Trade Centre, Pongŭnsa Temple has been relocated to the sterile southern part of Seoul (no doubt kicking and screaming all the way). A collection of important wood-block scriptures are housed in a small wooden structure next to the main temple. The original temple dates from the 8th century and in its time was an important Zen centre.

Olympic Stadium

The '88 Olympics held in Seoul was an event of great consequence for South Korean national pride, and the slogan 'keep the Olympic torch burning' crops up frequently in tourist literature. Despite all the hype, it is doubtful whether it is worth heading down to the Olympic Stadium for a look; when all's said and done it's just what its name suggests. Granted, with seating for 100,000 it's big, but it's a bit of an anticlimax. Don't confuse the Olympic Stadium with the adjacent Baseball Stadium. Entrance to the Olympic Stadium is through Gate 1-14. The best way to get there is from Sports Complex subway station on line No 2.

Lotte World

If you are a fan of mall culture you'll love Lotte World. It is a city within a building and includes an ice skating rink, the Hotel Lotte World, Lotte Department Store, Lotte Super Store, Lotte World Shopping Mall, Lotte World Sports, Lotte World Swimming and Lotte World Plaza. If this is not enough, there's a Disneyland look-alike next door in Lotte World Adventure with Magic Island and the Lotte World Folklore Museum.

It would easily be possible to spend an entire rainy day exploring the place, and it would be ideal for children (you could probably leave them there for good and they'd never miss you).

The basic admission fee to Lotte World Adventure doesn't include the rides or the Folklore Museum, which all carry steep surcharges. The admission fees are as follows:

	Adults	Students	Children
All-round ticket	W20,000	W17,000	W13,000
Big 5	W16,000	W13,000	W10,000
Admission	W7000	W5000	W4000
After 6:00 pm			
All-round ticket	W11,000	W9000	W7000
Big 5	W9000	W7000	W5000
Admission	W4000	W3000	W2000

Admission to the Folklore Museum is extra: W3500 for adults, W2500 for students and W1800 for children.

The vast majority of the shops and the department store are closed on Monday, though the ice skating rink and restaurants around it remain open.

Chamshil subway station on line 2 has clearly marked signs to Lotte World.

Olympic Park

Not far from the Olympic Stadium, Olympic Park is a more interesting outing than the former. Its grounds contain numerous sporting facilities from the '88 Olympics. There are also the remains of the Paekche dynasty (4th century) Mongch'on fortress, which are preserved as a museum.

Within the park's grounds there are numerous sculptures which offer a serene if somewhat bizarre sight against the background of sporting facilities.

The park is a short walk from Songnae or Chamshil subway stations on line No 2.

There is no admission fee to the park itself, but the Olympic Cultural Centre charges W4000 for the puppet shows, W4500 for the Space & Dinosaur Hall and W8000 for the sledding slope.

Children's Grand Park

Out near the Sheraton Walker Hill Hotel in eastern Seoul, Children's Grand Park has plenty to keep the kids amused. There are rides, play areas, fountains and ponds, and even a small zoo. The park is open daily from 9 am to 7 pm, and on summer weekends this is extended to 9 pm. Entry is W900 for adults, W500 for students and free for children under 12 or over age 65. It is a 10-minute walk north of Konkuk University subway station.

Yŏŭi-do Island

Subway line 5 can take you to Yŏŭi-do Island, touted as Seoul's answer to Manhattan. There are a few sights here, but nothing to hold your interest for long. During office hours the streets are eerily deserted but that changes dramatically on Sundays, when the enormous Yŏŭi-do Plaza fills up with Seoulites on an afternoon outing. Stalls are often set up and many people zip around on the

The Big 'I Do'

Despite the cries to 'keep the Olympic torch burning', the Seoul Olympic Stadium is now looking more than a little forlorn and is generally deserted except for the occasional tourist or two. But it may be that the stadium has found a new lease of life...in the mass wedding industry.

On 25 August 1995 the stadium was host to the largest mass wedding in history. A total of 720,000 members of the Unification Church (whose followers are better known as 'Moonies' after their spiritual leader and self-styled Son of God, the Reverend Moon Sun-myung) collectively said 'I do' at the ceremony.

The participants were by no means all Korean. The Unification Church is not even particularly popular in the Reverend Moon's homeland. At the Olympic Stadium itself only 35,000 couples were married that day – the remainder participated in the ceremony via satellite links. In fact, the brides and grooms were as international as the Olympic competitors for which the stadium was originally built and hailed from more than 160 nations worldwide. It wasn't the first such mass wedding conducted by the Unification Church, either – Reverend Moon married 20,825 couples by the same procedure in 1992.

If this all seems a little curious, the pairing up procedure before the wedding was even more bizarre. The Reverend Moon and his confidants matched spouses according to the compatibility of facial features by means of photographs. As it turned out, many of the matched couples could not even speak the same language. But 'love conquers all' as they say.

Naturally such a specialised match-making service is not without its costs. Participants were billed on a sliding scale according to nationality, with (surprise, surprise) Japanese heading the list at US$29,000. The high cost raised more than a few eyebrows – 80 South Korean Protestant organisations banded together to denounce the mass weddings as a scheme to make Reverend Moon rich.

And what about the mass honeymoon? Well, it was put on hold. Moonie weddings are followed by 40 days of celibate contemplation before knuckling down to the less contemplative business of creating 'blessed families'. ■

---

bicycles that are available for hire. In fact, it's about the only safe place in Seoul for cycling. There are plans afoot to tear up the asphalt and convert the plaza into a forested park.

In October the plaza hosts a major **ceramics market** where potters set up stalls and sell their products at prices much cheaper than elsewhere around town.

The only way to see Yŏŭi-do Island is on foot. Things to see include the **National Assembly** building, the **Full Gospel Church** and the outdoor **Korean War Museum**.

Also on the island is the **Korea Stock Exchange**. There's a free observation room on the 4th floor where explanations of stock exchange activities are provided in English through phones. It is a slightly sleepy place, though there are the obligatory scraps of paper scattered across the floor and staff making the occasional phone call.

Towards the south-eastern end of the island is the **DLI 63** building. Despite the name, it's only 60 storeys tall (they count three levels in the basement to make it seem higher). Nevertheless, it's Korea's tallest building, though it will soon be superseded by a new 102-storey monolith. The top floor has an observation deck, but the views here aren't as good as from Seoul Tower. The building also contains an aquarium and the Imax theatre. The latter offers a viewing screen 10 times larger than the average cinema and an excellent sound system. The ground level sports a wide selection of restaurants.

Close to the DLI 63 building is the **Riverside Park**. It no doubt holds great promise, but for the moment it is a vast expanse of lawn (pity the poor soul who has to cut it). It can be packed with picnickers on Sunday when the weather is fine – be careful at such times or you risk being impaled on a barbecue skewer. Along the shoreline you'll find a pier where there are ferry tours of the Han River. The boats run on the following routes:

ROBERT STOREY

CHRIS TAYLOR

ROBERT STOREY

CHRIS TAYLOR

A	C
B	D

Seoul
A: Korean Christmas preparations
B: Golden Lotte Department Store

C: Brick pattern, Tŏksugung Palace
D: Silhouette of the legendary Admiral
   Yi Sun-shin

Seoul Subway Network

Not to Scale

Route	Duration	Fare
Yŏŭi-do-Ttuksŏm-Chamshil	70 min	W4390
Yŏŭi-do-Ttuksŏm	60 min	W3730
Ttuksŏm-Chamshil	10 min	W700
Yŏŭi-do-Tongjak Bridge-Yŏŭido	60 min	W3730
Chamshil-Tongho Bridge-Chamshil	60 min	W3730
Ttuksŏm-Tongho Bridge-Ttuksŏm	60 min	W3730

Seoul National University Museum

Close to the main entrance of the campus is the Seoul National University Museum (π 880-5333). It displays ceramics, earthenware and farming implements It's open Monday through Friday, except public holidays.

Although rioting is a traditional spring and summer sport at this campus, there was a particularly violent student riot in mid-August 1996. The protest started as a pro-reunification rally and things went downhill from there. The students occupied one of the campus buildings, the police surrounded the place and the siege lasted for 10 days. As usual, the festivities included bricks, fire bombs, iron bars and tear gas. One policeman was killed, about 700 people were injured (on both sides) and more than 5000 students were arrested (about 2000 escaped). In the process, the students torched the building they'd been occupying, as well as tearing down a few walls with pickaxes in order to obtain bricks to throw at the police. Repairing the damage to the building is expected to cost US$12 million.

Strange as it may sound, the authorities are now considering not repairing the damage at all. Instead, there has been a proposal to preserve this trashed building as a **Student Riot Museum**. At the time of this writing, tours of the buildings were being given to groups by appointment only. No phone number for the 'museum' is currently available – ask around the campus to see if anyone knows anything about it. Don't expect the KNTO to have any tour information – the purpose of the museum is to show other

Koreans that the students can behave even worse than the police. It's not really meant as a tourist attraction for foreigners. Having an unbiased tour guide who is well versed in the events of the time would make the visit much more interesting.

ACTIVITIES

English is spoken at the International Outdoor Club (π 319-9917, 777-4188), which runs various hiking, sightseeing and other outdoor excursions. 'Cross-cultural' talks are held twice weekly in Seoul.

Archery

Both traditional Korean-style archery and the western form are practised in South Korea. Archery ranges are usually located out of town. More information can be obtained by contacting the Korea Amateur Sport Association (π 420-3333), 888 Oryundong, Songp'a gu, Seoul.

Buddhist Studies

The Lotus Lantern Buddhist Centre (π 735-5347) is the place to meet the expat Buddhist community for worship and study. There are Buddhist ceremonies in English every Sunday at 6.30 pm.

Computer Club

The Seoul Computer Club is an English-speaking organisation inside the US military base in Yongsan. You don't have to be a member of the military to participate in club activities. If you have a computer and modem you might want to ring up the club's electronic bulletin board service (BBS) (π 7913-6821/22).

Golf

There are 39 golf courses in the province of Kyŏnggi-do which surrounds Seoul, but only two within the Seoul city limits: Namsungdae (π 403-0071) and Taenung (π 972-2111).

A golf practice range can be found southeast of It'aewon and just one block west of Hannam railway station. This new, large multi-level facility actually has greens suspended from the top.

Miniature golf is much more accessible to those on a budget. About the only venue for this at present is in Seoul Dream Land.

Hang Gliding

Hang gliding has taken off in Korea and there are a number of commercial agencies trying to milk the market. Your best bet is to contact the Hang Gliding Association (☎ 514-7760, 783-3645) in Seoul.

Paragliding is a variation on the theme. There are numerous venues for this, but in Seoul try ringing up Mirae (☎ 771-4267) or the KRA (☎ 585-3002).

Hiking

While most of the really good hikes are further out of town, there are several worthwhile mountains within Seoul city limits.

Inwangsan There are a number of ways of approaching the summit, but the easiest is to first follow the road (Inwangsangil) on the west side of Sajik Park, then as you get to within sight of the peak take one of the obvious paths off to your left. Along the route you'll probably encounter a few soldiers or plainclothes police – the area is a little bit sensitive because it overlooks the Blue House, where the president lives. If you reach the summit (338m) and the weather co-operates you'll be rewarded with sweeping views of the city.

Kwanaksan Straddling the southern boundary of metropolitan Seoul and Kyŏnggi-do, Kwanaksan is a popular hiking spot. The summit is a moderate 632m above sea level, but the mountain is extremely rocky and rugged.

You reach the peak starting from the campus of Seoul National University. To get there, take subway line 2 to Seoul National University station, and from there a bus southwards about another two km to the campus. From the campus, Kwanaksan is the large and obvious peak to the south-east.

There are a number of hiking trails and students will point out the way.

Ice Skating

Lotte World offers year-round indoor ice skating, but avoid it on weekends when the ice is hidden under a mass of squirming arms and legs.

Squash

Squash hasn't really taken off in South Korea and the same goes for other countries in the region. If you want a game of squash, your best bet is the luxury-class hotels.

Swimming

Seoul residents complain that swimming pools are only open for the brief summer season and are horribly crowded. The Chamshil Indoor Swimming Pool is in the Seoul Sports Complex. Olympic Park also has an indoor swimming pool and classes are offered (☎ 410-1353). Most of the luxury hotels have swimming pools of both the indoor and outdoor varieties.

T'aekwondo

This traditional Korean form of self-defence evolved from an earlier form called t'aekkyŏn. Nowadays, almost all Korean males are inducted into the army and are taught t'aekwondo as part of their training – as a result, bar room brawls in Korea can be pretty nasty.

T'aekwondo also has a following in the west and serious students make the long journey to South Korea to study it. The headquarters of the World T'aekwondo Federation is in Seoul. More information regarding study and competitions can be obtained by calling them on 566-2505. Information can also be provided by the Korea T'aekwondo Association (☎ 420-4271).

ORGANISED TOURS

Seoul plans to start a new municipal tour system and it will probably be in operation by the time you read this. Initial plans call for opening four tour circuits. The tour buses will depart from the Yongsan bus terminal (take subway line 1 to Yongsan station). Ask at KNTO or the Seoul City Tourist Information Centre for additional details.

SPECIAL EVENTS

Seoul Citizens Day is officially 28 October every year. It's a big, free gala held in a stadium (not necessarily the same one every year). Since 1996 part of the events have included a 'Festival to Entertain Foreign Residents' at Taehangno (University St), including a Parade of Foreign Residents in 'traditional costume' (your one chance to dress like a slob and be admired for it?).

PLACES TO STAY
Places to Stay – bottom end

The definition of 'bottom end' in Seoul should be any hotel where it is possible to get a room for W25,000 or less. Almost all the budget places are in the central Seoul area.

Seoul Station Area This area has some of the cheapest yŏinsuk in Seoul but conditions are very basic and foreigners are thin on the ground. There are three alleys to the south-east of Seoul station harbouring 11 yŏinsuk and two yŏgwan (see the Central Seoul map). All rooms cost about W8000, but many places are grim, windowless shacks. Look at the closet-sized hovels first before you hand over the cash.

On the north alley you'll find *Sŏjŏng Yŏinsuk*, run by a kind woman who is used to dealing with foreigners. Nearby *Kwangju Yŏinsuk* (☎ 753-8460) is friendly and charges W8000 for a single but, incredibly, asks W16,000 for two people inside the same cupboard-sized room! *Shinhŭng Yŏinsuk* is not too receptive to foreigners and *Hanwon Yŏinsuk* seems to be full of long-term boarders. At the end of the alley is *Choil Yŏgwan* which costs W20,000 for a room with a bath. Neighbouring *Tŏksŏng-jang Yŏgwan* costs W20,000 for matchbox-sized rooms with attached bath, but the tariff rises to W25,000 on weekends.

The tiny eastern alley has *Kwangshin Yŏinsuk*, which is run by a friendly old man. The ajumma at *Migyŏng Yŏinsuk* is also

friendly to foreigners, but *Sŏngnam Yŏinsuk* is rather xenophobic.

In the south alley, *Kyŏnggi Yŏinsuk* (☎ 752-5272) boasts a friendly ajumma and her son speaks English – the only drawback is when the ajumma cooks fish (it smells bad). Both *Songrim Yŏinsuk* and *Hyŏndae Yŏinsuk* accept foreigners. At *Myŏngshin Yŏinsuk* the landlord seems to be permanently unavailable.

Kwanghwamun Area Urban renewal has swept through central Seoul, taking with it a lot of the old buildings and the cheap yŏgwan once common in this area. The cheapest remaining is *Inn Daewon* (☎ 735-7891), 26 Tangju dong, Chongno-gu. A bed in a shared oxygen-free room costs W7000 and your own private cubicle costs W11,000. All rooms share one grotty washroom with barely functional plumbing. Check the place out carefully before you pay – it looks like it's ready to collapse.

The same family that operates Inn Daewon also runs the *Inn Sung Do* (☎ 737-1056, 738 8226), 120 Naesu-dong, Chongno-gu. This place is in considerably better condition than its close cousin and is only slightly more expensive. Singles/doubles with shared bath cost W11,000/12,000 and a double with private bath costs W16,000. There are no dormitories here. The yŏgwan is hidden in a small alley but it's clearly marked with a sign in English.

Just next door to the Inn Sung Do is the *Inn Sam Sung* (☎ 737-2177). Rates are exactly the same as its neighbour's.

T'apkol Park Area A popular guesthouse which packs in the backpackers is *Munhwa Yŏgwan* (☎ 765-4659), located at 69 Unni-dong, Chongno-gu. It's built in traditional style with a pleasant courtyard, though like all such old places the rooms are small. It has such nice amenities as a washing machine and hot water for making tea. Singles/doubles with shared bath are W11,000/15,000. It's easy to miss this place as the sign over the door displays only Chinese characters and the English word 'hotel'.

Just a few doors south of the Munhwa is the *Motel Jongrowon* (☎ 745-6876). Beautiful rooms with private bath go for W20,000.

A little north of Chongno 3-ga subway station and just west of Chongmyo (Royal Shrine) is an alley where you'll find *Sun Ch'ang Yŏgwan* (☎ 765-0701). At W12,000 it's cheap, though the rooms are small. There is a small courtyard and the ajumma is very nice.

Just opposite the Sun Ch'ang Yŏgwan is the very clean *T'aeyang-jang Yŏgwan*, which costs W20,000 and boats a nice view of Chongmyo from the top floor. A few steps to the north, the *Taerim-jang Yŏgwan* charges W18,000 to W20,000 for a room with attached bath.

On the right-hand side as you face the YMCA you'll find an alley. If you head up this alley you'll find a sign in English saying 'Hotel'; at the end of the alley indicated by the arrow is the *Taewon Yŏgwan* (☎ 730-6244). Doubles with shared bath at this popular place cost W12,000.

Other alleys behind the YMCA contain a thick concentration of yŏgwan which all charge W18,000 to W20,000 for a double with private bath. Those charging W18,000 include the *Wongap Yŏgwan* (☎ 734-1232), *Unjong-jang Yŏgwan* (☎ 733-0959) and *Insŏng Yŏgwan*. In the same neighbourhood is *Chongno Yŏgwan*, which costs W20,000 on weekdays and W25,000 on Saturday night.

The *Yong Jin Hotel* (☎ 765-4481), 76 Nakwon-dong, Chongno-gu, is in an alley on the east side of the Nakwon arcade. Pleasant rooms with a private bath cost W16,000. Directly opposite is the *Hwasŏng-jang Yŏgwan* (☎ 765-3834) which costs W20,000 except on Saturday night, when it costs W25,000.

In the same alley is the *Emerald Hotel* (☎ 743-2001), 75 Nakwon-dong, Chongno-gu. A comfortable double with private bath goes for W23,000 on Sunday through Friday and W25,000 on Saturday night. Be sure not to confuse this place with the super-expensive Emerald Hotel in the Kangnam district.

A couple of alleys to the south is the *Sŏngbo-jang Yŏgwan*, which costs W20,000 on weekdays and W25,000 on Saturday night.

Close by is the *Tongnam-jang Yŏgwan*, which gets rave reviews from travellers. It's W20,000 a night, but for long-termers it's discounted to W450,000 per month.

To the west of Tonhwamunno is the *Seahwa-jang Hotel* (☎ 765-2881) which houses numerous foreigners working in Seoul. Rooms with attached bath cost W20,000 per night – but W400,000 per month, which works out to a very reasonable W13,300 when calculated on a daily basis. It's a good place for long-termers.

There are several yŏgwan hidden in the alleys running off Insadonggil, but most are run by avaricious owners whose overcharging may well be illegal. The favourite with foreigners in this area is the *Hanhŭn-jang Yŏgwan* (☎ 734-4265), 99 Kwanhun-dong, where a double room with an attached bathroom costs W20,000. The nearby *Kwanhun-jang Yŏgwan* costs W20,000 if you check out by 8 am, but W25,000 if you leave at noon. The *Shingung-jang Yŏgwan* (☎ 733-1355) costs W25,000 but the owner will give a 'discount' if you check out by 9 am. The *Poch'on-jang Yŏgwan* should be avoided at all costs – the owner demands W30,000 only if you arrive after 6 pm and depart at 8 am, but otherwise wants W50,000!

Shinch'on Since this is one of Seoul's premier nightlife areas, staying in Shinch'on is worth considering – although few travellers do so.

There are a couple of yŏgwan just northeast of Shinch'on subway station. Perhaps the best is the *Hyŏndae Yŏgwan* (☎ 313-6871), which costs Y20,000 and features a very hospitable ajumma. Just opposite is the similarly-priced *Mijin-jang Yŏgwan*.

In the same area is the well-appointed *Royal Park Motel* (☎ 393-6430), where doubles cost W23,000 on weekdays but W30,000 on Saturday night. Just opposite is the similar *Lucky Motel*. You'll find several other yŏgwan in nearby alleys.

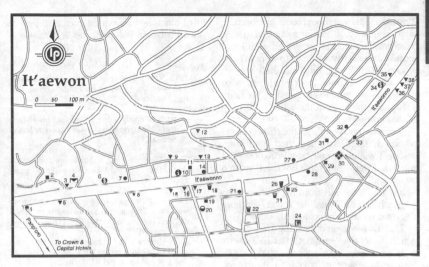

It'aewon 이태원

PLACES TO STAY
2 Ihwa-jang Yŏgwan
  이화장여관
11 Hamilton Hotel &
  Chohung Bank
  해밀턴호텔, 조흥은행
19 Kwangsŏn-jang Yŏgwan
  광선장여관
25 Hilltop Motel
  힐탑여관
29 Hannam Yŏgwan
  한남여관
31 Holiday It'aewon Hotel
  홀리데이이태원호텔
33 Mido Hotel
  미도여관

PLACES TO EAT
3 Pizza Hut
  피자 헛
5 McDonald's
  맥도날드
8 Popeye House
  파파이 하우스
9 Moghul Restaurant
  파키스탄 전문 음식점
12 Chalet Swiss Restaurant
  스위스식 산장

13 It'aewon Garden
  Restaurant
  이태원 갈비
15 Wendy's
  웬디스
16 Nashville
  내슈빌 클럽
17 Burger King
  버거킹
35 Pizza Hut
  피자 헛
36 Deutches Haus
  독일 호프
37 New York Pizza
  뉴욕 피자
38 Old Germany
  올드 저머니

OTHER
1 O&J Travel &
  Honey Bee Club
  오제이항공
4 Post Office
  이태원1동우체국
6 Korea Exchange Bank
  외환은행
7 All That Jazz
  올 댓 재즈
10 Tourist Information Booth
  관광안내소

14 Hollywood Club
  할리우드 클럽
18 Just Blues &
  Cowboy Saloon
  카우보이 싸롱
20 Bus Stop (Nos 23 & 401)
  버스 정류장 (23 & 401)
21 Las Vegas Rock & Disco
  라스베가스 디스코
22 King Club
  킹 클럽
23 Grand Ole Opry Bar
  그랜드 올 오프리
24 Korean Islam Mosque
  이슬람교중앙서원
26 Stomper Bar
  스톰퍼 바
27 NASA Disco
  나사 디스코
28 Rush Rock Disco
  러쉬 디스코
30 Viva Department Store
  비바 백화점
32 Catch-Me Disco
  케치미 디스코
34 Commercial Bank
  of Korea
  한국상업은행

It'aewon This neighbourhood has become increasingly less attractive as a place to stay. Yŏgwan here tend to be packed with long-term boarders (five or more to a room) and reports of pickpocketing and theft are not uncommon. Rampant prostitution also means that rooms can be rented by the hour.

Right in the heart of the action, at the top of that infamous stretch of alleyway known by locals as 'hooker hill', is the *Hilltop Motel* where doubles with attached bathroom, colour TV and air-con cost W20,000. The sign is in English and some English is spoken by the staff too.

Just down the hill from the Hilltop is an alley where you'll find the *Kwangsŏn-jang Yŏgwan*; rooms here cost W20,000.

Back on the main drag is the *Mido Hotel*, which in fact is a yŏgwan. Closet-like hovels with an attached bathroom cost W20,000. Nearby is the similar *Hannam Yŏgwan* which has an English sign saying simply 'Motel'.

At the western end of It'aewonno up on a hill is the *Ihwa-jang Yŏgwan*, which is much like the others.

Kangnam The *Olympic Parktel Hostel* (☎ 410-2114; fax 410-2100) is the only official hostel in Seoul, but it's hardly worth seeking out. While the facilities are comfortable, it's inconveniently located and not worth the price at W10,000 a bed. But if you're determined to try it, take subway line No 2 to Songnae station and walk ½ km. There are 1234 beds and the building is closed from 10 am to 3 pm.

Places to Stay – middle

The bottom end of the mid-range has to be the *YMCA* (☎ 732-8291; fax 734-8003) – it's a huge building with an English sign outside (see the T'apkol map). Rooms here are no better than the nearby yŏgwan, but some of the staff speak English. Singles, doubles and twins cost W32,000, W40,000 and W48,000 respectively, with the 20% tax and surcharge included. Check in on the sixth floor.

3rd Class Hotels The following are all third-class hotels, which means they are priced between W40,000 and W50,000:

Astoria
　13-2 Namhak-dong, Chung-gu (five-minute walk west from Ch'ungmuro station on subway line 3 or line 4) (☎ 268-7111; fax 274-3187)
Boolim
　620-27 Chŏnnong 2-dong, Tongdaemun-gu (just west of Ch'ŏngnyangni subway station on line 1) (☎ 962-0021)
Central
　227-1 Changsa-dong, Chongno-gu (one block south of the Chongno 3-ga subway station on line 1) (☎ 265-4121)
Chonji
　133-1 Ŭlchiro 5-ga, Chung-gu (five-minute walk west from Tongdaemun Stadium subway station on line 2) (☎ 265-6131; fax 279-1184)
Daehwa
　18-21 Ŭlchiro 6-ga, Chung-gu (three-minute walk west of Tongdaemun Stadium subway station on line 2 or line 4) (☎ 265-9181; fax 277-9820)
Eastern
　444-14 Ch'angshin-dong, Chongno-gu (one-minute walk east from Tongdaemun subway station on line 1 or 4) (☎ 741-7811; fax 744-1274)
Jeonpoong
　58 Tosŏn-dong, Sŏngdong-gu (km east of Sang-wangshimni subway station on line 2) (☎ 295-9365)
Kaya
　98-11 Kalwol-dong, Yongsan-gu (one-minute walk south of Namyŏng station, one stop south of Seoul station on subway line 1 and very close to the USO) (☎ 798-5101; fax 798-5900)
Rio
　72-7 Kwanghui-dong 1-ga, Chung-gu (five-minute walk west of Tongdaemun Stadium subway station on line 2 and line 4) (☎ 278-5700; fax 275-7207)
Samho
　436-73 Ch'angshin-dong, Chongno-gu (300m east of the Tongdaemun subway station on line 1 and line 4) (☎ 741-7080; fax 743-5981)
Samhwa
　527-3 Shinsa-dong, Kangnam-gu (just north of Shinsa subway station on line 3) (☎ 541-1011)
Tiffany
　132-7 Ch'ŏngdam-dong, Kangnam-gu (about ½ km north of the Samsŏng subway station on line 2) (☎ 545-0015)

2nd Class Hotels The following hotels are rated 2nd class, which means they are priced in the range of W51,000 to W80,000:

Bukak Park
113-1 P'yongch'ang-dong, Chongno-gu (10 minutes by bus from Kwanghwamun on bus Nos 135 or 135-1, seven-minute drive north of Kyŏngbokkung subway station on subway line 3) (☎ 395-7100; fax 391-5559)

City Palace
497-23 Tapshimni 5-dong, Tongdaemun-gu (five-minute walk from Tapshimni subway station on line 5) (☎ 244-2222; fax 246-6542)

Clover
129-7 Ch'ongdam-dong, Kangnam-gu (a five-minute taxi ride north from Samsŏng subway station on line 2) (☎ 546-1411; fax 544-1340)

Dynasty
202-7 Nonhyon-dong, Kangnam-gu (15-minute walk north on Kangnamdaero from Kangnam subway station on line 2, then east on Pong-ŭnsaro) (☎ 540-3041; fax 540 3374)

Hilltop
151-30 Nonhyŏn-dong, Kangnam-gu (five minutes from Shinsa station on subway line 3 south on Kangnamdaero then east on Haktongno) (☎ 540-3451)

Kims
66-50 P'yŏngch'ang-dong, Chongno-gu (10 minutes by bus from Kwanghwamun on bus Nos 135 or 135-1, seven-minute taxi ride north of Kyŏngbokkung subway station on subway line 3) (☎ 357-0520)

Metro
199-33 Ŭlchiro 2-ga, Chung-gu (two-minute walk south-east from Ŭlchiro-1 station on subway line 2) (☎ 752-1112; fax 757-4411)

Mirabeau
104-36 Taehyŏn-dong, Sŏdaemun-gu (between Ehwa Women's University and Shinch'on subway stations on line 2) (☎ 392-9511)

New Hilltop
152 Nonhyon-dong, Kangnam-gu (five minutes from Shinsa station on subway line 3 south on Kangnamdaero then east on Haktongno) (☎ 540-1121; fax 542-9491)

Prince
1-1 Namsan-dong 2-ga, Chung-gu (two-minute walk south of Myŏngdong station on subway line 4) (☎ 752-7111; fax 752-7119)

Savoy
23-1 Ch'ungmuro 1-ga, Chung-gu (two-minute walk north-west from Myŏngdong subway station on line 4) (☎ 776-2641; fax 755-7669)

Seoul
92 Ch'ongjin-dong, Chongno-gu (three-minute walk west on Chongno from Chonggak subway station on line 1, then north in first alley) (☎ 735-9001; fax 733-0101)

Sunshine
587-1 Shinsa-dong, Kangnam-gu (10-minute walk south from Apkujong subway station on line 3) (☎ 541-1818; fax 547-0777)

1st Class Hotels The following hotels are rated 1st class which means the price range is W81,000 to W110,000:

Crown
34-69 It'aewon-dong, Yongsan-gu (just south of It'aewon tourist zone) (☎ 797-4111; fax 796-1010)

Dong Seoul
595 Kuui-dong, Songdong-gu (one-minute walk north from Tong-Seoul bus terminal) (☎ 455-1100; fax 455-6311)

Green Grass
141-10 Samsŏng-dong, Kangnam-gu (five-minute walk east from Sŏllŭng subway station on line 2) (☎ 555-7575; fax 554-0643)

Hamilton
119-25 It'aewon-dong, Yongsan-gu (in It'aewon tourist zone) (☎ 794-0171; fax 795-0457)

Holiday It'aewon
737-32 Hannam-dong, Yongsan-gu (in It'aewon tourist zone) (☎ 792-3111; fax 798-8256)

Manhattan
13-3 Yŏŭido-dong, Yongdungp'o-gu (on Yŏŭi do Island) (☎ 780-8001, fax 784 2332)

New Kukje
29-2 T'aep'yongno 1-ga, Chung-gu (five-minute walk from City Hall subway station, one block north of City Hall) (☎ 732-0161; fax 732-1774)

New Seoul
29-1 T'aep'yongno 1-ga, Chung-gu (five-minute walk from City Hall subway station, one block north of City Hall) (☎ 735-9071; fax 735-6212)

Pacific
31-1 Namsan-dong 2-ga, Chung-gu (two-minute walk south from Myŏng-dong subway station on line 4) (☎ 777-7811; fax 755-5582)

Poongjun
73-1 Inhyon-dong 2-ga, Chung-gu (two-minute walk south-west from Ŭlchiro 4-ga subway station on line 2) (☎ 266-2151; fax 274-5732)

Prima
52-3 Ch'ongdam-dong, Kangnam-gu (five-minute taxi ride north from Samsŏng station on subway line 2) (☎ 549-9011; fax 544-8523)

Samjung
604-11 Yŏksam-dong, Kangnam-gu (10 minutes north on Nonhyŏnno from Yŏksam station on subway line, then west on Pong-ŭnsaro) (☎ 557-1221; fax 556-1126)

Seokyo
354-5 Sŏgyo-dong, Mao'o-gu (south-west of Hongik University station) (☎ 333-7771)

Seoul Rex
　65 Hoehyŏn-dong, Chung-gu (five-minute walk from Hoehyŏn subway station on line 4 – east on T'oegyero then south in first alley) (☎ 752-3191)

Yoido
　10-3 Yŏŭido-dong, Yongdungp'o-gu (on Yŏŭi-do Island right on Yŏŭi-do Plaza) (☎ 782-0121; fax 785-2510)

Youngdong
　6 Nonhyŏn-dong, Kangnam-gu (short walk north-east of Shinsa subway station on line 3) (☎ 542-0112)

Places to Stay – top end

Deluxe Class The following hotels are rated as deluxe class, which means they charge from W111,000 to W160,000:

Amiga
　248-7 Nonhyŏn-dong, Kangnam-gu (15-minute walk from Sŏllŭng subway station – west one block then north two blocks) (☎ 511-4000; fax 545-9353)

Capital
　22-76 It'aewon-dong, Yongsan-gu (in It'aewon tourist zone) (☎ 792-1122; fax 796-0918)

Emerald
　129 Ch'ongdam-dong, Kangnam-gu (north of Samsŏng subway station on line 2) (☎ 514-3535; fax 515-3309)

King Sejong
　61-3 Ch'ungmuro 2-ga, Chung-gu (just north-east of Myŏng-dong subway station on line 4) (☎ 773-6000)

Koreana
　61-1 T'aep'yongno 1-ga, Chung-gu (five-minute walk north of City Hall) (☎ 730-9911; fax 734-0665)

New World
　112-5 Samsong-dong, Kangnam-gu (10-minute walk from Sŏllŭng subway station on line 2) (☎ 557-0111; fax 557-0141)

Novotel Ambassador
　603 Yŏksam-dong, Kangnam-gu (five-minute taxi ride from Kangnam subway station on line 2 – north on Kangnamdaero then east on Pong-ŭnsaro) (☎ 567-1101; fax 562-0120)

President
　188-3 Ŭlchiro 1-ga, Chung-gu (five-minute walk one block south of City Hall) (☎ 753-3131; fax 752-7417)

Ramada Olympia
　108-2 P'yongch'ang-dong, Chongno-gu (10 minutes from Kwanghwamun on bus Nos 135 or 135-1; seven-minute taxi ride north of Kyŏngbokkung subway station on subway line 3) (☎ 287-6000; fax 353-8118)

Riviera
　53-7 Ch'ongdam-dong, Kangnam-gu (10-minute taxi ride north of Samsŏng station on subway line 2) (☎ 541-3111; fax 541-6111)

Royal
　6 Myŏngdonggil 1-ga, Chung-gu (five-minute walk north from Myŏng-dong subway station on line 4) (☎ 756-1112; fax 756-1119)

Sofitel Ambassador
　186-54 Changch'ung-dong, Chung-gu (three-minute walk north-west from Dongguk University subway station on line 3) (☎ 275-1101; fax 272-0773)

Tower
　San 5-5 Changch'ung-dong 2-ga, Chung-gu (10-minute walk south of Dongguk University station on subway line 3, near National Theatre) (☎ 236-2121; fax 235-0276)

Super Deluxe Class The following hotels are rated super deluxe class and priced from W161,000 to W300,000:

Grand Hyatt
　747-7 Hannam-dong, Yongsan-gu (short walk east of It'aewon) (☎ 797-1234; fax 798-6953)

Hilton International
　395 Namdaemunno 5-ga, Chung-gu (10-minute walk east from Seoul station) (☎ 753-7788; fax 754-2510)

Inter-Continental
　159-8 Samsong-dong, Kangnam-gu (three-minute walk north-west from Samsong subway station on line 2) (☎ 555-5656; fax 559-7990)

Lotte World
　40-1 Chamshil-dong, Songp'a-gu (two-minute walk from Chamshil subway station on line 2) (☎ 419-7000; 417-3655)

Lotte
　1 Sogong-dong, Chung-gu (two-minute walk south from Ŭlchi 1-ga subway station on line 2) (☎ 771-1000; fax 756-8049)

Plaza
　23 T'aep'yongno 2-ga, Chung-gu (two-minute walk from City Hall subway station on lines 1 or 2, one block south of City Hall) (☎ 771-2200; fax 755-8897)

Ritz-Carlton
　602-4 Yŏksam-dong, Kangnam-gu (near the Yŏksam subway station on line 2) (☎ 3451-8000)

Seoul Renaissance
　676 Yŏksam-dong, Kangnam-gu (five-minute walk from Kangnam subway station on line 2 – one block north on Kangnamdaero then east on Pong-ŭnsaro) (☎ 555-0501; fax 553-8118)

Sheraton Walker Hill
　San 21 Kwangjang-dong, Songdong-gu (two km east of Children's Grand Park) This place boasts Seoul's only casino. (☎ 453-0131; fax 452-6867)

Shilla
> 202 Changch'ung-dong 2-ga, Chung-gu (five-minute walk south from Dongguk University subway station on line 3) (☎ 233-3131; fax 233-5073)

Swiss Grand
> 201-1 Hong-un-dong, Sodaemun-gu (10-minute walk from Hongje station on subway line 3 – north on Üijuro then west on Yönhüiro) (☎ 356-5656; fax 356-7799)

Westin Chosun
> 87 Sogong-dong, Chung-gu (two-minute walk south-east from City Hall subway station on lines 1 and 2) (☎ 771-0500; fax 752-1443)

PLACES TO EAT
Breakfast & Snacks

The best place to start is at the beginning – with breakfast. If you're on a tight budget but can't get going in the morning without a coffee, try the *7-Eleven stores* or some of its competitors (*Family Mart*, *Circle K*, etc). They have fresh, percolated coffee for W400 and sell doughnuts for the same price. Alternatively look out for coffee-vending machines; prices range from W150 to W300 and they are common throughout Seoul. Of course, making your own instant coffee is cheapest, if you happen to have a source of hot water.

Just west of the Kwanghwamun intersection (near Inn Daewon) is a *Hardee's Hamburgers*, but for breakfast try the huge *bakery* next door. This is one of the few bakeries in Seoul which has seats, so you can sit and enjoy sweet breads along with coffee, tea, milk or juice.

The Japanese fast-food coffee chain *Doutor* has caught on in a big way in Seoul. Doutor has American coffee and café au lait for W900, and sells pastries and muffins for the same price. Most branches open between 8 and 9 am in the morning. The Doutor phenomenon has also spawned numerous imitations; *Caravan*, *Mr Coffee* and *Jardin* are a few examples.

Just opposite (south side) of the Sejong Cultural Centre is *Paris Baguette* which has great pastries and coffee. Within the bowels of Anguk subway station is *Paris Croissant*, a fine bakery with coffee, pastries and a place to sit down and enjoy it all.

Fast Food

Seoul has become a boom town for the fast food industry. All the familiar western chains (*McDonald's*, *Pizza Hut*, *Hardee's*, *Burger King*, etc) are omnipresent. The quality of the food and the plastic enamel furniture is identical to what you'll find back home.

Koreans are proud of *Lotteria*, their home-grown fast food mega-chain (even though they lament that the boss of the company lives in Japan).

Pelicana Chicken is Korea's answer to Colonel Sanders – not bad really, and cheap at about W5000 for half a chicken.

El Taco is currently the only Mexican fast food chain in Seoul. There is one branch at Hongik University subway station (take exit 6) on line 2 and another in the food court of Hyundai department store – at Samsöng subway station on line 2. In the same neighbourhood as the latter (near the Korean World Trade Centre) is *LA Palms*, which has not-bad Mexican food but is a little pricey.

The *USO* (☎ 795-3028/63) is operated by the US military, though you don't have to join the army to eat here. The food is American style all the way: fried chicken, hamburgers, French fries and ice cream for dessert. Prices are reasonable and you can pay in either Korean won or US dollars. The best deals are the breakfast and lunch specials. The USO is within walking distance of Namyong station on subway line 1.

Similarly, you don't have to join the army to eat at the restaurant inside the *Dragon Hill Lodge*, which is reputed to have the best Mexican food in Seoul. However, it's inside the US military base at Yongsan, so you will need a pass or someone with a pass to get you inside. On some days it's open to outside guests when a special event is on.

If you're in the vicinity of a large university you can eat well for about W1500 to W2000 at the student cafeterias, though this doesn't apply at some of the aristocratic schools like Ehwa Women's University, where the food is pricey and the portions are stingy. University cafeterias are normally open from about 10 am to 6 pm, but some only serve food from noon to 1 pm and 5 to 6 pm.

Self-Catering

The 24-hour convenience stores are a possibility for a cheap lunch or dinner. These places invariably sell instant noodles packaged in a styrofoam bowl. Most (but not all) have hot water, disposable chopsticks and a table (no chairs though), so you can consume your instant banquet on the premises. This should cost between W500 and W700 in *7-Eleven* or *Family Mart*, but a staggering W1000 to W1500 in *Bestore*.

If you're in the Kwanghwamun area (near Inn Daewon), you should definitely visit *Koryŏ Supermarket* (no English sign). The lunch counters are hidden in the back and to your right – you can eat well for around W1500. The supermarket itself is one of the cheapest in Seoul and has sustained many a budget traveller.

The *Agricultural Cooperative Supermarket* is not one market, but rather a chain store with branches throughout Seoul (and indeed, throughout Korea). Aside from a wide selection of food, this is the cheapest place to buy dried ginseng and other herbs, such as ganoderma mushrooms and mugwort. In the

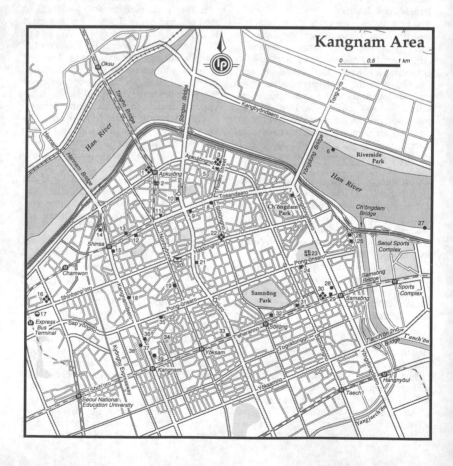

central part of Seoul, one branch of this market is labelled *Hanaro Mart* (☎ 720-0094); it's on Sambonggil one block north of the YMCA (see the T'apkol Park Area map). There are also numerous branches of the *Agricultural Cooperative Bank* (Nonghyŏp Bank) – although no food is on sale, they usually have a small counter selling herbs.

Jell Delicatessen is up the hill near the Grand Hyatt Hotel in It'aewon. Outside of US military bases, this deli offers the widest selection of rare items from the west (pancake mix, muesli, salami, cheeses, etc).

Korean Food

As for Korean food, the bottom end is occupied by the ubiquitous *kimbap* (sushi) and *dumpling* (mandu) *shops*. One roll of kimbap or a plate of dumplings can be had for about W1500. Most of these shops also offer noodle dishes for around W3000.

You should also check out the basements of large *department stores*, where you can usually find supermarkets and lunch counters. In the central area of town, the *Saerona Department Store* is a personal favourite mainly because it's relatively uncrowded. The *Shinsegae Department Store* has some cheap lunch counters in the basement, though the selection is limited. The *Lotte Department Store* is largest but very crowded. The *Printemps Department Store* has excellent restaurants in the basement and on the 7th floor.

The best kimbap in all of Korea can be had at *Iga Kimbap* just east of the YMCA on Chongno. The sign above the door is in Chinese characters, but there's no mistaking this place

---

– look through the large plate glass window to see the kimbap-making operation in progress. There are a wide variety of kimbap fillings available – everything from cheese to tuna.

On the first major street to the east of T'apkol Park are a few Korean-style chicken places. *Kentucky Chicken* is no relation to Colonel Sanders; nor is the nearby *P'ungch'a Hof*, which is open only in the evenings. At W5000 for a half chicken or W8000 for the whole bird, both places are a bargain.

Coco Fried Rice is another chain store, with about 30 branches in Seoul. Specialties are a sort of Korean-Chinese fast food, which isn't bad at all. One of the more accessible branches is in the Taehangno nightlife district near Hyehwa subway station on line 4.

You can easily find delectable Korean stews being sold on *small side streets* all over Seoul. Often the shop will set the stews simmering in miniature clay pots either outside or in the window. Good areas for searching out *small restaurants* specialising in stews include the alleys running parallel to the north side of Chongno and the restaurant street in Tongdaemun market.

Insadonggil (the trendy 'culture street' north-west of T'apkol Park) has many excellent Korean restaurants hidden away in the small alleys. The *Youngbin Garden Restaurant* is a good one for foreigners to try because there's an English sign outside and some menu items are also in English. You can find all the standard Korean dishes here, like pulgogi and pibimbap.

Almost next door to the foregoing, the *Airirang Restaurant* does traditional Korean food; there are only two items on the menu (both 15-course extravaganzas).

Just above Airirang is the *Yet Ch'at Chip Teashop* which is well worth stepping into – live birds flutter around the shop as you drink your tea. Some recommended beverages to try here include the honey and plum tea, citron tea and cold fruit punch tea served with a dried persimmon.

Vegetarian Food
The best-known of these restaurants is *Sanch'on* (☎ 735-0312). Sanch'on specialises

in Buddhist temple vegetarian cuisine – the W25,000 special full course allows you to sample 15 courses that include such oddities as acorn jelly and wild sesame gruel. Seating is on cushions on the floor, and there are traditional dance performances every evening from 8 to 9 pm to the twingings and twangings of Korean stringed instruments. This place has been getting packed out lately with Japanese tour groups – it's advisable to get there between 7 and 7.30 pm to stake out your turf. Sanch'on is down a small alley off Insadonggil, but it's easy to find because of the English sign out on the street.

Chinese Food
A cheap eats option that gets neglected by many travellers is Chinese food. You should be able to pick up a bowl of noodles with beef sauce *(tchajang myŏn)* for as little as W2000. Of course, you can fork out a little more for the more exquisite dishes. *Tongsŏnggak Chinese Restaurant* is a fine eatery tucked into an alley just south of the Sejong Cultural Centre. *Tonghaeru Chinese Restaurant* is just to the west of Sejong Cultural Centre.

The area around the Chinese Embassy in Myŏng-dong is another good place to look for Chinese food. This small collection of restaurants and one or two bookshops is about as close as Seoul gets to a Chinatown. Easiest to find is the *Wonsan Chinese Restaurant* opposite the CPO. *Shillawon Chinese Restaurant* (☎ 752-2396) is much favoured by the embassy staff and features (surprise!) an English menu.

Western Food
Just opposite the Lotte Hotel is *La Cantina* (☎ 777-2579), an outstanding Italian restaurant with an intimate atmosphere and English-speaking staff. It's downstairs in the basement (which it shares with a barbershop). This won't be a cheap evening out.

Up the hill a little in the direction of the Hyatt is the *Chalet Swiss* (☎ 796-6379). It's easy to find – the building even looks Swiss. Chalet Swiss is open from noon to 10 pm and reservations (☎ 797-0664) are necessary for dinner.

Up the far end of It'aewon is *Old Germany* (☎ 795-8780). The interior is tastefully decorated and the designers took great care to achieve an old German look. Main courses range from W5000 to W17,000.

Just a little up the road is another German restaurant: *Deutches Haus*. It has a pleasant roomy interior and main courses ranging from W7000 to W15,000. It also has set lunches at W5000. Also nearby, and less expensive, is *New York Pizza*.

Hugo's, at the Grand Hyatt Hotel, is regarded as one of the best western restaurants in Seoul and offers excellent smorgasbord lunches. Also in the Hyatt are *Akasaka*, a Japanese restaurant, and *Sansu* (☎ 797-1234), a Chinese restaurant that has Cantonese, Sichuan and dim sum dishes.

Bennigan's on the north-east side of Taehangno (subway line 4 to Hyehwa station) has a Boston theme, though there are some good Mexican dishes on the menu. The restaurant is on the 2nd floor. In the same neighbourhood is *El Paso*, which also does adequate Mexican food.

The Kangnam area can boast three branches of *TGI Friday's* (Thank God it's Friday's), the American bistro known for fine food and far-out interior decorating (aeroplane parts, baby carriages, etc). Mexican food is a significant part of the menu but it's pricey. The Yangjae branch (☎ 565-2961) is adjacent to Yangjae subway station on line 3; the Taechi branch (☎ 538-2532) is on Yŏngdongdaero, a few blocks south of Samsŏng subway station on line 2; the Nonhyŏn branch (☎ 512-7211) is on Tosandaero nearly two km east of Shinsa subway station on line 3; and there is a Sadang branch (☎ 587-0141), in the nearby Sŏch'o district, at Sadang station (both subway lines 2 and 4).

Tony Roma's (☎ 3443-3500) is a superb upmarket western restaurant. You'll find it on Tosandaero, about half way between Apkujong and Shinsa subway stations on line 3.

Indian Food

In It'aewon there are a few restaurants specialising in food from the subcontinent.

The major ones are the *Ashoka* (☎ 792-0117) on the third floor of the Hamilton Hotel, and *Moghul* (☎ 796-5501) which is behind the Hamilton Hotel store. They both have all-you-can-eat luncheon smorgasbords for W15,000. Evening meals at either, however, are even more expensive. Up the road in the nightclub area, a few more Indian restaurants have sprung up, catering largely to the Indian and Pakistani guest workers who live in the neighbourhood.

ENTERTAINMENT
Cinemas
Plenty of western movies play in Seoul. The biggest challenge is to find out what's on and where. The Friday entertainment section of the English-language newspapers is a good place to start. Also take a look at the magazines *Seoul Scope* and *Log-In Seoul*.

Cyber Cafes
You can cruise in cyberspace at the *Net Cyber Cafe* (☎ 733-7973; fax 738-5794; email council@net.co.kr). It's in a small alley just behind Kyobo Book Centre (see the Kwanghwamun Area map). The cafe is on the 2nd floor and a sign in English points the way.

South of the river is *Net Plaza* (☎ 3453-4802) which is open every day but Sunday. It's on the 3rd floor above Ponse Coffee Shop, in an alley on the north-east corner from Kangnam subway station on line 2.

Off in the north-east fringe of Seoul, *Virus II* (☎ 762-2989) is around the corner from Hansong University station on subway line 4 (take exit 3). It's open from 10 am to midnight and features a vegetarian menu. Another neat idea is the 'Salvation Army table' where you can drop off things you no longer want (old clothes, music tapes, books, etc) and pick up something you need.

Discos
The trendiest scene is centred in the luxury hotels, which means that you can expect pretty steep cover charges and high drink prices. Good places for a dance include *Chou Chou* at the Hamilton Hotel in It'aewon, *Olympia* at the Ramada Olympia, *Starland*

at the Royal Hotel in Myŏng-dong, *Pharaohs* at the Hilton and *Bistro* at the Hotel Lotte. The most in vogue clubs in the fashionable Kangnam district are *Chichi* at the Dynasty Hotel, *Coma* at the Novotel Ambassador, *Juliana* at the Emerald Hotel and *Lotus* at the Sunshine Hotel.

It'aewon chips in with a number of small clubs, including *Catch-Me*, *Rush*, *NASA* and *Las Vegas*.

Pubs

Take subway line 2 and get off at Shinch'on station. Just to the north-west of the station, in the alleys behind the Grace Department Store, is one of Seoul's prime pub districts. Here you'll find *Woodstock* (☎ 334-1310) where a foreign clientele is attracted to the 1960s classic rock music. A lot of people walk upstairs in the same building to *Don Quixote* (☎ 322-5065), which features a different selection of music and cheap beer.

A lot of people really like the *Golden Helmet*. It's near Hongik University's main gate (Chungmun). This place is below street level and looks like someone's unfinished basement with exposed pipes in the ceiling. To get there, start at the 7-Eleven across from the Hongik University main gate (take subway line 2 to Hongik station then walk up the hill). The 7-Eleven is next to a Burger King. Turn right out of the 7-Eleven and turn right again at the big intersection (with traffic signals). Walk 20 steps past the bank of public telephones ahead of you to a small alley on the right. Enter the alley and you'll see an electric sign with a picture of a black and white cat. In small letters, the sign says 'The Golden Helmet'. From 7 Eleven to the bar takes about one minute – any more and you're lost.

If you take subway line 2 and get off at Hongik University you can wander over to *Boston* (☎ 335-7927), a very popular expat bar near the campus front entrance. The music is often Latin or salsa, rather unusual in Korea. Also close by is *Heaven* (☎ 324-4725), an interesting reggae bar hidden in a small alley. *Joker* is another hot spot – it's two blocks up from the front gate of Hongik University towards the main road and subway station.

It'aewon is home to several legendary pubs. The *Hollywood Club* (☎ 749-1659) is one of the most popular spots for expat English teachers. It has American movie videos every Saturday and Sunday afternoon, music videos and classic-oldies rock in the evenings, plus there are billiards tables and darts. It's 50m east of the Hamilton Hotel on the same side of the street. Also in It'aewon is the excellent *Just Blues* (☎ 749-0906), which features some of the finest bands in Korea. There are heaps of other bars here which draw heavily on the US military market, including *King Club*, *Heavy Metal*, *All That Jazz* and *Nashville*.

Apkujŏng is the most expensive area in Seoul for nightlife. This is the favourite hangout of the rich kids, known to Koreans as the 'Orange Gang'. Most Koreans profess to hate the Orange Gang, but they all love to hang out with them. Being a member means you must spend at least US$200 a night on entertainment. Apkujŏng's action centres on dozens of so-called 'rock cafés' found just behind a McDonald's opposite the Galleria Department Store. Adjacent to McDonald's is 'Rodeo St', known for its pubs and high-fashion boutiques. One place to try here is *Rush Hour* (☎ 514-3380), adjacent to McDonald's and on the 2nd floor.

The area behind Tower Records (Kangnam subway station on line 2) is a vibrant nightlife area. A locals' club here which also attracts some foreigners is *Lexus*. In the alley on the opposite side of the street from Tower Records and near the Die Hard Cafe is *Woodstock II* (☎ 556-9774) – yes, it is related to the other bar called Woodstock in Shinch'on.

Taehangno literally means 'University St' because it was the former campus of Seoul National University. The university has long since moved, but the area has evolved into Seoul's trendiest café, pub, video parlour, karaoke and theatre district. Take subway line 4 to Hyehwa station.

Hotel Bars

A hot spot is *JJ Mahoney's* inside the Grand Hyatt. This place is renowned as Seoul's yuppie bar and has a clientele that is about half expat and half Korean.

Pharaoh over at the Hilton Hotel (just to the east of Seoul station) is a pub and disco: a raging place with expensive drinks.

Seoul's only Irish bar, *O'Kim's*, is in the basement of the Westin-Chosun hotel. Aside from the booze, there's pricey food available, such as burgers and French fries for W10,000.

Traditional Arts

The National Centre for Korean Traditional Performing Arts (☎ 580-3037) has a different performance of opera, music, etc every Saturday from 5 to 6.30 pm; it costs W5000. Don't confuse this place with the Seoul Arts Centre next door. Take subway line 3 to Nambu Bus Terminal station.

Korea House (☎ 266-9101) has similar performances to those of the Seoul Arts Centre, but they are performed every evening at 7.20 and 8.40 pm. Unfortunately, these shows are expensive at W15,000. This place is also a restaurant (not cheap) at night – you can eat and watch a performance. It's on the north side of Namsan Park – take subway line No 3 or 4 to Ch'ungmuro station.

The National Theatre (☎ 274-1172) is on the slopes of Namsan Park behind Dongguk University and right across from the Shilla Hotel. Every Saturday from 6 to 7.30 pm there is a free performance of traditional opera and dance. Admission is free.

Sejong Cultural Centre (☎ 399-1576) does modern performances and exhibits – classical music, art exhibitions, piano recitals, etc. During the warm weather, amateur troupes give free outdoor performances almost daily at noon for the benefit of office workers. For W2000 there is a performance of traditional music on Saturday between 3 and 5 pm.

The Seoul Nori Madang (☎ 414-1985) is an open-air theatre for traditional dance performances. It's just behind the Lotte World shopping complex near Chamshil subway station (subway line No 2). There are free performances every weekend and holidays according to the following schedule: during

April and October from 2 to 4 pm; in May from 3 to 5 pm; June, July and August from 5 to 7 pm; and during September from 4 to 6 pm.

Concerts

Western bands occasionally drop in on Seoul. The usual venue for these concerts is the Seoul Olympic Gym (☎ 700-7500) or the Hilton Hotel Convention Centre (☎ 388-3411).

The Seoul Arts Centre (☎ 585-3151), 700 Socho-dong, Socho-gu, is the best place to see western-style classical orchestras or operas. Take subway line 3 to Nambu bus terminal station – from there it's about a 15-minute walk.

THINGS TO BUY
Namdaemun Market

The Namdaemun (South Gate) Market is about half indoors and half in the open. It's Korea's largest market and a major drawcard for tourists and locals alike. The Koreans say you can get great deals here, but you wouldn't know it by the price tags. Bargaining is necessary, at least for clothing and shoes.

If you really feel you've been ripped off, there is a Consumer Protection Centre (☎ 752-5728) in the centre of the market. How much they can do about overcharging is debatable – they are mainly watching for counterfeit goods.

In Namdaemun, look for camping gear on the south side of the market (facing Hoehyŏn subway station on line 4). Also within Namdaemun is Namraemun, two floors underground, where black market goods (smuggled off US military bases) are sold. It's one of the few places in Seoul where you can buy deodorant, but you pay a premium. Namdaemun Market is near the Seoul Central Post Office.

All of the shops are closed on Sunday, but the street market operates daily.

Tongdaemun Market

The market is right near Chongno 5-ga subway station on line 1. Of special note are the camping stores – *the* place to hunt for very cheap rucksacks, tents, etc. Tongdaemun

Market is also a good place to pick up more fancy travel bags and suitcases. The market is closed on Sunday.

Herbal Medicine Arcade
On the north side of Chongno just opposite Tongdaemun Market is the Herbal Medicine Arcade *(yakryŏng shijang)*. Everything from ginseng to dried sea horses is for sale here, not to mention mundane western medicines.

Kyŏngdong Market
This is even better than the aforementioned Herbal Medicine Arcade. There are about 1000 stalls in Kyŏngdong Market. The specialty here is herbs and one alley specialises in spices – enthusiasts of Korean food may want to stock up on chilli powder and try their hand at creating homemade kimch'i.

Kyŏngdong Market is open from 7 am to 7 pm daily, except on the 1st and 3rd Sundays of every month. It's very close to Chegi subway station near the eastern end of line 1.

Hwanghak-dong Flea Market
This is perhaps the most important shopping area for newly-arrived shoestring travellers looking to get set up in Seoul: virtually anything can be bought here. The market is east of Tongdaemun. Take the line 2 subway to Shindang station and walk north. You will first encounter the Chung'ang Market, which basically sells food (even live chickens and dogs). Continue north for another block and you'll find the flea market – if you've passed the elevated roadway then you've gone too far.

It'aewon
The nearby US military base has made It'aewon a shopping district second to none. On the downside, every third person you encounter in this neighbourhood greets you by saying 'leather jacket' or 'custom-made suit'. Another specialty are T-shirts with unusual slogans ('North Korea – Where's the Beef?').

In this neighbourhood try the Hamilton Department Store (attached to the Hamilton Hotel). It stocks lots of things that interest tourists (ginseng, pottery, clothes, etc). The

vendors seem a bit desperate (too much competition) and can quickly be bargained down to the real price.

Insadonggil
This traditional shopping street is north of the YMCA. It's a popular place for buying antiques, arts and crafts, but shuts down every other Sunday. Just to the west of the top of Insadonggil on Yulgongno is the Korea Ginseng Centre.

Chang-an-dong Antique Market
Korea's largest antique market has about 150 stores. Just be sure that whatever you buy isn't a 'cultural treasure' and can be legally taken out of the country. This market is open from 10 am to 8 pm, but closed on Sunday.

Get there by taking subway line 5 to Tapshimni station.

One of the many antique shops in
Chang-an-dong Antique Market

Yongsan Electronics Market
This area just to the west of It'aewon is a good place to look for all manner of electronic wizardry – computers (including software), tape players, Nintendo games, etc. You can reach the market by taking the Suwon train on subway line No 1 and getting off at Yongsan station – from there follow the elevated walkway over the tracks. The first

part of the electronics market which you encounter is in an enormous building with the Yongsan bus terminal on the ground floor. However, a neighbouring building called 'Electroland' actually has a wider selection of goods. The electronics market continues to grow and has spilled out into the side streets.

The company which supplied the software used in creating this book was Jin Com Soft Company (☎ 706-2043) in Electroland, shop B-316. The staff speak English and are willing to order software from abroad.

Department Stores

Although not the cheapest place to buy things, the large department stores near the CPO are worth exploring – at least to see what's available. Popular stores in this area include Lotte (closed Monday), Midopa (closed Wednesday), Saerona (closed Thursday) and Shinsegae (closed Thursday). Just east of the CPO is a shopping district called Myŏng-dong. It's expensive, but you can try bargaining. Printemps (closed 2nd & 4th Wednesdays) is at Ulchiro 3-ga station on subway line 2.

A little to the west of downtown is the trendy Shinch'on area. Take line 2 to Shinch'on station to find the Grace Department Store (closed 1st & 4th Mondays) and Grand Plaza (closed Thursday).

Moving to the south side of the Han River, Lotte World (closed Monday) at Chamshil subway station on line No 2 is one of the largest shopping malls in the world. Near Express Bus Terminal subway station on line 3 there's the New Core Shopping Centre (partially closed every Tuesday) and the Galleria Department Store is in the fashionable Apkujŏng area (closed 1st & 3rd Mondays).

GETTING THERE & AWAY

It's said that about two million Seoulites depart their city every Saturday for various destinations around the country, only to return on Sunday. It's like an immense tidal wave that rolls out and in again. The city itself is nearly deserted on weekends and

holidays, but every bus, train and plane resembles a moving sardine can.

Air

There are direct flights between Seoul and 13 other Korean cities. See the Getting Around chapter for domestic flight details.

If you've arrived in Korea with an onward ticket, you must reconfirm your reservation at least 72 hours before departure. The current list of airline offices in Seoul includes:

Airline	Code	☎
Aeroflot	SU	551-0321
Air Canada	AC	779-5654
Air China	CA	774-6886
Air France	AF	773-3151
Air New Zealand	NZ	779-1071
Alitalia	AZ	779-1676
All Nippon Airways	NH	752-5500
Ansett Australia	AN	723-1114
Asiana Airlines	OZ	774-4000
British Airways	BA	774-5511
Cathay Pacific	CX	773-0321
China Eastern	MU	518-0330
China Northern	CJ	775-9070
Continental	CS	773-0100
Delta	DL	754-1921
El Al	LY	778-3351
Garuda Indonesia	GA	773-2092
Japan Air System	JD	752-9090
Japan Airlines	JL	757-1711
KLM Royal Dutch	KL	755-7040
Korean Air	KE	756-2000
Lufthansa	LH	538-8141
Malaysian	MH	777-7761
Mongolian	OM	592-7788
Northwest	NW	734-7800
Philippine	PR	774-3581
Qantas	QF	777-6871
Singapore	SQ	755-1226
Swiss Air	SR	757-8901
Thai Airways	TG	754-9960
United	UA	757-1691
Uzbekistan	HY	734-5157
VASP Brazilian	VP	779-5651
Vietnam	VN	775-7666
Vladivostok Air	XF	323-0011

Bus

The main bus station is the Seoul express bus terminal (Seoul kosok t'ŏminŏl) which is also

SEOUL

called the Kangnam express bus terminal. It's on the south side of the Han River – take subway line No 3 and get off at Express Bus Terminal subway station. The terminal is very well organised, with signs in English and Korean over all the ticket offices and bus bays. This huge terminal actually consists of two buildings, Kyŏngbusŏn (☎ 782-5552) and Honam-Yŏngdongsŏn (☎ 592-0050). Kyŏngbusŏn is a ten-storey building with everything useful on the 1st floor; Honam-Yŏngdongsŏn is a two-storey structure with ticket offices and platforms on the 1st floor, and a cafeteria on the 2nd floor. These two buildings are a few hundred metres apart.

See the appendix at the end of this book for details of buses leaving from both buildings of the Seoul express bus terminal (add about 50% to the fares for 1st class express buses).

There are some night buses from Seoul to major cities like Pusan, Taegu and Kwangju. A 'night bus' is defined as one which runs between 10 pm and midnight. To date no night buses leave between midnight and 5.30 am, but that could change. All night buses are from the Seoul express bus terminal.

The Tong-Seoul (east Seoul) bus terminal (☎ 458-4851) is also very useful, especially for getting to places on the east coast or the central part of the country. See the appendix at the end of the book for details.

You can reach Tong-Seoul bus terminal by taking subway line 2 to Kangbyŏn station.

Sangbong bus terminal (☎ 435-2122), in the eastern suburbs, is most useful to people heading east. The terminal is connected by bus with Ch'ŏngnyangni railway station (next to Ch'ŏngnyangni subway station on subway line 1). From Ch'ŏngnyangni it takes 15 minutes to reach Sangbong on bus Nos 38-2, 165, 165-2, 166 and 522-1; or 50 minutes by bus from Chongno 1-ga on bus Nos 131 and 131-1.

From Sangbong terminal there are buses to dozens of obscure little towns – see the appendix at the end of the book for a list of major destinations only.

Other bus terminals in descending order of usefulness include:

Shinch'on bus terminal (☎ 324-0611) offers non-stop bus services to Kanghwa Island every 10 minutes from 5.40 am to 9.30 pm.

Nambu (south) bus terminal operates buses to destinations in Kyŏnggi-do, such as Kanghwa Island, Yong-in Everland and Ansung.

Sŏbu (west) bus terminal (☎ 355-5103) is easily accessible from subway line 3 and runs buses bound for the north-western part of the province of Kyŏnggi-do, including Freedom Bridge, Imjingak, Kwangt'an, Pogwangsa, Munsan, Munbong, Pobwonni, Choksong, Pyokche, Songch'u and Ŭijŏngbu.

Train

Most long-distance trains departing from Seoul leave from Seoul station. The one important exception is the train heading east towards Ch'unch'ŏn. For this, go to Ch'ŏngnyangni railway station, which you reach by taking subway line 1.

GETTING AROUND
The Airport

Kimp'o International Airport is 18 km west of the centre, and handles both domestic and international flights. An easy way to get there (and avoid Seoul's traffic) is to take subway line 5. From the centre this costs W500, rather than the usual W400 fare.

At present there are five kinds of buses going there and charging different prices. Some are express and some are not, but it makes little difference – traffic jams are the key factor in determining how long the journey takes. The fancier buses offer fancier facilities and extra room to store luggage.

Local buses are cheapest. These are more frequent than express buses and cost W400. The No 63 bus stops next to Tŏksugung and just north of the Koreana Hotel at the Donghwa Duty-Free Shop. The No 68 bus also stops close to City Hall and Midopa Department Store. The disadvantage of both these buses is that they will take on standing passengers and there is very little room for baggage. However, there is a fancy new blue and white bus No 63 which costs W1000, goes directly to the airport and does not accept standing passengers.

It's more comfortable to take bus No 1002, which costs W1000. It follows much the

Seoul – Getting Around 147

same route as the No 63 and stops at the same spots in the centre. Service is frequent.

Bus Nos 600 and 601 are express buses and guarantee a seat for all passengers. However, they are relatively scarce – you could wait 30 minutes for one to come along. The No 601 bus goes into central Seoul, stopping at Shinch'on subway station, the Koreana Hotel, Tŏksugung, Seoul station, Nandaemun, Chongno 3-ga, Chongno 6-ga and on to Tongdaemun Gate. The No 600 bus goes from Kimp'o into the areas south of the Han River, stopping at the National Cemetery, Palace Hotel, Seoul express bus terminal, Yŏngdong Market, Nam Seoul Hotel, KOEX, the Seoul Sports Complex and Chamshil subway station. There is also a bus No 600-2, which follows the same route as the 600 but terminates at the Seoul express bus terminal. These buses run from 6 am to 9 pm and cost W900.

Special airport express buses also travel between Kimp'o International Airport and the Korea City Air Terminal (KCAT) in the Korea World Trade Centre, south of the Han River. This service is more expensive than the express buses at W3000 and it is also less frequent, running every 10 to 15 minutes from 7.20 am to 9.40 pm. It is probably only useful to get to the Inter-Continental, Lotte World and Ramada Renaissance Hotels, all of which are in the vicinity. A note about Korea City Air Terminal – you can actually complete your entire check-in procedure here (as opposed to checking in at the airport), but it depends entirely on which airline you are flying with. The airlines offering this service periodically change, so ask first.

Crème de la crème of Seoul's airport transport is the KAL limousine bus. There is no saving in time, but you get cushy seats, air-conditioning, videos, cellular phones and cellular fax machines – just the thing for the executive on the go. All that's missing is the sauna. The price tag for this luxury is W4500. These buses run from 7 am to 10 pm, once every 20 to 30 minutes. There are five routes covering 19 luxury hotels – ask at the airport information desk (or your hotel service desk) if interested.

Taxis are convenient if you don't mind paying for one. There are often traffic police handing out official complaint forms at the taxi ramp outside the airport to discourage bad behaviour from the drivers, and most now seem resigned to using their meters. The trip into town should take around 30 minutes and cost W10,000 or so (without the meter expect to pay W20,000).

One of the confusing things about Kimp'o International Airport is that there are three terminals – two for international and one for domestic. The terminals are too far apart to walk from one to the other, but a free shuttle bus zips around the airport every few minutes. It's useful to know that buses heading into the airport first stop at international terminal 2, then the domestic terminal and finally international terminal 1 – tell the bus driver which one you want to get off at. It could change, but at the time of writing you'll find the airlines distributed as follows:

International Terminal 1: Aeroflot, Air Canada, Air France, All Nippon Airways, Ansett Australia, British Airways, Cathay Pacific, Delta, Japan Air System, Japan Airlines, KLM, Northwest, Mongolian, Philippine Airlines, Singapore Airlines, THAI Airways, United, VASP Brazilian Airlines

International Terminal 2: Alitalia, Air China, Air New Zealand, Asiana Airlines, China Eastern, China Northern, Continental, Garuda Indonesia, Korean Air, Lufthansa, Malaysian, Qantas, Swiss Air, Vietnam Airlines, Vladivostok Air

Bus

City buses run from approximately 5.30 am until midnight. The ordinary buses are colour-coded purple & white or blue & white, and cost W400 (exact change please) or W390 with a token (same word in Korean) bought from one of the bus token booths found at most major bus stops. The green & white *chwasŏk* buses (the ones with seats) cost W1000 and no tokens are available. The token booths sell a *Bus Route Guide (bŏsŭ nosŏn onnae)* for W1000; it's written entirely in Korean even though some editions have had an English title on the cover.

The bus most tourists have to deal with is

No 23, which goes to It'aewon. It runs along Chongno, stops outside the YMCA before travelling up to the Kwanghwamun Gate, then doubles back on Sejongno to stop on the east side of the Sejong Cultural Centre and opposite City Hall. When subway line No 6 opens (probably in 1997) there will be a stop for It'aewon and the bus will no doubt get less use.

Minibuses are privately owned and operate illegally, but are tolerated by the government because they provide services to isolated areas not reached by public transport. The fare depends on the distance travelled.

Underground

The Seoul subway system is modern, fast and cheap, but can be so crowded that if you drop dead you'll never hit the ground. Currently there are five lines in operation, all of them colour-coded. Lines 6, 7 and 8 will be opening during the next few years, probably within the lifespan of this book. When all eight lines are up and running the Seoul subway system will be one of the largest in the world.

The system is very user friendly, and finding your way around should be no trouble. Trains run at least every six minutes from 5 am until midnight.

The basic charge is W400 for Zone 1, which includes most of the city. The fare rises to W500 if you cross into Zone 2 – the machines where you buy tickets have a self-explanatory fare map, but you'll rarely need to go outside Zone 1 (the airport is in zone 2). Outside the Seoul city limits, the fare rises by W66 for each five km travelled, so a ride from Seoul to Suwon (in the suburbs) costs W900.

If you do much commuting you might want to buy a multiple-use ticket, which gains you a 10% bonanza: a W10,000 ticket actually costs W9000 and a W20,000 ticket can be purchased for W18,000.

Car

While driving your own vehicle in Seoul is not recommended, some are determined to do it. If this interests you, cars can be rented from any of the following companies:

88 (☎ 665-8881); Changwon (☎ 951-5001); Cheil (☎ 525-6011); Hanyang (☎ 3442-7882); Hertz Kŭmho (☎ 798-1515); Korea (☎ 585-0801); Korea Express (☎ 719-7295); Saehan (☎ 896-0031); Sambo (☎ 797-5711); Seoul (☎ 474-0011); Tonghwa (☎ 790-1750); VIP (☎ 838-0015)

If you want to travel in style, chauffeur-driven cars can be rented (W50,000 for 10 hours) by calling Korea Car Rental Union (☎ 533-2503).

Taxi

During rush hour, demand is so much greater than supply that you practically have to throw yourself in front of a cab to get a driver's attention. However, drivers of the deluxe (expensive) taxis are often on the prowl for foreigners.

As for the ordinary taxis, you'll have to fight it out (literally) with the Koreans. Remember that taxis can be shared – as the taxi goes sailing past you must look confident and shout your destination loudly. There is no room for the meek when it comes to trying to catch a cab in Seoul.

Taxis can be hailed by telephone (☎ 414-0150) but there is a substantial extra charge for this service. Actually, the official dispatching service charge is only W1000, but drivers expect a more-or-less mandatory tip of W10,000. Furthermore, any taxis dispatched by phone are likely to be the expensive deluxe taxis.

Kyŏnggi-do

The province of Kyŏnggi-do surrounds
Seoul and a part even pokes into North
Korea. You have about as much chance of
visiting the moon as you do of crossing the
Demilitarised Zone (DMZ), but all other
parts of Kyŏnggi-do can be reached from
Seoul as a day trip.

PUK'ANSAN NATIONAL PARK

Just to the north of Seoul is Puk'ansan
('north of the Han River mountains'). This
national park boasts many massive white
granite peaks, forests, temples, rock-cut
Buddhist statues and tremendous views from
various points.

Puk'ansan (837m) is the highest peak in
the area, but there are at least 20 others within
the park boundary. Other notable peaks near
Puk'ansan itself (and connected to it by
ridges) include Insubong, Mangyŏngdae,
Paekundae, Nojŏkbong, Pohyŏnbong,
Pibong and Wonhyobong. Insubong, (811m)
Mangyŏngdae (800m) and Paekundae
(836m) form a triangle which is named
Samgaksan (Triangle Mountain). The
rugged granite face of Insubong is a
challenge to rock climbers, and they turn out
in force whenever weather permits.

Insubong offers some of the best multi-pitch climbing
in Asia for free climbers. It has been referred to as
Asia's 'Little Yosemite' and has routes of all grades.
The local climbers are extremely friendly and enthusiastic, eager to introduce newcomers to their mountain. It is possible to hire a guide through one of the
climbing shops in Seoul or through the mountaineering clubs. Information is available from KNTO – it's
on the computer there too.

Darren DeRidder

At the northern end of the park is another
peak, Tobongsan (717m), which is joined
by ridges to Chaunbong, Manjangbong,
Soninbong and Obong.

In the south of the park is Puk'ansansŏng
(North Mountain Fortress). The fortress was
originally built during the Paekche dynasty,

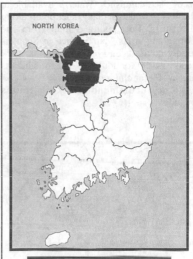

𝓗𝓘𝓖𝓗𝓛𝓘𝓖𝓗𝓣𝓢 HIGHLIGHTS

♦ Puk'ansan National Park, with its incredible granite peaks and the historic North
Mountain Fortress

♦ Seoul Grand Park, home to the National
Museum of Modern Art, a zoo, botanic
garden and hi-tech rides

♦ P'anmunjŏm, a sober reminder that the
Cold War is not yet over

♦ Korean Folk Village, a tasteful re-creation
of Korea's ancient past

♦ Paengnyŏngdo, a remote island just off
the coast of North Korea

about 1,700 years ago, but the present walls
date from the time of the Yi king, Sukchong,
who rebuilt the battlements in the 16th
century following invasions from China.
Sections of the wall were destroyed during
the Korean War but have since been restored.

As national parks go, it's fairly small
(about 78 sq km) but still large enough to get
lost in. There are a variety of well-marked
trails into the park and along the ridges, and

seven huts where simple accommodation is available (bring your own bedding) as well as a limited selection of canned and packaged foodstuffs. There are 32 officially recognised campsites. Water is available at the huts as well as at many other points along the trails. Purchasing a map from the Chung'ang Atlas Map Service in Seoul is highly advised. Entry to the national park costs W1000 for adults, W600 for students and W300 for children.

Some recommended hiking routes include:

South Area

North-South Route 1 (9.1 km) Ui-dong – U-i Hut – Paekundae – Taedongmun Gate – Kugi-dong

North-South Route 2 (8.5 km, 3.5hrs) Chŏngnŭng Resort – Pogukmun Gate – Yŏngammun Gate – Nojŏkbong – Paekundae

East-West Route 1 (6.5 km) Ui-dong – Paekun Hut – Taesomun Gate

East-West Route 5 (11 km, 4.5hrs) Puk'ansansŏng Fortress Entrance – Taesomun Gate – Paekundae – U-i Hut

Circular Route 1 (7.1 km) Ui-dong – Paekundae – Puk'ansan Hut – Chŏngnŭng Resort

Circular Route 2 (8.1 km) Ui-dong – Puk'ansan Hut – Paekundae – Ui-dong

Circular Route 3 (6.3 km, 3.5hrs) Ui-dong – Tosŏnsa – Paekun Hut – Paekundae – Nojŏkbong – Yŏngammun Gate – Ui-dong Resort
Circular Route 4 (5 km) Kugi-dong – Taesŏngmun Gate – Taedongmun Gate – 4.19 Memorial Tower
Circular Route 5 (7.5 km, 4hrs) Segŏmjŏng Resort – Munsusa Hermitage – Taenammun Gate – Pogukmun Gate – Chŏngnŭng Resort

North Area (Tobongsan)

East-West Route 2 (8.5 km) Tobong-dong, Podae Ridge, Obong, Ui-dong
East-West Route 3 (7.9 km) Tobong-dong – Tobong Hut – Kwanumam Hermitage – Ui-dong
East-West Route 4 (8.3 km) Tobong-dong – Kwanu mam Hermitage – Obong – Ui-dong
Circular Route 6 (6.7 km) Tobong-dong – Ch'ŏnch'uksa – Mangwolsa – Changsuwon

Getting There & Away

Getting to Puk'ansan by public transport is easy, though there are a number of entrances to the park. Some of the possibilities include:

City Hall – Ui-dong, bus Nos 6, 8 & 23 (50 minutes)
Chongno 1-ga – Chŏngnŭng Resort, bus No 5 (40 minutes)
Chongno 1-ga – Segŏmjŏng Resort, bus No 59 (20 minutes)
Sejong Cultural Centre – Puk'ansansông, bus No 156 (40 minutes)
Sejong Cultural Center – Ui-dong, bus No 8 (50 minutes)

Best of all, the newly-opened subway line 7 is a boon to hikers. Its last stop is Tobongsan station, near the northern end of the national park.

Alternatively, you could take subway line 3 to Kup'abal station, then go the last three km north-east towards the park by bus, taxi or on foot.

SURAKSAN MOUNTAIN

To the east of Puk'ansan National Park is Suraksan (638m) which is another attractive climbing area. It's not a national park, but it's still popular (too popular!) with weekend Seoulites trying to get away from it all.

Suraksan is just north of the Seoul city limits, but is connected by a ridge to Puramsan (508 metres) which is in Seoul.

Hiking along the ridge between the two peaks is recommended.

Access to Suraksan is possible from several angles, and it's not a bad idea to ascend and descend the mountain by different routes. A good way to begin would be to take subway line 4 to Sanggye station – Puramsan is two km to the east of this station. From Puramsan you can follow the ridgeline north about seven km to Suraksan. Along the way you must cross a small highway, and just off to the east is the interesting temple of Hŭngguksa, which is worth the small detour. From here there are several obvious trails down – one leads to Suraksan station on subway line 7, which will take you back to Seoul. Be warned that this is a long walk and will take a full day, so start early.

SEOUL GRAND PARK

In the suburbs south of the megalopolis is Seoul Grand Park (Sŏul Tae Kongwon), a huge sprawling affair with a number of attractions. Although it's largely geared towards kids, there are some sights for adults too. The park contains the National Museum of Modern Art, a major zoo with a botanic garden and Seoul Land, a hi-tech amusement park in the Disney tradition. If you don't want to be fighting with crowds all day, it is best to choose a weekday to visit.

The zoo has a good collection of animals, many of them in attractive roomy enclosures. There is even an ant ground. Dolphin shows take place three times daily at 11.30 am, 1.30 and 3.30 pm. Admission to the park costs W1150, plus there are additional fees for the zoo, dolphin show, exhibition halls and swimming pool.

Seoul Land is an afternoon out in itself. It has plenty of rides of the white-knuckle variety. General admission to Seoul Land is W3500 for adults, W2500 for students and W1500 for children, but there are steep extra charges for Tomorrow Land, Fantasy Land, Adventure Land and World Plaza. If you want to see it all, an all-inclusive ticket is W18,000 for adults, W15,000 for students and W11,000 for children.

Both Seoul Land and the zoo are open

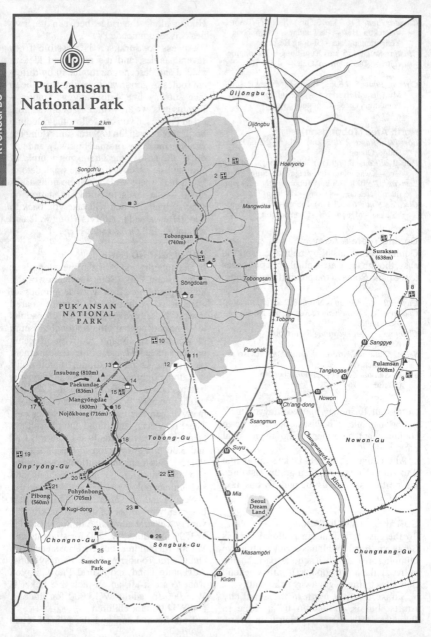

Puk'ansan
National Park

0   1   2 km

Ŭijŏngbu

Ŭijŏngbu

Songch'u

1

2

Hoeryong

3

Mangwolsa

Tobongsan
(740m)

4
5

Suraksan
(638m)

7

Sŏngdoam

6

Tobongsan

8

PUK'ANSAN
NATIONAL
PARK

Tobong

10

11

Panghak

Sanggye

12

Insubong (810m)

13

14

Paekundae
(836m)

15

Tangkogae

Pulamsan
(508m)

9

Mangyŏngdae
(800m)

16

Nojŏkbong (716m)

Ch'ang-dong

Nowon

17

18

Ssangmun

Tobong-Gu

Nowon-Gu

19

Suyu

Ŭnp'yŏng-Gu

20

22

21

Pibong
(560m)

Pohyŏnbong
(705m)

23

Mia

Seoul
Dream
Land

Kugi-dong

24

26

Chongno-Gu

Sŏngbuk-Gu

Miasamgŏri

Chungnang-Gu

25

Samch'ŏng
Park

Kirŭm

KYŎNGGI-DO

Puk'ansan National Park 북한산국립공원	23 Chŏngnŭng Resort 정릉유원지	10 Yongdŏksa Temple 용덕사
	24 Bugak Park Hotel 북악파크호텔	15 Tosŏnsa Temple 도선사
PLACES TO STAY 3 Songch'u Resort 송추유원지	25 Ramada Olympia Hotel 올림피아호텔	16 Yongammun Gate 용암문
5 Tobong Hut 도봉산장	**OTHER**	17 Taesŏmun Gate 대서문
6 Pomun Hut 보문산장	1 Sŏkch'ŏnsa Temple 석천사	18 Taedongmun Gate 대동문
11 U-i-dong Resort 우이동유원지	2 Hoeryongsa Temple 호룡사	19 Chingwansa Temple 진관사
12 Green Park Hotel 그린파크호텔	4 Ch'ŏnch'uksa Temple 천축사	20 Munsusa Hermitage 문수사
13 Insu Hut 인수산장	7 Naewonam Hermitage 내원암	21 Sŭnggasa Temple 승가사
14 U-i Hut 우이산장	8 Hŭngguksa Temple 흥국사	22 Hwagyesa Temple 화계사
	9 Pulamsa Temple 불암사	26 Kukmin University 국민대학교

daily from 9.30 am to 9 pm from May to August (to 10 pm on weekends and holidays), and from 9.30 am to 7 pm from September to April.

You can get to Seoul Land by taking the No 4 subway line to the Seoul Grand Park station.

SEOUL HORSE RACE TRACK

In order to project a family image, the race track (Sŏul Sŭngma Kongwon) is officially called the Seoul Equestrian Park (☎ 500-1273). Horse racing is one of the very few legal gambling activities open to Koreans, but the race season is deliberately kept short. The track is open to the public during December and January on Saturdays and Sundays only from 11 am to 6 pm. Admission costs W200 and bets range from a minimum of W100 to a maximum of W200,000. To give even more of a family image to this activity, baby carriages and children's bicycles are available for hire (but can't be ridden on the track). The races can also be viewed on large-screen TVs located at betting offices in downtown Seoul.

The race track is next door to the already-mentioned Seoul Grand Park. Take subway line 4 to Seoul Race Course station.

NAMHANSANSŎNG PROVINCIAL PARK

About 26 km south-east of Seoul is the peak of Namhansan. Like Puk'ansan, it's topped by a fortress (Namhansansŏng) originally built during the Paekche dynasty. However, the present walls are of more recent vintage (about 1626) and were constructed by the Yi rulers as protection against the Manchus. It was here, in 1637, that King Injo along with 14,000 of his troops was forced to surrender to an overwhelming Manchu invasion, which led to Korea being forced to accept the suzerainty of China. It's probably the nearest thing you'll find in Korea to the Great Wall of China. The stone walls and massive gates of this fortress snake for some eight km around the mountains above Sŏngnam City south-east of Seoul and are very popular as a picnic spot at weekends and public holidays. If you want to take in the ruins in peace, avoid these times.

Getting There & Away

Between 8.20 am and 7 pm, there are buses direct to the park once hourly from the Tong-Seoul bus terminal (subway line 2 to Kangbyŏn station).

Alternatively, bus No 66 from Ŭlchiro 6-ga runs about once every 10 minutes and takes about one hour for the ride. However, this bus takes you to Sŏngnam City rather than into the park. Just before entering Sŏngnam City, the bus will have to climb up a steep slope – get off at the next stop. From there, cross the street and hop on bus No 88 which will take you to the bottom of the hill on which the fortress is located – from there it's a 20 minute walk up the hill. Your other option is to grab a taxi in Sŏngnam City for the last stretch. Admission to the park costs W300.

SUWŎN

Suwŏn (population 650,000) is an ancient fortress city 48 km south of Seoul and is the provincial capital of Kyŏnggi-do. The walls were constructed in the later part of the 18th century by King Kongjo in an unsuccessful attempt to make Suwŏn the nation's capital. They once surrounded the whole city, but industrial and residential expansion in recent years have seen the city spill out beyond the enclosed area. The walls, gates, a number of pavilions and an unusual water gate have all been recently reconstructed along the original lines. It's possible to walk around almost all of the wall but the best point of entry is South Gate. From here, steps lead straight up to the pavilion at the top of P'altalsan. If you head off from here first to West Gate followed by North Gate and East Gate, you'll see most of the principal features of the fortifications.

Places to Stay

Dozens of yŏgwan and yŏinsuk are hidden in the back alleys clustered around the bus terminals (see map). More upmarket places to stay include the *New Arirang Hotel* and the *Brown Hotel* (☎ 464141), which is rated 2nd class.

Places to Eat

The small underground arcade right in front of Suwŏn train station has numerous stalls selling kimbap and noodles for W3000 or less.

Getting There & Away

Subway To get there take subway line 1

heading south all the way to the last stop, making sure the train is marked 'Suwŏn' (*not* Inch'ŏn or Ansan). The journey from Seoul takes about 45 minutes.

Bus The train service is so much easier and more convenient that the buses don't get much use. However, if you can find the express bus terminal (no mean feat in Suwŏn's twisted alleys) you can get to the following destinations:

Kwangju buses depart five times daily between 7 am and 6.30 pm. The fare is W13,300 (1st class) or W9000 (2nd class) and the journey takes 3¾ hours.
Taejŏn buses depart once hourly between 7.30 am and 7.30 pm. The fare is W6000 (1st class) or W4100 (2nd class) and the journey takes 1¼ hours.

Train Suwŏn is on the country's busiest railway and there are trains heading south to Taejŏn, Taegu and Pusan several times an hour.

KOREAN FOLK VILLAGE

The Korean Folk Village (Hanguk Minsok Ch'on) is tastefully done and well worth a day trip from Seoul. It's obvious that a lot of effort, attention to detail and sensitivity have gone into creating this village and it's as near to being as authentic as the thousands of tourists visiting it daily will allow.

If this model folk village had been built in China or Japan, no doubt there would be someone dressed in a Mickey Mouse or Bugs Bunny costume handing out balloons bearing the logo of some company. Indeed, most of the recreated 'traditional' tourist villages found elsewhere in the world are disastrously kitsch, but this one is a refreshing change.

The village has examples of traditional peasants', farmers' and civil officials' housing styles from all over the country as well as artisans' workshops, a brewery, a Confucian school, a Buddhist temple and a market place.

There are regular dance performances such as the farmers' dance at noon and 3.30 pm on weekdays and a wedding parade at

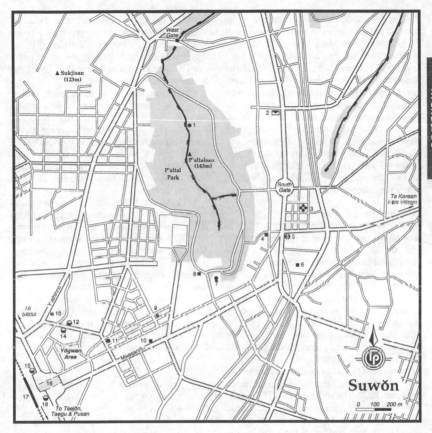

Suwŏn

0   100   200 m

Suwŏn 수원

PLACES TO STAY

4 Sŏksan Hotel
   석산 호텔
6 Brown Hotel
   브라운호텔
8 YMCA
   와이엠씨에이
9 P'unnyŏn-jang Yŏgwan
   풍년장여관
10 New Arirang Hotel
   뉴아리랑호텔
11 Kwibin-jang Yŏgwan
   귀빈장여관

13 Yŏngbin-jang Yŏgwan
   영빈장여관

OTHER

1 Sŏjangdae Command
   Post
   서장대
2 Central Post Office
   수원우체국
3 Shimin Department Store
   시민 백화점
5 Chohŭng Bank
   조흥은행
7 Confucian School
   향교

12 Express Bus Terminal
   고속버스터미널
14 Inter-City Bus Terminal
   시외버스터미널
15 Bus Nos 27 & 37 to
   Korean Folk Village
   성류상
16 Underground Arcade
   지하상가
17 Railway Station
   수원역
18 Shuttle Bus to Korean
   Folk Village
   민속촌을 위한
   버스정류장

1.30 and 4 pm on national holidays. Special request performances of the Lion Dance of Pukchong, the Mask Dance and rope walking are also available but there's a fee for these. The museum isn't just an artificial daytime affair – people live here and continue to practise traditional crafts though you shouldn't expect to see all the craftspeople hard at it when you visit. It's a good introduction to Korean culture, and if you enjoyed the National Folk Museum in Seoul then you should like this place. Entry to the village costs W7000 (W4000 for 12 to 24 year-olds, W3000 for children) and includes a free bus ride to and from Suwŏn.

Getting There & Away

To get to the village, first catch a train to Suwŏn. As you come out of the station you'll see the ticket office and bus stop on the right-hand side on the same side of the street. Buses to the village go every hour on weekdays and every half hour on weekends from 9 am to 5 pm. The last free bus back from the village is at 5 pm on weekdays and 6 pm on weekends and public holidays, but you can also take a regular local bus (bus No 27 or 37) and pay the fare. These regular buses run only once hourly until 8 pm.

Buses also go direct from Nambu bus terminal in Seoul to the village every 20 minutes between 10.20 am and 4.40 pm. If you use this option, there is no need to take the shuttle bus to and from Suwŏn. You can reach Nambu bus terminal by taking subway line 3 and exiting at Nambu Bus Terminal station.

From the big Chamshil intersection in Seoul, you can catch bus No 100-2 to the Korean Folk Village.

There are several bus companies in Seoul which offer tours of the village but they're pretty expensive. A half-day tour starts at W31,000, whereas the full-day itinerary is W42,000 (but at least you get a free lunch).

YONG-IN EVERLAND

Most people still know this place by its old name, the Yong-in Farmland (Yong'in Chayŏn Nongwŏn). Along with Children's Grand Park, Seoul Grand Park and Lotte World in Seoul, it's a good place to bring the kids. There's enough here to keep you busy all day.

Everland has a number of different mini-theme parks, including the jungle safari park, the Twilight Zone, Caribbean Bay, Everland Speedway and Global Village.

Caribbean Bay is a water park which boasts an indoor sandy beach, saunas and tanning rooms. Most interesting though is the wave pool – it's not Hawaii, but the waves reach two metres in height and you can 'surf'.

Everland Speedway is a racing track where automobile and motorcycle races are held. Intriguingly, it's also home to the Safe Driving School.

On a more dignified note, you might want to visit the **Hoam Art Museum**. This is a private collection of Korean art that is owned by the founder and chairman of the Samsung group. Sixty of the items on display here have been designated as national treasures. The collection is eclectic, featuring painting, sculpture, pottery, folk crafts and even prehistoric relics.

Aside from the general admission fee, there are extra charges for the various theme parks. Other options are to buy a 'big 5' or 'all-inclusive' ticket. The price breakdown is as follows:

	Adults	Students	Children
Admission	W7000	W5000	W1500
Big 5	W16,000	W13,000	W10,000
All-inclusive	W21,000	W18,000	W13,000

Yong-in Everland is open daily from 9.30 am to 9 pm (from 8.30 am to 11 pm on summer weekends and holidays). There are buses running out to Yong-in Everland from Suwon station. Alternatively, there are buses from Seoul express bus terminal every 15 minutes, taking 45 minutes for the journey.

ICH'ŎN

Just 50 km south-east of Seoul is the historic village of Ich'ŏn. Though perhaps it won't be much longer before the Seoul megalopolis swallows it up, at present Ich'ŏn is semi-rural and has several moderately interesting sights.

Ich'ŏn Ceramic Village

The Ich'ŏn Ceramic Village (Ich'ŏn Toye Ch'on) attracts a small but loyal following of pottery buffs. The Ich'on region has been the centre of the Korean ceramics industry since the Chosŏn dynasty (1392-1910). White porcelain is still a Korean export item, though these days there is heavy competition from low-wage sweatshops in China. Nonetheless, the ceramic kilns of Ich'ŏn are still of great historical importance to Korea.

Ich'ŏn is also the home of the Haegang Ceramics Museum (☎ 342226); admission is W1000.

Ich'ŏn Hot Springs

Though not the most spectacular hot springs in Korea, they're certainly among the most accessible. The water temperature is moderate 30°C. Ich'ŏn hot springs gained popularity during the Japanese colonial period from 1910 to 1945.

Perhaps this explains why hotels here charge Japanese prices – it's not the cheapest hot springs resort around. However, you needn't be a hotel guest to use the facilities, though of course you have to buy an admission ticket. Some of the cushy places where you can bathe or stay overnight include the *Solbong Hotel* (☎ 635-5701) which costs a mere W133,000 to W164,000. Or you could go downmarket and stay at the *Miranda Ich'ŏn Hotel* (☎ 332001) where doubles are W38,000 to W96,800.

Getting There & Away

There are at least two options for getting to Ich'ŏn. Perhaps easiest is from the Seoul express bus terminal – buses run once every 20 minutes from 6.30 am until 9.20 pm, taking just over an hour to make the journey. Buses are every 15 minutes from the Tong-Seoul bus terminal and take 50 minutes to do the trip. The fare is W2200.

You must tell the driver if you want to get off at the Ich'ŏn Ceramic Village rather than in Ich'ŏn itself which is about 10 km further down the highway. The Ceramic Village is actually about halfway between Ich'ŏn and Kwangju. Some tours (not many) take in both the Yong-in Everland and the Ich'ŏn Ceramic Village in one trip.

If you're going to the hot springs, take a taxi from central Ich'ŏn.

YŎJU

About two km to the east of the town of Yŏju is Shilŭksa, a magnificent temple built around 580 AD. The temple is open from 8 am to 4 pm.

A short bus ride to the west of Yŏju is Yŏngnŭng, where you can find the Tomb of King Sejong. The tomb site is open from 8.30 am to 6 pm, and there is a small museum on the grounds.

Yŏju is to the south-east of Seoul. You can get there by bus from Seoul's Sangbong bus terminal.

INCH'ŎN

Along with Pusan, Inch'ŏn (population 2.2 million) is one of Korea's two foremost seaports. As might be expected, it's not a port with quaint wooden sailing ships and fishing piers. Rather, it's a world of container ships and high-rise housing developments.

Inch'ŏn became well known to the rest of the world in 1950 when American General Douglas MacArthur led the UN forces in a daring landing here behind enemy lines. Military experts doubted such a tactic could succeed, but the general knew what he was doing and within a month the North Koreans were all but defeated. Unfortunately for the allies, the tide turned again in November of the same year when Chinese troops stormed across the border into Korea.

Most foreigners who come to Inch'ŏn only do so to catch a ferry to China, and it's unlikely you'll want to come here just to see the town. Having said that, Inch'ŏn does have a few charms.

Information

Tourist Office The Inch'ŏn Tourist Association (☎ 883-3068) operates a kiosk inside the International Ferry Terminal.

Chayu Park

At the centre of Chayu (Freedom) Park is a

KYǑNGGI-DO

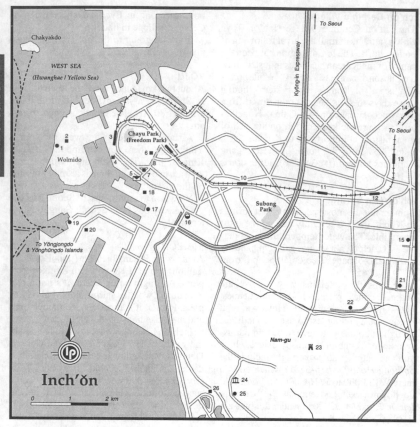

Chakyakdo

WEST SEA
(Hwanghae / Yellow Sea)

Wolmido

To Yǒngjongdo
& Yǒnghǔngdo Islands

Chayu Park
(Freedom Park)

Subong
Park

Nam-gu

Inch'ǒn

To Seoul

Kyǒng-in Expressway

To Seoul

0   1   2 km

statue of General MacArthur who led the famous Inch'ǒn landing during the Korean War. The park is right next to Inch'ǒn harbour.

Munhaksan Fortress

This was the seat of government of the old Paekche kingdom. Within the perimeters of the fort is a small lighthouse with a height of three metres. The surrounding park has an outdoor swimming pool.

The park is in the south side of the city in an area called Nam-gu.

Confucian School

First opened during the Koryǒ dynasty (918-1392), the school reached its height of glory during the Chosǒn dynasty (1392-1910) and was later annexed to a Confucian temple. These days the school serves as a shrine and no classes are held.

The Confucian School is just to the north of the Munhaksan Fortress.

Inch'ǒn Municipal Museum

There are about 1200 ancient artefacts on display, including some large temple bells from China. Next to the museum is the

Inch'ŏn 인천

PLACES TO STAY
2 Paradise & Habŏbu
   Motels
   파라다이스모텔,
   하버부모텔
4 Olympos Hotel
   올림프스호텔
6 Ch'ŏngma-jang & Yurim
   Park Yŏgwan
   청마장여관,
   유림파크여관
7 Taewon Hotel
   대원호텔
18 Muran-jang Yŏgwan
   모란장여관
20 Posŏng-jang &
   Ŭddŭm-jang Yŏgwan
   으뜸장어린,
   보성장여관
26 Songdo Resort
   송도유원지

OTHER
1 Wolmido Cultural St
   월미도문화의거리
3 Inch'ŏn Station
   인천역
5 Central Post Office
   인천우체국
8 Underground Arcade
   지하상가
9 Tonginch'ŏn Station
   동인천역
10 Chemulp'o Station
   제물포역
11 Chuan Station
   주안역
12 Kansŏk Station
   간석역
13 Tongam Station
   동암역
14 Paekun Station
   백운역
15 City Hall
   시청

16 Inter-City Bus
   Terminal
   시외버스터미널
17 International Ferry
   Terminal
   국제여객터미널
19 Yŏn'an Pier
   (Domestic Ferries)
   연안부두
21 Culture & Arts Hall
   종합문화회관
22 Confucian School
   향교
23 Munhaksan Fortress
   문학산성
24 Inch'ŏn Municipal
   Museum
   인천시립박물관
25 Inch'ŏn Landing
   Memorial Hall
   인천상륙작전기념관

Landing Commemoration Hall, another reminder of MacArthur's landing at Inch'ŏn.

The Municipal Museum is at the south end of town just east of Songdo Amusement Park.

Culture & Arts Hall
This brand new cultural centre has both indoor and outdoor performance halls for Korean dancing, drama, drum shows and the like. Art exhibits are also regularly presented here. The Culture & Arts Hall is roughly 1.5 km north-east of the Inch'ŏn Confucian School.

Shinp'odong Underground Arcade
If you exit the subway at Tonginchon station and descend through the Inch'ŏn Department Store, you will find yourself in one of Korea's longest underground malls. You're likely to spot plenty of foreigners here, mostly sailors on their off-day stocking up on electronics, chocolates, ginseng and other mementos of Korea.

Wolmido
This place was once an island, but land reclamation has turned it into a peninsula on the north-west side of Inch'ŏn harbour. Wolmido is a very trendy spot, boasting everything from raw fish restaurants to art galleries and, on summer weekends, street opera. Along the waterfront is the Wolmido Cultural St where various cultural performances are scheduled during summer weekends and holidays. There is also a small booth here dishing out tourist information. Locals claim that on a clear day you can see China – more likely some haze on the horizon which could be mistaken for China.

A large sightseeing cruise ship, the *Cosmos*, docks at Wolmido and offers dinner cruises with a view. The Inch'ŏn city government has plans to construct an Inch'ŏn Tower in this area to rival the one in Seoul.

Yŏn'an Pier
This is where you'll find some of the best fish markets and seafood restaurants in Korea. Yŏn'an Ferry Terminal (where you can catch ferries to the small islands just off the coast) is also here.

Songdo Resort
The resort boasts an amusement park atmosphere and is mainly geared towards locals

rather than tourists – when you see it, you'll understand why. Features include two artificial lakes and even an artificial beach. Think of it as a place for rowboats, paddleboats, drown-proof swimming and cotton candy. Overlooking the southern lake is the Hotel Songdo Beach.

Subong Park

The park is a good place for exercise, with its walking tracks and recreation facilities. The park has a war memorial, a Ferris wheel and other amusements for the kiddies. Subong Park is about three km east of Inch'ŏn harbour.

Islands

There are dozens of islands not far from Inch'ŏn, and some of them have decent beaches *(hesuyokjang)*. Just remember the rule about leaving the beaches as you've found them:

As I understood it, the park was not a national one, but still it's forbidden to pick up any stones from the beaches to take home with you. I didn't know about this rule, but became aware of it as some Korean rangers started to shout at me and rudely pulled my bag away and emptied it because of the few stones I had collected. I thought it would be OK to bring home some stones as souvenirs, but apparently that isn't allowed.

Astrid Trotzig

Chakyakdo This island is just three km north of Wolmido. In summer the landscape is decked with peonies *(chakyak* – thus the island's name. You can reach the island easily by taking a boat from Yŏn'an Ferry Terminal, on Yŏn'an Pier

Yŏngjongdo Ŭlwangni Beach on this island is the most accessible stretch of white sand in the Inch'ŏn area, but you'd better see it soon, before it's ruined. Yŏngjongdo Island will be the site of Seoul's new international airport, and when that airport opens (in the year 2002) the noise will no doubt make the beach far less desirable. A bridge to the island will also be constructed, bringing in heavy traffic (blissfully absent at present).

Yŏngjongdo Island is also known for Yŏngkungsa Temple. Ferries depart Inch'ŏn Ferry Terminal on Wolmido once hourly between 8 am and 9 pm and the journey takes 15 minutes. You land at Yŏngjongdo pier where there is a wonderful fish market (especially in the morning). From the pier you take a local bus (one hour) to Ŭlwangni Beach, on the opposite end of the island. There are no yŏgwan at Ŭlwangni but minbak are available.

Yŏnghŭngdo Shiplip'o Beach at the northwest corner of the island is 30 km from Inch'ŏn. The beach has a four-km long pebbly stretch and a one-km sandy stretch. Ferries to Yŏnghŭngdo depart Inch'ŏn about five or six times daily during summer, but it slows to two daily during winter. Ask a Korean speaker to call Wongwang Shipping Company (☎ (032) 882-1316/1714) for the current schedule. Ferries to Yŏnghŭngdo (and most other small islands) leave from the Yŏn'an Ferry Terminal on the south side of the harbour. Inch'ŏn city bus Nos 12, 14, 18 and 33 run out to the terminal.

Tokjokdo This is one of the more scenic islands reachable from Inch'ŏn, but it's a bit far for a day trip from Seoul. The ferry ride from Inch'ŏn takes one hour and 40 minutes. The island is 77 km from Inch'ŏn, and along it's southern shore is Sŏp'ori Beach which is two km long and is lined with a thick grove of pines. Much of the rest of the island has impressive rock formations, and it's worth climbing the highest peak, Pijobong (292 m). There are six yŏgwan on the island and at least 40 minbak. From Inch'ŏn's Yonan Ferry Terminal there are seven to eight ferries daily during summer (only one daily in winter). For further information contact Wongwang Shipping Company (☎ (032) 882-1316/1714).

Getting There & Away

Subway line 1 in Seoul connects to the trains heading to Inch'ŏn. The Inch'ŏn-Seoul journey takes about one hour.

MASON FLORENCE

MASON FLORENCE

MASON FLORENCE

MASON FLORENCE

MASON FLORENCE

MASON FLORENCE

A	B
C	D
E	F

Faces of Korea

A: A red hood for winter
B: Korean defence forces
C: Korean Monks

D: Confucian gentlemen chatting
E: Lotus elephant, Seoul
F: Street vendor, Seoul

ROBERT STOREY

CHRIS TAYLOR

ROBERT STOREY

ROBERT STOREY

A	B
C	D

Going Shopping

A: Masks, often used as props in traditional dance

B: Giant calligraphy brush, Insadong

C: Take your pick of baskets

D: Goddess of Mercy, Seoul

KYŎNGGI-DO

Getting Around
Subway Inch'ŏn is building a subway, but there is no word yet on when it will be finished.

Tour Bus Besides the baffling city bus system, there are also special tourist buses offering budget tours. These run twice daily at 11 am and 1 pm, and cost W4000. You catch these buses at the Wolmido Cultural St Tourist Information Booth.

Car Although self-drive transport is not especially recommended around the urban confines of Inch'ŏn, vehicles can be hired from the following companies:

Kyŏng-In (☎ 525 4444); New Inch'ŏn (☎ 882-0106); P'aldo (☎ 864 8680)

Boat Wolmido is also where you can take a cruise on the good ship *Cosmos*. This costs W4500 for a one-hour cruise, and the official departure times are as follows: 11 am, and 12.30, 2, 3.30, 5, 6.30 and 8 pm It's possible that this schedule is reduced during the off season (winter).

PAENGNYŎNGDO ISLAND
Far to the north-west of South Korea and within a stone's throw of North Korea is Paengnyŏngdo, a scenic island that is attracting an increasing number of tourists. The island is the westernmost point in South Korea and is notable for its remote location and dramatic coastal rock formations. Paengnyŏngdo is 12 km in length and about seven km wide.

Information
Korean speakers can try contacting the Paengnyŏngdo Government Office (☎ 436-0006).

Things to See & Do
There is a significant military presence on the island, a necessity with North Korea so close. This shouldn't interfere much with your enjoyment of the place, just don't climb over any barbed-wire fences.

A tour around the island by boat is one of those 'must do' activities. There are a few rare boats that also visit Taech'ŏngdo and Soch'ŏngdo, two smaller islands further south.

Sagot Beach is one of Paengnyŏngdo's unexpected sights. The beach is three km long and consists of sand packed so hard that people can (and do) drive cars on it. Some of the other beaches have a surface consisting of pebbles. The Koreans like to walk barefoot on the pebbles or even lie down on them because they believe that the resulting 'acupressure' is good for their health.

Aside from seafood, the island produces buckwheat which is used to make Korean buckwheat noodles. Fields of buckwheat flowers blooming in spring time can be a fantastic sight.

Places to Stay
Yŏgwan, yŏinsuk and minbak are easy to find – you should have some offers upon arrival at the ferry pier. *Hwanghae Yŏinsuk* (☎ 436-0333) is one of the cheapest at W15,000. Other places to consider are the *Ongjin Yŏgwan* (☎ 436-0163) and *Harbour Motel* (☎ 436-0354) at W20,000.

Getting There & Away
In summer there are about seven to eight boats daily between Paengnyŏngdo and Inch'ŏn. They depart from Yŏn'an Pier in Inch'ŏn and the journey takes four hours. Korean speakers can call Wongwang Shipping Company in Inch'ŏn (☎ 882-1316, 882-1714)

P'ANMUNJŎM
Situated about 56 km north-west of Seoul, P'anmunjŏm is the only location along the Demilitarised Zone (DMZ) where visitors are permitted. This is the truce village on the ceasefire line established at the end of the Korean War in 1953. It's in a building here that the interminable 'peace' discussions continue.

There's nowhere else in South Korea where you can get quite so close to North Korea without being arrested or shot, and the tension is palpable. In 1968, the crew of the American warship USS *Pueblo* (kidnapped at sea by the North Koreans 11 months earlier) were allowed to cross to the South here. In 1976, two American servicemen were hacked to death with axes by the North Koreans at P'anmunjŏm. It was also here that an American soldier peacefully defected to North Korea in 1983, and has never been heard from again. Just a year later, a Russian tourist defected to the South at P'anmunjŏm, triggering a gun battle that killed three North Koreans and one South Korean soldier.

P'anmunjŏm was also in the news in mid-1989. It was here that Lim Soo-kyong, a Hanguk University student, and the Reverend Moon Gyu-Hyon, a Catholic priest, were finally allowed to return to South Korea after protracted negotiations following Lim's visit to the Youth Festival in P'yŏngyang earlier in the year. Both were promptly arrested, whisked off to Seoul by helicopter and charged with violating the national security laws. Lim, a radical fervently committed to the reunification of Korea, had attempted to make the crossing several weeks before with the encouragement of the North Korean authorities but had been refused. The event made front-page news at the time, both in Korea and elsewhere.

P'anmunjŏm is perhaps overrated as a 'tourist attraction' but that doesn't seem to stop the hordes flocking here to gawk at this tense 'truce village', learn the history of the DMZ and come face to face with the stern-looking North Korean soldiers.

Part of the ongoing cold war between North and South is the existence of two civilian villages at P'anmunjŏm. On the southern side is Taesŏng-dong ('Great Success Village'), but the Americans call it 'Freedom Village'. It isn't terribly free for the villagers, as they must be out of the fields after dark and in their homes with doors locked by 11 pm. By way of compensation, it's a very prosperous agricultural community by South Korean standards – the villagers have plentiful land (though they don't own it), large homes and they are exempt from taxes. On the north side is Kijong-dong, which the Americans call 'Propaganda Village'. It differs from its southern counterpart in that it's uninhabited.

However, it would be fair to say that both villages exist mainly for no other purpose than propaganda. On the north side you can clearly see what is claimed to be the largest flagpole and flag in the world.

While you are permitted to take photos and use binoculars, there are a number of restrictions that visitors must adhere to. You must bring your passport; children under 10 years of age are not allowed; Korean nationals are not allowed unless special permission is obtained (a formidable bureaucratic procedure

Paradise in No-Man's-Land

The Demilitarised Zone (DMZ) separates North and South Korea. It's four km wide and 248 km long, surrounded by tanks and electrified fences, and virtually sealed off to all human beings. Ironically, this has made it something of an environmental paradise. Nowhere else in the world has a temperate habitat been so well preserved. This has been a great boon to wildlife – for example, the DMZ is home to a large flock of Manchurian Cranes. Environmentalists hope that if the two Koreas ever reunify, the DMZ will remain protected as a nature reserve. ■

which takes over a month). Furthermore, there is strict dress code which civilians must follow, and many travellers run afoul of this rule! Shaggy or 'unkempt' hair (especially on men) disqualifies some travellers. The military lists the following as examples of inappropriate clothing for this formal occasion:

- Shirts (top) without sleeves, T-shirts, tank tops and shirts of similar design
- Dungarees or blue jeans of any kind, including 'designer jeans'
- Shorts of any style, including hiking, Bermuda, cut-offs, or 'short-shorts'
- Miniskirts, halter tops, backless dresses and other abbreviated items of similar design
- Any item of outer clothing of the sheer variety
- Shower shoes, thongs or 'flip-flops'
- Items of military clothing not worn as an integral part of a prescribed uniform
- Any form-fitting clothing including tight-knit tops, tight-knit pants and stretch pants

In addition, you are warned:

- Visitors must remain in a group from the beginning to the end of the tour and will follow all instructions issued by their tour guide.
- Any equipment, microphones or flags belonging to the communist side in the MAC (Military Armistice Commission) conference room are not to be touched.
- Do not speak with, make any gesture toward or in any way approach or respond to personnel from the other side.
- Firearms, knives or weapons of any type cannot be taken into the Joint Security Area.

Getting There & Away

Access to P'anmunjŏm is permitted for tour groups only – this is not a do-it-yourself trip. In all cases, you must have your passport with you or you won't be allowed to board the bus. Your Korean tour guide will accompany you to Camp Bonifas on the southern side of the DMZ where the group eats lunch and you'll have a opportunity to play slot machines (the military must really need the money). You are then given a slide show and briefing by an American soldier, who will then accompany your group on a military bus into the Joint Security Area of P'anmunjŏm. All things considered, it's a good party.

Some tours take in a visit to the 'Third Tunnel of Aggression', which the North Koreans dug presumably to attack the South. The discovery of a fourth tunnel was announced in 1990 – this one large enough to accommodate trucks and tanks.

Commercial tours are available but they're expensive (though lunch is thrown in free). For some reason, all the commercial tour operators have their offices on the 3rd floor of the Hotel Lotte in Seoul. A recommended tour agency is Hanwha Travel Service (☎ 757-1232, 774-3226). Hanwha's tours take in both the DMZ and the Third Tunnel of Aggression for W42,000.

Korea Travel Bureau (☎ 585-1191) also has its office on the 3rd floor of the Lotte

On Burrowed Time

A brass plaque in P'anmunjŏm gives this account of the Third Tunnel of Aggression:

On 15 November 1974, members of a Republic of Korea Army (ROKA) patrol, inside the southern sector of the DMZ, spotted vapour rising from the ground. When they began to dig into the ground to investigate, they were fired upon by North Korean snipers. ROKA units secured the site and subsequently uncovered a tunnel dug by the North Koreans which extended 1.2 km into the Republic of Korea. On 20 November, two members of a United Nations Command (UNC) investigation team were killed inside the tunnel when dynamite planted by the North Koreans exploded. The briefing hall at Camp Kitty Hawk is named after one of the officers killed, Lieutenant Commander Robert N Ballinger. In March 1975, a second North Korean tunnel was discovered by a UNC tunnel detection team. In September of 1975, a North Korean engineer escaped and provided valuable intelligence concerning the communist tunnelling activities. Acting on the information, a tunnel detection team successfully intercepted a third tunnel in October 1978 less than two km from here. Today, the North Koreans continue to dig tunnels beneath the DMZ. The UNC and ROKA have fielded tunnel detection teams which drill around the clock in hope of intercepting these tunnels of aggression which threaten the security of the Republic of Korea. ∎

Hotel, but charges W48,000 and their tours skip the Third Tunnel. The tour cost is reduced to W30,000 if 'military or other official considerations prevent entry into the Joint Security Area'. The tours run daily and take seven hours. Departure is from the Lotte Hotel on Ŭlchiro, and you're expected to arrive 20 minutes before departure time.

Make sure when you book a tour that they are going to take you all the way to P'anmunjŏm and not just to the Odusan Unification Observatory on the southern side of the Imjin River. This can cost almost the same but it's essentially a ripoff.

Global Tour (☎ 335-0011) has a trip just to the Third Tunnel but skips P'anmunjŏm completely, and is therefore really not worth it. This tour costs W42,000. Global Tour is also in the Lotte Hotel.

Samhee Travel (☎ 757-1232) also avoids P'anmunjŏm, but takes in neighbouring sites such as Odusan Unification Observatory, the UN Korean War Monument, Freedom Bridge, the Third Tunnel, Imjingak Park and of course a restaurant for the requisite free lunch.

The cheapest tours by far to P'anmunjŏm are offered by the USO (☎ 795-3028), the US Army's cultural and social centre opposite Gate 21 of the Yongsan Army Base in Seoul. They have at least one tour (usually two) weekly and it costs US$25 or the equivalent in won, but doesn't include lunch or a visit to the Third Tunnel of Aggression. However, there are separate USO tours to the tunnels which are worthwhile, and Korean nationals may go on these. Because USO tours are cheap, they tend to be very heavily subscribed and you should book a few weeks in advance.

ODUSAN UNIFICATION OBSERVATORY

The Unification Observatory (T'ongil Chŏnmangdae) at Odusan is as close as most civilian Koreans can get to the DMZ. P'anmunjŏm, north of Seoul, is actually inside the DMZ and can be visited by foreigners, but Koreans are not normally allowed there.

Since the Unification Observatory does offer South Koreans a rare peek at the for-

bidden north, tourists by the bus load turn up here daily throughout the summer months. It isn't quite the same as going to P'anmunjŏm – there's little of the tension evident at P'anmunjŏm's 'Truce Village', since the Unification Observatory is actually a few km away from the DMZ. If you want to see anything at all (such as the UN post, the North Korean post and the North's propaganda signs) then you have to use the telescopes – at W500 a pop for 2½ minutes' viewing. It's essentially a non-event but it's a pleasant day out; there are no dress or age regulations; it's a little cheaper than going to P'anmunjŏm; and the government lays on a free slide show.

Admission to the Unification Observatory is W1200 for adults and W700 for students and seniors. It's open from 9 am to 6.30 pm in summer, or until 5.30 pm in winter.

Getting There & Away From Seoul Sŏbu bus terminal in Pulgwang-dong, take a bus to Kumch'on. These run every 15 minutes and the ride takes 50 minutes. Or from Seoul station, take a train to Kumch'on – these depart hourly and take one hour. From Kumch'on bus station, take a local bus to the Unification Observatory (these buses are marked Songdong-ri). The local buses depart once every 40 minutes and take ½ hour for the ride.

KANGHWADO ISLAND

West of Seoul and north of Inch'ŏn is Kanghwado, which played a significant part in Korean history. It's where the Koryŏ court took refuge during the Mongol invasions of the 13th century, and where the Koreans resisted American and French troops in the late 19th century. It is also where the second set of the 80,000 woodblocks of the Tripitaka Koreana were carved in the 14th century. They were later moved to another temple, Haeinsa, outside Taegu during the early years of the Yi dynasty.

Being an island fortress, Kanghwado has seen its fair share of fortifications, palaces and the like, but it's overrated as a tourist attraction. The tourist literature and some guide books to Korea go on at some length about Kanghwado's attractions, giving you the impression that the island is littered with fascinating relics and ruins. To a degree it is, but you'd have to be a real relic enthusiast to want to make the effort. One of the few redeeming features of a trip here is the temple of Pomunsa, but this is actually on a smaller island off the west coast of Kanghwado.

At the south-west tip of the island is Manisan (468m), which has on its summit a five-metre tall altar called Chamsongdan. This is dedicated to Tan'gun, the mythical first Korean born in 2333 BC. Koreans like to make the pilgrimage to the summit by foot from Chŏndŭngsa, a temple at the base of the mountain. This involves a five-km (each way) walk.

Kanghwa City

Despite all the hype, this city is a profound disappointment. True, the city gates still stand but the enclosing wall has disappeared. Likewise, the site of the Koryŏ court has a couple of traditional buildings of slight interest, but that's all and there's an admission fee to see it. If your time is limited, you can skip all this without feeling a deep sense of loss.

Pomunsa Temple

This important temple sits high up in the mountains on the island of Songmodo off the western coast of Kanghwado. The compound is relatively small but there is some superb and very ornate painting on the eaves of the various buildings and especially those of the bell pavilion. The famous grotto here is quite plain and uninteresting though it is a cool spot on a hot summer's day. One of the most interesting sights here is the 10m high rock carving of Kwansŭm Posal, the Goddess of Mercy, which stands below a granite overhang high above the temple compound. The carving was completed about 60 years ago and is quite unlike statues of the goddess to be seen elsewhere in Korea.

It's a steep walk up to the temple from where the bus drops you and there's a small tourist village with souvenir shops and restaurants at the bottom of the hill.

Getting There & Away

Buses to Kanghwado leave from the Shinchon bus terminal in the western part of Seoul. Take Subway line 2 to Shinch'on station and ask directions from there. It's a five-minute walk.

Buses leave every 10 minutes from 5.40 am to 9.30 pm, take one hour and cost W2300. The buses drop you at Kanghwa City bus terminal.

To get to Pomunsa from Kanghwa City, take a bus from the same bus station to Oep'ori. These depart every 20 minutes from 7.40 am to 6.40 pm, cost W400 and the ride takes 20 minutes. The bus will drop you in front of the main ferry terminal but this caters only for long-distance ferries and is not the one you want. Walk through to the front of the terminal, turn right and continue down the waterfront for about 100m. You'll see a concrete ramp going down to the water and another ferry terminal on the right. From here ferries run daily to Sŏkmo-ri on Songmodo approximately every hour from 7 am to 7 pm and they take both people and vehicles. It takes 10 minutes to cross the straits. Before buying a ticket you have to fill in a form (available in the ticket hall) stating your name, address and passport number (Kanghwado is very close to North Korea). The form is collected before you board the ferry.

On the opposite side there are buses to Pomunsa which take about half an hour.

SONGT'AN

To the south of Suwon and along the main rail line is Songt'an. The town's main claim to fame is that it's outside the enormous Osan US Air Force base.

In the not-too-distant past when South Korea was poor, Songt'an had a notorious reputation as a red light district. However, times change – Korea has become wealthy and the brothels have shut down.

Although Songt'an is considerably tamer these days, there is still a very active nightlife scene. Many Koreans come here to party along with the US military personnel. Expats of a non-military background come down on Friday and Saturday too, though this will often involve an overnight trip since it's rather far from Seoul to dash back after midnight.

In the confines of about six blocks there are about 25 to 30 expat bars. On the main street outside the base is the *Golden Gate*, *Dragon Lodge*, *Eagle Club* and *Stereo Club*. On several side streets radiating off from the main road there are many others including *Juliana's*, *Phoenix*, *Youn Chun* and the *UN Club*. There's even a strip of American-style 'biker bars' (but still fairly tame).

In short, Songt'an is probably as close as you'll come in Korea to finding a raging nightlife district. Beer and other alcohol is notably cheaper than what you'd pay in Seoul. Although expat males outnumber females, many of these bars are still acceptable places for women to comfortably enjoy a drink. Many Korean women also come here for an evening out.

Getting There & Away
Songt'an is on the main rail line and there are something like 80 trains daily from Seoul between the hours of 9 am and midnight. The ride takes about 45 minutes from Seoul, or only 15 minutes from Suwon.

SANJŎNGHO LAKE RESORT
This small but lovely alpine lake is adjacent to the border with Kangwon-do and not far from North Korea. Indeed, North Korea's former dictator Kim Il-sung is said to have briefly used the resort for some relaxation during the Korean War when the North controlled this area.

Nowadays, it's getting a bit commercialised and should be avoided on weekends and holidays. However, it can be most enjoyable when the masses are busy working or in school. You can expect a wide range of facilities, including a marina and mini-amusement park.

Nearby sights include Chainsa, a small temple. Also close by are three waterfalls, Tungnyong, Pison and Sanjŏng. Climbers may wish to challenge nearby Myŏngsŏngsan (924m), which is four km to the north and just across the border in Kangwon-do.

Places to Stay
Budget travellers can make use of the *Sanjŏng Campground*. Alternatively, there are a number of yŏgwan all charging around W20,000 for a double, though expect to pay more on holidays (if you can find a rooms at all!). The selection of yŏgwan includes:

Cheil-jang (☎ 326118); *Sanho Pake* (☎ 340081); *Sŏul-jang* (☎ 344590); *Shilla-jang* (☎ 325604); *Sopyong-yang* (☎ 325064); and *Yŏnghwa-jang* (☎ 325616)

Those requiring cushy facilities might want to check out the *Sanjŏnghosu Hotel* (☎ 344061) which has double rooms ranging from W35,000 to W55,000.

Getting There & Away
The nearest town is Unch'on. Buses between Unch'on and Sanjŏng Lake run every 30 minutes from 7 am to 7.50 pm. The journey takes 15 minutes and costs W400.

To reach Unch'on from Seoul, you can take a bus from Sangbong bus terminal. These run every 15 minutes between 5.20 am and 8.35 pm. The ride takes 1½ hours.

Kangwon-do

The north-east province of Kangwon-do is one of the least populated, most mountainous and scenic in South Korea. It's here that you'll find numerous opportunities for hiking and winter skiing.

CH'UNCH'ŎN

Ch'unch'ŏn (population 300,000) is the provincial capital of Kangwon-do and the urban centre of Korea's northern lake district, which includes lakes Soyangho and P'aroho. It's a very beautiful mountainous area and one of its principal attractions is the boat trips on the lakes. The town itself is fairly pleasant and is a major educational centre, with two universities and a teachers' college.

It's unlikely you'd come to Ch'unch'ŏn for the sake of the city itself, but it is a good stopover en route to Sŏraksan National Park if you'd prefer to take a bus and boat rather than just taking a bus all the way. The express buses from Seoul to Sŏraksan do not take the scenic route through the park from Inje to Yangyang. Instead, they use the Seoul to Kangnŭng (Yongdong) Expressway.

Orientation

An American military base, Camp Page, takes up a large slice of the town. This would be of no particular interest to travellers if it wasn't directly opposite Ch'unch'ŏn railway station. This means you step out of the station and find yourself one km from the nearest yŏgwan, restaurants and bus station. Buses to the railway station are infrequent and you may have to opt for a taxi or a long walk.

Nam Ch'unch'ŏn railway station is better situated, at the southern end of town, though still a long way from the centre and the bus station.

Information

There is a small (and not always open) information booth at the Folk Museum between

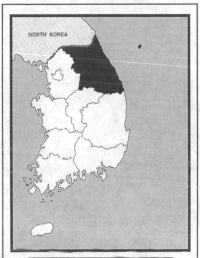

𝌆𝌆𝌆𝌆 HIGHLIGHTS 𝌆𝌆𝌆𝌆

- ◆ Sŏraksan National Park, the most scenic spot in South Korea
- ◆ Odaesan, home to South Korea's premier ski resort
- ◆ Samaksan, a weekend mountain retreat not too far from Seoul
- ◆ The coast south of Samch'ŏk, which has a scenic stretch of little-known beaches hidden in coves
- ◆ Ch'iaksan, a haven for technical rock climbers
- ◆ T'aebaeksan, one of Korea's three most sacred mountains to Shamanists

Ch'unch'ŏn Stadium and the express bus terminal.

Confucian School

Like virtually everywhere else in Korea, Ch'unch'ŏn has a Confucian School which taught the Chinese classics until the government examination system was abolished in 1894. It was originally built during the

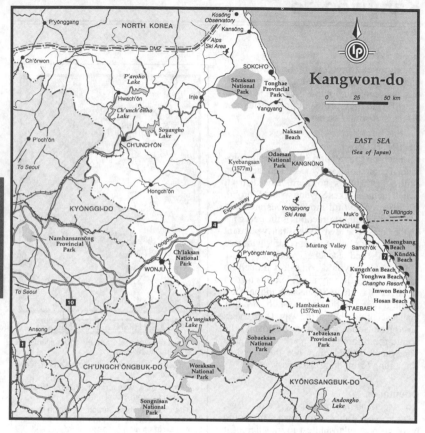

Chosŏn dynasty, but the Japanese burnt it and much of Korea down in 1592 during an invasion. It was rebuilt in 1594 and today serves as a shrine.

The Confucian School is just east of City Hall.

Ŭiam Lake

For some rest and relaxation you could do worse than spend a lazy afternoon rowing around Ŭiam Lake. Boats can be hired down by Ethiopia House, which is under the railway bridge from the inter-city bus terminal, and cost around W3000 per hour.

Kugok Waterfall

The waterfall is about 20 km south-west of the city and has the requisite cafes and snack bars.

The best way to get there is to take bus No 50 from the bus stop on the main street near the post office. These go every 40 minutes from 6.45 am to 6.15 pm; the trip takes about 20 minutes and the fare is W400. The last bus back from the waterfall is at 6.50 pm. After that you will have to take a taxi. The waterfall is the last stop for the bus so you can't go wrong. From where it drops you it's a 10 to 15-minute walk to the waterfall.

West of Ch'unch'ŏn on the other side of the lake is another waterfall, Tungson Pokpo.

Samaksan Mountain
For a panoramic view of Ch'unch'ŏn and the lake, you can make the steep climb up Samaksan. Take bus No 81 from near Ethiopia House in the direction of Seoul. After 15 minutes the bus crosses a bridge and turns right – the entrance to Samaksan is 50m down the road. Admission costs W1000.

The ascent is steep, but goes past a temple and is well worth it for the views. Down the other side you pass another temple and enter a beautiful narrow gorge. Follow it down to the road and catch a local bus (any will do) back upstream to Ch'unch'ŏn.

If you stay on the No 81 bus past Samaksan and get off at the last stop, you'll find the huge grave site of General Shin off to the right. About 1000 years ago, this general disguised himself as the king and as a consequence was killed by the enemy. The king had the tomb built out of gratitude for this act of sacrifice and loyalty.

Chŏngt'osa Temple
Slightly to the north-east of Camp Page is Chŏngt'osa temple, on the lower slopes of Pongŭisan. The temple is nestled between some trees and houses, and offers a good view of Ŭiam Lake. The caretakers live in the house just below and you have to go through their gateway to get to the temple.

Places to Stay – bottom end
The main place for cheap yŏinsuk is just to the north-east of the inter-city bus terminal, on the way to the post office. There are plenty of more expensive yŏgwan (W20,000) near the bus terminal itself; good ones include Ch'ŏnghwa-jang Yŏgwan and Yŏŭn-jang Yŏgwan.

The other option is out near Nam Ch'unch'ŏn railway station, though most travellers will find this location a little remote.

Places to Stay – top end
The Rio Hotel (☎ 562525; fax 558400), 300-3 Samch'on-dong, has 60 western-style and 18 Korean-style rooms. Korean-style costs W63,000 for two people. In the western rooms, doubles are W58,000 and suites can cost up to W125,000. Rated 2nd class.

The Ch'unch'ŏn Hotel (☎ 553300; fax 553372), 30-1 Nakwon-dong, is a recently remodelled place. Room rates for doubles are W38,000 to W50,000. Rated 2nd class.

The Sejong Hotel (☎ 521191; fax 543347), San 1, Pongui-dong, is considered the best in town. Doubles cost W40,000 while twins go for W45,000 to W55,000. Rated 1st class.

Places to Eat
Pyŏldang Makguksu (☎ 549603) is famous in Ch'unch'ŏn for having the best buckwheat noodles. There are many other fine dishes on the menu and the atmosphere is very pleasant.

Puil Shikdang boasts a quaint environment and marvellous Korean food. For some odd reason this place is always empty, but it's been around for years despite the lack of clientele.

Ethiopia House is more memorable for its fine lakeside aspect than for its food, but it's worth a try.

Entertainment
Ch'unch'ŏn's nightlife scene is decidedly small. About the most hip place in town is the Hard Rock Cafe (☎ 243-0516) which bears no relation to a cafe chain of the same name. There is a billiards table, and cocktails and imported beers for W4000. It's outside the north gate of Kangwon University, one alley east from the main road and slightly north of the gate.

Getting There & Away
Bus There are two terminals in Ch'unch'ŏn, one for express and the other for inter-city buses. Only a few buses depart from the express bus terminal, as follows:

Kwangju buses depart twice daily at 7 am and 5 pm. The fare is W17,500 (1st class) or W11,800 (2nd class) and the journey takes 5½ hours.
Pusan buses depart three times daily between 7 am and 5 pm. The fare is W21,900 (1st class) or W14,600 (2nd class) and the journey takes 6½ hours.

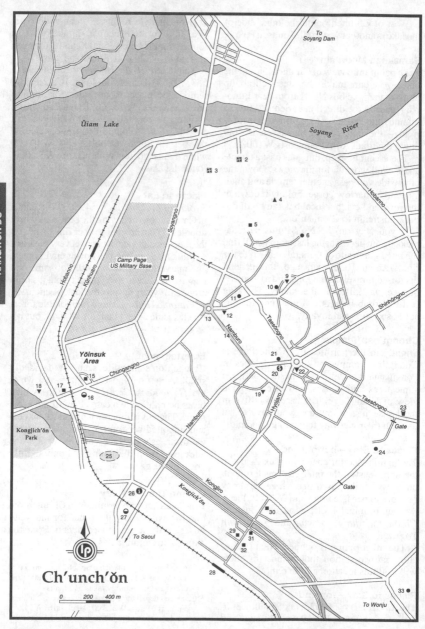

Ch'unch'ŏn

Ch'unch'ŏn 춘천

PLACES TO STAY
5 Sejong Hotel
세종호텔
15 Yŏŭn-jang Yŏgwan
여은장여관
17 Ch'ŏnghwa-jang Yŏgwan
청화장여관
29 P'yŏngnam Yŏinsuk
평남여인숙
30 Yunil-jang Yŏgwan
윤일장여관
31 Kangnam-jang Yŏgwan
강남장여관
32 Kŭmsu-jang Yŏgwan
금수장여관

PLACES TO EAT
9 Puil Shikdang
부일식당
12 Chester Fried Chicken
체스터 후라이드 치킨
18 Ethiopa House
에니오피아의집
19 Pyŏldang Makguksu
Restaurant
벌당막국수

22 Pelicana Fried Chicken
페리카나치킨

OTHER
1 Local Ferry Terminal
서면배터
2 Chŏngt'osa Temple
정토사
3 Sŏgwangsa Temple
석왕사
4 Pongŭisan (302m)
봉의산
6 Hallim University
한림대학교
7 Ch'unch'ŏn Railway
Station
춘천역
8 Central Post &
Telephone Office
우체국, 전화국
10 Confucian School
향교
11 City Hall
시청
13 Myŏngdong Shopping
Area
명동

14 Underground Arcade
지하상가
16 Inter-City Bus Terminal
시외버스터미널
20 Korea Exchange Bank &
Palace Buffet
외환은행, 파레스
21 Agricultural Cooperative
Supermarket
농협 수퍼마켓
23 Hard Rock Cafe
하드록까페
24 Kangwon University
강원대학교
25 Ch'unch'ŏn Stadium
춘천공설운동장
26 Folk Museum &
Tourist Information
향토박물관
27 Express Bus Terminal
고속버스터미널
28 Nam Ch'unch'ŏn Railway
Station
남춘전역
33 Ch'unch'ŏn National
Teachers' College
춘천교육대학

KANGWON-DO

Taegu buses depart three times daily between 6 am and 5 pm. The fare is W16,600 (1st class) or W11,100 (2nd class) and the journey takes 5½ hours.

The majority of departures and arrivals use the inter-city bus terminal. From here some of the places you can get to include:

Ch'ŏngju buses depart four times daily between 7.30 am and 3.55 pm. The fare is W9400 and the journey takes 3¾ hours.
Kangnŭng buses depart 26 times daily between 7 am and 6.30 pm. The fare is W8600 and the journey takes just over four hours.
Pusan buses depart six times daily between 7.40 am and 3.10 pm. The fare is W19,700 and the journey takes seven hours.
Seoul buses depart every 10 minutes from 5.15 am to 9.30 pm. The fare is W3900 and the journey takes 1¾ hours. These buses depart Seoul at Sangbong bus terminal, which is near Ch'ŏngnyangni subway station.
Sokch'o buses depart 17 times daily between 6 am and 6.50 pm. The fare is W8300 and the journey takes four hours. The buses follow a beautiful route via Inje.

Taegu buses depart 10 times daily between 7.10 am and 5.10 pm. The fare is W15,100 and the journey takes 5¾ hours.
Taejŏn buses depart 17 times daily between 6.55 am and 4.35 pm. The fare is W10,400 (there's another bus once a day for W8500) and the journey takes 5¾ hours.
Wonju buses depart every 10 minutes from 6.05 am to 9 pm. The fare is W4100 and the journey takes 1¾ hours.

Train Trains to Ch'unch'ŏn depart from Seoul's Ch'ŏngnyangni station at the terminus of subway line No 1. Unfortunately, Ch'unch'ŏn's two railway stations are both equally far from the inter-city bus terminal, so you'll need to deal with the city buses, take a taxi or walk about 1½ km. Please see the timetable appendix at the end of the book for the complete schedule from Seoul.

SOYANGHO LAKE
East and north-east of Ch'unch'ŏn there are two huge artificial lakes: Soyangho and

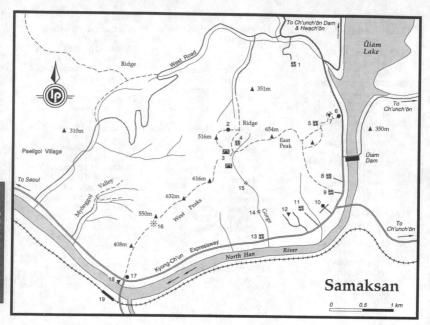

P'aroho. Soyangho is Korea's largest lake, and Soyang Dam (123m high) was the largest dam in Asia at the time of its completion in 1973. From December to March, the part of the lake near Kunchukgyo Bridge and Pupyong-ri is completely frozen and you can see people ice fishing here.

The lake is a favourite recreation spot for Koreans. Ferries run along it to Shinnam throughout the year and go the full 37 km to Inje when the water level allows. The level of water in Soyangho is lowered before the summer monsoon to accommodate the extra water which flows into it, so for part of the year the ferries only run from Ch'unch'ŏn to Shinnam. The boat-bus combination from Ch'unch'ŏn to Inje and the east coast via Shinnam is a popular way of travelling this part of Korea.

It's also possible to take these ferries if you're heading for Yanggu, but they will drop you at the Yanggu wharf and from there you must take a bus the remaining 13 km into Yanggu.

Ferries leave from Soyang Dam wall; to get there from Ch'unch'ŏn, take bus Nos 11 or 12 from the city centre; these run every 10 minutes and do the journey in 25 minutes. The buses will drop you at the top of the dam wall and from there it's a short walk down to the ferry piers. Only buses are allowed up to the top of the dam wall, so if you have your own transport you must leave it in the car park at the checkpoint and take a bus from there.

There are also speed boats for hire at the dam wall to take you to Ch'ongpyongsa, a Buddhist temple up in the hills north of the lake. These are six-seaters and the cost is shared by the number of people in the boat. Larger boats leave every 40 minutes and take 20 minutes to make the journey; they run from 9.30 am until 5.30 pm. From where the boat drops you it's a four km hike to the temple, so make sure you're wearing suitable footwear.

To Yanggu, there are slow ferries to Yanggu wharf at 9 and 11 am and 4 pm in the

Samaksan 삼악산

PLACES TO STAY
10 Wiam Mountain Hotel
위암산장

PLACES TO EAT
7 Rest House
휴게소
12 Valley of Restaurants
레스도랑
18 Kangchon House Restaurant
강촌의집

OTHER
1 Pongdŏksa Temple
봉너사
2 Rock Wall
산성
3 Picnic Areas
야영장
4 Hŭngguksa Temple
흥국사
5 Sangwonsa Temple
상원사
6 East Gate (Tioket Booth)
동문
8 Chŏngyangsa Temple
전안사
9 Tongch'ŏnsa Temple
동천사
11 Shinhŭngsa Temple
신흥사
13 Kŭmsŏnsa Temple & South Gate
금선사, 남문
14 Tŭngsŏn Waterfall
등선폭포
15 Pisŏn Waterfalls
비선폭포
16 Scenic Overlook
전망대
17 West Gate (No Tickets)
서문
19 Kangch'on Railway Station
강촌역

low season, and every hour from 8 am to 6 pm in the high season. In the opposite direction, they leave Yanggu wharf at 10.20 am, and 12.20 and 5.20 pm in the low season, and every hour from 8 am to 6.20 pm in the high season.

There are also fast boats to Yanggu wharf which leave at 9 and 11 am, 1 and 4 pm. In the opposite direction they leave at 10.20 am, 12.20, 2.20 and 5.20 pm.

Ferries to Shinnam leave at 11 am, 1 and 3 pm and return from Shinnam at 1.20, 2.30 and 4.30 pm.

P'AROHO LAKE

This large reservoir was created when the Hwach'on Dam was built in 1944. One of the fiercest battles of the Korean War was fought here and even today South Korean soldiers are a common sight in the area because North Korea is less than 50 km away. The lake shore is heavily forested and nearby attractions include the **P'astang Valley**, **Maitreya Rock**, and **Chikyon Falls**. The only yŏgwan are found in the nearby town of Hwach'on.

There are buses to Hwach'on from Seoul's Sangbong bus terminal every 40 minutes between 6.15 am and 6.40 pm, taking three hours for the trip. It's another 20 minutes from Hwach'on to P'aroho – only four buses run daily between the hours of 10 am and 5 40 pm. Two direct buses from Sanbong terminal to P'aroho depart daily at 7 am and 11 pm.

HONGCH'ŎN HOT SPRINGS

This new hot springs resort is 35 km southeast of Ch'unch'ŏn along highway 5. Pretty hills surround the site, which is on a bend in the river.

Currently there is one public bath inside a temporary but adequate building. It's not too popular yet, though a big resort complex is under construction and that will surely change. At present, the entrance fee is a very reasonable W1500.

Getting There & Away

Buses between Hongch'ŏn and Ch'unch'ŏn run every 10 minutes from 7.10 am to 10.20 pm, take 50 minutes for the journey and cost W1800. Buses also connect Hongch'ŏn to Sokch'o every 20 minutes from 6.40 am to 10.20 pm, take three hours and cost W6500.

You'll have to take a taxi from Hongch'ŏn to the springs or else face a 15-minute walk from where the local bus drops you off. It's likely that direct buses will become available when the resort complex is completed.

KANGWON-DO

SŎRAKSAN NATIONAL PARK

Top of the charts in the Korean national park scene, Sŏraksan ('snowy crags mountains') is spectacular. It's a land of high craggy peaks, lush forests, tremendous waterfalls, boulder-strewn white water rivers and old temples and hermitages whose roots go back to the Shilla era. It's at its colourful best in mid-October, when the leaves begin to change hue and the mountainsides are transformed into a riot of colour. Actually, a visit is rewarding at any time of the year. The nearby coast has some of Korea's best beaches.

Unfortunately, Sŏraksan's attractiveness is its biggest problem. It's easily Korea's most popular national park and on holidays you could be forgiven for thinking that they should have named this place Sŏraksan National Car Park. Even beyond the highways, the crunch of hikers can be oppressive. At times you will literally have to queue to get on the various trails leading to the waterfalls and peaks. Under the impact of so many feet, the park service has had no choice but to build concrete paths and steps – it's a wilderness with hand rails and public toilets.

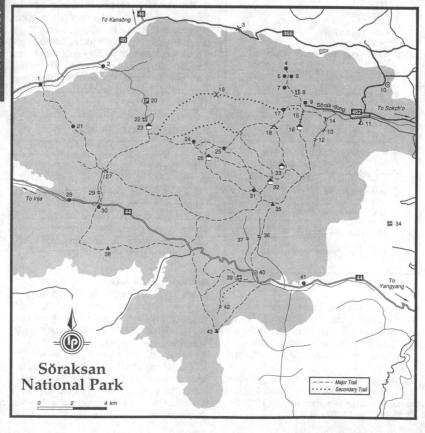

Sŏraksan
National Park

The peak season is summer, though the mid-October leaf-changing show also attracts busloads of weekend trippers. If you prefer to take in nature in more tranquil conditions then you have little choice but to visit during non-holiday times when the students are still in school. You can also escape some of the crowds by heading for remote trails far from the entrance roads.

Arriving at the park entrance to Sŏrakdong one might be a bit let down by the crowds, even during the cold season. But persevere! After about an hour of hiking up the paved trails the terrain suddenly gets rough and most of the day-trippers disappear.

The other drawback to visiting Sŏraksan during the peak season (July, August and mid-October) is that the cost of accommodation skyrockets and you'll find yourself having to pay up to three times the normal rates. Even a simple room in a minbak can cost you W30,000. Officially this is illegal since room rates are government-controlled, but it happens every year. Only in Sokch'o will you be able to find a room at a reasonable price and even then rates are still higher in summer.

A Sŏraksan Marathon is held every autumn (normally September). If you wish to participate, ask the KNTO in Seoul for details.

Information & Orientation

The park is divided into three sections: Outer Sŏrak, Inner Sŏrak and South Sŏrak. Inner Sŏrak is furthest inland and Outer Sŏrak is closest to the sea – the two are separated by a jagged ridge of mountains. South Sŏrak is divided from the rest of the park by highway 44.

KANGWON-DO

Sŏraksan National Park
설악산국립공원

PLACES TO STAY
9 Sŏrak Tourist Hotel
   설악관광호텔
11 Camping Ground
   야영지
16 Kwonkŭmsŏng
   권금성산장
23 Paekdam Hut
   백담산장
26 Surŏmdong Shelter
   수렴동대피소
32 Hŭiungak Shelter
   희운각 대피소
33 Yangpuk Hut
   양푹산장

OTHER
1 Namgyo
   남교
2 Yongdae-ri
   용대리
3 Mishinyŏng Pass
   미시령
4 Ulsanbawi Rock
   울산바위
5 Kyejo'am Hermitage
   계조암

6 Tottering Rock
   흔들바위
7 Naewon'am Hermitage
   내원암
8 Shinhŭngsa Temple
   신흥사
10 Ch'ŏksan Hot Spring
   적산온천
12 T'owangsŏng Waterfall
   토왕성폭포
13 Piryong Waterfall
   비룡폭포
14 Yukdam Waterfall
   육담폭포
15 Cable Car
   케이블카
17 Pisŏndae (Slick Rock)
   비선대
18 Kamganggul (Cave)
   감강굴
19 Chohangnyŏng Pass
   저항령
20 Parking Lot
   주차장
21 Shibisŏnnyŏt'ang Valley
   십이선녀탕 계곡
22 Paekdamsa Temple
   백담사
24 Yŏngshi'am Hermitage
   영시암
25 Ose'am Hermitage
   오세암

27 Taesŭngryŏng Pass
   대승련
28 Ongnyŏt'ang
   옥녀담
29 Taesŭng Waterfall
   대승폭포
30 Changsudae Rest Area
   장수대휴게소
31 Pongjŏng'am Hermitage
   봉정암
34 Yŏnghyŏlsa Temple
   영혈사
35 Taech'ŏngbong (1708m)
   대청봉
36 Sŏrak Waterfall
   설악폭포
37 Tokju Waterfall
   독주폭포
38 Karibong (1519m)
   가리봉
39 Sŏngguksa Temple
   성국사
40 Osaek Hot Springs
   오색약수
41 Mullebanga Rest Area
   물레방아 휴게소
42 Ongnyŏ Waterfall
   옥녀폭포
43 Chŏmbongsan (1424m)
   점봉산

Outer Sŏrak is the most accessible, and therefore the most crowded, area of the park. The chief town is Sŏrak-dong: a modern tourist resort in every respect, with deluxe hotels, restaurants and souvenir shops.

Inner Sŏrak is the least commercialised area of the park, though no doubt the day will come when the developers move in. There are three entrance points to Inner Sŏrak. Most accessible is Changsudae on highway 44. The second most popular entrance is by Paekdamsa, a remote temple area hidden in a large valley. The third entrance point is at Shibisŏnnyŏt'ang Valley, which is reached by a hiking trail running off highway 46 at the north-west corner of the park.

The main tourist spot in South Sŏrak is known as the Osaek ('five colours') area because of its proximity to Osaek Hot Springs – the major hot springs resort in the park. The Osaek area is also famous for impressive peaks, thick forests and numerous waterfalls.

The goal of many hikers is the highest peak in the park, Taech'ŏnbong (1708m). It can be most easily reached from either Sŏrak-dong or Osaek Springs – it's a very long way from Inner Sŏrak. However, even by the shortest route it's still a strenuous hike – start out early if you plan to get back before dark!

Serious hikers should pick up a good map of the park in Seoul from Chung'ang Map & Atlas Service or from various big city bookstores (see the Seoul chapter for details). No maps seem to be available for sale at the park, though there is a free tourist pamphlet which includes a basic hiking map.

What the maps don't show is that many of the trails are periodically closed. This usually occurs during spring, when the danger of forest fires is highest. There is also a campaign to close Sŏraksan's most popular trails for a full three years on a rotating basis. This is to allow the wilderness to recover from being trampled by the hordes of summer hikers.

If the weather is cold you'll almost certainly see kiosks at lower elevations renting strap-on ice cleats for about W1000. These are absolutely essential in the cold season because the higher elevations get icy and dangerously slippery. Don't be deceived just because the low end of the trail is initially easy – temperatures drop rapidly as you gain altitude.

The entry fee to Sŏraksan National Park varies according to where you enter: W1800 for Outer Sŏrak, W800 for Inner Sŏrak and W700 for South Sŏrak. There are discounts for students.

Kwonkŭmsŏng

Almost everyone begins their tour at Outer Sŏrak, and a good way to get a perspective on the place is to take the 1100m cable car to Kwonkŭmsŏng. It's good value at W1500 one way (W2800 return) and you'll be rewarded with amazing views if the weather is clear – expect mist to shroud the summit for much of the day. Cars go every 20 to 30 minutes. From where the cable car drops you it's a 10-minute walk to the summit.

This cable car gives immediate access to the trail which leads to Inner Sŏrak, but only if the trail is open. In fact, it has been closed numerous times because of landslides and there's no way to predict the situation. You'll easily discover if the trail is open or not: when it's closed, you will only be sold a return ticket on the cable car even if you request a one-way fare.

Tottering Rock

Known in Korean as *hŭndŭlbawi*, this is another of those 'must-see' spots in Outer Sŏrak. You'll see photographs of this large rock in just about all the tourist literature for the region. It's famous because it can be rocked to and fro by just one person. In fact, it's surprising it hasn't been rocked off its base by now since half the population of Korea must have had a go! There can't be a single family in the whole of Korea that has visited this place and not had their photograph taken pushing this rock. Almost adjacent to the rock is Kyejo'am, a small cave temple.

The hike up to the rock from Sŏrak-dong takes 1½ hours.

Shinhŭngsa Temple

Just to the west of downtown Sŏrak-dong is Shinhŭngsa, the oldest continually-used Zen meditation temple in Korea. It was first constructed in 653 AD, but later burnt to the ground; it was rebuilt in 1645 and burnt again in the Korean War, but has been nicely reconstructed. A giant sitting bronze Buddha was recently built between the temple and the main tourist plaza – rather garish!

Ulsanbawi Rock

From Tottering Rock you can climb another 20 minutes to Ulsanbawi Rock. More than just a rock, it's in fact a mountain (873m) with a huge granite cliff face which can be seen from many parts of the park. A steel staircase has been built up the cliff face. It's hard going, but the summit, which actually consists of six separate peaks, offers some spectacular views.

Yukdam, Piryong & T'owangsŏng Falls

Another short trip in the tourist zone of Outer Sŏrak is to the waterfalls. These are all along the same trail and the T'owangsŏng falls are particularly impressive. The trail is well marked and involves crossing many suspension bridges and climbing flights of steel stairs. There are various soft drink and snack stalls along the way. The most convenient entrance to this trail is across the bridge which spans the river a few hundred metres before you get to the cable car station.

Osaek Springs

This is in the southern part of the national park and approached by a different route (highway 44) from the one to Sŏrak-dong (highway 462). Osaek Springs boasts both a cold mineral spring (for drinking) and a hot spring (for soaking). The hot spring is arguably the best in Korea. There may be other spas in the country which claim to have fancier facilities (probably true) or better quality water (debatable), but none can match Osaek's combination of delightful hot springs and great scenic beauty. As elsewhere in Korea, the hot springs have been taken over by hotels and you won't find

natural pools in the wilderness for bathing. But there is little to complain about. The Greenyard Hotel is acknowledged as having the best bathing facilities and you do not need to be a hotel guest to use the pools (of course, you still must pay an admission fee).

There are also spectacular hiking opportunities in the vicinity, such as the climb up to Chŏmbongsan (1424m). Nearby waterfalls which can be reached on foot include Yongso and Sibi falls. The great attraction of the Osaek area is that you can hike to your heart's content and then collapse into a steaming pool of hot water. Not surprisingly, there are several restaurants here which lay on big meals of health food featuring wild mountain herbs (ask the price first!).

Treks

It's nearly impossible to describe all the various treks in the park, but the accompanying map should give you a good idea of the scope. Since it is limited by its small size and black and white print you shouldn't take the map as anything other than a rough guide. Detailed large-sized colour topographic maps are available (see the Information & Orientation section). The park service can tell you which trails are closed.

There are several shelters at various points along the hiking trails where you can stay overnight but most are closed in winter. Accommodation is on bare boards at about W3000 per night and you'd better have your own sleeping bag (blankets are occasionally available, but don't count on it). In most cases you'll have to do your own cooking too, so come prepared. A limited range of canned, bottled and packeted goods is for sale at higher than normal prices. Plenty of water is available at all the huts – either pump-fed or spring-fed. The shelters are marked on the tourist maps of the area.

Places to Stay – bottom end

For Outer Sŏrak, the centre for accommodation is Sŏrak-dong. For South Sŏrak, Osaek Springs has similar facilities plus there are minbak at Ongnyŏt'ang ('jade angel bath' – two km west of Changsudae on highway 44).

Tourist facilities are less developed at Inner Sŏrak but there is a shelter at Paekdamsa, and minbak at Yongdae-ri (the entrance road to Paekdamsa) and at Namgyo (the entrance point at the north-west corner of the park, near Shibisŏnnyŏt'ang Valley).

A minbak is the cheapest alternative but prices can be high: expect to pay around W15,000 per room on average out of season, but three times that amount during July and August. A platoon of ajummas plugging minbak tend to meet the buses, but if you don't find them just look for the signs – they are conspicuous enough.

For those with camping equipment, there's a huge camp site in both Sŏrak-dong and Osaek Springs; both have good facilities and cost W3000 to W6000 per site. In the high season it's like a rock festival site, with about a metre between tents. The camping grounds are open from 1 June to 31 December.

As an alternative to Sŏrak-dong, you could stay at the youth hostel or beach houses at Naksan nearby on the coast, or a yŏgwan or yŏinsuk in Sokch'o. Frequent local buses connect Naksan and Sokch'o with Sŏrak-dong.

Places to Stay – middle
Sŏrak-dong Despite the large number of hotels, the number of visitors is even larger so it's an hotelier's market in season – prices are high. For yŏgwan, expect to pay W25,000 minimum in the low season.

Most of these hotels are clustered together on the opposite side of the river from the main road and are adjacent to the camp site (that is, east of the park entrance). There's not a lot to choose between them – all are of much the same standard – but they're often booked out in advance during the high season. Get there early in the day if you want a sporting chance of finding a room at that time of year.

Some mid-range yŏgwan to consider include the following: *Haedong* (☎ 347791), *Ihwasan-jang* (☎ 347113), *Kinyang* (☎ 347178), *Korea* (☎ 347282), *Sansu-jang* (☎ 347167), *Sorim* (☎ 347171) and *Tongsan-jang* (☎ 347339).

Osaek Area There are several yŏgwan, all charging roughly W20,000 to W25,000 when it's not a weekend or holiday. The choice includes the *Hyundai Onch'on-jang* (☎ 672-1717), *Manggyong-jang* (☎ 672-8881), *Osaek Onch'on-jang* (☎ 672-3635), *Sorak Onch'on-jang* (☎ 672-2645), *Winners Onch'on-jang* (☎ 672-4111) and *Yongch'on-jang* (☎ 672-3791).

Places to Stay – top end
Sŏrak-dong There are several top-end hotels in Sŏrak-dong and one – the Sŏrak Park Hotel – distinguishes itself by having a casino. Add 20% tax and surcharge to the room rates of the following hotels:

Korea Condominium (☎ 347661; fax 348274), W86,000 for non-members with 30% discount on weekdays; rated deluxe.
New Sŏrak (☎ 347131; fax 347150), doubles W65,000 to W120,000, suites W135,000; rated 1st class.
Sŏrak Park (☎ 347711; fax 347732), twins W68,000 to W120,000, suites W180,000 to W1,200,000; rated deluxe class.
Sŏraksan (☎ 347101; fax 347106), Korean-style W35,000 (twins W45,000), suites W120,000; rated 3rd class.

Osaek Area There are fewer accommodation choices in South Sŏrak. The line-up of hotels includes:

Greenyard (☎ 672-8500; fax 672-0480), Osaek Hot Springs; W79,000 to W410,000
Nam Seoul (☎ 672-2101), W60,000 to W120,000

Getting There & Away
The main entry to Outer Sŏrak is via the tourist village of Sŏrak-dong, which is at the end of the road branching off from the coast road, about halfway between Naksan and Sokch'o. Frequent buses leave from both Yangyang, a few km south of Naksan, and from Sokch'o – every five to 10 minutes from around dawn to 9.30 pm. From Sokch'o catch bus No 7, which starts from the second-class bus terminal and passes by the Korean Air ticket office and the express bus terminal; the fare is W600 from Sokch'o to Sŏrak-dong. If you're not planning to stay in

Sŏrak-dong but only visiting for the day, get off the bus at the very last stop, about three km beyond the main part of the tourist village. This will save you a bit of walking. There are also direct buses to Seoul three times daily from Sorak-dong.

Local buses running between Yangyang and Inje stop at Osaek Springs in southern Sŏrak. The same buses also stop at Changsudae, which is the southern entry point for Inner Sŏrak, and at Ongnyŏt'ang, two km west of Changsudae (the trail head for climbing Karibong in southern Sŏrak).

You can also enter Inner Sŏrak via a narrow surfaced road that starts at Yongdac-ri and runs 8½ km up a lovely valley to the temple of Paekdamsa. Sokch'o-Ch'unch'ŏn long-distance buses follow highway 46 and stop at Yongdae-ri (8½ km from Paekdamsa) – tell the bus driver you want to get off at the '*Paekdamsa Ipgu*' (Paekdamsa entrance). Sokch'o-Ch'unch'ŏn buses also stop at Namgyo – tell the driver you want to get off at the *Shibisŏnnyŏt'ang Kyegok Ipgu* (Shibisŏnnyŏt'ang Valley entrance).

NAKSAN

Naksan is a pleasant but crowded summer resort by the sea, east of Sŏraksan.

Naksan Provincial Park

Naksan's major attractions are in Naksan Provincial Park just outside of town. This park is also known as Tonghae (East Sea) Provincial Park. Whatever you call it, it's famous for its temple, Naksansa, and its huge white statue of Kwanum, the Goddess of Mercy, which looks out to sea from atop a small, pine-covered rocky outcrop. The temple was built in 671 AD, rebuilt in 858 and burnt to the ground during the Korean War. It was reconstructed in 1953 along the original lines. The 15m-high statue of Kwanum is more recent and was completed only in 1977. The stone arch at the entrance to the temple with a pavilion built on top dates from 1465.

Entry to the park costs W1300 (W750 for students). It's a beautiful spot and very peaceful in the early mornings before the

tour groups arrive. It's also one of the very few Korean temples which overlooks the sea. Don't forget to visit the Uisang Pavilion which sits right on top of a cliff next to the ocean, shaded by an old (and ailing) pine tree.

Down below the temple is Naksan Beach, which is one of the best in the area, but unbelievably crowded during July and August.

Places to Stay

There's plenty of accommodation at Naksan, ranging from simple minbak to more expensive yŏgwan. As elsewhere around Sŏraksan, however, prices can triple in the high season.

A cheap alternative here is the *Naksan Youth Hostel* (☎ 672-3416). This is situated on the same hillock as Naksansa and there's a large sign on the coast road in English and Korean at the turn-off. Like other youth hostels in Korea this is a huge, plush place with its own restaurant, coffee shop, etc. There are five dormitory rooms here with varying numbers of beds costing W5000 a bed. They also have more expensive private rooms for W30,000 to W55,000. It's a spotless, beautifully furnished place where English is spoken. Booking in advance is essential in the high season.

The *Kwandong Yŏgwan* (☎ 672-2371) is also in the vicinity and costs W20,000 to W35,000.

If you want to rub elbows with the upper crust, the 1st class *Naksan Tourist Hotel* (☎ 672-4000; fax 742-9900) has rooms priced from W65,000 to W245,000.

Getting There & Away

All the local buses plying between Sokch'o and Yangyang pass Naksan and there's one every 10 to 15 minutes. Bus No 9 runs between Sokch'o and Yangyang and costs W600.

There are also nine direct buses daily between Naksan and Seoul's Sangbong bus terminal; they take 4¼ hours to make the journey and cost W10,500.

SOKCH'O

Sokch'o is a sprawling town north of Sŏraksan almost entirely surrounding a lagoon with a narrow outlet to the sea. Fishing used to be the major industry here, but tourism has proven far more lucrative and is now the No 1 cash cow. There's nothing particularly interesting about the town itself, but for the traveller it's a useful base for exploring Sŏraksan. Yŏgwan are everywhere and there is an abundance of places to eat. For the Koreans, the seafood restaurants are a major drawcard.

Ch'ŏksan Hot Springs

Just four km west of the lagoon is a major hot springs resort complex. It's actually just inside Sŏraksan National Park, though it's *not* at the main tourist village of Sŏrak-dong. You'd be hard pressed to find a better place to spend an evening in Sokch'o. These hot springs are extremely popular with hikers who come to soak away their aches and pains after a hard day scaling the heights.

Places to Stay – bottom end

The heavy volume of tourist traffic tends to keep accommodation pricey, though the tariff drops in the winter season.

Most of the cheap yŏinsuk are clustered around the inter-city bus terminal in the centre of town. The *Hyŏndae Yŏinsuk* and *Ŭngwang Yŏinsuk* are found here and you can expect to find doubles for around W15,000. About the cheapest yŏgwan in this area is *Ilhŭng-jang Yŏgwan* (☎ 333855) at W20,000, but next door is that fiendish creation of the devil, a karaoke lounge (though the noise volume is tolerable *if* your room faces the car park in the rear of the building).

The express bus terminal is five km further south, and you may actually find it more convenient to stay in this area as it's closer to Sŏraksan and the beaches. Here you'll find the *Myŏshi Yŏinsuk* where rooms are just W15,000. A woman hangs around here offering minbak.

More expensive yŏgwan can be found around the express bus terminal. Cheapest of the lot in this neighbourhood is *Usŏng-jang*

Yŏgwan, which costs W20,000, but the rooms are grotty and hardly worth it. Conditions are somewhat better at the nearby *Royal-jang Yŏgwan*, which costs W22,000. Across the street, the very plush *Tongsŏ-jang Yŏgwan* is also very friendly, but at W30,000 it stretches the definition of 'budget accommodation'.

Places to Stay – middle & top end

About one km north of the inter-city bus terminal you'll find the *Sorak Beach Hotel* (☎ 318700; fax 316758). Doubles are W65,000 and up.

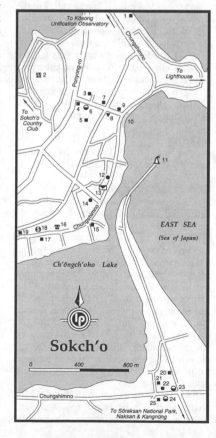

Getting There & Away

Air Korean Air is the only carrier flying to Sokch'o. There are several flights daily between Sokch'o and Seoul. There are also Sokch'o-Kwangju and Sokch'o-Taegu flights via Seoul.

Bus There are two bus stations in Sokch'o – the inter-city bus terminal in the centre of town and the express bus terminal far from the centre on the south-eastern side of the lagoon. Local bus No 2 connects the two terminals. Buses to Sŏrak-dong and Naksan start from the inter-city bus terminal, but can also be caught outside the express bus terminal. Neither of the terminals has lockers for storing gear.

From the express bus terminal buses depart to the following locations:

Seoul every 30 minutes from 6.30 am to 6.40 pm. The fare is W13,900 (1st class) or W9400 (2nd class) and the journey takes 5¼ hours.
Tong-Seoul (east Seoul) buses depart every 2½ hours from 7 am to 6.30 pm. The fare is the same as the preceding.

The inter-city bus terminal has frequent departures, including the following:

Ch'unch'ŏn buses depart 17 times daily from 6.40 am to 6.15 pm. The fare is W8300 and the journey takes two to four hours, depending on the route.
Kangnŭng buses depart every 25 minutes between 6.10 am and 8.30 pm. The fare is W3500 and the journey takes 1¼ hours.
Pusan buses depart 10 times daily between 6.40 am and 1.40 pm. The fare is W22,000 and the journey takes 7½ hours.
Seoul Sungbong buses depart 26 times daily between 6 am and 6 pm. The fare is W10,500 and the journey takes five hours.
T'aebaek buses depart eight times daily between 8.08 am and 6.12 pm. The fare is W8600 and the journey takes six hours.
Taegu buses depart 13 times daily between 6.10 am and 2.45 pm. The fare is W19,600 and the journey takes 8½ hours.
Tong-Seoul buses depart 11 times daily between 7.10 and 5.10 pm. The fare is W10,500 and the journey takes five hours.
Wonju buses depart four times daily between 7.45 am and 6.30 pm. The fare is W8800 and the journey takes four hours.

All the buses which depart from the inter-city bus terminal can also be picked up at Yangyang, south of Naksan.

Local buses to Sŏrak-dong and Naksan also start from the inter-city bus terminal, but you can easily pick them up anywhere along

---

Sokch'o 속초

PLACES TO STAY
1 Sŏrak Beach Hotel
  설악비치리조텔
3 Ilhŭng-jang Yŏgwan
  일흥장여관
4 Tonggyŏng-jang Yŏgwan
  동경장여관
5 Hyŏndae &
  Ŭngwang Yŏinsuk
  현대여인숙,
  은광여인숙
7 Shingwang-jang Yŏgwan
  신광장여관
9 Petel-jang Yŏgwan
  뼬엘장여관
15 Sokch'o Hotel
  호텔속초

17 Ŭnsŏng-jang Yŏgwan
  은성장여관
19 Nakch'ŏn-jang Yŏgwan
  낙천장여관
20 Usŏng-jang Yŏgwan
  우성장여관
21 Royal-jang Yŏgwan
  로얄장여관
22 Myŏshi Yŏinsuk
  머시여인숙
25 Tongsŏ-jang Yŏgwan
  동서장여관

OTHER
2 Pogwangsa Temple
  보광사
6 Inter-City Bus Terminal
  시외버스터미널
8 Pelicana Chicken
  페리카나치킨

10 Pagoda Park
  탑공원
11 Lighthouse
  등대
12 City Hall
  시청
13 Post Office
  우체국
14 Korean Air
  대한항공 매표소
16 Telephone Company
  전화국
18 Chohŭng Bank
  조흥은행
23 Express Bus Terminal
  고속버스터미널
24 Bus Stop
  (To Sŏraksan & Naksan)
  정류장 (설악산, 낙산)

their route – including outside the express bus terminal.

Boat Sokch'o is one of the places where you can catch a boat to the island of Ullŭngdo off the east coast. A timetable and other relevant details are provided in the Ullŭngdo section of the Kyŏngsangbuk-do chapter.

Getting Around
The Airport The airport is just south of town, about 15 to 20 minutes by bus. Buses to the airport run from both bus terminals and cost W400. Taxis charge W6000 from the inter-city bus terminal, or W5000 from the express bus terminal.

NORTH OF SOKCH'O
Beaches
There are a number of sheltered sandy coves and beaches north of Sokch'o. They're far less crowded than those to the south, though you're only allowed on them at certain points and at certain times of year. In the low season the endless razor wire fence which stretches along the whole of the east coast of Korea is firmly sealed and you'll be arrested (or, worse, shot at) if you venture onto the beaches.

The best of the coves are to be found at Taejin, north of Kansong. Taejin is a small fishing village which doubles as a laid-back resort during the summer months. You can rent a room at a minbak and there are a few relatively cheap yŏgwan with the usual facilities. The nearest sandy beach to Taejin is called Kŏjin Beach; it can be reached by bus from Sokch'o via Kansong. These buses leave every half hour from 6.30 am to 7.20 pm and take 70 minutes.

The most touristy beach north of Sokch'o is Songjiho.

Kosŏng Unification Observatory
On Korea's west coast there is a Unification Observatory (at Odusan, near P'anmunjŏm). Now the east coast has one too, but if you've already seen P'anmunjŏm don't be afraid to give this place a miss.

The Unification Hall to your left is sur-rounded by a sort of tourist village (souvenir shops, restaurants and the like) and vast car parks. There are plenty of souvenir Korean flags on sale and binoculars for voyeurs wanting a closer look at the forbidden North. Line up for the slide show which takes place every half hour or so and lasts about 20 minutes. As long as war doesn't break out, it's a good party.

Getting There & Away Local buses run between Sokch'o and the Unification Security Centre every five minutes between 6.30 am and 8.40 pm. The journey takes 1½ hours and costs W1500. From the Unification Security Centre, you have to take another bus for the 15-minute ride to the observatory. This is a tour of sorts costing W2000, and there are normally only five of these buses running daily between 9.40 am and 3 pm.

An alternative is to join an organised bus tour. A number of commercial tour companies in Sokch'o and Sŏrak-dong, including Sŏrak Tourist Company (☎ 328989), put on coach tours to the Observatory. The round trip costs W12,000 and takes about five hours.

The final option is to have your own set of wheels. The roads are excellent and the various obstacles designed to bring a rapid halt to any attempted invasion by North Korea are formidable. The guards will salute you as you pass through the last checkpoint.

ODAESAN NATIONAL PARK
Like Sŏraksan, Odaesan ('five platforms mountain') is another high-altitude massif where nature reigns supreme. There are excellent hiking possibilities and superb views. It also hosts one of Korea's foremost winter skiing resorts – at Yongpyong south of the park. Deep inside the western section of the park are two prominent Buddhist temples, Wolchŏngsa and Sangwonsa.

Pirobong (1563m) is the highest peak in the park. It's connected by hikable ridges to neighbouring peaks, such as Horyŏngbong (1563m) to the south and Sangwangbong (1493m) to the north. Both peaks are about an hour's walk from Pirobong.

As with Sŏraksan, the best times to visit are late spring (May and June) and early to mid-autumn (September and October), when the colours of the landscape are at their best. Entry to Odaesan National Park costs W1600.

Wolchŏngsa Temple

This temple was founded by the Zen Master Chajang-yulsa in 654 AD, during the reign of Queen Sondok of the Shilla dynasty, to enshrine relics of Sakyamuni (the historical Buddha). Over the next 1300 years or so it went through various trials and tribulations and was destroyed by fire on at least three occasions: notably in 1307, during the Koryŏ dynasty, and again during the Korean War in 1950. Yet today you would hardly suspect these disasters had ever happened. Reconstruction work was done in 1969 and again in 1996 – the result is simply magnificent and the internal painting of the main hall containing the Buddha image is a masterpiece of religious art. Not even in Tibet will you find anything quite as intricate, well-balanced and spellbinding as this.

Luckily, not everything was destroyed in the various disasters which have befallen this temple. Prominent remains from the Koryŏ era include a kneeling – and smiling! – stone Bodhisattva and a number of interesting stone stupas. There's also a unique, octagonal, nine-storeyed pagoda, dating from the same period, which is classified as a national treasure.

Sangwonsa Temple

Another 19 km beyond Wolchŏngsa at the end of a well-maintained road is Sangwonsa, the most popular trail head for hikers. From here you can ascend Pirobong and its two neighbouring peaks.

Aside from the hiking possibilities, the temple is a famous attraction in its own right. Like Wolchŏngsa, it has seen its share of hard times: it was last burnt to the ground in 1949 and reconstructed the following year. There's one gold-plated statue here plus four bronze ones. One image is of Mansuri (the Boddhisattva of Wisdom), but the temple's most famous possession is its bronze bell – one of the oldest and the second largest in

Korea (after the Emille Bell in the Kyŏngju National Museum). It was cast in 663, one year after construction of the temple commenced.

Sokŭmgang Valley

The most beautiful section of Odaesan park is hidden away in the north-east corner. Take a bus from Kangnŭng or Chinbu along national highway 6 and get off at Ch'wisŏn'am hermitage (by the Kŭmgamggyo Bridge). From there, catch another bus south on the small road to the car park with restaurants, yŏgwan and yŏinsuk (about four km) – hiking starts from here.

About an hour of walking brings you to a small temple, Kŭmgangsa. After that, the route is an orgy of waterfalls, cliffs and boulders (about two hours walking). Stunning! If you've still got the strength, it's another two km (two hours) hard climbing up to the summit of Noinbong (1338m). There is a hut just before the peak where you can sleep (and maybe eat, but bring food just in case). There's not much of a view from the peak itself because there are too many trees. From there you can head down by a different route to Chingogae Hut. Doing this whole walk in one day would really be a killer – day trippers should probably head back after the waterfall orgy.

Kyebangsan Mountain

Odaesan has some of the highest peaks in the nation, though they tend to be rounded rather than sharply spectacular, as in Sŏraksan. Just west of the park is Kyebangsan (1577m), one of South Korea's highest peaks. It was originally left out of the park because the military placed it off-limits to civilians, but this rule has now been relaxed and it is possible to walk to the summit.

A trail follows the ridge between Kyebangsan and Pirobong (the highest peak in Odaesan National Park). The walk is spectacular but it's 15 km – too far for a day's hike – with no established campgrounds in between.

Fortunately, there's a much easier route to the summit. You can approach Kyebangsan from the top of the 1100m pass on highway

Odaesan National Park

To
Kyebangsan

0   10   20 km

Hajinbu Village

31. From there it's only a net elevation gain of 477m, making it feasible for day hikers.

At the time of writing the area was closed to visitors because of a massive manhunt for three North Korean commandos who slipped into the south aboard a submarine (see the Kangnŭng section in this chapter for details).

Places to Stay
Back-country cooking and camping are currently prohibited. There are a number of yŏgwan and minbak, and a camping ground just a few km to the south of Wolchŏngsa. Further up the same road, about half way to Sangwonsa, the *Odaesan Hut* (☎ 326818) can accommodate 150 persons (bring your own sleeping bag) and there is an adjacent camping ground that charges W3000 for a site. This hut is the beginning of the trail for Horyŏngbong (1560m) and Tongdaesan (1433m) peaks.

On another highway to the south-east is the *Chingogae Hut* (☎ 329755) but ring up to make sure it isn't full.

Getting There & Away
A trip to Odaesan starts in Kangnŭng and there's a choice of direct buses or local buses

Odaesan National Park
오대산국립공원

PLACES TO STAY
5 Odaesan Hut
   오대산 산장
6 Camping Ground
   아영지
8 Chingogae Hut
   진고개 산장
10 Camping Ground
   아영지
12 Noinbong Hut
   노인봉산장

OTHER
1 Turobong (1422m)
   두로봉
2 Pirobong (1563m)
   비로봉

3 Horyŏngbong (1560m)
   호령봉
4 Sangwonsa Temple
   상원사
7 Tongdaesan (1433m)
   동대산
9 Wolchŏngsa Temple
   월정사
11 Noinbong (1338m)
   노인봉
13 Nagyŏng Waterfall
   나영폭포
14 Iryŏn Waterfall
   이련폭포
15 Ch'ŏngshimdae Waterfall
   청심대폭포
16 Kŭmgangsa Temple
   금강사
17 Bus Stop
   전류잘

18 Ch'ungmu Waterfall
   중무폭포
19 Ch'wisŏn'am Hermitage
   취선암
20 Maebong (1173m)
   매봉
21 Koshinbong (1131m)
   곤신봉
22 Pohyŏngsa Temple
   보형사
23 Pogwangsa Temple
   보광사
24 Taegwanryŏng Rest Area
   대관령휴게소
25 Hoenggyŏ Bus Stop
   횡거정류장
26 Yongpyŏng Ski Resort
   용평스키산

which involve a change at Chinbu, just off the expressway.

There are direct buses from Kangnŭng to Wolchŏngsa every hour from 6.10 am to 6.45 pm for most of the year (less in winter) and the journey takes about 1½ hours. These buses will have Wolchŏngsa on their destination indicator.

Alternatively, take a bus from Kangnŭng to Chinbu (this is what they will have on the destination indicator). These buses leave every five minutes from the inter-city bus terminal. At Chinbu change to a local bus, which will have Sangwonsa on the destination indicator. There are seven of these buses per day (fewer in winter) and the last bus from Sangwonsa to Chinbu runs at 5.30 pm. This journey takes about half an hour, and the ride between Wolchŏngsa and Sangwonsa takes a further 20 to 25 minutes. As their direction indicates, they terminate at Sangwonsa. There's no need to get off the bus at the entrance to the national park to pay the entrance fee – an official will get on the bus to sell you a ticket.

KANGNŬNG
Kangnŭng is the largest city on the north-east coast of Korea (population 225,000); it's

worth an overnight stay if you have an interest in Confucianism but is otherwise unremarkable. Most travellers simply pass through it en route to somewhere else, such as Sŏraksan, Odaesan or points further south.

Kangnŭng made world headlines in September 1996 when a North Korean spy submarine carrying 26 commandos beached here. One commando was captured, 11 others died in gun battles with South Korean troops, 11 are known to have committed suicide to avoid capture and (at the time of writing) three still remain unaccounted for. Several South Korean troops died in these gun battles too, and the North Koreans also murdered at least three civilian hikers in the Kyebangsan area near Odaesan National Park.

After five days of silence on the issue, North Korea suddenly demanded return of the submarine, explaining that it had drifted across the border because of engine trouble while on a routine training mission. This explanation didn't cut much ice with the South Koreans as the search for the commandos around Kyebangsan continued. Although the North eventually apologised, relations between the two Koreas reached an all-time low.

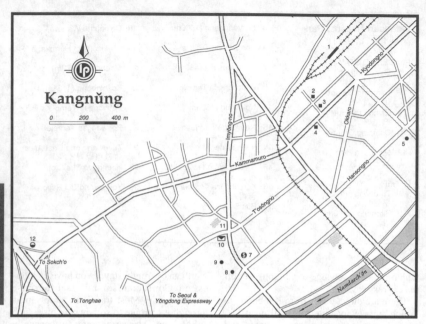

Information

The Kangnŭng City Tourism Bureau (☎ 436487) has a branch in the Kangnŭng bus terminal.

Tano Festival

Probably the only time you would come to Kangnŭng for its own sake is to see Tano, the Shamanist festival which takes the city by storm for a whole week from the 5th day of the 5th lunar month (for exact dates, see the 'Public Holidays & Special Events' section in the Facts for the Visitor chapter).

People flock to the city from all over the surrounding area for this festival and a tent city rises to accommodate them. Circus and carnival acts, folk operas, farmers' bands and all manner of stalls and hawkers create an atmosphere redolent of a medieval fair. It's also the nearest you'll get to seeing aspects of Korea's original religion unless you have contacts who can put you in touch with its practitioners.

Ojuk'ŏn Confucian Shrine

About 3½ km north of Kangnŭng, this is the birthplace of Shin Saimdang (1504-51) and her son, Yi Yul-Gok (or Yi-Yi) (1536-84). Shin Saimdang was an accomplished poet and artist while Yi Yul-Gok was one of the most outstanding Confucian scholars of the Chosŏn period.

Yi Yul-Gok learned the classics from his mother while very young and subsequently won first prize in the state examinations for prospective government officials in 1564. After that he served in various government posts. Along with his contemporary, Yi Toegye, another famous Confucian scholar, he wielded great influence among the various political factions at the royal court and was instrumental in advising the king to raise an army of 100,000 men to prepare for a possible invasion by Japan. His advice was tragically ignored, since only eight years after he died the Japanese did indeed invade and the peninsula was devastated.

Kangnŭng 강릉

1 Railway Station
   강릉역
2 Chongno-jang & Kŭraendŭ-jang Yŏgwans
   종로장여관, 그랜드장여관
3 Pando-jang & Uri-jang Yŏgwans
   반도장여관, 우리장여관
4 Hwanghae Yŏgwan
   한해여관
5 Yongjigak Pavilion
   농지각
6 Chung'ang Market
   중앙시장
7 Bank of Korea
   한국은행
8 City Hall
   시청
9 Kaoksamun (Gate)
   객사문
10 Central Post & Telephone Office
   우체국, 전화국
11 Sŏbu Market
   서부시장
12 Bus Terminal
   고속/시외버스터미널

The Yulgok-jae Festival is held annually here on 26 October, when traditional rituals are enacted and classical Korean music is played.

A small museum forms part of the complex and houses examples of painting, calligraphy and embroidery executed by Shin Saimdang and Yi Yul-Gok.

Local buses (Nos 1, 2 and 3) will take you to the shrine from Kangnŭng city centre. The shrine is open daily from 9 am to 5 pm.

Kaeksamun Gate

This gateway stands at the back of the main post office, close to the telephone and telegraph office, and has been declared a national treasure. The gate is all that remains of an official government inn which was built in 936, in reign of King Taejo during the Koryŏ dynasty. Known as Imyonggwan, the inn was eventually converted into an elementary school in 1929 and later demolished by Japanese occupation authorities. The gateway is a fine example of Koryŏ architecture, with tapered wooden columns and an unusual gabled roof instead of the normal hipped roof. It's also one of the few such structures from that period which was never painted.

Kyŏngp'o Provincial Park

This is another beachside park, but it's very developed, commercialised and touristy. It's six km north of Kangnŭng and can be reached by city bus.

Places to Stay

In 1996 Kangnŭng's bus terminal moved to a new facility far from the centre. As a result there are not as yet any yŏgwan near the terminal, though no doubt this will change. Almost all the hotels and guesthouses are to be found in the vicinity of the defunct bus terminals (which are not far from the railway station). Some of the yŏgwan in this neighbourhood include the *Chongno-jang*, *Kŭraendŭ-jang*, *Pando-jang*, *Uri-jang* and *Hwanghae*. Expect to pay at least W20,000 in all these places.

Getting There & Away

Air Asiana Airlines and Korean Air both have flights connecting Kangnŭng to Seoul and Pusan.

Bus Kangnŭng's express bus terminal and inter-city bus terminal are both in the same building, a shiny new facility near the freeway entrance. As yet there are no lockers in this huge building, an oversight which will hopefully be corrected soon.

Express buses which depart from this terminal include the following:

Seoul buses depart every 10 to 20 minutes between 6 am and 7.40 pm. The fare is W10,900 (1st class) or W7400 (2nd class) and the journey takes 3¾ hours.
Taejŏn buses depart 10 times daily between 8 am and 6.40 pm. The fare is W12,800 (1st class) or W8600 (2nd class) and the journey takes four hours.
Tong-Seoul (east Seoul) buses depart every 45 minutes between 6.30 am and 7.40 pm. The fare is W10,900 (1st class) or W7400 (2nd class) and the journey takes 3½ hours.
Wonju buses depart every 1¼ hours from 6.30 am to 6.20 pm. The fare is W5800 (1st class) or W4000 (2nd class) and the journey takes 2¼ hours.

Inter-city buses which depart from this terminal go to the following destinations:

Ch'unch'ŏn buses depart every 30 minutes from 6.30 am to 6 pm. These cost W8600 and take four hours.
Odaesan (buses terminate at Wolchŏngsa) leave every hour between 6.10 am and 6.45 pm; the journey takes 1½hours.
Pusan non-stop express buses depart every hour from 8.10 am to 4 pm, costing W16,500 and taking six hours. There are also slightly slower inter-city buses on this route which stop at east coast towns such as Uljin, P'ohang and Kyŏngju. These buses leave every hour from 6.20 am to 2.58 pm. The fare is the same as the express buses to Pusan, but they take 7½ hours.
Seoul buses depart every 30 minutes from 8.45 am to 5.30 pm, costing W7400 to W9900 and taking four hours.
Sokch'o buses depart every 10 minutes from 5.40 am to 9.30 pm. These cost W3500 and take 1½ hours.
T'aebaek buses depart every hour between 6 am and 2.50 pm. The fare is W5500 and the journey takes four hours.
Wonju buses depart every 30 minutes between 6.20 am and 7.10 pm. The fare is W5300 and the journey takes 2½ hours.

Train T'ong-il class trains depart Seoul's Ch'ŏngnyangni station twice daily at 10 am and 11 pm and the journey takes seven hours.

Getting Around
The Airport Taxis to the airport take 15 minutes and cost W5000. Buses take up to 30 minutes and cost either W400 (standing bus) or W1000 (seat bus).

TONGHAE
This small and pleasant coastal city (population 100,000) is mostly visited by travellers planning to catch a boat to Ullŭngdo. The nearby Murŭng Valley is also very much worth a visit.

Places to Stay
Tonghae's guesthouses are fairly expensive, at least during the summer tourist season: it's hard to find anything for under W30,000.

There are a few yŏgwan right in the centre of town near the Hanil Bank and Muk'o railway station, but it's a fairly crowded and noisy area. It's much more pleasant to stay

out near the express bus terminal, where you'll find plenty of yŏgwan. Right next to the terminal is *Tongho-jang Yŏgwan* (☎ 314310), which is quiet and relatively cheap (W30,000) by Tonghae's standards.

Getting There & Away
Bus Tonghae sits on the main east coast highway, so bus connections are fairly good. Places you can get to by express bus include:

Tonghae 동해

PLACES TO STAY
2 Haengbok Yŏgwan
   행복여관
8 Ch'ŏngwon-jang & Royal-jang Yŏgwan
   청원장여관, 로얄장여관
9 Hansŏng Yŏgwan
   한성여관
11 Taemyŏng-jang Yŏgwan
   대명장여관
13 Tongho-jang Yŏgwan
   동호장여관
15 Tongch'ŏn-jang Yŏgwan
   동천장여관
17 New Tonghae Tourist Hotel
   뉴동해관광호텔

OTHER
1 Taewonsa Temple
   대원사
3 Muk'o Post Office
   묵호 우체국
4 Hanil Bank
   한일은행
5 Muk'o Railway Station
   묵호역
6 Muk'o Ferry Terminal
   묵호여객선터미널
7 Muk'o Port Station (Freight Only)
   묵호항역
10 Telephone Office
   전화국
12 Express Bus Terminal
   동부고속버스터미널
14 Tonghae Hospital
   동해병원
16 Inter-City Bus Terminal
   시외버스터미널
18 City Hall
   시청
19 Kamch'usa Temple
   감추사

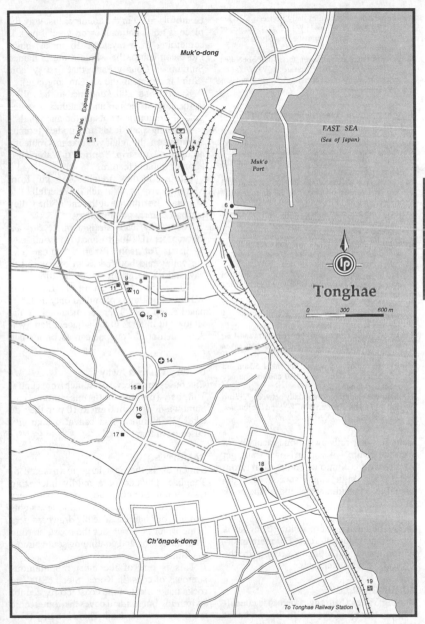

Muk'o-dong

Tonghae Expressway

EAST SEA
(Sea of Japan)

Muk'o
Port

Tonghae

0   300   600 m

Ch'ŏngok-dong

To Tonghae Railway Station

Seoul buses depart 22 times daily between 6.30 am and 7.10 pm. The fare is W12,700 (1st class) or W8600 (2nd class) and the journey takes 4½ hours.

Tong-Seoul buses depart seven times daily between 7.40 am and 6.50 pm. The fare is W12,700 (1st class) or W8600 (2nd class) and the journey takes 4¼ hours.

Tonghae is connected by inter-city bus to the following places:

Kangnŭng buses depart every 10 minutes from 6.15 am to 10.20 pm. The fare is W1700 and the journey takes 40 minutes.

Pusan buses run 15 times daily between 7 am and 3.44 pm. The fare is W14,800 and the journey takes 6½ hours.

Samch'ŏk buses depart every 10 minutes between 6 am and 10.20 pm. The fare is W700 and the journey takes 20 minutes.

Seoul buses depart 13 times daily between 8.29 am and 5.52 pm. The fare is W8600 and the journey takes about five hours.

Sokch'o buses depart 12 times daily between 8.10 am and 7.40 pm. The fare is W5200 and the journey takes 2½ hours.

T'aebaek buses depart seven times daily between 7.55 am and 7.10 pm. The fare is W3500 and the journey takes 3½ hours.

Taegu buses run 28 times daily between 6 am and 4.50 pm. The fare is W15,800 and the journey takes 6½ hours.

Ulsan buses depart only twice daily – at 11.52 am and 2.08 pm. The fare is W14,000 and the journey takes 3⅓ hours.

Wonju buses depart three times daily between 7.57 am and 10.56 am. The fare is W7000 and the journey takes 3½ hours.

Train Tonghae railway station is actually far from the centre – if you arrive by train, get off at Muk'o station. Trains start from Seoul's Ch'ŏngnyangni station. See the timetable appendix at the end of the book for details.

Ferry The main point of visiting Tonghae is to catch the Ullŭngdo ferry. For more information see the Ullŭngdo section in the Kyŏngsangbuk-do chapter.

MURŬNG VALLEY

Murŭng Valley (Murŭng Kyegok) is considered by many Koreans to be *the* most

beautiful valley in the country! Just why the place is not a national or provincial park is something of a mystery. To make things more confusing, the whole thing is named Suinumsan County Park (that first syllable 'Suin' is unique in the Korean language).

Kwanŭmsa, at the entrance to the valley, is the largest temple and features a seated golden Buddha just outside the main hall.

A hiking path leads to another temple, **Samhwasa**, though if you take this route it's an up and back trip. **Yongch'u Waterfall** is another notable feature.

Murŭng Valley stretches 2½ km from Murungbansok to Yongch'u Waterfall. The **Mirukam hermitage** at the end of the valley has particularly good scenery.

The valley leads straight up to a peak, **Chŏngoksan** (1404m), and to the south-east of that is **Tut'asan** (1353m). You can hike the valley and both peaks in one very full day, and it's definitely worth the effort.

Admission to Murŭng Valley costs W1000. Cooking is permitted only in designated camp sites. There are no hotels in the valley, but minbak in the adjacent Samhwadong district of Tonghae can accommodate you.

Getting There & Away

City buses run every 10 minutes from central Tonghae (passing both bus stations) to Samhwa-dong from 6 am to 10 pm; the ride takes 25 minutes. You can also take city buses from Samch'ŏk.

SAMCH'ŎK

Samch'ŏk is the next large town south of Tonghae. Outside of a mildly interesting Confucian School and the Chosŏn era Chsuksŏru Pavilion, the town has few sights to hold your interest. The big drawcard here is the beaches which dot the coast, starting from Samch'ŏk and continuing south almost to Uljin.

This is one of the most mountainous stretches of coast in Korea. Steep cliffs and rocks make most of the coast too rugged for swimming but in small coves there are scenic stretches of white sand. There is a tiny town

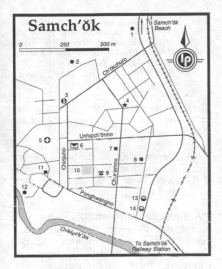

Samch'ŏk

0   250   500 m

To Samch'ŏk Beach

Ch'ŏkchuro

Ushipch'ŏnno

Chinjuro

Churanno

Ponghwangno

Oshipch'ŏn

To Samch'ŏk Railway Station

adjacent to most beaches where you can find meals and a minbak if you wish to spend the night.

Even if you don't care to swim, this bit of coastline should not be missed. Highway 7 hugs the coastline and makes for an interesting drive. Ideally, you would have your own transport, stopping off at any scenic coves which look appealing. There are local buses for those who don't have their own wheels, but sometimes there's a long wait before one comes by. A 10-speed (or better) bicycle would be a great way to travel, but be careful on the narrow, twisting highway. Traffic is not heavy here (except on holidays), but it only takes one cement truck to ruin your whole day. Sadly, nobody seems to rent out bicycles so you'll need to bring your own. For the less fit, a motorbike would no doubt be great fun. Hitchhiking is another possibility as long as you can accept the risks it entails.

A run down of the beaches from north to south follows. Bear in mind that there are more beaches than those listed here – not all of them have a name, nor are they all developed.

Samch'ŏk Beach

This beach is two km north of the town centre; although not the prettiest it's the most accessible. You could walk there if you're ambitious, otherwise simply take a taxi.

Maengbang Beach

About 12 km down the coast from Samch'ŏk is Maengbang Beach, one of the more popular spots. The water is very shallow here, making it a big hit with families with young children. There is also a small freshwater creek nearby which is OK for light swimming. Local buses from Samch'ŏk run about once every 20 minutes between 5.50 am and 9.10 pm.

Kŭndŏk Beach

Just south of Maengbang, Kŭndŏk Beach is where highway 7 swings inland. Getting to the beach requires a short drive or walk from the main road. The scenery is terrific.

KANGWON-DO

Kungch'on Beach

One of the larger developments on this section of coast, Kungch'on is trying to become a classy resort. So far, it's got a long way to go. The resort is about 20 km down the coast from Samch'ŏk. Minbak are available. There are 15 buses daily to Kungch'on from Samch'ŏk, taking 40 minutes to make the journey.

Yonghwa Beach

This beach 25 km south of Samch'ŏk has good sand and a background of pine trees. The beach is 800m long and there is a freshwater stream here. There are plenty of minbak and seafood is a local speciality.

Changho Resort

This is the most developed of the beach areas along this stretch of coastline. The beach is crescent-shaped and is well protected from the wind.

Imwon Beach

This small beach is only 200m long, but has a dramatic setting in a cliff-lined cove. Hwabanggul sea cave, Sobongsanjong Pavilion and a freshwater creek are nearby; there are some minbak in the vicinity.

Hosan Beach

The southernmost beach in Kangwon province, Hosan is about one km in length and has good white sand. There is a pine tree grove next to the beach and camping in the area is popular.

Places to Stay

Obviously, it's much more interesting to stay in a minbak out by the beach. But there are plenty of yŏgwan in Samch'ŏk within easy walking distance of the bus station. The *Sambo-jang* (☎ 731918), *Sanho-jang* and *Taedong-jang Yŏgwan* all charge pretty much the same – about W20,000 for a room.

Getting There & Away

Bus Departures from Samch'ŏk's express bus terminal include the following destinations:

Seoul buses depart every 1½ hours between 6.30 am and 6.50 pm. The fare is W13,300 (1st class) and W9000 (2nd class) and the journey takes five hours.

Tong-Seoul buses depart every 2½ hours between 6.30 am and 6.40 pm. The fare is W13,300 (1st class) and W9000 (2nd class) and the journey takes 4½ hours.

The inter-city bus schedule is almost identical to Tonghae's. See the Tonghae section for details.

Train The schedule is the same as for Tonghae, but with trains from Seoul arriving in Samch'ŏk about 15 minutes earlier than they do in Tonghae.

T'AEBAEKSAN PROVINCIAL PARK

At 1568m T'aebaeksan ('big white mountain') is the sixth highest mountain in South Korea. The mountain actually consists of two peaks, 1568m-high Changgunbong and its neighbour, Munsubong (1546m).

T'aebaeksan is also one of Korea's three most sacred mountains to Shamanists. On the summit is the Ch'onjedan Altar, where religious ceremonies are occasionally held.

Not surprisingly, the park has a number of temples, including Manggyongsa, Paektansa, Yuilsa and Mandoksa.

Tanggol – situated in a large valley – is the park's main entrance and also a magnet for pilgrims. There is a shrine here called Tan'gunsong which is dedicated to Tan-gun, the mythical progenitor of the Korean race.

Places to Stay

There are many minbak inside the park at Tanggol. For yŏgwan and hotels, you'll have to stay in the town of T'aebaek.

Getting There & Away

Bus The town of T'aebaek (population 105,000) is 15-20 minutes by bus from the national park. These run every 10 minutes between 6.20 am and 11 pm. Many of these buses are marked 'Tanggol' or 'Sododanggol' (the small town at the entrance to the park).

T'aebaek is connected to the outside world with bus services to many places, including:

CHRIS TAYLOR

CHRIS TAYLOR

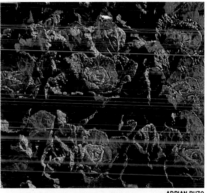

ADRIAN BUZO

CHRIS TAYLOR

MASON FLORENCE

Food
A: Corn cobs, Korean Folk Village
B: Fresh from the sea, Jinbu, Odaesan

C: Red chillis
E: Green lettuce
D: Orange mandarins

ROBERT STOREY

ADRIAN BUZO

ROBERT STOREY

碑詩圃蓮

물 네 방 아

ROBERT STOREY

A		C
B		D

Art

A: Lick the dirt, Taehangno 'art street', Seoul

B: Bas-relief of peasant

C: Traditional painting

D: Poem in stone, Kyŏngbokkung Palace

CHRIS TAYLOR

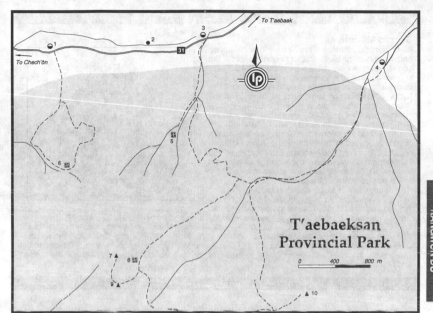

T'aebaeksan Provincial Park
태백신도립공원

1   Bus Stop
    정류장
2   Chŏngji-ri
    정기리
3   Bus Stop
    정류장
4   Bus Stop
    정류장
5   Paektansa Temple
    백단사
6   Yuilsa Temple
    유일사
7   T'aebaeksan (1567m)
    태백산
8   Manggyŏngsa Temple
    망경사
9   Ch'ŏnjedan (1561m)
    전제단
10 Munsubong (1517m)
    문수봉

Andong buses depart three times daily between 10.40 am and 4 pm. The fare is W7400 and the journey takes 2¾ hours.

Ch'unch'ŏn buses depart four times daily between 6.20 am and 2.30 pm. The fare is W12,200 and the journey takes 5¾ hours.

Kangnŭng buses depart 21 times daily between 5.40 am and 7.30 pm. The fare is W5500 and the journey takes 2½ hours.

P'ohang buses depart three times daily between 9.55 am and 11.55 am. The fare is W10,800 and the journey takes five hours.

Pusan buses depart three times daily between 6.30 am and 1.25 pm. The fare is W15,800 and the journey takes seven hours.

Seoul buses depart 20 times daily between 6 am and 5.20 pm. The fare is W11,000 and the journey takes 5½ hours.

Sokch'o buses depart eight times daily between 7.40 am and 4.40 pm. The fare is W8600 and the journey takes 4¼ hours.

Taegu buses depart 23 times daily between 7.30 am and 6.55 pm. The fare is W11,300 and the journey takes 5½ hours.

Train Trains depart from Ch'ŏngnyangni

Sacred Mountains

All of Korea's mountains are sacred in some sense and each has its own *sanshin* (mountain god). But some mountains are more sacred than others.

Those with major temples are more sacred to the Buddhists. Good examples are Namsan, south of Kyŏngju, and Palgongsan, north of Taegu. For the Shamanists, Paekdusan in North Korea is now number one, not only because of its large volcanic crater-lake and the fantastic legend of Tan-gun (see the Paekdusan section in the North Korea chapter), but also because of the reunification issue. Hallasan on Cheju is considered by some as an opposite-end counterpart to Paekdusan because it's also an old volcano with a (small) lake, and also because Cheju has a rich tradition of Shamanism.

T'aebaeksan in south-east Kangwon-do is also holy to Shamanists; it's the temporary home for many of them and an alternative site for the Tan-gun legend. Other mountains famous for Shamanism, magical events and powerful sanshins are: Myohyangsan and Kŭmgangsan in North Korea; Chirisan at the intersection of three southern provinces; Kyeryongsan west of Taejŏn; Moaksan in Chŏllabuk-do; Mudŭngsan outside Kwangju; Inwangsan in west-central Seoul; Puk'ansan to the north of Seoul; and Manisan on Kanghwa Island (the third major Tan-gun-worship site). All are important to Buddhists too, except Hallasan, Mudŭngsan, Inwangsan and Manisan. ■

---

railway station in Seoul. See the timetable appendix at the end of the book.

WONJU

This nondescript town (population 225,000) is mainly of interest to travellers wanting to visit nearby Ch'iaksan National Park.

Getting There & Away

Express buses depart Wonju for the following destinations:

Kangnŭng buses depart every 50 minutes between 6.30 am and 7 pm. The fare is W5800 (1st class) or W4000 (2nd class) and the journey takes 2½ hours.

Seoul buses depart every 10 to 15 minutes between 6 am and 9 pm. The fare is W5500 (1st class) or W3800 (2nd class) and the journey takes 1¾ hours.

Inter-city buses departing Wonju go to a number of destinations, including the following:

Andong buses depart seven times daily between 8.28 am and 6 pm. The fare is W8200 and the journey takes 3¼ hours.

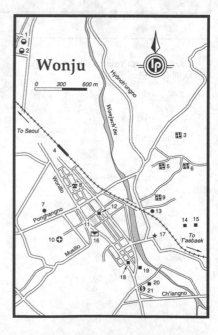

Ch'ŏngju buses depart 33 times daily between 6.45 am and 7.30 pm. The fare is W5200 and the journey takes 3¼ hours.

Ch'unch'ŏn buses depart 84 times daily between 6 am and 9.10 pm. The fare is W3700 and the journey takes 2¼ hours (or 1½ hours for the express).

Kangnŭng buses depart 29 times daily between 6 am and 7.30 pm. The fare is W4000 and the journey takes 2¾ hours.

Pusan buses depart six times daily between 9.40 am and 5.10 pm. The fare is W15,600 and the journey takes five hours.

Seoul buses depart around twice hourly between 6.20 am and 9.10 pm. The fare is W3800 and the journey takes 1¾ hours.

T'aebaek buses depart 25 times daily between 7 am and 8.20 pm. The fare is W8300 and the journey takes four hours.

Taegu buses depart eight times daily between 9.10 am and 7.10 pm. The fare is W11,000 and the journey takes 3½ hours.

Taejŏn buses depart every 30 minutes from 9.50 am to 6.30 pm. The fare is W6300 and the journey takes three hours.

Sokch'o buses depart four times daily between 5.40 am and 4.27 pm. The fare is W8800 and the journey takes four hours.

Train Trains to Wonju depart from Seoul's Ch'ŏngnyangni railway station. See the timetable appendix at the end of the book.

CH'IAKSAN NATIONAL PARK

Ch'iaksan ('magpie crags mountains') is just east of Wŏnju. The highest peak is Pirobong (1288m), but there are a number of other high peaks (over 1000m) along a north-south axis. They include Unbong, Maehwabong, Namdaebong and Hyangnobong. Ch'iaksan is close enough to Seoul to attract the usual horde of technical rock climbers who come to challenge the unusual rock formations in this park.

The northern part of Ch'iaksan National Park harbours a fairly large temple called Kuryongsa. Another notable temple here is Sangwonsa.

There is a touristy resort area at the southern end of the park, called Kŭmdae, which you might either enjoy or wish to avoid.

Admission to the Kuryongsa area costs W1400 while other areas of the park cost only W800.

Getting There & Away

Bus From Wonju inter-city bus terminal you can catch a city bus to Kuryongsa inside the park. These buses run every 25 minutes between 6 am and 9 pm. The cost is W670 and the journey takes 45 minutes.

Wonju 원주

PLACES TO STAY

12 Wonju Hotel
     원주호텔
14 Won'gyŏngsa
     원경사
15 Ch'ŏnwangsa
     전왕사
18 Taehŭng-jang Yŏgwan
     대흥장여관
19 Songdo-jang Yŏgwan
     송도장여관
20 K'ŭraun-jang Yŏgwan
     크라운장여관

OTHER

1 Express Bus Terminal
    고속버스터미널
2 Inter-City Bus Terminal
    시외버스터미널
3 Yŏngch'ŏnsa Temple
    영천사
4 Railway Station
    원주역
5 Ilgwangsa Temple
    일광사
6 Solimsa Temple
    소림사
7 City Hall
    시청
8 Telephone Office
    전화국
9 Pomunsa Temple
    보문사
10 Wonju Christian Hospital
     원주기독병원
11 Central Market
     중앙시장
13 Wonju University
     원주대학교
16 Post Office
     우체국
17 Police
     경찰서
21 Kangwon Bank
     강원은행

KANGWON-DO

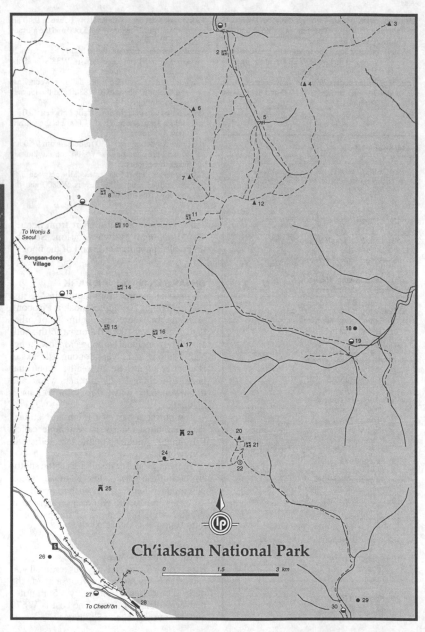

Ch'iaksan National Park

Ch'iaksan National Park
치악산국립공원

1 Bus Stop
정류장
2 Kuryongsa Temple
구룡사
3 Maehwabong (1084m)
매화봉
4 Ch'ŏnjibong (1086m)
천지봉
5 Seryŏm Waterfall
세렴폭포
6 T'oggibong (887m)
토끼봉
7 Sambong (1072m)
산봉
8 Pŏmmunsa Temple
범문사
9 Bus Stop
정류장

10 Sŏkgyŏngsa Temple
석경사
11 Ipsŏksa Temple
입석사
12 Pirobong (1288m)
비로봉
13 Bus Stop
정류장
14 Kwanŭmsa Temple
관음사
15 Kukhyangsa Temple
국향사
16 Pomunsa Temple
보문사
17 Hyangnobong (1042m)
향로봉
18 Pugok-ri
부곡리
19 Bus Stop
정류장
20 Namdaebong (1101m)
남대봉

21 Sangwonsa Temple
상원사
22 Spring
쌍룡수
23 Yŏngwonsansŏng
Fortress
영원산성
24 Yŏngwonsa
영원사
25 Haemisansŏng
(Old Fortress)
해미산성
26 Kŭmdae-ri
금대리
27 Bus Stop
정류장
28 Ch'iak Railway Station
치악역
29 Cŏngnam-ri
성남리
30 Bus Stop
정류장

KANGWON-DO

Kyŏngsangbuk-do

TAEGU

As the country's third largest city, Taegu (population 2.5 million) is an important industrial and commercial centre. The city itself has little to offer in the way of scenic attractions, but Taegu is a useful staging point for reaching one of the country's most famous temple-monastery complexes: Haeinsa in Kayasan National Park.

Herbal Medicine Market

In the central area about one km south of Taegu station is the Herbal Medicine Market *(yakryŏng shijang)*. This is one of the largest such places in Korea and if you've missed the one in Seoul than you should come here for a look. Stock up on everything from lizards' tails to magic mushrooms.

Turyu Park

In the south-west part of the city is Turyu Park. The prime feature here is Taegu Tower – an attempt (not too successful) to compete with Seoul Tower. Other amenities in the park include a swimming pool, roller skating rink, the Culture & Arts Hall, a soccer pitch, baseball field and Songding Lake.

Apsan Park

At the southern end of the city is Taegu's largest park, Apsan Park. The most notable attraction here is the cable car running 800m to the summit of Apsan, but you can walk up by following a four km trail. Near the base of the cable car ride is the Memorial Museum of Victory in Naktonggang, which celebrates a victorious (for the South) battle by the Naktong River during the Korean War. there is also an archery range, horse riding grounds and a swimming pool; and two temples, Taesŏngsa and Taedŏksa.

Places to Stay – bottom end

The *Taeyŏng-jang Yŏgwan* is one of several relatively cheap (around W20,000) places near the centre. However, most travellers

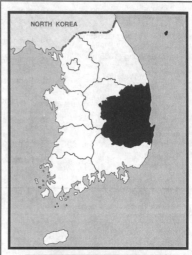

HIGHLIGHTS

- ◆ Kyŏngju, the historic ancient capital of the Shilla kingdom

- ◆ Andong, where much of Korea's traditional culture is still intact

- ◆ Haeinsa, the repository of the Tripitaka Koreana

- ◆ P'algongsan Provincial Park with its fine mountains and large temple, Tonghwasa

- ◆ Ullŭngdo, a remote, rugged and incredibly scenic island in the storm-lashed sea between Korea and Japan

overnighting in Taegu will probably prefer to stay near one of the bus terminals.

There are plenty of yŏgwan around the express bus terminal and the Tongdaegu railway station. The north side of this railway station has the thickest concentration of yŏgwan, examples being the *Shinra-jang Yŏgwan*, *Tongdaegu-jang Yŏgwan*, *Hyŏndae-jang Yŏgwan* and *Pyŏl-jang Yŏgwan*. Prices for doubles start around W18,000.

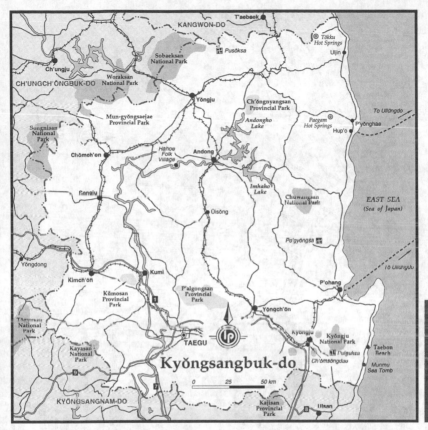

KANGWON-DO

T'aebaek

Sobaeksan
National Park

Pusŏksa

Tŏkku
Hot Springs

Uljin

Ch'ungju

CH'UNGCH'ŎNGBUK-DO

Woraksan
National Park

Yŏngju

Ch'ŏngnyangsan
Provincial Park

To Ullŭngdo

Mun-gyŏngsaejae
Provincial Park

Andongho
Lake

Paegam
Hot Springs

P'yŏnghas

Songnisan
National
Park

Hup'o

Hahoe
Folk
Village

Chŏmch'on

Andong

Sangju

Imhaho
Lake

Chuwangsan
National Park

EAST SEA
(Sea of Japan)

Ŭisŏng

Po'gyŏngsa

Yŏngdong

To Ullŭngdo

Kimch'ŏn

Kumi

Kŭmosan
Provincial
Park

P'algongsan
Provincial
Park

P'ohang

LP

Yŏngch'ŏn

Kyŏngju

Chirisan
National
Park

Kayasan
National
Park

TAEGU

Kyŏngju
National Park

Taebon
Beach

Kyŏngsangbuk-do

Pulguksa

Ch'ŏmsŏngdae

Munmu
Sea Tomb

0   25   50 km

KYŎNGSANGNAM-DO

Kajisan
Provincial
Park

Ulsan

KYŎNGSANGBUK-DO

Over at the east inter-city bus terminal there are only three yŏgwan: *Tonggŭng-jang Yŏgwan*, *Tongshin Yŏgwan* and *Taesŏng-jang Yŏgwan*. A room with attached bath can be had for W18,000.

Places to Stay – middle
3rd Class Hotels rated 3rd class in Taegu typically cost from W28,000 to W45,000. Some hotels in this category include:

Emerald (☎ 951-3031; fax 951-3035), 459-7 Pokhyon-dong, Puk-gu
Empire (☎ 555-3381), 63 Pisan-dong, Sŏ-gu

New Chongno (☎ 252-4101; fax 252-4568), 23 Chongno 2-ga, Chung-gu
Royal (☎ 253-5546), 24-4 Namil-dong, Chung-gu
Tongsan (☎ 253-7711; fax 253-7717), 360 Tongsan-dong, Chung-gu

2nd Class Hotels rated 2nd class in Taegu typically cost from W33,000 to W55,000. Some hotels in this division include:

Arirang (☎ 624-4000; fax 624-4240), 474-5 Turyu 3-dong, Talsŏ-gu
Hilltop (☎ 651-2001; fax 651-2006), 3048-35 Taemyong-dong, Nam-gu.

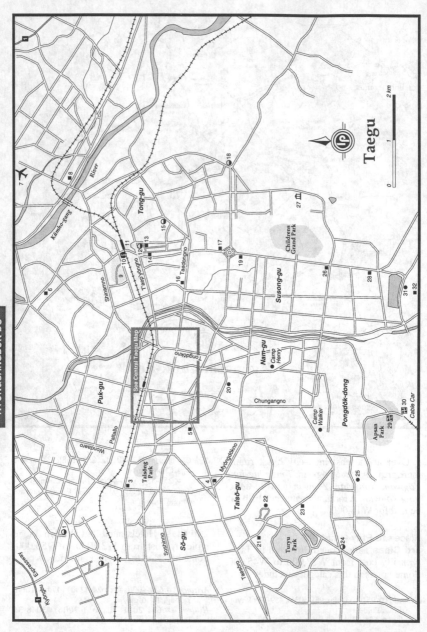

Taegu

See Central Taegu Map

Tong-gu

Susong-gu

Children's
Grand Park

Nam-gu

Camp
Henry

Camp
Walker

Chungangno

Pongdŏk-dong

Apsan
Park

Cable Car

Puk-gu

Taesŏng Park

Talsŏ-gu

Sŏ-gu

Turyu
Park

River

Kŭmho-gang

Shinamno

Taebyŏngno

Taebŏngno

Tongdŏkno

Pallialo

Wondaero

Soshinno

Taesŏno

Myŏngdŏkno

Kyŏngbu
Expressway

Riverside (☎ 982-8877; fax 982-7311), 1006-34 Ipsok-dong, Tong-gu

Tongin (☎ 426-5211; fax 423-7400), 5-2 Samdok-dong 1-ga, Chung-gu (500m from Taegu station)

1st Class Hotels rated 1st class in Taegu typically cost from W57,000 to W80,000. Hotels classified in this category include:

Crown Tourist (☎ 755-3001; fax 755-3367), 330-6 Shinch'ŏn-dong, Tong-gu (just behind the express bus terminal)

Crystal (☎ 252-7799), 1196-2 Turyu 1-dong, Talsŏ-gu

Garden (☎ 268-9911), 688 1 Pongdŏk-dong, Nam-gu

Hwangshil (☎ 751-2301; fax 751-2305), 45-1 Shinch'on 3-dong, Tong-gu (near the express bus terminal)

New Yŏngnam (☎ 752-1001; fax 755-0000), 177-7 Pomo-dong, Susong-gu

Tongdaegu (☎ 757-6141; fax 756-6623), Shinch'ŏn-dong, Tong-gu; just behind the express bus terminal

Places to Stay – top end

Deluxe Four hotels in Taegu are rated deluxe class and priced from about W93,000 to W100,000. Those in this range include:

Grand (☎ 742-0001; fax 756-7164), 563-1 Pomo-dong, Susŏng-gu

Kŭmho (☎ 252-6001; fax 253-4121), 28 Haso-dong, Chung-gu

Prince (☎ 628-1001), 1824-2 Taemyŏng 2-dong, Nam-gu

Soosung (☎ 763-7311; fax 764-0620), 888-2 Tusan-dong, Susong-gu

Entertainment

In Taegu most of the English-teaching crowd hang out at the *Texas Club* in Pongdŏk-dong, at the southern end of town. The nearby *MVP Club* is also popular but caters more to American soldiers.

Things to Buy

Aside from the herbal medicine market,

Taegu 대구

PLACES TO STAY
3 Empire Hotel
   엠파이어호텔
4 Crystal Hotel
   크리스탈호텔
5 Tongsan Hotel
   동산호텔
6 Emerald Hotel
   애머랄드호텔
8 Riverside Hotel
   리버사이드호텔
9 Yŏgwan Area
   여관지역
13 Crown Tourist Hotel
   크라운관광호텔
14 Tongdaegu Hotel
   동대구호텔
16 Hwangshil Hotel
   황실호텔
17 New Yŏngnam Hotel
   뉴영남호텔
19 Grand Hotel
   그랜드호텔

21 Arirang Hotel
   아리랑호텔
23 Hilltop Hotel
   힐탑호텔
26 Hwangkŭm Hotel
   황금호텔
28 Hotel Ariana
   아리아나호텔
32 Susŏng Hotel
   수성호텔

OTHER
1 West Taegu (Sŏdaegu)
   Express Bus Terminal
   서대구고속버스터미널
2 North (Pukbu) Inter-City
   Bus Terminal
   북부시외버스터미널
7 Airport
   공항
10 Tourist Information Kiosk
   관광안내소
11 Tongdaegu Railway Station
   동대구역

12 Express (Kosok)
   Bus Terminal
   고속버스터미널
15 East (Dongbu) Inter-City
   Bus Terminal
   동부시외버스터미널
18 South (Nambu) Inter-City
   Bus Terminal
   남부시외버스터미널
20 Confucian School
   향교
22 Taegu Tower
   대구탑
24 West (Sŏbu) Inter-City
   Bus Terminal
   서부시외버스터미널
25 Horse Riding Stables
   승마장
27 National Taegu Museum
   국립대구박물관
29 Taesŏngsa
   대성사
30 Taedŏksa
   대덕사
31 Susŏng Resort
   수성유원지

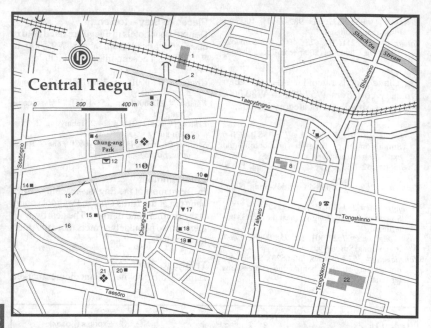

Central Taegu

0   200   400 m

Sex Town

In late 1996 Korean newspapers reported that the Taegu city government was studying a plan to create a 'sex town' in what is currently the Chagalmadang red light district. Facilities for visitors will include several adult movie houses, live nude shows, erotic dancing and sex shops. The idea of an 'adult entertainment centre' (Korea's first) was just one of several in a five-year tourist development plan presented to the mayor's office. Another part of the plan included the promotion of Katpawi Rock, on P'algongsan mountain, which is believed to bring baby boys to pregnant women.

Even as things stand the Chagalmadang district is something of a bizarre tourist attraction. It's one of the 'big three' such places in Korea, the other two being Wansol-dong in Pusan and Ch'ŏngnyangni in Seoul. All three cater to domestic business – there's scarcely a foreigner in sight. Taking a look at these places can be an interesting experience, even for women. The brothels look like nothing you've seen in the west and you might better describe them as 'display cases'. Each one fronts the street with a huge plate-glass window behind which, under intense pink lighting, up to two dozen women made up in traditional costume sit waiting for a client to choose them. These are not strictly *kisaeng* (the Korean equivalent of the Japanese *geisha*) since real kisaeng would be horrified by such indiscretion. Nevertheless, this is no bawdy sleaze-bag environment – everyone is on their best behaviour (after all, they are Koreans).

Not surprisingly, the proposal to create a 'sex town' has generated powerful opposition from feminist groups, church leaders and others who are concerned that the new 'tourist attraction' will tarnish Korea's image. Public hearings are planned on the new project – expect some raucous debate. More than likely, the whole idea will come to naught. Indeed, given the fact that Korea is rather conservative among North-East Asian countries, one has to question why the proposal was even made in the first place. Perhaps a colourful publicity stunt? Surely it could not have hurt real estate values. ■

Central Taegu
대구중심부

PLACES TO STAY

3 New Taegu Hotel
  뉴대구호텔
4 Savoy Hotel
  사보이호텔
7 Taeyŏng-jang Yŏgwan
  대영장어관
14 Kŭmho Hotel
  호텔금호
15 New Chongno Tourist
  Hotel
  뉴종로관광호텔
18 Kukje Hotel
  국제호텔
19 Tongin Hotel
  동인호텔

20 YMCA
  와이엠씨에이

PLACES TO EAT

17 Maxim's Restaurant
  맥심

OTHER

1 Taegu Railway Station
  대구역
2 Taegu Station
  Underground Arcade
  대구역 지하상가
5 Taebo Department Store
  대보 백화점
6 Korea First Bank
  제일은행
8 City Hall
  시청

9 East Taegu Telephone
  Office
  동대구 전화국
10 Korean Air
  대한항공
11 Korea Exchange Bank
  외환은행
12 Taegu Post Office
  대구 우체국
13 Central Underground
  Arcade
  중앙 지하상가
16 Herbal Medicine Market
  약령시장
21 Tonga Shopping Centre
  동아쇼핑센타
22 Kyŏngbuk Hospital
  경북대병원

Taegu's other unique shopping area is oppo-site the front gate of Camp Walker. The large military contingent stationed here makes this a sort of mini-It'aewon.

There are a couple of interesting under-ground arcades in the centre. Easiest to find is the Taegu station arcade. A bit to the south is Central Arcade, Taegu's largest.

Getting There & Away

Air Both Asiana and Korean Air have fre-quent flights between Taegu and Seoul, and between Taegu and Cheju. Korean Air offers a Sokch'o-Taegu flight, though this is in fact via Seoul.

Bus Taegu is something of a transport night-mare. There are six bus terminals spread around the city, each one offering buses to different destinations. You can easily spend over an hour hassling with city buses trying to get from one terminal to the next. The six bus stations are as follows: express bus ter-minal *(kosok t'ŏminŏl)*; east inter-city bus terminal *(tongbu shi'oe t'ŏminŏl)*; west inter-city bus terminal *(sŏbu shi'oe t'ŏminŏl)*; west express bus terminal *(sŏ kosok t'ŏminŏl)*; south inter-city bus termi-nal *(nambu shi'oe t'ŏminŏl)*; north inter-city bus terminal *(pukbu shi'oe t'ŏminŏl)*.

Local buses which connect the east inter-city bus terminal with Tongdaegu railway station and the west inter-city bus terminal include bus Nos 1, 12, 22, 126 and 127. Two other buses which you can use between the east and west inter-city bus terminals but which don't go past the railway station are bus Nos 33 and 120. In addition, bus No 76 connects Tongdaegu station with Taegu station and the west inter-city bus terminal. Should you be anywhere else in the city and want to get to the west inter-city bus terminal then bus Nos 1, 12, 31, 32, 35, 71, 75, 88, 89 and 101 will get you there. Bus No 26 con-nects the east inter-city terminal with the north inter-city terminal.

Some buses from the express bus terminal depart to the following destinations:

Kwangju buses depart every 30 minutes from 6.30 am to 6.30 pm. The fare is W9900 (1st class) or W6800 (2nd class) and the journey takes 3¾ hours.

Kyŏngju buses depart every 15 to 30 minutes from 6.50 am to 9.10 pm. The fare is W3000 (1st class) or W2100 (2nd class) and the journey takes under one hour.

Pusan buses depart every 15 minutes from 5.40 am to 9 pm. The fare is W6200 (1st class) or W4200 (2nd class) and the journey takes 1¾ hours.

Seoul buses depart every five to 10 minutes from 6 am to 8 pm. The fare is W13,200 (1st class) or W8900 (2nd class) and the journey takes 3¾ hours.

Taejŏn buses depart every 20 minutes from 6 am to 8.30 pm. The fare is W6800 (1st class) or W4600 (2nd class) and the journey takes two hours.

Tong-Seoul buses depart every 30 minutes between 6 am and 8 pm. The fare is W13,700 (1st class) or W9300 (2nd class) and the journey takes 3¾ hours.

Buses from the east inter-city bus terminal go to the following cities:

Kangnŭng buses depart every 40 minutes from 5 am to 2.50 pm. The fare is W16,100 and the journey takes 7½ hours.

Kyŏngju buses depart every eight minutes from 4.30 am to 10 pm. The fare is W2100 and the journey takes under one hour.

P'ohang buses depart every five minutes from 6.30 am to 9 pm. The fare is W3900 and the journey takes 1½ hours.

Sokch'o buses depart every 40 minutes from 7 am to 2.20 pm. The fare is W19,600 and the journey takes seven hours.

Buses from the west inter-city bus terminal go to the following destinations:

Chinju buses depart 29 times daily between 6.30 am and 7.30 pm. The fare is W4500 and the journey takes two hours.

Chŏnju buses depart 17 times daily between 7.24 am and 5.58 pm. The fare is W6800 and the journey takes four hours.

Haeinsa (temple) buses depart every 42 minutes between 6.30 am and 8 pm. The fare is W2500 and the journey takes 1½ hours.

Yŏsu buses depart six times daily between 8.20 am and 6.20 pm. The fare is W9500 and the journey takes four hours.

Buses from the north inter-city bus terminal go to the following destinations:

Andong buses depart every 10 minutes between 6.10 am and 9.10 pm. The fare is W3800 and the journey takes 1¾ hours.

Ch'unch'ŏn buses depart 12 times daily between 7.10 am and 5.10 pm. The fare is W15,100 and the journey takes 5¾ hours.

Chech'ŏn buses depart 12 times daily between 5.55 am and 5.20 pm. The fare is W10,100 and the journey takes five hours.

Kimch'ŏn (for Chikchisa and Sudosan) buses depart every seven minutes from 6.10 am to 10.30 pm. The fare is W2700 and the journey takes just over one hour.

Kuinsa buses depart four times daily between 7.22 am and 4.24 pm. The fare is W9800 and the journey takes five hours.

Kumi buses depart every seven minutes from 6.09 am to 10.20 pm. The fare is W1800 and the journey takes 45 minutes.

Songnisan buses depart seven times daily between 5.45 am and 12.03 pm. The fare is W8400 and the journey takes 3½ hours.

T'aebaek buses depart every 45 minutes between 7.40 am and 10.10 pm. The fare is W11,300 and the journey takes 5¼ hours.

Wonju buses depart 12 times daily between 7.10 am and 5.10 pm. The fare is W11,00 and the journey takes 3½ hours.

The south bus terminal offers little for the visitor; Kyŏngju (though the express bus terminal is better) and a couple of temples can be reached from here, including:

P'yoch'ungsa buses depart six times daily between 9.16 am and 6.20 pm. The fare is W4500 and the journey takes 1¾ hours.

Unmunsa buses depart every 20 minutes from 7.15 am to 7.50 pm. The fare is W2700 and the journey takes 1¼ hours.

Train Taegu station in the town centre is for local trains only and, unless you want to stay in the downtown area, don't get off the train here! Express trains stop at the Tongdaegu station on the east side of the city and in most cases this is where you should get off. The schedule of trains departing Seoul for Tongdaegu can be found in the timetable appendix at the end of the book.

Getting Around
The Airport Taegu's airport is north-east of the city about two km from the express bus terminal. Bus No 31 (W400) follows a circuitous route to the airport and can take 45 minutes. There are also seat buses from the centre that cost W1000 and cover the distance in 30 minutes. A taxi from the airport

to the centre will cost around W4000 and takes about 20 minutes.

Subway Taegu is currently building a subway and it might be in operation by the time you read this. No maps of the subway system were available at the time of writing.

Car If you feel the urge, cars can be rented at Yŏngil Rent-A-Car (☎ 952-1001).

P'ALGONGSAN PROVINCIAL PARK

Just 20 km north of Taegu's urban sprawl is P'algongsan Provincial Park. Pirobong (1192m) is the highest point in the park, and is connected by ridges to Tongbong (East Peak, 1155m) and Sohong (West Peak, 1041m). However, this is not a wilderness park and the splendid scenery is somewhat marred by an 18-hole golf course, numerous luxury hotels and a large gondola.

A major feature of the park is Tonghwasa, a large temple whose history stretches back over 1000 years. Even more conspicuous is the nearby Grand Stone Buddhist Image for Unification Desire. This is the largest statue of Buddha in Korea.

Places to Stay

Aside from the requisite yŏgwan, the *Hillside Hotel* (☎ 982-0801) near Tonghwasa charges W52,000 for a double and the *P'algong Hotel* (☎ 985-0802) is W37,000.

Getting There & Away

City bus Nos 76 (standing) or 376 (seat bus) from Tongdaegu (east railway station area) can take you to P'algongsan. These buses run at least once every 30 minutes from 5 am until 10 pm and take 50 minutes for the journey; the cost is W400 standing and W700 for a seat.

KYŎNGSAN HOT SPRINGS

These are also known as Sangdae hot springs because they're located in Sangdae-ri, 30 km south-east of Taegu. These are not the most spectacular hot springs in Korea, but it's a major place of recreation for Taeguites

(Taeguans?). The water temperature is a mellow 30°C.

If you stay in the *Sangdae Hot Springs Hotel* (☎ 823001) you can take advantage of their free shuttle bus from Taegu. Rooms here cost W28,000 to W50,000.

If you're not staying at this hotel, then catch a bus from Taegu's south inter-city bus terminal. There are departures for Sangdae-ri every 30 minutes between 6.20 am and 9 pm and the ride takes one hour.

KAYASAN NATIONAL PARK

This national park straddles the border between two provinces, Kyŏngsangbuk-do and Kyŏngsangnam-do.

Hikers will no doubt want to challenge Kayasan, a pretty peak 1430m in elevation. It is even possible to walk from here along a 22 km trail to Sudosan (see the Sudosan section in this chapter).

The most famous attraction in the park is Haeinsa, on the Kyŏngsangnam-do side of the border. This is the repository of the Tripitaka Koreana – more than 80,000 wood blocks on which are carved the complete Buddhist scriptures, as well as many illustrations remarkably similar to those you're likely to see in Nepal. Like Pulguksa near Kyŏngju, UNESCO has declared Haeinsa an international treasure. The blocks are housed in two enormous buildings complete with a simple but effective ventilation system to prevent their deterioration.

The buildings are normally locked, though it's possible to see the blocks through the slatted windows and one of the friendly monks may open them up if you show an interest. Even if you don't manage to get into the library there's plenty of interest in the other buildings of the complex.

The wood blocks which you see today are actually the second set. They were carved during the 14th century when a Koryŏ king, Kojong, was forced to take refuge on Kanghwa Island during the Mongol invasion of the mainland. The first set, completed in 1251 after 20 years' work, was destroyed by the invaders. The Tripitaka was moved from

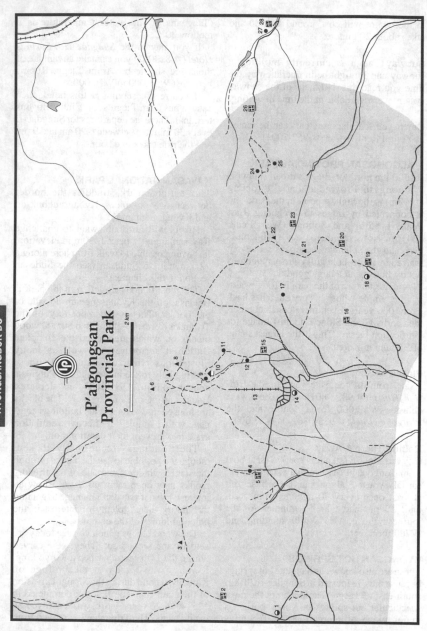

P'algongsan
Provincial Park

P'algongsan Provincial Park 팔공산도립공원	9 Yŏmbulam Hermitage 염불암	19 Poǔnsa Temple 보은사
1 Bus Stop 정류장	10 Shelter 대피소	20 Kwanamsa Temple 관암사
2 P'agyesa Temple 파계사	11 Yangjinam Hermitage 양진암	21 Nojŏkbong (887m) 노적봉
3 P'agyebong (991m) 파계봉	12 Pudoam Hermitage 부도암	22 Inbong (898m) 인봉
4 Samsŏngam Hermitage 삼성암	13 Cable Car 팔공스카이라인	23 Sŏnbonsa Temple 선본사
5 Puinsa Temple 부인사	14 Bus Stop 정류상	24 Chungangam Hermitage 중앙암
6 P'algongsan (1192m) 팔공산	15 Tonghwasa Temple 동화사	25 Myobongam Hermitage 묘봉암
7 Tongbong (1155m) 동봉	16 Pukjijangsa Temple 북지장사	26 Paekhŭngam 백흥암
8 Yŏmbulbong (1121m) 염불봉	17 Country Club 팔공컨트리클럽	27 Paeknyŏnam Hermitage 백년암
	18 Bus Stop 정류장	28 Ŭnhaesa Temple 은해사

Kanghwa Island to Haeinsa in the early years of the Yi dynasty.

Haeinsa itself has origins going back to the beginning of the 9th century, when it was founded by two monks, Sunung and Ijong, after many years of study in China. It was not until the early days of the Koryŏ dynasty in the mid-10th century that it attained its present size.

The main hall, Taejkwangjon, was burnt down during the Japanese invasion of 1592 and again (accidentally) in 1817, though miraculously the Tripitaka escaped destruction. The hall was reconstructed again in 1971. Other reconstruction has been undertaken since, principally on the monks' quarters, and all of it, naturally, along traditional lines.

Haeinsa is one of the most beautiful temples in Korea, but part of its appeal lies in its natural setting of mixed deciduous and coniferous forest. It's a romantic's paradise in wet weather, when wisps of cloud drift at various levels through the forest.

Entry to the temple costs W2100 and you have to pay W500 for entry to the national park. The temple is about 20 minutes' walk from where the bus drops you.

Places to Stay

Most people visit as a day trip from Taegu, but it is pleasant and worthwhile to spend the night. Accommodation is available in the tourist village below the temple, and ranges from minbak to yŏgwan. You won't have to look hard – ajummas meet arriving buses with offers of places to stay. In the off-season you can easily do some productive bargaining.

The top-end place to stay is the *Haeinsa Hotel* (☎ 332000) where doubles are W67,000.

Getting There & Away

The best way to go by far is from Taegu. Buses depart Haeinsa for the following destinations:

Chinju buses depart once hourly between 7 am and 5.50 pm. The fare is W5000 and the journey takes two hours.
Masan buses depart twice daily at 11 am and 5.15 pm. The fare is W5500 and the journey takes two hours.
Pusan buses depart once daily at 4 pm. The fare is W7200 and the journey takes 2½ hours.
Taegu buses depart every 20 minutes between 6.30 am and 7.50 pm. The fare is W2500 and the journey takes 1¼ hours. The bus terminates at Taegu's west inter-city bus terminal.

The obscure town of Kŏch'ang has buses to

KYŎNGSANGBUK-DO

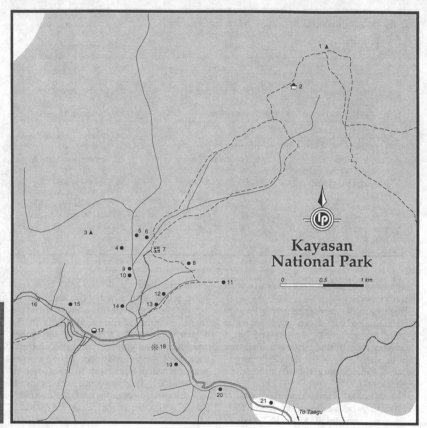

Kayasan National Park
가야산국립공원

1 Kayasan (1430m)
가야산
2 Shelter
대피소
3 Pibongsan (858m)
비봉산
4 Wondangam
Hermitage
원당암

5 Hŭngjeam
Hermitage
흥제암
6 Yongt'apsŏnwon
Hermitage
용탑선원
7 Haeinsa Temple
해인사
8 Chisokam
Hermitage
지족암
9 Kŭmsŏnam
Hermitage
금선암

10 Samsŏnam
Hermitage
삼선암
11 Paekryŏnam
Hermitage
백련암
12 Kukilam Hermitage
국일암
13 Yaksuam Hermitage
약수암
14 Pohyŏnam
Hermitage
보현암

15 Ch'iin-ri
치인리
16 Yongmun Waterfall
용문폭포
17 Bus Stop
정류장
18 Observatory
관광전망대
19 Kilsangam
Hermitage
길상암
20 Resthouse
농산정
21 Ticket Booth
매표소

Taegu which stop at Haeinsa en route. These depart Kŏch'ang every 40 minutes from 6.30 am to 8.50 pm.

KIMCH'ŎN

Kimch'ŏn is a useful staging point on a visit to nearby Chikchisa (a temple) and Sudosan (a mountain). There's little of cultural interest in Kimch'ŏn itself; it was completely destroyed during the Korean War and is totally modern, but it's pleasant enough for spending the night.

Places to Stay – bottom end

On the back side (north side) of the railway station there's a collection of yŏgwan and yŏinsuk.

Places to Stay – middle

There are at least two places in town which qualify as mid-range accommodation. One is the *Kimch'on Tourist Hotel* (☎ 329911) on the east side of Chasan Park near the river. On the west side of town is the equally salubrious *Grand Tourist Hotel*. Both places have doubles starting at W35,000 plus 20% tax and surcharge.

Getting There & Away

Bus Kimch'ŏn has both an express bus terminal and a more popular inter-city bus terminal. The railway station is sandwiched between the two bus terminals and all three places are within walking distance of each other. Buses from the inter-city bus terminal go to the following destinations:

Andong buses depart every 40 minutes from 6.20 am to 7 pm. The fare is W6000 and the journey takes three hours.

Chikchisa (temple) buses depart every 10 minutes between 6.20 am and 10.40 pm. The fare is W480 and the journey takes 25 minutes.

Kŏch'ang (for Haeinsa & Kayasan National Park) buses depart every 30 minutes from 6.20 am to 9 pm. The fare is W3500 and the journey takes 1¼ hours.

Kumi buses depart every 10 minutes from 6 am to 10.25 pm. The fare is W1200 and the journey takes 30 minutes.

Kyŏngju buses depart four times daily between 8.05 am and 4.52 pm. The fare is W5200 and the journey takes 1⅓ hours.

P'ohang buses depart seven times daily between 7.22 am and 4.52 pm. The fare is W6600 and the journey takes 3⅓ hours.

Taegu buses depart every seven minutes between 6.30 am and 9.50 pm. The fare is W2700 and the journey takes just over one hour.

Taejŏn buses depart 15 times daily between 7.20 am and 7.30 pm. The fare is W3300 and the journey takes just over one hour.

Train The train schedule on the Seoul-Kimch'ŏn route can be found in the appendix at the end of this book.

CHIKCHISA TEMPLE

Situated in the foothills of Hwang'aksan west of Kimch'ŏn, Chikchisa is one of Korea's largest and most famous temples. It was first constructed during the reign of the 19th Shilla king, Nul-ji (417-458 AD), which makes it one of the first Buddhist temples built in Korea. It was rebuilt in 645 AD by a priest, Chajang, who had spent many years studying in China and brought back to Korea the first complete set of the Tripitaka Buddhist scriptures. Further reconstruction was done in the 10th century but the temple was completely destroyed during the Japanese invasion of 1592. Though there were originally over 40 buildings at Chikchisa, only 20 or so remain, the oldest of which date from a reconstruction in 1602.

Chikchisa's most famous son is Sa-myong or Son'gun, a militant monk who spent many years in Kŭmgangsan (the Diamond Mountains in North Korea). He organised troops to fight against the Japanese in 1592 and later became the chief Korean delegate to the Japanese court when a peace treaty was negotiated in 1604. Following the completion of the treaty, Sa-myong returned to Korea with over 3000 released prisoners of war.

Entry to the temple costs W1100. It's very popular, especially at weekends, so if you don't like crowds go there during the week.

The actual temple compound is quite a walk from where the buses stop – about

KYŎNGSANGBUK-DO

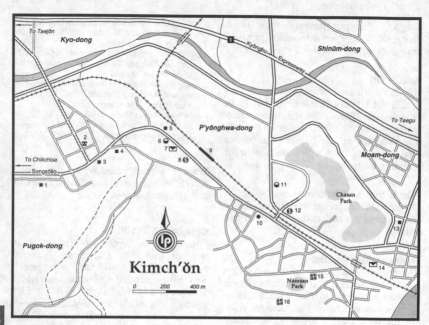

Kimch'ŏn 김천	5 Ŭhwa-jang Yŏgwan 으화장여관	7 Post Office 우체국	12 Bank 은행
PLACES TO STAY	13 Kimch'ŏn Tourist Hotel 김천관광호텔	8 Bank 은행	14 Central Post Office 김천우체국
1 Grand Tourist Hotel 그랜드관광호텔		9 Railway Station 김천역	15 Kwanŭmsa Temple 관음사
3 Tong'il-jang Yŏgwan 동일장여관	**OTHER** 2 Telephone Office 전화국	10 City Hall 시청	16 Kaeunsa Temple 개운사
4 YMCA 와이엠씨에이	6 Express Bus Terminal 고속버스터미널	11 Inter-City Bus Terminal 시외버스터미널	

1½ km – so in summer it's a good idea to get an early start to avoid the mid-day heat.

Places to Stay & Eat

If you don't want to stay in Kimch'ŏn you can stay close to the temple – there's a well-established tourist village where the buses stop, with a range of minbak, yŏgwan and restaurants.

Getting There & Away

There are local buses from Kimch'ŏn bus terminal to Chikchisa every nine minutes from 6.20 am to 10.40 pm; they cost W480 and take about 25 minutes.

SUDOSAN MOUNTAIN

Due south of Kimch'ŏn is Sudosan (1317m) The mountain is also known as Pulyongsan and the summit is called Shinsondae. When the weather is clear you can see the peaks in nearby Kayasan National Park.

Enchanting mountain scenery like this would not be complete without a temple, and Sudosan pitches in with Ch'ongamsa at the base of the mountain. The temple is at the mouth of Sudo Valley, from where you can hike up to Sudoam hermitage near the summit.

Near the temple is *Ch'ong'am Yŏgwan* (☎ 390194) where you can find comfortable double rooms for W20,000. Otherwise, stay in Kimch'ŏn.

Buses between Kimch'ŏn and Sudosan (Ch'ongamsa) run eight times daily between 7.30 am and 6.50 pm. The fare is W1800 and the ride takes 1½ hours.

ANDONG

Andong (population 200,000) is north of Taegu and Kyŏngju. The whole area surrounding Andong is notable for having preserved much of its traditional character. Though Andong itself is not particularly interesting, there are a few interesting spots on the edge of town and numerous places to visit in the vicinity.

Most of Andong's sights are outside the city – some of them a considerable distance away – and getting to them requires a series of bus rides.

Andong Folk Village

Almost within walking distance of Andong proper is the Andong Folk Village. It's nowhere near as large as its cousin outside Suwon, south of Seoul, but it serves a different purpose. Andong Folk Village was built to house all the cultural assets which were moved to prevent them from being drowned by the reservoir when Andong Dam was built in 1976.

Here you'll find a series of relocated and partially reconstructed traditional-style buildings, ranging from simple thatched peasants' farmhouses to the more elaborate mansions with multiple courtyards of government officials and the like.

Where this village differs from the one at Suwon is that many of the houses are also

restaurants, and for atmosphere and quality of food it cannot be beat. Koreans have already discovered this and it's a very popular place to go for lunch or dinner. You'll find both the people who run the restaurants and their guests very friendly indeed. It has to be *the* place to meet people in Andong. Not only that, but the prices of meals here are very reasonable; the two simpler restaurants near the top of the hill are the cheapest.

The village is situated about three km east of Andong, close to the dam wall on the opposite side of the river from the road which runs beside the railway track. A concrete bridge connects the two sides at this point. Note this is not the first bridge across the river at the smaller dam on the outskirts of Andong but the one beyond it. Local bus No 3 from the city centre will get you here.

Chebiwon (Amitaba Buddha)

Andong is also famous for the huge rock-carved Amitaba Buddha, also known as Chebiwon, some five km north of town on the road to Yŏngju. Its body and robes are carved on a boulder over 12m high topped by two separate pieces of rock on which is carved the head and hair. There's a very small temple nearby close to the highway which is attended by a nun. Entry is free.

To get there take bus No 54 from the main street in Andong. Buses are very frequent (usually every five minutes) and take about 10 minutes to get there. Local buses to Yŏngju can also drop you off by Chebiwon.

Places to Stay

There is a good selection of yŏgwan and a couple of grotty yŏinsuk close to the express and inter-city bus terminals on Hwarangno.

More expensive yŏgwan face the inter-city bus terminal. The top-notch place in town is the *Park Tourist Hotel* (☎ 859-1500), where twin rooms cost W55,000 and suites are W80,000 (plus 20% tax and surcharge).

The other cushy accommodation in town is the *Andong Hotel*.

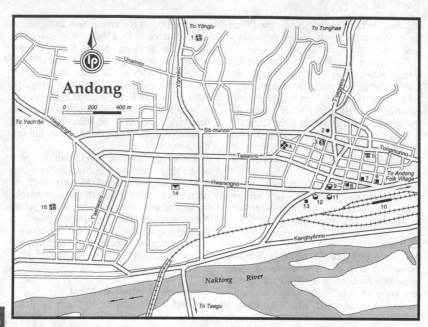

Andong 안동

1 Haedongsa Temple
해동사

2 City Hall
시청

3 Bank
주택은행

4 Saeandong Department
Store
새안동 백화점

5 Telephone Office
전화국

6 Park Tourist Hotel
파크관광호텔

7 Andong Hotel
안동호텔

8 Tongch'un-jang Yŏgwan
동춘장여관

9 Bus Stop (Hahoe Folk
Village & Chebiwon)
정류장 (하회마을,
제비원)

10 Railway Station
안동역

11 Bus Stop (Tosan Sŏwon)
& Shinho-jang Yŏgwan
정류장 (도산서원),
신호장여관

12 Inter-City Bus Terminal
시외버스터미널

13 Yŏngdong Yŏinsuk
영동여인숙

14 Central Post Office
우체국

15 Sŏaksa Temple
서악사

Getting There & Away

Air Although there is no airport in Andong, there is one at nearby Yech'on. Asiana and Korean Air fly between Seoul and Yech'on. Korean Air also has Yech'on-Cheju flights.

Bus The inter-city bus terminal serves both express and regular buses. Some of the buses to

Seoul also stop at Tanyang, a useful destination for exploring central Korea. From Andong, there are buses to the following destinations:

Ch'ŏngsong (Chuwangsan National Park) buses depart every hour between 6.55 am and 8.40 pm. The fare is W2700 and the journey takes one hour.

P'ohang buses depart nine times daily between 6.19 am and 5.54 pm. The fare is W7000 and the journey takes 2½ hours.

Pusan buses depart 23 times daily from 6.19 am to 5.22 pm. The fare is W8300 and the journey takes 4½ hours.

Seoul buses depart 24 times daily between 7 am and 6.45 pm. The fare is W12,000 and the journey takes over four hours.

Taegu buses depart every seven minutes from 6.40 am to 9.10 pm. The fare is W3800 and the journey takes 1¾ hours.

Taejŏn buses depart once every 1¼ hours from 7.25 am to 3.50 pm. The fare is W7800 and the journey takes 4½ hours.

Tanyang buses depart eight times daily between 7.40 am and 3.19 pm. The fare is W4700 and the journey takes about two hours.

Yŏngju buses depart 20 times daily between 7.30 am and 11.35 pm. The fare is W2100 and the journey takes one hour.

Train Trains run from Seoul's Ch'ŏngnyangni railway station to Andong. The train schedule on the Seoul-Andong route is in the appendix at the end of this book.

Getting Around
The Airport By bus between the airport and Andong takes nearly an hour and costs W2200. By taxi it's a 40-minute trip and costs around W18,000.

HAHOE FOLK VILLAGE
Hahoe Folk Village (*Hahoe Maŭl*) is as close as you'll find to a 16th-century Korean settlement. Unlike the folk village at Suwon, which is basically a tourist production, this is a genuine village with roots going back some 600 years. This is one of Korea's most picturesque villages; apart from the refrigerators, TVs and various other electrical appliances in the houses precious little has changed for centuries. Not only do the residents want to keep it that way, but the government actually funds the costs of preservation and restoration. At present there are about 130 traditional houses here.

Hahoe is a favoured location for shooting historical films and has also been discovered by the tour bus companies, so during the summer holidays it can be overrun with day-trippers. The only way to partially avoid the hordes is to stay overnight and try not to visit on a weekend. Outside the holiday season there are no drawbacks of this nature.

The admission fee to the village is W1500. You can visit various houses at no additional charge, but remember to respect people's privacy if you step beyond the entrance gates. These are their homes, after all. The most important of the houses usually have a sign outside describing their history.

The makkoli here is about the strongest alcohol in Korea – really knocks your socks off.
Richard Watson

Places to Stay
A number of minbak are available in Hahoe – mostly around where the buses stop – which cost W15,000 per room on average. Some have signs (and there's even one in English saying 'Welcome Foreign Visitors'!) but if you're not sure ask around. Dinner can usually be provided on request.

Camping is permitted. There are no regular yŏgwan or yŏinsuk.

Getting There & Away
Hahoe is about 24 km west of Andong, from where there are only five buses daily. The fare is W1000 and the journey takes 50 minutes. If you miss the bus or you're in a hurry a taxi costs W9000 one way.

If you have your own transport keep your wits about you because there are no signs for Hahoe on the main roads. Take route No 34 out of Andong towards Yech'on and turn off left along the 916 just past Pungsan. From there you drive a further five to six km and again turn to the left.

TOSAN SŎWON CONFUCIAN INSTITUTE
This is some 28 km north of Andong on the road to T'aebaek and Tonghae. It was founded in 1557 AD by Yi Toegye, Korea's foremost Confucian scholar (whose portrait appears on the W1000 banknote), during the reign of King Sonjo. For several centuries it was the most prestigious school for those who aspired to high office in the civil service

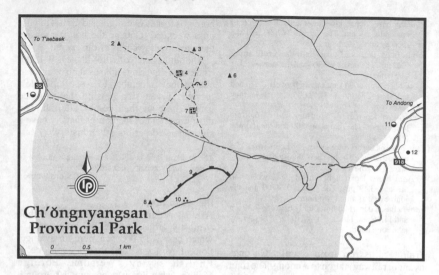

Ch'ŏngnyangsan
Provincial Park

and it was here that the qualifying examinations took place. Confucianism is no longer taught at the Institute and the buildings and grounds have been converted into a museum which is open to the public every day. It's a particularly beautiful spot and often used by Korean film directors for making historical documentaries and the like.

A brochure (partially in English) is available but perhaps only worth buying for the photographs. Entry costs W300 (less for students and those under 24 years old).

Getting There & Away
Catch a city bus from the main street in front of the inter-city bus terminal in Andong. There are 20 buses daily, but don't take the first one because the institute doesn't open until 9 am. The fare is W1000 and the journey takes about 40 minutes. These buses take you direct to the village. You can also take local bus No 66 (W400) but it will drop you two km before the village and from there you'll have to walk or take a taxi.

CH'ŎNGNYANGSAN PROVINCIAL PARK
Just north of Tosan Sŏwon is Ch'ŏngnyangsan Provincial Park. Its most notable

feature is Ch'ŏngnyangsan (870m), the summit of which is called Kumt'apbong. There are 11 other scenic peaks, eight caves and Kwanjang Waterfall. The largest temple in the park is Ch'ongnyangsa and there are a number of small hermitages.

There are no hotels in the park (most visitors stay in Andong) but there is a restaurant and store.

Getting There & Away
The park can be approached by bus from either Andong or the obscure town called Ponghwa. From Andong there are five buses daily between 5.50 am and 5.10 pm and the ride takes 1½ hours. From Ponghwa there are five departures daily between 7.50 am and 6.20 pm and the ride takes just over one hour.

PUSŎKSA TEMPLE
Another very much out-of-the-way place that's worth visiting is Pusŏksa, a temple about 60 km north of Andong between Yŏngju and T'aebaek. This temple was established in 676 AD by a monk, Uisang, who returned to Korea from China bringing the teachings of Hwaom Buddhism. Though burnt to the ground in the early 14th century by invaders, in 1358 it was

Ch'ŏngnyangsan Provincial Park
청량산도립공원

1 Bus Stop
   정류장
2 Ch'ŏngryŏngsan (870m)
   청량산
3 Posalbong (845m)
   보살봉
4 Naech'ŏngryangsa Temple
   내청량사
5 Kimsaenggul Cave
   김생굴
6 Kyŏngilbong Peak
   견일봉
7 Oech'ŏngryangsa Temple
   외청량사
8 Ch'ukyungbong (845m)
   축융봉
9 Ch'ŏngryangsansŏng Fortress
   청량산성
10 Kongminwang Ruins
   공민왕딩
11 Bus Stop
   정류장
12 Nammyŏn-ri
   남면리

reconstructed and escaped destruction during the Japanese invasions under Hideyoshi at the end of the 16th century.

This stroke of good fortune has resulted in the preservation of the beautiful main hall (Muryangsu-jon) to this day, making it the oldest wooden structure in Korea. It also has what are considered to be the oldest Buddhist wall paintings in the country and a unique gilded-clay sitting Buddha.

Getting There & Away
Transport to Pusŏksa is from Yŏngju or P'unggi, and in either case takes about one hour. From Yŏngju there are buses every 50 minutes between 6.40 am and 7.20 pm. From P'unggi buses are hourly between 7 am and 7.40 pm.

CHUWANGSAN NATIONAL PARK
Far to the east of Andong and almost by the coast is Chuwangsan National Park. In the past, Chuwangsan was known as Sokpyong-san, which means 'stone screen mountain'. As the name suggests it's a rocky peak, with some vertical faces, and like most of Korea's national parks it boasts the requisite temples, hermitages, valleys, forests and waterfalls. The park gets its share of the summer stampede trying to get away from it all.

There are a number of yŏgwan in the park, these include *Jinbo-jang* (☎ 729595), *Kukil* (☎ 873-2218), *Munhwajang* (☎ 729900) and *Sambojang* (☎ 874-2088); all charge around W20,000 for a double.

The most upscale hotel in the park is the *Chuwangsan Hotel* (☎ 726801) which has rooms costing from W32,000 to W52,000.

In order to give the environment a chance to heal itself, camping and cooking in the park are currently prohibited.

Admission to the park for adults costs W1400.

Getting There & Away
Getting to Chuwangsan is a two-stage process. You first have to get to the small town of Ch'ŏngsong which is due west of the park. Buses from Ch'ŏngsong run on the following schedule:

Andong buses depart once hourly between 6.55 am and 8.40 pm. The fare is W2700 and the journey takes one hour.
Kyŏngju buses depart eight times daily between 7.20 am and 5.10 pm. The fare is W7400 and the journey takes three hours.
Seoul buses depart five times daily between 8.50 am and 5.29 pm. The fare is W15,400 and the journey takes 5¾ hours. In Seoul, these buses arrive and depart at the Tong-Seoul terminal only.
Taegu buses depart every 48 minutes between 6.05 am and 6.55 pm. The fare is W6600 and the journey takes 2¾ hours.

Once you've arrived in Ch'ŏngsong it's another 20 minutes by bus to Chuwangsan. These buses are frequent: there are 65 per day between 6.30 am and 8 pm, and the fare is W750.

PAEGAM HOT SPRINGS
A small town called P'yŏnghae is right on the east coast and Paegam hot springs is 14 km to the west. It's one of Korea's more

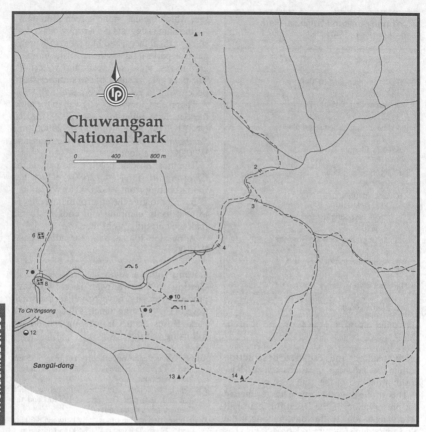

Chuwangsan National Park
주왕산국립공원

1 Kŭmŭngwangi (812m)
   금은광이
2 3rd Waterfall
   제삼폭포
3 2nd Waterfall
   제이폭포

4 1st Waterfall
   제일폭포
5 Yonhwagul Cave
   연화굴
6 Kwangamsa Temple
   광암사
7 Paekryŏnam Hermitage
   백련암
8 Taejŏnsa Temple
   대전사
9 Mujanggul
   무장굴

10 Chuwangam Hermitage
   주왕암
11 Chuwanggul Cave
   주왕굴
12 Bus Stop
   정류장
13 Chuwangsan (720m)
   주왕산
14 K'aldŭnggogae (732m)
   칼등고개

isolated and lesser known springs and the setting is still very rural, though that doesn't mean it's not developed! It's thronged with tourists during weekends. Water temperature is a very warm 46°C. Paegamsan (1004m) is a nearby peak that would be a moderately vigorous climb.

Places to Stay

At the bottom end there are some guesthouses in the W25,000 to W35,000 range, such as the *Paegam Koryo Yŏgwan* (☎ 787-3158) and *T'aebaek-jang Yŏgwan* (☎ 787-3881). More upmarket are the *Songnyu Park Hotel* (☎ 787-3711), where doubles are W61,000, and the *Paegam Hotel* (☎ 787-3500), which charges W80,000. At the top of the market is the *Paegam Hanhwa Condominium* (☎ 787-7001), where rooms are W110,000.

TŎKKU HOT SPRINGS

Unlike Paegam, Tŏkku is relatively undeveloped. But nothing stays the same for long in Korea – by next year perhaps there will be a Holiday Inn here. In the meantime, it's a reasonably unspoiled area with good walks further up the valley. The water temperature is a toasty 43°C.

There are a couple of yŏgwan priced at around W20,000. The *Tŏkku Sama Condominium* (☎ 830811) is more fancy and W70,000 for a double.

The hot springs are on the far north-east coast of Kyŏngsangbuk-do, near the small city of Uljin. There are four buses daily from Uljin to Tŏkku between 10.06 am and 4.08 pm. The ride takes 40 minutes and costs W1200.

P'OHANG

P'ohang (population 510,000) is the largest city on the east coast and an important industrial centre. The city's claim to fame is POSCO (P'ohang Iron and Steel Company), the world's second largest steel maker. Unless you have a particular interest in steel smelters, you are only likely to use P'ohang as a transit point to Ullŭngdo or Po'gyŏngsa temple.

Songdo Beach

The closest beach to the centre, this is something of a local summer resort area. A row of pine trees has been planted next to the beach, making an attractive background. There are complete facilities here, including lifeguards and a resort hotel. Seafood restaurants can dish up raw fish which costs the earth.

Pukbu Beach

This beach three km to the north of P'ohang is 1.7 km long, making it the longest sandy beach on Korea's east coast. City bus Nos 101 and 105 (W400) go to Pukbu Beach from P'ohang about once every 10 minutes between 6 am and 10.30 pm; the journey takes around 20 minutes.

Po'gyŏngsa Temple

P'ohang is a convenient place from which to visit Po'gyŏngsa, 30 km north of the city. This area boasts 12 splendid waterfalls, gorges spanned by bridges, hermitages, stupas and the temple itself. The scenery is impressive enough to draw large numbers of Koreans during the summer holidays and you'd be well advised to visit during off-peak times to escape these crowds.

Hikers may wish to challenge Naeyonsan (930m). The summit itself is called Hyangnobong and the return trip on foot from Po'gyŏngsa is 20 km (taking around six hours).

The temple is close to where the buses from P'ohang terminate and there's the inevitable tourist village with the usual collection of souvenir shops, restaurants, minbak and yŏgwan. There's also a camping ground beyond the ticket booth for the temple. Entry to the temple costs W1000.

The trail to the gorge and waterfalls branches off from the tourist village and is well maintained. It's about 1½ km to the first waterfall, Ssangsaengp'ok, which is five metres high. The sixth waterfall is called Kwanump'ok and is an impressive 72m high. It has two columns of water with a cave behind it. The seventh waterfall is called Yonsanp'ok and is a respectable 30m high.

As you head further up the trails the going

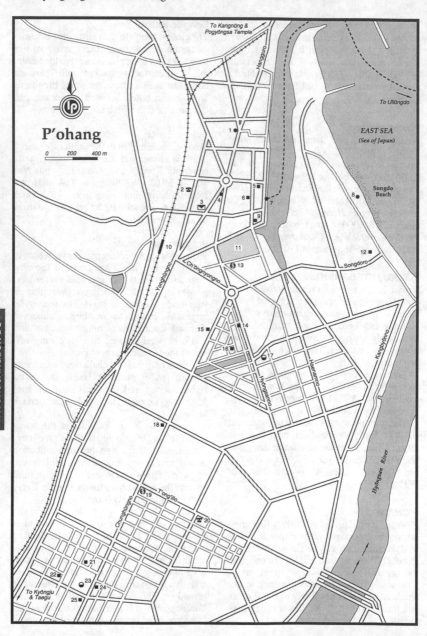

P'ohang 포항

PLACES TO STAY
4 Seraton Hotel
   쉐라톤호텔
5 New Hilton-jang Yŏgwan
   뉴힐튼장여관
6 Kimgang Hotel
   김강호텔
9 Palace Hotel
   팔레스호텔
12 Songdo Beach Tourist
   Hotel
   관광호텔
14 Mandarin Hotel
   만다린호텔
15 Paekma-jang Yŏgwan
   백마장여관
16 Savoy Hotel
   사보이호텔

18 Ocean Park Hotel
   오션파크호텔
21 Namjin-jang Yŏgwan
   남진장여관
22 Taedŏk-jang Yŏgwan
   대덕장여관
24 Hayat'ŭ-jang &
   Kŭraendŭ-jang Yŏgwans
   하아트장여관,
   그랜드장여관
25 New Korea-jang Yŏgwan
   뉴코리아자어관

OTHER
1 City Hall
   시처
2 Telephone Office
   전화국
3 Post Office
   우체국

7 Ullŭngdo Ferry Terminal
   포항-울릉도여객터미널
8 Songdo Resort
   송도국민관광지
10 Railway Station
   포항역
11 Chukto Market
   죽도시장
13 Korea Exchange Bank
   외환은행
17 Express Bus Terminal
   고속버스터미널
19 Bank of Korea
   한국은행
20 Telephone Office
   전화국
23 Inter City Bus Terminal
   시외버스터미널

---

gets difficult and the ascent of Hyangnobong should only be attempted if the day is young.

There are six buses daily from the inter-city bus terminal in P'ohang to Po'gyŏngsa from 10.40 am to 5.10 pm. The fare is W1400 and the journey takes 30 minutes. It's also possible to visit Po'gyŏngsa as a day trip from Kyŏngju.

Places to Stay – bottom end
There are plenty of yŏgwan and yŏinsuk in the streets going back from the Ullŭngdo ferry terminal. Most cater for the overnight ferry trade and there's not a lot to choose between them.

Another neighbourhood to consider staying in is near the inter-city bus terminal. There must be about two dozen yŏgwan here, with rooms typically going for W20,000.

Places to Stay – middle & top end
One of the top-rated accommodations in P'ohang is the 1st class *Ocean Park Hotel* (☎ 775555), though it's *not* near the ocean.

If you do want to be near the ocean, then you can try the *P'ohang Beach Tourist Hotel* (☎ 411401; fax 427534) which is rated by the government as 2nd class.

Another 2nd class place is the *Mandarin Hotel* (☎ 736666) near the express bus terminal.

There are a number of hotels downtown in the 3rd class category including the *Palace* (☎ 424242), *Seraton* and *Kimgang* hotels.

Getting There & Away
Air Asiana and Korean Air both fly Seoul-P'ohang. Asiana also operates a flight between P'ohang and Cheju.

Bus There are two bus terminals in P'ohang, the express bus terminal and the inter-city bus terminal. Buses from the express bus terminal go to the following destinations:

Kwangju buses depart every 2½ hours from 8 am to 6 pm. The fare is W14,200 (1st class) or W9600 (2nd class) and the journey takes 2¾ hours.
Seoul buses depart every 20 minutes from 6.30 am to 6 pm. The fare is W17,500 (1st class) or W11,700 (2nd class) and the journey takes five hours.
Taejŏn buses depart every 2¼ hours from 7 am to 6.10 pm. The fare is W11,200 (1st class) or W7600 (2nd class) and the journey takes 3¼ hours.

All other buses go from the inter-city bus terminal; destinations include:

Andong buses depart every 15 minutes between 8.10 am and 6.30 pm. The fare is W7000 and the journey takes 2½ hours.

Kangnŭng buses depart every 30 minutes from 4.40 am to 5.39 pm. The fare is W12,200 and the journey takes four hours by express or 5½ hours on the non-express.

Pusan buses depart every 10 minutes from 6.45 am to 8.30 pm. The fare is W4300 and the journey takes 1½ hours.

Sokch'o buses depart 15 times daily between 8.28 am and 3.56 pm. The fare is W15,600 and the journey takes 7¾ hours.

Taegu buses depart every nine minutes from 5.30 am to 10 pm. The fare is W3900 and the journey takes 1½ hours.

All buses going to Pusan, Taegu and Seoul go via Kyŏngju, so you can take any of these to get there so long as they're not express buses. The journey takes 40 minutes.

P'ohang's inter-city bus terminal is notable for being one of the few (or maybe the only one) which has ticket machines with destinations written in both Korean and English.

Train There are a few trains from Pusan, though buses are certainly more convenient. Seoul-P'ohang *saemaul* class trains cost W30,600, run twice daily and take 4¾ hours to make the journey.

Ferry For details of ferries to Ullŭngdo, refer to the appendix at the back of the book.

Getting Around
The Airport The airport bus costs W1000 and takes 25 minutes. A taxi covers the distance in less than 20 minutes and costs W6000.

ULLŬNGDO ISLAND
Isolated about 135 km east of the Korean peninsula, this spectacularly beautiful island is all that remains of an extinct volcano that

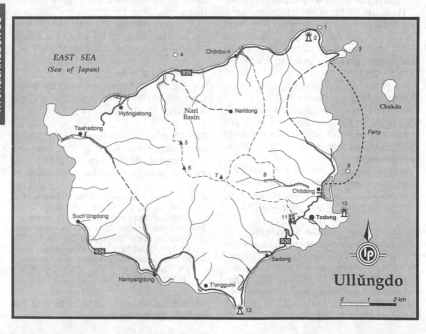

towers over the storm-lashed East Sea (Sea of Japan).

The island was captured from pirates on the orders of King Chijŭng (500-514 AD), the 22nd king of the Shilla dynasty, to secure the east coast of the peninsula. Ullŭngdo essentially remained a military outpost until 1884, when migration to the island was sanctioned by the government.

Rugged forested mountains and dramatic cliffs rise steeply from the sea, so don't expect sandy beaches. Snorkelling and scuba diving off the rocks is stunning, thanks to the clear water and abundant sea life, but the rip-tides can be powerful and the water is always cold. In short, diving in Ullŭngdo is not an activity for a novice.

Thanks to the rugged topography and isolation, the island is only sparsely inhabited and farms are tiny. Out of a population of 20,000, 10,000 live in Todong, another 5000 in Chŏdong and perhaps 1000 in Sadong. Most of the people are concentrated in small villages along the coast and make their living from summer tourists and by harvesting fish. Everywhere you look there are racks of drying squid, seaweed and octopus. Other industries include the production of pumpkin taffy and carvings made from native Chinese juniper. These products are for sale at the island's many souvenir shops, along with plenty of other tourist kitsch, much of which is made in China.

A popular slogan promoted by the local chamber of commerce is that Ullŭngdo lacks three things – thieves, pollution and snakes.

Information

There's a small Tourism Bureau (☎ 791-2191, ask for *kwangwanggyŏ*) near the ferry terminal. There's no English sign identifying the office, but the staff can speak some English and supply you with a useful brochure and tourist map. More detailed maps of the island can be purchased from tourist shops.

There are no banks on Ullŭngdo so take enough local currency with you (including enough to see you through a typhoon)

Todong

Todong is the island's administrative centre and largest town. It is almost hidden away like a pirate outpost in a narrow valley between two craggy, forested mountains and its very narrow harbour front makes it visible only when approached directly.

Boat Trips

Most visitors seem to agree that a boat trip around the island (about 56 km in all) is mandatory. The coast is spectacular, but the sightseeing boats are horribly overcrowded in summer and you mostly see seasick Korean tourists.

Enormous stacks rise vertically from the depths and reach for the clouds. Kong'am (Elephant Rock) is perhaps the most famous of these; the peculiar weathered appearance of the rock is not unlike the skin of an elephant.

In summer at least two tourist boats depart Todong daily at 9 am and 4 pm. On summer

---

Ullŭngdo 울릉도

1　Samsŏn'am Rock
　　삼선암
2　Lighthouse
　　영금정
3　Kwanŭmdo
　　관음도
4　Kong'am (Elephant Rock)
　　공암
5　Mirŭksan (900m)
　　미륵산
6　Hyŏngjebong (915m)
　　형제봉
7　Sŏnginbong (984m)
　　성인봉
8　Pongnae Waterfall
　　봉래폭포
9　Sea Stack
　　북저바위
10　Lighthouse
　　영금정
11　Taewonsa Temple
　　대원사
12　Lighthouse
　　영금정

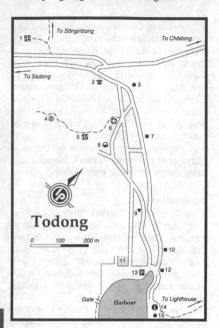

Todong 도동

1 Taewonsa Temple
   대원사
2 Korea Telecom
   한국통신
3 Ullŭng School
   울릉국교
4 Todong Mineral Springs
   도동약수터
5 Haedosa Temple
   해도사
6 Hospital
   병원
7 Ullŭng Hotel
   울릉호텔
8 Bus Stop
   정류장
9 Pizza Daily
   피자데인리
10 Pongnae Yŏgwan
   봉래어관
11 Park
   공원
12 Ullŭng Beach Hotel
   울릉비치호텔
13 Car Park
   주차장
14 Tourist Office
   여행사
15 Ferry Terminal
   여객선터미널

weekends there might be three boats, departing at 9 am, 3 and 4 pm. Tickets cost W8000.

Smaller boats depart from Chŏdong at odd times – make local inquiries.

In both Todong and Chŏdong you'll see plenty of fishing boats docked during the day. They don't generally take tourists, but it is interesting to watch them in the evening when they head out to sea with their brilliant lanterns glaring. The bright lights draw squid to their doom, just as a moth is drawn to a candle.

Pongnae Waterfall

As Ullŭngdo gets more than its fair share of rain, it naturally has a number of streams and waterfalls. Pongnae Waterfall is the easiest to reach: it's about five km from Todong and just 1½ km from Chŏdong. A frequent bus from Todong can drop you off near the ticket office, after which it's a steep one km walk along a very scenic path.

On the walk up to the falls you'll soon come to an outdoor cafe where you can visit a glass-enclosed room and experience a natural rock 'refrigerator': fanned by a draft of cold air from far underground, drinks can be kept very cool here without electricity.

Swimming is not allowed in the pools under the waterfall because some of the water is used to supply Chŏdong.

Todong Mineral Spring Park

There are some mineral springs halfway between Todong and Ch'ont'aejong. Near the park's entrance are monuments dedicated to General An Yong-bok and Kim Ha-woo. A stele displays a poem dedicated to the island. There is also a small history museum displaying artefacts from early residents of Ullŭngdo.

Drinking the spring's waters is claimed to have all sorts of medicinal benefits. The is a big deal to Koreans rather than for foreigners, but it's worth the short walk up here just to enjoy the party atmosphere.

Taewonsa Temple

This small Buddhist temple is hidden in the forest just off the main road that leads from Todong to Chŏdong. From the ferry pier at Todong it's about a 20-minute walk. The path is only signposted in Korean. The temple is not stunning, but the bell is finely crafted and the setting is very mellow.

Sŏnginbong Peak

This is the highest peak (984m) on the island and the summit of a dormant volcano. Various pathways lead up to the summit; for the main one take the path from Todong to Taewonsa – just before you reach the temple there is a fork in the trail and a sign (in Korean) pointing the way to Sŏnginbong. From Todong, the whole up and back trip takes about seven hours, so get an early start. You can't count on finding water along the route so bring plenty.

From the summit you can also descend to Nari Basin and walk back along the coast road, but it's a very long hike and you'll need to camp overnight.

Nari Basin

This valley is on the north slope of Sŏnginbong. It's the only place on the island that's reasonably flat, so there are several farms here. All around the valley there are thickly-forested slopes which are very photogenic.

Nari Basin is most readily reached on foot by hiking down from Sŏnginbong.

Namyang

The small fishing village of Namyang, south-west of Todong, is also worth a visit. Half the fun is getting there – the road from Todong follows a tortuous path along the coastal cliffs. This could raise the hair on your head or cause you to go prematurely grey, but there's no denying that it's spectacular. When you finally get to the village,

you may find yourself the local tourist attraction – foreigners rarely get this far.

The journey can be made by public bus or taxi. Along the way there are opportunities to stop off in Sadong and T'onggumi.

Places to Stay

Yŏgwan prices in Ullŭngdo rise steeply in the summer peak season (July and August), when the island is thronged with Korean vacationers. But even on a Saturday night you can find a place to stay, though top end accommodation tends to book out with tour groups.

Every ferry is met by a gaggle of ajummas, all of them extolling the virtues of their minbak. By all means go and have a look at what's on offer, but don't settle for anything you're not satisfied with – there are plenty of good ones to choose from. In the peak season minbak generally go for W20,000.

For campers with their own tents, there's a landscaped site just below the mineral springs which costs W3000 per tent. A shower and toilet block are on site.

Yŏgwan are ubiquitous in Todong. You can figure on W30,000 during summer. Closest to the ferry pier is the *Pongnae Yŏgwan*. For a little more money, there is the *Ullŭng Hotel* (☎ 791-6611) which boasts 36 double rooms at W40,000. For the same price you can also stay at the 30-room *Ullŭng Beach Hotel* (☎ 791-3132).

Even if you are staying in a room with a bath/shower and you have been hiking around the island, it is worth paying a visit to the *mokyokt'ang* (bath-house) in Todong, which accommodates both men and women. For W3000 you'll be given soap, shampoo, body lotion, a towel and a body scrubber and your introduction to a room full of madly splashing bodies. The bath-house is on the main street a few doors up from the harbour on the left hand side.

In Chŏdong there are also numerous accommodation possibilities.

At the top end of the market is the *Ullŭng Marina Hotel* (☎ 791-0020) in Sadong. Doubles begin at W55,000.

KYŎNGSANGBUK-DO

Places to Eat

Outdoor *seafood stalls* are ubiquitous in Ullŭngdo and you have to be careful not to trip over a squid.

If you're in the mood for something western, *Pizza Daily* in downtown Todong does a decent pulgogi pizza for W10,000 to W17,000 (depending on size). The small ones are easily enough to satisfy all but the most voracious appetites.

There are a few scattered *kimbap shops* where you can eat for as little W1500.

Entertainment

Karaoke lounges create a bit of noise pollution during the summer months. It can be fun if you're into it, though most westerners swear that the wailing sounds like a sonic representation of the island's chief product – squid.

Getting There & Away

You need your passport to enter Ullŭngdo, so be sure to bring it along.

Helicopter Citiair flies helicopters between Kangnŭng on the Korean peninsula and the hamlet of Sadong on Ullŭngdo. The one-way fare is W90,000 and the flight takes 50 minutes. You can call for bookings in Seoul (☎ 3272-8120), Kangnŭng (☎ 648-7626) or Ullŭngdo (☎ 791-1146).

Boat You can get to Ullŭngdo by ferry from P'ohang, Hup'o, Sokch'o and Tonghae. The good ship *Sun Flower* from P'ohang is the largest and most comfortable boat and it's the only possibility if you want to bring a vehicle to the island. In summer when the sea is relatively calm, many tourists prefer the smaller boats from Sokch'o, Tonghae or Hup'o.

Ferries are cancelled when the weather is rough, even during the summer peak season. If you happen to be on Ullŭngdo when the weather turns foul, you may have to spend more time on the island than you had originally planned.

Booking in advance may be necessary during July and August, but otherwise you can buy your ticket at the boat terminal. Advance bookings and news about cancelled ferries (in English) can be obtained in Seoul by ringing up Seoul Daea Express (☎ 514-6766). You can also ring up the passenger terminals at the various ports: P'ohang (☎ 425111); Hup'o (☎ 787-2811/2); Tonghae (☎ 315891); Ullŭngdo (☎ 791-0801); Sokch'o (☎ 636-2811).

Some travel agents also make reservations and get tickets, though you might have to book a tour through them. Departure times are shown in the appendix at the back of this book.

Getting Around

Bus There are few roads and overland public transportation is limited to three buses which all charge W800.

Todong-Chŏdong-Naesujŏn, departures every 30 minutes from 6 am to 8 pm; a 10-minute drive

Todong-Chŏdong-Pongnae Waterfall, departures every 10 minutes (in summer tourist season) from 6 am to 7.30 pm; a 15-minute drive

Todong-Sadong-T'onggumi-Namyang, departures every 40 minutes from 6 am to 7.40 pm; a 30-minute drive

Taxi The ring road which circumnavigates the island is approximately 40 km long, but has not yet been completed. Parts of it are little more than jeep trail. Jeep taxis can be chartered (at negotiable prices) for a tour over most of the island's roads, but for some areas you have to take the ferry from Chŏdong to Sŏmmok. For short distances, flagfall begins at W1000.

Bike Nobody as yet rents mountain bikes or motorcycles, though you can carry one on the large boat from P'ohang.

Boat A commuters' ship connects Chŏdong and Sŏmmok. This service will probably be snuffed when the highway is brought up to scratch.

Kyŏngju

Previous page:
Shinsŏnsa temple

Right: Dramatic
performance at
Pomun Lake
amphitheatre

Below: Autumn at
Pulguksa temple

For almost 1000 years Kyŏngju was the capital of the Shilla dynasty; for nearly 300 years of that period, following Shilla's conquest of the neighbouring kingdoms of Koguryo and Paekche, it was the capital of the whole peninsula. It had its origins way back in 57 BC, at the same time Julius Caesar was subduing Gaul, and survived until the 10th century AD when it fell victim to division from within and invasion from without. A time span like that is rare for any dynasty.

Following its conquest by Koryŏ in 918, after which the capital of Korea was moved far to the north, Kyŏngju fell into a prolonged period of obscurity. It was pillaged and ransacked by the Mongols in the early 13th century and by the Japanese in the late 16th century. Despite these ravages and the neglect of centuries the city survived to experience a cultural revival which began early this century and continues today. A great deal of restoration work has been accomplished, all of it to original specifications, and almost every year archaeologists uncover more treasure-troves of precious relics which help throw light on life during Shilla times.

Today Kyŏngju is an expanding city, though still relatively small (population 300,000); its major drawcard is that it's literally an open-air museum. In whatever direction you care to walk you will come across tombs, temples, shrines, the remains of palaces, pleasure gardens, castles, Buddhist statuary and even an observatory. It's an incredible place where the examples of Shilla artistry in the valley are only the most conspicuous and accessible of the sights. Up in the forested mountains which surround the city there are thousands of Buddhist shrines, temples, inscriptions, rock carvings, pagodas and statues. Just how much you enjoy Kyŏngju really depends on your interests: enthusiasts can and do spend weeks wandering around these places; other visitors may quickly tire of what appears, at first glance, to be mediocre rubble.

The dictator Park Chung-hee did his bit to preserve Kyŏngju – he set up strict limits on building heights and required houses to have curly roofs. In this era of democracy, the restrictions have been relaxed, to the delight of real estate developers but much to the chagrin of traditionalists.

Orientation

Central Kyŏngju is a fairly compact city. About five km east of town is Pomun Lake, a resort area with a country club, golf course, luxury hotels, condominiums and posh restaurants with all the trimmings.

A 16-km drive from the centre to the south-east brings you to Pulguksa, one of Korea's most famous temples and a major tourist drawcard. Next to the temple is the resort village of Pulguk-dong.

Kyŏngju National Park surrounds Kyŏngju city. It's not one contiguous park, but numerous separate districts: to the east is the largest district, T'ohamsan; due south of downtown Kyŏngju is the Namsan District, another significant piece of the park; the Hwarang and Sŏak Districts are to the west; and to the north-east is the Sokŭmgang District. Other pieces of the park lie further afield on the coast near Taebon.

Information

There is a tourist information kiosk (☎ 772-9289) outside the Kyŏngju bus terminal with English-speaking staff. This place also dishes out decent maps of the area. There is a similar information booth (☎ 772-9289) in front of the railway station.

If you're going to spend a lot of time exploring Kyŏngju and the surrounding area, and are interested in the legends, a detailed history and current archaeological debate about the Shilla remains, then it's

Ram figure of the zodiac from the tomb of General Kim Yu-sin.

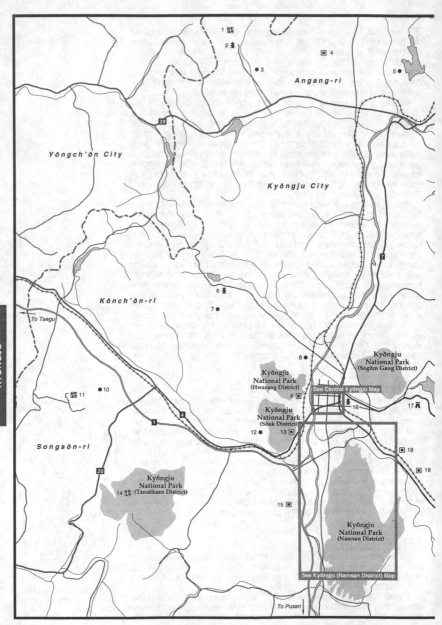

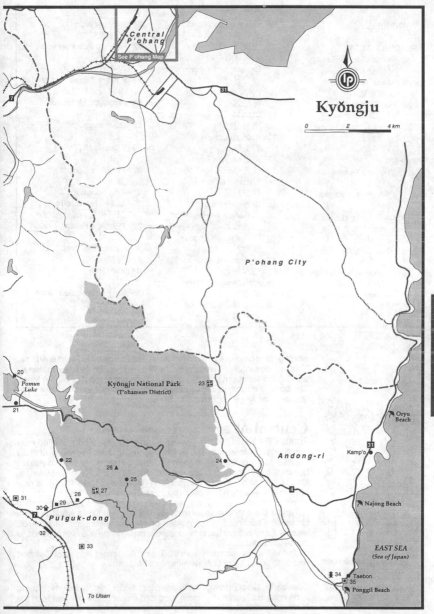

Kyŏngju

Central
P'ohang
See P'ohang Map

P'ohang City

Kyŏngju National Park
(T'ohamsan District)

Pomun
Lake

Andong-ri

Oryu
Beach

Kamp'o

Najong Beach

Pulguk-dong

EAST SEA
(Sea of Japan)

Taebon

Ponggil Beach

To Ulsan

KYŎNGJU

Kyŏngju 경주

PLACES TO STAY

20 Pomun Tourist Resort
　　보문관광단지
28 Kolon Hotel
　　코롱호텔
29 Hot Springs Hotel
　　온천호텔
30 Kyŏngju Youth Hostel
　　경주유스호스텔

OTHER

1 Todŏksa Temple
　　도덕사
2 Chŏnghyesa Pagoda
　　정혜사
3 Oksan Sŏwon &
　　Tongnaktang
　　옥산서원, 동낙당
4 King Hŭngdŏk's Tomb
　　흥덕왕능
5 Yangdong Folk Village
　　양동민속마을
6 Namsarisa Pagoda
　　남사리사

7 Yongdamjŏng Pavilion
　　용담정
8 Dongkuk University
　　동국대교경주분교
9 General Kim Yu-shin's Tomb
　　김유신장군묘
10 Poktu'am Hermitage
　　복두암
11 Chusasa Temple
　　주사사
12 Kyŏngju University
　　경주대학교
13 King Muyol's Tomb
　　태종무열왕능
14 Shinsŏnsa Temple
　　신선사
15 King Minae's &
　　Hŭigang's Tombs
　　민애왕능, 희강왕능
16 Punhwangsa Pagoda
　　분황사
17 Myŏnghwal Fortress Site
　　명활산성
18 King Hyogong Tomb
　　효공왕능
19 King Shinmu Tomb
　　신무왕능

21 Kyŏngju World
　　경주월드
22 Kyŏngju Folk Handicraft
　　Village
　　경주민속공예촌
23 Kirimsa Temple & Waterfall
　　기림사, 기림폭포
24 Kolgul'am Hermitage
　　골굴암
25 Sŏkkuram Grotto
　　석굴암
26 T'ohamsan (745m)
　　토함산
27 Pulguksa Temple
　　불국사
31 King Sŏngdŏk's &
　　Queen Hyoso's Tombs
　　성덕왕능, 효소왕능
32 Pulguksa Railway Station
　　불국사역
33 Kwaenŭng Tomb
　　괘릉
34 Kamŭnsa
　　감은사
35 King Munmu Sea Tomb
　　문무왕해중릉

worth getting hold of a copy of *Korea's Golden Age* by Edward B Adams. This is a beautifully illustrated guide to all known Shilla sites written by a man who was born in Korea and who has spent most of his life there. The book is difficult or impossible to buy in Kyŏngju, so pick up a copy at one of the large bookshops in Seoul.

Central Area

Tumuli Park Right in the heart of Kyŏngju City is a huge walled area containing 20 tombs of the Shilla monarchs and members of their families. Many of them have been excavated in recent years and yielded fabulous treasures which are now on display at the National Museum. One of the tombs, the Ch'ŏnmach'ong (Heavenly Horse Tomb), is now open in cross-section to show its method of construction. This huge tomb, 13m high and 47m in diameter, was built around the end of the 5th century AD and is the only one so far excavated which contains a wooden burial chamber. Facsimiles of the golden crown, bracelets, jade ornaments, weapons and pottery found here are displayed in glass cases around the inside of the tomb.

Tumuli Park is open daily from 8.30 am to 6.30 pm (1 April to 31 October) and 8.30 am to 5 pm (1 November to 31 March).

Tombs in Nosŏ-dong There are other Shilla tombs, for which there is no entry fee, across the main road and closer to the city centre in the Nosŏ-dong district. Sŏbongch'ong and Kŭmgwanch'ong are two adjacent

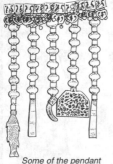

Some of the pendant decorations adorning a gold belt fashioned by the skilled goldsmiths of the Shilla era.

tombs, built between the 4th and 5th centuries AD, that were excavated between 1921 and 1946. The finds included two gold crowns. Across the road Ponghwadae, the largest extant Shilla tomb, is 22m high and 250m in circumference. Adjoining Ponghwadae is Kŭmnyongch'ong. Houses covered much of this area until 1984, when they were removed. It's tempting to climb to the top of one of these tombs, but if you do you'll have park guardians chasing you and blowing whistles! And that's despite the fact that hundreds of similarly minded people have done just that, judging from the bare tracks up the side of the tombs.

Ch'ömsöngdae A few hundred metres from Tumuli Park is Ch'öm-söngdae, a stone observatory constructed between 632 and 646 AD. Its apparently simple design conceals an amazing subtlety. The 12 stones of its base symbolise the months of the year and, from top to bottom, there are 30 layers – one for each day of the month. Altogether there are 366 stones used in its construction, roughly one for each day of the year. There are numerous other technical details relating to the tower's position, angles and the direction of its corners in relation to certain stars.

Ch'ömsöngdae – this unassuming structure houses one of the oldest observatories in East Asia

Panwolsong A little further on from Ch'ömsöngdae on the right side, at the junction with the main road, is Panwolsong (Castle of the Crescent Moon). Panwolsong was once the royal castle and the site of a fabled palace which dominated the whole area. There's hardly anything left of this fortress today except Sökbinggo or 'Stone Ice House' which was once used as a food store. There's no entry charge.

Anapji Pond Across the other side of the road (on the left hand side) is Anapji Pond, constructed by King Munmu in 674 AD as a pleasure garden to commemorate the unification of Shilla. Today there are only remnants of the palace which once stood here, but when the pond was drained for repair in 1975 thousands of relics were dredged up, including a perfectly preserved royal barge now displayed in the National Museum.

KYŎNGJU

National Museum Continuing a little further along the main road you come to the National Museum. This beautiful new building, whose design is based on classical Korean architecture, houses the best collection of historical artefacts of any museum in Korea, including the National Museum in Seoul.

Outside the main building in its own pavilion hangs the Emille Bell, one of the largest and most beautifully resonant bells ever made in Asia. It's said that its ringing can be heard over a three-km radius when struck only lightly with the fist. Unfortunately, you won't be allowed to test this claim! The museum is open during the same hours as Tumuli Park.

Punhwangsa Pagoda Completing this circuit is the Punhwangsa Pagoda. It was built in the mid 600s AD, during the reign of Queen Sondok, and is the oldest pagoda in Korea which can be dated. It originally had nine storeys but only three are left today. The magnificently carved Buddhist guardians and stone lions are a major feature of the pagoda.

To get there follow the willow-lined road across from the National Museum until you reach the first intersection. Turn right here then take the first lane on the right. The walk takes 20 to 25 minutes in all.

Shilla royalty was crowned with gold. This example was created about 14 centuries ago.

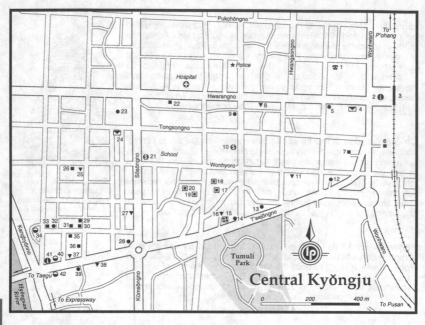

This 1300-year-old carved tortoise is all that remains of the stele at King Muyol's tomb.

West Area

King Muyol's Tomb The main tomb of the Muyol group is that of King Muyol who, in the mid-7th century, paved the way for the unification of Korea by conquering the rival Paekche Kingdom. Just as you enter the tomb compound there is an interesting monument to his exploits in the form of a tortoise carrying a capstone finely carved with intertwined dragons symbolising the power of his position.

General Kim Yu-shin's Tomb Back towards town and along a branch road which initially follows the river is the tomb of General Kim Yu-shin. He was one of Korea's greatest military heroes and led the armies of both Muyol and his successor, Munmu, in the 7th-century campaigns which resulted in the unification of the country. Though smaller in scale than the tomb of King Muyol, the tomb of General Kim is much more elaborate and surrounded by finely carved figures of the zodiac. The tomb stands on a wooded bluff overlooking the city.

The tomb of General Kim Yu-shin is typical of the many tumuli that dot the Kyŏngju landscape.

KYŎNGJU

KYŎNGJU

South-East Area

Pulguksa Built on a series of stone terraces about 16 km south-east of Kyŏngju is Pulguksa ('Buddha nation temple'), the crowning glory of Shilla temple architecture. It really is magnificent. Korea has never gone in for huge, monolithic (though magnificent) temples like the Potala Palace in Lhasa; instead it concentrates on the excellence of its carpentry, the incredible skill of its painters and the subtlety of its landscapes.

Originally built in 528 AD during the reign of King Pob-hung then enlarged in 751, it survived intact until destroyed by the Japanese in 1593. It languished in ruins, although a few structures were rebuilt, and didn't regain its former glory until 1970, when the late President Park Chung-hee ordered its reconstruction along the original lines. Work was completed in 1972.

Standing on the highest level and looking down you are presented with a rolling sea of tiles formed by one sloping roof after the next. The painting of the external woodwork and of the roofs should be one of the Seven Wonders of the World. Down in the courtyard of the first set of buildings are two pagodas which survived Japanese vandalism and which stand in complete contrast to each other. The first, Tabo t'ap Pagoda, is of plain design and typical of Shilla artistry; the other, Sokkatap Pagoda, is much more ornate and typical of those constructed

This lion guards one of the approaches to the superb Tabo t'ap Pagoda at Pulguksa.

in the neighbouring Paekche Kingdom. Copies of these two pagodas stand outside the main building of the Kyŏngju National Museum. Entry to the temple costs W2500 (less for students).

To get to Pulguksa from the city, take bus Nos 11, 12, 101 or 102. Bus Nos 12 and 102 go via Pomun Lake on the way out, and via Namsan Village on the way back. Bus Nos 11 and 101 do the opposite. The fare on bus Nos 11 and 12 is W400. Bus Nos 101 and 102 are express buses which take 35 minutes for the ride and cost W700. The buses drop you at the car park in Pulguk-dong (Pulguk Village), just below the temple.

Sŏkkuram Grotto High up in the mountains above Pulguksa, reached by a long, winding sealed road, is the famous Sŏkkuram Grotto. Here a seated image of the Sakyamuni Buddha looks out over the mountainous landscape towards the distant East Sea. Constructed in the mid-8th century out of huge blocks of granite – quarried far to the north at a time when the only access was a narrow mountain path – it bears a striking resemblance to similar figures found in China and India (especially those at Badami, north of Mysore).

When the Koryŏ dynasty was overthrown and Buddhism suppressed during the Yi dynasty the Sŏkkuram fell into disrepair. It was forgotten until accidentally rediscovered in 1909, during the Japanese occupation, and had the regional governor had his way it might very well have ended up in a Japanese museum. Luckily the local Korean authorities refused to co-operate in its removal and in 1913 a two-year restoration was undertaken. Unfortunately, incompetence resulted in the destruction of much of the superstructure at this time, but in 1961 a more thorough restoration was begun under the auspices of UNESCO (United Nations Educational Scientific & Cultural Organisation). It was completed three years later.

The one disappointing thing about Sŏkkuram Grotto is that the Buddha is encased in a shiny, reflective glass case and photographs are not permitted. Entry to the grotto costs W2500.

Both Pulguksa and Sŏkkuram Grotto literally crawl with tourists every day of the week during the summer months and the place can take on the air of a mass barbecue, so don't expect a wilderness experience.

The placement of the main Buddha in the Sŏkkuram Grotto conveys harmony and tranquility.

To get to the grotto from Pulguksa, take one of the frequent tourist buses which leave from the tourist information pavilion (☎ 746-4747) in the car park below the temple. The return fare is W2000 and there are departures every 50 minutes throughout the day. The buses terminate at a car park and from there it's a 400m walk along a shaded gravel track to the grotto. You get 40 minutes to visit the grotto before the bus returns, but if you miss it you can take any bus back without paying an additional fare. Alternatively, there's a well-marked hiking trail from the grotto to Pulguksa (about 3.2 km long) which is a much more interesting way to return.

Kwaenŭng Tomb Several km further to the south-east along the main road is Kwaenŭng Tomb. It is worth visiting for the unusual carved figures which line the approaches – military guards, civil officials, lions and monkeys. The military figures are quite unlike any others around Kyŏngju, with wavy hair, heavy beards and prominent noses. It's said they represent the Persian mercenaries who are known to have served the court of Shilla. The tomb itself is decorated with carved reliefs of the 12 animals of the zodiac. This tomb compound is rarely visited.

To reach Kwaenŭng Tomb from Pulguksa, take bus No 12, which will take you to the junction with the main road where the Pulguk railway station is. Change here for a bus going along the main road and tell the driver where you are heading. It's usually four or five stops from here, depending on who wants to get off or on. Where you get off there is a billboard at the side of the road with an illustration of Kwaenŭng Tomb on it. Take the tarmac road on the left hand side and follow it for about one km. It takes you directly to the tomb.

There are frequent buses back into Kyŏngju from the main road which go via the National Museum and the railway station – bus Nos 15 and 35 are two which cover this route. Simply flag them down. The fare is W400.

Places to Stay – bottom end

The *Hanjin Hostel* (☎ 771-4097; fax 772-9679), also known as the *Hanjin-jang Yŏgwan*, is two blocks north-east of the bus terminal and easily identified by a large sign in English on the roof. The congenial owner, Mr Kwon Young-joung, speaks good English and Japanese, hands out free maps and is very knowledgeable about local sights. The management seems to understand the needs of travellers – there is hot water for making tea and noodles; a meeting room for socialising with other travellers; and a courtyard where you can hang out in the evening and watch the stars. Surprisingly, for a yŏgwan, there is a satellite dish and English-language STAR TV from Hong Kong. This place has become a sort of backpackers' unofficial travel and information centre for Kyŏngju. Guests can use the washing machine and refrigerator, and you can receive faxes here. Prices for doubles with shared bath are W18,000; doubles with private bath costs W20,000 to W25,000. For a third person it costs 30% more. The price remains the same all year round.

There are heaps of other yŏgwan near the bus terminal, all charging similar or higher prices. Closest to the railway station is the *Buhojang Hotel*, which charges W25,000 for a double. The same price is charged at the nearby *Kirin Hotel. Seorimjang Hotel* asks W30,000 and *Oksanjang Yŏgwan* costs W28,000.

There are other places to stay near the railway station. You can try the *San-jang Yŏgwan, Myŏngji Yŏgwan* and *Hwanggŭm-jang Yŏgwan*.

The *Kyŏngju Youth Hostel* (☎ 421771) is far out of town near Pulguksa. This place tends to pack out with youth groups – be sure you have a reservation if you plan to stay.

The craftsmanship of Kyŏngju architecture even extended to the intricate detail of rooftiles.

KYŎNGJU

Places to Stay – middle

3rd Class Hotels rated 3rd class in Kyŏngju typically cost from W28,000 to W45,000. Some hotels in this category include:

Hyŏpsŏng (☎ 413335), 130-6 Nosŏ-dong (in central Kyŏngju)
Kyŏngju Park (☎ 428804), 170-1 Nosŏ-dong (in central Kyŏngju)

2nd Class Hotels rated 2nd class in Kyŏngju typically cost from W33,000 to W55,000. Some hotels in this division include:

Pulguksa Tourist (☎ 746-1911; fax 746-6604), 648-1 Chinhyŏn-dong (at Pulguk-dong near Pulguksa temple)
Kyŏngju (☎ 745-7123), 645 Shinp'yŏng-dong (near Pomun Lake)

1st Class Hotels rated 1st class in Kyŏngju typically cost from W57,000 to W80,000. The *Kyŏngju Spa Hotel*, also known as the *Hot Springs Hotel* (☎ 745-6661; fax 746-6665) is in this category; its official address is 145-1 Kujŏng-dong, but it's close to Pulguksa.

Places to Stay – top end

Super-Deluxe All the hotels in Kyŏngju rated super-deluxe are by Pomun Lake or Pulguksa. Rooms carry a price tag from about W93,000 to W100,000. Hotels in this range include:

Chosun (☎ 745-7701; fax 408349), San 410, Shinp'yŏng-dong (by Pomun Lake)
Concorde (☎ 745-7000; fax 745-7010), 410 Shinp'yŏng-dong (by Pomun Lake)
Hilton (☎ 745-7788; fax 745-7799), 370 Shinp'yŏng-dong (by Pomun Lake)
Hyundae (☎ 748-2233; fax 748-8234), 477-2 Shinp'yŏng-dong (by Pomun Lake)
Hyundai (☎ 748-2233), 477-2 Shinp'yŏng-dong (by Pomun Lake)
Kolon (☎ 746-9001; fax 746-6331), 111-1 Ma-dong (near Pulguk-dong); this place boasts Kyŏngju's only casino

Places to Eat

There's an excellent choice of *restaurants* in Kyŏngju, including Korean, Chinese, Japanese, western and seafood; seafood restaurants, as elsewhere in Korea, tend to be very expensive.

There are plenty of *bakeries* about town; *England Bakery* is notable for its enormous size and selection.

If you'd like a break from Korean food then the *Shiga Restaurant & Bar* on Tongsongno is a good place to go. It offers a range of western-style food, including such things as spaghetti with meat sauce. This restaurant is easy to miss; it's on the 1st floor and there's no sign in English though it does say in English underneath the *hangŭl* 'Western Restaurant'.

Taesong Shikdang on Sosongno is a popular restaurant doing Korean dishes. The food is good – the pulgogi is excellent – and the prices reasonable.

The *Grand Buffet Restaurant* is on the 2nd floor, just above the aforementioned Taesong Shikdang. You can enjoy all you can eat for W5000 and there are normally about 20 dishes on offer.

Chicky Chicky Fried Chicken (☎ 749-7279) serves – well, you guessed it. A half chicken costs W4500 and a whole bird is W8000. If you ring up, they can deliver a fried fowl to your door.

Just next door to Chicky Chicky is *Kwangrim Shikdang*, another fine Korean-style restaurant.

Going up somewhat in price, the *Grand Restaurant* enjoys a well-deserved reputation for its pulgogi, though they also serve a good range of other dishes. The menu is in both English and Korean.

Sarangch'ae Restaurant is an upscale traditional Korean restaurant with all the trimmings. It's just to the west of Pŏpchangsa (a small temple) and City Hall.

Entertainment
Soju tents set up in the evening along the riverbank to the north of town. This is a good place to enjoy snacks and alcoholic drinks at reasonable prices.

If you'd prefer something non-alcoholic, *Yurim Teahouse* is off the eastern end of Taejŏngno in a small alley.

Things to Buy
The price tags in many shops are geared to the Japanese tourist market – you can often get a 30% discount simply by pointing to the price tag and saying, 'I'm not Japanese'.

A shop called *Ch'ŏn Ma Dang* on Hwangrangno near the railway station (see the Kyŏngju map) is significantly cheaper than the souvenir shops around temples and other tourist sights. Items for sale include antiques, dance masks, lacquerware and paintings.

Carved wooden dance masks have been used since ancient times in court and popular plays.

Getting There & Away
Air There is no airport at Kyŏngju itself, but the busy airports at Pusan and P'ohang are readily accessible. P'ohang's airport is closer and therefore preferable, though you'll have to go to Pusan for flights to Japan. See the following Getting Around section for information on airport transport.

Kyoungbuk Travel Service (☎ 412311) in the centre of town is the only travel agency in town which books international air tickets. Another travel agency, just east of the inter-city bus terminal, only books domestic flights.

Bus Kyŏngju has an express bus terminal and an inter-city bus terminal, conveniently adjacent to one other. Buses depart the express bus terminal for the following destinations:

Kwangju buses depart twice daily at 6.30 am and 6.30 pm. The fare is W12,800 (1st class) or W8600 (2nd class), and the journey takes 3¾ hours.
Pusan buses depart every 30 minutes from 7 am to 7.30 pm. The fare is W3600 (1st class) or W2500 (2nd class), and the journey takes one hour. This bus does *not* stop at T'ongdosa (a temple) halfway between Kyŏngju and Pusan; you need the regular inter-city bus for this.
Seoul buses depart every 35 minutes from 7 am to 6.10 pm. The fare is W15,900 (1st class) or W10,700 (2nd class), and the journey takes 4¼ hours.
Taegu buses depart every 20 minutes from 6.50 am to 9.10 pm. The fare is W3000 (1st class) or W2100 (2nd class), and the journey takes 50 minutes.
Taejŏn buses depart every three hours between 8.20 am and 6 pm. The fare is W9700 (1st class) or W6600 (2nd class), and the journey takes 2¾ hours.

Buses depart from the inter-city bus terminal to the following destinations:

Andong buses depart 16 times daily from 7.15 am to 6.16 pm. The fare is W6700 or W8400 and the journey takes three hours.
Kangnŭng buses depart every 30 minutes from 6 am to 4 pm. The fare is W13,600 and the journey takes 6½ hours.

Kimch'ŏn (for Chikchisa) buses depart four times daily between 9.25 am and 5.20 pm. The fare is W5200 and the journey takes 2¼ hours.

P'ohang buses depart every 10 minutes from 5.30 am to 10.50 pm. The fare is W1400 and the journey takes about 40 minutes.

Pusan buses depart 15 times daily from 6.20 am to 9.40 pm. The fare is W2500 and the journey takes one hour. This is the bus to take if you intend to visit T'ongdosa, a temple halfway between Kyŏngju and Pusan.

Taegu buses depart every 10 minutes from 6.20 am to 10.50 pm. The fare is W2100 and the journey takes one hour.

Ulsan buses depart once hourly from 6.30 am to 9.50 pm. The fare is W2200 and the journey takes one hour.

Train Trains connecting Seoul to Kyŏngju are infrequent and you'll probably do better travelling by bus. Departures are from Seoul station, except for the T'ongil train which departs from Ch'ŏngnyangni station. There are also trains between Pusan and Kyŏngju, but, again, buses are more frequent. The train schedule on the Seoul-Kyŏngju route can be found in the appendix at the end of this book.

Getting Around

The Airport Direct buses now link Kyŏngju with both P'ohang Airport and Kimhae Airport (Pusan). The P'ohang Airport bus costs W4500, but the one to Kimhae Airport is W9000. The current departure times are as follows:

Kyŏngju	P'ohang Airport	Kyŏng-ju	Kimhae Airport
6.20 am	8.30 am	8.10 am	10.00 am
9.20	10.50	9.10	11.00
10.30	11.40	1.10 pm	3.00 pm
12.10 pm	1.30 pm	2.10	4.30
2.20	3.40	5.10	6.30
3.30	5.00	6.30	8.10
4.50	6.10		
6.20	7.30		

Bus Many local buses terminate in the road outside the inter-city bus terminal alongside the river, but these are mostly relatively long-distance local buses. For the shorter routes (eg to Pulguksa) buses can be picked up along Sosongno and Taejŏngno.

Four of the most important buses for travellers are Nos 11, 12, 101 and 102; these are the buses you need for Pomun Lake, Pulguksa and Namsan Village. Bus Nos 12 and 102 go Kyŏngju, Pomun Lake, Pulguksa, Namsan Village, Kyŏngju. Bus Nos 11 and 101 go Kyŏngju, Namsan Village, Pulguksa, Pomun Lake, Kyŏngju. Bus Nos 11 and 12 are standing buses and the fare is W400. Bus Nos 101 and 102 are seat buses and the fare is W700. All four buses pass the National Museum on their way out and on their way back. One of these buses comes along about once every five minutes.

Bicycle Hiring a bicycle for a day or two is an excellent way of getting around the sites in the immediate vicinity of Kyŏngju. There are some bike trails around Pomun Lake, which make for pleasant riding.

There are two bike rental shops along Taejŏngno (see map), though no doubt there are other sources. None of their bicycles have gears so going uphill can be hard work. A full-day rental costs W7000.

Ancient harness pieces from the Kaya era, a southern people whom the Shilla conquered.

Around Kyŏngju

SOUTH OF KYŎNGJU

There are literally thousands of other relics from the Shilla Kingdom scattered over the mountains all the way from Kyŏngju to P'ohang on the eastern seaboard, to Taegu in the west and to Pusan in the south. There are also many other places of interest dating from the Chosŏn period and some spectacular geographical beauty.

Namsan

One of the most rewarding areas to explore within easy reach of Kyŏngju is Namsan, a mountain south of the city. Not only is it worth hiking around this area purely for its scenic beauty but the mountain is strewn with royal tombs, pagodas, rock-cut figures, pavilions and the remains of fortresses, temples and palaces. There are hundreds of paths which you can follow along the streams which come tumbling down the mountain. The 'Namsan Skyway' is a winding gravel road which starts out close to P'osŏkjŏngji (bower), skirts the ridges of Namsan and ends up at Namsan Village near T'ongiljŏn (Unification Hall). The paths and tracks are all well-trodden and you cannot get lost, though at times you will need to scout around for relics which are not immediately visible (few are signposted). Whichever point you decide to take off from you're in for an exhilarating experience.

Buses which get you to the Namsan area include Nos 6, 23, 25, 27, 48, 49 and 51.

Visitors to Kyŏngju can experience colourful performances of traditional dance and music.

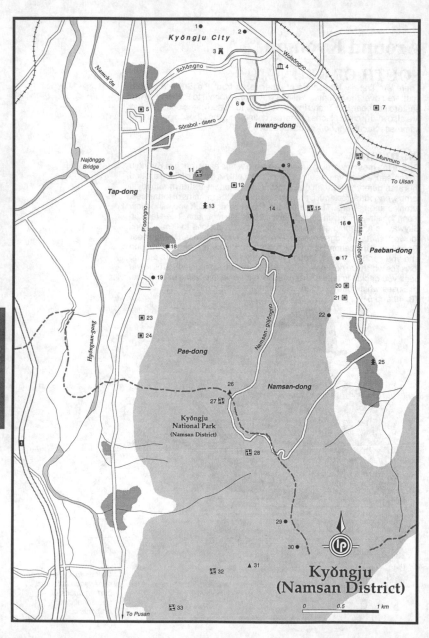

KYŎNGJU

Kyŏngju
(Namsan District)

0   0.5   1 km

Kyŏngju (Namsan District)
경주남산

1 Ch'ŏmsŏngdae
Observatory
첨성대

2 Sŏkbinggo Stone Reservoir
석빙고

3 Panwolsŏng Fortress
반월성

4 National Museum
경주박물관

5 Onŭng Royal Tombs
오릉

6 Sangsŏjang
상서장

7 King Sŏndŏk Tomb
선덕여왕릉

8 Mangdŏksaji
(Old Temple Site)
망덕사지당간지주

9 Maaejosanggun
(Carved Figures)
마애조상군

10 Najŏng Well
나정

11 Namgansaji (Temple Site)
남간사지

12 King Ilsŏng Tomb
일성왕릉

13 Ch'angnimsaji Pagoda
창림사지삼층석탑

14 Namsansŏngji (Castle Site)
남산성지

15 Porisa Temple
보리사

16 Kyŏngbuk Forest
Research Institute
경북임업시험장

17 Hwarang Education Centre
화랑교육원

18 P'osŏkchŏngji Bower
포석정시

19 Triple Buddhas
삼존석불

20 King Hŏngang Tomb
헌강왕릉

21 King Chŏnggang Tomb
정강왕릉

22 T'ongiljŏn (Unification Hall)
통일전

23 Samnu'ŭng (Three Tombs)
삼릉

24 King Kyŏng'ae Tomb
경애왕릉

25 Namsanni Pagoda
남산사지석탑

26 Namsan (466m)
남산

27 Sŏkkasaji (Temple Site)
석기시지

28 Yongjangsaji (Temple Site)
용장사지

29 Stone Buddha
신선암마애보살반가상

30 Stone Carved Buddhist
Images
칠불암마애석상

31 Kŭmosan (495m)
금오산

32 Ch'ŏngsa Temple
천용사

33 Waryongsa Temple
왈용사

Onŭng Tombs Going south from the city over the first river bridge you will come to the Onŭng tombs. These are five of the most ancient tombs in the area and include the 2000-year-old tomb of the kingdom's founder.

P'osŏkjŏngji Further down the road (quite a walk) is P'osŏkjŏngji bower, a banquet garden set in a glade of shade trees (not the originals) where there remains a fascinating reminder of Shilla elegance. This is a curious granite waterway (bower), carved in the shape of an abalone, through which a stream once flowed. The stream is still there but its course is now too low to feed the bower. Entry costs W300.

Bottoms Up

Legend has it that the king, in the company of his concubines and courtiers, would sit beside the waterway while dancers performed in the centre. One of the favourite games played here was for the king to recite a line of poetry and command one of his guests to respond with a matching line, at the same time placing a cup of wine on the water. If the guest couldn't come up with a matching line by the time the cup reached him then the guest was required to drain it to the last drop. Although there are records of similar entertainments in imperial China, P'osŏkjŏngji bower is the only banquet garden left in the world. ■

KYŎNGJU

*One of the Bodhisatvas
flanking the central figure
of the Triple Buddhas.
All three face east –
towards the rising sun.*

Triple Buddhas Less than one km down the road from P'osŏkjŏngji, on the left hand side, there are three mysterious statues known as the Triple Buddhas. Discovered only in 1923, it's not known how they came to arrive here since they are not of Shilla origin and display the massive boldness characteristic of the Koguryo style.

Samnŭng Last on this circuit, just a few minutes' walk past the Triple Buddhas, there's a group of four tombs known as Samnŭng. The one which stands separate from the rest is the burial place of King Kyong'ae, who was killed when a band of robbers raided P'osŏkjŏngji during an elaborate banquet. Nearly 1000 years separate these tombs from those in the Onŭng compound.

Trip No 1 If your time is limited, you could try this full-day itinerary. Take a bus from the inter-city bus terminal and get off at P'osŏkjŏngji (bower) on the west side of Namsan (or at the Samnŭng tombs if you've already visited P'osŏkjŏngji). From P'osŏkjŏngji walk to the Samnŭng tombs (about one km) via the Sambulsa triangle. From the Samnŭng tombs take the track which follows the stream up the side of Namsan to the crest of the mountain. On the way up there you will pass many freestanding and rock-cut images and a small hermitage near the summit where an old bearded monk lives. Follow the trail along the saddle until it joins the Namsan Skyway – the views from the saddle might inspire you to become a monk up here.

Carry on south along the Skyway towards Namsan Village for about half a km until the road makes a sharp turn to the left. A detour straight on from this point will bring you to two pagodas. Neither of these are visible from the road and the trail leading to them is somewhat indistinct. Also, the pagoda furthest from the road is not visible until you are just past the first so it's easy to miss. From here, backtrack to the Skyway and continue down to Namsan Village, where you should visit the twin pagodas and Sochulji (a pavilion and adjoining pond). The latter is an idyllic little spot described in legends going back to the early days of Shilla. If you've had enough for one day at this point you can catch local bus Nos 12 or 102 back to Kyŏngju from Unification Hall. If not, you could carry on south past Namsan Village to the seven Buddha reliefs of Chilbul'am. From there you would have to return to Namsan Village and take a bus back to Kyŏngju.

Trip No 2 Here's another possibility for a full-day trip. Take local bus No 11 and get off as soon as the bus crosses the river – about 2½ km past the National Museum. From here you can visit Porisa in the Miruk Valley; it's a beautifully reconstructed nunnery, set among old conifers, with a number of ancient free-standing images. It is possible to make your way over the hill at the back of this temple to Pagoda Valley but it's a rough climb. If you don't have the right footwear it's perhaps easier to backtrack down to the bridge over the river and turn left there. Take the track along the west side of the river for several hundred metres until you come to a small village. Turn left here and head up Pagoda Valley. The first temple you come to is Okryongsa. Just beyond it you will find the greatest collection of relief carvings anywhere in Korea, as well as a pagoda.

Returning to the river bridge and looking across to the main road to Ulsan you will see two stone pillars standing in a thicket of trees in the middle of paddy fields. These pillars are all that remain of what was once a huge temple complex during Shilla times. If you like fossicking for ancient reliefs then this is the spot to do it. If that doesn't particularly interest you then head off down to Namsan Village and take any of the trails which lead up into the mountains. ■

Above: Fierce
warriors guard
Kirimsa Temple

Left: Colouful god
at Pulguksa
temple

Below: The
silence of the
Shilla tombs ·

GEOFF CROWTHER

RUSTY CARTER

Above Left:
Green eaves,
Pulguksa

Above Right:
Pots and pots,
Folk Handicrafts
Village

Right: Golden
Buddha,
Pulguksa

DEANNA SWANEY

Above: Beating the drum, Pomun Lake amphitheatre

Left: Pavilion beside Anapji Pond

Below: Fan dance butterfly, Pomun Lake amphitheatre

Above Left:
A cloud of cherry
blossoms

Above Right: In
traditional
costume at
Pulguksa

Right: Arched
stone bridge
at Pulguksa

EAST OF KYŎNGJU

There are a number of interesting places to visit along or not far off the road between Kyŏngju and Taebon on the east coast, and the road which takes you there passes through a beautiful and thickly forested section of Kyŏngju National Park.

Kirimsa

This is the first place of interest once you've descended from the pass which takes you through Kyŏngju National Park. The temple was one of the largest complexes near the Shilla capital and its size (14 buildings in all) compares with that of Pulguksa. Yet it is rarely visited by foreigners. You can enjoy this temple in peace and quiet, without the picnicking multitudes common at Pulguksa.

The temple has its origins back in early Shilla times, when a monk named Kwangyu arrived from India and acquired a following of some 500 devotees. Known originally as Imjŏngsa, its name was changed to the present one in 643 AD, when the temple was enlarged. The present buildings date from 1786, when Kirimsa was rebuilt.

There are the beginnings of a small tourist village at the entrance to the temple and minbak rooms are available if you want to stay for the night.

If you have the time, check out the rock-cut image of the Buddha at **Kolgul'am** hermitage off to the west along a footpath (two km) closer to the turn-off from the main road. It will take you about 25 minutes to get to the image.

Getting There & Away Getting to Kirimsa requires a degree of perseverance since there are no direct buses from Kyŏngju. What you have to do is take a bus from the inter-city bus terminal in Kyŏngju to Taebon and ask the driver to drop you off at Andong-ri, where the turn-off to the temple goes off on the left hand side. From here to the temple it's about six km along a paved road. There are local buses from Andong-ri to the temple but they only go four times daily – at 6.20, 10.10 am, 1.10 and 6 pm. These buses originate in Kamp'o, about eight km up the coast from Taebon. For the rest of the day you'll either have to walk, hitch a ride or take a taxi.

Kamunsa

About one km back from Taebon Beach along the main road to Kyŏngju stand the remains of what was a large temple in Shilla times. All that is left are two three-storeyed pagodas – among the largest in Korea – and a few foundation stones. The pagodas are prototypes of those constructed following the unification of Shilla. A huge bell, four times larger than the Emille bell in the National Museum at Kyŏngju, once hung in Kamunsa. In 1592 it was stolen by the Japanese when they invaded; they tried to take it back to their homeland, but didn't get far and the bell was lost in the ocean close to Taebon. An unsuccessful search was made for the bell several years ago by a team from Kyŏngju National Museum and there are plans to try again.

Munmu Sea Tomb

The small, rocky islet 200m off the coast at Taebon is the site of the famous underwater tomb of the Shilla king, Munmu (661-681 AD). It's perhaps the only underwater tomb in the world and at low tide it can be seen through the clear water of the pool in the centre of the islet.

Munmu had made it known that on his death, he wished his body to be burned and the ashes buried at sea close to a temple, Kamunsa. The idea behind these unusual funeral rites was that his spirit would become a dragon and protect the eastern shores of the Shilla Kingdom from Japanese pirates. His wishes were carried out by his son, Shinmu, who became the next Shilla king.

The tomb was not rediscovered until 1967. There is speculation that the rock visible in the pool is actually a stone coffin, but most experts dismiss this as a flight of fantasy though no investigations have been carried out.

It used to be possible to hire boats at the beach to take you out to the islet but access is now restricted to protect the site. You need special permission to go out there, and even if this is granted you'd have to be an enthusiast to pay at least W5000 just to see a stone slab in the middle of a rock pool.

North of Taebon is Taebon Beach, and to the south is Ponggil Beach. Both are popular with Koreans, especially during the summer holiday period, but there's nothing special about this stretch of coastline. The inevitable barbed wire fence lines the beach.

Places to Stay Camping along the beach is prohibited, but you can set up your tent along the banks of the river back from the town where the bridge crosses it. Taebon itself has a number of minbak.

There are a number of *restaurants* along the beaches at Taebon which specialise in seafood but they're ridiculously expensive at W30,000 for a meal! Ask the price of seafood first, or suffer indigestion when you get the bill.

Getting There & Away To get to Taebon from Kyŏngju you must take a bus going to Kamp'o. These leave from the inter-city bus terminal (bay No 2). There are buses every 20 minutes from 6.10 am to 10 pm daily; The fare is W1960 and the journey takes about one hour.

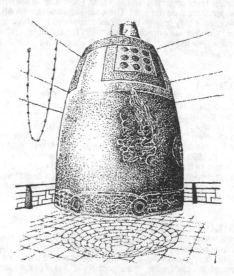

The massive Emille Bell, created in 771 AD, is one of the world's largest and oldest temple bells. Folklore has it that a child was thrown into the molten bronze when the bell was cast, and the sound the bell makes when struck evokes the child's cries for its mother ('Emi' in Korean).

NORTH OF KYŎNGJU

The places of interest north of Kyŏngju are perhaps best seen as two separate day trips; it's possible to see them all in a single day so long as you make an early start.

Yangdong Folk Village

Having steeped yourself in Shilla history it's now time to immerse yourself in a different period of Korea's past which has escaped the ravages of modernisation. Yangdong is a beautiful and peaceful Yi dynasty village full of superb traditional wooden houses and mansions. It's been designated as a preservation area, like Hahoe outside Andong and Sŏng-ŭp on Chejudo, and presents an excellent opportunity to soak up the atmosphere of a Korean village before the advent of concrete and corrugated iron.

The village was established in the 15th and 16th centuries, and consists of around 150 large and small houses typical of the *yangbang class* – a largely hereditary class based on scholarship and official position as opposed to wealth. It was the birthplace of Son-so (1433-84), a scholar-official who was one of the key figures involved in quashing the revolt against King Sejo in 1467. It was also the birthplace of Sŏn Chung-ton (1463-1529), otherwise known as Ujae, and of Yi On-jok (1491-1553), a famous Confucian scholar during the early years of the Yi era, more widely known by his pen name Hoejae.

Most of the houses here are still inhabited so you need to observe the usual courtesies when looking around, but the larger mansions stand empty and are open to the public. There's a plaque outside the more important structures on which you'll find the name of the building and an account of who built it, and in what year. Most of these mansions are left open but there may be one or two which are locked. If that's the case, ask for the key at the nearest house. There are no entry fees to any of the buildings.

Of the larger buildings, make sure you see the Yi Hui-tae House, Shimsujong and Hyangdam House. There's a booklet for sale with a map and coloured photographs (entirely in Korean) at the general store at the entrance to the village. It's worth picking up even if you can't read Korean as it gives you a good idea of the layout of the village. A half hour's walk from the village stands Korea's second largest Confucian study hall, built in honour of Yi On-jok and completed in 1575.

You're very unlikely to come across any other tourists in this village as it rarely features in any of the tourist literature. Possibly as a result, the people who live here are very friendly: it's easy to strike up a conversation and be invited to take tea and snacks. You should plan on spending several hours here.

There are no restaurants in Yangdong but two general stores sell snacks, cold drinks and the like.

Getting There & Away From Kyŏngju, bus Nos 1, 2, 18, 55, 57 and 88 will all get you to within 1½ km of Yangdong. These local buses go down the main road to Kyŏngju-P'ohang then turn around after they've crossed the large river bridge. They then turn off to the right just before the bridge and head for Angang-ri. A little way down this road is another fork to the right and this is where the buses will drop you. From here it's 1½ km to Yangdong, initially following the railway line and then going under it. You can't get lost as there's only the one road into the village.

No local buses go directly into Yangdong from Kyŏngju, but bus No 1 from Angang-ri (not the same as the No 1 from Kyŏngju) goes there three times daily. This bus returns to Angang-ri from Yangdong at around 11 am, 5 and 7.50 pm.

Return a friendly smile in Yandong Folk Village, and you may find yourself invited in for a cup of tea or rice wine.

KYŎNGJU

To get back to Kyŏngju from Yangdong simply walk back to the turn-off where the bus originally dropped you. There are plenty of buses from there back to Kyŏngju. Alternatively, if it's early enough in the day, take a bus to Angang-ri from the turn-off and another bus from there to Oksan Sŏwon (see next section), west of Angang-ri.

Oksan Sŏwon

Oksan Sŏwon was once one of the two most important Confucian schools in Korea and like its counterpart, Tosan Sŏwon outside of Andong, one of the few such scholarly institutes to escape the destruction wrought on them by the father of King Kojong in the 1860s. It was established in 1572 in honour of Yi On-jok (1491-1553) by another famous Confucian scholar, Yi Toegye, and enlarged in 1772. A fire accidentally destroyed some of the buildings here early this century and today only 14 structures remain.

When first established in the 1500s, these *sŏwon* quickly became the centres of learning – and political intrigue – and their alumni were numbered in the thousands. They rapidly became so powerful that the Yi kings lost their supremacy over the Confucian scholars, who thenceforth effectively controlled the country's economy and political direction. Were a scholar to commit a crime, he was tried not by the state but by the Confucian college. The Korean kings were not to regain their supremacy until several centuries later.

These days, though they no longer function, the sŏwon are regarded as an important part of the country's cultural heritage since it was at these schools that most of the calligraphy and paintings of the Yi dynasty's last three centuries were produced.

Oksan Sŏwon is in a sublime setting surrounded by shade trees and overlooking a stream with a waterfall and rock pools – an ideal place for contemplation and study. The main gate is usually unlocked so you can wander at will through the walled compound. Only one building is presently occupied, by a family which looks after the place. There's no entry fee.

During the summer holiday period the banks of the stream are a popular camping spot; you can swim in the rock pools below the waterfall.

Tongnaktang A 10-minute walk beyond Oksan Sŏwon along the main road up the valley will bring you to Tongnaktang hall, built in 1516 as the residence of Yi On-jok after he left the government service. Like the sŏwon, it has a timeless and relaxing atmosphere, as well as a beautiful pavilion which overlooks the stream. The walled compound is partly occupied by a family which looks after the place, but you can wander at will through the rest of it. The main entrance gate is usually unlocked and there's no entry fee.

Chonghyesa Beyond Tongnaktang and off to the left surrounded by rice fields is Chonghyesa, a huge, 13-storied stone pagoda. Its origins are somewhat obscure but it is generally agreed that it dates from the unified Shilla period. The temple of which the pagoda once formed part was destroyed during the Japanese invasion of 1592.

Todŏksa About 2¼ km beyond Chonghyesa, high up in the forested mountains near the end of the valley, is a small temple called Todŏksa. It's a beautiful little place perched on a rocky outcrop from which two springs emerge, and the views are magnificent. There are five buildings in all including a tiny hermitage above the temple itself, complete with its own ondol heating system. It's a steep walk up from the main road along a well-worn path but definitely worth the effort. It's about as far as you can get from the madding crowd and hardly anyone ever comes up here except the monks and the family who look after the cooking and cleaning. If male travellers were to bring their own food and drink, the monks would undoubtedly offer them somewhere to sleep.

To get to Todŏksa, take the main tarmac road up the valley past Tongnaktang, ignoring the gravel road which forks off to the right just after you cross the first bridge. Several hundred metres beyond this you come to a second bridge where the tarmac ends. A little further on from here you'll see a rusty sign on the left hand side with a painting of a temple on it and a zigzag path leading up to it. This is where you turn off and head up the mountain. It's about 900m from here to the temple. Don't be put off by the steepness of the path as it gets gentler further up. You'll know you're on the right track when you come across a rock in the middle of the track saying (in Korean), 'Todŏksa 700m'. There's a similar sign at the 500m point. For most of the way the path is shaded by trees so you can come up here even on a hot day. It's possible to hitch a ride with trucks along the main tarmac road as there's a quarry up near the end of the valley – you may hear the occasional explosion when blasting is in progress.

Getting There & Away The best way to get to Oksan Sŏwon from Kyŏngju is to take the bus to Angang-ri, which conveniently stops at Oksan Sŏwon. The bus leaves Kyŏngju every 30 minutes between 7.25 am and 10.30 pm and the journey take about 30 minutes.

There are also local buses between Angang-ri and Oksan Sŏwon other than the one from Kyŏngju. The stop for these buses in Angang-ri is close to the post office and opposite a supermarket on the road to Yŏngch'ŏn. It's about seven km from Angang-ri to Oksan Sŏwon. A taxi from Angang-ri to Oksan Sŏwon will cost about W5000.

King Hŭndŏk's Tomb

The furthest of the royal tombs from central Kyŏngju, this was also one of the last ones constructed during the Shilla dynasty. It's one of the most complete tombs and has a pretty setting among the trees.

The tomb is four km north of Angang-ri, about half way between Oksan Sŏwon and Yangdong Folk Village.

Yongdamjŏng

Along a minor road in the heart of the countryside stands Yongdamjŏng, the temple complex of the Chundo'kyo (Heavenly Way) religion. This unique Korean religion was founded by Choe Che-woo in 1860 and incorporates aspects of Confucianism, Buddhism and Taoism. Choe was regarded by the Yi authorities as a troublesome subversive at a time when Korea was attempting to shut out foreign influences. He was martyred in Taegu in 1864 and the buildings of this temple were burned to the ground. His followers were a determined bunch, however, and, despite further repression, rebuilt the temple – only to have it burned yet again. The most recent reconstruction was in 1960, this time with government assistance after the area had been made part of the Kyŏngju National Park. It's a beautiful, tranquil area of wooded mountains and terraced rice fields where farmers continue to cultivate the land in the traditional manner.

Within walking distance is the **Namsarisa 3-Stone Pagoda** which is worth a visit if you have the time.

As well as this unique feature of 19 carved niches holding the central figure of Buddha flanked by his attendants, this site gives you a great view and a glimpse of Kyŏngju in the distance.

Getting There & Away To get there take bus No 5 from the inter-city bus terminal in Kyŏngju and ask the driver to drop you at the turn-off for the temple. It's a short walk from where the bus drops you.

WEST OF KYŎNGJU
Poktu'am
Reaching this place involves a steep hike up thickly forested Obongsan mountain. Close to the summit is Poktu'am, a hermitage where you will find a huge rock face out of which 19 niches have been carved. The three central niches hold a figure of the historical Buddha flanked by two bodhisattvas (Munsu and Pohyon) while the remainder house the 16 arhat. The carving is of recent age and, although there's an unoccupied house up here, the actual hermitage which used to stand here was burned down in 1988 after an electrical fault started a blaze. There's also a recently erected statue of Kwanseum, the Goddess of Mercy, just beyond the rock face.

The trail is well maintained and easy to follow, but bring your own liquid refreshments as there are no springs along the way. The walk up will take around 1½ hours and somewhat less coming back down.

Getting There & Away Bus No 28 from Kyŏngju will take you direct to the village of Songsŏn-ri which is where the trail starts up the mountain. There are buses at 9.15, 10 and 11.27 am and the buses will say Sannae-ri in the front window.

If you can't find one of these buses, then take any bus along the old highway to Taegu and get off at the bus station in Kŏnch'ŏn. These buses are very frequent and the fare to Kŏnch'ŏn is W600. From the bus station in Kŏnch'ŏn take one of the frequent local buses to Songsŏn-ri village (about 2½ km, W300).

Where the bus drops you, you'll see a blue and white sign saying 'Songsŏn-ri' and a pedestrian crossing painted across the road. A few metres up from these a river comes down the valley to your right. Take the gravel road on the far side of this river until you get to the point where it crosses the river by a concrete causeway (less than one km). Take the left hand fork before the causeway and after a few metres you'll see a small temple off to the right. The trail to Poktu'am bears off to the left at this point and is well marked with Korean characters painted on rocks. It's impossible to get lost.

Chusasa Temple
This temple is on the opposite side of the valley from Poktu'am, high up on a ridge of Obongsan. The temple was founded by a monk, Uisang, some 1300 years ago and has provided a home for several famous monks.

To get to this temple use the same buses to get to Songsŏn-ri as you would for Poktu'am and take the same gravel road up into the valley, but instead of turning off at the concrete causeway cross it and continue up the other side of the valley. About halfway between the causeway and Chusasa, some 200m off the main gravel road, is Mankyo'am hermitage.

Shinsŏnsa Temple
This is about a two km hike from Poktu'am. This remote temple near the top of Tansŏksan (827m) was once used by General Kim Yu-shin in the 7th century – it has seen a bit of renovation work since then. About 50m to the right as you face the temple are some ancient rock carvings in a small grotto – it's believed to be one of the oldest cave temples in Korea.

Kyŏngsangnam-do

To many people Kyŏngsangnam-do means 'Pusan', the large port city which transcends its surroundings just as Seoul overshadows Kyŏnggi-do. Yet, if you dig a little deeper Kyŏngsangnam-do offers some surprises, including attractive temples, mountains, beaches, hot springs and the two best bird sanctuaries in South Korea.

PUSAN

Pusan is the second largest city (population 3.9 million) and principal port of South Korea. It was the only major city to escape capture by the communists during the Korean War although at the time its population was swelled by an incredible four million refugees. Pusan has a superb location nestled in between several mountain ridges and peaks, but this makes for a very spread-out city and, away from the subway line, it takes a lot of time to get from one place to another.

Many travellers regard Pusan as a concrete jungle to be passed through quickly: a place from which to take the ferries to Yŏsu, Cheju-do or Shimonoseki (Japan), or for domestic and international flights from Kimhae International Airport. This is a great pity as it has a cosmopolitan ambience all of its own, quite distinct from Seoul's, even though it doesn't have the old temples and palaces surrounded by areas of wooded tranquillity right in the heart of the city. It's a city which can grow on you if you're prepared to spend the time exploring, and if you're looking for wooded tranquillity then there are endless possibilities in the mountains which separate the various parts of the city.

Its distinct ambience is the result of constant exposure to sailors from all over the world. As far as seaports go, it's a *relatively* safe place to explore, but you should exercise a bit of caution in the central area at night. There is a huge number of Russian sailors in Pusan, especially in the area just west of Pusan railway station. All are poorly paid

ᏞᏞᏞᏞ HIGHLIGHTS ᎶᎶᎶᎶ

- ◆ Pusan, South Korea's largest and busiest seaport
- ◆ Pŏmŏsa, Pusan's best temple, more than 1300 years old
- ◆ The bird sanctuaries at Ŭlsukdo and Ch'angwon-gun, often visited by foreign conservation groups
- ◆ T'ongdosa, Korea's largest and most famous Buddhist temple
- ◆ Kajisan, a rocky mountain retreat which reaches an elevation of 1240m
- ◆ Chirisan, Korea's first national park and still one of the best

and many are prone to heavy drinking – this can be a formula for trouble if you're wandering around alone in 'their' neighbourhood at midnight.

Orientation

The central part of the city is squeezed into a narrow strip of land between a series of mountain peaks and steep slopes and the

Kyŏngsangnam-do

harbour. The ferry terminals, central business district, CPO, Pusan railway station and a collection of hotels and yŏgwan can be found in this area. The main subway stop here is Chung'ang-dong, which means 'central district'.

A little to the north is Sŏmyŏn, a trendy shopping and nightlife district which rivals downtown. To get there, simply take the subway to Sŏmyŏn station.

The bus terminals, of which there are three in total, are all a long way from this area. The main two of interest to travellers – the express bus terminal and the east inter-city

bus terminal – are about 11 km to the north but within easy reach of the subway. The east inter-city bus terminal is right outside Myŏngnyun-dong subway station and the express bus terminal is a 12-minute walk from Tongnae station.

Information
Tourist Office Pusan City Tourist Information Centre (☎ 462-9734) is in the Pusan City Hall – this place can give you information about tours.

KNTO (☎ 973-1100) has a tourist information kiosk at Kimhae International

Airport. There is also an information kiosk outside Pusan railway station (☎ 463-4938) and at the Pukwan ferry terminal (☎ 465-3471) where you catch ferries to Japan.

Foreign Consulates Consulates which are represented in Pusan include:

China
 1-207, 2-dong, Ch'oryang-dong, Tong-gu (☎ 441-8749)
Japan
 1147-11 Ch'oryang-dong, Tong-gu (☎ 465-5101)
Russia
 8th floor, Korea Exchange Bank Building, 89-1 Chung'ang-dong 4-ga, Chung-gu (☎ 441-9904)
USA
 American Consulate Building, 24 Taej'ŏng-dong 2-ga, Chung-gu (☎ 246-7791)

There is also a British Council (☎ 807-4612) at Pomnakoel.

Money In addition to all the usual Korean banks, there is an American Express Bank (☎ 244-0017) on the 8th floor of the Korea Development Bank Building, 44-1 Chung'ang-dong 2-ga, Chung-gu. If the door is locked that doesn't necessarily mean it's closed – try ringing the buzzer.

Bookshops Compared to Seoul, Pusan's bookshops offer lean pickings when it comes to English-language literature. The market seems to be sewn up by a chain store called Mun Woo Dang (☎ 245-3843). Only one branch of this store stocks English-language books and magazines. This store is on Chung'angno halfway between Chagalch'i and Nampo-dong subway stations. This small store is not conspicuous – it's on the 2nd floor above a camping supply store. There's a sign in English, but you have to look hard for it.

There is also the Mun Chang bookshop about one block from Mun Woo Dang in the direction towards City Hall. It has six floors, some of which contain English books.

Pŏmŏsa

This is Pusan's best temple by far, and perhaps the best sight in the city. Pŏmŏsa was founded in 678 by priest Uisang during the reign of King Munmu, one of the greatest of the Shilla rulers. Uisang himself is revered as one of the greatest of the early Buddhist scholars and spent some 10 years of his life studying in China following his entry into the priesthood. Despite its proximity to Pusan, Pŏmŏsa is a world away from the concrete jungle down at sea level. Surrounded by peaceful deciduous forest, it is one of the largest temples in Korea – and one of the most beautiful. The Chogyemun Gate, Belfry and Main Hall, in particular, are all sublime examples of Korean Buddhist art and architecture. A visit here on Buddha's birthday is an absolute must (see the Facts for the Visitor chapter)!

A great part of the original temple was destroyed during the Japanese invasion of 1592-93, but not before priest Sosan had defeated a Japanese army at this very same spot. Quite a few things remain from the Shilla period, including pagodas, stone lanterns and pillars. The rest of the temple was reconstructed in 1602 and there were other renovations in 1613 and 1713.

Immortality for W10,000
At major temple sites (Pulguksa in Kyŏngju, Pŏmŏsa in Pusan, etc), you may see stacks of large black tiles piled up near the side of the buildings. Each tile has some writing painted on it, usually in hangŭl but sometimes in Chinese characters or (rarely) English.
 The tiles are in fact building materials used by the temples for their continuous maintenance and expansion plans. The white writing is simply the names of people who have donated the money to buy the tile. You can have your name written on a tile for W10,000, but if you can't afford this then two people (or a group) can share one tile. Your small donation will immortalise your name within the temple structure and no doubt earn you some good karma. ■

KYŎNGSANGNAM-DO

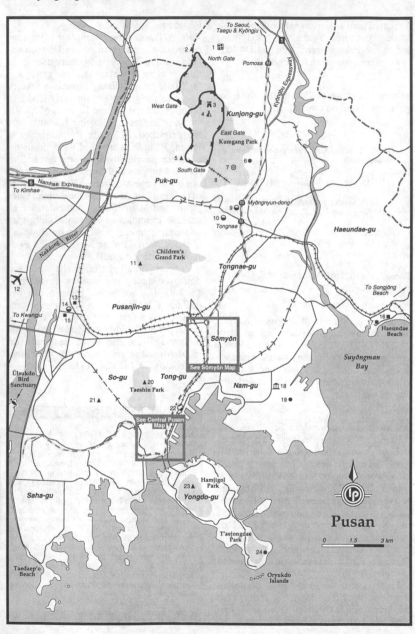

KYŎNGSANGNAM-DO

Pusan 부산

PLACES TO STAY
4 Kŭjŏng Camping Ground
   금정 야영지
13 Oriental Hotel
   오리엔탈호텔
15 Paragon Hotel
   파라곤호텔
16 Hyatt Regency Hotel
   하얏트리젠시부산호텔
17 Westin Chosun Hotel
   조선비치호텔

OTHER
1 Pŏmŏsa Temple
   범어사
2 Kŭmjŏngsan (790m)
   금정산

3 Kŭjŏngsansŏng (Fortress)
   금정산성
5 Sanghaksan (638m)
   상학산
6 Pusan National University
   부산대학교
7 Tongnae Hot Springs
   동내온천
8 Cable Car
   케이블카
9 East Inter-City Bus
   Terminal
   농부시외버스터미널
10 Express Bus Terminal
   고속버스터미널
11 Paegyangsan (642m)
   백양산
12 Kimhae International
   Airport
   김해공항

14 West Inter-City Bus
   Terminal
   서부시외버스터미널
18 Municipal Museum &
   Cultural Centre
   부산시립박물관,
   부산시문화회관
19 UN Cemetery
   UN 군묘지공원
20 Kubongsan (422m)
   구봉산
21 Kudŏksan (565m)
   구덕산
22 Japanese Consulate
   & YMCA
   일본영사관
23 Pongnaesan (395m)
   봉래산
24 T'aejongdae
   태종대

Getting there is simple enough. Take the subway and get off at Pŏmŏsa station. From there it's about 2½ km. Bus No 90 runs up to the temple – catch this bus from a small terminal just one block west of the station. Alternatively, take a taxi. This will cost W5000 (drivers don't expect to pick up a return passenger from the temple, so they won't use the meter. W5000 is the approximate cost of a round trip).

There is a W500 admission fee to the temple. Plenty of pricey souvenirs are on sale at the temple's shop (which itself looks like a temple).

Kŭmjŏngsansŏng

This walled mountain fortress is the biggest in Korea. It's located to the north-west of the northern suburb of Tongnae and perched high on the ridges of Kŭmjŏngsan (790m) and Sanghaksan mountains. To see it properly you really need to put aside a whole day, though you could combine it with a visit to the Buddhist temple of Pŏmŏsa, a little beyond the northern extremity of the fortress. The walls of this impressive fortress are more than 17km long; cover an area of more than eight sq km; and feature four imposing gates in the traditional style. Construction of the fortress began in 1703 and

was not completed until 1807. It's a popular place for weekend picnics and, weather permitting, the views from various points are terrific.

The best way to start a trek around this mountain fortress is to take the subway to Myŏngnyun-dong station and either walk to the park entrance from there (about 20 minutes) or take a taxi. As you leave the subway station, if you look straight ahead and a little to your right, you can see the cable car installations on the mountainside. This is where you're heading. Whether you take a taxi or walk, first cross the pedestrian bridge to the other side of the road and stay to the right-hand side of the east inter-city bus terminal. Walkers should follow this road down to the first junction, bear right and continue on past a large concrete and brick church (on the left hand side) and then take the next left. At the end of this road turn right in front of a (signposted) three-storey stone pagoda and then take the next left up a fairly steep hill. This road veers to the right and you'll find yourself outside the park entrance gate.

At the park entrance there's a Buddhist temple, pavilions, an aquarium, zoo, botanic gardens, folk art exhibition hall, restaurants, a children's playground and the cable car station. Take the cable car to the top (W1600

KYŎNGSANGNAM-DO

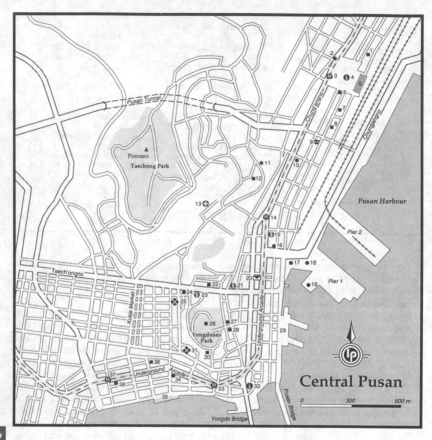

one way, W2200 return). It operates daily every 20 to 30 minutes (depending on demand) from 9 am to 7 pm. The ride takes you up 540m over a total distance of 1260m. Once at the top you can start walking, or pause for a drink or meal at one of the two restaurants. Of course, you don't have to take the cable car – masochists can make the steep ascent on foot.

Tongnae Hot Springs

The hot springs are close to the lower cable car station on Kŭmjŏngsan. Being the only hot springs in Korea right in the middle of a major city, it's not surprising that Tongnae has been overdeveloped to such an extent that the water temperature has fallen. Still, there are plenty of hotels in Pusan's Tongnae district (Tongnae-gu) offering hot spring water piped into pools or bathtubs. While soaking in a tub is not a bad way to relax in winter, don't expect to find a natural outdoor atmosphere at this spa.

Pusan Tower

If you've seen Seoul Tower, you've got the idea. Pusan Tower in Yongdusan Park is 118m high and offers reasonably good

Central Pusan
부산중심부

PLACES TO STAY
1 Kwangjang Hotel
   광장호텔
6 Arirang Hotel
   아리랑호텔
7 Hansŏng-jang &
   Monak'o Yŏgwan
   한성장여관,
   모나코여관
8 Plaza Hotel
   프리자호텔
11 Hillside Hotel
   힐사이드호텔
12 Commodore Hotel
   코모도호텔
22 Sorabol Hotel
   서라벌호텔
27 Tower Hotel
   타워호텔
28 Pusan Hotel
   부산호텔
30 Royal Hotel
   로얄호텔
36 Phoenix Hotel
   피닉스호텔

OTHER
2 Ch'oryang Foreigners'
   Shopping Area
   초량외국인상가
3 Pusan Subway Station
   부산역
4 Tourist Information Kiosk
   관광안내소
5 Pusan Railway Station
   부산역
9 Telephone Office
   전화국
10 Korean Air
   대한항공
13 Maryknoll Hospital
   메리놀병원
14 Chung'ang-dong
   Subway Station
   중앙동
15 Korea Exchange Bank
   외환은행
16 Asiana Airlines
   아시아나항공
17 Customs Office
   부산세관
18 Immigration Office
   출입국관리사무소
19 Kukje Ferry Terminal
   연안여객선터미널
20 Central Post Office
   중앙우체국
21 Korea First Bank
   제일은행

23 Bank of Korea
   한국은행
24 USIS
   미국문화원
25 Yuna Department Store
   유나백화점
26 Pusan Tower
   부산타워
29 Pukwan
   (International Ferries)
   부관훼리터미닐
31 Mihwadang Department
   Store
   미화당백화점
32 City Hall & Tourist
   Information Centre
   시청
33 Namp'o-dong
   Subway Station
   님포동
34 Mun Woo Dang
   Bookstore
   문우당서점
35 Chagalch'i Fish Market
   자갈지시상
37 Chagalch'i
   Subway Station
   지갈치
38 Agricultural Cooperative
   Supermarket
   논협수퍼마켓

views. Activities include visiting the aquarium, getting your photo taken, eating ice cream cones and buying tacky souvenirs. Admission costs W1600. The tower is right in central Pusan, about five minutes' walk from City Hall.

Chagalch'i Fish Market
Pusan's huge fish market is worth a visit for those who enjoy watching catches unloaded from the boats and the haggling which goes on between the fishing boat captains and the buyers. It's on the harbour front south of the central business district. Get there *early* though! Things quieten down by the time office workers are on their way to work. There are heaps of seafood restaurants here.

Haeundae Beach
Some 14 km north-east of the city centre are

Pusan's beach resorts, the main one of which is Haeundae. No doubt the beaches are a welcome sight for those who live and work in Pusan, but this certainly isn't Bali.

Haeundae is regarded as the most popular beach in all of Korea. So popular, in fact, that you'll have to slither through a mass of squirming bodies greased with suntan oil (could be fun) to reach the water. Haeundae Beach is 1¼ km long and is open from late June to early September. All the usual facilities from changing rooms to hot dog vendors are much in evidence. There are sightseeing boats on the east end of the beach.

Haeundae is the only beach resort in Korea which can also boast hot springs. This means that visiting in the winter when the beach is closed is not actually as ridiculous as it sounds!

KYŎNGSANGNAM-DO

Windsurfing on Suyŏngman Bay (which faces Haeundae Beach) has become a popular summer activity. The equipment is available for rent.

Not far north of Haeundae is a less well-known beach, Songjŏng. It looks more or less like Haeundae but is less famous and therefore less crowded.

Buses go direct from Pusan railway station to Haeundae every 10 minutes. The journey takes 50 minutes and costs W750.

T'aejongdae Park

If the Korean Riviera doesn't appeal, try a day out at T'aejongdae Park on Yongdo just across the bridge from City Hall. Once past the suburbs, it's a very pleasant place with beautiful views out to sea. It's not a national park so there are no entry fees. To get there take bus No 30 from the city centre, which takes about 20 minutes. If you take a taxi you have to pay a W2000 toll on top of the meter fare.

Taeshin Park

This park, high up above the city on Kubongsan (north-west of Pusan railway station), offers a complete contrast to the frenetic commercial and industrial activity below. And, weather permitting, the views are superb! The park is densely wooded with huge conifers and there are medicinal springs as well. The simplest way to get there is to take a local bus to Dong-A University's Taeshin campus and walk from there. Alternatively, take the subway to Sŏdaeshin-dong station and walk from there.

Oryukdo

Just off the headland to the south-east of Pusan are five tiny islands called Oryukdo. However, at high tide one of the islands (Pangp'aesom) is partially submerged and looks like two separate islands. Hence the name Oryukdo, meaning 'five or six islands'. One of the islands features a lighthouse.

The islands are hardly stunning, but for Koreans this is a 'must see' spot. There are regular cruises to the islands (☎ 742-2525) on the boat *Camellia 2000*. The boats run several times daily in summer between 7.40 am and 6.40 pm and the ride takes 40 minutes. The fare is W6000 for adults and W3000 for students.

Ŭlsukdo Bird Sanctuary

This is a large, flat sedimentary island in the mouth of the Nakdong River and is home to more than 100,000 migratory birds. More than 50 species have been identified, including the white-necked crane, spoonbill and white-tailed eagle which spend the winter here. The area is well known to international birdwatching groups such as the Audubon Society.

The island is to the south-west of Pusan. Actually there are several islands here, but the largest and most easily accessible can be reached by a bridge. The *Ŭlsukdo Kalbi Restaurant* is on the north side of the island, but fortunately no birds are on the menu.

If you contemplate coming here, remember that birds will be birds – their migratory patterns are seasonal and they won't pose for the camera. Your chance of seeing some interesting creatures depends on the time of year, the time of day, the weather and luck. Don't forget your binoculars and telephoto lenses.

Despite being a protected nature reserve, there seems to be a massive reclamation project going on in the area.

Getting There & Away From Pusan's Hadan subway station, it's a 20 minute walk west across the bridge to the Ŭlsukdo rest area, which is on the main island. Alternatively, bus Nos 2, 59 and 240 from Pusan railway station go to the Hadan five-road intersection. You can also take city bus Nos 58, 58-1 or 58-2 and get off at Ŭlsukdo rest area, or just take a taxi (W6000 from central Pusan). Most of the birds are south of the rest area – follow the rough road and hug the estuary for about one km. Still further south are some other islands, but these can only be reached by small boat.

Other Attractions

The **Pusan Municipal Museum** (☎ 624-6341) is not stunning, but it has a good collection of ancient Korean artefacts. It's open from 9 am to 5.30 pm (4.30 pm in winter) daily except Monday. Admission costs W200.

The museum is right beside the **UN Cemetery**, worth a visit to see approximately 2000 graves of soldiers from 16 nations who died in the Korean War.

The **Pusan Cultural Centre**, which has nightly performances, is also nearby. Every Saturday from 3 pm to 5 pm there is traditional theatre with music, dancing and drumming – really interesting. The Tourist Information Office in City Hall has the complete rundown.

For all three of these places, take bus Nos 25, 68 or 134 from Pusan railway station.

Places to Stay – bottom end

There are no yŏinsuk around the bus terminals, but heaps of yŏgwan costing around W18,000 to W22,000. Staying near the east inter-city bus terminal is convenient because it's near a subway station. Some yŏgwan in this neighbourhood include: *Taedŏk-jang Yŏgwan*, *Misŭng-jang Yŏgwan* (☎ 554-9558), *Arŭm-jang Yŏgwan*, *Ch'owon-jang Yŏgwan*, *Pusan-jang Yŏgwan* (☎ 556-0674) and *Tongon-jang Yŏgwan* (☎ 554-8781).

By the express bus terminal there are even more yŏgwan. Places to stay include the *Samu-jang Yŏgwan*, *Poksŏng-jang Yŏgwan*, *P'yŏnghwa-jang Yŏgwan*, *Kosok-jang Yŏgwan* and *Nakwon-jang Yŏgwan*.

The west inter-city bus terminal also has its fair share of yŏgwan, mostly on the north side of the terminal building. Examples include the *Sanho-jang*, *Cheil-jang* and *Horim-jang Yŏgwan*. Most travellers find this a much less interesting neighbourhood to stay in as it's far from downtown and not near the subway. However, it is a short taxi ride from the airport.

Places to Stay – middle

In many respects, the Sŏmyŏn area is a more attractive place to stay than central Pusan.

3rd Class Hotels rated 3rd class in Pusan typically cost from W28,000 to W45,000. Some hotels in this category include:

Daea (☎ 806-3010), 257-3 Pujŏn-dong, Pusanjin-gu (Sŏmyŏn area)
Hillside (☎ 464-0567), 743-33 Yŏngju 1-dong, Chung-gu (central area)
Kaya (☎ 803-2700), 520-19 Pujŏn-dong, Pusanjin-gu (Sŏmyŏn area)
Korea City (☎ 643-7788), 830-65 Pŏmil-dong, Tong-gu (Sŏmyŏn area)
Kwangjang (☎ 464-3141), 1200-17 Ch'oryang 3-dong, Tong-gu (Pusan railway station area)
Mokhwa (☎ 642-9000), 830-124 Pŏmil 2-dong, Tong-gu (Sŏmyŏn area)
More (☎ 803-0070), 226-5 Pujŏn 2-dong, Pusanjin-gu (Sŏmyŏn area)
New Life (☎ 634-3001), 830-172 Pŏmil 2-dong, Tong-gu (Sŏmyŏn area)
Woojeong (☎ 807-2222), 523-1 Pujŏn 2-dong, Pusanjin-gu (Sŏmyŏn area)

2nd Class Hotels rated 2nd class in Pusan typically cost from W33,000 to W55,000. Some hotels in this division include:

Moonhwa (☎ 806-8001), 517-65 Pujŏn 2-dong, Tong-gu (Sŏmyŏn area)
Oriental (☎ 314-0022), 536-7 Kwaebŏp-dong, Sasang-gu (near west inter-city bus terminal)
Plaza (☎ 463-5011), 1213-14 Ch'oryang-dong, Tong-gu (near Pusan railway station)
Shinshin (☎ 816-0360), 263-11 Pujŏn 1-dong, Pusanjin-gu (Sŏmyŏn area)
Tower (☎ 241-5151), 20 Tonggwang-dong 3-ga, Chung-gu (central area)

1st Class Hotels rated 1st class in Pusan typically cost from W57,000 to W80,000. Hotels in this category include:

Arirang (☎ 231-1300), 1204-1 Ch'oryang-dong, Tong-gu (near Pusan railway station)
Crown (☎ 635-1241), 830-30 Pŏmil 1-dong, Tong-gu (Sŏmyŏn area)
Kukche (☎ 642-1330), 830-62 Pŏmil 2-dong, Tong-gu (Sŏmyŏn area)
Paragon (☎ 328-2001), 564-25 Kwaebŏp-dong, Sasang-gu (near west inter-city bus terminal)
Phoenix (☎ 245-8061), 8-1 Namp'o-dong 5-ga, Chung-gu (central area)
Royal (☎ 241-1051), 2-82 Kwangbok-dong 2-ga, Chung-gu (central area)

Places to Stay – top end

There are a couple of top-end hotels in central Pusan, but most are now out to the east at Haeundae Beach.

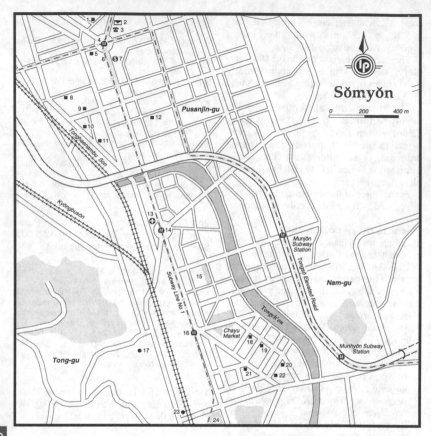

Sŏmyŏn

0   200   400 m

Pusanjin-gu

Tonghaenambu Sŏn

Kyŏngbusŏn

Subway Line No 1

Munjŏn Subway Station

Tongso Elevated Road

Nam-gu

Tongch'ŏn

Chayu Market

Munhyŏn Subway Station

Tong-gu

Deluxe Hotels in Pusan rated deluxe class range in price from about W93,000 to W100,000. They include:

Commodore (☎ 466-9101), 743-80 Yŏngju-dong, Chung-gu (central area)
Sorabol (☎ 463-3511), 37-1 Taech'ŏng-dong 1-ga, Chung-gu (central area)

Super Deluxe There are four hotels in Pusan rated super deluxe class. They are priced from about W100,000 to W170,000. Hotels in this range include:

Hyatt Regency (☎ 743-1234), Haeundae-gu (Haeundae Beach)
Paradise Beach (☎ 742-2121), Haeundae-gu (Haeundae Beach)
Westin Chosun Beach (☎ 742-7411), Haeundae-gu (Haeundae Beach)

Entertainment
There are two bars – *Monk* and *Guru* – which are very popular with expatriate English teachers. Both are right by the Pusan University subway station (not to be confused with the Teachers' College station). You can reach them by getting off at the north end of the station and walking up the street on the left

Sŏmyŏn 서면	19	Mokhowa Hotel 목화호텔	7	Bank of Korea 한국은행
PLACES TO STAY	20	Crown Hotel 크라운호텔	13	Pŏmch'onch'unhae Hospital 범천춘해병원
1 Shinshin Hotel 신신호텔	21	Kukche Hotel 국제호텔	14	Pŏmnaegol Subway Station
5 Daea Hotel 대아호텔	22	Korea City Hotel 코리아시티호텔		범내골 지하철역
8 Kaya Hotel 가야호텔			15	Chung-ang Market 중앙시장
9 Moonhwa Hotel 문화호텔	**OTHER**		16	Pŏmil-dong Subway Station
10 Woojeong Hotel 우정호텔	2	Post Office 부산진 우체국		범일동 지하철역
11 Oscar Hotel 오스카호텔	3	Telephone Office 부산진 전화국	17	Porim Theatre 보림극장
12 More Hotel 모아호텔	4	Sŏmyŏn Subway Station 서면 지하철역	23	Samil Theatre 삼일극장
18 New Life Hotel 뉴라이프호텔	6	Underground Arcade 지하상가	24	Pusanjin Market 부산진시장

side of the tracks. At the top of the street turn right and walk another two blocks. Monk is on the right side and Guru is in a narrow alley directly opposite Monk. Monk often has a jazz band while Guru plays rock music. There are rumours that Guru is going to be torn down, but at the time of writing it was still there.

O'Kim's at the Westin Chosun Hotel at Haeundae Beach is an excellent though pricey pub, and there seems little danger that it will be torn down to make way for another office tower.

The gaggles of heavily made-up mini-skirted girls who hang around outside the doors to the clubs in the 'Russian sector' (just west of Pusan railway station) might remind you of the raucous beer-swilling fleshpots of Thailand or the Philippines, but actually, not all these places are fronts for prostitution. Most of these clubs simply push overpriced food, beer and vodka on their clients. Interestingly, some of the prostitutes who ply their trade here are Russian women, not Korean.

Things to Buy

The Ch'oryang Foreigners' Shopping Area caters to the non-Korean market. This used to be the haunt of American soldiers and was known as 'Texas St'. These days it's Russian sailors and you'll see plenty of signs written in Cyrillic script. You can watch the sailors hauling away everything from fake Reeboks to Swiss watches and Mitsubishi refrigerators. However, there isn't really much to interest the average backpacker.

The enormous underground arcade between the Chung'ang-dong and Namp'o-dong subway stations is like one big fashion parade – row after row of clothing stores. Other items of interest here include electronics (reasonably priced), cameras (expensive), and heaps of places selling fast food and ice cream.

There is a smaller underground arcade at the Sŏmyŏn subway station.

The Kukje Market is Pusan's answer to Namdaemun in Seoul. It's definitely worth a stroll.

Pusan has the usual collection of department stores (with requisite restaurants and supermarkets in the basements). Some you might want to check out include Mihwa-dang, Yuna and Shinch'ŏnji.

Getting There & Away

Air Pusan has one of South Korea's three international airports (the other two being in Seoul and Cheju). Most of the international flights go to five cities in Japan – Tokyo, Nagoya, Osaka, Fukuoka and Sendai. There are also flights to Guam and Saipan in the western Pacific. As in Seoul, be sure to confirm onward flights. Three international

KYŎNGSANGNAM-DO

carriers fly from Pusan: Asiana Airlines (☎ 972-2626), Korean Air (☎ 972-0111) and JAL (☎ 972-1821).

As for domestic flights, the Seoul-Pusan route is one of Korea's busiest. There are also frequent flights between Pusan and Cheju. Infrequently-used domestic routes are the Kwangju-Pusan flight offered by Asiana Airlines, and Pusan-Kangnŭng on both Asiana Airlines and Korean Air.

Bus Both the express bus terminal (*kosok t'ŏminŏl*) and the east inter-city bus terminal (*tongbu shi'oe t'ŏminŏl*) are out in Tongnae-gu, a long way from the city centre. The east inter-city bus terminal is more convenient, being right next to Myŏngnyun-dong subway station. The express bus terminal is about one km west of the Tongnae subway station. Tongnae is the first subway station which is above ground going north so you can't miss it, and Myŏngnyun-dong is the next station going north.

If you can find one, local bus No 57 connects the express bus terminal with Tongnae subway station, but you'll probably wind up walking or taking a taxi.

There is one other bus terminal and that is the west inter-city bus terminal (*sŏbu shi'oe t'ŏminŏl*) in the Puk suburb in the western part of the city, about halfway to Kimhae International Airport. The only time you'd be likely to use this station is if you want to go to small towns and cities to the west of Pusan (especially Chinju). Local bus No 15 connects this terminal with the city centre, or take bus No 110, which connects the east and west inter-city bus terminals.

It's easy to find the bus you want at the express bus terminal since all the signs are in both Korean and English. This is not the case at the other two terminals, where all the signs are in Korean.

From the express bus terminal, there are buses to the following destinations:

Chinju, every 15 minutes from 6 am to 9 pm. The fare is W5200 (1st class) or W3600 (2nd class) and the journey takes 2¼ hours.

Ch'ŏngju, every 1⅓ hours from 7 am to 6 pm. The fare is W14,100 (1st class) or W9500 (2nd class) and the journey takes 4½ hours.

Chŏnju, every 1¼ hours from 7.30 am to 5.30 pm. The fare is W14,300 (1st class) or W9600 (2nd class) and the journey takes 5¼ hours.

Ch'unch'ŏn, three times daily between 7 am and 5 pm. The fare is W21,900 (1st class) or W14,600 (2nd class) and the journey takes 6½ hours.

Inch'ŏn six times daily from 7 am to 5 pm. The fare is W19,800 (1st class) or W13,300 (2nd class) and the journey takes 6½ hours.

Kwangju, every 20 minutes from 6 am to 6.20 pm. The fare is W12,100 (1st class) or W8200 (2nd class) and the journey takes 4¼ hours.

Kyŏngju, hourly from 7 am to 7.30 pm. The fare is W3600 (1st class) or W2500 (2nd class) and the journey takes one hour.

Seoul, every five to 10 minutes from 6 am to 6.40 pm. The fare is W18,700 (1st class) or W12,600 (2nd class) and the journey takes 5¼ hours.

Seoul Sangbong, every two hours from 6 am to 9 pm. The fare is W19,200 (1st class) or W12,900 (2nd class) and the journey takes 5¼ hours.

Sunch'ŏn, every 40 minutes from 7 am to 7 pm. The fare is W8900 (1st class) or W6100 (2nd class) and the journey takes three hours.

Taegu, every 15 minutes from 5.40 am to 9 pm. The fare is W6200 (1st class) or W4200 (2nd class) and the journey takes 1¾ hours.

Taejŏn, every 50 minutes from 6 am to 6.30 pm. The fare is W12,600 (1st class) or W8500 (2nd class) and the journey takes 3½ hours.

Tong-Seoul, every 30 minutes from 6 am to 6.40 pm. The fare is W19,200 (1st class) or W12,900 (2nd class) and the journey takes 5¼ hours.

Yŏsu, every 50 minutes from 6 am to 6.10 pm. The fare is W10,200 (1st class) or W7000 (2nd class) and the journey takes 3½ hours.

Some useful buses departing from the east inter-city bus terminal include the following:

Andong, eight times daily between 8.30 am and 3.50 pm. The fare is W9200 and the journey takes four hours.

Ch'unch'ŏn, every 1¾ hours between 7.40 am and 4 pm. The fare is W19,700 and the journey takes eight hours.

Kangnŭng, 16 times daily between 7 am and 3.20 pm. The fare is W16,500 and the journey takes six hours.

Kyŏngju, every 10 minutes between 5.30 am and 9 pm. The fare is W2500 and the journey takes one hour.

P'ohang, every 10 minutes between 5.30 am and 9 pm. The fare is W4300 and the journey takes 1¾ hours.

Sokch'o, eight times daily between 7 am and 2 pm. The
   fare is W20,000 and the journey takes 7½ hours.
T'aebaek, once daily at 9.50 am. The fare is W15,800.
Taegu, 11 times daily between 8.10 am and 7 pm. The
   fare is W4500 and the journey takes 1¾ hours.

Some buses from the west inter-city bus terminal depart for the following destinations:

Chinhae, every 15 minutes between 6 am and 9.30
   pm. The fare is W2300 and the ride takes one
   hour.
Chinju, every 10 minutes between 5.40 am and 9.30
   pm. The fare is W3600 and the ride takes 1¼
   hours.
Haeinsa, once daily at 9.50 am. The ride costs W7200
   and takes 2½ hours.
Hwaŏmsa (Chirisan National Park), once every hour
   between 6.40 am and 5 pm. The fare is W8100
   and the ride takes 3¼ hours.
Masan, every four minutes between 5.40 am and
   10.30 pm. The fare is W2000 and the ride takes
   45 minutes.
Ssanggyesa (Chirisan National Park), four times daily
   between 10.35 am and 6.10 pm. The fare is
   W7300 and the ride takes 2¾ hours.
Taewonsa (Chirisan National Park), once every 50
   minutes between 6.55 am and 7.22 pm. The fare
   is W6100 and the journey takes 2¾ hours.

Train The Seoul-Pusan line is one of Korea's
busiest. The schedule can be found in the
appendix at the end of this book.

Ferry Details of the international ferries
from Pusan to Shimonoseki and Hakata
(Fukuoka) can be found in the Getting There
& Away chapter at the beginning of this
book. Details of Pusan-Cheju ferries are in
the appendix at the end of the book.

Student discounts are available on domestic ferries.

The journey between Pusan and Yŏsu via
the Hallyŏ Haesang National Park on the
Angel hydrofoil is a popular trip in this part
of Korea, but you should be aware that the
ferries are completely enclosed by glass
windows. There are no open decks and you
must occupy a seat, which may face backwards. There's usually no need to book in
advance, but if you want to be certain then
give the company a ring – English is spoken.
The boats are operated by the Semo Marine
Company in Pusan (☎ 463-2255) and the
summer-season schedule and fares are listed
in the table below:

Schedule – summer season

Pusan	Kohyŏn	Sŏngp'o	T'ongyŏng	Saryangdo	Samch'ŏnp'o	Namhae	Yŏsu
10.20 am	11.40 am	11.55 am	12.20 pm	12.50 pm	-	-	-
2 pm	-	3.15 pm	3.40 pm	4.10 pm	4.35 pm	5.05 pm	5.40 pm
4 pm	5.20 pm	5.35 pm	6 pm	-	-	-	-

Yŏsu	Namhae	Samch'ŏnp'o	Saryangdo	T'ongyŏng	Sŏngp'o	Kohyŏn	Pusan
-	-	-	-	8.10 am	8.30 am	8.50 am	10 am
9.10 am	9.50 am	10.20 am	10.45 am	11.15 am	11.40 am	-	12.50 pm
-	-	-	12.50 pm	1.20 pm	1.45 pm	2 pm	3.10 pm

Fares
Pusan

W10,400	**Sŏngp'o**					
W13,000	W2820	**Ch'ungmu**				
W16,100	W4160	W2490	**Saryangdo**			
W18,700	W6320	W4750	W2290	**Samch'ŏnp'o**		
W22,000	W8290	W6720	W4350	W2080	**Namhae**	
W25,600	W11,530	W9950	W7420	W5090	W4220	**Yŏsu**

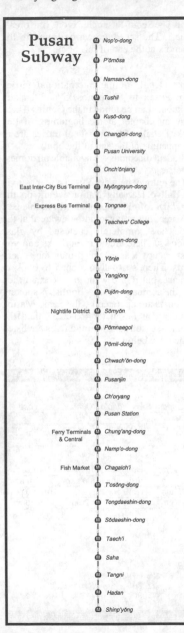

Pusan Subway

- Nop'o-dong
- P'ŏmŏsa
- Namsan-dong
- Tushil
- Kusŏ-dong
- Changjŏn-dong
- Pusan University
- Onch'ŏnjang
- Myŏngnyun-dong — East Inter-City Bus Terminal
- Tongnae — Express Bus Terminal
- Teachers' College
- Yŏnsan-dong
- Yŏnje
- Yangjŏng
- Pujŏn-dong
- Sŏmyŏn — Nightlife District
- Pŏmnaegol
- Pŏmil-dong
- Chwach'ŏn-dong
- Pusanjin
- Ch'oryang
- Pusan Station
- Chung'ang-dong — Ferry Terminals & Central
- Namp'o-dong
- Chagalch'i — Fish Market
- T'osŏng-dong
- Tongdaeshin-dong
- Sŏdaeshin-dong
- Taech'i
- Saha
- Tangni
- Hadan
- Shinp'yŏng

Getting Around

The Airport Two airport terminal shuttle buses connect Kimhae International Airport with the city. Bus No 201 runs from the airport terminal to Chung-gu (the city centre) via Kupo, Sasang, Sŏmyŏn, Pusan railway station and City Hall. Bus No 307 runs from the airport terminal to Haeundae Beach via Kupo, Mandok, the express bus terminal, Tongnae hot springs, Allak Rotary and the Yachting Centre. The fare on either is W1000. Both buses leave every 10 minutes from 5 am to midnight. The journey time from either to the city centre is one hour, but it's only 40 minutes from the express bus terminal.

Pusan Subway 부산지하철

Nop'o-dong	노포동
P'ŏmŏsa	범어사
Namsan-dong	남산동
Tushil	두실
Kusŏ-dong	구서동
Changjŏn-dong	장전동
Pusan University	부산대학교
Onch'ŏnjang	온천장
Myŏngnyun-dong (East Inter-City Bus Terminal)	명륜동
Tongnae (Express Bus Terminal)	동래
Teachers' College	교육대학
Yŏnsan-dong	연산동
Yŏnje	여제
Yangjŏng	양정
Pujŏn-dong	부전동
Sŏmyŏn	서면
Pŏmnaegol	범내골
Pŏmil-dong	범일동
Chwach'ŏn-dong	좌천동
Pusanjin	부산진
Ch'oryang	초량
Pusan Station	부산역
Chung'ang-dong (Ferry Terminals & Central)	중앙동
Namp'o-dong	남포동
Chagalch'i (Fish Market)	자갈치
T'osŏng-dong	토성동
Tongdaeshin-dong	동대신동
Sŏdaeshin-dong	서대신동
Taech'i	대치
Saha	사하
Tangni	당리
Hadan	하단
Shinp'yŏng	신평

KYŎNGSANGNAM-DO

Special airport limousine buses run between the airport and the city centre. These take 40 minutes and cost W3800.

There are also buses directly from the airport to Kyŏngju (see Kyŏngju section for details).

A taxi from the airport to the city centre takes around 40 minutes and will cost about W8000. Right outside the airport terminal is a large sign (in English) that lists taxi fares to various points in the city.

Bus Buses which run down Chung'angno as far as City Hall include Nos 26, 34, 42, 55, 127 and 139. The fare is W400.

Subway The subway is an excellent way of getting around Pusan though there is only one line, which basically follows the main north-south road through the city. Fares depend on the distance travelled – W400 for one sector or W450 for two sectors.

Car Car enthusiasts can hire vehicles at one of the following agencies in Pusan: Hankuk (☎ 205-3240), Pusan (☎ 469-1100), or Youngnam (☎ 469-5000).

KAJISAN PROVINCIAL PARK

This park has three separate sections.

Soknamsa

The northernmost section is known for its rocky terrain. This is where you'll find Kajisan (1240m), the highest peak in the park. Most hikers start their ascent from Soknamsa (the northern park's main temple and where the bus terminates). A good 20 km walk (around 12 hours) would be from Soknamsa to Kajisan, returning via Oksan, Taebisa (another temple) and Unmunsa.

Admission to the park and temple complex costs W600.

Getting There & Away From Pusan's east inter-city bus terminal, there is just one bus daily to Soknamsa. It departs at 3.15 pm and takes just over an hour.

Buses are much more frequent from Ulsan. These depart 11 times daily between

8.20 am and 4.15 pm. Tickets cost W2800 and the journey takes just over an hour.

T'ongdosa

This Buddhist temple, the biggest in Korea, is in the park's middle section. It was founded in 646 AD during the reign of Queen Sondok of the Shilla dynasty and is one of the most famous in Korea. Like many other Buddhist temples in Korea, such as Pŏpchusa, Kapsa, Pulguksa and Haeinsa, it's situated in beautiful surroundings amid forested mountains and crystal-clear streams. There are some 65 buildings in all, including 13 hermitages scattered over the mountains behind the main temple complex.

The temple's founder, priest Chajang, studied Buddhism for many years in China before returning to Korea and making T'ongdosa the country's foremost temple. He also brought back with him from China what were reputed to be part of the Buddha's relics, including his yellow robe. They were enshrined in the elaborate tomb known as the Sokka Sari-tap, which is the focal point of T'ongdosa.

There are some exceptionally beautiful buildings here and it's well worth making the effort to stop here on the Pusan – Kyŏngju trip. There are usually some 200 monks in residence, so it's more than likely that a ceremony or chanting will be going on when you arrive. This is traditionally a Zen temple.

Getting There & Away There are two ways to get to T'ongdosa. The first way is to take the Pusan-Taegu inter-city (not express) bus from either Pusan or Kyŏngju. Tell the ticket office where you want to go and they'll make sure you get on the right bus, which makes a number of stops at places just off the freeway between Pusan and Kyŏngju, including T'ongdo. From where the bus drops you it's less than one km into T'ongdo. You'll probably have to walk this stretch. At the village you have the choice of taking a taxi or walking to the temple, which is about 1½ km away. If you have the time it's worth walking as the road follows a beautiful mountain stream with many rock carvings along the way.

There's also a direct bus to T'ongdo from the east inter-city bus terminal in Pusan. This saves you the walk from the freeway to the village. There are regular buses from the village to both Pusan and Ulsan. If you don't want to carry your pack to the temple you can leave it at the bus terminal.

Naewonsa

South-east of T'ongdosa on the opposite side of the freeway is Naewonsa, another temple complex in the park's southernmost section. There is a nunnery here with some 50 Buddhist nuns and one priest. You get there by bus from T'ongdo, followed by a walk along a picturesque mountain stream. You can swim in the stream in summer.

Getting There & Away There are direct buses from the east inter-city bus terminal in Pusan to Naewonsa every hour from 7 am to 7 pm. The journey takes about one hour.

CHUNAM LAKE BIRD SANCTUARY

To the west of Chinyŏng is a remarkable bird sanctuary. Chunam Lake is most famous for holding up to 80% of the world's Baikal teal, which breed in Siberia and winter in South Korea. It is also a place to see white-naped cranes.

There is a small tourist information office at the lake and cheap minbak. This place is not well known and so far is reasonably free of the ravages of commercial tourism (but for how much longer?).

MAGŬMSAN HOT SPRINGS

Of the big four hot springs resorts in this province, this one is the most rural. However, this is not to say it's in a wilderness area. Magŭmsan is just to the west of Chunam Lake bird sanctuary. Water temperatures average 35°C to 55°C.

Getting There & Away

City buses run to Magŭmsan hot springs about once every 20 minutes from Ch'angwon and Masan.

PUGOK HOT SPRINGS

A major tourist resort in the countryside, Pugok is one of the hottest of Korea's hot springs (water temperature 58°C to 78°C). The rural environment is pretty, but the area has been developed for mass market tourism. The largest project is 'Pugok Hawaii' – with indoor and outdoor swimming pools, a huge bath house, a theatre, a botanic garden and a zoo. There is a golf course nearby.

Places to Stay

There are a few budget places such as the *Shilla-jang Yŏgwan* (☎ 365565), where rooms are W20,000. The *Hansong Hotel* (☎ 365131) has rooms starting at W35,000.

There are plenty of pricier hotels including:

Ilsong Pugok Condominium (☎ 369870), doubles from W75,000
Pugok Crown (☎ 366263), doubles from W44,000
Pugok Garden (☎ 365771), doubles from W49,000
Pugok Hawaii (☎ 366331), doubles from W62,000
Pugok Park (☎ 366311), doubles from W44,000
Pugok Royal (☎ 366661), doubles from W57,000
Pugok Tourist (☎ 365181), doubles from W67,000

Getting There & Away

From Pusan's west inter-city bus terminal there are buses that pass by Pugok hot springs. These depart every 30 minutes throughout the day.

From Taegu's west bus station there are buses to Pugok every 30 minutes. From Masan there are buses every 40 minutes, and from Miryang there are buses once every 40 minutes.

There is just one bus daily direct between Pugok and Seoul's Nambu bus terminal.

CHINJU

Chinju (population 340,000) is on the Namhae Expressway and is one possible base from which to explore the eastern side of Chirisan National Park. Kurye, however, is a more convenient base for the western side, which is where the famous temples are sited (see the Chŏllanam-do chapter).

Chinju lies on both sides of the large Nam River, which is dammed upstream at the confluence with the Dokchon River. It's a pleasant city with a history going back to the Three Kingdoms period. There's quite a large, partially forested hillock overlooking the river on which most of the historical relics and sites of the city are to be found.

Information

The Chinju Culture & Tourism Centre (☎ 426456) is at the entrance of the pavilion at Ch'oksŏngnu.

Chinju Fortress

The most interesting part of Chinju is the hillock which is actually the remains of Chinju Fortress. This was once a walled fortress built during the Koryŏ dynasty, but it was partially destroyed during the Japanese invasion of 1592-93. It was here that one of the major battles was fought in which some 70,000 Korean soldiers and civilians lost their lives. The wall was rebuilt in 1605 by the provincial commander in chief, Lee Su-ill, and it's the remains of this which you see today.

Inside the walls are several places of interest as well as a number of traditional gateways and shrines.

Chinju National Museum

Inside the fortress is the Chinju National Museum, a modern structure done in traditional style. The museum specialises in artefacts from the Kaya period though it also has many objects dating from the time of the Japanese invasion in 1592. It's open every day except Monday.

Ch'oksŏngnu

Overlooking the river is Ch'oksŏngnu, a large pavilion first built in 1368 during the Koryŏ dynasty and used as an exhibition hall for the poems of famous scholars and civil officials. Despite surviving the turbulent years of the Japanese invasion, it was finally burnt down during the Korean War. Various efforts were made to repair it after that event, but it has now been completely rebuilt in the original style.

Also worth noting are the impressive gates to the Chinju Fortress, including Sojangdae, Pukchangdae and Yongsam Pojongsa. The latter served as the front gate for the Kyŏngnam provincial government during the days of the Yi dynasty when its headquarters were inside the fortress.

Confucian School

Just outside the city on the hillside to the east is the Confucian School. This was founded in 987 during the reign of the Koryŏ king, Songjong, as a local school. Scholars of the Chinese classics and medicine lectured there. The school is open to the public.

Chinyangho

About five km west of Chinju is the huge Namgang Dam which was constructed from 1962 to 1969. The dam wall is 21m high and one km in length.

On the northern side of the dam there is a recreational and resort area known as Chinyangho (Chinyang Lake). There are lookout platforms, hotels, coffee shops and restaurants. You can hire motor boats and launches.

To get there from Chinju, take local bus No 16 from the centre (Unyolno). The fare is W400.

Places to Stay

A delightful thing about Chinju is the line-up of yŏgwan along the riverfront, close to the inter-city bus terminal. Rooms with a river view cost about W20,000 at the *Tongch'ŏnjang*, *Koch'ŏn-jang*, *Kaya-jang* and *Mujinjang Yŏgwan*. If the view is not so important, there are several yŏinsuk just on the west side of the bus terminal where rooms are W12,000.

A good mid-range hotel with a river view is the *Tongbang Hotel*.

The railway station area is a less interesting area to stay, but if you want to be in that neighbourhood then consider the *Pŭraja Hotel*.

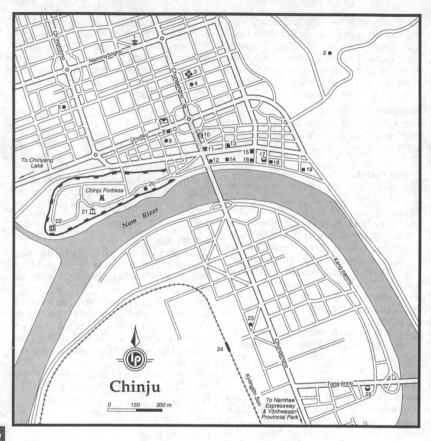

Chinju

0   150   300 m

Getting There & Away

Air Small as it is, Chinju boasts an airport.
There are flights to Chinju from Seoul on
both Asiana and Korean Air. There is also a
Cheju-Chinju flight with Korean Air.

Bus Both the railway station and the express
bus terminal are in the section of the city
south of the Nam River, about 1½ km from
the centre. Take local bus No 15 if you don't
want to walk.

Buses depart from the express bus terminal to the following destinations:

Kwangju buses depart every two hours from 7 am to
   7 pm. The fare is W7500 (1st class) or W5200
   (2nd class) and the journey takes 2¾ hours.
Pusan buses depart every 15 minutes from 6 am to 9
   pm. The fare is W5200 (1st class) or W3600 (2nd
   class) and the journey takes 1¾ hours.
Seoul buses depart every 30 minutes from 6.30 am to
   6 pm. The fare is W18,200 (1st class) or W12,200
   (2nd class) and the journey takes five hours.
Taegu buses depart every 40 minutes from 6.40 am to
   7 pm. The fare is W6500 (1st class) or W4500
   (2nd class) and the journey takes 2¼ hours.

The inter-city bus terminal is close to the
centre on the northern side of the river. Buses

Chinju 진주

PLACES TO STAY
12 Tongch'ŏn-jang Yŏgwan
동천장여관
14 Koch'ŏn-jang & Kaya-jang
Yŏgwan
고천장여관,
가야장여관
15 Yŏinsuk Area
여인숙지역
16 Mujin-jang Yŏgwan
무진장여관
18 Sŏrim jang Yŏgwan
서림장여관
19 Tongbang Hotel
동방호텔
23 Puruja Hotel
프라자호텔

OTHER
1 Telephone Office
전화국
2 Confucian School
향교
3 Chinju Shopping Centre
진주쇼핑센타
4 Chung'ang Market
중앙시장
5 Sŏbu Market
서부시장
6 Underground Arcade
지하상가
7 Post Office
우체국
8 Lotteria
롯데리아
9 City Hall
시청

10 Korea Exchange Bank
외환은행
11 Donky Chicken
동키치킨
13 Asiana Airlines
아시아나항공
17 Inter-City Bus Terminal
시외버스터미널
20 Ch'oksŏngnu Pavilion
촉석루
21 National Museum
진주박물관
22 Hoguksa
호국사
24 Railway Station
진주역
25 Express Bus Terminal
고속버스터미널

depart from this terminal to the following destinations:

Haeinsa buses depart every hour from 6.40 am to 5.30 pm. The fare is W5000 and the journey takes 2½ hours.
Kwangju buses depart five times daily from 9 am and 6.30 pm. The fare is W5200 and the journey takes 2¾ hours.
Okch'ŏnsa (Yŏnhwasan Provincial Park) buses depart hourly between 7.40 am and 8.40 pm. The fare is W1500 and the journey takes 1½ hours.
Pusan buses depart every 10 minutes from 5.50 am to 9.10 pm. The fare is W3600 and the journey takes 1½ hours.
Seoul buses depart four times daily between 8 am and 3.20 pm. The fare is W12,200.
Ssanggyesa buses depart hourly between 7.31 am and 4.15 pm. The fare is W3700 and the journey takes 2½ hours.
Taegu buses depart every 30 minutes between 6.30 am and 7.40 pm. The fare is W4500 and the journey takes two hours.
Taejŏn buses depart 10 times daily between 7.40 am and 5.40 pm. The fare is W9900 and the journey takes 4½ hours.
Taewonsa buses depart every 40 minutes from 7.15 am to 9 pm. The fare is W2200 and the journey takes 1¼ hours.
Yŏsu buses depart twice daily at 7 am and 1.50 pm. The fare is W5200 and the journey takes 2½ hours.

Train A railway snakes its way between Chinju and Pusan, and another line offers a more direct route to Seoul. The train sched-

ule on the Seoul-Chinju route can be found in the appendix at the end of this book.

Getting Around
The Airport Local buses to the airport cost W800 and take 40 minutes to make the journey. Airport limousine buses cost W2600 and take only 15 minutes. A taxi costs W8000.

YŎNHWASAN PROVINCIAL PARK
This small park south-east of Chinju offers pleasant scenery and is home to a temple, Okch'ŏnsa, and three hermitages, Paeknyon'am, Ch'ongnyon'am and Yondae'am.

There are two hiking trails which take you to the summit of Yŏnhwasan (477m); one starts from Yesong-ri, goes to Okch'onsa, Songgogae Pass and Odoro. This route is 4.2 km long and takes about two hours.

You could also start from Yesong-ri, then walk to the hermitage at Paeknyon'am, on to Okch'ŏnsa and then finally the summit of Yŏnhwasan. This walk is 4.7 km and takes about 2½ hours.

Access to the park is by inter-city bus from Chinju. Buses depart Chinju inter-city bus terminal for Okch'ŏnsa once hourly between 7.40 am and 8.40 pm. The ride takes 1½ hours and costs W1500.

KYŎNGSANGNAM-DO

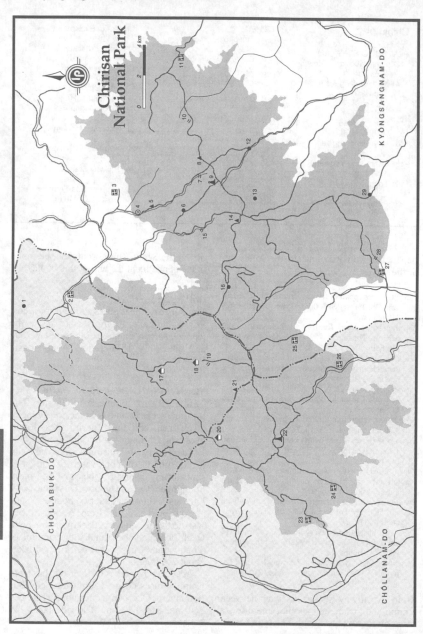

Chirisan National Park
지리산국립공원

1　Paekjam'am Hermitage
　　백장암
2　Shilsangsa Temple
　　실상사
3　Pyŏksongsa Temple
　　벽송시
4　Ch'ilsŏn Spring
　　칠선약수
5　Sŏnnyŏt'ang Hill
　　선녀탕
6　Hadongpawi Boulder
　　하동바위
7　Tŭngsŏn Waterfall
　　등선 폭포
8　Ch'onwangbong (1915m)
　　천왕봉
9　Chesŏktan Shrine
　　제석단

10　Mujaech'igi Waterfall
　　　무재치기 폭포
11　Taewonsa Temple
　　　대원사
12　K'albawi Boulder
　　　칼바위
13　Sesŏkp'yongjŏn Field
　　　세석평전
14　Yŏngshinbong (1651m)
　　　영신봉
15　Kanaeso Waterfall
　　　가내소 폭포
16　Pyŏksoryŏng Crag
　　　빅소령
17　T'akyongso Shelter
　　　탁용소
18　Pyŏngp'ungso Shelter
　　　병풍소
19　Tanchim Waterfall
　　　단심 폭포
20　Yongso Shelter
　　　용소

21　Panyabong (1751m)
　　　반야봉
22　Nogodan Shrine
　　　노고단
23　Ch'ŏnŭnsa Temple
　　　천은사
24　Hwaŏmsa Temple
　　　화엄사
25　Ch'ilbulsa Temple
　　　칠불사
26　Yŏngoksa Temple
　　　연곡사
27　Ssanggyesa Temple
　　　쌍계사
28　Pulil Waterfall
　　　불일 폭포
29　Ch'ŏnghakdong
　　　(Old Village)
　　　정학동 도인촌

CHIRISAN NATIONAL PARK

Straddling the border of three provinces is Chirisan National Park, which offers some of Korea's best hiking opportunities. This was Korea's first national park and is still one of the best.

Mountaineers are delighted with the place. Chirisan is honeycombed with well-maintained trails which will take you up to the ridge that forms the backbone of the park. Up here are many peaks over 1500m high, including South Korea's second highest mountain – Ch'onwangbong, at 1915m.

Within the park there are seven shelters where dormitory accommodation is available. All these shelters are situated along the saddle of the ridge. You need to bring your own bedding and food, though there is a limited range of canned and packaged foods for sale at inflated prices at the shelters. All the shelters have access to spring water.

If you're going to do some trekking get hold of a copy of the National Parks Authority's leaflet, 'Chirisan National Park', which has a map of the area indicating the road-heads, trails, camp sites, shelters, temples and other points of interest. It's sufficient for most purposes, though if you intend to get off the marked trails you'll need one or more of the topographical maps produced by the national cartography service – available from Chung'ang Atlas Map Service in Seoul.

There are three principal areas of the park, each with its own temple. Two of the three temples, Taewonsa and Ssanggyesa, lie in Kyŏngsangnam-do. A third, Hwaŏmsa, can be is approached from Kurye in Chŏllanam-do (see the Chŏllanam-do chapter for details).

Taewonsa

At the extreme eastern end of Chirisan National Park is Taewonsa, which is the most accessible part of the park from Chinju.

The Taewonsa entrance to the park offers the most direct route for the assault on Ch'onwangbong, Chirisan's highest peak. The lower part of the route follows a stream decorated with boulders, pools and small waterfalls – the largest of which is known as Mujaech'igi Waterfall.

Entry to Taewonsa costs W1000 for adults.

Places to Stay Camping offers the cheapest option. Second cheapest is minbak, and one place in this league is *Sakkun Minbak* (☎ 721212) where rooms start at W12,000.

KYŎNGSANGNAM-DO

Yonhwa Yŏgwan (☎ 729054) offers rooms for W18,000. Nearby is the plusher *Kwonhu-jang Yŏgwan* (☎ 729036) where doubles cost W20,000.

Getting There & Away Buses from Chinju to Taewonsa run once every 40 minutes between 7.15 am and 9 pm. The ride takes 1¼ hours and costs W2200.

Ssanggyesa

In the south-eastern part of the park is Ssanggyesa, one of the principal temples of the Chogye order of Korean Buddhism. The temple was originally built in 722 AD to enshrine a portrait of monk Yukcho which two Shilla monks brought back with them from China. The temple was originally named Okch'ŏnsa, but received its present name from Chonggang-wang around 886 in tribute to the Zen monk, Chingam-sonsa, who enlarged the temple in 840 after he returned from studying in China. Chingam-sonsa was also responsible for establishing the tea plantations on the slopes of Chirisan using seeds which he brought back from China. The temple has been renovated several times by a number of prominent monks and there are several national treasures listed here.

This temple has a sublime setting amid steep forested hillsides and is entered by a series of massive gateways housing the various guardians of the temple. A crystal-clear rocky stream spanned by a bridge divides the compound into two and, if you follow the path which crosses this stream further up into the mountain, it will take you to the waterfall of Pulil-pokpo. It's about two km from Ssanggyesa to the falls.

Entry to the temple costs W1700 (less for those under 24 years old).

Places to Stay & Eat Buses to Ssanggyesa terminate in a small village on the opposite side of the main river from the temple, so to get to the temple you first have to cross the river bridge. There are restaurants, souvenir shops and minbak both in the village where the buses stop and alongside the tarmac road which leads to the temple, plus one yŏgwan. Expect to pay around W20,000 for a room at a minbak. You can camp in the village where the buses stop (thus avoiding repeated entry fees) or alongside the stream below the temple compound.

Getting There & Away There are buses from Chinju to Ssanggyesa hourly between 7.31 am and 4.15 pm. The fare is W3700 and the journey takes 2½ hours.

From Yŏsu there are direct buses to Ssanggyesa four times daily between 5.30 am and 2.25 pm. The fare is W4700 and the journey takes 2¼ hours.

From Pusan's west inter-city bus terminal, there are buses to Ssanggyesa four times daily between 10.35 am and 6.10 pm. The fare is W7300 and the ride takes 2¾ hours.

There are buses direct from Kurye (in Chŏllanam-do province) to Ssanggyesa every 25 minutes between 8.15 am and 6.10 pm – the journey takes 35 minutes and costs W1000. There are local buses every 30 minutes between Ssanggyesa and Hadong (south-east of the temple).

Chŏllanam-do

The south-west corner of Korea is notable for its dramatic rocky coastline. The province is also known for its rocky politics – political dissent has a long history here. Aside from the annual spring riots, the province is a pleasant place to travel. There is plenty of good beachside scenery as well as the requisite Buddhist temples and hermitages.

KURYE

Kurye is probably the best gateway to Chirisan National Park – at least for the southern part of the park. It's a small town just south of the western end of the park and connected to Kwangju, Yŏsu and Chinju by frequent buses. There's also a railway station, with connections from Chŏnju and Sunch'ŏn, but it is some seven km south of the town. In Kurye, there's a good selection of yŏinsuk, yŏgwan, restaurants and shops where supplies can be obtained.

Getting There & Away

Not surprisingly, Kurye has only one bus terminal. Buses depart from Kurye to the following places:

Hwaŏmsa (Chirisan National Park) buses depart every 20 minutes from 8 am to 8 pm. The fare is W450 and the ride takes about 15 minutes.

Kwangju buses depart every 20 minutes from 6.30 am to 8.10 pm. The fare is W3500 and the journey takes 1½ hours.

Pusan buses depart every 30 minutes from 7 am to 6.40 pm. The fare is W7800 and the journey takes 3½ hours.

Seoul buses depart twice daily at 10 am and 4.10 pm. The fare is W12,800 and the journey takes four hours.

Ssanggyesa (Chirisan National Park) buses depart nine times daily between 6.15 am and 6.10 pm. The fare is W1000 and the ride takes 35 minutes.

Yŏsu buses depart 30 times daily between 5.40 am and 8 pm. The fare is W3700 and the journey takes two hours.

HWAŎMSA

One the three famous temples in Chirisan National Park and certainly one of the oldest,

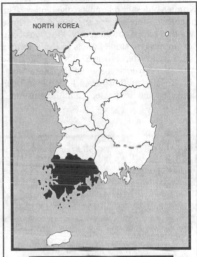

▚▚▚▚ HIGHLIGHTS ▚▚▚▚

- ◆ Tadohae Haesang National Park, a marine park consisting of over 1700 islands and islets
- ◆ Hwaŏmsa, a temple which has survived five major devastations and was last rebuilt in 1636
- ◆ Chogyesan Provincial Park, home to the Chogye Buddhist sect and the location of Songgwangsa, their most cherished temple
- ◆ Turyunsan Provincial Park, where you'll find Taehŭngsa, a major Zen meditation temple
- ◆ Chindo, a scenic island known for its bizarre 'Landing Tide Phenomenon'
- ◆ Pogildo, an island boasting three fine sandy beaches

Hwaŏmsa was founded by priest Yongi in 544 AD after his return from China and is dedicated to the Virochana Buddha. The temple has suffered five major devastations including the Japanese invasion of 1592, but luckily not everything was destroyed. It was last rebuilt in 1636.

The most famous structure surviving from the old days is a unique three-storey pagoda supported by four stone lions as well as Korea's oldest and largest stone lantern. The huge two-storey Kakwang-jŏn Hall, whose wooden pillars tower nearly 49m, was once surrounded by stone tablets of the Tripitaka Sutra (made during the Shilla era) but these were destroyed during the Japanese invasion. Many of the pieces have since been collected and are preserved at the museum.

Entry to Hwaŏmsa costs W1900 (less for students and those under 24 years old).

The tourist village below the temple has the usual collection of souvenir shops, restaurants, minbak and yŏgwan. You can camp if you have your own tent.

Getting There & Away

Most visitors get to Hwaŏmsa from Kurye. However, there are also direct buses from Sunch'ŏn to Hwaŏmsa three times daily between 10.35 am and 4.25 pm. From Pusan's west inter-city bus terminal, there

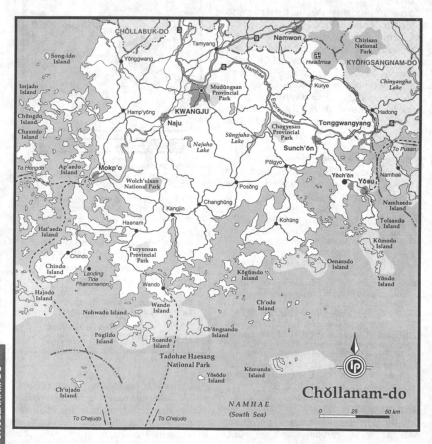

Medicinal Water

Korea's mountains are mostly granite, an excellent stone for filtering water. From cracks in the cliffs or under boulders issues spring water of excellent quality. Every Buddhist temple or hermitage in rural areas is built around, or next to, a spring which visitors may sample by employing the plastic ladle hanging there, often scooped from a granite tub carved with dragon designs. Some of the springs, more mineral-rich than most, are thought to have the power to cure various illnesses. There are many famous Korean folk tales of cures involving a monk, sage, or royal figure, led to a spring by magic or prophecy.

Long accustomed to such excellent water, the modern city-dwelling Koreans have a particular distrust of the government-supplied variety that issues forth from a pipe. You'll see patient lines of urbanites with large plastic containers filling up at mountain springs. Sometimes retired grandparents take on the role of daily water-carrier, to do something useful for the family and to get exercise.

Travellers should sample the waters as they travel around the nation – you may be surprised at the variety of tastes. In general, the higher the altitude, the purer it is. Most mountain springs are referred to by locals, and on signs, as *yaksut'ŏ* (medicinal water source).

In former times, the Koreans held annual *San Yaksu Che* (Sacrificial Ceremony for the Spring Waters) to offer gratitude for the gift of pure water. Only one such yearly event is still held, at Hwaŏmsa temple in Chirisan National Park. ∎

---

are buses to Hwaŏmsa once hourly between 6.40 am and 5 pm.

YŎSU

Yŏsu (population 180,000) lies about halfway along the mountainous and deeply indented southern coastline of Korea. It's a spectacularly beautiful area peppered with islands and peninsulas. A large part of the area between Yŏsu and Pusan now makes up the Hallyŏ Haesang National Park. One of the most popular trips in this part of the country is the hydrofoil from Yŏsu to Pusan (or vice versa) via Namhae, Samch'ŏnp'o, Ch'ungmun and Sŏngp'o.

Orientation

Owing to the mountainous terrain of the peninsula on which Yŏsu stands, the city is divided into a number of distinct parts, though the centre essentially consists of the area between the railway station and the passenger ship terminal. The bus terminal is a long way from the centre (about 3½ km) along the road to Sunch'ŏn so you'll need to take a local bus or taxi between the two. The airport is even further out, but a shuttle bus operates into the centre whenever there are flights. The fare is W1000.

The Korean Air office is about halfway between the city centre and the bus terminal.

There are *no* lockers available at either the bus terminal or the railway station. This is a real drag if you just want to stop off at Yŏsu for a few hours

Chinnamgwan

Right in the centre of town stands the huge Chinnamgwan, one of the longest pavilions in Korea. It's a beautiful old building, with massive poles and beams, which was originally constructed for receiving officials and holding ceremonies and later used as military quarters.

In the summer months it's used by the old men of the town as a place to gather and talk and perhaps throw down a bottle of *soju*. They're a friendly bunch and will probably draw you into conversation since very few westerners ever visit Yŏsu.

Ch'ungminsa

High up on the hill which overlooks the area between City Hall and the railway station is the Ch'ungminsa Shrine dedicated to Admiral Yi. It was built in 1601 by another naval commander, Yi Si-ŏn, though it has been renovated since then. There are great

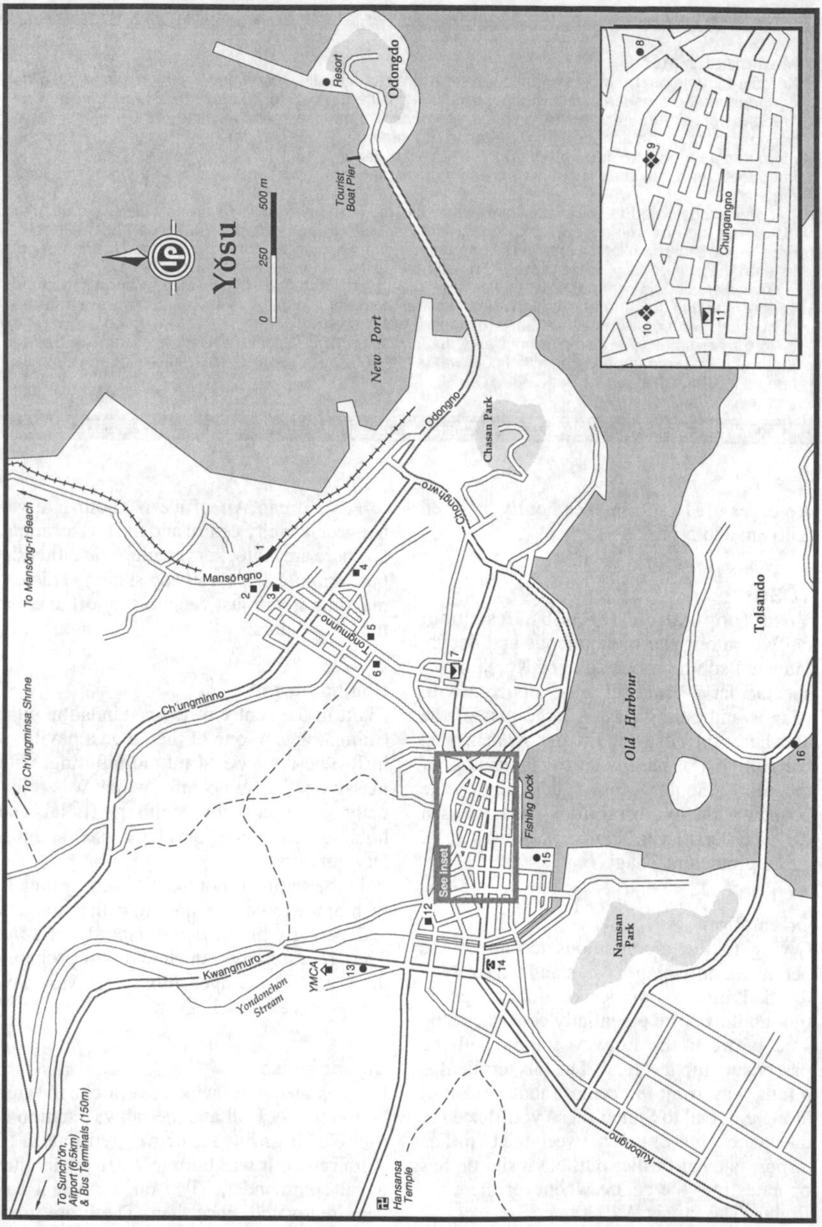

Yŏsu
0
250
500 m
Resort
Odongdo
Tourist Boat Pier
New Port
Odongno
Chasan Park
Chonghwaro
Mansŏngno
To Mansŏng-ri Beach
Tongmunno
Ch'ungminno
To Ch'ungminsa Shrine
Old Harbour
Tolsando
Fishing Dock
See Inset
Namsan Park
Kwangmuro
YMCA
Yondonchon Stream
Hansansa Temple
Kubongno
To Sunch'ŏn, Airport (6.5km) & Bus Terminals (150m)
Chungangno
1
2
3
4
5
6
7
8
9
10
11
12
13
14
15
16

Yŏsu 여수

PLACES TO STAY

2 Osŏng &
   Taedong Yŏinsuks
   오성여인숙,
   대동여인숙
3 Kungsil-jang &
   Kwangsŏng-jang
   Yŏgwans
   군실장여관,
   광성장여관
4 Yŏsu Hotel
   여수호텔

5 Sejong Hotel
   세종관광호텔
6 Yŏsu Park Hotel
   여수파크호텔
12 Yŏsu Beach Hotel
   여수비치호텔

OTHER

1 Railway Station
   여수역
7 Yŏsu Post Office
   여수우체국
8 Chinnamgwan Pavilion
   시남관

9 Samoa Department Store
   사모아백화점
10 Citizens Department
   Store
   시민백화점
11 Kyodong Post Office
   교동우체국
13 Korean Air
   대한항공 매표소
14 Telephone Office
   전화국
15 Ferry Terminal
   여객선터미널
16 Turtle Ship
   거북선

views over Yŏsu and the harbour area but it's a steep climb.

Odongdo

Another popular spot in Yŏsu is Odongdo, which is linked to the mainland by a 730m-long causeway. Odongdo is a craggy, tree- and bamboo-covered island with a light-house, picnic spots and walking trails. The best time to see the island is spring, when it's covered with camellia blossoms. Entry costs W800 - Odongdo is actually part of the Hallyŏ Haesang National Park. Local bus Nos 1 and 2 will take you there from the centre of town. The fare is W400.

A restaurant complex has been built on the island and the specialty is fresh seafood. Check the prices or you may choke when you get the bill.

One of the most enjoyable things to do here is to take the tourist launch around the island. The launches are berthed halfway along the causeway and drop you off next to the restaurant complex. The trip costs W2000 and the launches leave whenever there are sufficient passengers.

Admiral Yi's Turtle Ship

Yŏsu's historical claim to fame is in connection with Admiral Yi, who routed the Japanese navy on several occasions during the 16th century. On display in Yŏsu is a full-size re-creation of one of the admiral's famous iron-clad war vessels, known as turtle ships (kŏbuksŏn).

The ship can be found on the island of Tolsando, which is south of town and connected to the mainland by an enormous suspension bridge. From the bridge you can see dozens of souvenir stalls, or maybe even the ship itself – it's moored in the water and you can go inside. Tolsando has an abundance of bird life, particularly doves and pheasants.

Hansansa

If you're up to a more substantial trek there is Hansansa, a temple high up on the wooded mountain slopes to the west of Yŏsu. The temple was built in 1194 by a high priest named Bojo during the reign of the Koryŏ king, Myŏngjong.

The trail up to the temple is well marked and the views are superb. The best view of all is not from the temple itself, however, but from a point five minutes' walk away.

To get there, take the trail through the woods to the right of the temple as you face it and descend onto a small platform where the local people do their washing. Then turn left up through an area dotted surrealistically with gym equipment and posters telling you how to do push-ups, and on to the highest point, which is a grassy cliff-top. The views are practically 180°. At the laundry trough you may be lucky enough to come across a Shamanistic performance.

CHŎLLANAM-DO

Mansŏng-ri Beach

Mansŏng-ri Beach is almost unique in Korea because of its black sand. The black sand soaks up the sun's summer rays and gets quite hot, and Koreans are fond of burying themselves up to the neck and letting themselves cook – this is supposed to relieve all those aches and pains. Whether or not you wish to bake yourself in a sand cast, the beach is about 300m long and fine for swimming. Mansŏng-ri is three km north of Yŏsu and can be reached by frequent city buses, which run between 5.40 am and 8.30 pm and cost W400.

Places to Stay – bottom end

The majority of yŏgwan and yŏinsuk are clustered along the road which connects the harbour front to the railway station. The cheapest places near the railway station are the *Osŏng Yŏinsuk* and *Taedong Yŏinsuk*. Also near the railway station but decidedly higher priced are the *Kungsil-jang Yŏgwan* and *Kwangsŏng-jang Yŏgwan*.

There are three relatively upmarket yŏgwan near the bus station: the *Ŭnsu-jang Yŏgwan*, *Po'ŭn-jang Yŏgwan* and *Tŏkwon-jang Yŏgwan*.

Places to Stay – middle

Yŏsu Beach Hotel (☎ 632011; fax 631625) is on the west side of town and not on the beach at all. Nonetheless, it's still a nice place to stay. Doubles cost W45,000, twins W48,000 and suites W90,000, plus 20% tax and surcharge.

The *Sejong Hotel* (☎ 626111; fax 621929) is a somewhat older place about ½ km south-west of the railway station. Room rates here are doubles W40,000, twins W46,000 and suites W85,000 plus 20%.

Almost directly opposite the Sejong Hotel is the *Yŏsu Park Hotel* (☎ 632334; fax 632338). Doubles cost W30,000, twins W45,000 and suites W68,000, plus 20%.

The *Yŏsu Hotel* (☎ 623131; fax 623491) is another 3rd class hotel near the railway station. Room prices for twins are W35,000 to W50,000 and suites cost W63,000, plus the requisite 20%.

Getting There & Away

Air There are direct flights between Yŏsu and Seoul, and also Yŏsu and Cheju.

Bus The express and inter-city bus terminals are next to each other on the north-western side of the city on the road out to Sunch'ŏn and the airport.

The only buses departing from the express bus terminal go to Seoul. These depart 18 times daily from 6.10 am to 5.50 pm and take 5½ hours. The fare is W16,800 (1st class) or W11,300 (2nd class).

Buses departing from the inter-city bus terminal include the following:

Chinju buses depart three times daily between 10.15 am and 6.50 pm. The fare is W5200 and the journey takes 2¼ hours.
Chŏnju buses depart six times daily between 7.10 am and 6.15 pm. The fare is W8300 and the journey takes 3¾ hours.
Hwaŏmsa buses depart five times daily between 7.25 am and 3.07 pm. The fare is W4000 and the journey takes 2¼ hours.
Kwangju buses depart 25 times daily between 6.10 am and 8.40 pm. The fare is W5300 and the journey takes about two hours.
Mokp'o buses depart 16 times daily between 5.50 am and 6.10 pm. The fare is W8500 and the journey takes 3¾ hours.
Pusan buses depart 18 times daily between 6 am and 10.40 pm. The fare is W10,200 (1st class) or W7000 (2nd class) and the journey takes 3½ hours.
Seoul buses depart 10 times daily between 6 am and 5.50 pm. The fare is W12,800 and the journey takes 5½ hours.
Ssanggyesa (Chirisan National Park) buses depart four times daily between 7.30 am and 2.25 pm. The fare is W4700 and the journey takes 2¼ hours.
Taegu buses depart six times daily between 7.25 am and 5.25 pm. The fare is W9500 and the journey takes five hours.
Taejŏn buses depart twice daily at 8.20 am and 1.55 pm. The fare is W11,300 and the journey takes five hours.

Train You can get to Yŏsu by train from Kwangju, Pusan or Seoul. The train schedule on the Seoul-Yŏsu route can be found in the appendix at the end of this book.

Boat All boats into and out of Yŏsu dock at

the large passenger ship terminal at the western end of the old fishing dock. You can get boats here to many of the islands off the south coast and to the east of Yŏsu. There are no ferries to Chejudo from here.

The main ferry of interest to travellers is the *Angel* hydrofoil to Pusan via Namhae, Samch'ŏnp'o, Saryangdo, Ch'ungmu and Sŏngp'o. Except during the holiday season (July and August) it isn't necessary to book in advance. The schedule for the hydrofoil is in the Pusan section.

Getting Around

The Airport If you arrive by air, the airport is about seven km north of town on the way to Sunch'ŏn. The airport is served by local buses and there's no need to take a taxi – simply walk the few metres from the terminal buildings to the road and wait for a bus which will have 'airport' in the front window. The fare is W400 on a standing bus (W1000 on a seat bus) and the journey to the express bus terminal takes about 40 minutes.

A taxi between the airport and Yŏsu will cost around W10,000.

Bus The express and inter-city bus terminals are far to the north of the city. City bus Nos 3, 5, 6, 7, 8, 9, 10, 11, 13 and 17 go past the two bus terminals but probably the most useful is bus No 11, which connects the bus terminals with the railway station via the centre of town.

SUNCH'ŎN

Sunch'ŏn is a pleasant city to the north of Yŏju. Travellers mainly use it as a base for exploring Chogyesan Provincial Park.

Chuktobong Park

On the east side of the Tongch'on River is Chuktobong Park. As in Chinju, Sunch'ŏn has its Cherry Blossom Festival sometime in April when the trees co-operate, and if you happen to be here at that time then check out Chuktobong Park. The park has the requisite observation tower, though it isn't likely to provide serious competition to Seoul Tower

or Pusan Tower. The archery range looks like it would be fun, but it's for members only.

Confucian School

On the west side of town is the Confucian School. The school was founded in 1407, but moved several times before reopening at its present location in 1801. As with other such places in Korea, Sunch'ŏn's Confucian School became a shrine after the government examination system was abolished in 1894.

Nagan Fortress Folk Village

About 12 km west of Sunch'ŏn is the Nagan Fortress Folk Village whose 108 households live in traditional Korean style. If you've already seen the Korean Folk Village in Suwon or the Hahoe Folk Village near Andong, you've got the idea.

Of greater interest is the annual **Namdo Food Festival**, usually held here in early October. There are traditional cultural events put on, along with displays of about 300 kinds of Korean food. Livening up the atmosphere are eating contests. Typically, at least 200,000 persons attend and the number grows every year. However, the location of the festival has moved from time to time. To get the latest information, check with the KNTO in Seoul or the Tourism Promotion Department in Kwangju (☎ 222-0101).

From Sunch'ŏn bus terminals there are buses every 30 minutes throughout the day during the festival. At other times buses go via Pŏlgyo.

Places to Stay

Yŏinsuk around the railway station are reasonably plush – some rooms for W12,000 even come with private bath. There are not nearly so many yŏinsuk near the bus terminal. Most inter-city buses make a stop near the railway station, so it might be wise to get off there if you want to look for cheap accommodation. Otherwise, you'll have to take a city bus or taxi to commute between the inter-city bus terminal and the railway station.

More upmarket accommodation can be found at the *Kŭmgang Hotel* (☎ 528301; fax

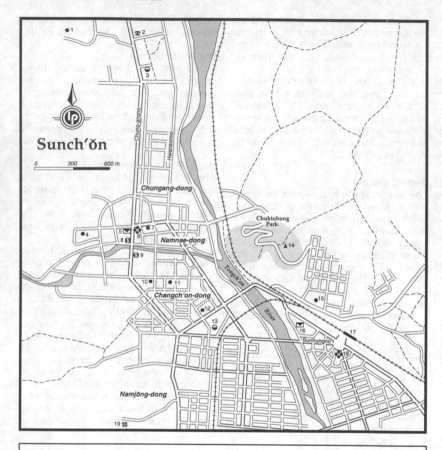

Sunch'ŏn 순천	2	Telephone Office 전화국	11	City Hall 시청

PLACES TO STAY

7	Kŭmgang Hotel 금강호텔
10	Namho Hotel 남호호텔
12	Royal Hotel 로얄호텔

OTHER

1 Sunch'ŏn National University
국립순천대학교

2 Telephone Office
전화국

3 Express Bus Terminal
고속버스터미널

4 Confucian School
향교

5 Post Office
우체국

6 Hwangkŭm Department Store
황금백화점

8 Bank
은행

9 Bank
은행

11 City Hall
시청

13 Inter-City Bus Terminal
시외버스터미널

14 Chuktobong (102m)
죽도봉

15 Sunch'ŏn Sports Park
순천체육공원

16 Central Post Office
순천우체국

17 Railway Station
순천역

18 Chŏngho Department Store
정호백화점

19 Namhŭngsa Temple
남흥사

529193). Doubles here cost W55,000 to W65,000 and suites are W80,000, plus 20% for tax and surcharges.

The other fancy place in town is the *Royal Hotel* (☎ 741-7000; fax 741-7180) with twins for W45,000 to W50,000 and suites for W65,000 to W240,000, plus 20%.

Getting There & Away
Air Sunch'ŏn shares an airport with the neighbouring town of Yŏsu. There are direct flights between Sunch'ŏn-Yŏsu and Seoul, and also Sunch'ŏn-Yŏsu and Cheju.

Bus There is an express bus terminal and an inter-city bus terminal. Buses departing from the express bus terminal go to the following cities:

Pusan buses depart every 30 minutes from 7.20 am to 7.10 pm. The fare is W8900 (1st class) or W6100 (2nd class) and the journey takes three hours.

Seoul buses depart every 45 minutes from 6.30 am to 6 pm. The fare is W17,700 (1st class) or W11,900 (2nd class) and the journey takes 5¼ hours.

Taegu buses depart seven times daily between 7.30 am and 6 pm. The fare is W9900 (1st class) or W6700 (2nd class) and the journey takes 3½ hours.

Some useful buses depart from the inter-city bus terminal, going to the following destinations:

Chindo buses depart six times daily between 10.42 am and 3.42 pm. The fare is W8200 and the journey takes 3¾ hours.

Chinju buses depart every 30 minutes from 7 am to 7.40 pm. The fare is W3400 and the journey takes 1½ hours.

Chŏnju buses depart once hourly from 7.45 am to 7 pm. The fare is W6500 and the journey takes three hours.

Hwaŏmsa (Chirisan National Park) buses depart three times daily between 10.35 am and 4.25 pm. The fare is W2200 and the journey takes 1½ hours.

Kurye (for Chirisan National Park) buses depart once hourly from 6.05 am to 8.10 pm. The fare is W1900 and the journey takes one hour.

Kwangju buses depart every 15 minutes from 6.30 am to 9.40 pm. The fare is W3900 and the journey takes 1½ hours.

Mokp'o buses depart every 1⅓ hours from 6.40 am to 7.05 pm. The fare is W6800 and the journey takes 2¾ hours.

Pusan buses depart every 20 minutes from 9.30 am to 7 pm. The fare is W6100 and the journey takes three hours.

Songgwangsa (for Chogyesan Provincial Park) buses depart every 40 minutes from 6.50 am to 6.35 pm. The fare is W1900 and the journey takes 1¼ hours.

Ssanggyesa (Chirisan National Park) buses depart six times daily between 7.25 am and 3.10 pm. The fare is W2900 and the journey takes two hours.

Taegu buses depart 15 times daily between 7 am and 7.10 pm. The fare is W7700 and the journey takes four hours.

Taejŏn buses depart three times daily between 9.15 am and 2.45 pm. The fare is W9500 and the journey takes 4½ hours.

Wando buses depart nine times daily between 7.34 am and 6.35 pm. The fare is W7200 and the journey takes 3½ hours.

Yŏsu buses depart every 10 minutes from 6.10 am to 11.30 pm. The fare is W1800 and the journey takes 50 minutes.

Train The schedule for trains on the Seoul-Sunch'ŏn route is virtually the same as for Seoul-Yŏsu.

CHOGYESAN PROVINCIAL PARK
This provincial park is somewhat special. Songgwangsa, located in this park, is the main temple of the Chogye sect, the largest subgroup by far of Korean Buddhists. On the other side of the mountain is another temple, Sŏnamsa. There is a spectacular hike over Changgunbong (884m), the peak which separates the two temples. The walk takes six hours if you go over the peak, or four hours if you go around it. Either route is fantastic.

There is an entry fee of W800 for Songgwangsa, W700 for Sŏnamsa.

Places to Stay
Yŏgwan at Songgwangsa charge a fairly standard price of W20,000 for doubles. Some of the yŏgwan available here include the *Chogyesan-jang* (☎ 532130), *Kŭmgang* (☎ 532063) and *Songgwang* (☎ 532122).

It's a similar story at Sŏnamsa. Some good yŏgwan here are the *Chowon-jang* (☎ 545811), *Hyondaesan-jang* (☎ 549102), *Kwankwang-jang*

Chogyesan
Provincial Park

0   400   800 m

(☎ 546350); you could also try *Namilgak* (☎ 546188), *New Chogyesan-jang* (☎ 519121) and *Sonamgak* (☎ 546029).

Getting There & Away

From Kwangju there are buses to Songgwangsa nine times daily between 8.45 am and 9 pm taking 1½ hours for the journey. From Kwangu there are also buses to Sŏnamsa once daily at 7.50 am.

From Sunch'ŏn and Yŏsu there are buses to Songgwangsa every 40 minutes from 6.50 am to 6.35 pm, taking 1¼ hours for the journey. From Sunch'ŏn there are also buses to Sŏnamsa three times daily between 9.35 am and 4.45 pm, taking 30 minutes for the journey.

KWANGJU

Though Kwangju (population one million) has been the provincial capital of Chŏllanam-do for centuries and is the fifth largest city in Korea, there is precious little left of its traditional heritage. This is a sprawling, all-modern, concrete and glass city with few redeeming features. It's not surprising that most travellers give it a miss

Chogyesan Provincial Park
조계산도립공원

1 Bus Stop
   정류장
2 Kamnoam Hermitage
   감로암
3 Songgwangsa Temple
   송광사
4 Yŏksanbong (851m)
   역산봉
5 Changgunbong (884m)
   장군봉
6 Hangnoam Ruins
   항로암터
7 Chukhak-ri
   죽학리
8 Bus Stop
   정류장
9 Namamjae (537m)
   남암재
10 Ch'ŏnjaamsan
    천자암산
11 Ch'onjaam Hermitage
    천자암

or, at the most, spend a night here en route to somewhere else.

Recently it has acquired a reputation for its student and industrial worker radicalism,

CHŎLLANAM-DO

complete with at least one riot every 18 May. All this has its roots in the 'Kwangju massacre': A series of events here in 1980 (see the History section in the Facts about the Country chapter) led to large scale student protests against the government. On 18 May 1980 the military moved into Kwangju – and used bayonets to murder dozens of protesters. Outraged residents broke into armories and police stations, and used the seized weapons and ammunition to drive the military forces out of the city. The city of Kwangju enjoyed nine days of freedom before the brutal military response came. On 27 May soldiers armed with M16 rifles retook the city and leaders of the protests were summarily shot. Critics of the government put the death toll at more than 2000, but the government put the number at only 180. An independent count made after President Kim Young-sam came to power put the death toll at around 200 and this figure has been accepted by the opposition. At present, 130 bodies have been accounted for and are buried in a special commemorative cemetery.

The chief culprits behind these tragic events were two generals, Chun Doo-hwan and Roh Tae-woo, both of whom later were to serve as president. Student protesters have long made prosecution of these two men their key demand. As a result, Kwangju-massacre protests have been staged in the central area of the city every 18 May.

Chun Doo-hwan voluntarily stepped down as president in 1988, and part of the deal he made was that there would be no prosecutions over the Kwangju incident. Therefore, many considered the students' cause to be hopeless. But in 1996 President Young-sam surprised everybody by giving the green light to the prosecutors. In effect, he reneged on the deal he had made with Chun, but his move proved politically popular. In 1996, Roh was sentenced to 22 years in prison while Chun was given the death penalty.

Now that the students' key demand has been met, one might think that the Kwangju protests will be cancelled. But the harsh sentences are being appealed and few believe

that Chun's execution will ever take place. Demands for his death ought to be good for another 15 years of rioting. All this means that it might still be prudent to avoid Kwangju on 18 May.

Information
The Kwangju Tourist Association (☎ 224-3702) has a branch in Kwangju Airport.

Kwangju National Museum
Just about the only sight worth seeing is the Kwangju Museum. It was built mainly to house the contents of a Chinese Yuan dynasty junk. The junk sank off the coast some 600 years ago and was only rediscovered in 1976. Exhibits include celadon vases, cups and apothecaries' mortars and pestles, almost all of them in perfect condition. The rest of the museum is taken up by 11th- to 14th-century Buddhist relics, scroll paintings from the Yi dynasty and white porcelain.

The Kwangju National Museum is open daily, except Mondays, from 9 am to 5 pm (winter) and 9 am to 6 pm (summer).

The museum is to the far north of the city centre, north of the Honam Expressway. City buses (W400) run from the railway station to the museum every 10 minutes, taking about 15 minutes for the journey. The alternative is to go by taxi.

Mudŭngsan Provincial Park
Overlooking Kwangju is Mudŭngsan Provincial Park, the summit of which reaches 1187m. At the base of the mountains there's a resort area and further up the slopes is Chungshimsa, a picturesque Buddhist temple surrounded by a tea plantation. This plantation, established initially by an artist of the Yi dynasty at the end of the 19th century, is famous for its green tea and there are two nearby processing factories. Another temple in the park is Wonhyosa and there is also Yaksa'am, a small Buddhist hermitage.

Although it's not one of Korea's most spectacular parks, Mudŭngsan's thick forests offer a splendid display of colours during autumn. There are plenty of streams through the forest and it's popular hiking country.

Kwangju

Kwangju 광주

PLACES TO STAY
3 New Seoul-jang Yŏgwan
   뉴서울장여관
5 Paekrim-jang Yŏgwan
   백림장여관
6 Royal-jang Yŏgwan
   로얄장여관
7 Kwangch'ŏn-jang Yŏgwan
   광천장여관
11 Koreana Hotel
   코리아나호텔
12 Tonggung-jang Yŏgwan
   동궁장여관
13 Yŏinsuk Area
   어인숙지역
15 Kŭmsujang Hotel
   금수장호텔
19 Taewon Hotel
   대원호텔
26 Riverside Hotel
   리버사이드호텔
29 Grand Tourist Hotel
   그랜드관광호텔

PLACES TO EAT
18 Haniljŏng Restaurant
   한일정식당
21 Tongwon Restaurant
   동원식당

OTHER
1 Bus Terminal
   광주종합버스터미널
2 Agricultural Cooperative
   Supermarket
   농협수퍼마켓
4 Post Office
   우제국
8 Shinsegae Department
   Store
   신세계백화점
9 Telephone Office
   선화국
10 Railway Station
   광주역
14 City Hall
   시청

16 Yangdong Arcade
   양동상가
17 Bus Stop for Mudŭngsan
   정류장 (무등산)
20 Hwani Department Store
   화니백화점
22 Bank of Korea
   한국은행
23 Korean Air
   대한항공
24 Garden Department Store
   가든백화점
25 Kwangju Department
   Store
   광주백화점
27 Central Post Office
   광주우체국
28 Kaiserhof
   키이제르 호프
30 Zoo
   동물원

A recent addition has been a 'sculpture park' – some post-modern bits of concrete, bent tubes and welded iron bars among the trees and grass.

To get to the entrance of the park take local bus No 18 from the inter-city bus terminal (or from the bus stop on Chebongno). The bus costs W400 and takes about 40 minutes.

Tamyang Bamboo Crafts Museum
North of Kwangju is the obscure town of Tamyang; it's unremarkable except for its Bamboo Crafts Museum. The Koreans claim that this is the first museum dedicated solely to the art of bamboo craftwork. Including the basement, the museum contains three floors and harbours the requisite souvenir shop.

The Bamboo Crafts Museum (☎ 757-0086) is open from 9 am to 6 pm.

A bamboo products market operates on the 2nd, 7th, 12th, 17th, 22nd and 27th day of each month.

Buses to Tamyang run from Kwangju every 10 minutes between 5.30 am and 10.45 pm. The journey takes 30 minutes and tickets cost W1100.

Places to Stay – bottom end
The bus terminal area in the west of town is the most convenient for places to stay. Just to the north of the bus terminal and across the street is a plethora of yŏgwan tucked away in the small alleys. Some are fairly expensive (W35,000 for cushy rooms), but you can do all right for W25,000 at the *New Seoul-jang Yŏgwan*. Similar prices are charged at the nearby *Paekrim-jang Yŏgwan* (☎ 363-0356), *Royal-jang Yŏgwan* (☎ 369-9600) and the *Kwangch'ŏn-jang Yŏgwan* (☎ 362-2350).

The alleys opposite the railway station have some yŏinsuk (increasingly scarce) plus a number of yŏgwan. In this area you will find the comfortable *Tonggung-jang Yŏgwan* (☎ 524-7314), which costs about W22,000.

Places to Stay – middle & top-end
As always, figure on an additional 20% tax and surcharge at mid-range and upmarket places. The *Taewon Hotel* in the centre has rooms starting at W38,000. Other hotels in the central area include:

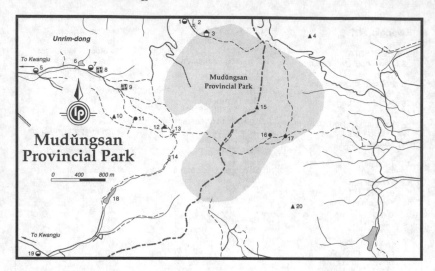

Grand Tourist (☎ 224-6111; fax 224-8933), 121 Pullo-dong, Tong-gu. Room rates are doubles W45,600, twins W55,000, suites W95,000 to W260,000.

Koreana (☎ 526-8600; fax 526-8666), 120-9 Shinan-dong (one block from the railway station). Room rates are doubles W65,000, twins W75,000, suites W125,000.

Palace (☎ 222-2525; fax 224-9723), 11-4 Hwang-gum-dong, Tong-gu. Room rates are doubles W52,000, twins W60,000, suites W100,000 to W140,000.

Riverside (☎ 223-9111; fax 223-9112), 72-1 Honam-dong, Tong-gu. Room rates are doubles W38,000 to W45,000.

On the eastern outskirts of Kwangju and about halfway up Mudŭngsan is the city's most plush accommodation, the *Mudŭngsan Spa Resort* (☎ 226-0026). There are hot springs baths here in both public pools and private rooms. The price range for double rooms is W93,000 to W100,000.

Places to Eat

The bus terminal area will do nicely for all but the fussiest eaters. The huge *Shinsegae Department Store* next to the terminal has all sorts of restaurants – the basement has a huge supermarket, bakery and pizza restaurant; the ground floor has *Hardee's Hamburgers* while up on the 8th floor are classier restaurants and a frozen yoghurt shop. There is a *Paris Baguette* in the bus terminal itself, along with other restaurants.

Entertainment

Many expat English teachers congregate at *Kaiserhof* (☎ 232-5787), mostly on Friday nights. To find it, start on Kŭmnamno near the Bank of Korea. Take the street which goes to the post office, and continue down, pass three lanes until you come to *The Ministop* – take a right down that alley. Other clues – it's directly beside the *New Zealand Club* which has a sign in English (the sign for *Kaiserhof* is in Korean only).

Getting There & Away

Air There are Kwangju-Seoul and Kwangju-Cheju flights on both Asiana and Korean Air. Asiana also operates a flight between Kwangju and Pusan.

Bus Kwangju is unique among large Korean cities in that the express bus and inter-city bus terminals are in the same building. The terminal is out in the west end of town, and

Mudŭngsan Provincial Park 무등산도립공원	6 No 1 Reservoir 제1저수지	14 Yongch'u Waterfall 용추폭포
1 Bus Stop 정류장	7 Bus Stop 정류장	15 Chŏnwangbong (1187m) 천왕봉
2 Seshim Waterfall 세심폭포	8 Munbinjŏngsa Temple 문빈정사	16 Sŏkbulam Hermitage 석불암
3 Mudŭng Hut 무등산장	9 Chungshimsa Temple 증심사	17 Kyubongam Hermitage 규봉암
4 Puksan (782m) 북산	10 Saeinbong (490m) 새인봉	18 No 2 Reservoir 제2저수지
5 Bus Stop 정류장	11 Yaksaam Hermitage 약사암	19 Bus Stop 정류장
	12 Shelter 대피소	20 Anyangsan (853m) 안양산
	13 Chungmŏrijae Pass 중머리재	

city bus Nos 7, 9, 13, 17, 36 and 101 connect the bus terminal with the railway station area. The bus station has a travel agency which can do marvellous things like selling air tickets to Cheju or Seoul.

Bus service is outstanding in Kwangju. Express buses depart for the following destinations:

Chinju buses depart twice daily at 6.30 am and 5.30 pm. The fare is W7500 (1st class) or W5200 (2nd class) and the journey takes 2¾ hours.

Ch'ŏngju buses depart eight times daily between 6 am and 7 pm. The fare is W9300 (1st class) or W6400 (2nd class) and the journey takes 2¾ hours.

Chŏnju buses depart every 20 minutes from 6.30 am to 8.30 pm. The fare is W4800 (1st class) or W3300 (2nd class) and the journey takes 1½ hours.

Ch'unch'ŏn buses depart three times daily from 7 am to 5 pm. The fare is W17,500 (1st class) or W11,800 (2nd class) and the journey takes 5½ hours.

Inch'ŏn buses depart seven times daily from 7 am to 6 pm. The fare is W15,300 (1st class) or W10,300 (2nd class) and the journey takes about four hours.

Kyŏngju buses depart only twice daily at 9.40 am and 4.40 pm. The fare is W12,800 (1st class) or W8600 (2nd class) and the journey takes 5¼ hours.

P'ohang buses depart only twice daily at 8 am and 5 pm. The fare is W14,200 (1st class) or W9600 (2nd class) and the journey takes 3½ hours.

Pusan buses depart every 20 minutes from 6 am to 6.20 pm. The fare is W12,100 (1st class) or W8200 (2nd class) and the journey takes 4¼ hours.

Seoul buses depart every five to 10 minutes from 5.30 am to 8 pm. The fare is W14,200 (1st class) or W9600 (2nd class) and the journey takes about four hours.

Seoul Sangbong buses depart hourly from 6 am to 7.40 pm. The fare is W14,200 (1st class) or W9600 (2nd class) and the journey takes about four hours.

Suwon buses depart every 50 minutes from 7 am to 6.30 pm. The fare is W13,300 (1st class) or W9000 (2nd class) and the journey takes 3¾ hours.

Taegu buses depart every 50 minutes from 6.30 am to 6 pm. The fare is W9900 (1st class) or W6800 (2nd class) and the journey takes 3¾ hours.

Taejŏn buses depart every 20 to 30 minutes from 6 am to 8 pm. The fare is W8400 (1st class) or W5800 (2nd class) and the journey takes 2¾ hours.

Tong-Seoul buses depart every 30 minutes from 6 am to 7.30 pm. The fare is W14,600 (1st class) or W9800 (2nd class) and the journey takes about four hours.

A small sampling of the inter-city buses departing Kwangju includes:

Chindo buses depart every 40 minutes from 5.10 am to 7.45 pm. The fare is W7400 and the journey takes three hours.

Haenam (for Turyunsan Provincial Park) depart every 20 minutes from 5 am to 9.30 pm, taking 1¾ hours for the journey and costing W4800.

Kurye (transfer point for Hwaŏmsa & Chirisan National Park) buses depart every 20 minutes from 6.15 am to 8.10 pm. The fare is W3500 and the ride takes 1½ hours.

Mokp'o buses depart every 10 minutes between 5.20 am and 10 pm. The fare is W3600 and the journey takes 1¾ hours.

Paegyangsa (Naejangsan National Park) buses depart every 50 minutes from 6.15 am to 7.50 pm. The fare is W2100 and the journey takes one hour.

Songgwangsa (Chogyesan Provincial Park) buses depart nine times daily between 8.45 am and 9 pm. The fare is W3100 and the journey takes 1½ hours.

Ssanggyesa (Chirisan National Park) buses depart twice daily at 6.50 am and 2.10 pm. The fare is W4500 and the journey takes two hours.

Tamyang (Bamboo Museum) buses depart every 10 minutes between 5.30 am and 10.45 pm. The fare is W1100 and the ride takes 30 minutes.

Wando buses depart every 30 minutes from 4.50 am to 7.45 pm. The fare is W6900 and the journey takes 2¾ hours.

Yŏsu buses depart every 15 minutes between 5.30 am and 9 pm. The fare is W5300 and the journey takes 2½ hours.

Train The train schedule on the Seoul-Kwangju route can be found in the appendix at the end of this book.

Getting Around

The Airport Local buses from the railway station area and bus terminal cost W400 and take 40 minutes to reach the airport. Seat buses cost W1000 and take 30 minutes. A taxi between the airport and the centre costs around W5500 and takes 20 minutes.

Car Cars can be hired from Hanjin Rent-A-Car (☎ 696-3167).

MOKP'O

The fishing port of Mokp'o (population 260,000) is at the end of the railway line near the south-western tip of mainland Korea. Mokp'o is a departure point for some of the cheapest ferries to Chejudo (the other place being Wando, further south) and for ferries to the islands west of Mokp'o, the most interesting of which is Hongdo.

The town itself is of little interest and most travellers only stay overnight. If you have some time to spare it's worth wandering along the waterfront near the ferry terminal to see the incredible number of octopuses for sale – kept alive writhing and slithering in aerated plastic tubs and bowls. It's also worth walking around Yudal Park, dominated by the rocky hill Yudalsan (229m) which affords good views and sunsets. Up here are a number of small temples, pavilions, a botanic garden and a modern 'sculpture park'. Along the south side of Yudalsan is a

---

Mokp'o 목포

1 Mokp'o Post Office
   목포우체국
2 Korea Exchange Bank
   외환은행
3 Kukto Cinema
   국도극장
4 Bus No 1 Bus Stop
   정류장 (시외터미널)
5 Railway Station
   목포역
6 Cheil Department Store
   제일백화점
7 Ch'angp'yŏng Post Office
   창평우체국
8 Telephone Office
   전화국

---

road which leads to Yudal Beach on the west side of town.

Places to Stay

The most convenient yŏgwan and yŏinsuk in Mokp'o are to be found in the streets on the south side of the railway station since these are within walking distance of the ferry terminal. The line-up here includes *Wando Yŏinsuk* (☎ 428105), *Oddugi Yŏinsuk* (☎ 449411) and *Kwangju Yŏinsuk* – all three places charge W12,000. More expensive yŏgwan include the *Sŏhae-jang Yŏgwan* (☎ 435300) which charges W20,000, and the *Kukje P'ak'ŭ Hotel* (☎ 245-2281), which asks W22,000 for a double.

There are three yŏgwan adjacent to the bus station charging W20,000 for a double: *Kŏbuk-jang Yŏgwan*, *Porim-jang Yŏgwan* and *Yurim-jang Yŏgwan*. However, few travellers wish to stay so far from the centre.

Getting There & Away

Air Both Asiana and Korean Air fly the Seoul-Mokp'o route. Korean Air also flies between Mokp'o and Cheju.

Bus There's only one bus terminal in Mokp'o and it services both express and regular inter-city buses. It's some distance from the centre of town so take a local bus (No 1) or a taxi into the centre.

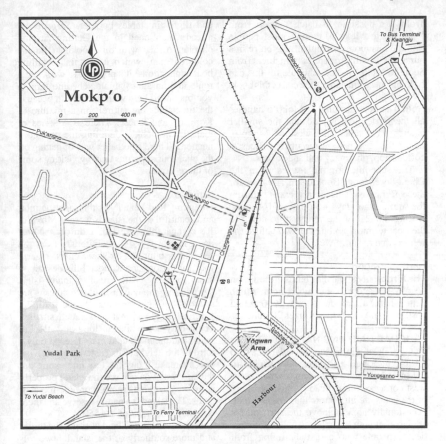

Mokp'o

Buses depart Mokp'o for the following places:

Chindo buses depart every 40 minutes from 6.40 am to 7.20 pm. The fare is W5100 and the journey takes two hours.

Chŏnju buses depart hourly from 8.10 am to 5.45 pm. The fare is W7000 and the journey takes 3½ hours.

Haenam (for Turyunsan Provincial Park) buses depart every 20 minutes from 6.40 am to 8 pm. The fare is W2500 and the journey takes one hour.

Kwangju buses depart every 15 minutes from 5.15 am to 10 pm. The fare is W3600 and the journey takes 1½ hours.

Pusan buses depart nine times daily between 7.50 am and 3.30 pm. The fare is W12,900 and the journey takes 6½ hours.

Seoul express buses depart every 30 minutes between 6 am and 6.30 pm. The fare is W16,800 (1st class) or W11,300 (2nd class) and the journey takes 5¼ hours.

Taehŭngsa (Turyunsan Provincial Park) buses depart four times daily between 8.50 am and 4.15 pm. The fare is W3000 and the journey takes 1½ hours.

Wando buses depart nine times daily between 7.55 am and 5.40 pm. The fare is W5000 and the journey takes 2¼ hours.

Yŏsu buses depart once hourly from 6.15 am to 6.50 pm. The fare is W8500 and the journey takes 3½ hours.

Train It's possible to catch a train from Kwangju to Mokp'o, though most people find the bus more convenient. If you're in a hurry, it's possible to catch a train direct from Seoul to Mokp'o – the schedule for this can be found in the timetable at the end of this book.

Boat The boat terminal at Mokp'o handles all the ferries to Chejudo and the smaller islands west and south-west of Mokp'o. Inside the terminal are the ticket offices, a coffee shop, pharmacy and snack bars.

The schedule for the ferries is in the Cheju-do chapter. Booking in advance for these ferries isn't necessary except during the summer holidays – July to mid-August. During the rest of the year just go down to the boat terminal an hour or two before the ferry is due to sail.

Getting Around
The Airport Local standing buses to the airport cost W900 and take nearly an hour. Much better are the airport buses for W2000. A taxi costs around W12,000 and takes 20 minutes.

TADOHAE HAESANG NATIONAL PARK
Consisting of more than 1700 islands and islets, Tadohae Haesang ('archipelago marine') National Park occupies the south-west corner of the Korean peninsula. Many of the islets are little more than rocks which occasionally appear above the surf, others are large enough to support small communities of people who earn their living from fishing and catering to summer tourists.

There are scores of local ferries from Mokp'o to the larger islands. The most popular islands with Korean tourists are Hongdo and Hŭksando. Indeed, Hongdo is so popular with holidaymakers during July and August that it's often difficult to get on a ferry and equally difficult to find accommodation if you want to stay on the island overnight. During July your only option may be to camp.

These are not the only islands you can visit, of course, but if you're planning a trip around the lesser-known ones you really need a copy of the national bus, boat, train and flight timetables booklet *(Shigakp'yo)* already mentioned in the Getting Around chapter. Armed with this booklet (and the coloured maps which it contains detailing boat connections) it's possible to work out a route and an approximate schedule though you may need help with translation because the timetables are entirely in a mixture of Korean and Chinese. There is a series of maps in the booklet detailing the boat connections. There's no better way of getting off the main tourist circuits than by visiting some of these islands.

Hongdo
Hongdo ('Red Island') is the most popular and beautiful of the islands west of Mokp'o. It's comparable with Ullŭngdo off the east coast in that it rises precipitously from the sea and is bounded by sheer cliffs, bizarre rock formations and wooded hillsides cut by steep ravines. There are also many islets surrounding the main island and sunsets are spectacular on clear days. Where it differs from Ullŭngdo is that it is much smaller, being only some six km long and 2½ km wide, and the main land mass rises to only a third of the height of its eastern cousin. That doesn't make it any the less interesting but the only way you can see the island properly is by boat as there are no shoreline roads or paths. The island is a nature reserve and there is an admission fee of W1550.

Ferries to Hongdo land at Il-gu, the larger and more southerly of the island's two villages, and the one where the minbak, yŏgwan and telephone office are situated. It's also the only village where electricity is available, thanks to a small generator. Like I-gu, its smaller neighbour to the north, there's a tiny cove which provides shelter to fishing boats. The two villages are connected by a footpath which follows the high ground and walking between the two places will take you about one hour.

Places to Stay There's a good choice of minbak, yŏinsuk and yŏgwan in Il-gu at the usual prices (except during the summer holiday period when prices can double). For minbak, expect to pay W20,000 in summer (about W30,000 for yŏgwan).

Getting There & Away Hongdo is 115 km west of Mokp'o, and there are four ferries making the Mokp'o-Hongdo run during summer. Expect the schedule to be cut back in the winter season.

Namhae Star takes 2¼ hours to make the one-way journey. In the summer months there are two departures daily from Mokp'o (7.50 am, 1 pm) and Hongdo (10 am and 4 pm). The fare is W21,100. For more details, you can ring up Namhae Star Ferry in Mokp'o (☎ 449915) or Hongdo (☎ 743977).

The *Namhae Queen* departs Mokp'o at 7.50 am and 1.50 pm. It leaves Hongdo at 10.20 am and 4.20 pm. The ride takes 2¼ hours and costs W21,100. Ring up in Mokp'o (☎ 449915) or Hongdo (☎ 743977) for details.

Tongyang Gold departs Mokp'o twice daily at 8.10 am and 2.10 pm. It departs Hongdo at 10.20 am and 4.20 pm. It costs W21,100 and takes 2¼ hours. Ring up in Mokp'o (☎ 432111) or Hongdo (☎ 777201).

The *Dong Won No 1* ferry is the slow boat, taking 5½ hours to cross the waters. It runs just once daily, departing Mokp'o at 9 am. The fare is W14,700. For details, ring up Dong Won Ferry in Mokp'o (☎ 440005) or Hongdo (☎ 743977).

Hŭksando

Hŭksando is a small group of islands to the east of Hongdo, the largest of which is called Taehŭksando ('great Hŭksando'). Taehŭksando is larger and more populous than Hongdo; it is reminiscent of Chejudo in that the numerous stones littered the island have been used to build dry-stone walls that enclose the fields. Attached to rope, these stones are also used to hold down thatch roofs in windy weather. There are several villages on Taehŭksando and, since the island doesn't rise anywhere near as steeply from the sea as Hongdo, farming is possible on the coastal fringes. The villages are connected by trails and you can walk around the island in a day if you make an early start.

The largest village, Ye-ri, has an excellent harbour and was formerly a whaling post. It's also where the ferries from the mainland dock and where most of the island's accommodation is. There's a sizeable fishing fleet which moors here. The other village is Chin-ni.

Places to Stay & Eat Unlike on Hongdo, you shouldn't have any problems finding accommodation on this island even during the summer holiday period. Ye-ri has a good selection of minbak for around W20,000. One is run by the *Fisheries Cooperative* (☎ 759253). You can also try the *Taedo Yŏinsuk* and the *Yusong Yŏinsuk* which are close to each other opposite the train (there's no railway on the island but an engine, coal tender and passenger car have been set up here as a kind of children's playground).

In Chin-ni there are at least two minbak, the *Chin-ni 1-gu* (☎ 759229) and *Chin-ni 2-gu* (☎ 759414).

With a substantial fishing fleet, you might expect that cheap seafood is available on Hŭksando but, as elsewhere in Korea, this isn't necessarily the case. Be sure to ask the price of a meal before you order because it can be very expensive.

Getting There & Away All the ferries from Mokp'o to Hongdo call at Hŭksando so you can use any of them to get to this island. The fast ferry from Mokp'o takes 1½ hours and costs W16,800. Hongdo-Hŭksando takes about 30 minutes and costs W5500.

WOLCH'ULSAN NATIONAL PARK

This park is small enough to hike from the east to the west in a day if you start early. The ascent is steep, but you'll be rewarded with great views for your efforts.

Wolch'ulsan ('moon rising mountains') is reminiscent of Taedunsan Provincial Park near Taejŏn (see the Ch'ungch'ŏngnam-do chapter). There are crags and spires, steel stairways on the trail and even a steel bridge crossing a huge gap between rocks.

The park's highest peak, Ch'onwangbong, reaches a modest 813m. Nonetheless, the area boasts beautiful, rugged rock formations.

CHŎLLANAM-DO

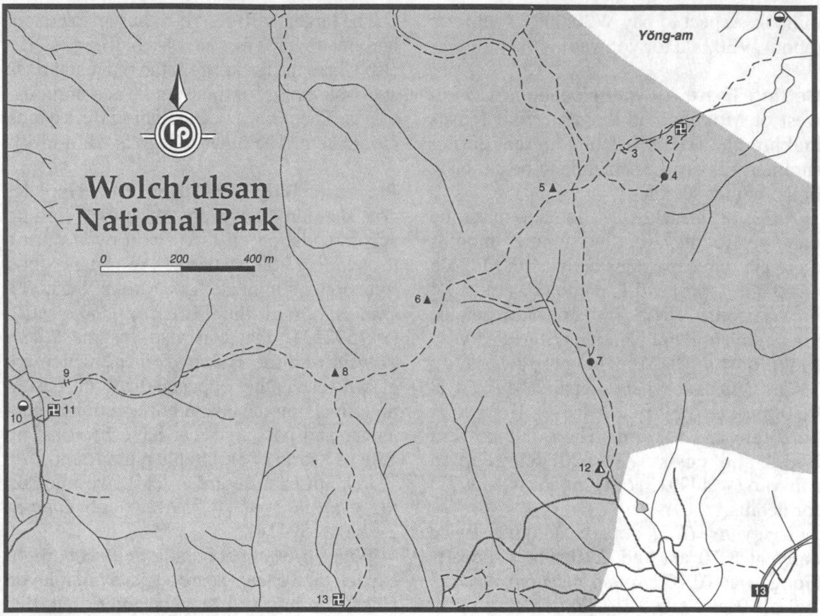

Wolch'ulsan National Park
월출산국립공원

1 Bus Stop
정류장
2 Ch'ŏnhwangsa Temple
천황사
3 Param Waterfall
바람폭포

4 Suspension Bridge
구름다리
5 Ch'ŏnhwangbong (812m)
천황봉
6 Hyangnobong (743m)
향로봉
7 Kŭmrŭnggyŏng Pavilion
금릉경포대
8 Palbong Peak
발봉

9 Yongsu Waterfall
용수폭포
10 Bus Stop
정류장
11 Togapsa Temple
도갑사
12 Camping Ground
청소년야영장
13 Muwisa Temple
무위사

The park's three principal temples are Ch'onhwangsa (north-east area), Togapsa (west area) and Muwisa (south area). While the temples are not spectacular, they do add a nice touch to this scenic area.

Admission to Wolch'ulsan National Park costs W1000.

Places to Stay

There is a designated camping area and you are not permitted to camp back-country. Near Togapsa is the *Injong Minbak* (☎ 720432) which costs W15,000. Near Ch'onhwangsa are the *Pausan-jang Minbak* (☎ 733784) and *Sanjang Minbak* (☎ 734900).

Getting There & Away

The small community of Yŏng-am has buses directly to Ch'onhwangsa inside the park. These buses run only three times daily between 6.20 am and 4.30 pm, taking 10 minutes for the journey and costing W400.

CHŎLLANAM-DO

CHRIS TAYLOR

CHRIS TAYLOR

CHRIS TAYLOR

CHRIS TAYLOR

MASON FLORENCE

A	C
	D
B	E

Details, details
A: Paper window, Tŏksugung Palace, Seoul
B: Chongmyo (Royal) Shrine, Seoul
C, D & E: Wall, window and door

CHOE HYUNG PUN

CHRIS TAYLOR

DAVID MASON

ROBERT STOREY

DAVID MASON

A	C
	D
B	E

The North

A: Pavilion at Naksan Temple
B: Sŏraksan National Park
C: Command Post, Sŭwongsŏng Fortress, Suwŏn

D: Green ridgeline, Ch'iaksan National Park
E: Blue roofs, Ch'iaksan National Park

If you miss the bus, you should be able to catch a taxi.

Kurim-ri is the entrance to the park for Togapsa, but it's four km from the temple. Buses from Yŏng-am to Kurim-ri run every 20 minutes between 6.20 am and 4.30 pm, taking 15 minutes for the ride.

Buses run from Kwangju to Yŏng-am every 10 minutes between 5 am and 10 pm, taking one hour for the journey.

There are buses from Wando to Yŏng-am departing every 20 minutes from 5.45 am to 7.40 pm. The fare is W4000 and the journey takes 1½ hours.

TURYUNSAN PROVINCIAL PARK

Turyunsan is a great place and not to be missed, but you should probably see it soon because there are nasty plans to develop a hot springs resort here. That will probably turn this place into just another Korean resort village.

Here you'll find Taehŭngsa, a major Zen meditation temple. There are dramatic views from the temple – you can see all the way to the ocean.

Places to Stay

Free camping is permitted in the park. Otherwise, you'll find a scattering of minbak. Some people prefer to stay in Haenam, where there are three yŏinsuk right around the corner from the bus terminal.

Getting There & Away

Access to the park is from the nearby town of Haenam. Local buses depart Haenam for Taehŭngsa every 30 minutes between 6 am and 7.30 pm, taking 20 minutes for the journey and costing W450.

The bus schedule from Haenam is as follows:

Kwangju buses depart every 20 minutes between 7.40 am and 8.50 pm. The fare is W4800 and the journey takes 1¾ hours.

Mokp'o buses depart every 30 minutes between 6.50 am and 8.10 pm. The fare is W2500 and the journey takes one hour.

Pusan buses depart hourly between 8.40 am and 4.25 pm. The fare is W11,600 and the journey takes six hours.

Wando buses depart every 30 minutes between 6.20 am and 9.10 pm. The fare is W2600 and the journey takes one hour.

Yŏsu buses depart every hour between 5.35 am and 7 pm. The fare is W7200 and the journey takes 3¼ hours.

WANDO

The island of Wando (population 100,000) is off the south-western tip of the mainland and is famous throughout Korea for the quality of its seaweed *(kim)*. At certain times of the year you'll see this seaweed drying in racks around the island in much the same way as squid are dried on Ullŭngdo and along the north-east coast.

The town of Wando has a quiet, rural atmosphere and a look of benign neglect about it. Unfortunately most of the traditional tile-roofed buildings have disappeared but the narrow streets are still there. In fact they are so narrow that the somewhat decrepit local buses only go down one street. It's a very small town so you can't get lost.

There are both sandy and pebble beaches on the island. These days, the island is connected to the mainland by bridge and there is a ferry service to Chejudo.

Ch'ŏngdo-ri

Ch'ŏngdo-ri is the main pebble beach on the island and it is very attractive. From the town of Wando, take a local bus from the centre close to the ferry terminal and get off at Sajong-ri. From there it's a one-km walk to the beach. There's a small cafe on the beach which sells beer and soft drinks but no food.

Myŏngsashim-ri

Myŏngsashim-ri (otherwise known as Myongsajang) is the main sandy beach and is very beautiful. At certain times of the year it's a little harder to get to than Ch'ŏngdo-ri since it involves a trip by local ferry which only operates if there's sufficient demand.

The ferries leave from the local ferry terminal which is about one km from the main terminal serving the Chejudo ferries. The

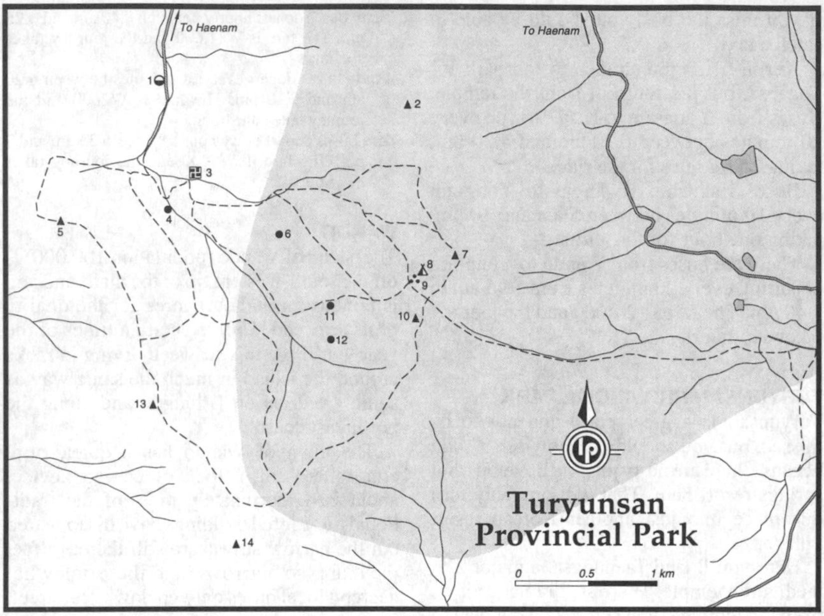

Turyunsan Provincial Park
두륜산도립공원

1 Bus Stop
정류장
2 Kogyebong (638m)
고계봉
3 Taehŭngsa Temple
대흥사

4 Ch'ŏngshinam Hermitage
청신암
5 Hyŏlmangbong (379m)
혈망봉
6 Iljiam Hermitage
일지암
7 Karyŏnbong (703m)
가련봉
8 Camping Ground
야영지

9 Manilam (Ruins)
만일암터
10 Toryunbong (630m)
두륜봉
11 Chinbulam Hermitage
진불암
12 Sangwonam Hermitage
상원암
13 Yŏnhwabong (613m)
연화봉
14 Taedunsan (671m)
대둔산

fare is W400 and the trip takes about half an hour. There are three to four ferries per day when there are sufficient passengers. Buses wait for the ferries at the far end and take you from there to the beach.

Places to Stay

There's a good choice of yŏinsuk in Wando and they all charge more or less the same. The *Tongmyon Yŏinsuk* in front of the post office is good value at W12,000 a double. Next door is the *Sujong Yŏinsuk* which is similar and charges the same price. At the back of the post office is the *Kwangju Yŏinsuk*.

More upmarket yŏgwan charge from W20,000 to W25,000 for a double. Yŏgwans in this class include the *Tongrim-jang* (☎ 544040), *Ch'onji-jang* (☎ 542569) and *Yurim-jang* (☎ 523360).

The *Wando Garden Hotel* (☎ 525001) offers deluxe accommodation, W35,000 to W40,000 for a double room.

Getting There & Away
Bus You can catch a bus from Wando to the following locations:

Haenam (for Turyunsan Provincial Park) buses depart every 30 minutes from 6.45 am to 7.10 pm. The fare is W2600 and the journey takes one hour.

Kwangju buses depart about every 20 minutes from 5.44 am to 7 pm. The fare is W6900 and the journey takes 2½ hours.

Mokp'o buses depart every 50 minutes from 8 am to 6.40 pm. The fare is W5000 and the journey takes 1¾ hours.

Pusan buses depart once hourly from 7.25 am to 3.10 pm. The fare is W14,100 and the journey takes almost seven hours.

Seoul buses depart four times daily between 8.50 am and 5.30 pm. The fare is W13,100 and the journey takes 6 hours.

Yŏng-am (for Wolch'ulsan National Park) buses depart every 20 minutes from 5.45 am to 7.40 pm. The fare is W4000 and the journey takes 1½ hours.

Yŏsu buses depart twice daily at 11.17 am and 4.20 pm. The fare is W9000 and the journey takes three hours.

Ferry Wando is connected to Chejudo by ferry. The schedule is in the Cheju-do chapter.

If you want to explore some of the nearby islands there are ferries going from Wando to Ch'ŏngsando, Noktongdo, Nohwado, Chodo and Sokhwapo.

To Ch'ŏngsando there is a slow boat (1½ hours) and a fast boat (30 minutes). Similarly, to Noktongdo there is a slow boat (3½ hours) and a fast boat (2¼ hours). To Chodo by one of these boats takes 3¾ hours and to Sokhwapo it is one hour.

If you're heading for Mokp'o from Wando and would prefer to go by sea rather than by bus, there is a daily ferry which leaves Wando at 8 am and takes seven hours. The ferry calls at many places en route.

Getting Around
The bus terminal is a long way from the centre of town (about 1½ km). If the walk doesn't appeal to you there are local buses and taxis into the centre.

POGILDO
An island to the south-west of Wando, Pogildo boasts three fine beaches. The popular sandy spot is Chungni Beach, also known as Pogildo Beach. Yesong-ri Beach at the southern end of the island is a pebbly beach that boasts a dramatic evergreen forest, and a temple called Namunsa. The other beach is called Soanp'o Beach.

Pogildo is the old home of Yun Son-do, a famed poet of the Chosŏn dynasty. The story goes that Yun Son-do took temporary shelter from a typhoon here while on his way to Chejudo. He was so impressed by the beauty of the island that he decided to stay for the next 10 years. During that time, he is said to have built 25 buildings on the island, and also penned some of his best poems, such as 'Fisherman's Prose'.

Pogildo is very much a summer resort, which means it can get a bit packed out at such times. On the other hand, visiting during the winter wouldn't be much fun and most hotels will close then anyway. You might try to hit it in June or September, which will just miss the tourist crunch season.

The Festival of Admiral Chang Po-ko is held here on the 15th day of first moon, though you aren't likely to visit at that time unless you're a member of the Polar Bear Club.

Getting There & Away
There are ferries five times daily between Wando and Pogildo, starting at 8 am and ending at 5.40 pm. The journey takes 1½ hours and costs W4000. Between 15 July and 20 August the schedule is increased to eight times daily.

CHINDO
This is another large island (population 70,000) south of Mokp'o and is connected to the mainland by a bridge. The most remarkable thing to see here is the dramatic rise and fall of the tides, which are some of the largest

such changes in the world. There is an island far off the south-east coast of Chindo which, in early March of every year, can be reached on foot during the low tide by crossing a spit of tidal land 2.8 km in length and 40m wide.

The experience is officially known as the Landing Tide Phenomenon *(kanjuyuk kyedo)*. This phenomenon was witnessed in 1975 by the French ambassador to Korea, who later described it in a French newspaper as 'Moses' Miracle.' The name easily stuck as South Korea has a very large population of Christians, and some view this parting of the seas as akin to the great biblical miracle that allowed the Jews to escape from ancient Egypt. Not surprisingly, large numbers of people come to view this event, and what you often get to see is a line of people 2.8 km in length seemingly walking on water!

As you will no doubt be told by locals,

Chindo is home to a unique breed of dog simply known as the 'Chindo dog' *(Chindo kae)*.

Getting There & Away
Bus Buses depart Chindo for the following places:

Kwangju buses depart every 30 minutes from 6.05 am to 7.35 pm. The fare is W7400 and the journey takes 2½ to three hours.
Mokp'o buses depart 12 times daily from 6.34 am to 7 pm. The fare is W5100 and the journey takes 2¼ hours.
Pusan buses depart twice daily at 6.15 am and 12.45 pm. The fare is W14,100 and the journey takes 6¾ hours.
Seoul express buses depart four times daily between 8 am and 5 pm. The fare is W20,000 (1st class) or W13,400 (2nd class).
Yŏsu buses depart twice daily at 11.25 am and 3 pm. The fare is W9800 and the journey takes four hours.

Cheju-do

Eighty-five km off the southernmost tip of the peninsula lies Korea's windswept island of myth and magic. Isolated for many centuries from developments on the mainland, it acquired its own history, cultural traditions, dress, architecture and even dialect.

There is also the enigma of the *harubang*, or grandfather stones: they were carved from lava, but their purpose is still debated by anthropologists. Parallels easily could be drawn between these and the mysterious statues found on Easter Island and Okinawa, but debates about whether they once represented the legendary guardians of the gates to Cheju's ancient towns seem largely irrelevant as you stand next to them in the gathering twilight at Sŏng-ŭp, Cheju's ancient provincial capital. But what can be said for sure is that no other symbol personifies Cheju-do so completely as the harubang. They're even painted on the sides of the local buses. Not surprisingly, the production of imitation harubang for sale to tourists has been a lucrative growth industry. Indeed, so many harubang are being carted home by foreign tourists that archaeologists of the future may well wonder if harubang were not part of some worldwide religious movement.

All of the foregoing is not to suggest that Cheju-do doesn't share in the Korean cultural tradition, since it clearly has done so for millennia, but the differences are sufficiently evocative to draw people from all over Korea in search of legend.

A remote provincial outpost it may have been until recently, but over the last two decades Cheju-do has changed radically. The catalyst was tourism. Cheju-do began as the favoured honeymoon destination for Korean couples, lured by the warm south and the difficulties of obtaining a passport which would have allowed them to go further afield. The honeymooners still arrive in droves, though more and more are taking their romantic interlude in Guam (which is cheaper).

HIGHLIGHTS

- ◆ Hallasan, a volcanic peak that is South Korea's highest mountain
- ◆ Manjanggul Caves, at seven km in length the longest lava tube in the world
- ◆ Sŏng-ŭp Folk Village and Cheju Folk Village, for a look at Korea's past
- ◆ San'gumburi, the largest volcanic crater on the island
- ◆ Sunrise Peak (Sŏngsan-ilch'ubong), a spectacular volcanic cone whose sides plunge vertically into the surf

Adding to the tourist boom are the Japanese who arrive by the plane-load direct from Japan into Cheju-do's flashy international airport. Cheju is rapidly becoming Korea's second busiest airport and a whole new suburb (Shinjeju) consisting of pricey hotels, restaurants and associated services has been built next to it to milk the tourist market.

Chejudo is touted in the tourist literature as Korea's Hawaii and it does have some

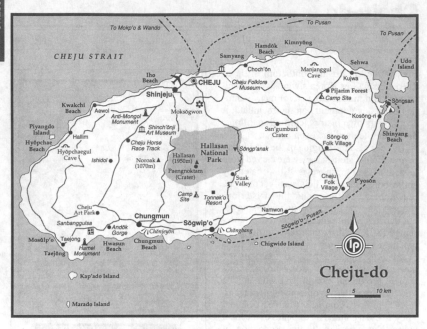

CHEJU STRAIT

To Mokp'o & Wando
To Pusan
To Pusan

Udo Island

Hamdŏk Beach
Kimnyŏng
Samyang
Choch'ŏn
Manjanggul Cave
Sehwa
Kujwa

CHEJU
Iho Beach
Cheju Folklore Museum
Pijarim Forest
Camp Site
Sŏngsan

Shinjeju
Moksŏgwon
Kosŏng-ri
Shinyang Beach

Kwakchi Beach
Aewol
Anti-Mongol Monument
Shinch'ŏnji Art Museum

Piyangdo Island
Hallim
Cheju Horse Race Track
San'gumburi Crater
Sŏng-ŭp Folk Village

Hyŏpchae Beach
Hyŏpchaegul Cave
Ishidol
Noroak (1070m)
Hallasan National Park
Hallasan (1950m)
Sŏngp'anak
Paengnoktam (Crater)

Suak Valley
Cheju Folk Village
P'yosŏn

Camp Site
Tonnek'o Resort
Namwon

Cheju Art Park
Chungmun
Sŏgwip'o
Chŏngbang
Sŏgwip'o-Pusan

Sanbanggulsa
Andŏk Gorge
Chŏnjiyŏn
Mosŭlp'o
Taejong
Hwasun Beach
Chungmun Beach
Chigwido Island

Hamel Monument
Taejŏng

Kap'ado Island

Marado Island

Cheju-do

0   5   10 km

Tolharubang 'grandfather' statues were traditionally placed at the village gate to protect those within.

Hawaiian-style geographical features. For example, there is the almost 2000m-high extinct volcano called Hallasan, the highest mountain in South Korea, with its own crater lake and several well-marked hiking trails. Then there are the beaches dotted around the island; the impressive Chŏngbang and Ch'ŏnjiyŏn waterfalls at Sŏgwip'o on the south coast; the famous volcanic cone at Sŏngsan which rises sheer from the ocean on the eastern tip of the island; and the lava-tube cave of Manjanggul, whose humid, 9°C average temperature will make you wish you were back in the balmy warmth on the surface. At dusk, bats swoop out of the caves by the ten thousand, sometimes even blackening the sky over Cheju City.

The coastal lowlands are dominated by small fields of barley, wheat, corn and vegetables, but further inland there are enormous pastures where horses and cattle graze. It's also the only place in Korea where citrus fruit, pineapples and bananas can be grown though, regrettably, that doesn't mean they're cheap!

The climate here is significantly different from the Korean peninsula – you can even find palm trees. But all the subtropical greenery comes at a price – Chejudo is the rainiest place in Korea, typically recording only 60 clear days annually. Try to visit during autumn, when downpours are least likely.

Another feature which Chejudo shares with Hawaii is its rapid commercialisation. While the place has not yet been 'ruined', it's certainly no wilderness. Especially during summer holidays, you trip over so many newly-weds and rental cars that you begin to wonder if the entire population of Seoul hasn't been relocated here.

Another possible annoyance is the bird hunters who descend on the island in winter from 1 November until the end of February. Although there are no recorded cases of travellers getting blown away by bird hunters, the sound of shotguns blasting can detract from your enjoyment of the back country. It's probably no coincidence that the bird hunting season is during the winter, when visitors to Chejudo are fewest.

In spite of these minor negative points, you shouldn't miss Chejudo when you come to Korea. This place has a very different flavour from the mainland and is definitely worth exploring. There are also a number of sporting activities to keep you amused, such as hiking, golf, snorkelling, scuba diving, windsurfing, sailing, fishing, hang gliding and horse riding.

CHEJU CITY

It might be worth explaining that 'Cheju' is actually three places. There is Cheju-do (the province) and Chejudo (the island, spelled without a hyphen). And finally there is Cheju City, the island's capital.

To further complicate the picture, Cheju City (population 250,000) is actually two places – Kujeju (Old Cheju) and Shinjeju (New Cheju). If you tell a taxi or bus driver that you want to go to Cheju City, it's generally assumed that you mean Old Cheju.

Information

At least four places in Cheju City dish out pamphlets and other tourist paraphernalia. The KNTO has a branch in the international terminal of the airport (☎ 420032), in the Cheju Ferry Terminal (☎ 587181) and also in the Changmun Tourist Complex (☎ 381201).

Kwandŏkjŏng Pavilion

This 15th-century pavilion is one of Cheju's most interesting buildings, complete with harubang. It's the oldest building of its type on the island and draws a steady flow of domestic tourists out to get a perfect photo of themselves standing in front of something.

In the morning an interesting and extensive daily market sets up nearby. It sells everything from clothes to apples which are grown on Hallasan's southern slopes.

Cheju Folkcraft & Natural History Museum

The Cheju Folkcraft & Natural History Museum, up on the hill at the back of town and close to the KAL Hotel, is excellent. It features an authentic replica of a traditional thatched house in the local style, local crafts, folklore and marine displays. There's also a film about the island (in Korean) which is shown five times daily for no extra charge. Entry costs W600 and the museum is open daily (except Monday) from 9 am to 5 pm.

Samsŏnghyŏl

Nearby is Samsŏnghyŏl, a Confucian-style mausoleum which has now become a shrine. Essentially it's just an empty house, like many other such shrines on the mainland, and it's touch and go whether or not it's worth the W900 admission fee.

Yongdu'am Rock

Yongdu'am ('dragon's head rock') on the seashore to the west of town is eulogised in all the tourist literature. It might be worth a visit if you have nothing to do for a couple or hours, but you can place it at the bottom of your priority list. On the other hand, no Korean honeymoon is complete without a photograph of the newly-weds taken at this spot.

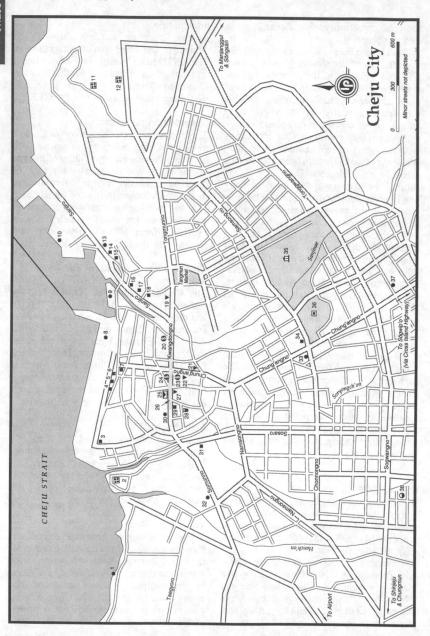

Confucian School

Cheju City's Confucian School was originally built in 1392, but it has seen a bit of renovation work since then. A ceremony is held here twice annually, in spring and autumn (see Facts for the Visitor under Public Holidays & Special Events).

Cheju World

We can't say too much about this place because it was under construction at the time of our visit. When completed, Cheju World will aspire to be Cheju's answer to America's Disney World. Expect Ferris wheels, aquariums, cotton candy (fairy floss) and balloons for the kiddies.

Cheju World is along the waterfront just west of the ferry harbour.

Moksŏgwon Garden

About six km outside Cheju City on the No 1 cross-island highway is Moksŏgwon, a natural sculpture garden of stone and wood. If you've ever found yourself taking home interesting-looking pieces of wood and stone which have been carved by the elements you'll love this place.

The collection at Moksŏgwon was put together over many years by a local resident. It comprises objects found all over the island, many of which originated from the roots of the jorok tree. The jorok is found only on Chejudo; its wood is very dense – it even sinks in water – and in times gone by it was used to make combs and tobacco boxes. Along with the natural objects, the garden features assorted old grinding stones and even harubang. The collection is now main-

---

Cheju City 제 수

PLACES TO STAY

3 Oriental Hotel
제 주 오 리 엔 달 호 텔
4 Beach Hotel
비 치 호 텔
5 Cheju Seoul Hotel
제 주 서 울 관 광 호 텔
6 Seaside Hotel
해 상 호 텔
7 Namgyŏng Hotel
남 경 호 텔
14 Yangsando, Hanil &
Yonan Yŏinsuks
양 산 도, 한 일,
연 안 여 인 숙
15 Namyang Yŏinsuk
남 양 여 인 숙
16 Kŭmsan-jang Yŏgwan
금 산 장 여 관
17 Sujŏng-jang Yŏgwan
수 정 장 여 관
18 Hwangkŭm-jang Yŏgwan
황 금 장 여 관
29 Robero Hotel
호 텔 로 베 로
31 Lagonda Hotel &
Mugunghwa-jang
Yŏgwans
호 텔 라 곤 다,
무 궁 화 장 여 관

34 KAL Hotel
KAL 호 텔

PLACES TO EAT

19 Bakery
베 이 커 리
21 Nammun Barbecue
Chicken
남 문 숯 불 바 베 큐
22 Joong Ang Bakery
중 앙 양 곽
27 Lotteria
롯 데 리 아

OTHER

1 Yongdu'am Rock
용 두 암
2 Yongaksa Temple
용 악 사
8 Cheju World
제 주 월 드
9 Fish Market
어 시 장
10 Ferry Terminal
어 객 선 터 미 널
11 Sarasa Temple
사 라 사
12 Moch'ungsa Shrine
모 충 사
13 Kosa Mart (24 hour
Grocery)
수 퍼 마 켓 협 동 조 합

20 Korea First Bank
젤 은 행
23 Korea Exchange Bank
외 환 은 행
24 Hanil Bank
안 일 은 행
25 Post Office
우 제 쿡
26 Underground Arcade
지 하 상 가
28 The Doors Pub
도 어 스 클 럽
30 Kwandŏkjŏng Pavilion
관 덕 정
32 Confucian School
향 교
33 Korean Air
대 한 항 공 매 표 소
35 Folkcraft &
Natural History Museum
민 속 자 연 사 박 물 관
36 Samsŏnghyŏl Shrine
삼 성 혈
37 City Hall
시 정
38 Inter-City Bus Terminal
시 외 버 스 터 미 널

tained by the government. Admission to the garden costs W600.

To reach Moksŏgwon take the city bus bound for Cheju National University. The journey takes 30 minutes and costs W500.

Places to Stay – bottom end

Since Cheju-do is such a popular place for honeymooners and young people on holiday, there is an excellent choice of reasonable places for most of the year. However, you

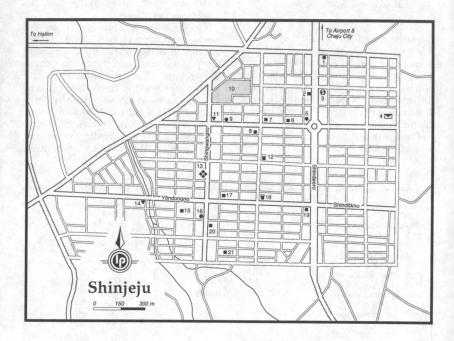

Shinjeju 신제주

PLACES TO STAY
1 Marina Hotel
   마리나호텔
2 Hyundai Hotel
   현대호텔
6 Country Tourist &
   Cheju Garden Hotels
   커트리관광호텔,
   호텔제주가든
7 Holiday Inn Crowne Plaza
   홀리데이호텔
8 Sŏwon Hotel
   서원호텔
12 Cheju Royal Hotel
    제주로얄호텔

15 Grand Hotel
    그랜드호텔
17 Milano Hotel
    미라노호텔
19 Cosmos Hotel
    코스모스호텔
20 Mosu Hotel
    모수관광호텔
21 Hawaii Hotel
    하와이관광호텔

OTHER
3 Korea First Bank
   제일은행
4 Post Office
   우체국

5 Asiana Airlines
   아시아나항공 매표소
9 Cheju Rent-A-Car
   제주렌트카
10 Sammu Park
    삼무공원
11 Grand Durant Restaurant
    그란드 드랑 식당
13 Lotte Champion
    Department Store
    롯데참피온백화점
14 939 Pizza
    939 피자
16 Halla Rent-A-Car
    한라렌트카
18 Bebeto's Pub
    베베토

may have to do a little bit of legwork during July and August when it gets quite crowded and prices tend to rise. Most of the cheapies are on or off Sanjiro, and between this road, Kwandongno and the sea front.

If you arrive by boat you'll probably be met by people from the various yŏgwan and yŏinsuk offering you a room. If anything sounds like a good deal go and have a look. Most yŏinsuk cost around W10,000.

The *Yangsando Yŏinsuk* (☎ 589989), only a stone's throw from the boat terminal on Sanjiro, has been a popular place to stay for years. It's very clean and has hot water in the communal bathroom. The owners are very friendly and helpful. Ask for a room on the top floor, which has an open flat roof, good views and is quiet.

Also good value is the *Hunil Yŏinsuk* (☎ 571598). All the rooms have fans, there is hot water in the showers and guests can use the kitchen facilities.

The *Namyang Yŏinsuk* (☎ 589617) is similar and very clean. Hot water is available in the showers, but there's only one bathroom and it's inadequate to cope with the demand when the yŏinsuk is full. The manager speaks excellent English and is helpful. Guests have the use of a washing machine.

Also in this same area, just off the main road, is the *Yonan Yŏinsuk* (☎ 559345); it is clean, quiet and friendly, and costs W10,000 a double. There's no hot water but there are laundry facilities.

You'll find more creature comforts around the corner for W20,000 at the *Kŭmsan-jang Yŏgwan*.

Hwangkŭm-jang Yŏgwan (☎ 582440) is in an alley off Sanjiro and has excellent facilities. Rooms which feature a private bath, fridge, satellite TV and a decent view cost W25,000.

Places to Stay – middle

The only 3rd class hotel in Old Cheju is the *Seaside Hotel* (☎ 520091; fax 525002), 1192-21 Samdo 2-dong. As the name implies it was built right on the seaside, but a new land reclamation scheme puts the hotel more than 100m back from the waterfront. Facilities include a karaoke lounge.

2nd Class Upmarket accommodation is pricier in Chejudo than on the mainland. Rooms at 2nd class hotels cost between W60,000 and W78,000. Hotels which fall into this category include the following:

Continental (☎ 473390; fax 468847), 268 Yon-dong, Shinjeju. Facilities include a restaurant, bar and beauty shop.
Grace (☎ 420066; fax 437111), 261-23 Yon-dong, Shinjeju.
Hawaii (☎ 420061; fax 420064), 278-2 Yon-dong, Shinjeju. Facilities include a cocktail lounge, coffee shop, restaurants and banquet hall.
Marina (☎ 466161; fax 466170), 300-8 Yon-dong, Shinjeju.
Milano (☎ 420088; fax 427705), 273-49 Yon-dong, Shinjeju.
Raja (☎ 474030; fax 469731), 268-10 Yon-dong, Shinjeju.
Simong (☎ 427775; fax 467111), 260-9 Yon-dong, Shinjeju.
Tamra (☎ 420058; fax 424551), 272-29 Yon-dong, Shinjeju. Facilities include restaurant and bar.
VIP Park (☎ 435530; fax 435531), 917-2 Nohyong-dong, Old Cheju City.

1st Class On Chejudo, rooms in 1st class hotels cost between 68,000 and W121,000. Hotels in this category include:

Cheju Seoul (☎ 522211; fax 511701), 1192-20, Samdo 2-dong, Old Cheju City.
Country Tourist (☎ 474900; fax 474915), 291-41 Yon-dong, Shinjeju. Facilities include a sauna, game room and beauty salon.
Green (☎ 420071; fax 420082), 274-37 Yon-dong, Shinjeju. Facilities include a banquet hall, night-club, health club and sauna.
Honey (☎ 584200; fax 584303), 1315 Ido 1-dong, Old Cheju.
Island (☎ 430300; fax 422222), 263-12 Yon-dong, Shinjeju. Facilities include a cocktail lounge, coffee shop, restaurants, sauna, games room, karaoke bar, beauty salon and shops.
Mosu (☎ 421001; fax 427466), 274-13 Yon-dong, Shinjeju. Facilities include a sauna, barbershop, beauty salon, games room, nightclub and bowling alley.
Palace (☎ 538811; fax 538820), 1192-18 Samdo 2-dong, Old Cheju. Facilities include a sauna and game room.

Pearl (☎ 428871; fax 421221), 277-2 Yon-dong, Shinjeju.
Robero (☎ 577111; fax 559001), 57-2 Samdo 1-dong, Old Cheju
Royal (☎ 432222; fax 420424), 272-34 Yon-dong, Shinjeju. Facilities include restaurants, bar, nightclub and sauna.

Deluxe Class Rooms at deluxe hotels cost between W147,000 and W160,000. Some hotels in this range include:

Holiday Inn Crowne Plaza (☎ 424111; fax 464111), 291-30 Yon-dong, Shinjeju. Facilities include a casino, health club, indoor swimming pool and sauna.
KAL (☎ 536151; fax 524187), 1691-9 Ido 1-dong, Old Cheju. Facilities include restaurants, sauna, health club, indoor swimming pool, casino and nightclub.
Lagonda (☎ 582500; fax 550027), 159-1 Yongdam 1-dong, Cheju City. Facilities include a cocktail lounge, banquet hall, sauna and shopping arcade.
Oriental (☎ 528222; fax 529777), 1197 Samdo 2-dong, Cheju City. Facilities include banquet hall, casino, bowling alley, sauna, shopping arcade and games room.

Super-Deluxe Hotels in this category charge between W184,000 and W295,000. Currently, the only super-deluxe accommodation in this part of the island is the *Grand Hotel* (☎ 475000; fax 470278), 263-15 Yon-dong, Shinjeju. Facilities include a casino, health club, swimming pool, nightclub and sauna.

Places to Eat

As elsewhere in Korea, the biggest problem with finding a place to eat is knowing where to start – there is a cornucopia of restaurants and you'd have to take up permanent residence on the island to get through them all.

One place to start looking for budget meals in Old Cheju is in the Underground Arcade which runs under Kwangdongno. In the eastern part of the arcade you'll find *Disney's Land*, which features western-style fast food such as fried chicken (good), pizza (not bad), sandwiches (awful), hamburgers (acceptable) and ice cream in cones (OK). At the western end of the arcade is *Pizzeria*.

Nammun Barbecue Chicken is a Korean-style place. You can eat half a roast chicken for W5000 or a whole one for W8000.

Cheju City seems to be thick with bakeries – *Joong Ang Bakery* is the largest and has tables where you can sit down and enjoy your pastries with coffee, tea or milk. The other bakeries around town are all take-aways.

To eat well, you really should hop over to Shinjeju. The *Grand Durant Restaurant* has the best western food on the island and is reasonably priced.

The *Lotte Champion Department Store* has an excellent supermarket in the basement. There's a Korean restaurant here, as well as a *Lotteria* fast food shop and a *Baskin-Robbins* ice cream parlour.

You'll find a Harley-Davidson motorcycle parked indoors at *939 Pizza*. The motorcycle is used by the owner, though not for delivering pizzas. The pizza here is reputed to be the best in town.

Entertainment

Cheju abounds with nightclubs which lay on live bands and karaoke sessions, though most of them are to be found in the large

---

Dishes That Never Say Die

The Korean government cracked down some time ago on the practice of eating endangered species – restaurants no longer dish up bear paws and tiger meat. However, some Koreans travelling abroad (especially in China) have been known to partake in an endangered species barbecue.

Two creatures which do not get protection are the lowly octopus and the giant prawn. The problem isn't that the world faces an octopus or shrimp shortage, it's that at least some Koreans like to eat these creatures before they're dead! The prawns squirm, but live octopus tentacles make a meal that literally fights back. Diners need to be skilled with chopsticks to pry their squiggling delicacies off the plate, plus they need to chew fast to prevent the suckers from sticking to their teeth. While there can be no doubt about the freshness, this is a meal that might haunt you in your sleep. ■

hotels and cater to people with money to burn. Ditto for casinos, which suck in money from (mostly Japanese) foreign tourists.

In Cheju City, check out *The Doors*. This place has a fabulous CD collection.

Over in Shinjeju, *the* place to go is *Bebeto's Pub*. It's a good bar with imported beer. You'll find it on the 4th floor and there's a sign in English.

Around the Island

SŎGWIP'O
On the south coast of Cheju-do, Sŏgwip'o (population 85,000) is the island's second largest town and is connected to the rest of Korea by ferries from Pusan. It's more laid back than Cheju City and its setting at the foot of Hallasan, whose lower slopes are covered with citrus groves, is quite spectacular. You'll also see plenty of greenhouses in the area – this is where Korea's bananas are raised.

Information
Unusually for Korea, the town of Sŏgwip'o seems to be almost totally devoid of public toilets – not even the bus terminal has one. Only the ferry terminal at the southernmost end of town has a public toilet. If you're not near there find some bushes.

Chŏngbang Waterfall
This waterfall is 23m high and claimed in the tourist literature to be the only waterfall in Asia which falls directly into the sea. This isn't quite correct, since the Toroki Falls on the south coast of Yaku-shima in Japan also do this and are even larger than Ch'ŏnjiyŏn. All the same, these falls are a very impressive sight and are only a 10 to 15-minute walk from the centre of town. Just off the coast you can see several small, partially forested and very rocky islands. Entry costs W1000.

Ch'ŏnjiyŏn Waterfall
This waterfall is on the other side of town at the end of a beautifully forested and steep gorge. Like the Chŏngbang Waterfall,

Ch'ŏnjiyŏn is a 10 to 15-minute walk from the centre of town down by the fishing harbour. Entry costs W1100.

Places to Stay – bottom end
There are quite a few yŏgwan in the small streets around the centre of town. Some reasonable places include the *Manbu Yŏgwan* and nearby *Namyang-jang Yŏgwan*, where rooms cost W22,000.

Places to Stay – middle & top end
In the last few years, Sŏgwip'o has become a resort town in its own right and there are a number of top-end hotels to choose from. The line-up includes:

KAL (☎ 329851; fax 323190), 486-3 T'op'yong-dong, Sŏgwip'o. Twins W150,000 to W160,000. Facilities include a casino, indoor & outdoor swimming pools, tennis courts, nightclub, sauna, shopping arcade and golf course. Rated deluxe class.
Lions (☎ 335651; fax 333617), 803 Sogwi-dong, Sŏgwip'o. Twins W60,000. Facilities include a nightclub and bar. Rated 3rd class.
New Kyungnam Tourist (☎ 332121; fax 332129), 314-1 Sogwi-dong, Sŏgwip'o. Doubles cost W110,000. Facilities include a restaurant, bar, shops, beauty salon, sauna and games room. Rated 2nd class.
Paradise (☎ 632100; fax 329355), 511 T'op'yong-dong, Sŏgwip'o. Doubles cost W100,000. Facilities include a health club, outdoor swimming pool, sauna and karaoke bar. Rated 1st class.
Park (☎ 622161; fax 332882), 674-1 Sogwi-dong, Sŏgwip'o. Doubles W52,000 to W60,000. Facilities include a nightclub, sauna and indoor swimming pool. Rated 3rd class.
Prince (☎ 329911; fax 329900), 731-3 Sohong-dong, Sŏgwip'o. Rated deluxe class.
Sun Beach (☎ 322612), 820-1 Sogwi-dong, Sŏgwip'o. Twins cost W90,000. Facilities include banquet hall and game room. Rated 2nd class.

Getting There & Away
Helicopter For a mere W30,000, you can fly for 25 minutes from Cheju Airport to Sŏgwip'o. Bargain hunters may want to fly from Cheju Airport to Ch'uja-dong, which takes 20 minutes and costs W20,000.

Bus Bus No 600 runs from the airport to

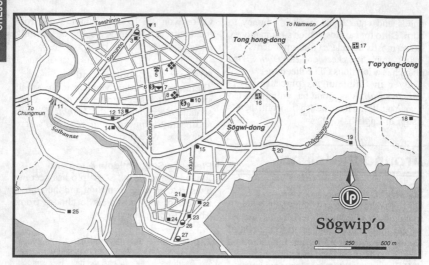

Sŏgwip'o

0   250   500 m

Sŏgwip'o 서귀포

PLACES TO STAY

3 Mansu-jang Yŏgwan
   만수장여관
10 Kŭmwu Hotel
   금우호텔
12 New Kyungnam Tourist
   Hotel
   신균남관광호텔
13 Sun Beach Hotel
   호텔서비치
14 Lions Hotel
   라이온스호텔
18 KAL Hotel
   KAL호텔
19 Paradise Hotel
   파라다이스호텔
21 Koreana Hotel
   호텔코리아나
22 Manbu Yŏgwan
   만부여관

23 Namyang-jang Yŏgwan
   남양장여관
24 Park Hotel
   파크호텔
25 Prince Hotel
   프린스호텔

OTHER

1 Winchell's Donut House
   윈첼도넛하우스
2 Inter-City Bus Terminal
   시외버스터미널
4 Mokhwa Department
   Store
   목화백화점
5 Telephone Company
   전화장
6 Hanil Bank
   한일은행
7 Post Office
   우체국

8 Tongmyŏng Department
   Store
   동명백화점
9 Bank
   국민은행
11 Ch'ŏnjiyŏn Waterfall
   천지연폭포
15 City Hall
   시청
16 Chŏngbangsa Temple
   정방사
17 Pŏpryunsa Temple
   법륜사
20 Chŏngbang Waterfall
   정방폭포
26 Airport Bus Stop
   정류장 (공항)
27 Ferry Terminal
   서귀항터미널

Sŏgwip'o (W3300) via the Chungmun Resort (W2200).

From the inter-city bus terminal in Cheju City, there are buses to Sŏgwip'o (W2500) via Chungmun (W1900) every 12 minutes from 6.20 am to 9.30 pm.

CHUNGMUN RESORT

Chungmun is Cheju's largest resort and has a number of super-deluxe hotels, condominiums, restaurants and a marine park. It also gets very crowded during the summer holiday season. While the much-touted beach is no big deal, it's worth visiting the **Chonjeyon Waterfall** (not to be confused with the Ch'ŏnjiyŏn Waterfall in Sŏgwip'o); it's a 20-minute walk back from the beach up to the bridge on the coastal highway.

Overlooking the beach itself is the **Royal Marine Park**, which contains a dolphinarium, aquarium and restaurant complex. If you're interested in seeing performing dolphins, after all the research that's been done into the effects of captivity on these animals, then there are shows at 11 am, and at 1.30, 2.40 and 4.30 pm daily. If you're not interested in seeing this sort of thing, the aquarium itself isn't worth the entry fee. Entry to the park costs W4000.

Places to Stay & Eat

This is the territory of the rich and famous. There are a couple of yŏgwan in Chungmun Village itself, but it's quite a walk from the beach and along the highway. Unless you've got the money for the golf course, tennis courts, horse riding and other amenities, there's really no reason to stay in Chungmun.

If price is no object, Chungmun can accommodate you in style. There's at least one high-priced restaurant in every hotel. The more upmarket places include:

Green Villa (☎ 389990), 2812-10 Saektal-dong, Sŏgwip'o. Rated deluxe class.
Hyatt Regency Cheju (☎ 331234; fax 322039), 3039-1 Saektal-dong, Sŏgwip'o. The facilities include a casino. Rated super-deluxe class.
Korea Resort Condominium (☎ 384000; fax 323493), 2822-5 Saektal-dong, Sŏgwip'o (Chungmun). Facilities include a disco, outdoor swimming pool and video rental shop.
Shilla (☎ 384466; fax 383982), 3039-3 Saektal-dong, Sŏgwip'o. Facilities include a casino. Rated super-deluxe class.

Getting There & Away

Bus No 600 runs between the airport and Sŏgwip'o, stopping at Chungmun en route. It runs every 15 minutes between 6.20 am and 9.50 pm, and takes 45 minutes for the journey. The fare to the airport is W2200.

From the inter-city bus terminal in Cheju City there are buses to Chungmun every 12 minutes from 6.20 am to 9.30 pm.

BEACHES

To read the raves in the tourist literature, you might be forgiven for thinking Chejudo's beaches rival those of Hawaii, Australia, Thailand or Indonesia. Unfortunately, the tourism bureau folks tend to get carried away with their own rhetoric. True, there are a number of sandy beaches tucked away in coves which can be pleasant places to enjoy the sun and surf. But as beaches go Chejudo's are hardly world class.

If you've got the time the beaches are worth exploring, but as they are 33½° north of the equator July and August are the only months when the water is warm enough for pleasant swimming.

Some of the beaches have yŏgwan, yŏinsuk or minbak. Certainly it's more relaxing to stay in these places than in downtown Cheju City.

While none of the beaches are truly outstanding, some are better than others. Starting from Cheju City and moving in a clockwise direction around the island, the following will give you an idea of what's on offer.

Hamdŏk Beach

This beach is 14 km east of Cheju City. It's ¾ km in length, has good quality sand and a pretty pine grove at the east end. Adjacent to the beach are fields where watermelons are grown. In summer the big hotels set up tarpaulins where their guests can escape the sun and slurp cold drinks.

The beach area is fairly commercialised and you won't have to go far to find drinks, restaurants, changing rooms and showers. Lifeguards are on duty during the summer months.

You can reach Hamdŏk Beach by inter-city bus. There are buses every 20 minutes and the ride takes ½ hour.

Shinyang Beach

Near the eastern end of the island, Shinyang Beach is shaped like a half moon and is about 1½ km in length. It's the most sheltered beach on the island and there is a place here where you can rent sailboats and take lessons on how to use them. This is a good staging post for climbing nearby Sunrise Peak (see the Sŏngsan section for details).

There are numerous yŏgwan and minbak in Sŏngsan-ri just to the north of the beach. Rates are typically W15,000 to W20,000.

This beach is a bit remote. Buses from Cheju City do not go directly to Shinyang Beach. First take a bus to Kosŏng-ri – these run about once every 20 minutes from 5.45 am to 9.40 pm and take 1¼ hours. The hard part is the last two km from Kosŏng-ri to the beach. You could take a taxi or walk it if your bags aren't too heavy; otherwise there is a bus once an hour from 6.15 am to 9.12 pm which takes just six minutes.

During the summer months the beach is patrolled by lifeguards and small kiosks sell drinks and snacks.

Western culture is making an impression, but many Koreans adhere to traditional values and at heart are deeply conservative.

Hwasun Beach

This unusual beach features black volcanic sand. It's 250m in length with good scenery. On a clear day you can easily see the islets of Hyŏngjedo, Kapado and Marado.

There are about 15 minbak in the vicinity and free camping near the beach.

The beach is 67 km from Cheju City via the west coastal highway, 23 km west of Sŏgwip'o and 10 km west of Chungmun Resort.

Buses from Cheju City's inter-city bus terminal run every 40 minutes. Or get a bus in Sŏgwip'o – these run every 30 minutes.

Hyŏpchae Beach

This is not one of the island's stellar beaches, but Hyŏpchae has shallow water and therefore is a big hit with little kids. There are, of course, lifeguards on duty during the summer months. There is an attractive grove of pine trees lining the back of the beach.

Hyŏpchae Beach is 32 km west of Cheju City. Buses depart every 20 minutes between 5.45 am and 9.20 pm. The journey takes 50 minutes.

Kwakchi Beach

The consensus is that Kwakchi Beach, at the north-west of the island, has the best sand, surf and scenery. The beach is only ¼ km in length – this isn't Bali, but at a pinch it will do nicely.

Kwakchi is 23 km west of Cheju City. By bus from the inter-city bus terminal the trip takes about 40 minutes.

There is a minbak at Kwakchi operated by a Mr Hong Song-ok (☎ 990587).

Iho Beach

This is the nearest beach to Cheju City (eight km), which accounts for its popularity. The swimming is OK here, but the area attracts plenty of Koreans trying to fish from the shore. In other words, watch out for fish hooks! The beach has lifeguard patrols, abundant shops, a changing room, showers, beach umbrellas for hire and even a camping ground.

SŎNG-ŬP FOLK VILLAGE
A short bus ride north of P'yosŏn lies Cheju-do's former provincial capital. It was founded in the 13th century, became the provincial headquarters in 1423, during the reign of King Sejong, and remained as such until 1914. Today it's designated a folk village, and its traditional architecture and character have been preserved with government assistance.

If you want to see what Cheju's villages looked like before concrete and corrugated iron transformed the Korean landscape, then Sŏng-ŭp is definitely worth a visit. There's a good collection of original harubang here and much more recent harubang are on display in the nearby souvenir shops. Other modern intrusions include the provision of a parking lot for coaches and cars, and a number of tourist restaurants.

A large sign in English and Korean in the centre of the village, where the buses stop, describes the main features of the village and the history of the principal sites, so take time to have a look at it. Otherwise, take off down the narrow lanes and discover the place for yourself. Remember that most of the houses are still occupied so observe the usual courtesies regarding privacy. There are no entry fees to any of the buildings.

Places to Stay & Eat
There's a reasonable selection of restaurants, ranging from simple to more elaborate, along the main street of Sŏng-ŭp but no yŏgwan as such. If you'd like to stay here for the night then you'll have to ask around for a minbak.

Getting There & Away
The schedule for the buses from Cheju City to P'yosŏn via San'gumburi and Sŏng-ŭp can be found in the Getting Around section of this chapter. The bus timetable board in Sŏng-ŭp itself indicates there are buses from Cheju City to Sŏng-ŭp and P'yosŏn every half hour from 6 am to 10 pm, and from P'yosŏn to Sŏng-ŭp and Cheju City every half hour from 6.30 am to 10 pm. Locals dispute the existence of the later buses and say they don't always arrive. What they do

agree on is that there are buses from Sŏng-ŭp to Cheju City every half hour from 7 am to 8 pm, so it's best to assume that the last bus back to Cheju City is at 8 pm. These are the same buses which run past San'gumburi.

CHEJU FOLK VILLAGE
In addition to Sŏng-ŭp, there is a specially built folk village just outside P'yosŏn and close to the town's fine beach. It re-creates 19th-century Cheju, showing the different lifestyles of people living on the coast, plains and mountains. There's a Shamanistic area and official buildings to house magistrates, government officials and records. Though essentially a modern creation, all the construction here is authentically traditional; some of the cottages were brought intact from other areas and are 200 or 300 years old. There's also a performance yard where folk songs and legends are enacted.

Like other such folk villages, there are a number of restaurants offering traditional food as well as makkoli (white rice wine), beer and soft drinks.

The Cheju Folk Village is open daily from 9 am to 6 pm and entry costs W2500.

SAN'GUMBURI CRATER
The huge San'gumburi volcanic crater lies right by the side of the road on the way from Sŏng-ŭp to Cheju City. Larger than the one at Sŏngsan, this crater is some 350m in diameter and around 100m deep. The floor of the crater is covered with grass, but the steep sides are densely forested with evergreen oak and other broad-leaved trees, as well as a few pine trees. Craggy rocks line the rim. The crater is home to deer, badgers, reptiles and many species of bird. There's a trail you can walk along which follows the rim, but you're not allowed down in the crater itself.

Buses from Cheju City to Sŏng-ŭp and P'yosŏn pass right by the gate and will stop if you want to get off. You can't miss this place as it's fronted by a huge parking lot and a tourist village by the entrance gate.

Entry to the crater costs W1000 (W500 for students and children, free for seniors).

Beware the Giant Snake

Chejudo's lava tubes are linked to an ancient legend of a huge snake which supposedly lived in them. In order to placate this snake and prevent harm befalling the nearby farms and villages, a 15 or 16-year-old virgin girl was annually sacrificed by being thrown into the cave. This horrific practice was stopped in 1514 when a newly-appointed magistrate persuaded the reluctant villagers to perform their customary ritual, but to omit the sacrifice. At this, the story goes, the angry snake emerged and was killed by the villagers then burnt to ashes. Soon afterwards the magistrate inexplicably fell ill and died, but there was no reappearance of the snake. ■

MANJANGGUL LAVA CAVES

East of Cheju and about 2½ km off the coast road from Kimnyŏng Beach are the caves of Manjanggul. The main section of the caves is almost seven km long (!!) with a height and width varying from three to 20 metres, thus making it the longest known lava tube in the world. If you've never seen one of these before then make sure you visit this place.

Take a sweater with you and a reasonable pair of shoes. It's damp down there (87% to 100% humidity) and the temperature rarely rises above a chilly 9°C. The cave is well-lit as far as a huge lava pillar (about one km from the entrance) which is as far as you're allowed to go without special permission. The caves are open every day from 9 am to 6 pm and entry costs W1600.

Much closer to the turn-off from the main highway, but alongside the same road which leads to the Manjanggul Caves, there's another series of lava tubes known as the Kimnyŏngsagul Caves. They're not as long as the Manjanggul Caves – 700m divided into four parts – but they're almost as spectacular; there are actually two tubes, one on top of the other, at this site. At the time of writing this cave was closed, though there is talk of reopening it.

Getting There & Away

To get to the Manjanggul and Kimnyŏng-sagul caves, take a bus from Cheju City going to Sŏngsan and get off at the Kimnyŏng turnoff (signposted for the caves). From here there are local buses to the Manjanggul Caves every 30 to 60 minutes between 7.50 am and 6.30 pm. There's a full schedule for the buses posted in the window of the ticket office at the Manjanggul Caves. Alternatively, you can hitch a ride or walk to the caves.

SŎNGSAN PEAK

Sŏngsan, at the eastern tip of Cheju-do, nestles at the foot of the spectacular volcanic cone known as Sunrise Peak (Sŏngsan-ilch'ubong), whose sides plunge vertically into the surf. The volcano is on a peninsula and only connected to the main island by a spit of sand. If conditions are favourable you can watch Cheju-do's famous diving women searching for seaweed, shellfish and sea urchins. The summit has a shallow crater, but unlike Hallasan there's no longer a lake there. The area below the jagged outer edges of the peak is continuously harvested for cattle fodder (it supports luxurious grass). It is definitely one of Cheju-do's most beautiful areas. If you want to catch the sunrise, you'll have to spend the night here in a local yŏgwan. Entry to Sunrise Peak costs W1000.

You can walk around the crater and boats can sail you around the peninsula, although they only go when demand is sufficient and the sea is calm. The price is W5000.

Places to Stay

Facing the road which leads up to the tourist complex and entrance gate to Sunrise Peak is the *Suji Yŏgwan*, where you can get a room with bath and hot water for W20,000. Round the corner from the Suji Yŏgwan is the *Sŏngsan Yŏinsuk* which also is OK.

Going up in price, there is the *Chaesong-jang Yŏgwan*, opposite the post office on the bottom road, which has rooms for W25,000.

Getting There & Away

There are frequent buses to Sŏngsan from Cheju City which take about 1½ hours. Make sure the bus you get on is going right into Sŏngsan and not just to Tongnam, the town on the main coast road where you have to turn off for Sŏngsan. If you get dropped here it's a 2½ km walk into Sŏngsan.

UDO ISLAND
North-east of Sŏngsan, just off the coast, is Udo (Cow Island). It is still very rural and there are no vehicles other than a few tractors and a single minibus; it's about as far as you can get from civilisation in this part of the world. There are superb views over to Sunrise Peak; two sandy beaches completely free of trash; and a community of *haenyo*, Cheju's famous diving women, who work in the cove below the lighthouse.

The island is a relaxing place to stay and several minbak are available.

Getting There & Away
There are ferries from the port at Sŏngsan to Udo. The ticket office and ferry pier are quite a way from the centre of Sŏngsan so leave yourself enough time to walk (about 15 minutes). From March to June and during October the ferries depart Sŏngsan at 10 am, noon, 3 pm and 6 pm, and from Udo at 8 am and 11 am, 2 pm and 5 pm. From July to September they depart Sŏngsan at 8.50 am and 10.30 am, 2 pm, 4 pm and 7 pm, and from Udo at 7.30 am and 9.30 am, 1 pm, 3 pm and 6 pm. From November to February the ferries leave Sŏngsan at 10 am, noon, 2 pm and 5 pm; and from Udo at 8 am and 11 am, 1 pm and 4 pm.

HYŎPCHAEGUL LAVA CAVE
About 2½ km south of Hallam on the north-western side of the island is a group of lava tube caves. The most famous of these, Hyŏpchaegul, is actually a system of several interconnected lava tubes that was only discovered in the 1950s. Although much shorter than the Manjanggul Cave, it is one of the few lava tubes in the world which has stalagmites and stalactites; these are usually only found in limestone caves. In Hyŏpchaegul the stalactites and stalagmites are caused by large quantities of pulverised shells in the soil above the cave, which have been blown up from the sea shore over thousands of

years. Entry to the caves costs W1600. It's advisable to hire an umbrella in wet weather, otherwise you'll be soaked to the skin. They're available at the cave entrance.

There's an extensive tourist complex and a mini folk village around the entrance. The paths into and out of the cave are tediously designed to force you to pass through as many souvenir shops as possible.

Also part of the complex is a subtropical **botanic gardens**, though entry to this costs a further W1000.

The other caves in this area are not commercialised and include Ssangynonggul, Hwanggumgul, Sŏch'ongul and Chogitgul. The largest and most spectacular of these is Sŏch'ongul, which measures some three km in length; its two entrances resemble a huge subterranean botanic garden.

Getting There & Away
To get there take a bus going along the west coast road. You can't miss the caves as the entrance is right by the side of the road and all the buses stop here.

SANBANGGULSA CAVE TEMPLE
About seven km east of Taejŏng rises the massive volcanic cone of Sanbangsan. Halfway up its southern slope overlooking the ocean is a natural cave which was turned into a temple by a Buddhist monk during Koryŏ times. It's quite a steep walk up, but although the grotto itself is only of marginal interest the views are worth the effort. Water dripping from the roof of the cave is said to be the tears of Sanbang-gok, the patron goddess of the mountain. Lower down, near the entrance, are two recently-built temples where there always seems to be something going on. There's a cafe about halfway up to the grotto which is a great place to sit and have a cold drink.

Entry to the site costs W1000 (W500 for those under 24 years old).

The entrance to the grotto is right beside the coast road so you can't miss it. Buses between Taejŏng and Sŏgwip'o will get you there.

HAMEL MONUMENT

Across the road from Sanbanggulsa is a rocky promontory where a plaque was erected by the Korean and Dutch governments to commemorate the shipwreck of the Dutch merchant vessel *Sparrowhawk* in 1653. Those who survived the wreckage were taken to Seoul by order of the Yi king and forced to remain there for the next 13 years until they escaped to Japan in a small fishing vessel. An account of those years written by one of the survivors, Hendrick Hamel, became a best seller in Europe at the time. It was the first accurate description of the so-called Hermit Kingdom that Europe had received until that date.

CHEJU ART PARK

Built on an open meadow near Sabangsan on south-west Chejudo, the Cheju Art Park features more than 180 pieces of sculpture in a natural setting of ponds and trails. The park is open from 9 am to 5.30 pm.

KAP'ADO & MARADO ISLANDS

South of Taejŏng (or Mosŭlpo, as the nearby beach is called) lie Kap'ado and Marado, the most southerly points of Korea. Both are inhabited. Kap'ado, the nearest and largest of the islands, is flat and almost without trees; crops are cultivated behind stone walls to protect them from the high winds which sweep the island. Many of the inhabitants earn their living by fishing.

Unlike Kap'ado, Marado rises steeply from the sea. It is only half the size of Kap'ado and there are only some 20 families living there. Its grassed top supports cattle grazing.

Getting There & Away

There are two ferries daily from Taejŏng to Kap'ado, at 8.30 am and 2.30 pm, which take about half an hour. To Marado there is one ferry daily from Taejŏng at 10 am which takes about 50 minutes. Neither of these ferries sails during rough weather.

The ferry terminal in Taejŏng is down by the fishing harbour and about one km from the centre of town, which is where the buses drop you. There are yŏinsuk, yŏgwan and restaurants in Taejŏng if you prefer to stay overnight in order to catch the morning ferry. It's possible to miss this ferry if you attempt to get to Taejŏng from Cheju City by early morning bus.

ANTI-MONGOL MONUMENT

Cheju-do was the last stronghold of a faction of the Koryŏ army which resisted the Mongols even after King Wonjong had made peace with the invaders and returned to his capital at Kaesong. In 1273, an elite military force built a six-km long dual-walled fortress near what is today the town of Aewol on the north-west coast of the island. The defenders were later slaughtered to a man by the Mongols. Although the effort proved futile, islanders have honoured their ancestors' bravery by erecting the Anti-Mongol Monument on the site of the battle.

Another relic is the **Wondangsa Temple** site, a five storey stone pagoda which has been designated local cultural property No 1. The Mongols built their own temple here when they ruled Chejudo; it was later destroyed and today only the pagoda remains.

HALLASAN NATIONAL PARK

Walking to the top of Hallasan is one of the highlights of a visit to Cheju-do, but at the time of writing the last few hundred metres of the trail were closed to give the summit a respite from the impact of hikers. It's scheduled to reopen in spring of 1999. Until then you can still do some good hikes close to the summit.

Whatever you do, make sure you get off to an early start. No matter how clear the skies may look in the morning, the summit is often obscured by cloud in the early afternoon – which is when you should be on the way down. Anyone reasonably fit can do this trek. No experience is necessary and no special equipment required. Just make sure you have a decent pair of jogging shoes or hiking boots and something warm (it gets chilly up there at nearly 2000m). Rain gear is also advised as the weather is very changeable on the mountain.

There are five well-marked trails: Yongshil (from the south-west side), Orimok

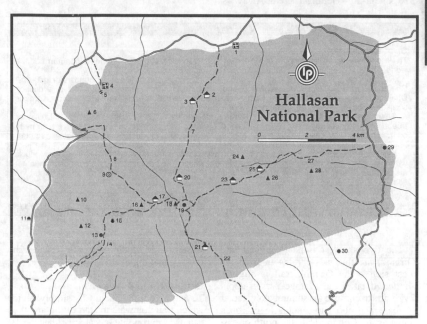

Hallasan National Park
한라산국립공원

1 Kwanŭmsa Temple
관음사
2 Red Cross Shelter
적십자 대피소
3 T'amna Gorge
Shelter
담라게곡 대피소
4 Ch'ŏnwangsa
Temple
천왕사
5 Sŏnnyŏ Waterfall
선녀폭포
6 Ŏsŭngsaengorŭm
(1169m)
어승생오름

7 Kwanŭmsa Trail
관음사 코스
8 Orimok Trail
오리목 코스
9 Spring
샘터
10 Ŏsŭllŏngorŭm
(1335m)
어슬렁오름
11 Sŏngnŏl Rest Area
(1100m)
1100고지휴게소
12 Pollaeorŭm
(1362m)
볼래오름
13 Rest Area
휴게소
14 Yongshil Trail
어실 코스

15 Yŏngshil Rocks
영실기암
16 Witsaeorŭm
(1714m)
윗새오름
17 Witsaeorŭm Shelter
윗새오름 대피수
18 Hallasan (1950m)
한라산
19 Paengnoktam
Crater
백록담
20 Yongchingak
Shelter
용진각 대피소
21 P'yŏngjigwe
Shelter
펑지케 대피소
22 Tonnaek'o Trail
돈내코 코스

23 Chindallae Shelter
신달래밭 대피소
24 Hukpulgŭnorŭm
(1391m)
흙붉은오름
25 Sara Shelter
사라 대피수
26 Saraorŭm (1338m)
사라오름
27 Sŏngpan'ak Trail
성판악 코스
28 Sŏngnŏlorŭm
(1215m)
성닐오름
29 Sŏngp'anak Rest
Area
성판악휴게소
30 Suak Gorge
수악계곡

(north-west side), Kwanŭmsa (north side), Tonnaek'o (south side) and Sŏngpan'ak (east side). Some are considerably more difficult than others. The trails all connect with one or other of the two cross-island highways. Entry to the national park costs W800 unless you arrive very early (before the ticket sellers come to work).

Spot the Mongol

The Mongols – who swooped out of Mongolia on horseback in the 13th century to conquer half the world – have a special (though not very happy) kinship with the people of Chejudo.

The Mongols stayed from 1276 to 1375 and evidence of their occupation still abounds. For instance, Chejudo's unique dialect was heavily influenced by the invaders. Though classified as a dialect, Chejudo's language is as different from Korean as Provençal is from French. Mainland Koreans sometimes have difficulty understanding what is being said on this island.

There are other reminders of the past. Koreans claim to be 'of the Mongolian race', and this is more true in Chejudo than anywhere on the mainland. Many natives of Chejudo are born with a birth mark on their buttocks. It's called a 'Mongolian spot' and it tends to fade with age. It's debatable whether or not the spot originated with Mongolians, but the mainlanders do not seem to have it.

One of the more aesthetic legacies from the Mongol occupation are the island's horses. It was the Mongols who first used Chejudo's pastures to graze these animals. The horses (or rather, their descendants) are still there, earning their living giving rides to paying tourists and posing for photo opportunities. ■

The two shortest trails (Yongshil and Orimok) are the ones coming in from the west side – the Orimok trail is slightly shorter. It takes the average person about 2½ hours to climb to the summit along either of these and about two hours to get back down again. Coming from the north or east side you should plan on about four or five hours to the summit. The Tonnaek'o, from the south, is the most difficult trail of all and should be avoided unless you're fit and experienced at climbing. If you have camping equipment there are several sites where you can pitch a tent, although in most cases the park service would prefer that you stay in the huts. These are indicated on the map. You can buy soft drinks, snacks and even soju near all the ticket offices.

Rock slides frequently close trails. You'll have to make local inquiries to find out which are open when you visit.

There's a large and active Buddhist monastery called Kwanumsa close to the trail of the same name.

Places to Eat

There are a number of *restaurants* at the start of some of the trails. The one at the start of the Sŏngkwanak trail is open year-round, as is the one at the '1100 Meter Rest Area' about halfway between the trail entry points on the western side of the mountain (on the 2nd cross-island highway).

Getting There & Away

To get there from Cheju City simply decide which trail you want to start off on and then take the appropriate bus along either the 1st or 2nd cross-island highway (see the Getting Around section). Tell the driver or conductor which trail you want to go on and they'll make sure you're put down at the right spot.

Getting There & Away

Air

Both Korean Air and Asiana Airlines operate domestic flights to Cheju-do – see the Getting Around chapter for routes and airfares.

There are international flights to Fukuoka and Sendai in Japan.

The main Korean Air office is opposite the KAL Hotel on Chung'angno. The Asiana Airlines main office is in Shinjeju. However, it's very easy to book tickets from numerous travel agents around town.

Ferry

There are ferries from Cheju City to Mokp'o, Wando, Pusan, Yŏsu and Inch'ŏn. On the southern coast there are ferries from

Sŏgwip'o to Pusan. Student discounts are available on all the ferries, but you have to ask for them. The seas in the straits between Cheju-do and the mainland are often quite rough – if you're not a good sailor it might be worth taking one of the faster ferries or even flying.

Schedules vary from one season to another. Not surprisingly, boats are most frequent during summer and the following schedules all assume you are travelling during peak times. If travelling off-peak it's a good idea to ring up first or check the schedule immediately upon arrival in the port city.

Pusan-Cheju There is a choice of four ferries to Cheju-do from Pusan – two to Cheju City and two to Sŏgwip'o via Sŏngsan (on the eastern tip of the island). All these ferries depart from the domestic ferry terminal in Pusan. The timetables at the terminal are in both Korean and English.

From Pusan to Cheju City, you can take the car ferry *Queen*. It sails from Pusan on Sunday, Tuesday and Thursday at 7 pm, and from Cheju City on Monday, Wednesday and Friday also at 7 pm. The journey takes about 12 hours and the fares are from W15,200 to W88,500. You can ring up for the latest schedules (☎ Seoul 755-2511, Pusan 263-0260, Cheju 564511).

Tongyang Car Ferry No 5 or *No 6* sails Pusan-Cheju daily except Sunday. Departures from Pusan or Cheju are at 5.30 pm and the journey takes 12 hours. Fares are from W15,200 to W37,800. You can telephone for information (☎ Seoul 730-7788, Pusan 463-0605, Cheju 511901).

The two ferries to Sŏgwip'o are the *Cheju Car Ferry No 1* and *No 3*, which alternate with each other. One or the other sails from Pusan daily except Saturday at 6.30 pm. From Sŏgwip'o there's a sailing daily except Saturday at 5 pm and the journey takes 15 hours. The one-way fares range from W15,400 to W40,200. For information, ring up (☎ Pusan 464-2228, Sŏgwip'o 320220).

Mokp'o-Cheju The boat *Democracy No 2*

departs Mokp'o daily at 1.40 pm, and from Cheju daily at 9.30 am. The journey takes slightly over three hours. Fares are W31,500 to W37,300. For information you can telephone in Mokp'o (☎ 245-3235) or Cheju (☎ 212171).

The *Kukje Express* runs daily except Monday in either direction. Departures from Mokp'o are at 9 am and departures from Cheju are at 5.30 pm. The journey takes 5½ hours and costs W10,200 to W28,000. For information you can ring up in Seoul (☎ 393-4841), Mokp'o (☎ 431927) or Cheju (☎ 212171).

Tongyang Car Ferry No 2 departs Mokp'o daily except Sunday at 3.30 pm. Departures from Cheju are daily except Monday at 5 pm. The journey takes 5½ hours and costs from W10,200 to W28,000. For the latest information, ring up (☎ Seoul 730-7788, Cheju 511901, or Mokp'o 432111).

Wando-Cheju *Hanil Car Ferry No 1* sails from Wando daily, except the first and third Saturday of each month, at 4 pm. In the opposite direction it departs Cheju at 7.20 am daily except the 1st and 3rd Sunday.

Hanil Car Ferry No 2 departs Wando at 5 pm daily except on the second and fourth Saturday of every month. It departs Cheju at 9.20 am daily except the second and fourth Sunday.

On either boat the schedule might be cut back during winter. Both boats take three hours to make the crossing. Car ferry No 1 costs from W9650 to W12,400; and car ferry No 2 from W9650 to W21,000. Call for the latest information (☎ Seoul 535-2101, Cheju 224170, Wando 543294).

Yŏsu-Cheju The good ship *Democracy No 3* departs Yŏsu daily at 9.10 am and leaves Cheju daily at 1.30 pm. The ride takes 3½ hours and costs from W28,050 to W33,550. For more details you can ring up in Yŏsu (☎ 632191) or Cheju (☎ 212171).

Inch'ŏn-Cheju It's a long boat ride, but some people like it. Departures from Inch'ŏn are on Monday, Wednesday and Friday at 5 pm; from Cheju it's on Tuesday, Thursday and Saturday at 2.20 pm. The journey takes 16½ hours and costs W29,600 to W55,000 depending on class. For further information, call Semo Express in Inch'ŏn (☎ 884-8700) or Cheju (☎ 212171).

Getting Around

The Airport

The airport is about two km west of the city. Bus No 100 costs W500 and takes 20 minutes between the airport and the ferry terminal via the inter-city bus station and Shinjeju. You can also use bus No 500 (W500) to get downtown though it doesn't go all the way to the ferry terminal. A taxi will cost W2000.

Bus

Arriving by boat, there's no need to take a taxi or bus since most of the cheap yŏgwan and yŏinsuk are only a few minutes' walk from the ferry terminal. You probably won't have to use Cheju city buses at all except to get to the airport or to the local bus terminal (about two km).

There are plenty of buses to most places of interest around the island. Provided you have your destination written down in Korean characters along with the route you want to take, it's very unlikely you'll be sold the wrong ticket or ever board the wrong bus. The people here are very helpful. But before heading out to explore the island by bus, consider the virtues of taking a tour (see the following 'Tours' section). A rough guide to the bus routes is as follows:

P'yosŏn via San'gumburi and Sŏng-ŭp. Buses terminate at Cheju Folk Village near P'yosŏn.
Sŏngsan via the eastern coast road.
Hallasan and Sŏgwip'o via No 1 cross-island highway.
Hallasan and Chungmun via No 2 cross-island highway.
Taejŏng and Hwasun via inland routes.
Chungmun and Sŏgwip'o via inland routes.
Sŏgwip'o via Hallim, Taejŏng, Hwasun and Chungmun along the western coast road.

Hallim and Sŏgwip'o partially via the western coast road and partially via inland routes.

The following is a more detailed description of the routes:

Coast Road – Soehaeson Route The coast road going west (known as the Soehaeson route) will give you the best selection of beaches on the island. These include Iho, Kwakchi, Hyŏpchae and, on the southern coast, Chungmun. Also along this coastal road are the Hyŏpchaegul Lava Caves and Sanbanggulsa Grotto. All buses along this road stop at both the lava tubes and the grotto.
Coast Road – Tonghaeson Route The coast road going east from Cheju City (known as the Tonghaeson Route) will take you to the beaches of Hamdok and Kimnyŏng, the turn-off for the Kimnyŏng and Manjanggul Caves and the volcanic cone of Song San Po.
Cross-Island Highway No 1 This road skirts the eastern side of Hallasan, passes three points at which you can start the trek to the summit and ends up at Sŏgwip'o.
Cross-Island Highway No 2 The other road is known as the 2nd cross-island highway. It passes two points at which you can start the trek up Hallasan and ends at Chungmun. Buses taking this route will have '2' in the window.
Tongbusan Route This is a minor route which connects Cheju City with P'yosŏn. It branches off from the No 1 cross-island highway on the lower northern slopes of Hallasan and goes past San'gumburi and Sŏng-ŭp to end at Cheju Folk Village (near P'yosŏn).

A few examples of schedules and fares:

Cheju City-Sŏgwip'o (via No 1 cross-island highway) There are buses every 12 minutes from 6 am to 9.30 pm which cost W2500 and take about one hour. Fares and journey times are proportionately less if you're getting off at the start of the Hallasan trekking trails.
Cheju City-Chungmun (via the 2nd cross-island highway) There are buses every 20 minutes from 6.20 am to 8 pm which take about one hour and cost W1900. Fares and journey times are proportionately less if you're getting off at the start of the Hallasan trekking trails.
Cheju City-Sŏng-ŭp-P'yosŏn (via the Tongbusan route) There are buses every 30 minutes from 6 am to 9 pm which cost W1700 to Sŏng-ŭp and W1200 to P'yosŏn. The journey to Sŏng-ŭp takes about one hour.

Cheju City-Sŏngsan (via the eastern coast road) There are buses every 20 minutes from 5.30 am to 9.40 pm which cost W2200 and take about one hour. These buses will drop you at the turn-off for the Manjanggul Caves.

Car

Given the rural nature of the island (though decidedly less so, year by year), renting a car almost makes sense. Most upmarket hotels also have a car-rental desk in the lobby. Or you can deal directly with the car rental agencies, as follows:

Asia (☎ 482290); Cheju (☎ 423301); Donga (☎ 431515); Green (☎ 432000); Halla (☎ 555000); Hansŏng (☎ 472100); Pŏmhan (☎ 484002); Sŏkkwan (☎ 482800); Sŏngsan (☎ 476661); Woori (☎ 529661).

Organised Tours

Even if you consider yourself a dyed-in-the-wool budget traveller, you might want to consider taking a tour of Chejudo. These tours are not expensive and can save you considerable hassle since the island's sights are so spread out. A free lunch is thrown in and the tour price includes all the admission fees.

If you're with a large group an English-speaking tour guide can be arranged, but otherwise you can expect the tour to be conducted in Korean only.

The cheapest and most readily available tours are those which can be booked right in Cheju Airport at the information counter. There are tours departing daily from the airport at 9 am and finishing around 6 pm. Most tours are in fact two days – west Chejudo is explored the first day and the east part of the island is covered on the second day. These two-day tours cost W43,000 (and do not include accommodation). A one-day tour is also offered which just covers west Chejudo and costs W25,800. You can arrange to be picked up and dropped off at your hotel.

Chŏllabuk-do

The western province of Chŏllabuk-do surprises you with its temples, high mountains and rocky seashore. Although a fairly small province it features a rich collection of national and provincial parks.

CHŎNJU

Chŏnju (population 530,000) is the provincial capital of Chŏllabuk-do. Other than its value as a major transit point, the town isn't likely to hold your interest for long.

The most interesting sights are south of the centre of town. These include the city's museum, P'ungnammun (a large gate) and the old Confucian School. At the southernmost extreme of town is Wansan Park, home to a few notable temples such as Anhaengsa and Ch'ilsŏngsa.

Places to Stay

There is a good collection of yŏgwan sandwiched between the express bus terminal and the inter-city bus terminal. Just opposite the latter is the *Munhwat'ang Yŏgwan* where rooms start at W20,000. Close to the railway station are numerous other yŏgwan in the same price range, such as the *Haekŭm-jang Yŏgwan*, *Wŏlgung-jang Yŏgwan* and *Riberi-jang Yŏgwan*.

The *Chŏnju Hotel* (☎ 832811; fax 834478) offers rooms at the following rates: singles W25,000, doubles W38,000, twins W42,000 and suites W75,000, plus 20% tax and surcharge.

The *Koa Hotel* (☎ 851100; fax 855707), also known as the *Core Hotel*, is the most upmarket place in town. Twins cost W75,000 and suites are W110,000 to W480,000, plus 20% tax and surcharge.

Getting There & Away

Bus From the express bus terminal, there are buses to the following places:

Inch'ŏn buses depart every hour from 6.30 am to 6.40 pm. The fare is W11,700 (1st class) or W7900 (2nd class) and the journey takes four hours.

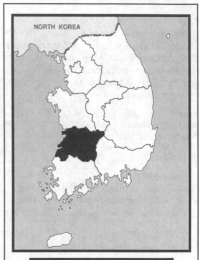

Kwangju buses depart every 20 minutes from 6.30 am to 8.30 pm. The fare is W4800 (1st class) or W3300 (2nd class) and the journey takes 1¾ hours.

Pusan buses depart 10 times daily between 7 am and 5.30 pm. The fare is W14,300 (1st class) or W9600 (2nd class) and the journey takes 5¼ hours.

Seoul buses depart every five to 15 minutes from 6 am to 8.30 pm. The fare is W10,500 (1st class) or W7100 (2nd class) and the journey takes 2¾ hours.

Seoul Sangbong buses depart every 1¾ hours from 6 am to 8 pm. The fare is W11,000 (1st class) or W7400 (2nd class) and the journey takes 2¾ hours.

Taegu buses depart every 1⅓ hours from 7 am to 6.40 pm. The fare is W9900 (1st class) or W6800 (2nd class) and the journey takes 3¾ hours.

Taejŏn buses depart every 30 minutes from 6.30 am to 8.30 pm. The fare is W4400 (1st class) or W3000 (2nd class) and the journey takes 1¼ hours.

Tong-Seoul buses depart every 40 minutes from 6 am to 8.20 pm. The fare is W11,000 (1st class) or W7500 (2nd class) and the journey takes 2¾ hours.

From the inter-city bus terminal you can get to a number of destinations including:

Chinan (for Maisan Provincial Park) buses depart every 10 minutes from 6.30 am to 9.30 pm. The fare is W1800 and the journey takes 50 minutes.

Chinju buses depart every 20 minutes from 6.34 am to 5.48 pm. The fare is W7900 and the journey takes 3½ hours.

Ch'ŏngju buses depart every 30 minutes from 7.30 am to 6.35 pm. The fare is W5000 and the journey takes two hours.

Hwaŏmsa (Chirisan National Park) buses depart every 20 minutes from 7 am to 6.10 pm. The fare is W4500 and the journey takes 3½ hours.

Koch'ang (for Sŏnunsan Provincial Park) buses depart every 30 minutes from 6.10 am to 8.30 pm. The fare is W3800 and the journey takes 1½ hours.

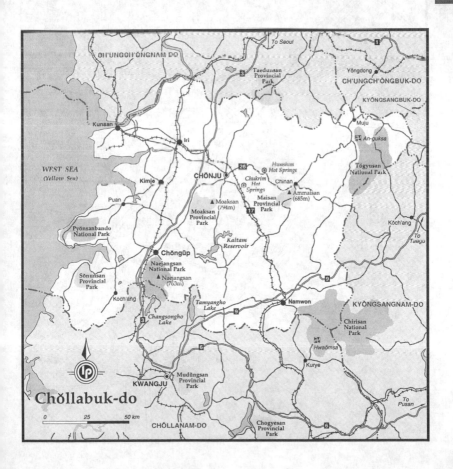

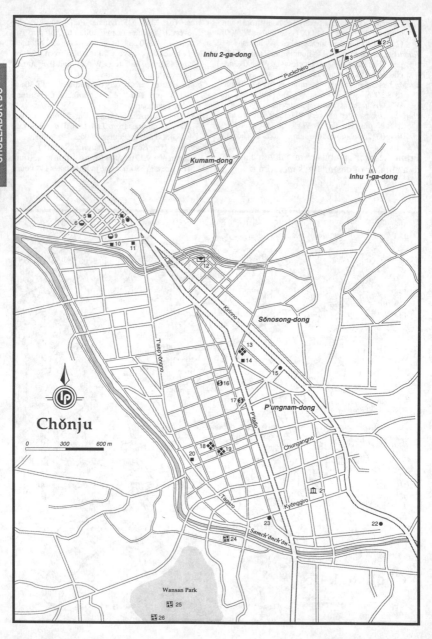

Chŏnju

0   300   600 m

Chŏnju 전주

PLACES TO STAY

2 Riberi-jang Yŏgwan
   리베리장여관
3 Wŏlgung-jang Yŏgwan
   월궁장여관
4 Haekŭm-jang Yŏgwan
   해금장여관
5 Paeknyŏn-jang Yŏgwan
   백년장여관
7 Yŏinsuk Area
   여인숙지역
10 Munhwat'ang Yŏgwan
    문화탕여관
11 Sŏngbuk-jang Yŏgwan
    성복장여관
14 Koa Hotel (Core Hotel)
    코아호텔

20 Chŏnju Hotel
    전주호텔

OTHER

1 Railway Station
   전주역
6 Express Bus Terminal
   고속버스터미널
8 Asiana Airlines
   아시아나항공
9 Inter-City Bus Terminal
   시외버스터미널
12 Post Office
    우체국
13 Core Department Store
    코아백화점
15 City Hall
    시청
16 Bank of Korea
    한국은행

17 Hanil Bank
    한일은행
18 Chŏnju Department Store
    전주백화점
19 Hanarŭm Department
    Store
    한아름백화점
21 Museum
    박물관
22 Confucian School
    향교
23 P'ungnammun Gate
    풍남문
24 Wŏngaksa Temple
    원각사
25 Anhaengsa Temple
    아행사
26 Ch'ilsŏngsa Temple
    칠성사

CHŎLLABUK-DO

Kurye (for Chirisan National Park) buses depart 25 times daily between 6.10 am and 6.10 pm. The fare is W4300 and the journey takes two hours.

Kwangju buses depart six times daily from 6.50 am to 6.20 pm. The fare is W3300 and the journey takes 1½ hours.

Mokp'o buses depart every 1¼ hours from 6.10 am to 4.10 pm. The fare is W7000 and the journey takes four hours.

Muju (for Tŏgyusan National Park) buses depart every 40 minutes from 6.20 am to 8.30 pm. The fare is W3900 and the journey takes 2½ hours.

Puan (for Pyŏnsanbando National Park) buses depart every 28 minutes from 6.15 am to 9 pm. The fare is W2100 and the journey takes 55 minutes.

Pusan buses depart 14 times daily between 6.44 am and 4.20 pm. The fare is W11,100 and the journey takes six hours.

Seoul buses depart four times daily between 7.58 am and 4.29 pm. The fare is W7100 and the journey takes 6½ hours.

Suwŏn buses depart 16 times daily between 8 am and 6.10 pm. The fare is W8100 and the journey takes three hours.

Taegu buses depart 25 times daily between 6.10 am and 6 pm. The fare is W6800 and the journey takes over three hours.

Yŏsu buses depart 11 times daily between 6.18 am and 6.10 pm. The fare is W8300 and the journey takes four hours.

Train The railway station is inconveniently far from the centre and not as useful as the bus terminals. The train schedule on the Seoul-Chŏnju route can be found in the appendix at the end of this book.

Getting Around

Bus No 79-1 goes from the bus terminal area to Moaksan Provincial Park, but it also goes to the centre so is useful for getting around town. Taxis are readily available.

CHUKRIM HOT SPRINGS

These small hot springs were discovered during drilling in the area, prompted by the calligraphy of Li Sam-man, who lived during the Chosŏn dynasty (1392-1910). Li wrote about women washing their hair with hot waters which flowed naturally from streams in the Chukrim area.

The springs were only opened for commercial development in 1993. The water here is very alkaline and is claimed to cure skin diseases. Bathing facilities are open from 6 am to 8 pm.

Places to Stay

Yŏgwan here charge about W30,000. Among the places on offer there are the *Songsan Motel* (☎ 882111), *Chukrim-jang Motel* (☎ 874061) and *Chukrim Onch'ŏn-jang* (☎ 879757).

Getting There & Away
The hot springs are 11 km from Chŏnju along Highway 17 to Namwon. Local city buses plying the Chŏnju-Namwon route can drop you off at the springs.

HWASHIM HOT SPRINGS
Another minor hot springs but one with a long history, mostly it attracts day-trippers rather than overnighters.

Attached to the resort is a restaurant doing superb bean curd vegetarian dishes. A specialty here is the medicinal wild herbs used in the cooking.

Getting There & Away
The springs are close to Maisan Provincial Park, 20 km from Chŏnju on highway 26 towards Chinan. From Chŏnju take city bus Nos 17, 39, 54, 55 or 726 to the springs.

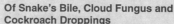

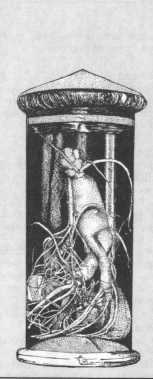

Of Snake's Bile, Cloud Fungus and Cockroach Droppings
Korea has two systems of medicine – western and *hanyak*, (traditional herbal medicine). Hanyak draws on Chinese tradition, though the Koreans have added their own ingredients to the herbal brew. If any herb is associated with Korea, it's ginseng (*insam*). There are two kinds of ginseng, red and white, and the red ginseng is by far the more expensive. It is possible to buy ginseng in a number of forms: in its raw state (in markets), in capsules, in tea, as a powder and as a liquid extract.

The second most popular herb in Korea is a mushroom called *yŏngji pŏsŏt*, known to westerners as *ganoderma lucidium karst*. It's expensive stuff, but claimed to be effective against everything from stomach ulcers to ageing. Considerably less expensive is another mushroom called *unji pŏsŏt*, which could be translated into English as 'cloud fungus'. This one has recently been touted as a possible cure for cancer.

There are many other types of herbal remedies. Possible ingredients – to name a few – include ginger, cinnamon, anise, nutmeg, the dried skins of fruits, powdered antlers, rhinoceros horn, cockroach droppings, dead bees and snake's bile.

Adherents of herbal medicine claim it's preferable to combine herbs, rather than use a single herb, to produce the desired result. When properly mixed, the herbs are believed to have a synergistic effect; that is, the whole is greater than the sum of its parts.

Another important property of herbal medicine is that the effects are supposed to be gradual, not sudden or dramatic. That is, you start taking herbs at the first sign of illness or as a preventive measure before you get sick. So in the cold and flu season you might start taking herbs so that you can build up resistance before your first cough or sniffle.

When reading the theory of herbal medicine, the word 'holistic' appears often. Basically, this means that herbal medicine seeks to treat the whole body rather than focusing on a particular organ or disease. Using appendicitis as an example, a doctor may try to fight the infection using the body's whole defences, whereas a western doctor would simply cut out the appendix. In the case of appendicitis, the western method might be more effective, but herbal medicine has sometimes proven better in treating chronic illnesses, such as migraine headaches and asthma. ■

Buses depart every 15 minutes and the ride takes 20 minutes.

MAISAN PROVINCIAL PARK

Maisan means 'horse ears mountain', a rough description of the shape of the two rocky outcrops which make up the twin peaks (Maibong). The east peak (Sutmaisan) is considered male and reaches a height of 678m. The west peak (Ammaisan) is regarded as female and is slightly taller at 685m.

T'apsa (Pagoda Temple) is stuck right between the two 'horse ears'. It's a temple of unique design, decorated by hundreds of stone formations created by stacking rocks on top of one another.

For the best views, climb up to the summit of Ammaisan via the small path which is to the left of the souvenir stands when coming down from the main temple.

There are two other temples on the mountain called Ŭnsusa and Kŭmdangsa. There is a campground just opposite Ŭnsusa.

Admission to Maisan Provincial Park costs W1000.

Getting There & Away

Bus transport is via the tiny town of Chinan at the park's entrance. From Chinan buses to the temple go every 30 minutes between 8 am and 6.20 pm and the ride takes 10 minutes. The bus schedule from Chinan is as follows:

Chŏnju buses depart every 10 minutes between 6.20 am and 9.50 pm. The fare is W1800 and the journey takes 40 minutes.

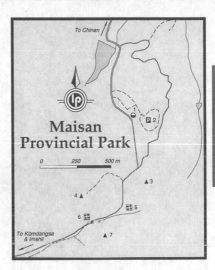

Maisan Provincial Park
마이산도립공원

1 Bus Stop
   정류상
2 Car Park
   수자상
3 Sutmaisan (678m)
   숫마이산
4 Ammaisan (685m)
   암마이산
5 Ŭnsusa Temple
   은수사
6 T'apsa Temple
   탑사
7 Nadosan Peak
   나도산

Seoul buses depart four times daily between 9.30 am and 3 pm. The fare is W8200 and the journey takes four hours.

Taegu buses depart every 30 minute between 7.10 am and 6.15 pm. The fare is W6500 and the journey takes four hours.

Taejŏn buses depart once hourly between 6.50 am and 5.45 pm. The fare is W3900 and the journey takes 2½ hours.

'Horse Ears Mountain'

CHŎLLABUK-DO

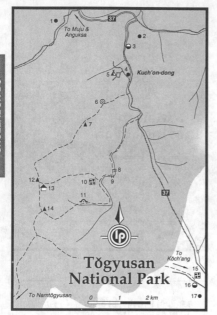

Tŏgyusan National Park
덕유산국립공원

1 Shimgok-ri
   심곡리
2 Samgong-ri
   삼공리
3 Bus Stop
   정류장
4 Wolhat'an Pavilion
   월하탄
5 Tŏkyudae Camping Ground
   덕유대야영장
6 Spring
   칠봉약수
7 Ch'ilbong (1305m)
   칠봉
8 Kuch'ŏn Rapids
   구천폭
9 Yŏnhwa Rapids
   연화폭
10 Paekryŏnsa Temple
    백련사
11 Osujagul Cave
    오수자굴
12 Tŏgyusan (1614m)
    덕유산
13 Hyangjŏkbong Hut
    향적봉산장
14 Chungbong (1594m)
    중봉
15 Songgyesa Temple
    송계사
16 Bus Stop
    정류장
17 Sojŏng-ri
    소정리

TŎGYUSAN NATIONAL PARK

The park's most significant geographical feature is Tŏgyusan (1614m), the fourth tallest peak in South Korea. Kuch'on-dong is the main tourist village, located at the southern (upper) end of a 30-km valley. From Kuch'on-dong you can walk six km to the south (uphill) along the valley to Paengnyonsa, a small temple from where you begin the ascent of Tŏgyusan.

The two main temples in this park are Anguksa and Chonggyesa. You can hike from Kuch'on-dong to Anguksa (18 km, seven hours) over a beautiful footpath, but there is no back-country trail to Chonggyesa. These two temples are not that famous in Korea, so they tend to be less packed out than other large temples.

Tŏgyusan is also home to the Muju Resort, which during the winter becomes a popular ski area.

Admission to the national park costs

W1300 for adults, W750 for students and W380 for children.

Places to Stay

There are two camping grounds in the park, one at Samgong-ri (near Kuch'on-dong) and a larger one at Tŏgyu, at the eastern edge of the park near Songgyesa. Back-country camping and cooking are prohibited.

Samgong-ri is one km north of Kuch'on-dong and there are yŏgwan here costing around W15,000.

More expensive yŏgwan are in Kuch'on-dong, close to the bus stop and tourist shops. Expect to pay W20,000 to W30,000.

Minbak are on offer, and chances are good

MARTIN MOOS

ROBERT STOREY

MARTIN MOOS

RICHARD I'ANSON

H GOOSSENS

A	C
B	D
	E

The South

A: Floodlit Old City gate, Chŏnju
B: T'apsa temple, Maisan PP
C: Fishing boats, Ullŭngdo Island

D: Pŏmŏsa Temple, near Pusan
E: Near Haeinsa Temple, Kayasan
National Park

PATRICK HORTON

PATRICK HORTON

PATRICK HORTON

ROBERT STOREY

PATRICK HORTON

North Korea

A: Tower of the Juche Idea, P'yŏngyang

B: Great Leader, Kim Il-sung

C: Victorious workers, near the Great Leader

D: Mausoleum or P'yŏngyang subway?

E: Preaching the message in the countryside

that you'll be greeted at the stop by various *ajumma* offering you a place to stay for around W15,000.

Upmarket accommodation is offered at the *Muju Resort* (☎ 324-9000) where rooms are a mere W150,000. The resort is four km from Kuch'on-dong and can be reached by bus.

Getting There & Away

Bus Muju is the main gateway to the park, though you can also get there from Yŏng-dong in Ch'ungch'ŏngnam-do. Buses frequently depart Muju for Kuch'on-dong though you can do this same trip by taxi for around W18,000.

The bus schedule from Muju is as follows:

Chŏnju buses depart 23 times daily between 6.25 am and 5.50 pm. The fare is W4700 and the journey takes 2½ hours.

Kuch'on-dong buses depart 38 times daily between 7.10 am and 9.45 pm. The fare is W1700 and the journey takes 50 minutes.

Kwangju buses depart 23 times daily between 6 am and 6.40 pm. The fare is W7400 and the journey takes 3¾ hours.

Seoul buses depart five times daily between 9.45 am and 5.45 pm. The fare is W9000 and the journey takes 3¼ hours.

Taegu buses depart nine times daily between 6.50 am and 6.37 pm. The fare is W6700 and the journey takes 2¾ hours.

Tuejŏn buses depart 30 times daily between 6.35 am and 8.05 pm. The fare is W3100 and the journey takes 1¾ hours.

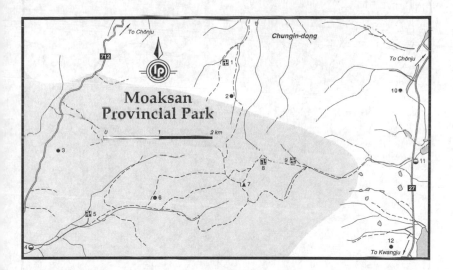

Moaksan Provincial Park
모악산도립공원

1 Kŭmsaŏnsa Temple
   금선사
2 Ch'ŏnhwangsa
   천황사
3 Ch'ŏngdo-ri
   정도리
4 Bus Stop
   정류장
5 Kŭmsansa Temple
   금산사
6 Shimwonam Hermitage
   심원암
7 Moaksan (794m)
   모악산
8 Suwangsa Temple
   수왕사
9 Taewonsa Temple
   대원사
10 Tuhyŏn-ri
    두현리
11 Bus Stop
    정류장
12 Hangga-ri
    항가리

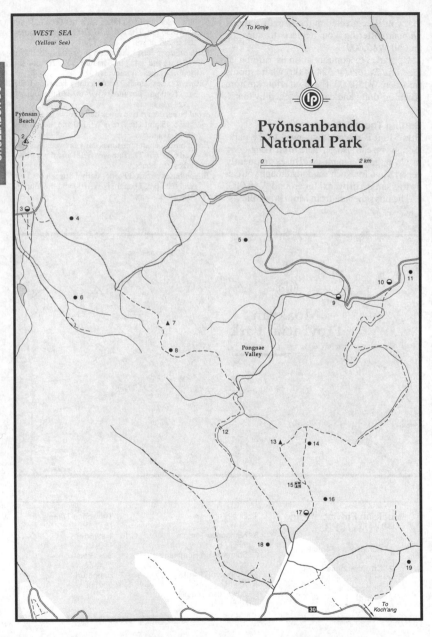

Pyŏnsanbando National Park
변산반도국립공원

1 Taehang-ri
대항리
2 Camping Ground
아영지
3 Bus Stop
정류장
4 Chisŏ-ri
지서리
5 Chunggye-ri
중계리

6 Unsan-ri
운산리
7 Ssangsŏnbong (459m)
쌍선봉
8 Wolmyŏngam Hermitage
월명암
9 Bus Stop
정류장
10 Bus Stop
정류장
11 Ch'ŏngrim-ri
청림리
12 Chikso Waterfall
직소폭포

13 Kwanŭmbong Peak
관음봉
14 Ch'ŏngryŏnam Hermitage
청련암
15 Naesosa Temple
내소사
16 Chijangam Hermitage
지장암
17 Bus Stop
정류장
18 Sŏkp'o-ri
석포리
19 Chinsŏ-ri
진서리

Yŏng-dong buses depart 18 times daily between 7.24 am and 8.20 pm. The fare is W1300 and the journey takes 35 minutes.

Train You can't get a train to the park, but trains run from Seoul to Yŏng-dong. See the time table in the appendix at the end of this book.

MOAKSAN PROVINCIAL PARK

There are nice views from Moaksan (794m), but the big attraction here is the temple of Kŭmsansa. The temple was built in 599 AD. There are a number of unusual buildings on the temple grounds, including the curiously shaped pagoda in front of the main hall. The main hall itself is home to two huge golden Buddhas. There is also a row of golden Buddhas in the second main hall.

Admission to Moaksan Provincial Park costs W1000.

Places to Stay

There is a camping ground near Kŭmsansa near the Maningyo Bridge. Minbak are readily available for around W15,000. Yŏgwan are also easy to find – try the *Moaksan-jang* (☎ 434411) which has rooms from W20,000.

Getting There & Away

It is most convenient to get there from Chŏnju. Catch bus No 79-1 to Kŭmsansa – this runs every 30 minutes between 6.20 am

and 8.45 pm. The fare is W1000 and the ride takes 25 minutes.

PYŎNSANBANDO NATIONAL PARK

The park occupies a peninsula in the extreme western part of Chŏllabuk-do. It's dotted with temples such as Naesosa (the largest) and Kaeamsa. The park's highest peak is Sabyŏnsan (492m).

On the north side of the park is Pyŏnsan Beach, one of the cleanest sandy beaches on the west coast. It's absolutely amazing to see the change of tides here – at low tide you can almost walk to distant offshore islands.

At the west end of the park is Ch'aesŏkkang, where a cliff drops straight into the sea. It really isn't all that impressive, but it attracts large numbers of Korean tourists.

There are camping grounds, but backcountry camping and cooking are prohibited in the park. Yŏgwan cost from W20,000 to W25,000 for a double. There are yŏgwan near Naesosa and also at Pyŏnsan Beach.

Admission to the park costs W900.

Getting There & Away

From Chŏngŭp there are buses to either Naesosa or Ch'aesŏkkang; the latter take longer since they go by way of Shint'aein and Puan (though the scenery is fine). Puan is a major transit point. The buses going by way of Puan stop at Pyŏnsan Beach and then terminate at Ch'aesŏkkang. At Ch'aesŏkkang you can change to a bus heading for

Naesosa. Buses from Puan to Ch'aesŏkkang depart every 10 minutes from 7.15 am to 8.40 pm, taking 40 minutes for the journey and costing W1600.

You can get to Puan from Chŏnju, Chŏngŭp or Kimje. From Chŏnju, buses depart for Puan every 28 minutes from 6.15 am to 9 pm and take 55 minutes. From Chŏngŭp, buses go to Puan every 30 minutes between 7.30 am and 7.40 pm and take 40 minutes. From Kimje, buses depart for Puan every five minutes from 5.40 am to 9.50 pm and take 30 minutes.

CHŎNGŬP

The only likely reason you'd want to go to Chŏngŭp is to get to neighbouring Naejangsan National Park, or to Sŏnunsan Provincial Park which is slightly further afield.

Getting There & Away

Bus Chŏngŭp's express and inter-city bus terminals are right up against each other – basically opposite sides of the same complex. Nevertheless, there is a difference in where the buses go. From the express side of the bus terminal there are departures as follows:

Seoul buses depart every 20 to 30 minutes between 6 am and 8 pm. The fare is W11,900 (1st class) or W8000 (2nd class) and the journey takes 3¼ hours.

Tong-Seoul (East Seoul) buses depart every 1½ hours from 6.30 am to 6.40 pm. The fare is W12,400 (1st class) or W8400 (2nd class) and the journey takes 3¼ hours.

The inter-city side of the bus terminal has departures for the following destinations:

Chŏnju buses depart 44 times daily from 6.25 am to 8.45 pm. The fare is W1800 and the journey takes 1¼ hours.

Kimje (for Pyŏnsanbando National Park) buses depart once hourly from 7.40 am to 7.30 pm. The fare is W1800 and the journey takes one hour.

Koch'ang (for Sŏnunsan Provincial Park) buses depart every 10 minutes from 6.15 am to 9 pm. The fare is W1300 and the journey takes 40 minutes.

Kwangju buses depart every 10 minutes from 6.40 am to 9.50 pm. The fare is W2200 and the journey takes 1¼ hours.

Mokp'o buses depart five times daily between 8.05 am and 5.15 pm. The fare is W5400 and the journey takes 3½ hours.

Naejangsa (Naejangsan National Park) buses depart once hourly from 6.20 am to 7.20 pm. The fare is W600 and the journey takes 25 minutes.

Puan (for Pyŏnsanbando National Park) buses depart every 30 minutes from 7.30 am to 7.40 pm. The fare is W1700 and the journey takes 40 minutes.

Pusan buses depart five times daily between 8.40 am and 4.20 pm. The fare is W11,300 and the journey takes 4½ hours.

Taegu buses depart twice daily at 9.20 am and 3 pm. The fare is W9300 and the journey takes five hours.

Taejŏn buses depart 11 times daily between 8.30 am and 7 pm. The fare is W4100 and the journey takes 1¾ hours.

Train The train schedule on the Seoul-Chŏngŭp route can be found in the appendix at the end of this book.

NAEJANGSAN NATIONAL PARK

It's easy to see why this place was named Naejangsan ('inner hidden mountains') – the landscape is arranged like an amphitheatre. Once you've climbed to the rim, you can walk all the way to the other side, though it's strenuous. There are ladders to help hikers master the cliffs, and the views are just amazing all around. It takes at least three hours to walk the circuit, but try to allow more.

Temples in the park include Naejangsa and Paegyangsa. Other sights include Todokam hermitage, the Kumson and Wonjok Valleys, Todok waterfall and Yonggul cave. This park is famous for its beauty in autumn.

Admission to the park costs W1000. There are several yŏgwan in the tourist village of Naejang-dong inside the park.

Getting There & Away

You get to Naejangsan from Chŏngŭp (not to be confused with Chŏnju, which is further north). The bus drops you off in the tourist village, from where you have a 30-minute walk to Naejangsa temple and the start of the climb.

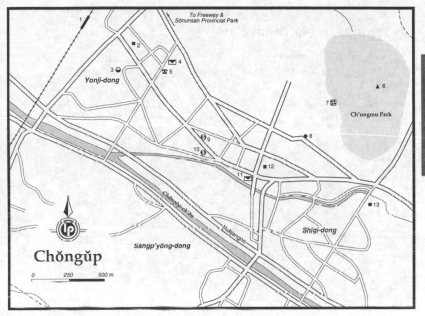

Chŏngŭp

Chŏngŭp 정읍

PLACES TO STAY
2 Songho-jang Yŏgwan
   송호장어관
12 Kŭmho Hotel
   금호호텔
13 Honam Tourist Hotel
   호남관광호텔

OTHER
1 Railway Station
   정주역
3 Bus Terminal
   시외-고속터미널
4 Post Office
   우체국
5 Telephone Office
   전화국
6 Sŏnghwangsan (177m)
   성황산

7 Ilgwangsa Temple
   일광사
8 City Hall
   시청
9 Bank
   주택은행
10 Bank
   전북은행
11 Central Post Office
   우체국

SŎNUNSAN PROVINCIAL PARK

Sŏnunsan is a gorgeous place which boasts a temple called Sŏnunsa, and small sub-temples perched all around a gorge near the sea. One enthusiastic traveller wrote 'this place is possibly the most beautiful spot in all Korea, if not the world'. Perhaps this is an exaggeration, but you'd have a hard time not enjoying this park.

As you follow the path past Sŏnunsa, take

a right once you see a little shop across the creek (to your left), then take a left at the next intersection and you'll come to a hermitage. There you will find a large image of Buddha engraved into the side of a cliff. To your right will be a stairway, which you can climb to reach a small image above the Buddha image. This Buddha image was made during the Paekche period by the Chinese – the artists of this masterpiece built a precarious

CHŎLLABUK-DO

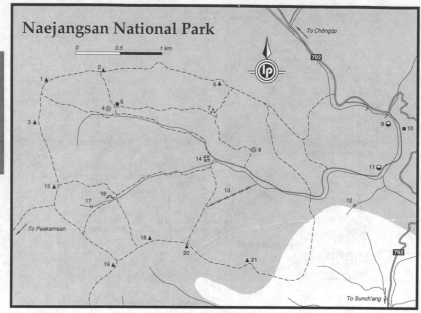

Naejangsan National Park

0   0.5   1 km

To Chŏngŭp

792

To Paekamsan

To Sunch'ang

792

Naejangsan National Park 내장산국립공원	5 Wonjŏkam Hermitage 원적암	14 Naejangsa Temple 내장사
PLACES TO STAY 10 Naejangsan Hotel 내장산관광호텔	6 Sŏraebong (622m) 서래봉 7 Paekryŏnam Ruins 백련암터	15 Kkach'ibong (717m) 까치봉 16 Yonggul Cave 용굴
OTHER 1 Manghaebong (650m) 망해봉 2 Pulch'ulbong (610m) 불출봉 3 Yŏnjibong (670m) 연지봉 4 Spring 산삼약수	8 Spring 백년수 9 Bus Stop 정류장 11 Shuttle Bus Stop 서틀버스정류장 12 Todŏk Waterfall 도덕폭포 13 Cable Car 케이블카	17 Kŭmsŏn Waterfall 금선폭포 18 Munp'ilbong (675m) 문필봉 19 Shinsŏnbong (763m) 신선봉 20 Yŏnjabong (673m) 연자봉 21 Changgunbong (696m) 장군봉

scaffolding of sticks and branches in order to perform this artistic feat.

Ch'ongnyongsan is the main peak, a six-km two-hour climb starting from Sŏnunsa. The other main hike is from the House of Nature to the top of Ch'onwangbong (three km, one hour).

Admission to the park costs W1000 for adults, W570 for students and W300 for children.

Places to Stay

There is a camping ground plus several minbak and yŏgwan in the park near Sŏnunsa. You can also stay in nearby Koch'ang, though there's little point unless you're enthused about the nearby Sokchong hot springs.

Getting There & Away

There are only five buses daily direct from Chŏngŭp to the park. Otherwise, get yourself to Koch'ang. Do not confuse Koch'ang with Kŏch'ang – the latter is in Kyŏngsangnam-do province, halfway between Kwangju and Taegu. The schedule for buses from Koch'-ang is as follows:

Chŏnju buses depart 44 times daily between 6.25 am and 8.45 pm. The fare is W2900 and the journey takes 1¾ hours.

Kwangju buses depart 34 times daily between 6.20 am and 8.30 pm. The fare is W2200 and the journey takes one hour.

Seoul buses depart 19 times daily between 7 am and 6 pm. The fare is W8700 and the journey takes 3¾ hours.

Sŏnunsa buses depart every 20 minutes between 7 am and 8 pm. The fare is W1000.

SOKCHONG HOT SPRINGS

The waters of the hot springs are touted as a cure for cancer, not to mention high blood pressure, diabetes, rheumatism, arthritis and nappy rash.

Places to Stay

The big hot springs resort is in the *Sokchong Onch'ŏn Resortel* (☎ 644441).

Getting There & Away

The hot springs are just outside the small city of Koch'ang, 20 km from Sŏnunsan Provincial Park.

Ch'ungch'ŏngnam-do

Less than two hours south of Seoul, booming Taejŏn is an easy-to-navigate city with a superb hot spring on one side and a beautiful national park on the other. The rest of the province doesn't disappoint either, with its numerous historical sites, temples, mountains and seashore.

TAEJŎN

This is Korea's sixth largest city, with a population of just over one million. You aren't likely to come here for the city itself, but Taejŏn is a very useful transit point for many interesting places in this part of Korea.

Information

There is a tourist office (☎ 632-1338) in a kiosk in the Taejŏn express bus terminal. There is also a tourist information booth (☎ 273-8698) in the forecourt of Taejŏn railway station.

Pomunsan

While Taejŏn isn't known for stunning scenery, the southern side of town boasts Pomunsan. This is a small mountain park dotted with temples and hermitages, and there is a short cable car ride to reach a scenic overlook. Some of the temples on the mountain's slopes include Wongaksa, Tŏksu'am, Songhaksa, Porimsa and Pokkŭn'am.

Taejŏn Expo Science Park

Taejŏn's claim to fame is Expo '93. Most of the Expo '93 exhibits have been preserved in one form or another. The park has been officially designated a 'special tourism zone' – whatever that means. It might be worth a visit if you have time to spare in Taejŏn. The **National Science Museum** is on the west side of the park. Even if science parks are not your cup of tea, there is an outstanding roller coaster.

The Expo site is on the far northern end of town, and there is even a separate Expo railway station *(eksŭpo yok)*. However, the Expo site is still about two km west of this station and you'll probably need a taxi to get there.

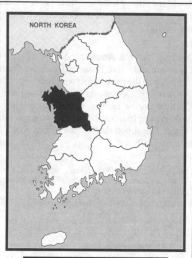

🔯🔯🔯 **HIGHLIGHTS** 🔯🔯🔯

- ◆ Taedunsan, a pocket-sized but amazingly scenic but amazingly rugged mountain area outside of Taejŏn
- ◆ Puyŏ, a quiet provincial town which is the site of the last capital of the Paekche Kingdom
- ◆ Kongju, the second capital of the Paekche Kingdom, which today houses a rich collection of tombs of the Paekche kings
- ◆ Kyeryongsan National Park, home of the temples Kapsa and Tonghaksa
- ◆ Tŏksan, a mountain of incredibly varied scenery that includes pretty valleys, pine forests, large boulders, rocks and waterfalls

Yusŏng Hot Springs

Just 10 km west of central Taejŏn near the Honam Expressway is the hot springs resort of Yusŏng. The water here is very good with a temperature range of 42°C – 55°C, and it's not hard to see what attracts the throngs of Korean and Japanese clientele. On the other hand, there really isn't much here for budget

travellers. Essentially, it's a collection of large, fancy hotels where you can soak in luxurious indoor pools. If you're not a guest at one of these palaces, you can still have a soak but expect to pay up to W8000. From Taejŏn you can reach Yusŏng by taking a 15-minute taxi ride from the centre.

Places to Stay – bottom end

Since the main reason for coming here is to get to someplace else, you'll do best to stay near the bus terminal from where you plan to depart. There are several bus stations, but the ones most used by travellers are the express and the east inter-city bus terminals. These two terminals are next to one another, a rare convenience in Korea. Steep competition keeps yŏgwan reasonable – around W18,000 for a double with private bath, W20,000 on weekends and holidays. Some options include *Yaksu-jang P'ak'ŭ Yŏgwan* (☎ 625-0240), *Pugok P'akŭ Yŏgwan* (☎ 627-7980) and *Honey Park Hotel*.

Places to stay in the centre are scarce, and are only worth considering if you're arriving or departing by train (or if you want to patronise the late-night *soju* tents by the river). If you'd like a room overlooking the river then try

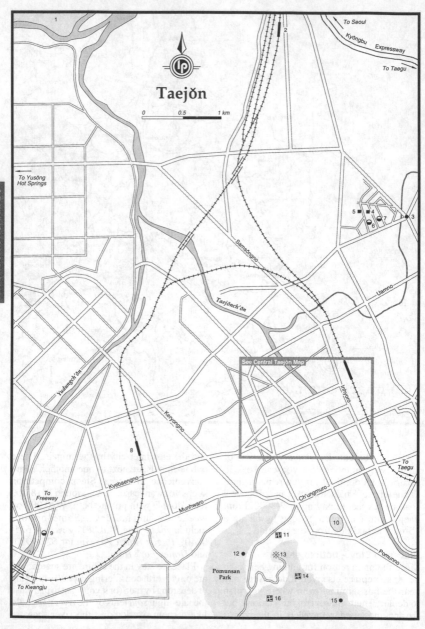

Taejŏn 대전

PLACES TO STAY
4 Pugok P'ak'ŭ &
Yaksu-jang P'ak'ŭ
Yŏgwans
부곡파크여관,
약수장파크여관
5 Honey Park Hotel
하니파크여관

OTHER
1 Taejŏn Expo Science
Park
대전엑스포

2 Expo Railway Station
엑스포역
3 Taejŏn Tower
대전탑
6 Express Bus Terminal
고속버스터미널
7 East Inter-City Bus
Terminal
동부시외버스터미널
8 Sŏdaejŏn Railway Station
서대전역
9 West Inter-City Bus
Terminal
서부시외버스터미널
10 Taejŏn Stadium
대전공설운동장

11 Wongaksa Temple
원각사
12 Tŏksuam Hermitage
덕수암
13 Pomunsan Scenic
Overlook
보문산전망대
14 Porimsa Temple
보림사
15 Pokkŭn'am Hermitage
복근암
16 Songhaksa Temple
송학사

either the *Ilshin-jang Yŏgwan* or *P'yŏng-hwa-jang Yŏgwan*. They're situated next to each other and have rooms for W20,000.

The YMCA in Taejŏn is not a place to stay – it is an activity centre.

Places to Stay – middle & top end
Closest to the railway station is the *Taejŏn Tourist Hotel* (☎ 273-8131; fax 273-0131) 20 16 Won-dong, Tong-gu. Doubles cost W35,000 to W38,000.

Very similar in style are the *Taerim Hotel* (☎ 255-2161) and *Central Hotel*, both close to the railway station.

Most of Taejŏn's middle-level hotels and all the top-end ones are 10 km to the west of the centre at Yusŏng hot springs. A smattering of what's on offer includes:

Adria (☎ 824-0211; fax 823-5805), 442-5 Pongmyong-dong, Yusŏng-gu, doubles W99,000, rated 1st class.
Hongin (☎ 822-2000; fax 822-9410), 536-8 Pongmyong-dong, Yusŏng-gu, doubles W95,590 to W99,100, rated 1st class.
Mugunghwa (☎ 822-1234; fax 822-1237), 549-1 Pongmyong-dong, Yusŏng-gu, doubles W75,500, rated 2nd class.
Onch'on (☎ 820-8888; fax 820-8270), 549-15 Pongmyong-dong, Yusŏng-gu, doubles W52,870, rated 3rd class.
Princess (☎ 822-9200; fax 823-9909), 536-3 Pongmyong-dong, Yusŏng-gu, doubles W75,500, rated 2nd class.

Riviera Yusŏng (☎ 823-2111; fax 822-0071), 444-5 Pongmyong-dong, Yusŏng-gu, doubles W110,000, rated deluxe class.
Royal (☎ 822-0720; fax 823-4019) 202-5 Pongmyong-dong, Yusŏng-gu, doubles W38,720 to W50,820, rated 3rd class.
Yusŏng (☎ 822-0711; fax 822-0041), 480 Pongmyong-dong, Yusŏng-gu, doubles W120,000, rated deluxe class.

Places to Eat
Halfway between the river and Inhyoro (the street on which the post office and the railway station are situated) is the *Central Market*. All around here are many different restaurants and street stalls where you can eat well and cheaply. However, some of the stalls don't smell too good, and the *dog restaurants* are not everybody's cup of tea. Still, it's a very colourful neighbourhood and worth a stroll even if you aren't hungry. People flock to this market every day of the week from all over the city and outlying areas but as the day starts early (usually by 6 am) many places close around 9.30 pm.

Foreign-owned fast food barns are notable for their absence in Taejŏn – it's still not Seoul or Pusan. But if you need something with cheese and tomato sauce, a good alternative is *Bears Cabin Pizza* (☎ 253-3343), on the 2nd floor just above the excellent *Eiffle Bakery*. This pizza place also does home (or yŏgwan) deliveries.

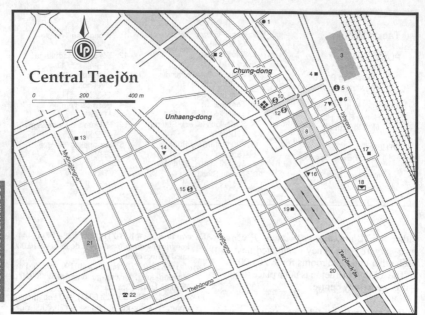

Central Taejŏn

0   200   400 m

Chung-dong

Unhaeng-dong

Just opposite the Eiffle Bakery is the *Agricultural Cooperative Supermarket*, a good stop for self-caterers.

Those less adventurous could do worse than eat at the restaurants in the basements of the department stores. One of the cheapest of these is in the basement of the *Tongyang Department Store*. It's a popular place with students, in part because dishes are so cheap (starting at around W1500). Very similar is

---

It's a Dog's Life

For the most part, Koreans treat animals as well as westerners do. Unlike in many other Asian countries, you will almost never see half-starved, diseased dogs wandering the streets of Seoul. Nor is there any evidence that Korean farm animals are treated any worse than their western counterparts.

Like the Chinese, the Koreans believe that eating dog meat has various medicinal properties and is good for health. Unlike the Chinese (who eat dog in winter to ward off colds and flu), the Koreans eat dog in summer. It's believed that *poshintang* (dog soup) makes you hot (certainly true with all those spices) and many Koreans think that sweating is healthy.

Ever since the 1988 Olympic Games in Seoul, the Korean government has been sensitive to western criticism about eating dog. Therefore, dog restaurants are no longer allowed to display signs in English and are restricted to back alley locations rather than main thoroughfares. Also, many Koreans do not admit to eating dog (at least in the presence of westerners) and profess to disdain this practice. They will also respect the hell out of you if you do it. This is largely a male activity - Korean men consider it one way to demonstrate their macho prowess. However, before ordering a plate of Fido fricassee, bear in mind that dog meat is expensive. Figure on W10,000 to W15,000 a bowl, though the portions are large. Like elsewhere in the world, you always pay a bundle for health food. ■

Central Taejŏn
대전중심부

PLACES TO STAY
2 Central Hotel
   중앙호텔
4 Hama-jang &
   Illyŏk-jang Yŏgwan s
   하마장여관.
   일력장여관
13 Taerim Hotel
   대림호텔
17 Taejŏn Tourist Hotel
   대전호텔
19 Ilshin-jang,
   P'yŏnghwa-jang Yŏgwans
   일신장여관.
   평화장여관

PLACES TO EAT
7 Bears Cabin Pizza &
   Eiffle Bakery
   에펠제과
14 Tongyang Department
   Store
   동양백화점
16 Taejŏn Department Store
   대전백화점

OTHER
1 YMCA
   와이엠씨에이
3 Taejŏn Railway Station
   대전역
5 Tourist Information Kiosk
   관광안내소
6 Agricultural Cooperative
   Supermarket
   농협수퍼마켓

8 Central Market
   중앙시장
9 Underground Arcade
   지하상가
10 Commercial Bank
   상업은행
11 Fashion Mall Department
   Store
   동양중앙점
12 Korea First Bank
   제일은행
15 Korea Exchange Bank
   외환은행
18 Central Post Office
   대전 우체국
20 Night-time Soju Tents
   포장마차
21 City Hall
   시청
22 Telephone Office
   대전 전화국

---

the restaurant in the supermarket basement of the *Taejŏn Department Store*.

Entertainment
Like all Korean cities, the centre of Taejŏn is peppered with beer bars and cocktail bars but most of them are a poor choice for meeting local people as they're broken up into a series of curtained partitions to give couples or small groups of friends a degree of privacy.

Far better is to spend the evening with the hordes of locals out drinking *makkoli* and soju (rice wine and potato vodka) on the benches in the sea of tents around the Hongmyŏng Arcade, by the river and opposite the Taejŏn Department Store. This is an extremely popular spot (even in the depths of winter!) and by the time you leave you'll have met half of Taejŏn. These places stay open until around midnight.

Getting There & Away
Bus There are three bus terminals in Taejŏn – the west inter-city bus terminal *(sŏbu shi'oe t'ŏminŏl)*, the east inter-city bus terminal *(tongbu shi'oe t'ŏminŏl)* and the express bus terminal *(kosok t'ŏminŏl)*. The latter two are located side by side on the eastern outskirts of town and are the most used by travellers.

Some useful buses from the express bus terminal go to the following destinations:

Ch'ŏnan buses depart every 30 minutes from 6.20 am to 9 pm. The fare is W3300 (1st class) or W2300 (2nd class) and the journey takes 1¼ hours.
Chŏnju buses depart every 20 to 30 minutes from 6.30 am to 8.30 pm. The fare is W4400 (1st class) or W3000 (2nd class) and the journey takes 1¼ hours.
Kangnŭng buses depart 10 times daily between 8 am and 6.40 pm. The fare is W12,800 (1st class) or W8600 (2nd class) and the journey takes four hours.
Kwangju buses depart every 40 minutes from 6.40 am to 7.10 pm. The fare is W8400 (1st class) or W5800 (2nd class) and the journey takes almost three hours.
Kyŏngju buses depart every three hours from 7.50 am and 5.30 pm. The fare is W9700 (1st class) or W6600 (2nd class) and the journey takes 2¾ hours.
P'ohang buses depart every two hours between 7 am and 7 pm. The fare is W11,200 (1st class) or W7600 (2nd class) and the journey takes 3¼ hours.
Pusan buses depart every two hours from 6 am to 6.30 pm. The fare is W12,600 (1st class) or W8500 (2nd class) and the journey takes 3¾ hours.
Seoul buses depart every five to 10 minutes from 6 am to 9.40 pm. The fare is W7000 (1st class) or W4800 (2nd class) and the journey takes 1¾ hours.
Seoul Sangbong buses depart every hour from 6 am to 9 pm. The fare is W7500 (1st class) or W5100 (2nd class) and the journey takes 1¾ hours.

Taegu buses depart every 20 minutes from 6.30 am to 8.30 pm. The fare is W6800 (1st class) W4600 (2nd class) and the journey takes two hours.

Tong-Seoul (east Seoul) buses depart every 30 minutes between 6 am and 8.30 pm. The fare is W7600 (1st class) or W5200 (2nd class) and the journey takes 1¾ hours.

The east inter-city bus terminal offers a side selection of buses, including those going to the following destinations:

Andong buses depart about once hourly between 6.25 am and 5.50 pm. The fare is W7800 to W9600 and the journey takes four hours.

Chinju buses depart 12 times daily between 7.40 am and 6.20 pm. The fare is W9900 and the journey takes four hours.

Ch'ŏngju buses depart six times daily from 6.30 am to 9.40 pm. The fare is W1600 and the journey takes 45 minutes.

Hongsŏng (for Tŏksan Provincial Park) buses depart every 14 minutes from 7 am to 7 pm (these buses terminate in Sŏsan, not Hongsŏng). The fare is W5800 and the journey takes 2¼ hours.

Kongju buses depart 26 times daily between 7 am and 7 pm. The fare is W1900 and the journey takes one hour.

Kŭmsan (for International Ginseng Market) buses depart every seven minutes from 5.45 am to 10 pm. The fare is W1700 and the journey takes 40 minutes.

Muju (for Tŏgyusan National Park) buses depart every 20 minutes between 6.20 am and 8.10 pm. The fare is W3100 and the journey takes two hours.

Songnisan National Park buses depart 36 times daily between 6.22 am and 8.10 pm. The fare is W3200 and the journey takes 1¾ hours.

Sudŏksa (Tŏksan Provincial Park) buses depart only once daily at 4.37 pm. The fare is W5900 and the journey takes 2½ hours.

T'aean (for T'aean Haean National Park) buses depart 34 times daily between 7 am and 6.47 pm. The fare is W8400 and the journey takes four hours.

T'aebaek (for T'aebaeksan Provincial Park) buses depart three times daily between 7.10 am and 1.43 pm. The fare is W14,700 and the journey takes five hours.

Taedunsan Provincial Park buses depart four times daily between 7.20 am and 2.50 pm. The fare is W1900 and the journey takes one hour.

Wonju buses depart every 30 minutes from 8 am to 5.10 pm. The fare is W6300 and the journey takes 2½ hours.

Buses from the west inter-city bus terminal go to the following destinations:

Ch'ŏnan (for Independence Hall) buses depart every 10 minutes from 6.30 am to 8.25 pm. The fare is W2300 and the journey takes 1¾ hours.

Ch'ŏngyang (for Ch'ilgapsan Provincial Park) buses depart 30 times daily between 6.30 am and 7.50 pm. The fare is W3700 and the journey takes two hours.

Chŏngŭp buses depart 12 times daily between 7.30 am and 6.40 pm. The fare is W2400 and the journey takes one hour.

Chŏnju buses depart every 20 minutes from 6.45 am to 6.11 pm. The fare is W3000 and the journey takes two hours.

Kapsa (Kyeryongsan National Park) buses depart seven times daily between 7.29 am and 5.50 pm. The fare is W2600 and the journey takes one hour.

Kimje buses depart 20 times daily between 6.55 am and 7.20 pm. The fare is W4000 and the journey takes 1½ hours.

Kongju buses depart every five minutes from 6.29 am to 10.30 pm. The fare is W1900 and the journey takes one hour.

Nonsan (for Kwanch'oksa) buses depart every five minutes from 6 am to 10 pm. The fare is W1900 and the journey takes 50 minutes.

Puyŏ buses depart every five minutes from 6 am to 9.35 pm. The fare is W2900 and the journey takes 1¼ hours.

T'aean (for T'aean Haean National Park) buses depart five times daily between 8.35 am and 4.31 pm. The fare is W8300 and the journey takes 3¾ hours.

Taedunsan Provincial Park buses depart 12 times daily between 7.30 am and 6.20 pm. The fare is W1500 and the journey takes 50 minutes.

Yesan (for Tŏksan Provincial Park) buses depart 39 times daily between 6.51 am and 7.03 pm. The fare is W4600 and the journey takes two hours.

Yŏsu buses depart twice daily at 9.20 am and 3.05 pm. The fare is W11,300 and the journey takes five hours.

Train There are two railway stations in Taejŏn. Taejŏn railway station in the centre of the city serves the main line between Seoul and Pusan and all trains en route to either of those cities stop here. The other station on the west of town is Sŏdaejŏn railway station. This station serves the line to Mokp'o via Iri, Kimje and Chŏngŭp, though if you're heading for Kwangju you must change at Yŏngsanpo.

The train schedule on the Seoul-Taejŏn route can be found in the appendix at the end of this book.

Getting Around

Bus The most important local bus as far as travellers are concerned is the No 841, which connects the east inter-city/express bus terminals with the west inter-city bus terminal via Taejŏn railway station and the city centre. Bus No 851 also connects Taejŏn railway station with the east inter-city/express bus terminals and No 714 connects Taejŏn railway station with the west inter-city bus terminal. The fare is W400 on all city buses.

Car Car rental agencies include the following:

Ch'ungnam (☎ 524-6568); Daesŏng (☎ 621-1785); Hyundai (☎ 825-5141)

KŬMSAN

In the south-east corner of Ch'ungch'ŏngnam-do is the obscure market town of Kŭmsan. This town wouldn't rate a mention in a guidebook to Korea if it were not for the fact that 80% of the nation's ginseng is collected and marketed here.

Overseas buyers who purchase in bulk come to Kŭmsan for one-stop shopping. Individual travellers with a particular interest in ginseng might want to come here and take a look, but all the retail ginseng products found in Kŭmsan are also available in other parts of Korea. The town's main ginseng markets include the Kŭmsan Ginseng International Market, Kŭmsan Undried Ginseng Centre, Kŭmsan Ginseng Shopping Centre and Kŭmsan Medicinal Herb Market.

The market functions on the 2nd, 7th, 12th, 17th, 22nd and 27th days of every month.

From 21 to 23 September, Kŭmsan is host to Korea's Ginseng Festival.

Not surprisingly, ginseng-based foods are a local speciality in Kŭmsan's restaurants. Ginseng chicken soup *(samgye t'ang)* is the most famous and perhaps healthiest of these dishes, but also look in the stores for tasty ginseng candy.

Getting There & Away

The easiest access is from Taejŏn's east inter-city bus terminal. From Taejŏn, buses to Kŭmsan cost W1700 and depart once every seven minutes between 5.45 am and 10 pm, taking 40 minutes for the journey.

TAEDUNSAN PROVINCIAL PARK

Yet another beautiful park, Taedunsan offers craggy peaks with spectacular views over the surrounding countryside. Although relatively small, it's one of Korea's most scenic mountain areas.

Aside from the views, the climb to the summit of Taedunsan (878m) along steep, stony tracks is an adventure in itself. Calm nerves are required since the ascent involves crossing a hair-raising steel rope bridge stretched precariously between two rock pinnacles. This is followed by an incredibly steep and long steel stairway. Those in search of a thrill have struck gold. Vertigo sufferers should go somewhere else for the day. It's a very popular place on weekends with local people as well as others from further afield huffing and puffing their way to the summit, and loaded with goodies for the inevitable picnic. On these precarious slopes you'll even meet amazing old grandfathers *(halabŏji)* and grandmothers *(halmŏni)* ascending the heights so rapidly that it makes the younger folks lose face *(ch'emyŏni ansokda)*.

For any reasonably fit person, the ascent will take between two and 2½ hours, and the descent about one hour. There are soft drink stalls at various places on the climb but prices tend to be double what you would pay in urban areas – not that that's going to deter you from digging deep if you go up there in the summer. For the determined budget traveller, fresh water is available free at certain points. Entry to the park costs W1000.

Places to Stay

There are a number of minbak available at the entrance to the park where the buses drop off passengers. Most of these are souvenir shops with one or two rooms to let, and you can figure on starting the bidding at W15,000.

Getting There & Away

Access to Taedunsan is from Taejŏn. From Taejŏn's east inter-city bus terminal there are departures four times daily between 7.20 am

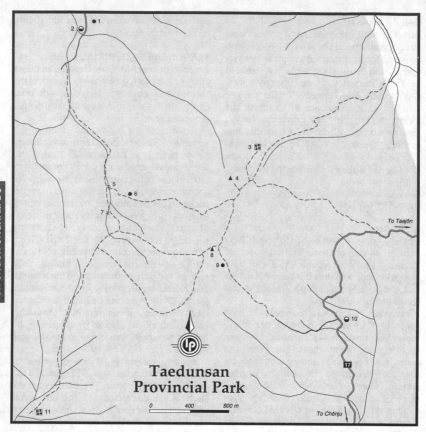

Taedunsan
Provincial Park

0   400   800 m

To Taejŏn

To Chŏnju

and 2.50 pm, costing W1900 for the one hour trip. From Taejŏn's west inter-city bus terminal, departures are 12 times daily between 7.30 am and 6.20 pm.

KWANCH'OKSA

This old Buddhist temple just outside Nonsan is famous throughout Korea for possessing the second largest Buddha in the country. It has some features unique in Korea, and is well worth a visit. The Unjin Miruk statue was built in 968 AD during the Koryŏ dynasty and stands 18m high. It's made out of three massive pieces of granite – one piece for the head and body and two pieces for the arms – and must have presented some interesting construction problems. The courtyard in which it stands is surrounded by typical Korean temple buildings as well as a five-storey pagoda and stone lanterns. If you're lucky, you may come across a small festival going on.

Places to Stay

There's a small yŏgwan just below the temple entrance, though most people just come here for the day. You might want to stay in nearby Nonsan rather than bustling Taejŏn.

Taedunsan Provincial Park
대둔산도립공원

1 Surak-ri
   수락리
2 Bus Stop
   정류장
3 T'aegosa Temple
   태고사
4 Nakjodae Summit
   낙조대
5 Hwarang Waterfall
   하랑폭포
6 Sŏkch'ŏnam Hermitage
   석천암
7 Kŭmgang Waterfall
   금강폭포
8 Taedunsan (878m)
   대둔산
9 Suspension Bridge
   구름다리
10 Bus Stop
   정류장
11 Anshimsa Temple
   안심사

Getting There & Away

Buses for Nonsan depart from Taejŏn's west inter-city bus terminal every five minutes from 6 am to 10 pm, and cost W1900 for the 50 minute ride. There are also frequent buses coming from Kongju, Puyŏ, Seoul and Chŏnju.When you arrive in Nonsan you will find yourself at the inter-city bus terminal. Walk out of the bus terminal onto the main street and turn right. Continue up the street

for about 500m and then take the road which forks to the right. A little way down this road you'll see a signposted bus stop for Kwanch'oksa. Wait here for the local bus which will take you direct to the temple. The buses also have the same destination sign on the front and run every 15 to 20 minutes. The fare is W400 and the journey takes about eight minutes. You'll also find other buses to Kwanch'oksa circling around the central area.

PUYŎ

Standing to the south of a wooded hill (Pusosan) around which the Paengma River makes a wide sweep, Puyŏ is the site of the last capital of the Paekche Kingdom. The capital was moved here from Kongju in 538 AD and flourished until destroyed by the combined forces of Shilla and the Tang dynasty of China in 660 AD. Today it's a quiet provincial town surrounded by wooded hills and paddy fields with a friendly and very traditionally minded people. Of the Paekche ruins, not a great deal remains save for the kings' burial mounds a little way out of town; a few foundation stones of the army's arsenal and foodstore on Pusosan; and a five-storey stone pagoda – one of only three surviving from the Three Kingdoms period. The main point of interest here is the museum, opened in 1971, which has one of the best collections of artefacts from the Paekche Kingdom you will find in Korea, as well as other exhibits from later periods in the country's history.

Detail of the painting in the main hall, Kwanch'oska

CH'UNGCH'ŎNGNAM-DO

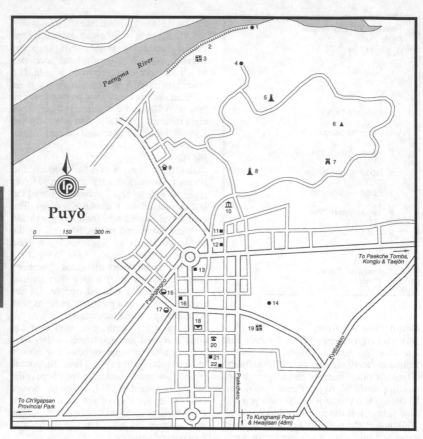

Information

There is a tourist information centre (☎ 302585) at the entrance to Pusosan.

Puyŏ National Museum

The museum houses bronze spearheads, daggers, pottery and musical instruments from the 5th to 4th centuries BC, Paekche dynasty jars, Buddha images and examples of roof tiles embossed with various designs, as well as a collection of celadon vases, funeral urns and bronze bells dating from the 6th to 14th centuries. There are also several interesting stone objects – baths, lanterns,

Buddha images, etc – in the gardens in front of the museum. Unfortunately, there's very little explanation of the various objects in the museum so it's of limited interest to those without a knowledge of Korean archaeology.

Also recently moved into the grounds of the museum are three Puyŏ county government offices dating from the late Chosŏn period. They include the county magistrate's office, his residence and a guesthouse for government officials.

The museum is open daily, except Mondays, from 9 am to 6 pm in summer and 9 am to 5 pm in winter. Entry costs W200.

Puyŏ 부여

PLACES TO STAY

9 Puyŏ Youth Hostel
부여유스호스텔
11 Pangsan-jang Yŏgwan
방산장여관
12 Kwibin-jang Yŏgwan
귀빈장여관
13 Purim-jang Yŏgwan
부림장여관
16 Ihak-jang Yŏgwan
이학장여관
21 Royal Hotel
로얄호텔
22 Seoul Hotel
서울호텔

OTHER

1 Ferry
나루터 (선착장)
2 Naghwa'am Cliff
낙화암
3 Koransa Temple
고란사
4 Sajaru Pavilion
사자루
5 Kungnyŏsa Shrine
궁녀사
6 Pusosan (94m)
부소산
7 Pusosan Fortress
부소산성
8 Ch'ungnyŏngsa Shrine
충렬사

10 Puyŏ National Museum
국립부여반물관
14 Confucian School
향교
15 Express Bus Terminal
고속버스터미널
17 Inter-City Bus Terminal
시외버스터미널
18 Post Office
우체국
19 Chŏngnimsa Temple Site
정림사
20 Telephone Office
전화국

Pusosan

The royal palace and fortress of the Paekche kings once stood on a pine-forested hill, called Pusosan, which rises behind the museum. It's now a popular park criss-crossed with paths and roads, and it contains a number of very attractive temples and pavilions with some excellent views over the surrounding countryside. Also on this hill are the ruins of the Paekche army's food store where, it's said, it is still possible to find carbonised rice, beans and barley.

Pusosan is associated with the legend of the 3000 court ladies who threw themselves onto the rocks from a high cliff – known as Naghwa'am – above the Paengma River, preferring death to capture by the invading Chinese and Shilla armies when the Paekche Kingdom finally came to an end. People come from all over Korea to see this spot. A stroll around this peaceful hillside, combined with a visit to the museum, is a pleasant and relaxing way to spend a morning or afternoon.

The park is open every day and entry costs W1200 (W500 for students and those under 24 years old). There is a detailed map of the hill at the entrance, though all the points of interest are marked in Chinese characters.

Chŏngnimsa

This small temple site near the centre of town contains a five-storey pagoda dating from the Paekche period and a weatherbeaten, seated stone Buddha from the Koryŏ dynasty. The latter is one of the strangest Buddhas you're ever likely to see and bears an uncanny resemblance to the Easter Island statues.

Kungnamji Pond & Pavilion

About one km past Chŏngnimsa and surrounded by paddy fields stands a pavilion which was originally constructed by King Mu of the Paekche Kingdom as a pleasure garden for the court ladies. Until a few years ago it stood in virtual ruins but restoration was then undertaken and the bridge which takes you across the pond to the pavilion is now in good repair. It's a beautiful place to sit and relax and watch the activity in the surrounding paddy fields.

Royal Paekche Tombs

About two km from Puyŏ along the road to Nonsan stands an extensive collection of Paekche royal tombs, dating from 538 to 660 AD, which are similar to those at Kongju. Most are open for viewing (though their contents have been removed so they're of limited interest). The wall painting in the 'painted tomb' is actually a modern reconstruction. What is worth seeing here is the museum, which has been designed to resemble a tomb. Inside are a number of scaled-down reproductions of the various tombs showing their manner of construction as well as a burial urn.

The area around the tombs has been landscaped and is a popular picnic spot.

The tombs are open daily and entry costs W450. To get there, take a local Puyŏ-Nonsan bus or hire a taxi (W2000). You can't miss the site as it's right next to the road on the left hand side.

Places to Stay

Close to the Puyŏ National Museum is the *Pangsan-jang Yŏgwan*. The ordinary rooms cost W20,000, rooms with air-con cost W22,000 and there's one room with a water bed for W28,000.

In the same neighbourhood is the *Kwibin-jang Yŏgwan* which has rooms for W20,000.

Just to the north of the inter-city bus terminal is the *Ihak-jang Yŏgwan* (☎ 835-4521) and neighbouring *Taemyŏng-jang Yŏgwan* (☎ 835-3877). Both offer rooms with traditional under-floor heating (*ondol*). Prices start at W20,000.

Getting There & Away

Buses depart from the inter-city bus terminal according to the following timetable:

Ch'ŏngju buses depart every 30 minutes from 7 am to 8 pm. The fare is W4000 and the journey takes two hours.

Chŏnju buses depart 10 times daily from 8.35 am to 6.35 pm. The fare is W3200 and the journey takes 1¾ hours.

Seoul buses depart 39 times daily between 7 am and 6.30 pm. The fare is W6600 and the journey takes three hours.

T'aean (for T'aean Haean National Park) buses depart four times daily between 8.20 am and 5.45 pm. The fare is W5400 and the journey takes three hours.

Taejŏn (via Nonsan, thus Kwanch'oksa) buses depart every eight minutes from 6.30 am to 9.40 pm. The fare is W2900 and the journey takes 1¼ hours.

Yesan (for Tŏksan Provincial Park) buses depart every 50 minutes from 7.30 am to 7.05 pm. The fare is W3000 and the journey takes two hours.

KONGJU

Established in 475 AD, Kongju was the second capital of the Paekche Kingdom after its first capital south of the Han River near Seoul was abandoned. Nothing remains of that first capital today except for a few artefacts preserved in the National Museum at Seoul. At Kongju, however, there are far more tangible remains in the form of a whole collection of tombs of the Paekche kings.

The tombs are clustered together on a wooded hillside outside Kongju. Inevitably, most of them were looted of their treasures over the centuries and nothing was done to preserve what remained until the Japanese carried out excavations there in 1907 and 1933. Even these excavations were marred by the looting which went on once the tombs were opened up, but in 1971, while work was in progress to repair some of the known tombs, archaeologists came across the undisturbed tomb of King Muryŏng (501-523 AD), one of the last monarchs to reign here. The find is one of Korea's greatest archaeological discoveries, and the hundreds of priceless artefacts that were unearthed form the basis of the collection at the National Museum in Kongju.

Kongju is today a fairly small provincial market town and educational centre, but its Paekche origins are celebrated with an annual festival held in mid-October which lasts for three to four days. It includes a large parade down the main street, fireworks, traditional dancing on the sands of the Kŭmgang River, traditional games and sports and various other events at local sites. If you're around at that time go to the Kongju City Hall for full details.

Information

There is a tourist information kiosk (☎ 856-7700) at the entrance to the west gate of Kongsan fortress.

Kongju National Museum

The museum, opened in 1972, was built to resemble the inside of King Muryŏng's tomb. It houses the finest collection of Paekche artefacts in Korea, including two golden crowns, part of a coffin, gold, jade and silver ornaments, bronze mirrors and utensils as well as Bronze Age daggers, arrowheads and axes, an Iron Age bell and a number of Buddhist images. Outside the museum is an interesting collection of stone images. The museum is open daily, except Mondays, from 9 am to 6 pm during the summer and 9 am to 5 pm in the winter.

King Muryŏng's Tomb

The Paekche tombs are clustered together on Sangsan-ni hill, a 20-minute walk from the centre of town. By the entrance to the site is the Muryŏng's Tomb Model Hall. The star attraction is, of course, King Muryŏng's tomb, but only three of the burial chambers are open for viewing at present. Previously it was possible to go into the chambers themselves but it was found that moist warm air entering from the outside was causing deterioration of the patterned bricks and tiles inside so they're now all protected by hermetically sealed glass windows.

Entry to the tombs costs W500 and it's open daily from 9 am to 6 pm.

Kongsansŏng

This mountain fortress was once the site of the Paekche Royal Palace, but now it's a park with pavilions and a temple. The castle walls, though they had their origin in Paekche times, are the remains of a 17th-century reconstruction.

Places to Stay & Eat

Because the two bus terminals both recently moved to the other side of the river, there is so far only one yŏgwan in the neighbourhood, the *Kŭmgangpak'ŭ Yŏgwan*. Undoubtedly more will be built as time goes on. The intercity bus terminal itself is a good place to eat, with a cheap *Chinese restaurant* upstairs.

Across the river in the town itself are many other reasonable places to stay. The selection includes the *Samwon Yŏinsuk* (☎ 552496), which is very clean and run by friendly people. It costs W12,000. There's a shady courtyard.

The *Kŭmho-jang Yŏgwan* (☎ 555305) offers excellent rooms for W18,000.

Those looking for accommodation among the mid-range hotels should try the *Kongju*

Tourist Hotel (☎ 554023; fax 554028) where twins cost W35,000 and suites are W58,000.

Getting There & Away

The express bus terminal and inter-city bus terminal are right next to each other on the north side of the river, opposite the town. You'll have to take a bus or taxi, or else walk about 1½ km to commute between the terminal and the town. Bus No 8 goes from the bus terminal to the centre, but you must return on bus No 1! Taxis charge around W1500.

Buses depart the express bus terminal for Seoul every 40 minutes from 7 am to 7 pm. The fare is W6000 (1st class) or W4100 (2nd class) and the journey takes 2¼ hours.

Buses depart the inter-city bus terminal for the following destinations:

Ch'ŏngju buses depart 45 times daily between 6.10 am and 9 pm. The fare is W2200 and the journey takes 1¼ hours.
Ch'ŏngyang (for Ch'ilgapsan Provincial Park) buses depart 51 times daily between 7.14 am and 8.04 pm. The fare is W1900 and the journey takes two hours.
Kapsa (Kyeryongsan National Park) buses depart nine times daily between 6.40 am and 4 pm. The fare is W900 and the journey takes 25 minutes. City bus No 2 is more frequent.
Puyŏ buses depart 65 times daily between 6.30 am and 9.45 pm. The fare is W1800 and the journey takes 45 minutes.
Seoul buses depart 91 times daily between 6.50 am and 7.30 pm. The fare is W4100 and the journey takes 2¼ hours.
Taejŏn buses depart 39 times daily from 6.40 am to 10 pm. The fare is W1900 and the journey takes one hour. Many stop at Nonsan (ask first), the stop for the temple of Kwanch'oksa.
Yesan (for Tŏksan Provincial Park) buses depart 42 times daily between 6.25 am and 8.15 pm. The fare is W2700 and the journey takes 1¼ hours.

KYERYONGSAN NATIONAL PARK

This park's unusual name means 'rooster dragon mountain', apparently because some locals thought the mountain resembled a dragon with a rooster's head. Regardless of what it's called, Kyeryongsan (845m) is a worthwhile peak to climb. This area of forested mountains and crystal clear streams between Kongju and Taejŏn is a popular

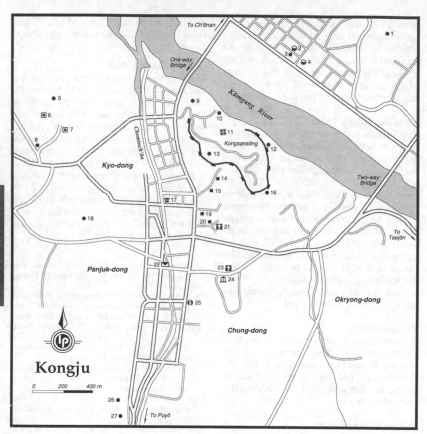

Kongju

```
0    200   400 m
```

To Ch'ŏnan

Kŭmgang River

Kongsansŏng

One-way Bridge

Two-way Bridge

Ch'ŏninch'ŏn

Kyo-dong

Panjuk-dong

Okryong-dong

Chung-dong

To Taejŏn

To Puyŏ

---

hiking spot and also contains within its boundaries two of Korea's most famous temples, Kapsa and Tonghaksa.

The best way to see the two temples is to set off early in the day and walk from one to the other. This takes about four hours at a comfortable pace. The trails are well marked and signposted but, other than a number of hermitages scattered over the mountain and the tourist villages at the temples themselves, there are no facilities so bring food and drink with you.

Entry to the national park costs W1600 (less for students and those under 24 years old).

Kapsa

At the western end of the park stands Kapsa, one of the oldest Buddhist temples in Korea dating back to the Unified Shilla period (8th to 10th centuries AD). Unlike many of the temples in Korea which have been either restored or completely rebuilt from time to time, some of the buildings here are original. Times are obviously changing, however, as there's now a souvenir stall in the temple compound itself – usually these things are found only in the tourist villages. The monks at this temple are not keen on people photographing the Buddhas in the main hall even when no one is praying, so ask first if that's what you want to do.

Tonghaksa

Although the buildings here are nowhere near as old as those at Kapsa, the complex is a large one and the setting is stunning. As at Kapsa, there's a small tourist village down the road from the temple with the usual facilities.

Places to Stay

There are small campgrounds at both Kapsa and Tonghaksa. Back-country cooking and camping are prohibited. Both temples have the requisite tourist villages with some pricey yŏgwans (W20,000 to W30,000). If you want to conserve funds, minbak are W15,000.

Getting There & Away

Bus From Kongju there are 13 buses daily to Kapsa between 6.40 am and 6 pm, taking 25 minutes for the ride. From Kongju you can also take city bus No 2. From Taejŏn's west inter-city bus terminal there are seven buses daily to Kapsa between 7.30 am and 5.50 pm. The buses terminate at the tourist village which is about one km below the actual temple.

Tonghaksa is best approached by city bus from Taejŏn. From Taejŏn, there are seat buses every eight minutes between 6.30 am and 11 pm, taking 40 minutes for the ride and costing W1000. Less expensive (W400) city buses go from Taejŏn every 30 minutes. There are only four buses daily from Kongju to Tonghaksa.

Taxi If you take a taxi to either of these temples the drivers will demand that you pay around 1½ to double the metered fare. The reason for this is that they can't be sure of getting a return fare. On the other hand, if you're coming back from either of the temples you can often get a taxi for much less than the normal fare for the same reason so it's worth considering if you can fill the taxi.

MAGOKSA

Another fairly remote and beautiful temple north-west of Kongju off the main road to Onyang is Magoksa. It was built by the Zen master Chajangyulsa during the reign of the first Shilla queen, Son-dok (632-647 AD), a major patron of Buddhism who introduced Chinese Tang culture into Korea. The temple was reconstructed during the middle years of the Koryŏ dynasty but since then, apart from additional structures erected during the

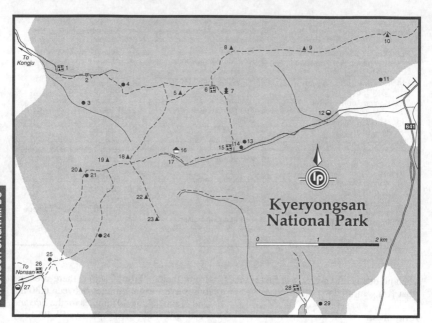

Kyeryongsan
National Park

0   1   2 km

middle of the Yi dynasty, precious little has changed so you're in for a real treat of genuine Koryŏ religious art.

Magoksa's Chonbul-jon hall, with its three huge golden buddhas, is simply incredible both in size and execution. That beams of this size were lifted into place in the days before cranes is almost beyond belief. Another gem at this temple is the Yongsan-jon hall with its three golden Buddhas flanked by four smaller Boddhisatvas and backed by a thousand pint-sized, white-painted devotees – all slightly different from each other. Entry to the temple costs W1000.

There's a small tourist village alongside the river before the temple entrance gate but not many places to stay. Some restaurants are attractively placed, overlooking the river. You can eat well and fairly cheaply at these, or sit and relax with a cold beer. If you want to stay overnight then the best place is the minbak across the other side of the river from the restaurants, reached by a footbridge.

Make arrangements early in the day as it only has a few rooms.

Getting There & Away
Kongju has city buses which go directly to Magoksa every 30 minutes between 6 am and 8 pm. The ride is 37 km and takes 40 minutes, costing W1000. A taxi from Kongju to the temple would cost around W11,000.

CH'ILGAPSAN PROVINCIAL PARK
The summit of Ch'ilgapsan is a modest 561m, but it's a pleasant area with hiking trails and forests. The main temple here is Changgoksa, and there is a smaller temple called Chonghyesa.

Getting There & Away
The small city of Ch'ŏngyang is the gateway to the park. From Ch'ŏngyang there are city buses to Changgoksa eight times daily between 8 am and 8.10 pm, taking 20 minutes for the ride which costs W750.

Buses depart Taejŏn's west inter-city bus

Kyeryongsan National Park
계룡산국립공원

PLACES TO STAY
16 Ŭnsŏn Hut
     은선산장

OTHER
 1 Kapsa Temple
     갑사
 2 Yongmun Waterfall
     용문폭포
 3 Taejaam Hermitage
     대자암
 4 Shinhŭngam Hermitage
     신흥암
 5 Sambulbong (775m)
     삼불봉
 6 Kyemyŏngjŏngsa Temple
     계명정사

 7 Onwit'ap Pagoda
     오뉘탑
 8 Shinsŏnbong (645m)
     신선봉
 9 Imgŭmbong (553m)
     임금봉
10 Changgunbong (510m)
     장군봉
11 Hakbong-ri
     학봉리
12 Bus Stop
     정류장
13 Munsuam Hermitage
     문수암
14 Mit'aam Hermitage
     미타암
15 Tonghaksa Temple
     동학사
17 Ŭnsŏn Waterfall
     은선산장
18 Chŏnmangdae Summit
     전망대

19 Munp'ilbong (756m)
     문필봉
20 Yŏnch'ŏnbong (738m)
     연천봉
21 Tŭngunam Hermitage
     등운암
22 Ssalgaebong (827m)
     쌀개봉
23 Kyeryongsan (845m)
     계룡산
24 Kowangam Hermitage
     고왕암
25 Sorimwon Hermitage
     소림원
26 Shinwonsa Temple
     신원사
27 Bus Stop
     전류장
28 Yonghwasa Temple
     용화사
29 Yongdong-ri
     용동리

terminal for Ch'ŏngyang 30 times daily between 6.30 am and 7.50 pm, taking two hours for the journey. From Kongju there are 51 departures daily for Ch'ŏngyang between 7.14 am and 8.05 pm, taking one hour for the trip.

CH'ŎNAN

The largest bronze statue of the Buddha in all Asia stands at the temple of Kagwonsa, (north-east of Ch'ŏnan). This, and the nation's biggest museum, the Independence Hall of Korea (about 10 km south-east of the city), are probably the only reasons you would come to Ch'ŏnan.

Information

There is a tourist information office (☎ 550-2438) outside the Ch'ŏnan railway station.

Independence Hall of Korea

The nation's largest museum, the Independence Hall of Korea, sees relatively few foreign visitors. Nevertheless, it *is* worth seeing, as much to watch the throngs of Korean visitors as to see the exhibits themselves.

The main hall is like something out of a science fiction movie. Built entirely out of concrete and tiles, it's a fine display of artistry and civil engineering skills. At the back of this hall is a whole complex of seven air-conditioned exhibition halls cataloguing the course of Korean history from the earliest recorded times up until the present. It's possibly the best museum in Korea – especially if you can read Korean. Unfortunately for foreign visitors, most of the explanations which accompany the exhibits are in Korean and there's very little English.

Entry to the Independence Hall costs W1500 (W1000 for students and W700 for children). Entry to the Circle Vision Theatre is an extra W1500. The Hall is open every day except Monday during March to October from 9 am to 6.30 pm (admission ends at 5.30 pm), and November to February from 9 am to 5.30 pm (admission ends at 4.30 pm). Strollers for babies can be rented at the entrance, but the lack of ramps makes them only partially useful.

The complex includes several restaurants, a bookshop, post office, souvenir shops and even a bank where you can change travellers' cheques. Smoking, eating and drinking are prohibited inside the halls. Indoor photography is also prohibited, though plenty of film is on sale at kiosks throughout the site.

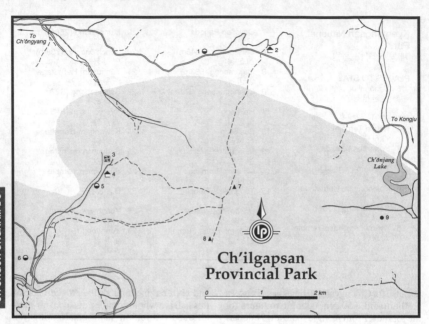

Ch'ilgapsan
Provincial Park

0   1   2 km

Ch'ilgapsan Provincial Park
칠갑산도립공원

PLACES TO STAY

2 Ch'ilgap Hut
   칠갑산장
4 Changgok Hut
   장곡산장

OTHER

1 Bus Stop
   정류장
3 Changgoksa Temple
   장곡사
5 Bus Stop
   정류장
6 Bus Stop
   정류장
7 Ch'ilgapsan (560m)
   칠갑산
8 Samhyŏngjebong Peak
   삼형제봉
9 Ch'ŏnjang-ri
   천장리

City buses shuttle between Ch'ŏnan and the Independence Hall every few minutes between 6 am and 8.50 pm. A convenient one is bus No 500, which stops opposite the Ch'ŏnan railway station. The ride takes 20 minutes and costs W700. There are also buses direct from the Seoul express bus terminal to Independence Hall every 40 minutes between 6.30 am and 7.20 pm, taking 1¾ hours for the journey.

Kagwonsa

Seven km north-east of Ch'ŏnan on the slopes of Taejosan stands Kagwonsa, a temple which has the largest bronze statue of the Buddha in Asia. It was erected in 1977 as a kind of plea for the reunification of Korea and is over 14m tall. The temple is Korea's second largest – only Pulguksa in Kyŏngju is bigger.

Local bus No 102 from Ch'ŏnan railway station area will take you to Kagwonsa, or look for bus No 46. Both are rather infrequent. From where the bus drops you it's a steep walk up just over 200 steps to the temple precincts.

Places to Stay

Heaps of yŏgwan are hidden behind Chohŭng Bank, which is opposite and slightly south of the railway station. Some of these places are real dumps – ask to see the room first. Double rooms with private bath cost W25,000.

Getting There & Away

Bus Express buses depart Ch'ŏnan according to the following schedule:

Seoul buses depart every 20 to 30 minutes from 6.40 am to 9 pm. The fare is W3800 (1st class) or W2400 (2nd class) and the journey takes one hour.

Taejon buses depart every 30 minutes from 6.20 am to 9 pm. The fare is W3300 (1st class) or W2300 (2nd class) and the journey takes one hour.

Some of the more useful inter-city buses depart Ch'ŏnan to the following destinations:

Hongsŏng (for Tŏksan Provincial Park) buses depart every 20 minutes from 6.40 am to 9.28 pm. The fare is W2000 and the journey takes one hour.

Seoul buses depart every 20 minutes from 6.35 am to 9.40 pm. The fare is W2600 or W3400 and the journey takes 1¼ hours.

Songt'an buses depart every 10 minutes from 5.50 am to 10.20 pm. The fare is W1700 and the journey takes 45 minutes.

Suwon buses depart every 10 minutes from 6.40 am to 9.40 pm. The fare is W2600 or W2800 and the journey takes one hour.

T'aean (for T'aean Haean National Park) buses depart every 20 minutes from 7.11 am to 7.55 pm. The fare is W5300 and the journey takes 2½ hours.

Taejŏn buses depart every 20 minutes from 6.30 am to 9.20 pm. The fare is W2300 and the journey takes one hour.

Wonju (for Ch'iaksan National Park) buses depart eight times daily between 7.30 am and 7.10 pm. The fare is W6300 and the journey takes 2¼ hours.

Yesan (for Tŏksan Provincial Park) buses depart every 20 minutes from 6.40 am to 9.28 pm. The fare is W2000 and the journey takes 1¼ hour.

Train Ch'ŏnan straddles one of the most heavily travelled railway lines in the country, but it can be difficult to get even a standing-room ticket on weekends. The train schedule on the Seoul-Ch'ŏnan route can be found in the appendix at the end of this book.

ONYANG HOT SPRINGS

Known variously as Onjong, Onsu and Onyang (foreigners just call it 'Onion'), this is

Monumental Hate

When it comes to nationalism, there is a competition of sorts between North and South Korea. Both have built gigantic statues, monuments, plazas, towers and other feel-good projects which are meant to eulogise the nation's integrity and the uniqueness of its culture. The main difference is that North Korea can't afford these projects but South Korea can.

Virtually every South Korean has visited the Independence Hall of Korea, and some have visited numerous times. It's quite apparent to the visitor that all stops were pulled out to make this an uncompromising totem to national sovereignty.

There's a high propaganda content to many of the exhibits which chart the course of late19th and 20th century Korean history; the Japanese and North Koreans come in for some particularly virulent condemnation. On any weekday you will see busloads of school children being run through this place accompanied by their teachers. Unfortunately, part of Korea's educational system includes a lengthy hate-mongering campaign against Japan – the 'Japanese Aggression Hall' is the most notorious example of the genre. Intriguingly, there seems to be official amnesia about China's nasty behaviour during the Korean War. Perhaps this is because China now has nuclear weapons and a willingness to use them.

Although Japanese travellers might be nonplussed by how they're portrayed in the history exhibits, travellers of other nationalities generally find this place enjoyable. There's also the Circle Vision Theatre which presents a 15-minute film displaying Korea's scenic beauty, traditions, customs and development using the latest high-tech audio-visual techniques. ■

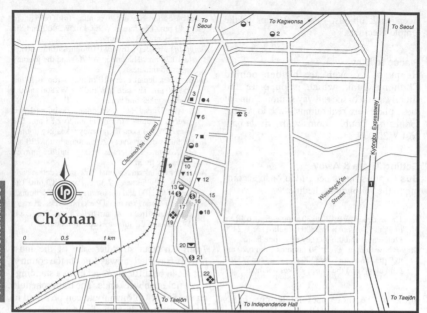

one of Korea's oldest and most heavily developed hot springs resorts. Its history goes back at least to the Chosŏn dynasty when kings came here to bathe. The water has a high sulfur concentration and reaches a temperature of 50°C. It's an intensively developed resort with over 150 hotels. Being easily accessible from Seoul it packs out on weekends.

Getting There & Away

Bus From Seoul express bus terminal there are departures every 20 minutes between 6.30 am and 9 pm, taking 1½ hours for the journey and costing W4200. From the Tong-

Seoul station there are 25 departures daily between 6.30 am and 9 pm.

Train Onyang is not exactly on the major north-south railway (as is nearby Ch'ŏnan), but it does have a direct service from Seoul (see the table below).

TOGO HOT SPRINGS

Togo is just 16 km south-west of Onyang which makes it convenient to handle some of the hot springs overflow crowds. The water temperature here is relatively low which puts some people off. Togo tries to

Class	Time	Frequency	Travel Time	Fare
Saemaul	9.30 am, 5.35 pm	2 daily	1 hr 10 mins	W5400
Mugungwha	7.35 am to 6.35 pm	7 daily	1 hr 25 mins	W2900
T'ongil	6.35 am to 7.35 pm	5 daily	1 hr 30 mins	W2100

Ch'ŏnan 천안

PLACES TO STAY
3 Onsŏng-jang Yŏgwan
온성장여관
7 Yongju-jang Yŏgwan
용주장여관
17 Yŏgwan Area
여관지역

PLACES TO EAT
6 Pelicana Fried Chicken
페리카나치킨
11 Paris Baguete
파리바게뜨
12 Wendy's Hamburgers
웬디스

OTHER
1 Ch'ŏnan Bus Terminal
천안버스터미널
2 Express Bus Terminal
고속버스터미널
4 Girls' Middle School
복지여중고교
5 Telephone Office
전화국
8 Bus No 102
(to Kagwonsa)
정류상 (각원사)
9 Railway Station
천인역
10 Central Post Office
천안우체국
13 Bus No 500
(to Independence Hall)
정류장 (독립기념관)
14 Chohŭng Bank
조흥은행
15 Underground Arcade
지하상가
16 Shinhan Bank
신한은행
18 City Hall
시청
19 Ch'ŏnan Department
Store
천안백화점
20 Post Office
오룡우체국
21 Bank
은행
22 Pagoda Department
Store
파고다백화점

make up for this with modern facilities such as a horse riding track and a golf course. The major resort here is the *Paradise Hotel*. All things considered, Korea definitely has better places to enjoy hot springs.

Getting There & Away
The town of Togo is 10 minutes away by city bus from the hot springs resort itself. There are also buses direct from Onyang. Some trains stop at the Togo Hot Springs station.

HONGSŎNG
This is the main staging post for a visit to Sudŏksa and Tŏksan Provincial Park. The town itself is not a major attraction, but it's pleasant enough and you might even want to spend the night. Hongsŏng is an old fortress town with parts of its city wall and one beautiful gate still remaining.

Getting There & Away
Bus There is only one bus terminal in town, handling both express and inter-city buses. Local city buses with the word 'Sudŏksa' (in Korean) on the windshield can get you to Tŏksan Provincial Park. Some useful buses go from Hongsŏng to the following places:

Ch'ŏnan buses depart every 10 minutes from 6.35 am to 9.32 pm. The fare is W3100 and the journey takes 1½ hours.

Ch'ŏngju buses depart nine times daily between 7.43 am and 6.30 pm. The fare is W4900 and the journey takes 2¾ hours.

Seoul buses depart every 40 minutes from 7.35 am to 7.15 pm. The fare is W6100 and the journey takes 2¼ hours.

Sŏsan (for T'aean Haean National Park) buses depart every 10 minutes from 6.40 am to 10.10 pm. The fare is W1800 and the journey takes 50 minutes.

Sudŏksa (Tŏksan Provincial Park) buses depart every 30 minutes from 7.45 am to 8.30 pm and the fare is W1050. The journey takes 40 minutes.

Taejŏn buses depart every 30 minutes from 6.30 am to 7 pm. The fare is W5800 and the journey takes 2¼ hours.

Train The railway station is a 15-minute walk east of the bus terminal. There are a few trains to Ch'ŏnan and Seoul, but in general you'll get around more quickly by bus.

TŎKSAN PROVINCIAL PARK
This park offers incredible scenery and should not be missed it you're in the area. Attractions include pretty valleys, pine forests, large boulders, rocks and waterfalls. There is also the peak of Tŏksungsan which is a modest 495m. The park is nicknamed 'little Kŭmgangsan' – Kŭmgangsan is in

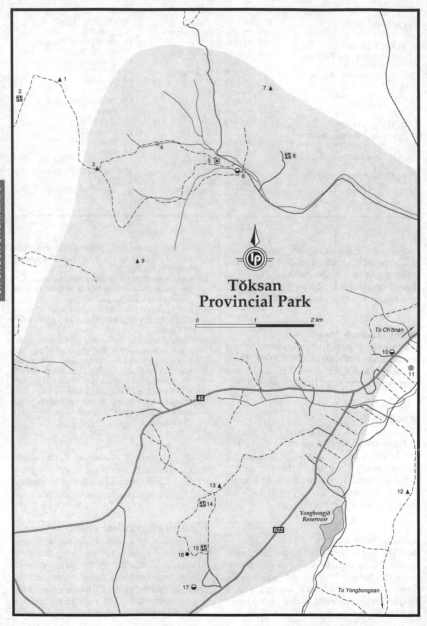

Tŏksan Provincial Park 덕산도립공원	6 Bus Stop 정류장	12 Suamsan (260m) 수암산
	7 Sŏwonsan (472m) 서원산	13 Tŏksungsan (495m) 덕숭산
1 Illaksan (521m) 일락산	8 Podŏksa Temple 보덕사	14 Chonghyesa Temple 정혜사
2 Illaksa Temple 일락사	9 Kayasan (677m) 가야산	15 Sudŏksa 수덕사
3 Sŏkmunbong (653m) 석문봉	10 Bus Stop 정류장	16 Kyŏnsŏngam Hermitage 견성암
4 Oknyŏ Waterfall 옥녀폭포	11 Tŏksan Hot Springs 덕산온천	17 Bus Stop 정류장
5 Namyŏn Tomb 남연군묘		

North Korea and is considered the country's most spectacular mountain range.

On the southern slope of Tŏksungsan is Sudŏksa, a Buddhist temple known for its large contingent of resident nuns. The other main temple in the park is called Chonghyesa.

Tŏksan hot springs is just on the eastern edge of the park in Sadong-ri. The water here has an eye-opening temperature of 52°C. There are developed pools for soaking and some yŏgwan such as the *Tŏksan Onch'ŏn-jang* (☎ 373535), which costs W20,000.

Admission to Tŏksan Provincial Park costs W800.

Getting There & Away

Access is either from Hongsŏng or Yesan (Hongsŏng is somewhat better). Buses depart Yesan for Sudŏksa 12 times daily between 8.20 am and 7.05 pm. The ride takes 50 minutes and costs W1000.

You can easily get to Yesan from Taejŏn's west inter-city bus terminal. You can also get to Yesan from Ch'ŏnan and Kongju.

From Seoul's Nambu bus terminal, buses leave daily for Sodŏksa at 7.20 am and 1.45 pm.

T'AEAN HAEAN NATIONAL PARK

T'aean Haean ('seashore') National Park offers some dramatic coastal scenery, four large sandy beaches and about 130 islands and islets. The largest island by far is Anmyŏndo, which can be reached by a bridge. From north to south, the four main beaches are Ch'ŏllip'o,

Mallip'o, Yŏnpo and Mongsanp'o. Mallip'o seems to be the most popular.

This is the nearest national park to Seoul offering beachside scenery. Not surprisingly, July and August are the peak months and the beaches can be wall-to-wall bodies and beach umbrellas. Visiting slightly off-season (June or September) is recommended.

Admission to the park costs W1000.

Places to Stay

There are plenty of minbak and yŏgwan, many built next to the beach with no thought given to aesthetics. These places can pack out during the July-August peak season, and you can forget it on weekends and holidays.

Getting There & Away

Access is from the town of T'aean, which is about 16 km from the beach at Mallip'o. Local city buses run out to the beaches.

Buses leave T'aean for the following:

Ch'ŏnan buses depart 41 times daily between 7.30 am and 7.40 pm. The fare is W5300, W5600 or W5800 and the journey takes 2¾ hours.
Seoul buses depart 48 times daily between 7.25 am and 7.35 pm. The fare is W7700 and the journey takes 3½ hours.
Taejŏn buses depart 27 times daily between 7 am and 5.20 pm. The fare is W8000, W8300 or W8500 and the journey takes 3¾ hours.

You can catch a train from Seoul to Hongsŏng then get a bus to T'aean.

Ch'ungch'ŏngbuk-do

A land of small towns, mountains, hot springs and forests, Ch'ungch'ŏngbuk-do is South Korea's most rural province. There are no large cities here, but plenty of opportunities for outdoor recreation. The province may be landlocked, but a tidal wave of Seoulites pours in on weekends and holidays – at other times, this is one of the most peaceful places in the country.

CH'ŎNGJU

Ch'ŏngju (population 465,000) is the provincial capital and a useful launchpad for nearby Songnisan National Park. The town has a few minor sights, but nothing to hold your interest for long.

Sangdangsansŏng

This huge fortress is just to the north-east of Ch'ŏngju on the slopes of Uamsan. Four gates are still standing and the wall is in good nick thanks to a recent renovation. It takes about 40 minutes to walk the length of the wall.

The history of the fortress is unclear. One legend claims that it was built in the Shilla dynasty by the father of Kim Yu-shin who was the leader of a military contingent called the *hwarang*. Another story says it was built by Kosŏng of the Paekche Kingdom. Whoever first built it, the fortress was falling apart until it was renovated in 1716. These days it's past its prime and, along with nearby Samil Park, serves as a weekend getaway for residents of Ch'ŏngju.

Sangdangsansŏng is not a major tourist attraction, but is one of the few quick journeys you can do out of town if you're spending the night in Ch'ŏngju.

The fortress is 30 minutes by city bus from the express bus terminal stop. It runs only about once hourly and is actually a minibus. Exact change or a bus ticket is available from a kiosk (fare is W410). The fortress is the terminus of the bus route.

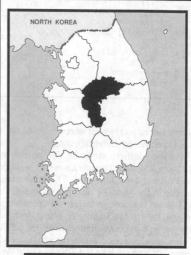

HIGHLIGHTS

- Songnisan, a national park that features fine scenery and the magnificent Pŏpchusa temple
- Tanyang, a beautiful mountain resort where you can boat on a lake, climb forested peaks and visit ancient Buddhist caves
- Sobaeksan, a magnificent national park, home of the huge Kuinsa temple
- Suanbo, known for its superb hot springs and fine winter skiing
- Woraksan, one of the less visited national parks, featuring thick forests which display magnificent colours in the autumn

Places to Stay

The best collection of yŏgwan is in an alley on the east side of the inter-city bus terminal (see the Ch'ongju map). There are fewer places near the express bus terminal.

Close to the express bus terminal is the upmarket *Ch'ongju Royal Tourist Hotel* (☎ 221-1300; fax 221-1319), 227-22 Somun-dong. Room rates are: doubles W42,000, twins W68,000 and suites W85,000, plus 20% extra for tax and service charge.

The plushest hotel is the *Ch'ongju Tourist Hotel* (☎ 642181; fax 668215) which is far out in the west end of town. Room rates are doubles W40,000, twins W42,000 to W60,000 and suites W86,000 to W160,000, plus 20%.

Getting There & Away

There is an express bus terminal and an inter-city bus terminal in Ch'ŏngju. Departures from the express bus terminal are as follows:

Kwangju buses depart every 1½ hours from 6 am to 7 pm. The fare is W9300 (1st class) or W6400 (2nd class) and the journey takes 2¾ hours.

Pusan buses depart every 1⅓ hours from 7 am to 6 pm. The fare is W14,100 (1st class) or W9500 (2nd class) and the journey takes 4½ hours.

Seoul buses depart every five to 10 minutes from 5.50 am to 10 pm. The fare is W5800 (1st class) or W4000 (2nd class) and the journey takes 1¾ hours.

Taegu buses depart 16 times daily between 7 am and 7.30 pm. The fare is W9000 (1st class) or W6200 (2nd class) and the journey takes 2¾ hours.

Tong-Seoul (East Seoul) buses depart every 30 minutes from 6 am to 9 pm. The fare is W4300 and the journey takes 1¾ hours.

CH'UNGCH'ŎNGBUK-DO

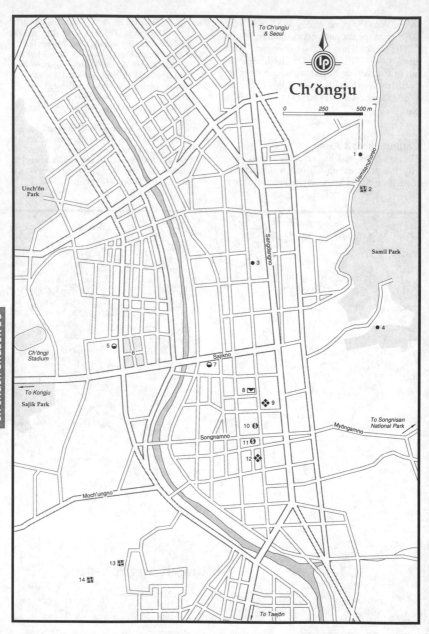

Ch'ŏngju

Ch'ŏngju 청주

1 Ch'ŏngju University
   청주대학교
2 Pohyŏnsa Temple
   보현사
3 City Hall
   시청
4 Confucian School
   향교

5 Inter-City Bus Terminal
   시외버스터미널
6 Yŏgwan Area
   여관지역
7 Express Bus Terminal
   고속버스터미널
8 Post Office
   우체국
9 Ch'ŏngju Department
   Store
   청주백화점

10 Commercial Bank
    상업은행
11 Chohung Bank
    조흥은행
12 Tonggwang Department
    Store
    동광백화점
13 Yonghwasa Temple
    영화사
14 Hwaŏmsa Temple
    화엄사

Departures from the inter-city bus terminal are as follows:

Chech'ŏn buses depart every 10 minutes from 6.20 am to 8 pm. The fare is W5700 and the journey takes three hours.

Chŏnju buses depart 20 times daily between 7.20 am and 6.35 pm. The fare is W5000 and the journey takes two hours.

Ch'unch'ŏn buses depart 12 times daily between 8.55 am and 5.55 pm. The fare is W9400 and the journey takes 3¾ hours.

Ch'ungju buses depart every 10 minutes from 6.15 am to 9 pm. The fare is W3300 and the journey takes 1¾ hours.

Tŏksan Provincial Park buses depart every 30 minutes between 6.20 am and 8 pm. The fare is W2000 and the journey takes 1¼ hours.

Muju (for Tŏgyusan National Park) buses depart five times daily between 7 am and 2.50 pm. The fare is W4900 and the journey takes 2½ hours.

Puyŏ buses depart every 40 minutes from 7 am to 7.15 pm. The fare is W4000 and the journey takes two hours.

Seoul buses depart 38 times daily between 6.30 am and 8.40 pm. The fare is W4000 and the journey takes 1¾ hours.

Songnisan National Park buses depart every 10 minutes from 6.30 am to 8.35 pm. The fare is W3400 and the journey takes 1½ hours.

Taejŏn buses depart every four minutes from 6.30 am to 9.40 pm. The fare is W1600 and the journey takes 35 minutes.

Tanyang buses depart 24 times daily between 6.37 and 4.53 pm. The fare is W6900 and the journey takes 3½ hours.

Wonju buses depart every 25 minutes from 7.30 am to 6.05 pm. The fare is W5200 and the journey takes 3¾ hours.

SONGNISAN NATIONAL PARK

Songnisan National Park is one of the finest scenic areas in central Korea. Not surprisingly, there are numerous excellent walks. A popular trail for hikers leads to the summit of Ch'unhwangbong (1058m), the park's highest point.

Although the area's great scenic beauty is a major attraction, Songnisan National Park is really distinguished by Pŏpchusa, one of the largest and most magnificent temple sites in Korea. Indeed, the park's name originated from Buddhist philosophy and literally means 'remote from the mundane world mountains'.

Construction of the temple was begun as early as 553 AD during the Shilla dynasty; this was when Pŏpchusa's Taeongbojŏn Hall, with its enormous golden buddhas, and the five-roofed Palsangjŏn Hall were constructed. At the time it was one of the largest sanctuaries in Korea. Repairs were undertaken in 776 AD but in 1592 it was burned to the ground during the Japanese invasion. Reconstruction began in 1624 and it's from this time that the present Palsangjŏn Hall dates, making it one of the few wooden structures at Pŏpchusa to survive since the 17th century. Most of the others were constructed or reconstructed towards the end of the Yi dynasty.

Pŏpchusa is famous for another reason. Until 1986, it had the largest Buddha statue in Korea – possibly in the whole of North-East Asia – and the 27m-high, concrete statue of the Maitraya Buddha dominated the temple compound. It took 30 years to build and was completed only in 1968. It featured prominently in all the tourist literature of this area. Unfortunately, by the 1980s the statue

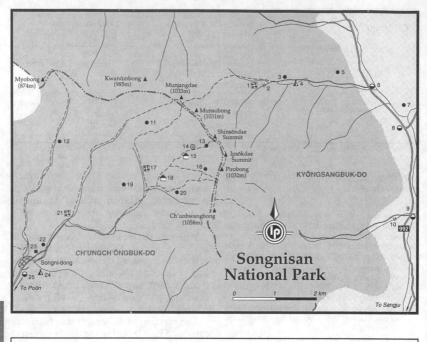

Songnisan National Park
속리산국립공원

1 Sŏngbulsa Temple
   성불사
2 Osong Waterfall
   오송폭포
3 Park Office
   공원관리사무소
4 Camping Ground
   야영지
5 Changam-ri
   장암리
6 Bus Stop
   정류장
7 Yongyu-ri
   용유리

8 Bus Stop
   정류장
9 Bus Stop
   정류장
10 Changgak Waterfall
   장각폭포
11 Chungsajaam Hermitage
   중사자암
12 Yŏjŏkam Hermitage
   여적암
13 Kyŏngopdae Rock
   경업대
14 Spring
   장수약수
15 Kŭmgang Shelter
   금강대피소
16 Sanggoam Hermitage
   상고암

17 Pokch'ŏnam
   복천암
18 Piro Hut
   비로산장
19 T'algolam Hermitage
   탈골암
20 Sanghwanam Hermitage
   상환암
21 Pŏpchusa
   법주사
22 Park Office
   공원관리사무소
23 Songnisan Tourist Hotel
   속리산관광호텔
24 Camping Ground
   야영지
25 Bus Stop
   정류장

had begun to crack and in late 1986 it was demolished. In its place has risen a new statue; 33m in height, this one is made of 160 tons of brass and sits on top of a massive white stone base containing a ground-level shrine. This gigantic project, which cost about US$4 million, was completed in late 1989.

There are many other interesting features at Pŏpchusa, including stone lanterns, a rock-cut seated Buddha, a huge bell, and an enormous iron cauldron, cast in 720 AD, which was used to cook rice for the 3000 monks who lived here during Pŏpchusa's heyday.

The magnificent temple buildings are surrounded by the luxuriously forested mountains of Songnisan National Park. Although at its best during autumn, it is beautiful at any time of the year. There are well-marked, scenic hiking trails in the mountains above the temple, and several hermitages where you may be able to stay for the night.

Admission fees are W1700 for adults, W950 for students and W600 for children.

Information

The national park headquarters are near the park entrance. You might be able to get a map from the staff, but don't count on it. Perhaps the most useful service this place offers is the baggage storage room; it is signposted in English.

Places to Stay & Eat

Like all important temple complexes in Korea, Pŏpchusa has its own tourist village (called Songni-dong) before the entrance to the national park – here it's more like a small town. There's a wide choice of places to stay but prices are pushed upwards by the fact that this is a resort area. Minbak with shared bath go for W20,000 while yŏgwan boasting a private bath start at W25,000. In the off season polite bargaining should gain you a 10% discount. The owners of minbak and yŏgwan hang out by the bus terminal and solicit business.

There is a *Youth Hostel* (☎ 425211) here with beds from W6600 and private rooms costing W40,000 to W115,000.

If you're looking for an upmarket place, Songni-dong can accommodate you. The best in town is the *Songnisan Tourist Hotel* (☎ 425281) where doubles go for a cool W64,000 to W116,000. Next to the best is the *Poŭn Hotel* (☎ 431818) with doubles for W31,000.

There's a free camp site (signposted 'Camping Ground' in English), which usually isn't crowded, on the opposite side of the river from the village. Facilities are good, and include clean toilets and wash basins.

Getting There & Away

The most useful direct buses go from Songnisan to Ch'ŏngju, Taejŏn and Seoul, but a few other destinations are also on the timetable. Some places you can get to directly from Songnisan include:

Ch'ŏngju buses depart 69 times daily between 6.10 am and 7.50 pm. The fare is W3400 and the journey takes 1½ hours.

Seoul buses depart 25 times daily between 6.30 am and 6.35 pm. The fare is W7400 and the journey takes three hours.

Suwon buses depart eight times daily from 7.30 am to 6.50 pm. The fare is W7500 and the journey takes three hours.

Taegu buses depart five times daily between 9.33 am and 6.26 pm. The fare is W4100 and the journey takes 3½ hours.

Taejŏn buses depart 33 times daily from 6.29 am to 7.56 pm. The fare is W3200 and the journey takes 1¾ hours.

CH'UNGJU

Ch'ungju (population 210,000) is an unremarkable town on the north slope of the Sobaek mountain range. If you're exploring Ch'ungch'ŏngbuk-do it's very likely you'll at least pass through Ch'ungju, but unlikely that you will need to spend the night. However, the town is the main jumping off point for Suanbo hot springs, Woraksan National Park, Ch'ungjuho (lake) and some ski resorts.

Getting There & Away

Bus Ch'ungju has only one bus terminal, conveniently located right in the centre of town. Local city buses can be caught across the street from the terminal and travel to some useful destinations, such as Suanbo hot springs, Ch'ungjuho and Woraksan National Park.

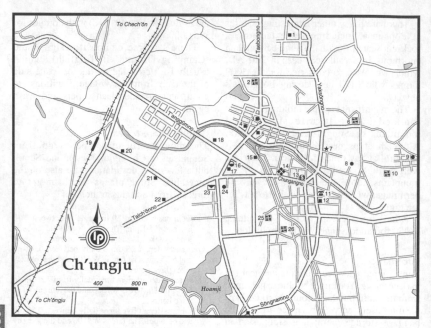

Ch'ungju

From the bus terminal itself, there are departures to the following destinations:

Andong buses depart eight times daily between 9.25 am and 6.05 pm. The fare is W7300 and the journey takes three hours.

Chech'ŏn buses depart every 20 minutes from 7 am to 8.35 pm. The fare is W2400 and the journey takes 1¼ hours.

Ch'ŏngju buses depart every seven minutes from 6.15 am to 9 pm. The fare is W3300 and the journey takes 1¾ hours.

Ch'unch'ŏn buses depart eight times daily from 9.30 am to 7 pm. The fare is W7000 and the journey takes 3½ hours.

Inch'ŏn buses depart every 15 minutes from 7.30 am to 7.30 pm. The fare is W6500 and the journey takes three hours.

Pusan buses depart three times daily between 10.03 am and 1.50 pm. The fare is W13,200 and the journey takes six hours.

Seoul buses depart every 15 minutes from 5.40 am to 8.35 pm. The fare is W4400 and the journey takes two hours.

T'aebaek buses depart only once daily at 9.05 am. The fare is W8900 and the journey takes four hours.

Taegu buses depart every 35 minutes from 6 am to 6.15 pm. The fare is W9800 and the journey takes 4¼ hours.

Taejŏn buses depart every 20 minutes from 7 am to 6.40 pm. The fare is W5000 and the journey takes two hours.

Wonju buses depart three times daily between 6.40 am and 8.15 pm. The fare is W2900 and the journey takes 1¼ hours.

Train There is one train daily from Seoul to Ch'ungju. It departs Seoul station at 6.40 pm, costs W5100 and takes 2¾ hours to reach Ch'ungju.

SUANBO HOT SPRINGS

The town of Suanbo is a resort village at the base of the Sobaek mountains, 21 km south of Ch'ungju. This is South Korea's pre-eminent hot springs resort, but is also known for its golf courses and skiing facilities.

Suanbo's amenities are no secret, and the area can be overrun with tourists at any time of year. On holidays it seems like half of

Ch'ungju 충주	20 Hwangshil-jang Yŏgwan 황실장여관	10 Samch'ungsa 삼충사
PLACES TO STAY	21 Sŏrin-jang Yŏgwan 서린장여관	11 Telephone Office 전화국
1 Mirim-jang Yŏgwan 미림장여관	22 Ch'ungju Hotel 충주관광호텔	13 Hanil Bank 한일은행
3 Urim Yŏgwan 우림여관	27 Hoam Tourist Hotel 호암관광호텔	14 Tongbu Department Store 동부백화점
4 Cheil-jang Yŏgwan 제일장여관		16 Bus Terminal 버스터미널
5 Ch'ŏnil-jang Yŏgwan 천일장여관	**OTHER**	19 Railway Station 중주역
12 Central Hotel 중앙호텔	2 Uamjŏngsa Temple 우암정사	23 Post Office 우체국
15 88 Yŏgwan 88 여관	6 Samjŏngsa 삼정사	24 City Hall 시청
17 Pastel Hotel 파스텔관광호텔	7 Police 경찰서	25 Taewonsa Temple 대원사
18 Wibin-jang Yŏgwan 귀빈장여관	8 Confucian School 향교	26 Yong'unsa Temple 용운사
	9 Confucian School 한교	

Seoul has migrated here in pursuit of pleasure and you'd be wise to schedule your visit when most of the Korean populace is at work. Another peak time is during the Suanbo Hot Springs Festival in October.

For those who can afford the ticket, Waikiki Suanbo can furnish the latest in recreational facilities (golf, skiing and others you haven't thought of). This place also organises boat tours on nearby Ch'ungjuho.

Nearby is another tourist complex under development, variously known as Nung-am, Tonsan and Ch'ung-on hot springs. Keep your eyes open for this one.

Places to Stay – bottom end

There are two youth hostels in Suanbo, though they are usually full. One is *Hanal* (☎ 846-3151) and the other is *Sajo Maŭl* (☎ 846-0750). Dorm beds are about W6000 but rates for private rooms are W22,000 to W48,000.

Of course, you don't need to stay in a youth hostel unless your budget is rock bottom. For around W20,000 you can get a decent double room in a yŏgwan, though prices can go higher on weekends and holidays when demand is high. There are far too many yŏgwan to list here.

Places to Stay – top end

Suanbo is hardly backpacker heaven – pricey hotels are available to all who can afford it. If you're flush with cash, consider the following:

Suanbo (☎ 846-2311; fax 846-2315), 50 rooms costing from W48,000 to W200,000
Suanbo Park (☎ 846-2331; fax 846-3705), 113 rooms costing from W58,000 to W363,000
Suanbo Plaza Condominium (☎ 846-8211), 72 rooms priced at W80,000
Suanbo Sangnok (☎ 845-3500), 101 rooms costing from W56,000 to W308,000
Waikiki Suanbo (☎ 846-3333; fax 846-0500), 102 rooms costing from W58,000 to W150,000

Getting There & Away

Bus There is a city bus from Ch'ungju going to Suanbo every 1¼ hours from 5.40 am to 8 pm. The ride takes 40 minutes and costs W1000. Long-distance inter-city buses depart Suanbo according to the following schedule:

Andong buses depart every 2½ hours. The fare is W6300 and the journey takes 2½ hours.
Ch'ŏngju buses depart every 40 minutes from 7.05 am to 7 pm. The fare is W3900 and the journey takes 1¾ hours.
Pusan buses depart twice daily at 10.33 am and 2.20 pm. The fare is W14,100.

Seoul buses depart every 30 minutes from 7.30 am to 7.40 pm. The fare is W6400 and the journey takes 2¼ hours.

Suwon buses depart 16 times daily between 7.05 am and 7.50 pm. The fare is W6200 and the journey takes three hours.

Taegu buses depart every 35 minutes from 6.30 am to 6.45 pm. The fare is W8800 and the journey takes 3¼ hours.

Taejŏn buses depart five times daily between 8.45 am and 5.40 pm. The fare is W5500 and the journey takes 2¾ hours.

Train Ch'olma Tourist Service (☎ 393-4841, 909-4412) in Seoul organises weekend and holiday tourist trains. The trains only go as far as Ch'ungju and the last leg of the journey is by tourist coach.

CHECH'ŎN

Chech'ŏn is another useful transit point in the northern part of Ch'ungch'ŏngbuk-do, but you aren't likely to come here just to enjoy the town.

Ŭirimji Pond

The nearest sight is Ŭirimji Pond, north-west of town. The 'pond' is in fact a small reservoir, two km in circumference. It's part of the oldest irrigation system in Korea and has been designated an historic monument. History aside, the pond is picturesque, surrounded by pines and willows. The scenery is dressed up by two pavilions, Kyonghoru and Yonghojong.

Local city buses run from the main streets of Chech'ŏn to Ŭirimji Pond every 10 minutes from early morning until late in the evening.

Places to Stay

With luck, you won't spend the night in Chech'ŏn, but there are plenty of yŏgwan if the need should arise. Prices are around W20,000 for a double. Typical of this genre is the *Sŏrin-jang Yŏgwan* (☎ 423663), about 500m north of the railway station.

Getting There & Away

Bus Chech'ŏn has two bus stations: the Tongbu express bus terminal and the inter-

city bus terminal. From the Tongbu express bus terminal there are buses to Seoul every 40 to 50 minutes between 6.30 am and 8 pm. The fare is W7200 (1st class) or W4900 (2nd class) and the journey takes 2¾ hours.

From the inter-city bus terminal there are buses to the following places:

Andong buses depart 16 times daily between 8.13 am and 7.05 pm. The fare is W6200 and the journey takes three hours.

Ch'ŏngju buses depart 15 times daily between 6.15 am and 7.40 pm. The fare is W5700 and the journey takes three hours.

Ch'unch'ŏn buses depart eight times daily between 9.52 am and 6.30 pm. The fare is W6200 and the journey takes three hours.

Ch'ungju buses depart every 10 minutes from 6.15 am to 8.10 pm. The fare is W2400 and the journey takes 1¼ hours.

Kangnŭng buses depart 16 times daily between 6.20 am and 6.44 pm. The fare is W7300 and the journey takes four hours.

Kuinsa buses depart 14 times daily between 7.10 am and 7.50 pm. The fare is W2500 and the journey takes 1¾ hours.

Pusan buses depart three times daily between 8.35 am and 12.10 pm. The fare is W14,600 and the journey takes seven hours.

Seoul buses depart 86 times daily between 6.55 am and 8 pm. The fare is W5800 and the journey takes three hours.

T'aebaek buses depart every 40 minutes from 9.10 am to 9.25 pm. The fare is W6500 and the journey takes 2¾ hours.

Taegu buses depart 13 times daily between 8.13 am and 7.05 pm. The fare is W10,100 and the journey takes five hours.

Taejŏn buses depart 27 times daily between 6.15 am and 5.40 pm. The fare is W7400 and the journey takes 3¾ hours.

Tanyang buses depart 71 times daily from 6.55 am to 9.10 pm. The fare is W1500 and the journey takes 50 minutes.

Wonju buses depart every 10 minutes from 6.55 am to 9.30 pm. The fare is W2000 and the journey takes one hour.

Yŏngju buses depart 38 times daily between 7.10 am and 8.40 pm. The fare is W4100 and the journey takes two hours.

Train Trains to Chech'ŏn depart from Seoul's Ch'ŏngnyangni station. The train schedule for the Seoul-Chech'ŏn route can be found in the appendix at the end of this book.

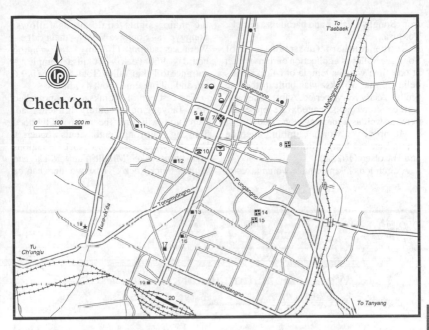

Chech'ŏn 제천

PLACES TO STAY
5 Tongshin-jang Yŏgwan
동신장여관
6 P'unggi-jang Yŏgwan
풍기장여관
11 Paeut'ang Yŏgwan
배우탕여관
12 Haengun Tourist Hotel
행운관광호텔
13 Sŏrin-jang Yŏgwan
서린장여관
16 Hotde-jang Yŏgwan
롯데장여관

17 Kadŭn-jang Yŏgwan
가든장여관
19 Kŭrin-jang Yŏgwan
그린상여관

OTHER
1 City Hall
시청
2 Tongbu Express Bus
Terminal
동부고속버스터미널
3 Inter-City Bus Terminal
시외버스터미널
4 Won'gaksa Confucian
School
원각사향교

7 Central Supermarket
중앙쇼핑
8 Pokch'ŏnsa Temple
복천사
9 Post Office
우체국
10 Telephone Office
전화국
14 Won'gaksa Temple
원각사
15 Hansansa Temple
한산사
18 Police
견찰서
20 Railway Station
제천역

WORAKSAN NATIONAL PARK

Woraksan ('moon crags mountains') gets relatively few visitors by Korean national park standards. While lacking the dramatic cliffs and spires found in some mountains, the park still offers fine hiking through pic-turesque forests. Songgye, a valley six km in length on the north slope of the park, forms the main entrance to the Woraksan area. At the northern end of the valley is Songgye-ri, a tourist village which offers basic facilities. Further south, Tŏkju Valley branches east from Songgye Valley and harbours a temple, Tŏkjusa.

At the southern (upstream) end of Songgye Valley is a collection of ruins which at one time was the temple of Mirŭksa. It's believed that Mirŭksa was built in the late Shilla or early Koryŏ period. A five-storey and a three-storey stone pagoda are preserved here, as well as a standing stone Buddha.

Major peaks worth climbing include Chuhulsan (1106m), Munsubong (1162m) and Hasolsan (1028m).

A circuitous hiking course which takes in the major sights could be as follows: Songgye-ri – Songgye Valley – main ridge – Woraksan summit (1093m) – information board – 960 Peak – Tŏkjusa (temple) – entrance to Tŏkju Valley. Total distance is 9.6 km and hiking time about 4½ hours.

The east end of Woraksan is approached from Tanyang on an entirely different road. Here you will find the much ballyhooed Tanyang P'algyong ('eight scenic wonders'). Essentially, these wonders are rock formations with names like 'Middle Fairy Rock' and 'Upper Fairy Rock'. These wonders can be

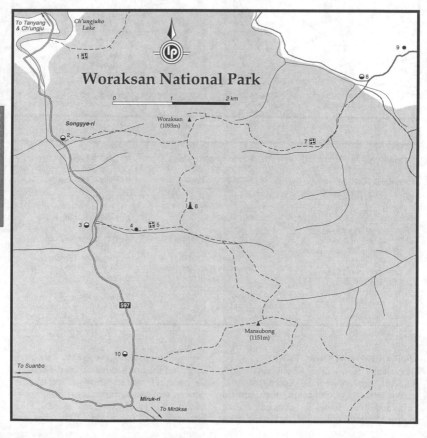

Woraksan National Park

reached by highway and are therefore more visited by windshield tourists. You'll get a better look at the park on foot.

Admission to Woraksan National Park costs W700.

Places to Stay & Eat

There are four tiny villages in the park (Worak-ri, Songgye-ri, Miruk-ri and T'anji-ri) which offer minbak; rooms are priced around W15,000 to W25,000, depending on the market. All the villages have a small assortment of *restaurants* and *grocery stores*. Back-country camping and cooking are prohibited in the park.

Getting There & Away

Local buses from Ch'ungju ply the route to Songgye-ri every 1¼ hours between 6.25 am and 5.45 pm. The journey takes 1¼ hours.

There are also four buses daily from Chech'ŏn to Songgye-ri between the hours of 7 am and 5.50 pm; the journey takes two hours and costs W2900.

TANYANG

Tanyang (population 65,000) is an up-and-

coming resort town nestled between Woraksan and Sobaeksan National Parks. It's a very relaxing place to spend a few days and there are plenty of interesting things to see and do in the area.

The town itself is completely modern; an old town of the same name was partially drowned by the waters of the Ch'ungju dam. Tanyang is actually called Shin Tanyang (New Tanyang) while the original (part of which still exists) is called Ku Tanyang (Old Tanyang).

Ch'ungju lake stretches almost all the way to Ch'ungju to the west. Like Lake Soyang, east of Ch'unch'ŏn, there are boats along the lake. There's also a very attractive bridge which connects the town to the eastern shore, where you'll find Kosu Donggul, some of Korea's most famous limestone caves, and where a very scenic route (No 595) branches off to Yŏngwol and the east coast.

Information

A tourist information kiosk (☎ 221146) is located on the eastern side of the bridge into town (on the way to Kosu Donggul), on which obviously quite a lot of money has been spent. They have precious little information other than a booklet (in Korean) containing colour photographs of places of interest in the area.

The terminal for ferries to Ch'ungju is on the lake's shore in the centre of town. It deals only with boats going to the dam wall (near Ch'ungju). You cannot pick up sightseeing boats here; they go only from Todam Sambong, a few km north of Tanyang.

The railway station is on the opposite side of the lake, over the road bridge (this is a different bridge from the one in the centre of town) about four km west of Tanyang, where the old town used to stand. Local buses run along the main road to the station at 8.05, 9, 10.15 am, noon, 2.15, 3.45, 4.30, 5.20 and 8.30 pm.

Kosu Donggul

Just across the bridge from the centre of Tanyang are some of Korea's most famous limestone caves. Koreans flock here by the

---

Woraksan National Park
월악산국립공원

1 Podŏkam Hermitage
  보덕암
2 Bus Stop
  정류장
3 Bus Stop
  정류장
4 East Gate
  동문
5 Tŏkjusa Temple
  덕주사
6 Tŏkjusa Buddha Statue
  덕주사지마애불
7 Shinruksa Temple
  신륵사
8 Bus Stop
  정류장
9 Tojŏn-ri
  도존리
10 Bus Stop
  정류장

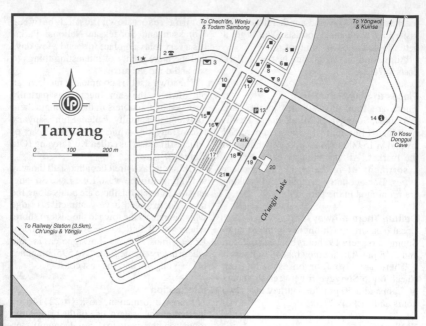

Tanyang 단양

PLACES TO STAY
4 Manli-jang Yŏgwan
    만리장여관
5 Sanho-jang Yŏgwan
    산호장여관
6 Hosusan-jang Yŏgwan
    호수산장여관
7 Yonhwabong Yŏgwan
    연화봉여관
8 Takhi Yŏinsuk
    탁희여인숙
10 Huimang Yŏinsuk
    희망여인숙
15 Taehŭng Yŏgwan
    대흥여관

18 Ch'ŏnil-jang Yŏgwan
    천일장여관
21 Lake Hotel
    라크장여관

PLACES TO EAT
9 Kunmun Shikdang
    Chinese Restaurant
    군문 중국집
16 Ace Club Pizza
    에이스클럽

OTHER
1 Police
    경찰서
2 Telephone Office
    전화국

3 Post Office
    우체국
11 Bus Stop
    정류장
12 Inter-City Bus Terminal
    시외버스터미널
13 Car Park
    주차장
14 Tourist Information Kiosk
    관광안내소
17 Central Market
    중앙시장
19 Ferry Terminal
    선착장
20 Boat Wharf
    선착장

thousands: during the summer holidays you literally cannot move for people and it takes an excruciating hour or more to walk round the system.

Kosu Donggul has spectacular and exten-

sive caves – or rather they must have been before the catwalks and miasmic spiral steel staircases were installed up the main vertical galleries. These aids to access (or was it commercial exploitation?) are thoroughly overdone. A considerable amount of vandalism is also apparent where the tips of stalactites and stalagmites are within reach of eager souvenir hunters. Nevertheless, it's perhaps worth visiting the caves if the crowds are not too great.

You should allow about one hour to get through the caves, which are about 1300m long. The entrance to the caves is obscured by an extensive tourist complex with yŏgwan, restaurants and souvenir shops. Prices here are well above average.

Ch'ŏngdong Donggul

About four km beyond Kosu Donggul, keeping left at the only road junction, is a smaller cave, Ch'ŏngdong Donggul, which is some 300m long and was only discovered in 1977. Unlike its larger cousin, which has both vertical and horizontal galleries, this cave is essentially a vertical drop. Entry costs W1200 (less for those under 24 years old).

There's the inevitable tourist village below the caves with yŏgwan, restaurants and a camp site.

There are local buses from Tanyang bus station to Ch'ŏngdong Donggul at 7.05, 8.30, 10.30, and 11.40 am, and at 12.30, 1, 1.50, 3, 3.50, 4.40, 5.40, 7 and 8 pm.

Nodong Donggul

Instead of keeping to the left at the road junction, if you turn right across the concrete bridge, continue up the hill and then down the other side, you'll arrive at a third set of caves. Nodong Donggul are the most recently discovered of the caves and are every bit as spectacular as Kosu Donggul. They're about one km in length, and there are the usual steel staircases and catwalks for access, but nowhere near the same number of people visit this cave so you don't get that feeling of claustrophobia that is possible in Kosu Donggul.

There are local buses from Tanyang to Nodong Donggul at 6.40, 8.50, 11 am, 1.40, 3.40, 5.45 and 8 pm.

Ch'ungjuho

When the water level is high (late summer),

Ch'ungjuho (Ch'ungju Lake) is an impressive body of water and a cruise can be very appealing. It's considerably less impressive in spring, when the water level drops and leaves an ugly 'bathtub ring' around the shore. Indeed, in central Tanyang the 'lake' reverts to being a river during much of the year.

All the pleasure craft are moored at Todam Sambong, about three km north of Tanyang via the lakeside road. You cannot board them at Tanyang itself because there is seldom enough water. Local buses run along the main street of Tanyang to Todam Sambong at 7.50, 10 am, 12.10, 1.30, 2.30, 5.10 and 7.40 pm. The buses will have Todam Sambong (in Korean) in the window and the journey takes about 10 minutes.

There are two varieties of boat which you can hire: speed boats taking up to six passengers, and slower open-decked boats which take many passengers.

The speed boats are good fun and the drivers really take them through their paces, but you won't have much time to take in the sights. They go when full and operate between 9.30 am and 5.10 pm. There are two options available: an eight-minute trip which visits the natural arch (Songmun) and goes around the island of Todam Sambong; and an 18-minute trip which goes down the lake as far as Tanyang then returns.

The slow boats are perhaps preferable as they are more mellow and you see far more of the sights along the lake. At least in theory, these go once an hour and operate between 9 am and 5 pm. Again, there are two options: an 18-km round trip taking nearly an hour; and a 40-km round trip that takes 2½ hours.

Places to Stay

Expect to pay around W20,000 to W30,000 for a yŏgwan, and W15,000 for a yŏinsuk. Just north and west of the bus terminal there are a couple of narrow lanes chock-a-block with yŏgwan. *Sanho-jang Yŏgwan* and *Hosusan-jang Yŏgwan* have some rooms with a sweeping view of the lake.

Another relative cheapie is the *Huimang Yŏinsuk*; it's on the top side of the main street

CH'UNGCH'ŎNGBUK-DO

near the junction with the road which crosses the bridge.

There are also scores of yŏgwan along the main street all the way down towards the bridge which leads to the railway station, but the most convenient places to stay are those between the main street and the riverside in the centre of town. Some of these places have rooms overlooking the lake, a good example being the *Ch'ŏnil-jang Yŏgwan*.

Places to Eat

As is typical in Korean resorts, you'll be tripping over restaurants every couple of metres. *Sambong Shikdang* does a mean pulgogi, or you can score excellent Chinese food at the *Kunmun Shikdang* opposite the inter-city bus terminal.

Ace Club Pizza (☎ 423-1486) will deliver right to your yŏgwan if you can make yourself understood on the telephone.

An excellent alternative to the restaurants in the evenings are the *roadside stalls* close to the ferry terminal. While not significantly cheaper than restaurants, dining outdoors on a warm summer evening is an enjoyable way to have a meal.

The two *bakeries* in the centre of town are not too good. Perhaps this will change if they get some more competition. Meanwhile, if you want some bread or pastries just buy the packaged stuff from a grocery store.

Getting There & Away

Bus The inter-city bus terminal is well-organised and even has a printed schedule of local buses. If you can read Korean and are planning on spending some time here then it's worth asking for a copy of this. Some buses which depart from the inter-city bus terminal go to the following destinations:

Andong buses depart 24 times daily between 8.55 am and 7.53 pm. The fare is W4700 and the ride takes two hours.

Chech'ŏn buses depart 71 times daily between 6.55 am and 9.15 pm. The fare is W1500 and the journey takes 50 minutes.

Ch'unch'ŏn buses depart four times daily between 8.10 am and 3 pm. The fare is W7600 and the journey takes 3¾ hours.

Kuinsa buses depart five times daily between 8.30 am and 8.30 pm. The fare is W1500 and the journey takes 45 minutes.

Pusan buses depart once daily at 9.20 am. The fare is W13,100 and the journey takes six hours.

Taegu buses depart 21 times daily between 7.50 am and 7.53 pm. The fare is W8900 and the journey takes 3¾ hours. These buses also stop in Andong.

Tong-Seoul buses depart seven times daily between 7.10 am and 7.15 pm. The fare is W7200 and the journey takes three hours.

Tonghae buses depart once daily at 1.45 pm. The fare is W13,800 and the journey takes six hours.

Train Trains from Seoul to Tanyang depart from Seoul's Ch'ŏngnyangni station. The train schedule on the Seoul-Tanyang route can be found in the appendix at the end of this book.

There are also special tourist trains which run only on weekends and holidays. These are geared towards group tours, but if you have an interest contact Ch'olma Tourist Service (☎ 393-4841) in Seoul.

Lake Ferry Ferries connect Tanyang with Ch'ungju at the western end of the lake (the dam wall is actually outside Ch'ungju but local buses connect the ferry pier to the centre of town).

The boats run between 8.30 am and 4.30 pm in summer (9.30 am to 3.30 pm in winter) and cost W8000 per person. The journey takes slightly over two hours. When the water level is down, you can catch the boats further downstream at Changhwa. This schedule is not engraved in stone, so it's prudent to have a Korean speaker ring up the Ch'ungjuho Ferry Company in Ch'ungju (☎ 851-5771) or in Seoul (☎ 532-3274) to get the latest information. There's a notice warning passengers (in English and Korean) that, 'Drinking, dancing, disturbances and demoralisation are not allowed on board'. Meals and drinks are available on these boats.

SOBAEKSAN NATIONAL PARK

Sobaeksan ('little white mountain') National Park is one of Korea's largest. It's on a par with the better-known Sŏraksan National Park, but lacks the latter's dramatic cliffs and

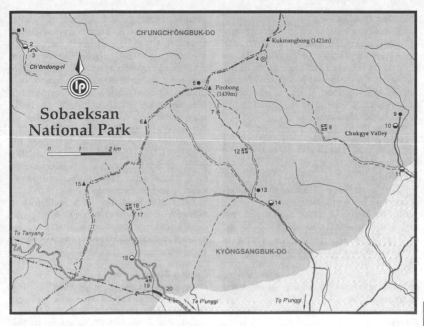

Sobaeksan National Park
소백산국립공원

1 Kŭmgok-ri
금곡리
2 Bus Stop
정류장
3 Ch'ŏndonggul Cave
천동굴
4 Spring
백호암약수
5 Redwood Grove
주목군락
6 No 1 Yŏnhwabong
(1394m)
제1연화봉

7 Piro Waterfall
비로폭포
8 Ch'oamsa Temple
소암사
9 Tŏkhyŏn-ri
덕현리
10 Bus Stop
정류장
11 Bus Stop
정류장
12 Pirosa Temple
비로사
13 Samga-dong Village
삼가동
14 Bus Stop
정류장

15 No 2 Yŏnhwabong
(1357m)
제2연화봉
16 Hŭibangsa Temple
희방사
17 Hŭibang Waterfall
희방폭포
18 Bus Stop
정류장
19 Paekryongsa Temple
백룡사
20 Hŭibang Railway Station
희방역

rock formations. Nevertheless, the park is rich in flora and offers good hiking trails through thick forests. The climbs are not particularly steep, difficult or dangerous, but certain areas of the park are periodically closed to hikers to give nature a chance to recover from human impact.

Admission to the national park costs W1100 for adults, W650 for students and W400 for children.

Climbing Routes

Sobaeksan can be approached from several different angles. Pirobong (1439m) is the highest peak and is most easily climbed from Ch'ŏndong-ri on the north-west side of the mountain. Ch'ŏndong-ri is a typical tourist village offering food, drink, accommodation, postcards, plastic toys, stuffed teddy bears and other necessities.

Besides Pirobong, other peaks worthy of note are Kukmangbong (1421m) and Yŏnhwabong (1394m).

Hŭibangsa

Hŭibang waterfall and Hŭibangsa (the adjacent temple) are in the south-west area of the park. The 28m-high waterfall is the largest in Korea. This area is also one possibility for scaling Sobaeksan. Below the temple is another tourist village offering all that is needed in life.

Hŭibang station is just four km south-west of Hŭibangsa, making feasible an approach by train.

Kuinsa

About 20 km north-east of Tanyang, off route No 595 to Yŏngwol and deep into the mountains, stands the headquarters of the Chontae sect of Korean Buddhism. This old order was re-established in 1945 by monk Sangwol Wongak. Its precepts are based on an interpretation of the Lotus Sutra made by an ancient Chinese monk named Chijang Taesa. Entirely modern (it's built in traditional Korean style but uses concrete instead of wood) the temple is conspicuously rich, and has a vast and obviously highly motivated band of devotees. This is real cult territory of the born-again kind. Devotees with name cards clipped to their shirts and dresses are very much in evidence, and that disgusting habit of smoking within temple precincts – which is permitted elsewhere – is totally prohibited here.

There are some 38 buildings at the temple, including gateways, dormitories, adminis-

tration blocks, halls dedicated to various bodhisattvas and an enormous five-storey main hall which, it is claimed, can accommodate up to 10,000 people. There's even a post office and bookshop! All these buildings are crammed into a steep, narrow and thickly wooded valley and wherever it's been necessary to contain runoff or to landscape you'll see beautiful examples of dry-stone walling. It's obvious that no effort has been spared to create the best. Indeed, no effort has been spared anywhere in this temple to produce what is a masterpiece of civil engineering, sculpture, traditional painting and landscaping.

Just below the temple is a small tourist village with restaurants, a couple of yŏgwan and a number of souvenir shops selling religious paraphernalia and ornaments made in Taiwan.

Getting There & Away

Local buses ply the route between Tanyang and Ch'ŏndong-ri about once hourly. If you get disgusted with waiting and want to take a taxi, it's about W4000 to go up to the village (regardless of the number of passengers) but only W1000 per person to return to Tanyang.

There are seven non-stop buses daily from Tanyang to Hŭibangsa between 9.40 am and 7 pm, taking 40 minutes for the journey. Local buses also run from P'unggi (in Kyŏngsangbuk-do) to Hŭibangsa every 30 minutes between 6.30 am and 7.10 pm, taking 30 minutes for the ride. And there are also 21 local buses daily from Yŏngju (also in Kyŏngsangbuk-do) to Hŭibangsa between 6.30 am and 7.10 pm which take 30 minutes for the journey.

Kuinsa is approached by a totally different road. There are five express plus 14 local buses daily from Tanyang to Kuinsa between 5.40 am and 8.30 pm, and the journey takes 40 minutes. There are also 13 buses daily from Chech'ŏn to Kuinsa, running between 7.10 am and 5.40 pm.

North Korea

More than 100 years ago Korea was known as the 'Hermit Kingdom' because it tried to shut out the rest of the world. These days South Korea is an open and modern nation, but in the North both the terms 'Hermit' and 'Kingdom' apply – in strange and novel ways.

While most other formerly hardline communist countries are opening up to market-based economic systems and some semblance of political pluralism, North Korea remains devoutly mired in a unique and highly organised way of life. No other country in the world maintains such a closed, rigid system.

This may not sound like a traveller's paradise. Indeed, it is entirely possible that North Korea hosts fewer foreign tourists than any other country on earth (just a few hundred per year). And those who do manage a visit are restricted to seeing certain places and must be accompanied by a government-employed tour guide at all times. Visitors also find that they are subjected to non-stop propaganda which borders on the comical; the 'US imperialist aggressors' and 'South Korean puppet stooges' are the favourite themes. And finally, all this costs plenty – North Korea is one of the most expensive countries to visit.

So why go? Simply put, North Korea is fascinating. Tourists are drawn to this country out of pure curiosity. Furthermore, it's an education you aren't likely to forget; many travellers have commented that their visit to North Korea was easily their most memorable journey. When asked to sum up their impressions of the country, visitors come up with phrases such as 'a Stalinist theme park', 'a dictatorship *par excellence* ' or 'too surreal to be believable'. On the other hand, North Korea contains stunningly beautiful mountains surrounded by verdant rural regions that have hardly been touched by commercial tourism.

Some travellers come away from North

HIGHLIGHTS

- ◆ P'yŏngyang, the national capital, with its larger-than-life monuments to the late Great Leader

- ◆ The Kŭmgang and Myohyang mountain areas, which offer spectacular and pristine scenery

- ◆ The northern side of P'anmunjŏn, your last chance to see the Cold War at full freeze

Korea impressed by the cleanliness and orderliness of the society. Many come away horrified. But the big question is whether or not you'll be able to go at all.

North Korea periodically opens and closes its doors to foreign tourists – the only thing predictable about it is its unpredictability. The country is in a desperate financial situation and badly needs every bit of hard currency that tourists bring. But at the same time North Korea is the world's most xenophobic country. All foreign tourists are regarded as potential spies and saboteurs.

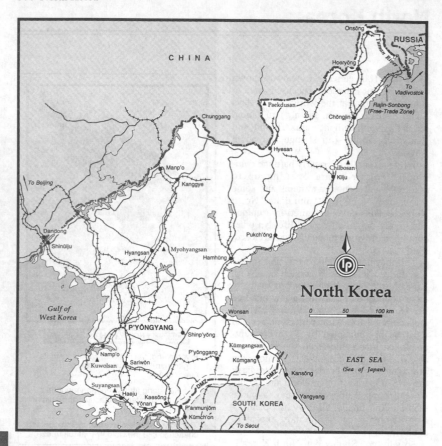

The government is especially paranoid that tourists might try to 'pollute' the people's minds with foreign ideas like free enterprise and democracy.

One might have thought the opening up of eastern Europe and the former Soviet Union would have encouraged some sort of reform efforts in North Korea, but the opposite has happened. Fearing similar unrest, the dictatorship has cracked down harder politically and threatened to resume the Korean War, while making only a few grudging and ineffective attempts at economic reform.

The recent absence of visible leadership, along with two summers in a row of heavy flooding resulting in severe food shortages, have put the survival of the regime in grave doubt. Predictions by journalists and others of a sudden catastrophic collapse have become all too common. More worryingly, some feel the regime would prefer to go down in flames rather than be peacefully taken over by the South – thus a renewed Korean War becomes a frightening if still unlikely possibility. So, 'see it while you can'!

Tourists hoping to get a glimpse of this unique country are officially welcome. They must keep in mind, however, that sudden crises caused by military, diplomatic or natural factors (all increasingly common these days) may force the cancellation of plans with little or no advance notice.

Facts about the Country

HISTORY
The North Korean Version
See the South Korean section of this book for general Korean history before 1945. An additional theme that is important for the traveller to remember is that the northern Koreans have a history of grievance against the southerners; their current troubles and attitudes are not as Cold War modern as one might think. They have felt politically oppressed, economically exploited and socially looked-down upon by the southerners for over 1300 years; a significant factor in the background to the past 50 years of national division and acrimony.

In 668, the far-south-eastern Shilla Kingdom, in alliance with Tang China, conquered the more sophisticated northern Koguryŏ Kingdom (the northern half of the peninsula and most of Manchuria), losing most of Koguryŏ lands to China in the process. From the northern point of view, this was only the first of a long string of betrayals of the Korean nation to foreign powers by southerners acting for their own benefit. Shilla proceeded to oppressively rule what remained of Koguryŏ for 250 years, sowing seeds of resentment that still bloom today. The subsequent Koryŏ dynasty was founded by a general of north-central origins, and some northern families gained importance in its government, but for the most part southern clans continued socio-economic dominance.

Northerners felt especially mistreated throughout the Chosŏn dynasty (1392-1910), when they were ruled by a clan from Chŏlla-do and their mostly southern cronies in an openly subservient relationship to China. Northerners had less chances to advance to the ruling classes and bore the brunt of frequent raids and invasions from Manchuria; in return for their onerous tax payments they saw very few benefits from the capital. Being less mountainous, warmer and better-watered, the south was naturally wealthier in an economy based on rice. Little was ever done to redress the imbalance or pull the northern populace back from the brink of starvation during frequent famines. The government only seemed to acknowledge the worth of the taller, stronger and tougher northern mountain-dwellers when they needed soldiers to fight off another 'barbarian' incursion.

During the 'Hermit Kingdom' phase of Chosŏn, one of Korea's first encounters with westerners was the ill-fated attempt of the American ship *General Sherman* to sail up the Taedong River to P'yŏngyang in 1866. It arrogantly ignored warnings to turn around and leave, insisted on trade, carried a Protestant missionary who illegally proselytised, and repeatedly abused riverside inhabitants. When it ran aground on a sand-bar just below P'yŏngyang, locals burnt it to the waterline and killed all on board. Although an American military expedition later pressed the Seoul government for reparations for these losses (and after that, this incident was otherwise virtually forgotten in the south) the northerners have always regarded it with great pride as their first of many battles with and victories over the hated Yankee imperialist enemy.

At the end of Chosŏn, after it opened up to foreign involvement, almost the only successful western economic venture was a large gold mine north of P'yŏngyang. By providing difficult and dangerous jobs for northern workers at very low wages, and sending all profits to Seoul and abroad, it came to be seen as foreign theft of the north's resources, sanctioned by the south. At the same time, American Christian missionaries found the northern regions to be fertile soil, rapidly gaining converts by exploiting the resentment of poor northerners against the corrupt and exclusive Confucian culture of the capital.

The Japanese imperial conquest of Korea

(1905-1945) was, in northern eyes, the result of yet another sellout of the national sovereignty by corrupt southern officials. Most of the guerrilla warfare conducted against the Japanese police and army happened in the northern provinces and neighbouring Manchuria; northerners are still proud of having carried a disproportionate burden in the struggle against Japan. In fact, modern history books from P'yŏngyang imply that Kim Il-sung defeated the Japanese nearly single-handedly (with a bit of help from loyal comrades and his infant son).

During the occupation the south remained mostly agricultural (and better-fed), while Japan partially industrialised the northern regions by exploiting their hydropower, logging and mining potential. This fostered a semi-urbanised, harshly-treated industrial working class in the north. This new class and the hungry farmers, both already primed to hopeful idealism by evangelical Protestantism, became fertile soil for another foreign ideology – Marxism.

The Democratic People's Republic

North Korea's history as a separate political entity begins from the end of WWII. The USA, the UK and the USSR had made a deal shortly after the Yalta Conference in the closing days of the war – the USSR was to temporarily occupy Korea north of the 38th parallel, while the USA would occupy the south, with the purpose of disarming surrendered Japanese troops and sending them home. This 'temporary' partitioning was also done to Germany, with the same tragic result.

Stalin sent a young Korean officer who called himself Kim Il-sung from a specially-trained unit of the Soviet Red Army to take charge of rapidly communising the north. 'Kim Il-sung' was the name of a famous anti-Japanese fighter in the 1910-1930 era who had disappeared in Manchuria; this officer (whose family name is believed to have originally been Kim) apparently borrowed the famous name (and exploits) to give himself instant legitimacy as a post-colonial leader.

This ambitious and ruthless man steadily ascended to the head of a separate government in North Korea, in defiance of the United Nations plan for nationwide democratic elections. In February 1946 a de facto separate northern administration, called the Interim People's Committee, was established in P'yŏngyang with quiet Soviet backing. It was initially comprised of communist, socialist and moderate figures, but Kim Il-sung was able to take full control and force the moderates out in less than a year. He created the pro-Soviet and revolutionary communist Korean Worker's Party as his personal political vehicle, and police and military forces to defend his takeover and implement his revolution. These institutions evolved into a government during 1947-48.

In May 1948 the South went ahead with UN-sponsored elections when the North refused to let UN personnel enter their territory. Negotiations failed to resolve the problem, and the temporary division became permanent because neither side was willing to yield; the higher population of the South would have ensured victory for the US-installed southern authorities. Elections were held in the north on 25 August 1948 in response to the southern elections and in September 1948 the Democratic People's Republic of Korea (DPRK) was proclaimed as the only legitimate government on the peninsula. Kim Il-sung took formal office as Prime Minister.

Both the USA and USSR had pulled most of their troops out of Korea by the end of 1948. However, the Soviets left their heavy equipment behind and gave Kim Il-sung other military assistance. On 25 June 1950, while US military aid to the southern government was still on the drawing boards and the US State Department was sending out signals that it had little further interest in Korea, the North Korean army invaded.

The Korean War

The North Koreans swiftly pushed the South Korean police forces (not much of an army yet) into a tiny enclave around Pusan. Under US prompting, the United Nations passed a resolution calling for other countries to send in troops to halt the aggression. The war effort took a dramatic turn when a 16-nation UN army, led by the legendary WWII General Douglas MacArthur, landed behind enemy lines at Inch'ŏn on 15 September. Within days they recaptured Seoul, cutting the enemy's supply lines; within a month they had routed the North Koreans, pushing them back to the Chinese border.

Fortunes changed again when China's Mao Zedong decided to support the North Korean effort in response to Kim Il-sung's pleas (Stalin had declined), sending in 180,000 Chinese 'volunteers'. UN forces were pushed back again to the 38th parallel. The war continued as a bloody stalemate in the centre of the peninsula while negotiations for a truce dragged on for two years.

During the entire war the US Army Air Force relentlessly bombed northern territory in an unsuccessful attempt to force a surrender; they targeted anything and everything, military or civilian. P'yŏngyang claims that by the end there was hardly a building left standing in all the North; their citizens and soldiers became accustomed to living underground and eating scraps. This bombing campaign was in fact heavier than either Japan or Germany had endured in WWII. The North Koreans still recall it with deep bitterness as a war crime.

In 1953 the war ended with a negotiated ceasefire treaty, signed only by P'yŏngyang, Beijing and the UN Forces (led by Washington, of course); Seoul refused to sign out of anger that America 'had not finished the job' of complete reunification. The Korean peninsula remained divided, split by the Demilitarised Zone (DMZ). The Korean War resulted in over two million deaths, a million separated families and the devastation of the economies and infrastructure of both countries – but with no political resolution at all.

North Korea, which refers to this conflict as the 'Fatherland Liberation War', gives a different account of how the Korean War started. Your guide and others may tell you repeatedly that American soldiers attacked them massively with tanks and bombers, but they – with no military preparation and fighting with sticks and rocks – defeated the invasion and massively counter-attacked into the South, finally attaining a great victory. One pamphlet, *An Earthly Paradise for the People*, has this to say about the war:

The US imperialists, who had boasted of being the strongest in the world, frantically pounced upon the Korean people in league with the south Korean puppet army plus the troops of 15 satellite countries.

However, the American imperialists who were assured of a glorious victory in this grim war were covered all over with wounds and surrendered to the heroic Korean people. As a result, the Korean people and their young People's Army held a military parade in honour of their victory in the presence of President Kim Il-sung, the ever-victorious and iron-willed brilliant commander.

This was a great victory and natural outcome attained under the wise leadership of the great President Kim Il-sung

Post-war Standoff

Using Stalinist-style purges, Kim Il-sung's one-man dictatorship evolved steadily out of the wartime collective leadership installed by the Soviets. In the first 10 post-war years the North Korean economy actually developed quite rapidly, building Soviet-style heavy industry on the foundations the Japanese had laid. North Korean people had some of their first schools, clinics, food reserves, labor rights and recreation facilities; life greatly improved for those not considered 'class enemies', while mortality rates nosedived. Development was much faster, and friendlier to common people, than in the South during those early days.

The *Juche* (self-reliance) ideology that Kim Il-sung created and installed as his nation's complete and only guiding thought never meant that he would refuse aid from Moscow and Beijing. In fact he used it quite successfully to play them off against each other, gaining massive assistance while maintaining independence from both – something no other country managed to do, except perhaps Albania. Meanwhile the Kim personality cult was rising; soon it began to rival that of Mao Zedong, and then it surpassed Mao by canonising most of Kim Il-sung's family too – especially his parents, ancestors and oldest son Jong-il. As just one example, Kim's great-grandfather was declared by North Korean historians to have been the leader of those who massacred the crew of the American ship *General Sherman* in 1866.

Constant provocation by the North and hard-line responses by the South have kept relations between them at the subzero level for nearly 50 years now. 'Negotiations' have mostly been exercises in rhetoric. Incidents of terrorism, assassination and armed incursion into the DMZ have bedevilled the South for decades, though P'yŏngyang consistently and angrily denies having anything to do with them.

North Korea's position regarding the USA and the present South Korean government is well summed up in the following quote from *Women of Korea* (1991, vol 2), a magazine published in P'yŏngyang:

The US imperialists have stationed more than 40,000 troops and more than 1000 nuclear weapons in south Korea, and they, with the nearly one million puppet troops, are preparing an invasion against north Korea...Their aim is to create 'two Koreas', to divide Korea permanently and to continuously occupy south Korea as their colony and, using south Korea as a bridgehead, to make an invasion of north Korea and the other countries of Asia.

Cold War Continues

The disintegration of the Communist bloc has left North Korea with very few friends. The former USSR established diplomatic relations with South Korea in 1990 and cut off most of its aid to the North. China followed suit in 1992, although it continues to grant small amounts of economic aid (and permits lots of cross-border smuggling) to keep their old ally afloat. Both Russia and China now trade far more with the South than with the North, and regularly exchange friendly diplomatic meetings at the highest levels. P'yŏngyang has reacted angrily and spitefully to these moves, and neither China nor Russia has been able to moderate the DPRK's recent behaviour.

In early 1991, the International Atomic Energy Agency (IAEA) declared that North Korea was suspected of developing nuclear weapons at its reactor near Yŏngbyŏn, north of P'yŏngyang. P'yŏngyang denied this but refused IAEA inspections, counter-claiming that the USA had over 1000 nuclear warheads based in the South. The crisis slowly escalated all year long until the USA surprised North Korea by withdrawing all nuclear weapons from the Korean Peninsula; those based elsewhere are now considered sufficient deterrent. Western military sources say that North Korea is developing long-range missiles and possesses huge quantities of chemical and biological weapons, with the potential to kill millions if ever launched against the South.

In spite of this tense international atmosphere, 1991 actually saw the first signs of a thaw in the icy relations between the two Koreas. Their prime ministers held high-level talks in P'yŏngyang and Seoul, which implicitly recognised each other's governments for the first time ever. To the great surprise of the rest of the world, they signed a non-aggression accord at the end of the year, providing for mutual nuclear inspections and various civilian exchanges. Optimists began to talk of the possibility of peaceful reunification of the peninsula.

In the end it was the pessimists who proved correct. An inspection team from the International Atomic Energy Agency (IAEA) was denied access to North Korean nuclear facilities in January 1993. Further pressure from IAEA caused P'yŏngyang to announce in March that it would withdraw from the Nuclear Non-Proliferation Treaty; they had already refused to implement their 1991 accord with South Korea. Negotiations accomplished nothing, with P'yŏngyang demanding the total withdrawal of US military forces from the Korean peninsula as the price of co-operation on the nuclear issue, while insisting that their nuclear reactors are for peaceful purposes only.

North Korea's apparent ambitions in nuclear weaponry brought harsh condemnation from the rest of the world. P'yŏngyang countered with threats, which resulted in a statement from US President Bill Clinton that a military strike from the North would result in 'the end of North Korea'. Even relations with China, North Korea's one remaining friend, deteriorated. A watered-down statement was issued by the United Nations in the spring of 1994, with Chinese co-operation, calling on North Korea to comply with the IAEA's nuclear safeguards. P'yŏngyang rejected the statement. World media speculated whether the two Koreas were sliding towards another 'inevitable' war.

A Rising Son
On 29 June 1994, after a personal visit by former American President Jimmy Carter, Kim Il-sung surprised everyone with an announcement that he would freeze North Korea's nuclear program and would meet with South Korean President Kim Young-sam for summit talks. The talks never happened because Kim Il-sung died of a heart attack on 8 July, after ruling the North for 46 years. A new era of greater uncertainty began.

Kim Il-sung (the 'Great Leader') had long planned that power should be passed to his son, Kim Jong-il (the 'Dear Leader'). Dynastic succession runs counter to Marxist theory

Kim Il-sung – North Korea's 'Great Leader'

– and this is the first such case in a communist society. If one is to believe the North Korean news media, Kim Junior has indeed smoothly assumed power, with no opposition from other possible contenders to the throne. However, many observers doubt this official line. The fact that Kim Junior has not assumed his father's title has left many wondering if he really is in power, or simply a figurehead.

Little is actually known about Kim Jong-il, but all accounts from the few who have met him indicate that he lacks the charisma of his father. Kim Junior is never seen publicly, not even for official functions held in his honour. He showed up for his father's funeral, but kept silent, looked dazed and feeble and made no statement. There is much speculation that he is in poor health or somehow handicapped; western intelligence reports indicate that he is heavily introverted and devotes much of his time to watching foreign videos. In the more than two years since the funeral, he has rarely been seen in public and has never given a public speech. He has yet to meet any foreign head of state and has not visited any other country since his father's death. As the North Korean economy sinks by an average 5% per year, and food and energy shortages grow ever more severe, the nation stumbles along without visible or consistent leadership.

Now What?
In the past three years the flow of refugees and defectors escaping from North Korea to Russia, China or other nations has noticeably increased, averaging maybe one person per week by 1996, from high-level diplomats to common fishermen. The policy of the Russian government is to permit North Korean defectors to leave the country as they wish. Those North Koreans who escape to China are sometimes not so lucky – the Chinese government has 'repatriated' some to horrific fates, such as torture and execution. China is now reportedly building a huge refugee camp outside Yanji near the border, to hold the soon-expected flood of starving refugees. Some South Korean churches have

established aid centres in North-East China close to the border to give aid to escapers. South Korea is reluctant to take in and support all these refugees, and recently has been reforming its laws on defectors to cope with the increasing flow.

As we go to press there are further signs of serious divisions of opinion within whatever group is now leading North Korea. In mid-September 1996 a UN-sponsored seminar for potential foreign investors (also attended by some foreign journalists and officials) was held in the Rajin-Sonbong 'Free Trade Zone'. This indicated a desire for economic reform and to 'open up'. But at the last minute, the invitation to half the South Korean delegation was revoked by the North Koreans, causing the other half to cancel. This indicated an absence of desire both for reconciliation with the South and for general involvement with the world. The industrial conglomerates of the South are most willing to invest in the DPRK, for obvious reasons; Japanese companies are No 2 and those of all other countries come in a distant third – most are waiting for the South Korean concerns to go in first and literally pave the way.

Relations between the two Koreas plummeted again in late 1996 after a North Korean submarine carrying heavily-armed commandos beached in Kangnŭng (South Korea). Firefights between the commandos and South Korean troops left several South Koreans dead. After a massive manhunt all the surviving commandos were killed or captured in the Odaesan area. Conservative politicians and social leaders in the South have called for a tougher policy against the North, and Seoul has suspended all food and energy aid efforts. South Korean and American troops resumed limited military exercises in late 1996 (previously suspended to improve relations with the North).

North Korea's true situation and intentions remain closely watched and intensely speculated upon. In 1997 the defection of a high-ranking North Korean caused much tension in the region, but anyone who tells you that they know what's *really* going on up there is either a fool or a liar. It's not even certain that the North Koreans know what their next move will be. The world can only watch and wait as the next act of the Korean drama unfolds.

The Price of Reunification

You would be hard-pressed to find anybody in Korea who does not support reunification of their divided country. Indeed, if there is anything that both North and South Korea can agree on, it is the 'burning desire of the Korean people for reunification'. Furthermore, every Korean agrees that the sooner the country can reunify, the better.

Or do they? Having witnessed the great financial burden that the former West Germany has incurred while absorbing the East, many South Koreans have started to ask just how much the family reunion is going to cost them. This question has sent economists scurrying for their computers and the price sticker they've come up with has raised more than a few eyebrows.

All figures are rough estimates, but it is thought that the cost of absorbing North Korea into the South Korean economy will require up to US$250 billion in direct government handouts, plus perhaps US$1 trillion in private investment. The high figures have much to do with the fact that North Korea is in far worse financial shape than the former East Germany ever was. And this is to say nothing of the potential social problems if millions of northern economic refugees pour into the South to search for better-paying jobs.

While you won't find many South Koreans opposing reunification, as it approaches many seem to be having second thoughts about its consequences. Even if the P'yŏngyang regime collapses, maybe that electric fence on the DMZ should be kept in place just a little bit longer? Southern politicians have indicated that the creation of one Korean nation out of the two may be 'too expensive' for now and should be postponed until some unspecified time in the future. Many youths now agree, openly saying that they don't want to pay the price. ∎

GEOGRAPHY

North Korea occupies 55% of the land area on the Korean peninsula. It is divided from China to the north by the Amnok (Amur) and Tuman (Tumen) Rivers, and from a sliver of Russia to the extreme north-east. The DMZ and an electrified fence mark the border with South Korea.

North Korea is estimated to be 80% uninhabitable mountains, compared to 70% for the South. The northern and eastern regions are mostly rugged mountains with dense forests, and are not well suited for agriculture. Resources include great mineral wealth (soft coal, iron, magnesium and a little gold), vast forests of both hardwoods and softwoods, hydropower sites and fisheries. Estuaries and marshes teem with migratory birds and other wildlife.

CLIMATE

The weather is similar to South Korea's, only colder and drier in winter. There are four distinct seasons. Autumn is the best time to visit, when there is crisp, dry weather and a chance to see the leaves changing colour. More than 60% of the annual rainfall falls from July to September. The average monthly temperatures and rainfall in P'yŏngyang are given in the climate chart below.

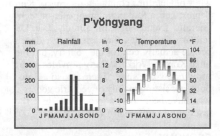

ECOLOGY & ENVIRONMENT

North Korea is interesting to compare to the South. While South Korea suffers from some serious environmental problems, there is little visible pollution in the North. The one thing which strikes most visitors to North Korea is its squeaky-clean appearance. This is not just because of a lack of consumer goods and packaging; official policies keep it that way: the streets are washed down twice a week and before dawn each day street cleaners are out sweeping up any litter or leaves they can find. You'd be hard pressed to find a single piece of paper on the streets despite the absence of litter bins. Even in the countryside, women are assigned a particular stretch of the main road to sweep up – each and every day.

The other major contrast is the lack of vehicular traffic. Most of what you'll see will be army vehicles. There are very few passenger cars. North Korea does not manufacture cars and must import all its vehicles. As a result, there's nothing remotely like the traffic congestion and exhaust pollution which now characterises many South Korean cities.

GOVERNMENT & POLITICS

The country's official name is the Democratic People's Republic of Korea (DPRK). The P'yŏngyang government has divided the republic into nine provinces and five 'Special Cities' (under direct control of the national government), exactly the same as in South Korea. The southern government holds to the pre-war view that North Korea consists of just five provinces (with no Special Cities), and so maps of North Korea made by the two sides look quite different (P'yŏngyang acknowledges the divisions of the South as the southern authorities have drawn them).

The reason for the expansion of northern administrative units to match those of the South (assuming it's not just a coincidence...) is to support North Korea's reunification proposals: P'yŏngyang proposes that it and the Seoul government share power equally through indirect democracy; having an equal number of provinces and special cities makes the two nations appear politically equivalent even though the population of the South is double the North's. Seoul rejects this administrative-division equivalence and insists on a whole-nation direct democracy

NORTH KOREA

Red Faces Over Running Dog

By early 1997 cracks were beginning to show in North Korea's once inscrutable facade and all bets were off in the perpetual game of brinkmanship. In February North Korea's top ideologue, Hwang Jang- yop, defected while in Beijing. Hwang and an aide sought asylum at the South Korean embassy just four days before the official celebration of the Dear Leader's Birthday back in P'yŏngyang, causing diplomatic embarrassment and tension around the region.

His defection placed Beijing in an awkward position between an old ally and bilateral trade with South Korea – worth US$20 billion per year. The US, which has 37,000 troops stationed on the peninsula, is watching the situation closely; attempts to defuse the North Korean nuclear program may be unravelled by Kim Jong-il's loss of face. Understandably, South Korea was nervous that P'yŏngyang's displeasure could have grave consequences, and on 15 February North Korean agents shot another prominent defector living in Seoul. But in a surprise statement three days later the Dear Leader said 'Those who are cowards, go if they want to go'. Both the US and Seoul have responded to P'yŏngyang's magnanimity with promises of increased food aid to the North.

It is no exaggeration to say Hwang was one of the men who ran North Korea: he was in charge of international relations in the North Korean Workers' Party and had accompanied the Great Leader on a visit to Beijing a few years previously. His was the first defection at such a high level.

Hwang claims he was motivated by the best of intentions and hoped his defection could save the North from war and famine. In a stunning display of candour, he dismissed left-wing demonstrators in Seoul as naive radicals. In his own words: 'How can there be a socialist society when [North Korea's] people, workers, peasants and intellectuals are dying of starvation?' ■

(in which the southerners would have an overwhelming advantage).

Kim Il-sung totally dominated the politics of North Korea from 1948 until his death in 1994. If anyone's personality cult outshone that of Stalin or Mao Zedong, then it was Kim Il-sung's. Huge statues and portraits of him litter North Korean cities, villages and parks; every home, store and office has pictures of him and his son mounted on the wall. Not only was his word considered as the Will of Heaven, but children are taught to sing hymns to him daily. He is still referred to as 'Our National Father, Who Shines On Us Like the Sun', 'Ever-Victorious Marshall', 'the Greatest Genius the World Has Ever Known', and so on.

His death has created a vacuum. Kim Il-sung ruled supremely and Kim Jong-il was expected to inherit the country. Confucian-style mourning for his father has now been semi-officially invoked to explain why Kim Jong-il has stayed out of sight and left the positions of President and Chairman of the Worker's Party vacant for more than two years. He is said to have thus 'achieved a new standard of morality that surpasses even our ancestors'. Recent slogans have transferred

the title of 'Great Leader' to Kim Jong-il and proclaimed that 'Kim Jong-il is the same as Kim Il-sung', a rather heavy-handed attempt to pass the mantle. No one knows to what extent the elite, the common people and, especially, the military accept the charisma-challenged Kim Junior as their leader.

As far as any outsider can understand North Korea's political system, its government continues as a closely-knit affair. It consists of Kim Jong-il and various relatives; a few old hardline comrades-in-arms of Kim Senior; and a few more pragmatic or technocratic friends of Kim Junior. The US military speculates that less than a dozen people actually control the country, but the huge Korean Workers' Party provides a sort of 'window-dressing'. There is also a Politburo, consisting mainly of geriatric generals who have been locked into office since the last Party Congress in 1980.

ECONOMY

Market freedom does not officially exist here, although elements of a barter capitalist underground economy have appeared in the past few years as the mainstream economy has steadily shrunk.

The nominally-Marxist centralised command economy established after 1945 has been distorted well beyond former Soviet Bloc levels by the additional imposition upon it of Kim Il-sung's ideology of Juche (self-reliance). The 40-year attempt at isolationist self-sufficiency resulted in the country spurning overseas aid and trade, especially from or with the west. Instead, North Korea has poured resources into the military, heavy industry and grandiose monuments and statues of the Great Leader – all at the expense of agriculture and consumer goods.

The ironic result of these policies is what has been called the world's most heavily industrialised nation – is estimated that an astounding 60% of North Korea's workforce is employed in industry (the Soviet Union at its peak had only 40%, while developed western countries average 20% or less).

Unfortunately, steel and bricks are not edible and heavy industry depends on input such as fuel and materials, which have grown steadily scarcer. Industry has been in a steep decline since subsidies from the former USSR ended in 1990. Nevertheless, the latest statistics from P'yŏngyang indicate an annual growth rate of about 1.5%. Credible outside sources claim the economy is now shrinking at a rate of at least 5% per year, though it is hard to see how the economy can decline much further since it is already close to subsistence-level. Severe energy shortages have led to the closure of more than half of all factories. The last furnace in their largest steel mill was shut down in March 1996. The North's total annual foreign trade equals less than four days' worth of South Korea's trade.

Catastrophic flooding in the summers of 1995 and 1996 ruined grain crops and destroyed prime agricultural land, resulting in widespread malnutrition; even soldiers are thought to be desperately short of food. Grain rations are reported to have sunk to 200g per person per day (the UN-set minimum is 500g) and that is often only coarse corn or millet. While the party elite remain well-fed, ordinary citizens have been reduced to foraging the hills for weeds to make soup, and hand-forging bits of scrap metal to make household and garden tools.

Officially unacknowledged, apparently unregulated markets have sprung up in the heart of major cities and towns, devoted as much to barter of food-for-goods as to cash sales. Your guide may deny their existence at first, but if you find one it seems all right for you to walk around. There are even some street vendors now; and travelling traders (mostly Korean-Chinese) are becoming a common sight in the far-northern provinces, often accepting household goods and clothing in exchange for Chinese-grown food.

North Korea owes more than US$8 billion in defaulted loans to European and Japanese banks – the country borrowed the money for manufacturing joint-ventures in the 1970s, then abruptly abrogated the contracts, kept the technology and simply refused to repay. As a result, North Korea cannot borrow additional funds for development projects, nor will most countries trade with it on anything other than a cash or barter basis. As for exports, the North has little to sell except for weapons (Africa has proven to be a particularly good market). North Korean artworks and antiques, some of 'national treasure' quality, have been quietly appearing for sale in Beijing and other cities of China.

In the early 90s North Korea passed a number of encouraging foreign investment laws, such as the Foreign Enterprise Act, which made it legal for wholly-owned foreign companies to set up operations in authorised 'free-trade zones'. To this end, zones were established with UN sponsorship in far north-eastern Korea along the Tuman River bordering Russia and China (called the Rajin-Sonbong region) and at Namp'o on the west coast. So far they have failed to attract much interest from foreign companies. Most South Korean companies have been excluded, although so far they are the only ones willing to make serious investments.

POPULATION & PEOPLE

The population is approximately 24 million – about half the population of the South. The government has encouraged population growth, which in 1990 was estimated at 2.1% per annum. There are serious concerns that this growth may now be slowing because of a rise in infant mortality.

You need never be in doubt as to whether someone is a North Korean or not. Everybody, young or old, at home or abroad, wears a small metal badge with the face of the 'Great Leader' on it, surrounded by a colour-coded rim indicating the wearer's social rank. There is no sign yet of these being replaced with 'Dear Leader' badges.

You won't see any minority groups; Korea is ethnically almost completely homogeneous.

ARTS

One thing you must say for Kim Il-sung – he promoted traditional Korean arts and culture, though his motives for doing so are debatable. Kim was a fierce nationalist who relentlessly emphasised the superiority of Korean culture: North Koreans are told they are ethnically superior, that their country is the best in the world and that Kim Il-sung was the greatest man that ever lived. The focus on Korea's cultural superiority reinforces the late Kim's position as 'the greatest leader of all time' and also helps divert attention from North Korea's serious economic problems.

Whatever ulterior motives the regime might have, tourists with an interest in traditional arts stand to benefit, and visits to performances of traditional Korean music, singing and dance can be arranged easily. Some even argue that in terms of traditional culture the North is the 'real Korea'. Exhibitions of traditional or modern-style pottery, sculpture, painting and architecture can be viewed upon request, and your guide will take you to films or theatre performances for a reasonable extra charge.

RELIGION

For Korea's general religious background before this century see the section on Religion in the South Korean Facts about the Country chapter.

In North Korea, all traditional religion is regarded according to Marxist theory as an expression of a 'feudal mentality', an obsolete superstitious force opposing political revolution, social liberation, economic development and national independence. Therefore, it has been effectively proscribed since the 1950s.

Christianity

By the end of the Chosŏn dynasty, the P'yŏngyang area and some other parts of northern Korea were the most successful centres for American Protestant missionary work. For centuries northerners had resented their relative poverty and oppression by the South; this made them more susceptible than the southerners to the missionary appeals to abandon traditional Buddhist, Confucian and Shamanist beliefs in favour of a relatively 'foreign' religion. The Protestants' belief in the essential equality of all human beings was a revolutionary notion in Korea; northerners were growing ripe for revolt, not only against foreign occupation but also the Neo-Confucian elitism, stagnation and corruption that were bringing it about.

P'yŏngyang was the epicentre of the 'Great Revival' of 1907 and the origin of the subsequent nationwide 'Million Member Movement'. These fevered evangelical outbreaks were partly an emotional response to the surrender of Korea's sovereignty to Japan in 1905; but regardless of cause they resulted in a heavy concentration of Christians in northern areas.

Until Kim Il-sung arrived from Russia, that is. The near total suppression of religion and traditional customs that he imposed from 1946 onwards led to an exodus of Christians – especially priests, ministers and lay leaders – to the South before and during the Korean War. Many of those who would not or could not flee were either summarily executed or died in hard-labour prison camps. One result of this was a strong anti-communist and anti-Kim Il-sung passion in South Korean Christian churches that persisted until the early 1990s.

Showcase Christians and churches have been exhibited to foreign visitors in the past five years in an effort to claim that North

Koreans enjoy religious freedom. These are part of a general strategy to head off human-rights accusations and woo sympathisers in the west. However, reporters and delegations of Christian visitors have noticed that the displayed churches, bibles and hymnals show few signs of use and the introduced 'Christians' seem remarkably unencumbered by biblical knowledge or doctrines.

Traditional Religions

The northern version of Korean Shamanism was individualistic and ecstatic, while the southern style was hereditary and based on regularly-scheduled community rituals. As far as is known, no Shamanist activity is now practiced in North Korea. Many northern shamans – and their enemies the Christians – have fled to the south, chased out along with the enduring popularity of the services they offer (such as fortune-telling). The near-destruction of Shamanism in South Korea by relentless modernisation has meant that only northern Korean Shamanist practices can now be witnessed in the South.

There were many important centres of Korean Buddhism in northern Korea from the 3rd century through the Japanese occupation. The Kŭmgangsan and Myohyangsan mountain areas hosted large Zen-oriented (Chogye) temple complexes left over from the Koryŏ dynasty. Buddhism in the north (along with Confucianism and Shamanism) suffered a fate identical to that previously described for Christianity.

Some important Buddhist temples and shrines still exist, mostly in rural or mountainous areas. The most prominent are the P'yohŏn temple at Kŭmgangsan; the Pohyŏn temple at Myohyangsan; and the Sŏng-gyungwan Confucian Shrine just outside of Kaesŏng. Most function only as tourist attractions or museums today, but many of the traditional arts associated with them are still practised. Most temples or shrines that a foreign traveller will be able see have been renovated to their original colourful state.

LANGUAGE

This is essentially the same as that of South Korea, but the North has developed a sharply different accent and vocabulary which has been influenced by China and Russia rather than Japan and America. It's getting a bit difficult for citizens of both sides to understand each other's casual speech. Very few people in North Korea outside of government service speak English or any other foreign language.

Facts for the Visitor

PLANNING
When to Go

North Korea's winters are long and Siberian-cold, but don't come for the ski resorts because there aren't any. Summers are generally hot, sticky and rainy. The best months to visit are May, June, September and October.

What to Bring

There is a shortage of basic consumer items. Bring everything you think you'll need, especially pharmaceutical items such as medicine, shaving cream, tampons and deodorant. Korean men smoke like chimneys and foreign cigarettes make good gifts; Marlboro reds are especially valued since they are not available in North Korea. If you can bring a Polaroid camera, instant photos make a great gift for the North Koreans you meet.

TOURIST OFFICES

Ryohaengsa, the government tourist agency, is also known as the Korea International Tourist Bureau. For information on their domestic and international offices see the Visas & Documents and Organised Tours sections following.

VISAS & DOCUMENTS

North Korea began to accept group tourism in 1986 and individual western travellers in 1989 (although their version of 'individual travel' requires the 24-hour escort of a government tour guide). Unfortunately, at the time of writing US passport holders were not being given tourist visas at all. All other nationalities (except South Korean) seem to be OK. It's still possible for anyone to get a business visa – those willing to invest in joint ventures are especially welcome.

To do it on your own, your best bet is to directly approach the tourism office in the North Korean embassy in Beijing (☎ 6532-4862; fax 6532-4862); Ryohaengsa is located here. The chances are far lower at other North Korean embassies or consulates. You choose a tour program and fill out a visa application which they then fax off to P'yŏngyang straight away. They can usually give you an approval or rejection within 10 minutes.

One of the first questions you will be asked is 'Are you a journalist?' If you really want to go to North Korea, you'd better say 'No', but we don't recommend you lie to get in. It is illegal to enter North Korea on a tourist visa if you are any sort of journalist or writer, and if caught you could be expelled at your own expense or worse. Whoever is travelling with you or has helped arrange your tour (a tour company) could also get in trouble, so keep the risk to them in mind as well. Journalists and other professional writers can apply to Ryohaengsa directly or through a well-connected travel agent for a special visa; approval or rejection will be according to their whim.

Ryohaengsa normally issues your visa as soon as you pay the full charge. You must pay for the entire trip in advance in hard currency before your visa is issued then arrange your own transport to North Korea and back. Two passport-type photographs are required and there is a US$10 visa fee.

The money you pay only covers your tour within North Korea. You still must book your transport to and from P'yŏngyang. The normal starting point is Beijing and you can book at China International Travel Service (CITS) Beijing Tourist Building (☎ 515-8570; fax 515-8603), 28 Jianguomenwai Dajie. You must then inform the North Korean embassy of your arrangements. They will call ahead to make sure your guide is there to meet you, your hotels are booked and that transport within Korea is arranged.

While buying your ticket to and from Beijing, keep in mind that success in booking your tour directly with the North Korean embassy is far from automatic. Some travellers have received a warm welcome at the embassy, while others have been told 'the person you need to see won't be back for two months'. Assuming they respond favourably, you may be issued the visa in anything from 10 minutes to three weeks. Changes in the precarious economic and political situations in North Korea may bring sudden, unannounced changes in their tourism and visa policies; at times they refuse all prospective travellers and give no reason. You should have a back-up plan for travel in China in case your bid for a North Korean visa fails.

There are no little tricks like entering on a transit visa then extending after arrival. Don't even think about sneaking across a border into North Korea. This is one country where you dare not thumb your nose at the authorities; you could be accused of 'espionage' and suffer the most severe consequences.

Getting your visa extended is easy as long as you pay. Just how much your extended stay will cost is subject to negotiation, but include in your calculations your hotel bill, meals and a service charge for your guide. If you want a visa extension and can come up with the cash your guide will make all the arrangements.

The visa is not stamped into your passport (which might prejudice future visits to the USA or South Korea), but on a separate sheet of paper which is retained by the immigration authorities on leaving North Korea. You can't keep it as a souvenir, unfortunately.

At the time of writing it was not possible to arrange North Korean visas and tours in Hong Kong. But now that Hong Kong has been handed back to China it might not be long before a North Korean consulate or visa office opens.

Most likely, you'll be entering and returning through China. This means you should get a double-entry or multiple-entry visa for China. Otherwise, you can get a re-entry permit from a CITS office in Beijing before leaving. If you fail to obtain one or other of these you may be turned back from North Korean immigration counters with no refund. In an emergency some travellers have managed to get a return visa at the Chinese embassy in P'yŏngyang; this can cost up to US$90.

If your time is limited and you want to arrange everything before arriving in China, there are a few travel agents (very few!) who deal with tours to North Korea. Making use of them is highly recommended, both to save money and to ensure a smooth and well-organised visit. See Organised Tours under the Getting There & Away section for names, addresses, details and costs.

EMBASSIES
North Korea Embassies Abroad
North Korea has tiny embassies in various European countries and Japan, but these are worthless to prospective visitors. Some Asian-based embassies and visa offices which might be of use include:

China
  Embassy of the Democratic People's Republic of Korea, Ritan Beilu, Jianguomenwai, Chaoyang District, Beijing (☎ 6532-1186); the Ryohaengsa travel office is within the Consular section (☎ 6532-4862), the entrance to which is on the east side of the building. There is a consulate in Shenyang, Liaoning Province and a branch of Ryohaengsa in Dandong, Liaoning Province
Russia
  ulitsa Mosfilmovskaya 72 (☎ 436249) (telex 413272 ZINGG SU); there is also a consulate in Nakhodka, ulitsa Vladivostokskaya 1
Macau Embassy of the Democratic People's Republic of Korea, 23rd floor, Nam Van Commercial Centre, 57-9 Rua da Praia Grande, Macau (☎ 333355; fax 333939).

Foreign Embassies in North Korea
There are about 25 foreign embassies in P'yŏngyang, but the only ones of significant size are those of China (☎ 390274) and Russia (☎ 813101). The rest are small offices staffed by one or two persons repre-

senting mostly third world nations in Africa, Asia and the Middle East. The only western countries with a full-time representative are Poland (☎ 817327), Germany and Sweden (no contact information available, curiously). The Swedish mission handles the interests of the USA and Canada.

CUSTOMS
North Korean Customs have received a wide variety of reviews. We were not hassled at all, but some other travellers have reported being gone over quite thoroughly. Bags are usually searched on the way in for illegal or 'subversive' materials (which may include religious documents and any products or papers from South Korea). Always be very polite and agreeable with the Customs officers, who understand and speak English reasonably well. Besides the usual prohibitions against firearms and narcotics, the government lists several other things which you may not bring in:

• Telescopes and magnifiers with over 6X magnification
• Wireless apparatus and their parts
• Seeds of tobacco, leaf tobacco and other seeds
• Publications, video tapes, recording tapes, films, photos and other materials which are hostile to our socialist system or harmful to our political, economic and cultural development and disturb the maintenance of social order.

Note that they are very serious about the last of these prohibitions, which may include any information printed abroad about either North or South Korea. It may even possibly include this guidebook, although we have never yet heard of one of our books being confiscated by the North Korean authorities. Bags rarely seem to be checked on the way out.

MONEY
Costs
All in all, it's going to be an expensive trip. You're looking at between US$100 and US$250 per day all-inclusive (not including transport to and from North Korea). There are also six price levels, depending on the number of persons in your group: one person

NORTH KOREA

(US$200+/day), two persons ($180), three to five persons ($160), six to nine persons ($130), ten to fifteen persons ($100), or sixteen and more persons ($70). In some cases you can save up to US$25 per day by choosing 'standard' accommodation rather than 'deluxe' and thus sleep and eat in lower-class hotels. Discounts may also be offered during the 'low' travel season (November-March); inquire with a travel agency.

Transport to/from P'yŏngyang costs extra. See the Getting There & Away section for details.

If it's any consolation, they do give very good service for the money.

Travellers' Cheques & Credit Cards

These are only useful at the big hotels. When changing money you will get a much better rate for cash rather than travellers' cheques. The policy on credit cards seems to change frequently; don't depend on being able to use them.

Currency

The unit of currency is the won (= 100 jon). There are bank notes for W1, W5, W10, W50 and W100, and coins for W1 and 1, 5, 10 and 50 jon.

There are three types of North Korean currency. The first is coloured green if you're converting hard currency; this is the only one you are likely to use. The second is coloured red if you're exchanging 'non-convertible' currency; this is mainly for Chinese tourists exchanging RMB (Chinese Yuan). The last is local currency for use by Koreans only. Local currency comes in both banknotes and coins whereas green and red currency comes only in banknotes. As a foreigner, you must pay for hotels, restaurants and goods bought in stores in green banknotes and change will be given only in the same.

Red currency is North Korea's way of saying it doesn't really want Russian roubles or Chinese yuan. There are certain limits on consumer goods that can be bought with red currency. There are also two sets of prices for certain goods – a green price and a red price.

The red price is often up to 10 times greater than the green price.

The only time you're likely to need local currency is if you use the Metro in P'yŏng-yang because the escalator down into it takes only coins. You'll also need coins if you want to make a call from a public pay phone.

Currency Exchange

Foreigners must exchange money at hotels. There's no black market but you can, with some people, swap green for red or local currency; be aware that this is illegal. Most Koreans would love to have the green currency since it can be used to buy rare imported goods.

Currency declaration forms are usually issued when you get your visa or at the port of entry and you must fill in an exit currency form when you leave. It's probably best to make sure you get a currency form to avoid hassles on leaving, but if you don't it seems that the guides assigned to you can generally sort things out without too much trouble.

The only currencies you are able to exchange easily are the Deutschmark, French franc, British pound, US dollar and Japanese yen. Exchange rates in won at the time of writing were as follows:

Country	Currency		W
Australia	A$1	=	1.75
Canada	C$1	=	1.64
China	Y1	=	0.26
France	FFr1	=	0.42
Germany	DM1	=	1.44
Japan	¥100	=	1.93
New Zealand	NZ$1	=	1.55
UK	UK£1	=	3.54
USA	US$1	=	2.20

The black market exchange rate in Chinese cities close to the border demonstrates the true value of North Korean currency; in September 1996 it was around US$1 = W180. Anywhere else in the world it is effectively zero. We advise that you do *not* buy North Korean currency in China and try to smuggle it in with you – at the least it will be confiscated and at the worst you will be arrested.

POST & TELECOMMUNICATIONS
Postal Rates
A postcard to Australia costs W1.30. To the USA it's W1.50. The postcards themselves cost W1 each.

Sending Mail
You needn't bother trying to track down the post office because most major hotels offer a postal service.

You're better off sending postcards so the authorities can read what you've said without having to tear open your letters. Saying a few nice things about how clean and beautiful North Korea is will increase the chances of your mail getting through.

Receiving Mail
You can forget about the central post office and poste restante. Given the short time you're likely to be spending in North Korea, it's hardly worth the bother of trying to receive letters. But if you want to try, the most likely place to receive mail is at the P'yŏngyang Koryŏ Hotel, Tonghung dong, Central District, P'yŏngyang; or care of the Korea International Tourist Bureau (Ryohaengsa), Central District, P'yŏngyang. There is a better than average chance that your letters will be opened and read.

Telephone
It's easy to book an overseas call from major hotels and some even offer international direct dialling (IDD) from your room. Phone calls usually go through without much trouble.

Public pay phones require 10 jon coins, so you'll need some local money if you want to use them. Coin-operated phones are not very common even in P'yŏngyang, but you probably won't find too many people to call anyway.

If you are dialling direct to North Korea from abroad, the country code is 850. A number of western countries still do not have direct phone or fax connections with North Korea, but making an IDD call from Beijing or Japan to P'yŏngyang is very easy. Of course, you cannot contact South Korea by any means from North Korea, and vice versa – it is illegal even to try.

Fax, Telex & Telegraph
Fax and telex services are readily available from major hotels like the Koryŏ in P'yŏngyang. A telegraph (cable) service is not available.

Rates per minute for international calls and faxes are: Australia W14; China W3; East Asia W10; Europe W11; Middle East W12; USA W15.

BOOKS & MAPS
Literature about North Korea is rare and tourist literature is even rarer. The easiest place to get travel brochures is from the DPRK Embassy in Beijing, if they are in stock. They are printed in several languages – English, German, French, Japanese and Chinese, and list all the major sites open to foreign tourists, the hotels, an airline schedule and a breakdown of suggested itineraries, ranging from three to 16 days.

As you enter the consular section of the embassy, there is a large waiting room dominated by a giant painting of a scene in the Diamond Mountains; a rack holds free copies of various glossy colour magazines, tourist guidebooks and books by or about Kim Il-Sung and Kim Jong Il. You may take these with you when you leave.

Another source of information is the book *Korean Review* by Pang Hwan Ju, which gives information on North Korea's flora, fauna, minerals, history, economy, politics and sightseeing.

Many scholarly works have been written on North Korean history, policies, and leadership; check your local library or university. Most of these can be found in Seoul. See the Books section in the South Korea Facts for the Visitor chapter for more titles which include discussions and travelogues on North Korea.

Numerous propaganda books and pamphlets are for sale fairly cheaply in North Korea. Though these have scant useful information, they are rare gems for collectors.

Maps of P'yŏngyang and Korea can be purchased at major tourist hotels.

As for getting a general feel for the place, what could be more relevant than George Orwell's *1984* or *Animal Farm*? Read these before or after you arrive, as it would not be wise to carry them through North Korean Customs.

Perhaps more to the point is a report on human rights in North Korea published jointly by Asia Watch (Washington DC, USA) and the Minnesota Lawyers International Human Rights Committee. A brief summary of this report, which appeared in the *Far Eastern Economic Review* on 19 January 1989, should be available from libraries in Hong Kong and elsewhere. North Korea has harshly denounced this report and its subsequent updates.

MEDIA

Information about the rest of the world is hard to come by in North Korea. The press is rigidly controlled and prints only what the government tells it to print: most stories are about contented workers, loyal soldiers, US imperialist aggressors, South Korean puppets, the superhuman feats of Kim Il-sung and 'new discoveries' about Kim Jong-il's mythical childhood. Likewise, TV programs are all designed to reinforce the reigning ideology. North Koreans cannot receive foreign news broadcasts because all radio and TVs are designed to only pick up the government broadcasting frequencies.

Newspapers & Magazines

No foreign publications are available, so if you want to read any you'll have to bring your own copies. By the way, these are hotly sought-after items by news-starved embassy staff in P'yŏngyang – you can quickly win some expat friends if you have a few extra magazines and books to give away.

As for local publications in English, the selection is severely limited. There are free magazines everywhere in a variety of languages, especially the colourful *Democratic People's Republic of Korea* magazine. This is filled with the usual tirades against US imperialists and South Korean puppets, plus articles about the Great Leader and Dear Leader. You'll also learn that 'the Juche idea' is a shining beacon of hope which has taken the world by storm. At the tourist hotels you can pick up a free weekly English-language

newspaper, the *P'yŏngyang Times*, but every issue is practically the same.

The *P'yŏngyang Times* reported that our 500-room hotel with 20 guests in residence was 'always full'.
Ron Gluckman

Radio & TV

There are two AM radio stations and two regular TV stations. It is said that there is a third TV station which broadcasts cultural events on holidays only, but we haven't seen it. The two TV stations broadcast from approximately 6 pm to 11 pm.

It's interesting to note that about one hour per week of North Korean TV is now shown in South Korea (heavily edited and with dubbed commentary). When this was first permitted, the South Koreans were fascinated, but they quickly grew bored with it. You can rest assured that the only South Korean TV shown in the North is news clips of student riots and labor violence.

PHOTOGRAPHY & VIDEO
Film & Equipment

You can buy colour print film at reasonable prices from the hard currency gift shops; everything else is expensive, so bring what you need. There are photo-processing facilities on the second floor at the Koryŏ Hotel, but you'd probably be better off waiting until you return to China, Hong Kong or elsewhere. This same place can do visa photos if you need them.

Restrictions

You are surprisingly free to photograph what you like, but ask first before taking pictures of soldiers or any military facilities – and obey the reply. In many cases, permission *will* be given. The only time we had a problem was when we tried to photograph a long queue of people trying to buy ice cream cones. A man jumped out of the crowd and put his hand over the lens.

TIME

The time in Korea is GMT/UTC plus nine hours. When it is noon in Korea it is 7 pm the previous day in Los Angeles or San Francisco; 10 pm the previous day in New York; 3 am in London; and 2 pm in Sydney or Melbourne.

ELECTRICITY

Electric power is 220 V, 60 Hz, though luxury hotels often have an outlet for 110 V. If so, it will be clearly labelled. All outlets are of the US type, with two flat prongs but no ground (earth) wire.

HEALTH

There seems to be no problem with food and most Koreans drink their water unboiled. You won't have to worry about eating from dirty street stalls either, because there aren't any.

That having been said, North Korea does not seem like a good place to get sick because there are shortages of basic western medicines. Traditional Korean medicine is similar to the Chinese variety.

WOMEN TRAVELLERS

We saw a few foreign women travelling in North Korea and they were always part of a group that included men. This isn't to say that a single woman or group of women couldn't travel without male companions, but it seems to be very rare. According to all we know you can expect complete safety. Neither did we see a female guide leading a tour group, though Ryohaengsa claims female guides are available. It's the opposite in South Korea, where most tour guides are women.

One thing we can say for sure – Korea is a male-dominated society. In spite of the regime's constant attempts to show complete equality between the sexes there are no women holding any positions of importance (except possibly Kim Song-ae, Kim Il-sung's widow). However, there are two North Korean women who are revered: the Great Leader's mother, Kang Ban-sok, sometimes referred to as the 'Mother of Korea', and Kim Jong-suk, mother of the Dear Leader.

DANGERS & ANNOYANCES

As far as we can tell crime is not a problem. The North Korean criminal laws, crime statistics and penal system are state secrets, but we'd be willing to guess that thieves are dealt with harshly (ie execution). This doesn't mean you should be careless with your valuables, but the chance of theft is probably lower than in most countries.

On the other hand, in 1996 there were reports from Japan of gang-robberies of Japanese-Koreans visiting their relatives in rural areas; given the extreme poverty and malnutrition of North Koreans in the past few years and the government-encouraged resentment of foreigners, it would be wise to keep alert to potentially dangerous situations while travelling outside P'yŏngyang. Social order has held up pretty well, but there is no guarantee that violence won't break out if food shortages persist.

The one thing which will get you into serious trouble fast is to insult the Great Leader or the Dear Leader. We know of one Austrian visitor who put out his cigarette butt on a newspaper, right on the face of a photo of Kim Il-sung. The maid found it in his hotel room and informed the police. This resulted in a frightening confrontation, with threats, shouting and pushing. The Austrian escaped prosecution but was quickly booted out of the country.

Climbing into the lap of a statue of the Great Leader for a photo is just not on (standing in front of it is OK). Avoid expressing disrespect for the nation's leadership in any way until you are safely back in China. You needn't be paranoid, but keep your political opinions to yourself. Assume your actions are being watched, that offensive activities will be reported, and that your hotel room has hidden microphones. The last thing you need in North Korea is to be accused of 'espionage'.

Male travellers should not even think about touching a North Korean woman regardless of how friendly, charming and receptive she might seem to be. Even something fairly innocent like shaking hands could be construed as an 'immoral act' and could result in serious punishment for both parties to this 'crime'. Relations between North Korean men and foreign women are a big unknown. Most North Korean men would probably not dare touch a foreign

NORTH KOREA

woman, but given the fact that Korea is a bastion of male chauvinism, it would probably be viewed less seriously than contact between a foreign man and a Korean woman.

Besides thinking about dangers to yourself, give some thought to the Koreans you meet. Giving them gifts like foreign coins or writings could have unpredictable consequences for them. What might seem like an innocent friendly act for you might result in them spending time in a concentration camp.

In general, if you aren't sure whether you should do something or not, ask your guide or just don't do it.

BUSINESS HOURS

Official working hours are Monday to Saturday from 9 am to 6 pm. In practice, business hours will matter little to foreigners.

PUBLIC HOLIDAYS & SPECIAL EVENTS

Public holidays in North Korea include:

New Year's Day, 1 January
Kim Jong-il's Birthday, 16 February
Kim Il-sung's Birthday, 15 April
Armed Forces Day, 25 April
May Day (international socialist workers holiday), 1 May
National Liberation (from Japan) *Day*, 15 August
National Foundation Day, 9 September
Korean Workers' Party Foundation Day, 10 October
Constitution Day, 27 December

Note that North Korea does not celebrate Christmas or the Lunar New Year, nor many of South Korea's major holidays.

Foreign tourists are usually not welcome around the birthdays of the Kims (16 February & 15 April) except by special invitation. In the first two years after Kim Il-sung's death, July 8 has been commemorated with ceremonies, speeches, public tears and wreath-laying observances, but has not yet been made into a public holiday. This may change when, and if, his son formally takes power.

By all means try to be in P'yŏngyang during May Day or Liberation Day. Both holidays are celebrated with huge extravaganzas featuring military-style parades and mass-gymnastics performances that rank among North Korea's most memorable sights.

WORK

Aside from investing in weapons sales, work opportunities are scarce in North Korea. A handful of foreigners have landed foreign-language teaching jobs, but such opportunities are rare and pay is at survival level. On the other hand, they reported that they were treated well.

ACCOMMODATION

Everywhere you go you will have to stay at designated hotels. Although they are modern, multi-star affairs built specifically for foreign tourists, this requirement limits where in the country you can travel. It would be illegal for you to stay anywhere else.

FOOD

Despite reports of severe food shortages, foreign visitors with US dollars eat very well. Your guide orders your food, so if you have any special requests, make them known early. The food is heavily based on meat, fish and poultry – vegetarians are liable to have a difficult time. There is a tendency to order western food for westerners, so if you want Korean food, ask for it.

DRINKS

Korean beer is not bad, but the hard liquors are often too 'exotic' for western tastes. Try the refined rice-wines and the *insam-ju* (Korean vodka infused with ginseng roots). Imported liquors are available at high prices. North Korea produces mineral water and some pleasant-tasting carbonated fruit drinks. Plenty of imported soft-drinks are available in hotels and hard currency shops.

Getting There & Away

AIR

The Chinese airline China Northern and the North Korean airline Koryŏ Air (also known as Chosŏnminhang) fly between Beijing and P'yŏngyang. The flights take less than two hours either way. China Northern flies a round-trip once weekly on Wednesdays.

Koryŏ Air flies twice weekly on Tuesdays and Saturdays. We found the staff at the Air China office in P'yŏngyang to be very friendly – though they were preoccupied with raising fish in the bathtub and vegetables on the terrace because they couldn't buy these things without hard currency.

Tickets cost US$156 one-way in either direction and US$296 return.

There are flights between P'yŏngyang and the Russian cities of Khabarovsk or Moscow in either direction, by either Aeroflot or Koryŏ Air. There are irregular flights from Bangkok via Macau and from Berlin via Moscow, but western tourists may not be able to use them.

You're advised to book as far in advance as possible, though most aircraft fly nearly empty. Occasionally, delegations of diplomats descend on P'yŏngyang for some special event and seats suddenly become scarce. Apparently, there never was a problem of getting bounced by the Great Leader – he was afraid of flying and all his journeys abroad were made overland.

Sunan International Airport is 30 km west of P'yŏngyang, which is about 20 minutes by car.

TRAIN

There are four trains per week in either direction between Beijing and P'yŏngyang via Tianjin, Tangshan, Jinxi, Dandong and Shinŭiju. They run Monday, Wednesday, Thursday and Saturday. On each day train No 27 leaves Beijing at 4.48 pm and arrives at P'yŏngyang the next day at 4.05 pm (about 23 hours). Going the other way, train No 26 departs P'yŏngyang at 11.50 am on the same four days, arriving in Beijing at 10 am. The one-way fare is US$66 in hard sleeper (economy class), US$92 in soft sleeper (first class) or US$108 in soft sleeper (deluxe).

Chinese trains are more comfortable than the North Korean ones. North Korean trains don't have air-conditioning, not even in the soft sleeper section, and the windows are locked, so ventilation is non-existent.

The North Korean train is actually just two carriages attached to the main Beijing-Dandong train; these are detached at Dandong (on the Chinese side) then taken across the Yalu River bridge to Shinŭiju (Korean side), where more carriages are added for local travellers. Non-Koreans remain in their original carriages.

The trains usually spend about four hours at the border for Customs & Immigration – two hours at Dandong and two hours at Shinŭiju. Customs & Immigration on both sides of the border are relatively casual: your passport will be taken away for stamping and you are permitted to wander around the stations. Obey the signs, officials and guides when going outside or taking any pictures.

Shinŭiju station will be your first introduction to North Korea and the contrasts with China are quite marked. Everything is squeaky-clean and there are no vendors plying their goods. A portrait of the Great Leader looks down from above this, and all other, railway stations in North Korea. You may wander around the station and take photos. One of the buildings is a rest area for foreign passengers and here you will encounter the first of many billboards with photos and captions in English: 'The US Aggression Troops Transferring Missiles'; 'South Korean Puppet Police'; 'US Imperialists and South Korean Stooges' etc.

Soon after departing Shinŭiju you will be presented with a dinner menu complete with colour photographs. The food is excellent and the service is fine. It's all very civilised. Make sure you have some small denomination US dollar bills to pay for the meal, as it is not included as part of the package deal you paid for in advance. There are no facilities for changing money at Shinŭiju or on the train. The dining car is for the use of non-Koreans only.

Your guide will meet you on arrival at P'yŏngyang railway station and accompany you to your hotel. Likewise, when you leave North Korea, your guide will bid you farewell at the station or the airport and you then travel to China unaccompanied.

When leaving North Korea, you could also link up with the Trans-Siberian train at Shinŭiju/Dandong in China. To make this

NORTH KOREA

connection you need to take the noon train from P'yŏngyang on Saturday, which arrives in Moscow the following Friday. There's also the possibility of crossing directly from North Korea into Russia in the north-east via Hasan and then taking the Trans-Siberian to Moscow. The P'yŏngyang-Moscow journey currently departs every Monday and Wednesday, takes seven days, and costs US$450 in a soft sleeper carriage. As an alternative, you could take the hard sleeper to Vladivostok in 30 hours for US$130.

A book published in August 1996 called *Russia By Rail*, by Athol Yates, contains much rare and valuable information about train travel in North Korea and the northern Far East in general (check out http://www.russia-rail.com on the web).

DEPARTURE

You should make your reservations for departure before you arrive in North Korea. Ryohaengsa can easily do this for you as long as you inform them in advance. Departure reservations can be reconfirmed through your guide; remember to ask.

If departing by air, your guide will accompany you to the airline office so you can buy your ticket or reconfirm your outbound flight. You must pay an airport departure tax of W22 or US$11 at the airport.

Money-changing facilities are available at the airport, but not at the railway station. There is no tax on departures by train.

Getting Around

Public transport isn't nearly as well developed in North Korea as it is in the South. However, you will have a few opportunities to use it, usually only when accompanied by your guide.

One thing you'll notice is the distinct lack of traffic in the cities and countryside. Most of the motor vehicles you'll see will be military transports. There are no regularly scheduled domestic flights.

BUS

There are hardly any public buses in the countryside or between major cities; North Koreans are not allowed to move freely around their own country without permission. Most of the time you'll travel by car with a driver and your guide. If you're with a larger group you'll ride in a specially arranged tourist bus. Naturally, this will limit your chances of meeting local people.

Children will wave at you as you pass by, while adults will smile and maybe even chat (in Korean) if you happen to stop and get out on the streets. They've been encouraged to give visiting foreigners a warm welcome.

TRAIN

You may be able to take the railway to visit some of the major tourist sites, such as Kaesŏng or Myohyangsan. If so, you'll ride in ornate 1950s sleeper cars rather than the dilapidated hard-seat carriages used by the masses. Indeed, the North Koreans sometimes put on separate trains just for foreigners.

BICYCLE

In a major contrast with China, there is a distinct lack of bicycles. There are almost none in P'yŏngyang and comparatively few elsewhere; outside P'yŏngyang most people walk. Presumably, the absence of bicycles in P'yŏngyang indicates a ban on their use. Occasionally, you'll come across a few in a department store, but they usually have no price tags on them. You cannot rent bikes anywhere.

Finally, even if you did have your own bike, you'd be hard-pressed to find your way around because there are no street signs in the cities or direction signs in the countryside, and road maps are almost impossible to find. The only street map you'll find is of P'yŏngyang.

ORGANISED TOURS

Ryohaengsa's representative in North Korea itself is known as SAM Travel Service, Korea International Travel Company, Central District of P'yŏngyang (☎ (8502) 817201; fax 817607). Five-day tours of

P'yŏngyang and Kaesŏng go for around US$600 all-inclusive (except for international travel).

Tours booked through a private travel agent are more expensive than booking directly with Ryohaengsa, but only slightly. Travel agents will shield you from all the hassles of dealing with the North Korean bureaucracy and China International Travel Service (CITS) in Beijing. They will ensure a smoother and safer tour, and act as a buffer zone between you and the authorities in P'yŏngyang.

If you book a tour through a travel agent you'll usually have to wait between one and four weeks for your visa application to be processed and your tour confirmed, you may have to leave your passport with them for a few days. P'yŏngyang's approval or rejection of your visa may be known in less than a week.

Koryo Tours (☎ (10) 6595-8357, 6592-2717; email jgreen@iuol.cn.net) is a company specialising in tours of North Korea. Write to their office in China at Kindly Commercial Centre, 9 Jianguomenwai Dajie, Beijing 100020, China. Their eight-page brochure makes interesting reading, and offers set-date four-day, eight-day and tailor-made tours, accompanied by their own experienced British guides. Prices are quite reasonable for their very good service and they offer semi-annual six-day tours arranged to include the May Day or Liberation Day festivities in P'yŏngyang at a discounted price.

In Australia, an agency with long experience at North Korea journeys is Red Bear Travel (☎ (03) 9824-7183; fax 9822-3956; email bmccunn@werple.net.au; http://www.travelcentre.com.au), 320 Glenferrie Rd, Malvern 3144. Red Bear has five to 10-day tours for US$1700 and US$2800 per person (twin share, including return transport from Beijing). Also available are individually-designed tours; recently Red Bear sent in a single person for 10 days and her cost was US$3800 all-inclusive.

These prices seem high by global standards, but keep in mind that they include

everything: all meals, most drinks and sightseeing, plus good quality accommodation, interpreters, private cars, trains and entrance fees. A similar packaged tour of South Korea would cost more.

Also in Australia are Passport Travel (☎ (613) 9867-3888, fax 9867-1055), Kings Cross Plaza, Suite 11, 401 St Kilda Rd, Melbourne, Victoria 3004; and Orbitours (☎ (02) 9221-7322), 7th floor, Dymocks Building, 428 George St, Sydney, NSW 2000. In Hong Kong, the agent specialising in North Korean trips is Wallem Travel (☎ 2528-6514), 46th floor, Hopewell Centre, 183 Queen's Rd East, Wanchai. In the UK, try Regent Holidays Ltd (☎ (0117) 921-1711; fax 925-4866), 13 Small St, Bristol BS1 1DE.

On the Internet, contact Russia-Rail Internet Travel Service; take a look at the web site at http://www.russia-rail.com.

You must be accompanied at all times by a Korean guide, whose fees you will already have paid (in addition to the guide provided by your travel agency, if any). This guide works for Ryohaengsa.

In a few places you are allowed to walk around alone (central P'yŏngyang and a few scenic spots) though this is only reluctantly conceded. Guides are available who can speak English, French, German, Chinese, Japanese and Russian, as well as a number of other languages; the guides we encountered all spoke English well. Never try to 'give your guide the slip' or disobey his instructions – both of you could get in serious trouble (and so could your travel agency).

There are a number of special interest tours, the per-day costs of which are all generally the same as quoted in the Costs section of this chapter; some may have higher rates. Special tours include Mountaineering (Paekdu, Myohyang & Kumgang mountains), Taekwŏndo (traditional martial art), Mud (spa) Treatment, Korean Language Study, Educational Establishments, Dance Notation, Golf, and Hunting and Biological or Geological Survey trips to Paekdusan (these last three would be more expensive).

NORTH KOREA

Another possibility is the 'Tour for Traditional Korean Medical Treatment'. This involves acupuncture, moxibustion, suction using vacuum flasks, manipulative (chiropractic) treatment and physical therapy. Cure rates of 90% are claimed for most illnesses. The additional costs for these treatments vary, but don't expect them to be cheap. Ryohaengsa can supply you with more details.

How much you enjoy your trip largely depends on your guide, so keep a good relationship. A few gifts (a carton of cigarettes, some chocolate bars) given early in the journey will ensure smooth relations. North Korean guides earn a pittance – consider giving them a tip at the end of the journey if you have received good service.

P'yŏngyang

Being the capital, P'yŏngyang is a superb example of the regime's determination to project its own image of progress, discipline and the well-being of its citizens. You won't find here the hustle and bustle, the noise and smells of other cities in Asia. North Korea's version of the model Communist capital excludes people with disabilities and attempts to limit the public appearance of the very old, bicycles, animals, street vendors and even pregnant women. All this has attracted a negatively-toned commentary from the foreign press and, possibly because of such criticism, these restrictions seem to have been relaxed a bit in recent years. One 'token' disabled man has been seen riding a modified bicycle near the Koryŏ Hotel (where most foreigners stay) and a few elderly persons have also appeared around there, but their numbers are exceedingly low.

It's said that only those with the proper 'class background' and proven records of unswerving loyalty to the country's leaders are allowed to live in P'yŏngyang. It is the showpiece of North Korea and is peppered with distinctive landmarks and monuments, many of them in honour of the Great Leader. A 13-lane boulevard connects the city centre

with the outer suburb of Kwangbok, more than three km away – quite an extravagance given the scarcity of traffic, though no more so than all the expensive monuments. Many of these monumental works are named after the Great Leader: Kim Il-sung Square, Kim Il-sung Stadium, Kim Il-sung University, Kim Il-sung Higher Party School, and so on.

Orientation

Like Seoul, the city is built on the banks of a major river – the Taedong. One of the amazing sights here is the two mid-river fountains which rise to a height of 150m. Your guide will proudly tell you they're the highest in the world and this may well be true. Most of the major monuments are near the banks of the Taedong.

Since P'yŏngyang is one of the few places where you may be allowed, with a little gentle but persistent persuasion, to walk around unaccompanied (it's a good idea to take this opportunity either before or after you've been chauffeured around the main sights. If you request it, you can, for instance, be dropped on the far side of the city at Liberation Tower and walk back from there to the centre, calling in at department stores along the way if you want.

Be careful not to jaywalk, even if there's not a car in sight! There are underground walkways or pedestrian crossings at all major intersections and *everyone*, without exception, uses them. There are also traffic police standing on wooden plinths at all such points. If you attempt to jaywalk the nearest one will give a sharp blast of her whistle (they're mostly women) and a smart remonstration which should quickly bring you back in line.

Things to See

Your first day out in P'yŏngyang will undoubtedly be a guided tour by car. One of the principal monuments is the **Tower of the Juche Idea**, a 170m-high needle on the east bank of the Taedong River. You can get to the top by an express lift for an unencumbered view of the city. The ride costs W20 or US$10, but is worth it on a clear day. In an alcove at the bottom are commemorative messages from various parts of the world hewn in stone and brick extolling the concept of Juche. As the plaques indicate, the Juche ideology is also referred to as *Kim Il-sungism*.

You will surely be taken to see the **Arch of Triumph**, which marks the spot where Kim Il-sung made his rallying speech following the departure of the Japanese, and you will be reminded that it is a full three metres higher than its counterpart in Paris. Nearby is the **Chollima Statue**, a bronze Pegasus representing the high-speed progress of the socialist reconstruction of North Korea, and the **Kim Il-sung Stadium**, one of the world's largest.

Dominating the huge plaza on Mansudae Hill (overlooking the Taedong River) is the 30 m-tall **Grand Monument**. This is a larger-than-life polished bronze statue of the Great Leader himself, right hand thrust out to the heavens, flanked by castings of previously oppressed but ultimately victorious follow

ers. Since Kim's death, visitors have been expected to 'pay respect' to the statue here, by standing still and quiet with a bowed head while a representative of your group lays a wreath or bouquet of flowers. Bouquets are available for W20 or so. No matter what you think of the man, in the eyes of the North Koreans it's not unreasonable that foreign visitors should pay at least this minimum level of respect for their fallen leader. If you refuse to participate it may cause very hard feelings with the authorities and could get your guide and tour company into trouble; think twice before standing on principle.

Behind the Grand Monument (Great Leader statue) on Mansudae Hill is the **Korean Revolution Museum**, founded on 1 August 1948. This has been declared 'a centre for education in the Juche Idea'. It contains exhibits covering the 'anti-Japanese struggle, the period of the anti-imperialist, anti-feudal democratic revolution carried out after liberation, the period of the Great Father Liberation War, the period of building

Visitors to P'yŏngyang will almost certainly be shown the Arch of Triumph.

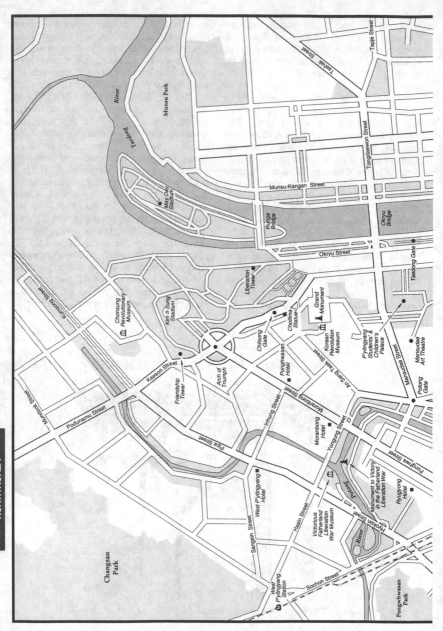

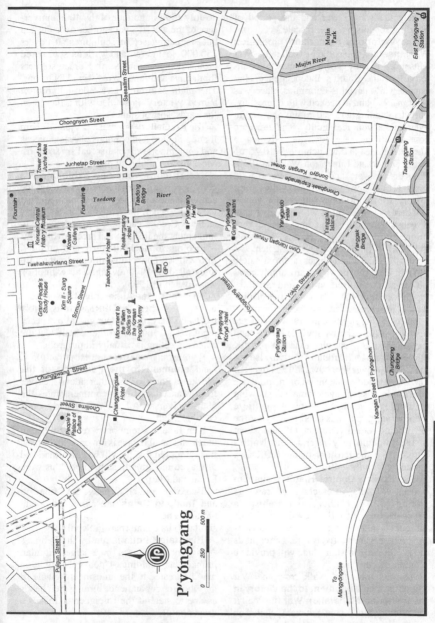

P'yŏngyang

0   250   500 m

socialism after the war and the period of building socialism on a full scale.'

The **Victorious Fatherland Liberation War Museum** (you could just call it the 'War Museum') is truly worth a visit. The counterpart of the South's Independence Hall outside Ch'ŏnan, this enormous place was built in 1953 and is packed with interesting, dull, frightening and sad rooms that might even make you feel guilty. The museum covers anti-Japanese guerrilla activities in northern Korea and Manchuria 1910-45 up to the Fatherland Liberation War (the 1950-53 Korean War) and gives a very good insight into how the DPRK views their history. It has brilliant displays by anyone's standards – battle scenes with moving three-dimensional models and images and very impressive panorama exhibits. It's very graphic and hero based. The basement has various US and allied planes (approximately 10) that were shot down but are largely complete, and captured tanks and artillery (approximately 40). It's a massive display which provides a very effective counter-balance to the glorification of war you see upstairs. The exhibits include MIGs and torpedo boats, all of which the three-storey building were built around. You can also see the US helicopter shot down in 1994 over the DMZ and read the statement of the pilot. Be sure not to miss the cyclorama hall showing the Battle of Taejŏn, a 360° revolving frieze incorporating real tanks and portraying the USA being routed yet again. Of note is that in the museum they refer to the North's retreat from the territory of the ROK as a 'strategic withdrawal'.

The **Korean Central History Museum** houses exhibits, artefacts and drawings tracing Korean history from prehistoric times right up to the revolution. This museum is mainly geared to locals and visits by foreigners are relatively rare. The exhibits are in Korean, but your guide will provide a running commentary.

Just five minutes' walk from the War Museum is the **Monument to the Victory in the Fatherland Liberation War** (just call it the 'Victory Monument'). It was unveiled on 26 July 1993 in honour of the 40th anniversary of the war. It's yet another over-the-top but staggering set of sculptures. It covers 150,000 sq metres and various sculptured groups depict heroic North Korean soldiers (both male and female) resisting UN troops. The main sculpture is a 30m-tall bronze named 'Victory' (a soldier with a flag in an 'onwards' sort of stance).

The **Art Gallery** is a must. It's just off Kim Il-sung Square and contains classical pieces and contemporary socialist realism sections. Most visitors find it stunning.

The **Three Revolutions Exhibition** is a good opportunity to get bored. It displays the achievements of the Korean people under the wise guidance of the Korean Workers' Party and the Great Leader in the endeavour to implement the line of the Three Revolutions – ideological, technological and cultural. You will see Three Revolutions street sculptures all over P'yŏngyang. The exhibition was opened in 1993.

The **Mansudae Assembly Hall** was built in 1984. It's where the DPRK state assembly meets. It's only open to tour groups by special request and you can forget about visiting when a meeting is actually in progress.

P'yŏngyang's newest tourist attraction is the **Monument to the Founding of the Worker's Party**, on the other side of the river from Mansudae Hill. It commemorates the 50th anniversary of the ruling party on 3 October 1995.

Kim Il-sung's temporary resting place in the Presidential Palace is not open to tourists. It is rumoured that he will be embalmed and displayed in a grandiose memorial, as were Lenin and Mao.

Two of the old city's gates, the **Chilsŏng** and **Taedong Gates**, are more traditional. nature. The latter has a two-tiered roof similar to its counterpart in Seoul.

The **State Circus** is run by the People's Army and is housed in a large, circular, immaculate building. Upon entering, you may be treated to the amusing spectacle of the whole circus audience turning their heads as one to stare at the foreigners – makes a great photo!

Eastern circuses have a high level of acrobatics, which is always great to watch, but they also have the inevitable animal acts – horses, boxing bears and even dogs doing tricks. The clowns came on dressed as clumsy South Korean soldiers, but the subsequent clownesque portrayal of an American soldier (complete with blond hair, sunglasses, big nose and swaggering walk) shall remain with me forever.

Paul E Bakker

The **Metro Museum** offers bizarre underground fun with the Great Leader. You can actually see the seat he sat in on the Metro. There are portraits of him offering on-the-spot 'guidance' to appreciative workers who built this underground transport system. For more information on the Metro, see the Getting Around section for P'yŏngyang.

Other institutions which may well be worth a visit include the **Students' & Children's Palace** and the **P'yŏngyang Embroidery Institute**. The former was established in 1963 as a centre for after-school activities. Here you can see students playing music and doing everything from ping pong to dance to gymnastics. At the Embroidery Institute you can see an exhibition of very impressive embroidery and prototype designs which are copied by manufacturers around the country.

Although **Kim Il-sung University** is not on every tour, you might want to pay it a visit. It is from here that Dear Leader Kim Jong-il graduated. The book *Kim Jong-il In His Young Days* makes it clear that the Dear Leader was the university's foremost scholar and was soon teaching his teachers. When the Dear Leader read his thesis about socialism, it was described thus:

The professors and scholars, who were so strict about scientific matters, could not suppress their surging emotions, and approached the author who made immortal theoretical achievements, shaking his hands and congratulating him heartily and warmly.

His thesis was highly assessed as an immortal document.

Another major site of interest is the western suburban district of **Mangyŏngdae** – the so-called 'Cradle of the Revolution' – where the Sunhwa River flows into the Taedong.

This is where Kim Il-sung allegedly was born and spent his childhood. His old thatched house, set in carefully tended gardens, has been turned into a shrine. It houses photographs of his family as well as a few everyday household items (Kim's straw sleeping mat, etc) to indicate his humble background. The surrounding pine woods hold the burial mounds of his relatives, all of whom are said to have been great anti-foreigner patriots and revolution-minded leaders of the lower classes. There's also a marble observation platform overlooking the Taedong River at the top of Mangyŏng Hill.

Near Mangyŏngdae are the **Revolutionary Museum** and **Revolutionary School**, and a giant fun fair. Guides claim that the entire complex receives over 100,000 visitors a day.

On the way back from Mangyŏngdae, it's worth making a detour to see **Kwangbok St**, a eerie modernistic suburb visible from high points in central P'yŏngyang. It's essentially a suburb of high-rise apartment blocks laid out in lines which stretch for over three km on either side of the virtually empty 13-lane highway.

Another worthwhile excursion is a visit to the **P'yŏngyang Movie Studio** out in the north western suburbs. This is not part of the standard tours, so you must request it if you want to go there. It is not difficult to arrange, but give your guide as much advance notice as possible. Like everything else in North Korea, the movie studio is very politicised. Most of the films are anti-US, anti-South Korean and anti-Japanese. Reel after reel, Kim Il-sung is credited with the almost single-handed defeat of Japan in WWII (the Allied war effort is never acknowledged). His mother and father are also depicted on screen as great revolutionaries. As part of the tour, they usually give you a sneak preview of films currently in production. Although the sound tracks are all in Korean, your guide will interpret for you. We were treated to one such film depicting former South Korean presidents Chun Doo-hwan and Roh Tae-woo as raving lunatics brandishing guns while screaming 'kill, kill, kill!' Fascinating stuff.

NORTH KOREA

The Legend of Tan-gun

In the year 2333 BC, a son of the Lord of Heaven named Hwanung descended from heaven with 3000 retainers to T'aebaeksan and established a 'City of God' on the summit. Modern scholars have been unable to unequivocally locate this 'T'aebaeksan', and Korean traditionalists have varying opinions: some favour the great mountain with the same name in Kangwon Province of South Korea; more favour Myohyangsan just north of P'yŏngyang; but most hold that Paekdusan must have been the spot, being closest to heaven and having such outstanding natural features (see the Paekdusan section).

Wherever it was, the myth continues: a bear and a tiger beseeched 'Heavenly King Hwanung' to turn them into humans. He gave them bundles of garlic and mugwort (a green medicinal herb, common in Korea) and directed them to eat those foods (the first kimch'i!) while avoiding the sun for 100 days. The tiger failed the test, but the bear succeeded and emerged from the cave as a young woman. She mated with Hwanung and produced a son named Tan-gun. He became the first Korean king, establishing his capital at 'the walled city of P'yŏngyang' (which is probably not the same place as the current North Korean capital city, although they now claim it is!). ∎

Foreign tourists are not usually taken out to the **Taesongsan Complex** north-east of the city, but you can request a visit if you have an extra day in P'yŏngyang. The dominant feature is the **Revolutionary Martyrs Cemetery** – very holy ground for the North Koreans and you may not be permitted to enter beyond the main gate. There is also a public amusement park; the **Central Zoo**; the small **Kwangbŏp Buddhist Temple**; two pretty lakes with nearby restaurants; and the huge and beautiful **Central Botanic Garden** which boasts two special hot-houses for the newly-developed *kimilsungia* and *kimjongilia* flowers!

The Tomb of Tan-gun

History continues to evolve in North Korea, and 'revolutionary discoveries' are made every year. The government announced in 1993 that its archaeologists had discovered the tomb of Tan-gun, the founder of the first Korean kingdom. Until that point, they had agreed with most scholars of Korean history that Tan-gun is a mythical figure: his kingdom of 'Kochosŏn' (ancient Korea), and its capitals 'P'yŏngyang' and 'Asadal', was located in North-East China – if indeed it ever existed. However, it's been recently 'discovered' that Kochosŏn was northern Korea; its ancient capital was right where P'yŏngyang now stands; and Tan-gun was a real person (they claim to have found his bones).

Those decayed bones (and those said to be of his wife) are on display at a grandly constructed tomb just outside of P'yŏngyang. A small museum nearby displays artefacts from Tan-gun's times said to have been found in and around the tomb. Books about the life and times of Tan-gun may be on sale.

Places to Stay

Wherever you choose to stay in P'yŏngyang it's going to cost you heavily, although the price is already included in your tour charge. There is a choice between Deluxe, Class A, Class B and Class C accommodation. You'll probably be pressured to stay at the deluxe *P'yŏngyang Koryŏ Hotel* (☎ 38106), a 45-storey tower with a revolving restaurant on top. It's a five-minute walk from the railway station and it's where most foreigners stay. The hotel has 500 rooms and, given the small number of tourists, it's unlikely you'll have to worry about making a reservation.

There are some other deluxe hotels, but most are inconveniently located. There's the *Tourist Hotel* and the *Angol Hotel*, both about seven km from the city centre, and the *Yanggakdo Hotel*, about four km from the centre.

Further down the scale in the B class are the *Potonggang Hotel* (☎ 48301), the *Sosan Hotel* and the *Ryanggang Hotel*, all around four km from the centre; and the *Youth Hotel*, about 10 km out.

The most popular C class hotel is the *Changgwangsan Hotel* (☎ 48366), with 326 rooms, less than two km from the railway station. In the heart of the city is the *P'yŏngyang Hotel* (☎ 38161) with 170 rooms, and the smaller *Taedonggang Hotel* (☎ 38346).

The skyline of P'yŏngyang is dominated by the incredible *Ryugyong Hotel*, a 105-storey pyramid with 3000 rooms and five revolving restaurants. Originally conceived (by Kim Jong-il himself) as the world's largest luxury hotel, the concrete pyramid was erected in 1989 four km from the city centre. Unfortunately, it seems the government ran out of money for the interior technology (such as high-speed elevators and water systems) before they could complete it. The building now sits as an empty shell and it's unlikely further work will be done unless there is a dramatic increase in tourism. Tourist pamphlets produced in North Korea often show the building photographed at night with lights on inside, a considerable feat since the building is not wired for electricity. It would make quite a tourist attraction in itself, but most requests to visit are denied. You'll probably have to be content photographing it with a long lens.

Places to Eat
You'll usually eat at your hotel, but eating elsewhere can be arranged. Many foreigners hang out in the coffee shop of the *Changgwangsan Hotel*, where prices are high. As for the 'local restaurants', these in fact cater to foreigners or privileged Koreans with access to hard currency. Don't think you'll ever be able to eat along with the working class. Just where the locals eat is a mystery – either they bring food from home or they're fed at the workplace, but there are very few of the pavement restaurants or food stalls you find in developing nations. If you want to eat outside your hotel for the sake of variety, your guide will arrange it upon request.

One recent traveller very much enjoyed a long and lavish dinner of dog, at a strangely decorated (and seemingly secret) speciality restaurant. Visiting such places can only be accomplished by making arrangements with your guide.

Entertainment
The streets are deserted at night. For North Koreans, the evening is presumably spent sitting by the radio or TV listening to testimonials by happy workers and reruns of profound speeches by the late Great Leader.

There are a few discos for decadent foreigners (no Koreans allowed). Don't get your hopes up though – the largest disco managed to attract 20 customers (19 males and one female) when we visited on a Saturday night during the peak summer season. The most popular disco is on the top floor of building No 2 in the Changgwangsan Hotel (☎ 48366). It's open from 9.30 pm until midnight and costs W5 to enter.

The Koryŏ Hotel has a dance-karaoke hall but the cover charge is W50, so it's usually empty except for a few Japanese karaoke enthusiasts. The 2nd floor of the same hotel has a billiards room which is a good place to socialise with embassy staff, journalists and whoever else happens to be in town.

Other possibilities for diversion include bowling, North Korean movies, rifle shooting, exercise, swimming, sauna and massage – ask your guide.

Things to Buy
There are plenty of hard currency souvenir shops at the main tourist venues carrying mostly Chinese-made goods. Out where the masses shop, there are scarcely any consumer goods on the shelves. Nevertheless, North Korea does offer plenty of unique souvenirs which make fantastic conversation pieces. Books and videos on the immortal achievements of Juche and its Great Leaders may be your best picks.

Just to the south of the P'yŏngyang Koryŏ Hotel on Changgwang St is a place selling postage stamps (sign in English) and it's well worth your time to stop in here. One postage stamp shows a crowd of angry Koreans beating a US soldier to death while someone sticks a knife through his throat. Another shows two soldiers, one Korean and one Chinese, standing shoulder to shoulder while brandishing AK-47s (symbolising socialist solidarity). You might enjoy the stamps depicting North Korea's version of the space shuttle, but even more bizarre are the stamps proudly displaying the British royal family. Just why Charles and Diana are more popular in North Korea than in the UK awaits some scholarly research. As for whose photo is displayed on the largest stamps, we'll let you guess.

Many tourists have expressed an interest in purchasing the metal badge depicting the Great Leader which every North Korean wears. Unfortunately, these are not for sale.

Ginseng is for sale in hotels, but prices seem ridiculously high. It's all claimed to be from Paekdusan; ginseng from there has high mythological value for all Koreans. You can buy all grades of ginseng much more cheaply in the South. If you're an aspiring acupuncturist, you can find acupuncture needles in the medicine shops at rock-bottom prices.

Getting Around

All public transport in P'yŏngyang costs 10 jon. They want it in coins, so you'll need local money. As a general rule, foreigners are discouraged from using the public transport system – except for the Metro (underground) which is something of a showcase – and forbidden to use it unless accompanied by their guide.

Bus It's unlikely you'll ever use the urban bus network because the queues are phenomenally long and the buses crammed to bursting point; buses run until 10 pm each day. Women with children form separate queues and have priority in boarding buses.

Tram P'yŏngyang's tram service began in 1991. It's not a bad way of getting around, but it's often extremely crowded and it is not recommended for foreigners unless accompanied by their guide. No maps of the tram routes are published; presumably they run to housing estates around the city.

Taxi You won't find taxis plying the streets as in Seoul, but you can book one from a tourist hotel. The word 'taxi' is not written on the car, nor will you see a meter, but the fare is based on distance. The fare is approximately W2 per km, depending on the type of vehicle (Mercedes are most expensive). The price also rises slightly late at night. In the rare event that you don't find a taxi waiting outside your hotel you can call one (☎ 10507).

Underground You should definitely visit a Metro station if only to see the extravagance with which they were constructed. Each station is designed differently, with varying bronze sculptures, murals, mosaics and chandeliers, and all the pillars, steps, corridors and platforms are fashioned in marble. The Metor stations have names which translate as 'Liberation', 'Reunification', 'Reconstruction', and so on. Being dim and dingy, the trains are nowhere near as impressive as the stations, but each car contains a portrait of you-know-who. There are 17 stations in all, served by two lines that cover a total length of 24 km; the present system was completed in 1978. There are grand plans to extend it to Mangyŏngdae (P'yŏngyang's western district) and eventually to Namp'o (P'yŏngyang's seaport). Each station has a map of the system indicating where you are. The cost of a ride on this system is a standard 10 jon and it's a very convenient way of quickly visiting different parts of the city.

Around the Country

What you get to see outside P'yŏngyang depends on what sort of itinerary you request and how much time you have. It will also be limited to the places where tourist hotels are located. The big five tourist destinations are Kŭmgangsan, Myohyangsan, Paekdusan, Kaesŏng and P'anmunjŏm.

Travellers who have 'been there done that' may wish to request visits to lesser sites, such as the Taesongsan Complex just outside

P'yŏngyang, Wonsan, Namp'o, Kuwŏlsan, Haeju-Suyangsan, Chilbosan and the Rajin-Sonbong Economic Zone.

NAMP'O

Namp'o is a dull port city but makes a good contrast with the model capital, P'yŏngyang, 55 km away.

On the way to Namp'o port you pass **Chollima Steel complex** and **Taean Heavy Machinery complex**, now looking derelict (the Russians are assisting with renovation).

The Namp'o **golf course** is by Japanese standards very good. It costs about US$100 a round including clubs and female caddies. Drinks are available at each tee. The course looks completely out of place in industrialised Namp'o, but a visit is an absolute must for the 10 or so westerners who might be in Pyongyang at any given time. Golfers from Hong Kong are enthralled with the place – it's cheaper than home, and where in Hong Kong can you play on an empty professional (Japanese designed) course?

The **West (Yellow) Sea Barrage** is a truly revolutionary feat and worth a visit. It's 13 km from Namp'o and the dam is eight km long. It's designed to stop the Taedong River from flooding P'yŏngyang (which it has done on several occasions) during high tides. It's like the Thames barrage in London but on a larger scale, with three locks and 36 sluices. It keeps the sea out and has turned the Taedong River to fresh water. It also helps the irrigation of the countryside and has reclaimed land for agriculture. There is a visitor centre here where you can buy souvenir stuffed pheasants. Swimming is also possible nearby.

KUWŎLSAN

Just across the mouth of the Taedong River from Namp'o City stands the '**Nine Moons Mountains**', the best set of peaks and valleys on the west coast. Several unpaved roads and hiking trails provide access to the 954m-high main peak and 800m Obong peak, two main valleys, three high waterfalls, five hot spring sources, restored mountain fortress walls and numerous sites of former shrines and hermitages. South of the main peak lies the **Samsong Pleasure Ground**, a favoured summer resort for North Korean citizens. Further south but still amid superb scenery is a reconstructed temple called **Woljongsa**, though it's an empty shadow of its former glory. The main attractions can be experienced in one long day of driving and hiking.

HAEJU

This port city is 130 km due south of P'yŏngyang. It has numerous islets which you can take a boat to. Haeju has a very high tidal range (6-7m) which means sandy beaches and crabs when the tide is out, but lots of rock when the tide is in. **Suyangsan** (946m) is eight km away and boasts a mountain fort pleasure ground with statues, slogans and other reminders of the Great Leader scattered everywhere.

WONSAN

Wonsan is on the east coast, 200 km from Pyongyang. It has good beaches and is a popular recreation resort for the boys in uniform. Wonsan is also a good staging point for Kŭmgangsan.

MYOHYANGSAN

The third most famous mountain in North Korea, behind Kŭmgangsan and Paekdusan, **Myohyangsan** ('mountain of mysterious fragrance') is well worth a leisurely visit. It is considered a sacred place by many Koreans and offers grand scenery, unspoiled nature, a dozen old Buddhist temples and countless waterfalls.

The main centre of non-natural interest in Myohyangsan is the **International Friendship Exhibition (IFE)** centre, about three or four km from the railway station. It's another of those monuments to the glory of the Great Leader and, to a lesser extent, of the Dear Leader. It's a six-storey building in traditional Korean style in a magnificent setting among densely wooded hills. It houses gifts given to Kim Il-sung and Kim Jong-il from all over the world.

You need to be on your best behaviour

here, as the building is officially a hallowed shrine. You must take off your hat if you have one, and shoe covers must be worn when walking around. You may be permitted to open the golden doors to the shrine, but you must put on a pair of gloves before touching the handles. During your tour, you'll be escorted by a woman in traditional Korean costume.

The list of donors reads like a roster of the dead and discredited: Stalin, Mao, Castro, Ceausescu, Honecker, Khaddafi, etc. The gifts themselves are quite fascinating: a bullet-proof Zil limousine from Stalin, a luxurious train carriage from Mao Zedong, a stuffed alligator from the Sandinistas, and carvings, pottery and paintings from all over the Third World. The gifts are arranged by country and each has a note, in Korean and English, of who sent them and when. There are 120 rooms in total and it's not possible to see them all in one day.

When you've seen enough of the IFE, it's possible to go for a three-km hike up the **Sangwon Valley** directly to the north-east. After climbing via a clearly defined pathway, stone steps and a suspension footbridge past the **Kŭmgang, Taeha, Ryongyon** and **Chŏnsin waterfalls**, (the **Sanju falls** are another option off to the right) and the humble **Sangwon Hermitage**, you'll arrive at the pretty **Chŏnsin Pavilion**. From there you can descend the same way or take an alternative eastern route up a bit more to the **Osŏn Pavilion** then back down to civilisation via **Pulyong Hermitage, Ryongju Peak** and **Poyun Hermitage**. If you're not yet tired and have plenty more daylight you can proceed three more km upwards from the Chŏnsin Pavilion past **Nungin Hermitage** to the **Pŏbwang Peak**, which offers an astounding view of the entire region.

At any rate don't miss **Pohyonsa**, the most historically-important Buddhist temple in western North Korea. It's just a short walk from the IFE at the entrance to Sangwon Valley, and features several small pagodas; a large hall housing images of the Buddha; and a museum which sports a collection of woodblock Buddhist scriptures. You may be told

that these wooden buildings are 950 years old and have never been rebuilt, although they certainly have been repainted and placed on a concrete foundation. It's almost possible that the building is really that old, but how it survived the American bombing is anybody's guess.

Theoretically, there are numerous trekking possibilities. However, you may not be permitted to put on your backpack and head into the hills. If you are allowed, there are three more great valleys nearby: Manp'ok Valley, leading to Hyangro Peak; Chŏnt'ae Valley, leading to Wonman Peak; and Chilsong Valley, leading to Pirobong (the highest, at 1909m).

Getting There & Away
A visit to Myohyangsan from P'yŏngyang can be done in a day trip, taking the train both ways. It's 160 km north of the capital.

The train leaves P'yŏngyang daily at 6 am and arrives at Myohyangsan at 9 am. Breakfast is taken on the train in a dining car reserved for foreigners. On the return journey, the train leaves Myohyangsan at 7 pm and arrives at P'yŏngyang at 10.20 pm.

The village of Myohyangsan itself consists of one main street lined by traditional Korean houses. The main tourist hotel in this vicinity is the *Hyangsan Hotel*, rated as class A; it's about halfway between the station and the IFE. There is also the class C *Chongbyong Hotel* and the class D *Chongchon Hotel*, both about one km from the railway station.

KAESŎNG
Kaesŏng has some 200,000 residents, but 800 years ago, when it was the capital of the Koryŏ dynasty, it had around four times as many. The Koryŏ dynasty took over after Shilla collapsed in the early 10th century. It then endured turbulent politics, Mongol invasion and domination and barely survived until the Chosŏn Kingdom replaced it in 1390. As a royal capital in the 11th century, however, it was a sumptuously wealthy and sophisticated metropolis crowded with Buddhist aristocrats enjoying the art and temples they patronised.

After centuries of neglect and three major wars, each of which left little but rubble, you won't see many relics of those happy times. At least there is the **Sŏnggyungwan Neo-Confucian College**, which was originally built in 992 and rebuilt after being destroyed in the Japanese invasion of 1592. Today it is host to the **Koryŏ Museum** of celadon pottery, pagodas and other Buddhist relics; Confucian ceremonies are sometimes re-enacted. The buildings surround a wide courtyard, dotted with ancient trees, and the grounds are very nice to walk around. It's a short drive north-east of town.

Kaesŏng may be your only chance while in the DPRK to see a Korean royal tomb. The best one by far is the **Tomb of King Kongmin** (the 31st Koryŏ king, who reigned between 1352 and 1374) and his queen, which is richly decorated with traditional granite facing and statuary. It's about 13 km west of the city centre at a very secluded site. Here there are splendid views over the surrounding tree covered hills from a number of vantage points.

The third great tourist site is the 37m-high **Pakyon Falls**, one of the three most famous in North Korea. It's found in a beautiful natural setting some 24 km north of town. In theory, some great hiking can be done from the falls to the **Taehungsan Fortress**, the mid-Koryŏ **Kwanŭm Temple** (with cave) and the **Taehung Temple**. In practice, however, you can only hike where the authorities say it's OK, which in most cases means being restricted to a few well-worn sites with lots of security.

Kaesŏng itself is a modern city with wide streets, but is of scant interest except for an interesting old part where traditional tile-roofed houses are sandwiched between the river and the main street. Within the town are a number of sights: the **Sonjuk Bridge**, a tiny clapper bridge built in 1216 and, opposite, the **Songin Monument**, which honours Neo-Confucian hero Chong Mong-ju in classic Korean style; the **Nammun** (South Gate), which dates from the 14th century and houses an old Buddhist bell; the **Sungyang Sŏwon** (Confucian Academy); and a peak,

Chanamsan, on the summit of which there's a massive bronze statue of – guess who?

To get to Kaesŏng you can take either the train or a car; the car is preferable if you want to see the towns en route. Driving time between P'yŏngyang and Kaesŏng is about 3¼ hours, including a tea stop at a tourist halt built on a rocky outcrop overlooking the Sohung River.

If you stay in Kaesŏng, you'll be based at either the *Chanamsan Hotel* near the Sonjuk Bridge or the *Kaesŏng Minsok* (Folk) *Hotel*. If you have a choice, opt for the latter; it is built in the traditional Korean yŏgwan style. Both hotels are rated class C.

P'ANMUNJŎM

A short drive south from Kaesŏng is one of the most morbidly fascinating sights in Korea. Even if you've visited this 'Truce Village' from the South, the trip from the northern side is well worth the effort.

The trip there is on the Reunification Highway, a six-lane freeway devoid of traffic with military checkpoints every 20 km. The freeway is supposed to connect P'yŏngyang to Seoul, and the last exit before the DMZ has a large sign saying 'Seoul 70 km'. You drive up to a sentry box at the entrance to the DMZ where a military officer gives you a brief introduction, after which you're escorted to the Joint Security Zone by military officers. From the car park, you enter a large building facing the row of huts which straddle the demarcation line. There you can exchange glances with burly US marines, South Korean soldiers and tourists on the other side in their pagoda viewing tower. Unless meetings are in progress, you'll be permitted to visit the very room where the endless armistice talks go on. After that, it's back to the main building for an exposition of the North Korean view of things.

The whole setting looks very serene, with well-tended gardens, trees, rice fields and chirping birds. However, all around you the countryside is bristling with camouflaged bunkers, tanks, artillery, nerve-gas and bio-logical-weapons shells, missile silos and land mines. If war were to break out during your visit, you'd be incinerated within a minute. Imagine that.

On the way out of the DMZ, you are given a chance to visit the gift shop. There are some real collectors' items here, including a classic propaganda book called *P'anmunjŏm* which is published in a variety of languages:

The US imperialist aggressors drew the Military Demarcation Line to divide Korea and her people by artificial means. P'anmunjŏm is a place through which the line runs and a court which exposes and vehemently denounces the US imperialist criminal aggression in Korea to the whole world. The US imperialists started a war of aggression (1950-53) in order to swallow up the whole of Korea. But here at P'anmunjŏm they went down on their knees before the Korean people and signed the Armistice Agreement.

The next stop on your tour is the **Korean Wall**. According to the North, the Americans and South Koreans have built a concrete wall all the way across the peninsula (248 km) along the southern side of the DMZ, similar to the former Berlin Wall, to prevent the citizens of both Koreas from effecting their reunification. In fact it is an anti-tank barrier which has been there for many years and attracted no attention whatsoever from the North until 1989, when the Berlin Wall was torn down. Suddenly the propaganda potential was recognised and even student protesters in Seoul organised demonstrations to demand that the 'Korean Wall' be torn down.

You'll be able to view the wall through telescopes from four km away. You'll then be taken into a room where you'll be shown a video and given a lecture on the burning desire of the Korean people for reunification. All very gripping stuff. Not much will be said about the triple 3000 V electric fence running along the northern side of the DMZ.

In the DMZ you are mostly able to photograph at will, but always ask your guide first if there is any uncertainty.

KŬMGANGSAN

In the far south-eastern corner of North Korea you'll find the most beautiful set of peaks and valleys of the entire peninsula –

Kŭmgangsan ('diamond mountains'). Despite the name, there are no diamond mines here – the region was named after the key Chinese Zen scripture *The Diamond-like Cutter of All Doubts Sutra*. It's just as well that there are no diamonds, because it would be a tragedy if this area were ever mined. As it stands, you'd be hard-pressed to find better scenery anywhere! During the Tang dynasty (618-907 AD) the famously ethnocentric Chinese were compelled to include these mountains among the five most impressive in the world – the other four are in China.

Kŭmgangsan is divided into Inner, Outer and Sea Kŭmgang regions. The main activities (at least theoretically) are hiking, mountaineering, boating and sightseeing. The area is peppered with former Buddhist temples and hermitages, waterfalls and mineral springs; there's also a pretty lagoon and a small museum. Maps of the area are provided by the park officials to help you decide where you want to go among dozens of excellent sites. The hiking trails around **Kŭmgangsan** (1639m) have been defaced with revolutionary slogans said to have been carved by the Great Leader himself.

If your time here is limited, the best places to visit are the **Samil Lagoon** (hire a boat and rest at the Tanp'ung Restaurant); the **Manmulsang** area (fantastically-shaped crags) and the **Kuryong** and **Pibong Falls** (a 4½ km hike from the Mongnan Restaurant) in the Outer Kŭmgang Region; and the impressive reconstruction of the **P'yohŏn Temple** (founded in 670 and one of old Korea's most important Zen monasteries) in the Inner Kŭmgang Region. Hiking in the valleys around P'yohŏnsa or, really, *anywhere* in the park would be rewarding and memorable. You won't need to carry much drinking water, but bring plenty of film. **Pirobong** (1639m) is the highest of at least a hundred peaks.

Getting There & Away

The usual route to Kŭmgangsan is by car along the new highway from P'yŏngyang to Onjong-ri, via Wonsan (around 315 km, a four-hour drive). Along the way to Wonsan

NORTH KOREA

your car or bus will stop off at a teahouse by Sinp'yŏng Lake. From Wonsan, the road more or less follows the coastline south, and you'll get glimpses of the double electric fence which runs the entire length of the east coast. There may be a stop for tea at Shijung Lake.

Your final destination is the village of Onjong-ri and the *Kŭmgangsan Hotel*, rated class B. The hotel is a rambling affair, consisting of a main building and several outer buildings which include chalets, a shop, a dance hall and a bath-house (fed by a hot spring). The food served here is good, especially the wild mountain vegetable dishes.

PAEKDUSAN

Beautiful Paekdusan straddles the Korean-Chinese border in the far north. At 2744m it's the highest peak on the whole Korean peninsula. An extinct volcano surrounded by vast wilderness, its name means literally 'White Head Mountain'; the main peak is covered year-round by whitish pumice and snow. Surrounded by bare rocky crags at the summit is a huge crater lake, called Chŏnji or 'Lake of Heaven'; it is some 14 km in circumference and reaches a maximum depth of 384m. This makes it one of the deepest alpine lakes in the world and, although it's fed by two hot springs, it's also one of the coldest.

Paekdusan is sacred to both North and South Koreans. According to Korean mythology, this is where the 'Son of the Lord of Heaven' descended to earth and the first Korean kingdom began (see the Tan-gun Legend aside). It should be no mystery, then, why the North Korean regime claims that Kim Jong-il was born here, even though all sources outside North Korea maintain that he was born in the Russian city of Khabarovsk. New official mythology even claims that flying white horses were seen in the sky after baby Kim entered the world.

North Korea's current history books also claim that Kim Il-sung established his guerrilla headquarters at Paekdusan in the 1920s and from there defeated the Japanese. As proof, you'll be shown revolutionary and anti-imperialist declarations which the Great

Leader and his comrades carved on the trees. You'll be told that more and more of these 'slogan-bearing trees' are being discovered every year; some of the carvings are so well preserved you'd almost think they were carved yesterday, if you didn't know better. Outside of North Korea, no history books claim that this mountain was ever a battlefield during WWII. Nevertheless, the North Korean book *Kim Jong-il In His Young Days* describes the Dear Leader's difficult childhood during those days of ceaseless warfare at Paekdusan:

His childhood was replete with ordeals.

The secret camp of the Korean People's Revolutionary Army in the primeval forest was his home, and ammunition belts and magazines were his playthings. The raging blizzards and ceaseless gunshots were the first sounds to which he became accustomed.

Day in and day out fierce battles went on and, during the breaks, there were military and political trainings. On the battlefield, there was no quilt to warmly wrap the new-born child. So women guerrillas gallantly tore cotton out of their own uniforms and each contributed pieces of cloth to make a patchwork quilt for the infant.

Visitors here will be shown those trees; the **Secret Camp**, featuring an equally newish looking log cabin beneath **Jŏng-il Peak** (said to be the Dear Leader's birthplace); and plenty of monuments commemorating patriotic fighters and glorious battles.

But the real reason to come here is the glories of nature – vast tracts of virgin forest, abundant wildlife, lonely granite crags, fresh springs, gushing streams and dramatic waterfalls. For those able to make the steep and treacherous climb, there's the astounding peak area where heaven indeed seems close and the mundane world so very far away. Few foreign travellers make it here at all, because of the formidable costs involved, and that is unlikely to change until a proper highway or railway line is built.

Places to Stay

Hotels to stay at in this area include the *Hyesan Hotel*, in the town of the same name; the *Samjiyon Sin Hotel*, some 67 km from

NORTH KOREA

Hyesan; the *Pegaebong Hotel*; and the *Onsupyong Hotel*. The first two are B class and the latter two C class.

Getting There & Away

Paekdusan is only accessible from around late June to mid-September; at all other times it is forbiddingly cold and stormy. Access to the mountain is by air only, followed by car. Charter flights are available to Paekdusan for US$3000 per round-trip flight, which can hold up to 30 people. At US$100 per person that isn't unreasonable, but it would be a rather significant expense if you were travelling solo! Unfortunately, this flight is currently the only transport offered to Paekdusan.

You can also visit the mountain and crater lake from the Chinese side – a trip that is now popular with tourists from South Korea. Paekdusan is called Changbaishan in Chinese and the crater lake is called Tianchi (Lake of Heaven).

CHILBOSAN

The 'seven treasures mountains' offer impressive scenery, although it is inferior to that found at Kŭmgangsan or Myohyangsan. They are located on the east coast at the southern end of North Hamgyŏng Province and, like Kŭmgangsan; they are divided into three sections: Inner Chilbo, Outer Chilbo and Sea Chilbo. The highest peak – Chonbul or 'Thousand Buddhas' – is only 659m high, but the steepness of the granite cliffs adds grandeur to the scenery. The 250 sq km Chilbosan area boasts enough valleys, crags, waterfalls, temple sites and mineral springs to keep a nature-loving traveller happy for several days. North Korea is planning to open the area to foreign tourists for the first time during 1997. The availability of hotels and restaurants is still unknown as we go to press.

RAJIN-SONBONG ZONE

This is a 746 sq km strip of land on the extreme north-eastern coast. A few years ago it was designated as an 'International Free-Trade Investment Zone', whatever that might mean in the context of North Korea. The UN has lobbied China, Russia and North Korea to set up a 'Golden Triangle' economic-growth area on the lower reaches of the Tuman River where the three nations meet; Rajin-Sonbong is P'yŏngyang's decidedly unimpressive contribution to the scheme. The other two prospective partners have shown even less enthusiasm for the venture, so the idea is so far going nowhere fast.

Travellers are unlikely to visit here, unless the North Korean authorities view them as potential joint-venture investors (or sympathetic business journalists). There is very little infrastructure here yet for business or tourism, for the obvious reason that multi-national companies have not exactly been breaking down the door to invest.

Those who do make it to Rajin-Sonbong (whether by train or car, from P'yŏngyang or Wonsan), may be able to enjoy 56 km of relatively unspoiled jagged coastline featuring sanctuaries for seabirds and seals, a few

The Lake of Heaven

Many legends spring from the Lake of Heaven. Dragons, and other things that go bump in the night, were believed to have emerged from the alpine waters. In fact, they're still believed to do so. There have been intermittent sightings of unidentified swimming objects – Asia's own Loch Ness beasties or aquatic yetis or what have you. Since the lake is frozen over in winter and temperatures are well below zero, it would be a pretty hardy monster that survives these conditions (even plankton can't). Sightings from the Chinese and North Korean sides point to a black bear, fond of swimming and oblivious to the paperwork necessary for crossing these tight borders. On a more symbolic note, Chinese and Korean couples throw coins into the water, pledging that their love will remain as deep as the lake, and as long-lived. ∎

visitable offshore islands and some quiet fishing villages. There are three pretty lakes and the Chogol Buddhist hermitage within the peninsular Tuman estuary at the far eastern end of the zone. Two hot spring 'spas' are said to exist within the zone, but we were unable to find any information about them; we suspect that they have not yet been developed for tourists.

Two or three small hotels were opened here for potential investor guests in 1996. A Hong Kong hotel company broke ground in 1997 for a $US50 million five-star casino-hotel complex on the beach within the free-trade zone. The Emperor Hotel is scheduled to begin accepting investors and tourists by the spring of 1998. There are a few Korean restaurants in the towns.

Crossing the border here into or from China doesn't seem to be possible for westerners now. Crossing the Tuman River into or from Russia (by train) is possible but difficult and rarely attempted; special visa and ticket arrangements must be made in advance. The border stations on both sides are heavily guarded and they still have a Cold War mentality – the paperwork is taken very seriously. Customs checks may be thorough, so be on your best behaviour and don't carry anything that might be objectionable to the officials of either side. Don't even pull your camera out when at the border, or your film may be confiscated. The border town of Tumangang is actually three km from the border (the Tuman River), and is the farthest point in the nation from P'yongyang.

Glossary

ajimah, ajumma – a married or older woman; a term of respect for a woman who runs a hotel, restaurant or other business
am – hermitage

bawi – large rock
bong – peak

ch'a – tea
ch'ang – traditional drama, resembling western opera
chaebol – huge corporate conglomerate
chihach'ŏl yŏk – subway station
chogye – principal Korean Buddhist sect, representing 95% of believers
chonhwa kadu – magnetic phone cards

dae – great, large
-do – province
do – island
donggul or **gul** – cave

-ga – section of a long street
gak, nu or **ru** – pavilion
gil – street
gung or **kung** – palace
-gu – urban district
gun – county

hae – sea
hagwon – private language school often employing foreign teachers
hangŭl – Korean phonetic alphabet
hanja – Chinese-style writing system
harubang – 'grandfather stones' found on Chejudo
hasukchip – boarding house
hesuyokjang – beach
ho – lake
hof, hop'ŭ – pub

insam – ginseng

jŏng – hall of a temple

kibun – a sense of well-being or harmony between people. In practice it resembles the Japanese notion of 'face'.
kimch'i – spicy fermented cabbage, the national dish
konghang – airport
kongwon – park
k'ŏpi syop – coffee shop
kugak – traditional music using stringed instruments, drums, cymbals, horns, chimes and flutes

maekju – beer
makkŏli – white rice wine
minbak – guesthouse, a private home with rooms for rent
minsogak – traditional folk music
mok yok t'ang – bathhouse
mudang – shaman; usually female
mun – gate
myŏn – township
myo or **tae** – shrine

nam – south
no or **ro** – large street, boulevard
nŭng or **rŭng** – tomb
nyŏng or **ryŏng** – mountain pass

onch'ŏn, wonch'ŏn – hot spring
ondol – underfloor heating

p'ansori – traditional stories told to the beat of a drum
p'okp'o – waterfall
p'yŏng – a unit of measure, one p'yŏng equals 3.3 sq metres
paduk – Korean chess, same as the Japanese game *go*
puk – north
pulgogi – barbecued beef & vegetables grilled at the table, the most popular dish with foreigners
pungsu – geomancy; the art of remaining in harmony with the universe

ri or **ni** – village
Ryohaengsa – North Korean government tourist agency, also known as Korea International Tourist Bureau

salpuri – traditional improvised dance
samsŏng-gak – Shamanistic hall found in the grounds of many Buddhist temples (literally three spirit hall)
sanjang – mountain hut
sansŏng – fortress built on a mountaintop
san – mountain
sa – temple
shich'ŏng – city hall
shi – city
soju – potato 'vodka'
sŏ – west
sŏwon – former Confucian academies which are now preserved as national treasures
ssirum – Korean wrestling, similar to Japanese sumo wrestling
sungmu – traditional drum dance

t'aekkyŏn – the original form of *t'aekwondo*
t'aekwondo – Korean martial arts
t'alchum – traditional mask dance
t'ap – pagoda

tchinjilbang – saunas, often converted bath houses
t'ongil – unification
tabang – tearoom
taepiso – mountain shelter
tong – east

ŭp – town

won – unit of Korean currency

yak – medicine
yŏgwan – small family-run hotel, usually with private bath
yŏinsuk – small family-run hotel with closet-sized rooms and shared bath

ACRONYMS
CPO – Central Post Office
DMZ – Demilitarised Zone
DPRK – Democratic People's Republic of Korea (North Korea)
KAL – Korean Air
KNTO – Korean National Tourist Organisation
NP – National Park
PP – Provincial Park
ROK – Republic of Korea (South Korea)
USO – United Services Organisation

Gazetteer

GENERAL TERMS

Airport	공항
Beach	해수욕장
Confucian School	향교
Folk Museum	민속박물관
Hot Springs	온천
Island	도
Market	시장
Museum	박물관
Pavilion	정
Temple	사
Timetable	시각표

SEOUL 서울

Ch'angdŏkkung	창덕궁
Ch'anggyŏnggung	창경궁
Chang-an-dong Antique Market	장안동시장
Changch'ung Park	장충공원
Children's Grand Park	어린이대공원
Chogyesa Temple	조계사
Chonggak	종각
Chongmyo	종묘
Department Stores	백화점
Herbal Medicine Arcade	한약상가
Hongik	홍익
Hwanghak-dong Flea Market	황학동시장
Insadonggil	인사동길
Inwangsan	인왕산
It'aewon	이태원
Kangnam	강남
Kimp'o International Airport	김포공항
Kwanaksan	관악산
Kwanghwamun	광화문
Kyŏngbokkung	경복궁
Kyŏngdong Market	경동시장
Kyŏnghŭigung	경희궁
Lotte World	롯데월드
Myŏng-dong	명동
Namdaemun	남대문
Namdaemun Market	남대문시장
Namsan Park	남산공원
National Folk Museum	국립민속박물관
Olympic Park	올림픽공원
Olympic Stadium	올림픽스타디움
Pongwonsa Temple	봉원사
Pongŭnsa Temple	봉은사

Poshingak Pavilion	보신각
Postal Museum	우체국박물관
Sajik Park	사직공원
Seoul Dream Land	서울드림랜드
Shinch'on	신촌
T'apkol Park	탑골공원
Taehangno	대학로
Tŏksugung	덕수궁
Tonam	도남동
Tongdaemun Gate	동대문
Tongdaemun Market	동대문시장
Unhyŏn-gung Palace	운현궁
War Memorial	전쟁기념관
Yŏŭi-do	여의도
Yongsan Electronics Market	용산전자상가
Yongsan Family Park	용산가족공원

KYŎNGGI-DO 경기도

Chakyakdo	작약도
Chayu Park	자유공원
Confucian School	향교
Culture & Arts Hall	종합문화회관
Ich'ŏn Ceramic Village	이천도예촌
Inch'ŏn	인천
Inch'ŏn Municipal Museum	인천시립박물관
Kanghwa City	강화시
Kanghwado	강화도
Korean Folk Village	한국민속촌
Kwanaksan	관악산
Munhaksan Fortress	문학산성
Namhansansŏng Provincial Park	남한산도립공원
Odusan Unification Observatory	오두산통일공원
P'anmunjŏm	판문점
Paengnyŏngdo Island	백령도
Pomunsa	보문사
Puk'ansan National Park	북한산국립공원
Sanjŏng Lake Resort	산정호수
Seoul Grand Park	서울대공원
Seoul Horse Race Track	서울승마공원
Songdo Resort	송도유원지
Songt'an	송탄
Subong Park	수봉공원
Suraksan	수락산
Suwon	수원
Tŏkjŏkdo	덕적도

Wolmido	월미도
Yi Dynasty Royal Tombs	이조왕릉
Yŏju	여주
Yŏn'an Pier	연안부두
Yŏnghŭngdo	영흥도
Yŏngjongdo	영종도
Yong'in Farmland	용인자연농원
Yong-in Everland	용인자연농원

KANGWON-DO	**강원도**
Beaches	해수욕장
Ch'iaksan National Park	치악산국립공원
Ch'unch'ŏn	춘천
Chŏngt'osa	정토사
Kaeksamun	객사문
Kangnŭng	강릉
Kugok Waterfall	구곡폭포
Kwonkŭmsŏng	권금성신장
Kyŏngp'o Provincial Park	경포누립공원
Kyebangsan	계방산
Murŭng Valley	무릉견찌
Naksan	낙산
Naksan Provincial Park	낙산도립공원
Odaesan National Park	오대산국립공원
Ojuk'ŏn Confucian Shrine	오죽헌
Osaek Springs	오색약수
P'aroho Lake	파로호
Samaksan	삼악산
Samch'ŏk	삼척
Sangwonsa	상원사
Sŏraksan National Park	설악산국립공원
Shinhŭngsa Temple	신흥사
Sokch'o	속초
Soyangho Lake	소양호
T'aebaeksan Provincial Park	테믈뿔도립겜왠
Tano Festival	단오제
Tonghae	동협
Tottering Rock	흔들바위
Unification Observatory	통일전망대
Wolchŏngsa	월정사
Wonju	왠凩
Yukdam, Piryong & T'owangsŏng Falls	육담폭포, 비롱폭포, 토왕성폭포
Ŭiam Lake	의암호

KYŎNGSANGBUK-DO	**경상북도**
Andong	안동
Andong Folk Village	안동민속촌
Apsan Park	앞산공원
Ch'ŏngnyangsan Provincial Park	청량산도립공원

Chebiwon (Amitaba Buddha)	제비원
Chikchisa	직지사
Chuwangsan National Park	주왕산국립공원
Hahoe Folk Village	하회마을
Herbal Medicine Market	약령시장
Kayasan National Park	가야산국립공원
Kimch'ŏn	김천
Namyang (Ullŭngdo)	남양동
Nari Basin (Ullŭngdo)	나리동
P'algongsan Provincial Park	팔공산도립공원
P'ohang	포항
Po'gyŏngsa	보경사
Pukbu Beach	북부해수욕장
Pusŏksa	부석사
Sŏnginbong (Ullŭngdo)	성인봉
Sokŭmgang Valley	소금강
Songdo Beach	송도해수욕장
Sudosan	수두신
T'onggumi	통구미
Taegu	대구
Taewonsa (Ullŭngdo)	대원사
Todong	도동
Tosan Sŏwon Confucian Institute	도산서원
Turyu Park	두류공원
Ullŭngdo	울릉도

KYŎNGJU	**경주**
Anapji Pond	안압지
Ch'ŏmsŏngdae	첨싱대
Chŏnghyesa	징혜사
Chusa'am	수사밤
General Kim Yu-shin's Tomb	김유신징군묘
Kamunsa	가문사
King Hŭngdŏk's Tomb	흥덕왕능
King Muyol's Tomb	태종무열왕릉
Kirimsa	기림사
Kwaenŭng Tomb	쾌릉
Munmu Sea Tomb	문무왕해중릉
Namsan	남산
National Museum	경주박물관
Oksan Sŏwon	옥산서원
Onŭng Tombs	오릉
P'osŏkjŏngji	포석정지
Panwolsong	반월성
Pokdu'am	복두암
Pomun Lake Area	보문호
Pulguk-dong	불국동
Pulguksa	불국사
Punhwangsa Pagoda	분황사
Samnŭng	삼능
Shinsŏnsa Temple	신선사

Sŏkkuram Grotto	석굴암
Todŏksa	도덕사
Tombs in Nosŏ-dong	노소동릉
Tongnaktang	동낙당
Triple Buddha	삼존석불
Tumuli Park	대릉원
Ura Village	우라마을
Yangdong Folk Village	양동
Yongdamjŏng	용담정

KYŎNGSANGNAM-DO 경상남도

Ch'oksŏngnu	촉석루
Chagalch'i Fish Market	자갈치시장
Chinju	진주
Chinju Fortress	진주성
Chinju National Museum	진주박물관
Chinyangho	진양호
Chirisan National Park	지리산국립공원
Haeundae Beach	해운대해수욕장
Kajisan Provincial Park	가지산도립공원
Kŭjŏngsansŏng	금정산성
Naewonsa	내원사
Oryukdo	오륙도
Pŏmŏsa	범어사
Pusan	부산
Pusan Tower	부산타워
Ssanggyesa	쌍계사
T'aejongdae	태종대
T'ongdosa	통도사
Taeshin Park	대신공원
Taewonsa	대원사
Yŏnhwasan Provincial Park	연화산도립공원

CHŎLLANAM-DO 전라남도

Admiral Yi's Turtle Ship	거북선
Ch'ŏngdo-Ri	정도리
Ch'ungminsa	충민사
Chindo	진도
Chinnamgwan	지남관
Chogyesan Provincial Park	조계산도립공원
Chuktobong Park	죽도봉공원
Confucian School	향교
Hansansa	한산사
Hongdo	홍도
Hwaŏmsa	화엄사
Hŭksando	흑산도
Kurye	구례
Kwangju	광주
Kwangju National Museum	국립광주박물관
Mansŏng-ni Beach	만성리해수욕장
Mokp'o	목포
Mudŭngsan Provincial Park	무등산도립공원
Myŏngsashim-ni	명사십리
Nagan Fortress Folk Village	낙안읍성

Odongdo	오동도
Pogildo	보길도
Sunch'ŏn	순천
Tadohae Haesang National Park	다도해해상 국립공원
Tamyang Bamboo Crafts Museum	담양대나무 박물관
Turyunsan Provincial Park	두륜산도립공원
Wando	완도
Wolch'ulsan National Park	월출산국립공원
Yŏsu	여수

CHEJU-DO 제주도

Ch'ŏnjiyŏn Waterfall	천지연폭포
Ch'ungmun Beach	중문해수욕장
Chŏngbang Waterfall	정방폭포
Cheju City	제주
Cheju Folk Village	제주민속촌
Cheju Folkcraft & Natural History Museum	민속자연사박물관
Chungmun Resort	중문관광단지
Hallasan National Park	한라산국립공원
Hyŏpchaegul	협재굴
Kap'ado & Marado	가파도, 마라도
Kwandŏkjŏng	관덕정
Manjanggul	만장굴
Moksŏgwon	목석원
Samsŏnghyŏl	삼성혈
San'gumburi	산굼부리 분화구
Sanbanggulsa	산방굴사
Sŏgwip'o	서귀포
Sŏng-Ŭp Folk Village	성읍민속촌
Sŏngsan	성산
Udo	우도
Yongdu'am	용두암

CHŎLLABUK-DO 전라북도

Chŏngju	정주
Chŏnju	전주
Maisan Provincial Park	마이산도립공원
Moaksan Provincial Park	모악산도립공원
Naejangsan National Park	내장산국립공원
Pyŏnsanbando National Park	변산반도 국립공원
Sŏnunsan Provincial Park	선운산도립공원
Tŏgyusan National Park	덕유산국립공원

CH'UNGCH'ŎNGNAM-DO 충청남도

Ch'ŏnan	천안
Ch'ilgapsan Provincial Park	칠갑산도립공원
Chongnimsa	정림사
Hongsŏng	홍성
Independence Hall Of Korea	독립기념관

Kagwonsa 각원사
Kapsa 갑사
King Muryŏng's Tomb 백제무령왕릉
Kongju 공주
Kongju National Museum 국립공주박물관
Kongsansŏng 공산성
Kungnamji Pond & Pavilion 궁남지
Kwanch'oksa 관촉사
Kyeryongsan National Park 계룡산국립공원
Kŭmsan 금산
Magoksa 마곡사
Pomunsan 보문산
Pusosan 부소산
Puyŏ 부여
Puyŏ National Museum 국립부여반물관
Royal Paekche Tombs 왕릉
T'aean Haean 태안해안
　National Park 국립공원
Taedunsan Provincial Park 대둔산도립공원
Taejŏn 내선
Taejŏn Expo Science Park 대전엑스포
Tŏksan Provincial Park 넉산노립공원
Tonghaksa 동학사
Yusŏng Hot Springs 뉴싱븐친

CH'UNGCH'ŎNGBUK-DO 충청북도
Ch'ŏngdong Donggul 청동동굴
Ch'ŏngju 청주
Ch'ungju 충주
Ch'ungjuho 충주호
Chech'ŏn 제천
Hŭibangsa 희방사
Kosu Donggul 고수동굴
Kuinsa 구인사
Nodong Donggul 노동동굴
Sangdangsansŏng 상당산성
Sobaeksan National Park 소백산국립공원
Songnisan National Park 속리산국립공원
Suanbo Hot Springs 수안보온천
Tanyang 단양
Woraksan National Park 월악산국립공원
Ŭirimji Pond 의림지

NORTH KOREA 북한
Haeju 해수
Kaesŏng 개성
Kŭmgangsan 금강산
Myohyangsan 묘향산
Namp'o 남포
P'anmunjŏm 판문점
P'yŏngyang 평양
Paekdusan 백두산
Rajin-Sonbong Zone 나진성봉
Wonsan 원산

Timetables

BUSES FROM SEOUL

Table 1 – Buses from Kyŏngbusŏn Building, Seoul Express Bus Terminal

Destination	1st Bus	Last Bus	Frequency	Fare (W)	Travel Time
Ch'ŏnan	6.30 am	9.20 pm	15 min	2600	1 hr
Ch'ŏngju	5.50 am	10 pm	10 min	4000	1¾ hrs
Chinju	6 am	6.30 pm	25 min	12,200	5½ hrs
Kimch'ŏn	7.10 am	6.50 pm	11 daily	7000	3 hrs
Kongju	6 am	11 pm	30 min	4100	2½ hrs
Kumi	6.50 am	7.40 pm	1¼ hrs	7700	3¼ hrs
Kŭmsan	7 am	6.40 pm	11 daily	6200	2¾ hrs
Kyŏngju	6.30 am	6.30 pm	30 min	10,700	4¼ hrs
Masan	6 am	9 pm	15 min	11,200	5 hrs
P'ohang	6 am	6.30 pm	20 min	11,700	5 hrs
Poŭn	7.10 am	6.50 pm	8 daily	6100	2½ hrs
Pugok	8 am	6 pm	2 hrs	10,400	4¾ hrs
Pusan	6 am	8.30 pm	15 min	12,600	5¼ hrs
Taegu	6 am	8.30 pm	5-10 min	8900	4 hrs
Taejŏn	6 am	9.55 pm	5-10 min	4800	2 hrs
Ulsan	6 am	6.30 pm	20 min	11,900	5 hrs
Yŏngdong	7.10 am	7.10 pm	8 daily	6400	2¾ hrs

Table 2 – Buses from Honam-Yŏngdongsŏn Building, Seoul Express Bus Terminal

Destination	1st Bus	Last Bus	Frequency	Fare (W)	Travel Time
Ch'ungju	6.20 am	8.30 pm	30 min	4500	2 hrs
Chech'ŏn	5.40 am	8.10 pm	40-50 min	4900	3¾ hrs
Chinan	9.35 am	4.35 pm	4 daily	8200	4 hrs
Chindo	7.35 am	4.20 pm	4 daily	13,400	6¼ hrs
Chŏngŭp	6 am	11 pm	30 min	8000	3¼ hrs
Chŏnju	5.30 am	11 pm	5-15 min	7100	2¾ hrs
Haenam	7.55 am	5.55 pm	6 daily	12,000	5½ hrs
Ich'ŏn	6.30 am	9.20 pm	20-30 min	2300	1 hr
Iksan	5.30 am	10.30 pm	30 min	7000	3 hrs
Kangnŭng	6 am	11.30 pm	15 min	7400	4½ hrs
Kimje	6.40 am	7.50 pm	1 hr	7400	3¼ hrs
Koch'ang	9.50 am	5.40 pm	30-60 min	8700	4 hrs
Kunsan	6 am	10.50 pm	20-30 min	7600	3¼ hrs
Kwangju	5.30 am	midnight	5-10 min	9600	4 hrs
Mokp'o	5.30 am	10.40 pm	30 min	11,300	5½ hrs
Namwon	6 am	10.20 pm	40 min	8800	4¼ hrs
Nonsan	7 am	7.50 pm	1¼ hrs	6400	2¾ hrs
Puan	6.50 am	7.30 pm	30-50 min	8300	3½ hrs
Sokch'o	6.30 am	11.30 pm	30-60 min	9400	5¼ hrs
Sunch'ŏn	6 am	10.50 pm	20-30 min	11,900	5¼ hrs
Tonghae	6.30 am	11.30 pm	30-60 min	8600	4¾ hrs
Wando	7.45 am	5.30 pm	4 daily	13,100	6 hrs
Wonju	6 am	9 pm	15 min	3800	1¾ hrs
Yong-in	7.30 am	9.30 pm	15-30 min	1300	40 min
Yŏju	6.30 am	9.20 pm	30-40 min	2700	1¾ hrs
Yŏngam	8.40 am	4.40 pm	4 daily	10,900	4¾ hrs
Yŏsu	6.10 am	10.40 pm	30-40 min	12,800	5½ hrs

Table 3 – Buses from Tong-Seoul Bus Terminal

Destination	1st Bus	Last Bus	Frequency	Fare (W)	Travel Time
Ch'ŏngju	6 am	9 pm	30 min	4300	1¾ hrs
Ch'ungju	6 am	8.40 pm	20 min	4480	3¾ hrs
Chŏnju	6 am	8.20 pm	40min	7500	3¼ hrs
Chŏngŭp	6.30 am	6.40 pm	6 daily	8400	3¼ hrs
Ich'ŏn	6.30 am	9.30 pm	1 hr	2200	1 hr
Kangnŭng	6 am	7.40 pm	45 min	7400	3½ hrs
Kuinsa	7.05 am	4.20 pm	7 daily	8200	4 hrs
Kwangju	6 am	7.30 pm	30 min	9800	4 hrs
Pusan	6 am	6.40 pm	30 min	12,900	5¼ hrs
Sokch'o	7 am	6.30 pm	4 daily	9400	5 hrs
Songnisan	7.30 am	6.20 pm	10 daily	7700	2¾ hrs
Taegu	6 am	8 pm	30 min	9300	3¾ hrs
Taejŏn	6 am	8 pm	30 min	5200	1¾ hrs
Tanyang	6.40 am	6.15 pm	6 daily	7200	3 hrs
Tonghae	7 am	6.40 pm	2 daily	8600	4¼ hrs
Wonju	7 am	8 pm	1 hr	3800	1¾ hrs
Yŏju	6.30 am	8.30 pm	40 min	2700	1¼ hrs
Yŏngju	9 am	4.30 pm	4 daily	11,000	3¼ hrs
Yŏngwol	7 am	7 pm	4 daily	6400	3 hrs

Table 4 – Buses from Sangbong Bus Terminal

Destination	1st Bus	Last Bus	Frequency	Fare (W)	Travel Time
Ch'iaksan	6.30 am	2.05 pm	4 daily	5900	2¼ hrs
Ch'unch'ŏn	5.15 am	9.30 pm	15 min	3900	1½ hrs
Inje	5.50 am	6.30 pm	30 min	7600	3½ hrs
Kangnŭng	6 am	6.30 pm	8 daily	10,100	4 hrs
Kwangju	6 am	7.40 pm	1 hr	9800	4 hrs
Pusan	6 am	9 pm	8 daily	12,800	5¼ hrs
Sokch'o	6 am	6 pm	26 daily	10,500	4½ hrs
Taegu	6 am	9 pm	8 daily	9200	3¾ hrs
Taejŏn	6 am	9 pm	1 hr	5100	1¾ hrs
Wonju	6 am	6.50 pm	1 hr	5500	2¾ hrs

TRAINS FROM SEOUL, CH'ŎNGNYANGNI

From Ch'ŏngnyangni to Ch'unch'ŏn

Class	Time	Frequency	Travel Time	Fare (W)
Mugunghwa	7.42 am-9.26 pm	6 daily	1 hr 30 min	3500
T'ongil	6.37 am-10.10 pm	9 daily	1 hr 50 min	2400
Pidulgi	6.10 am, 6.50 pm	2 daily	2 hr 10 min	1200

From Ch'ŏngnyangni to Tonghae

Class	Time	Frequency	Travel Time	Fare (W)
Saemaul	5 pm	1 daily	5 hr 30 min	20,700
Mugunghwa	2 pm	1 daily	5 hr 35 min	11,000
T'ongil	10 am, 11 pm	2 daily	6 hrs	7500

From Ch'ŏngnyangni to T'aebaek

Class	Time	Frequency	Travel Time	Fare (W)
Saemaul	5 pm	1 daily	4 hrs	17,300
Mugunghwa	2 pm	1 daily	4 hr 10 min	8800
T'ongil	10 am, noon	2 daily	5 hrs	6000

From Ch'ŏngnyangni to Wonju

Class	Time	Frequency	Travel Time	Fare (W)
Saemaul	9 am, 5 pm	2 daily	1 hr 30 min	8500
Mugunghwa	11 am-6 pm	3 daily	1 hr 40 min	3800
T'ong-il	10 am-11 pm	7 daily	1 hr 50 min	2600
Pidulgi	6.30 am-7 pm	4 daily	2 hr 30 min	1500

FERRIES & FARES TO/FROM ULLŬNGDO

P'ohang-Ullŭngdo

Period	P'ohang	Ullŭngdo	Frequency	Travel Time	Ship's Name
21 Aug-19 Jul	10 am	5 am	every 2 days	3 hours	Sun Flower
20 Jul-20 Aug	7 pm	2.30 pm	daily	3 hours	Sun Flower
21 Aug-19 Jul	10 am	3 pm	daily	4 hours	Sea Flower
20 Jul-20 Aug	9.30 am	4.30 am	daily	4 hours	Sea Flower

Hup'o-Ullŭngdo

Period	Hup'o	Ullŭngdo	Frequency	Travel Time	Ship's Name
25 Jul-15 Aug	6 pm	2 pm	daily	3 hours	Sea Flower
25 Jul-15 Aug	9 am, 7 pm	2 pm, 4.30 pm	2 daily	3 hours	Ocean Flower
16 Aug-30 Oct	noon	4 pm	daily	3 hours	Ocean Flower
1 Nov-31 Mar	noon	4 pm	Th & Sat	3 hours	Ocean Flower
1 Apr-24 Jul	noon	4 pm	daily	3 hours	Ocean Flower

Sokch'o-Ullŭngdo

Period	Sokch'o	Ullŭngdo	Frequency	Travel Time	Ship's Name
1 Mar-20 Jul	2 pm	9 am	daily	4 hours	Taewon
21 Jul-20 Aug	9 am	4 am	daily	4 hours	Taewon
21 Aug-31 Oct	2 pm	9 am	daily	4 hours	Taewon

Tonghae (Muk'o)-Ullŭngdo

Period	Tonghae	Ullŭngdo	Frequency	Travel Time	Ship's Name
21 Jul-20 Aug	9.30 am, 6 pm	5 am, 2.30 pm	2 daily	3 hours	Taewon
21 Mar-20 Jul	1 pm	8.30 am	daily	3 hours	Taewon
21 Aug-31 Oct	1 pm	8.30 am	daily	3 hours	Taewon
1 Nov-20 Mar	1 pm	10.30 am	Tue & Fri	3 hours	Taewon

Fares to Ullŭngdo (in W)

Route	Ship's Name	deluxe	1st class	Age 2-12	Age 05
Hup'o	Ocean Flower	31,000	28,300	14,150	21,000
P'ohang	Sun Flower	44,000	38,000	19,000	30,400
P'ohang	Sea Flower	38,300	34,800	17,400	27,800
Sokch'o	Taewon Catamaran		36,000	18,000	28,800
Tonghae	Taewon Catamaran		26,600	13,300	21,000

TRAINS TO KYŎNGSANGBUK-DO

Trains from Seoul to Tongdaegu

Class	Time	Frequency	Travel Time	Fare (W)
Saemaul	8 am-11.20 pm	16 daily	3 hrs	21,300
Mugunghwa	6.10 am-11.55 pm	28 daily	3 hr 40 min	11,400
T'ong-il	6.10 am-10.30 pm	14 daily	4 hrs	7800

Trains from Seoul to Kimch'ŏn

Class	Time	Frequency	Travel Time	Fare (W)
Saemaul	9 am, 5.30 pm	2 daily	2 hr 25 min	18,100
Mugunghwa	7.30 am-11.55 pm	28 daily	2 hr 50 min	8800
T'ongil	6.10 am-10.30 pm	14 daily	3 hr 10 min	6100

Trains from Ch'ŏngnyangni to Andong

Class	Time	Frequency	Travel Time	Fare (W)
Saemaul	9 am	1 daily	4 hrs	17,500
Mugunghwa	11 am, 6 pm	2 daily	4 hr 20 min	7400
T'ongil	1 pm-9 pm	3 daily	4 hr 40 min	5100

Trains from Seoul to Kyŏngju

Class	Time	Frequency	Travel Time	Fare (W)
Saemaul	9 am-6.30 pm	4/day	4 hr 10 min	26,800
Mugunghwa	9 pm	1 daily	5 hr 25 min	12,600

TRAINS TO KYŎNGSANGNAM-DO

Trains from Seoul to Pusan

Class	Time	Frequency	Travel Time	Fare (W)
Saemaul	7 am-11 pm	18 daily	4 hrs 10 mins	29,000
Mugunghwa	7.30 am-11.55 pm	25 daily	5 hrs	15,400
T'ongil	6.10 am-10.30 pm	11 daily	5 hrs 20 mins	10,600

Trains from Seoul to Chinju

Class	Time	Frequency	Travel Time	Fare (W)
Saemaul	9 am	1 daily	6 hrs	31,700
Mugunghwa	8.45 am, 10 pm	2 daily	6 hrs 15 mins	17,200
T'ongil	12.30 pm, 11.50 am	2 daily	6 hrs 40 mins	

TRAINS TO CHŎLLANAM-DO

Trains from Seoul to Yŏsu

Class	Time	Frequency	Travel Time	Fare (W)
Saemaul	9.40 am, 6.05 pm	2 daily	5 hr 30 mins	29,200
Mugunghwa	8.05 am-10.45 pm	5 daily	6 hrs	15,6800
T'ong-il	10.08 am-9.45 pm	2 daily	6 hr 40 mins	10,700

Trains from Seoul to Kwangju

Class	Time	Frequency	Travel Time	Fare (W)
Saemaul	9.05 am, 5.10 pm	2 daily	3 hr 40 mins	23,000
Mugunghwa	11.05 am-11.30 pm	4 daily	4 hr 10 mins	12,500
T'ong-il	8.20 am, 7.45 pm	2 daily	4 hr 30 min	8600

Trains from Seoul to Mokp'o

Class	Time	Frequency	Travel Time	Fare (W)
Saemaul	10.05 am, 4.05 pm	2 daily	4 hr 40 min	27,600
Mugunghwa	7.20 am-8.50 pm	4 daily	5 hr 30 min	14,500
T'ong-il	11.20 am-11 05 pm	4 daily	5 hr 50 min	10,000

TRAINS TO CHŎLLABUK-DO

Trains from Seoul to Chŏnju

Class	Time	Frequency	Travel Time	Fare (W)
Saemaul	9.40 am, 6.05 pm	2 daily	3 hrs	18,500
Mugunghwa	8.05 am-10.45 pm	5 daily	3 hrs 20 mins	9600
T'ong-il	10 08 am-11.50 pm	4 daily	3 hrs 30 mins	6600

Trains from Seoul to Yŏng-dong

Class	Time	Frequency	Travel Time	Fare (W)
Mugunghwa	7.30 am-11.55 pm	21 daily	2 hrs 20 mins	7400
T'ong-il	6.10 am-10.28 pm	9 daily	2 hrs 30 mins	5100

Trains from Seoul to Chŏngŭp

Class	Time	Frequency	Travel Time	Fare (W)
Saemaul	9.05 am-5.10 pm	4 daily	2 hrs 55 mins	17,500
Mugunghwa	7.20 am-11.30 pm	8 daily	3 hrs 25 mins	10,500
T'ong-il	8.20 am-11.05 pm	6 daily	3 hrs 55 mins	7100

TRAINS TO CH'UNGCH'ONGNAM-DO

Trains from Seoul to Taejŏn

Class	Time	Frequency	Travel Time	Fare (W)
Saemaul	8 am-11.20 pm	18 daily	1 hr 30 mins	16,000
Mugunghwa	7.30 am-11.55 pm	28 daily	1 hr 40 mins	5800
T'ong-il	6.10 am-10.30 pm	14 daily	1 hr 50 mins	4000

Trains from Seoul to Ch'ŏnan

Class	Time	Frequency	Travel Time	Fare (W)
Saemaul	9.30 am-11.20 pm	3 daily	1 hr	8500
Mugunghwa	7.20 am-11.55 pm	45 daily	1 hr 5 mins	3500
T'ong-il	6.10 am-11.50 pm	33 daily	1 hr 10 mins	2400

TRAINS TO CH'UNGCH'ŎNGBUK-DO

Trains from Ch'ŏngnyangni to Chech'ŏn

Class	Time	Frequency	Travel Time	Fare (W)
Saemaul	9 am	1 daily	2 hrs 15 mins	10,900
Mugunghwa	11 am, 6 pm	2 daily	2 hrs 20 mins	5400
T'ong-il	1 pm-9.30 pm	3 daily	2 hrs 30 mins	3700

Trains from Ch'ŏngnyangni to Tanyang

Class	Time	Frequency	Travel Time	Fare (W)
Saemaul	9 am, 5.25 pm	2 daily	2 hrs 20 mins	12,100
Mugunghwa	11 am, 6 pm	2 daily	2 hrs 50 mins	6200
T'ong-il	1 pm, 2 pm	2 daily	3 hrs	4300

Index

TEXT

Phrasebooks

Lonely Planet phrasebooks are packed with essential words and phrases to help travellers communicate with the locals. With colour tabs for quick reference, an extensive vocabulary and use of script, these handy pocket-sized language guides cover day-to-day travel situations.

- handy pocket-sized books
- easy to understand Pronunciation chapter
- clear & comprehensive Grammar chapter
- romanisation alongside script to allow ease of pronunciation
- script throughout so users can point to phrases for every situation
- full of cultural information and tips for the traveller

'...vital for a real DIY spirit and attitude in language learning'
– *Backpacker*

'the phrasebooks have good cultural backgrounders and offer solid advice for challenging situations in remote locations'
– *San Francisco Examiner*

Arabic (Egyptian) • Arabic (Moroccan) • Australian *(Australian English, Aboriginal and Torres Strait languages)* • Baltic States *(Estonian, Latvian, Lithuanian)* • Bengali • Brazilian • British • Burmese • Cantonese • Central Asia • Central Europe *(Czech, French, German, Hungarian, Italian, Slovak)* • Eastern Europe *(Bulgarian, Czech, Hungarian, Polish, Romanian, Slovak)* • Ethiopian (Amharic) • Fijian • French • German • Greek • Hebrew phrasebook • Hill Tribes • Hindi/Urdu • Indonesian • Italian • Japanese • Korean • Lao • Latin American Spanish • Malay • Mandarin • Mediterranean Europe *(Albanian, Croatian, Greek, Italian, Macedonian, Maltese, Serbian, Slovene)* • Mongolian • Nepali • Pidgin • Pilipino (Tagalog) • Quechua • Russian • Scandinavian Europe *(Danish, Finnish, Icelandic, Norwegian, Swedish)* • South-East Asia *(Burmese, Indonesian, Khmer, Lao, Malay, Tagalog Pilipino, Thai, Vietnamese)* • South Pacific Languages • Spanish (Castilian) *(also includes Catalan, Galician and Basque)* • Sri Lanka • Swahili • Thai • Tibetan • Turkish • Ukrainian • USA *(US English, Vernacular, Native American languages, Hawaiian)* • Vietnamese • Western Europe *(Basque, Catalan, Dutch, French, German, Greek, Irish)*

Lonely Planet Journeys

JOURNEYS is a unique collection of travel writing – published by the company that understands travel better than anyone else. It is a series for anyone who has ever experienced – or dreamed of – the magical moment when they encountered a strange culture or saw a place for the first time. They are tales to read while you're planning a trip, while you're on the road or while you're in an armchair in front of a fire.

These outstanding titles explore our planet through the eyes of a diverse group of international writers. JOURNEYS books catch the spirit of a place, illuminate a culture, recount a crazy adventure or introduce a fascinating way of life. They always entertain, and always enrich the experience of travel.

IN RAJASTHAN
Royina Grewal

As she writes of her travels through Rajasthan, Indian writer Royina Grewal takes us behind the exotic facade of this fabled destination: here is an insider's perceptive account of India's most colourful state, conveying the excitement and challenges of a region in transition.

SHOPPING FOR BUDDHAS
Jeff Greenwald

In his obsessive search for the perfect Buddha statue in the backstreets of Kathmandu, Jeff Greenwald discovers more than he bargained for ... and his souvenir-hunting turns into an ironic metaphor for the clash between spiritual riches and material greed. Politics, religion and serious shopping collide in this witty account of an enlightening visit to Nepal.

BRIEF ENCOUNTERS
Stories of Love, Sex & Travel
edited by Michelle de Kretser

Love affairs on the road, passionate holiday flings, disastrous pick-ups, erotic encounters ... In this seductive collection of stories, 22 authors from around the world write about travel romances. A tourist in Peru falls for her handsome guide; a writer explores the ambiguities of his relationship with a Japanese woman; a beautiful young man on a train proposes marriage ... Combining fiction and reportage, *Brief Encounters* is must-have reading – for everyone who has dreamt of escape with that perfect stranger.

Includes stories by Pico Iyer, Mary Morris, Emily Perkins, Mona Simpson, Lisa St Aubin de Terán, Paul Theroux and Sara Wheeler.

Lonely Planet Travel Atlases

Lonely Planet has long been famous for the number and quality of its guidebook maps. Now we've gone one step further and produced a handy companion series: Lonely Planet travel atlases – maps of a country produced in book form.

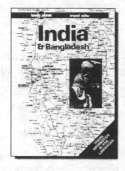

Unlike other maps, which look good but lead travellers astray, our travel atlases have been researched on the road by Lonely Planet's experienced team of writers. All details are carefully checked to ensure the atlas corresponds with the equivalent Lonely Planet guidebook.

- full-colour throughout
- maps researched and checked by Lonely Planet authors
- place names correspond with Lonely Planet guidebooks
- no confusing spelling differences
- legend and travelling information in English, French, German, Japanese and Spanish
- size: 230 x 160 mm

Available now: Chile & Easter Island ● Egypt ● India & Bangladesh ● Israel & the Palestinian Territories ● Jordan, Syria & Lebanon ● Kenya ● Laos ● Portugal ● South Africa, Lesotho & Swaziland ● Thailand ● Turkey ● Vietnam ● Zimbabwe, Botswana & Namibia

Lonely Planet TV Series & Videos

Lonely Planet travel guides have been brought to life on television screens around the world. Like our guides, the programs are based on the joy of independent travel, and look honestly at some of the most exciting, picturesque and frustrating places in the world. Each show is presented by one of three travellers from Australia, England or the USA and combines an innovative mixture of video, Super-8 film, atmospheric soundscapes and original music.

Videos of each episode – containing additional footage not shown on television – are available from good book and video shops, but the availability of individual videos varies with regional screening schedules.

Video destinations include: Alaska ● American Rockies ● Australia – The South-East ● Baja California & the Copper Canyon ● Brazil ● Central Asia ● Chile & Easter Island ● Corsica, Sicily & Sardinia – The Mediterranean Islands ● East Africa (Tanzania & Zanzibar) ● Ecuador & the Galapagos Islands ● Greenland & Iceland ● Indonesia ● Israel & the Sinai Desert ● Jamaica ● Japan ● La Ruta Maya ● Morocco ● New York ● North India ● Pacific Islands (Fiji, Solomon Islands & Vanuatu) ● South India ● South West China ● Turkey ● Vietnam ● West Africa ● Zimbabwe, Botswana & Namibia

The Lonely Planet TV series is produced by: Pilot Productions
The Old Studio
18 Middle Row
London W10 5AT, UK

FREE Lonely Planet Newsletters

We love hearing from you and think you'd like to hear from us.

Planet Talk

Our FREE quarterly printed newsletter is full of tips from travellers and anecdotes from Lonely Planet guidebook authors. Every issue is packed with up-to-date travel news and advice, and includes:

- a postcard from Lonely Planet co-founder Tony Wheeler
- a swag of mail from travellers
- a look at life on the road through the eyes of a Lonely Planet author
- topical health advice
- prizes for the best travel yarn
- news about forthcoming Lonely Planet events
- a complete list of Lonely Planet books and other titles

To join our mailing list, residents of the UK, Europe and Africa can email us at go@lonelyplanet.co.uk; residents of North and South America can email us at info@lonelyplanet.com; the rest of the world can email us at talk2us@lonelyplanet.com.au, or contact any Lonely Planet office.

Comet

Our FREE monthly email newsletter brings you all the latest travel news, features, interviews, competitions, destination ideas, travellers' tips & tales, Q&As, raging debates and related links. Find out what's new on the Lonely Planet Web site and which books are about to hit the shelves.

Subscribe from your desktop: www.lonelyplanet.com/comet

LONELY PLANET

Guides by Region

Lonely Planet is known worldwide for publishing practical, reliable and no-nonsense travel information in our guides and on our Web site. The Lonely Planet list covers just about every accessible part of the world. Currently there are thirteen series: travel guides, shoestring guides, walking guides, city guides, phrasebooks, audio packs, city maps, travel atlases, diving and snorkeling guides, restaurant guides, first-time travel guides, healthy travel and travel literature.

AFRICA Africa – the South • Africa on a shoestring • Arabic (Egyptian) phrasebook • Arabic (Moroccan) phrasebook • Cairo • Cape Town • Cape Town city map • Central Africa • East Africa • Egypt • Egypt travel atlas • Ethiopian (Amharic) phrasebook • The Gambia & Senegal • Healthy Travel Africa • Kenya • Kenya travel atlas • Malawi, Mozambique & Zambia • Morocco • North Africa • South Africa, Lesotho & Swaziland • South Africa, Lesotho & Swaziland travel atlas • Swahili phrasebook • Tanzania, Zanzibar & Pemba • Trekking in East Africa • Tunisia • West Africa • Zimbabwe, Botswana & Namibia • Zimbabwe, Botswana & Namibia travel atlas
Travel Literature: The Rainbird: A Central African Journey • Songs to an African Sunset: A Zimbabwean Story • Mali Blues: Traveling to an African Beat

AUSTRALIA & THE PACIFIC Auckland • Australia • Australian phrasebook • Bushwalking in Australia • Bushwalking in Papua New Guinea • Fiji • Fijian phrasebook • Islands of Australia's Great Barrier Reef • Melbourne • Melbourne city map • Micronesia • New Caledonia • New South Wales & the ACT • New Zealand • Northern Territory • Outback Australia • Out To Eat – Melbourne • Papua New Guinea • Papua New Guinea (Pidgin) phrasebook • Queensland • Rarotonga & the Cook Islands • Samoa • Solomon Islands • South Australia • South Pacific Languages phrasebook • Sydney • Sydney city map • Tahiti & French Polynesia • Tasmania • Tonga • Tramping in New Zealand • Vanuatu • Victoria • Western Australia
Travel Literature: Islands in the Clouds • Kiwi Tracks • Sean & David's Long Drive

CENTRAL AMERICA & THE CARIBBEAN Bahamas and Turks & Caicos • Bermuda • Central America on a shoestring • Costa Rica • Cuba • Dominican Republic & Haiti • Eastern Caribbean • Guatemala, Belize & Yucatán: La Ruta Maya • Jamaica • Mexico • Mexico City • Panama • Puerto Rico
Travel Literature: Green Dreams: Travels in Central America

EUROPE Amsterdam • Amsterdam city map • Andalucía • Austria • Baltic States phrasebook • Barcelona • Berlin • Berlin city map • Britain • British phrasebook • Brussels, Bruges & Antwerp • Budapest city map • Canary Islands • Central Europe • Central Europe phrasebook • Corsica • Croatia • Czech & Slovak Republics • Denmark • Dublin • Eastern Europe • Eastern Europe phrasebook • Edinburgh • Estonia, Latvia & Lithuania • Europe • Finland • France • French phrasebook • Germany • German phrasebook • Greece • Greek phrasebook • Hungary • Iceland, Greenland & the Faroe Islands • Ireland • Italian phrasebook • Italy • Lisbon • London • London city map • Mediterranean Europe • Mediterranean Europe phrasebook • Norway • Paris • Paris city map • Poland • Portugal • Portugal travel atlas • Prague • Prague city map • Provence & the Côte d'Azur • Romania & Moldova • Rome • Russia, Ukraine & Belarus • Russian phrasebook • Scandinavia & Baltic Europe • Scandinavian Europe phrasebook • Scotland • Slovenia • Spain • Spanish phrasebook • St Petersburg • Switzerland • Trekking in Spain • Ukrainian phrasebook • Vienna • Walking in Britain • Walking in Ireland • Walking in Italy • Walking in Switzerland • Western Europe • Western Europe phrasebook
Travel Literature: The Olive Grove: Travels in Greece

INDIAN SUBCONTINENT Bangladesh • Bengali phrasebook • Bhutan • Delhi • Goa • Hindi/Urdu phrasebook • India • India & Bangladesh travel atlas • Indian Himalaya • Karakoram Highway • Kerala • Mumbai • Nepal • Nepali phrasebook • Pakistan • Rajasthan • Read This First: Asia & India • South India • Sri Lanka • Sri Lanka phrasebook • Trekking in the Indian Himalaya • Trekking in the Karakoram & Hindukush • Trekking in the Nepal Himalaya
Travel Literature: In Rajasthan • Shopping for Buddhas

LONELY PLANET

Mail Order

Lonely Planet products are distributed worldwide. They are also available by mail order from Lonely Planet, so if you have difficulty finding a title please write to us. North and South American residents should write to 150 Linden St, Oakland, CA 94607, USA; European and African residents should write to 10a Spring Place, London NW5 3BH, UK; and residents of other countries to PO Box 617, Hawthorn, Victoria 3122, Australia.

ISLANDS OF THE INDIAN OCEAN Madagascar & Comoros • Maldives • Mauritius, Réunion & Seychelles

MIDDLE EAST & CENTRAL ASIA Arab Gulf States • Central Asia • Central Asia phrasebook • Hebrew phrasebook • Iran • Israel & the Palestinian Territories • Israel & the Palestinian Territories travel atlas • Istanbul • Istanbul to Cairo • Jerusalem • Jordan & Syria • Jordan, Syria & Lebanon travel atlas • Lebanon • Middle East on a shoestring • Syria • Turkey • Turkish phrasebook • Turkey travel atlas • Yemen
Travel Literature: The Gates of Damascus • Kingdom of the Film Stars: Journey into Jordan

NORTH AMERICA Alaska • Backpacking in Alaska • Baja California • California & Nevada • Canada • Chicago • Chicago city map • Deep South • Florida • Hawaii • Honolulu • Las Vegas • Los Angeles • Miami • New England • New Orleans • New York City • New York city map • New York, New Jersey & Pennsylvania • Pacific Northwest USA • Puerto Rico • Rocky Mountain States • San Francisco • San Francisco city map • Seattle • Southwest USA • Texas • USA • USA phrasebook • Vancouver • Washington, DC & the Capital Region • Washington DC city map
Travel Literature: Drive Thru America

NORTH-EAST ASIA Beijing • Cantonese phrasebook • China • Hong Kong • Hong Kong city map • Hong Kong, Macau & Guangzhou • Japan • Japanese phrasebook • Japanese audio pack • Korea • Korean phrasebook • Kyoto • Mandarin phrasebook • Mongolia • Mongolian phrasebook • North-East Asia on a shoestring • Seoul • South-West China • Taiwan • Tibet • Tibetan phrasebook • Tokyo
Travel Literature: Lost Japan

SOUTH AMERICA Argentina, Uruguay & Paraguay • Bolivia • Brazil • Brazilian phrasebook • Buenos Aires • Chile & Easter Island • Chile & Easter Island travel atlas • Colombia • Ecuador & the Galapagos Islands • Latin American Spanish phrasebook • Peru • Quechua phrasebook • Rio de Janeiro • Rio de Janeiro city map • South America on a shoestring • Trekking in the Patagonian Andes • Venezuela
Travel Literature: Full Circle: A South American Journey

SOUTH-EAST ASIA Bali & Lombok • Bangkok • Bangkok city map • Burmese phrasebook • Cambodia • Hanoi • Healthy Travel Asia & India • Hill Tribes phrasebook • Ho Chi Minh City • Indonesia • Indonesia's Eastern Islands • Indonesian phrasebook • Indonesian audio pack • Jakarta • Java • Laos • Lao phrasebook • Laos travel atlas • Malay phrasebook • Malaysia, Singapore & Brunei • Myanmar (Burma) • Philippines • Pilipino (Tagalog) phrasebook • Singapore • South-East Asia on a shoestring • South-East Asia phrasebook • Thailand • Thailand's Islands & Beaches • Thailand travel atlas • Thai phrasebook • Thai audio pack • Vietnam • Vietnamese phrasebook • Vietnam travel atlas

ALSO AVAILABLE: Antarctica • The Arctic • Brief Encounters: Stories of Love, Sex & Travel • Chasing Rickshaws • Lonely Planet Unpacked • Not the Only Planet: Travel Stories from Science Fiction • Sacred India • Travel with Children • Traveller's Tales

The Lonely Planet Story

Lonely Planet published its first book in 1973 in response to the numerous 'How did you do it?' questions Maureen and Tony Wheeler were asked after driving, bussing, hitching, sailing and railing their way from England to Australia.

Written at a kitchen table and hand collated, trimmed and stapled, *Across Asia on the Cheap* became an instant local bestseller, inspiring thoughts of another book.

Eighteen months in South-East Asia resulted in their second guide, *South-East Asia on a shoestring*, which they put together in a backstreet Chinese hotel in Singapore in 1975. The 'yellow bible', as it quickly became known to backpackers around the world, soon became *the* guide to the region. It has sold well over half a million copies and is now in its 9th edition, still retaining its familiar yellow cover.

Today there are over 350 titles, including travel guides, walking guides, language kits & phrasebooks, travel atlases, diving guides and travel literature. The company is the largest independent travel publisher in the world. Although Lonely Planet initially specialised in guides to Asia, today there are few corners of the globe that have not been covered.

The emphasis continues to be on travel for independent travellers. Tony and Maureen still travel for several months of each year and play an active part in the writing, updating and quality control of Lonely Planet's guides.

They have been joined by over 120 authors and 280 staff at our offices in Melbourne (Australia), Oakland (USA), London (UK) and Paris (France). Travellers themselves also make a valuable contribution to the guides through the feedback we receive in thousands of letters each year and on our web site.

The people at Lonely Planet strongly believe that travellers can make a positive contribution to the countries they visit, both through their appreciation of the countries' culture, wildlife and natural features, and through the money they spend. In addition, the company makes a direct contribution to the countries and regions it covers. Since 1986 a percentage of the income from each book has been donated to ventures such as famine relief in Africa; aid projects in India; agricultural projects in Central America; Greenpeace's efforts to halt French nuclear testing in the Pacific; and Amnesty International.

LONELY PLANET OFFICES

Australia
PO Box 617, Hawthorn, Victoria 3122
☎ 03 9819 1877 fax 03 9819 6459
email: talk2us@lonelyplanet.com.au

USA
150 Linden St, Oakland, CA 94607
☎ 510 893 8555 TOLL FREE: 800 275 8555
fax 510 893 8572
email: info@lonelyplanet.com

UK
10a Spring Place, London NW5 3BH
☎ 020 7428 4800 fax 020 7428 4828
email: go@lonelyplanet.co.uk

France
1 rue du Dahomey, 75011 Paris
☎ 01 55 25 33 00 fax 01 55 25 33 01
email: bip@lonelyplanet.fr
www.lonelyplanet.fr

World Wide Web: www.lonelyplanet.com *or* AOL keyword: lp
Lonely Planet Images: lpi@lonelyplanet.com.au